BUDDHISM AND COMPARATIVE CONSTITUTIONAL LAW

Buddhism and Comparative Constitutional Law offers the first comprehensive account of the entanglements of Buddhism and constitutional law in Sri Lanka, Myanmar, Thailand, Cambodia, Vietnam, Tibet, Bhutan, China, Mongolia, Korea, and Japan. Bringing together an interdisciplinary team of experts, the volume offers a detailed portrait of "the Buddhist-constitutional complex," demonstrating the intricate and powerful ways in which Buddhist and constitutional ideas merge, interact, and co-evolve. The authors also highlight the important ways in which Buddhist actors have (re)conceived Western liberal ideals such as constitutionalism, the rule of law, and secularism. Available Open Access on Cambridge Core, this trans-disciplinary volume is written to be accessible to a non-specialist audience.

TOM GINSBURG is the Leo Spitz Professor of International Law at the University of Chicago and a Research Professor at the American Bar Foundation.

BENJAMIN SCHONTHAL is Professor of Buddhist Studies and Head of the Religion Programme at the University of Otago, where he also co-directs the Otago Centre for Law and Society.

COMPARATIVE CONSTITUTIONAL LAW AND POLICY

Series Editors

Tom Ginsburg *University of Chicago*
Zachary Elkins *University of Texas at Austin*
Ran Hirschl *University of Texas at Austin*

Comparative constitutional law is an intellectually vibrant field that encompasses an increasingly broad array of approaches and methodologies. This series collects analytically innovative and empirically grounded work from scholars of comparative constitutionalism across academic disciplines. Books in the series include theoretically informed studies of single constitutional jurisdictions, comparative studies of constitutional law and institutions, and edited collections of original essays that respond to challenging theoretical and empirical questions in the field.

Books in the Series

Amending America's Unwritten Constitution edited by Richard Albert, Ryan C. Williams, and Yaniv Roznai

Constitutionalism and a Right to Effective Government? edited by Vicki C. Jackson and Yasmin Dawood

The Fall of the Arab Spring: Democracy's Challenges and Efforts to Reconstitute the Middle East Tofigh Maboudi

Filtering Populist Claims to Fight Populism: The Italian Case in a Comparative Perspective Giuseppe Martinico

Constitutionalism in Context David S. Law

The New Fourth Branch: Institutions for Protecting Constitutional Democracy Mark Tushnet

The Veil of Participation: Citizens and Political Parties in Constitution-Making Processes Alexander Hudson

Towering Judges: A Comparative Study of Constitutional Judges edited by Rehan Abeyratne and Iddo Porat

The Constitution of Arbitration Victor Ferreres Comella

Redrafting Constitutions in Democratic Orders: Theoretical and Comparative Perspectives edited by Gabriel L. Negretto

From Parchment to Practice: Implementing New Constitutions edited by Tom Ginsburg and Aziz Z. Huq

The Failure of Popular Constitution Making in Turkey: Regressing Towards Constitutional Autocracy edited by Felix Petersen and Zeynep Yanaşmayan

A Qualified Hope: The Indian Supreme Court and Progressive Social Change edited by Gerald N. Rosenberg, Sudhir Krishnaswamy, and Shishir Bail

Reconstructing Rights: Courts, Parties, and Equality Rights in India, South Africa, and the United States Stephan Stohler

Constitutions in Times of Financial Crisis edited by Tom Ginsburg, Mark D. Rosen, and Georg Vanberg

Hybrid Constitutionalism: The Politics of Constitutional Review in the Chinese Special Administrative Regions Eric C. Ip

Constitution-Making and Transnational Legal Order edited by Tom Ginsburg, Terence C. Halliday, and Gregory Shaffer

The Invisible Constitution in Comparative Perspective edited by Rosalind Dixon and Adrienne Stone

The Politico-Legal Dynamics of Judicial Review: A Comparative Analysis Theunis Roux

Constitutional Courts in Asia: A Comparative Perspective edited by Albert H. Y. Chen and Andrew Harding

Judicial Review in Norway: A Bicentennial Debate Anine Kierulf

Constituent Assemblies edited by Jon Elster, Roberto Gargarella, Vatsal Naresh, and Bjorn Erik Rasch

The DNA of Constitutional Justice in Latin America: Politics, Governance, and Judicial Design Daniel M. Brinks and Abby Blass

The Adventures of the Constituent Power: Beyond Revolutions? Andrew Arato

Canada in the World: Comparative Perspectives on the Canadian Constitution edited by Richard Albert and David R. Cameron

Constitutions, Religion and Politics in Asia: Indonesia, Malaysia and Sri Lanka Dian A. H. Shah

Courts and Democracies in Asia Po Jen Yap

Proportionality: New Frontiers, New Challenges edited by Vicki C. Jackson and Mark Tushnet

Constituents before Assembly: Participation, Deliberation, and Representation in the Crafting of New Constitutions Todd A. Eisenstadt, A. Carl LeVan, and Tofigh Maboudi

Assessing Constitutional Performance edited by Tom Ginsburg and Aziz Huq

Buddhism, Politics and the Limits of Law: The Pyrrhic Constitutionalism of Sri Lanka Benjamin Schonthal

Engaging with Social Rights: Procedure, Participation and Democracy in South Africa's Second Wave Brian Ray

Constitutional Courts as Mediators: Armed Conflict, Civil-Military Relations, and the Rule of Law in Latin America Julio Ríos-Figueroa

Perils of Judicial Self-Government in Transitional Societies David Kosař

Making We the People: Democratic Constitutional Founding in Postwar Japan and South Korea Chaihark Hahm and Sung Ho Kim

Radical Deprivation on Trial: The Impact of Judicial Activism on Socioeconomic Rights in the Global South César Rodríguez-Garavito and Diana Rodríguez-Franco

Unstable Constitutionalism: Law and Politics in South Asia edited by Mark Tushnet and Madhav Khosla

Magna Carta and Its Modern Legacy edited by Robert Hazell and James Melton

Constitutions and Religious Freedom Frank B. Cross

International Courts and the Performance of International Agreements: A General Theory with Evidence from the European Union Clifford J. Carrubba and Matthew J. Gabel

Reputation and Judicial Tactics: A Theory of National and International Courts Shai Dothan

Social Difference and Constitutionalism in Pan-Asia edited by Susan H. Williams

Constitutionalism in Asia in the Early Twenty-First Century edited by Albert H. Y. Chen

Constitutions in Authoritarian Regimes edited by Tom Ginsburg and Alberto Simpser

Presidential Legislation in India: The Law and Practice of Ordinances Shubhankar Dam

Social and Political Foundations of Constitutions edited by Denis J. Galligan and Mila Versteeg

Consequential Courts: Judicial Roles in Global Perspective edited by Diana Kapiszewski, Gordon Silverstein, and Robert A. Kagan

Comparative Constitutional Design edited by Tom Ginsburg

Buddhism and Comparative Constitutional Law

Edited by

TOM GINSBURG
University of Chicago

BENJAMIN SCHONTHAL
University of Otago

CAMBRIDGE
UNIVERSITY PRESS

CAMBRIDGE
UNIVERSITY PRESS

Shaftesbury Road, Cambridge CB2 8EA, United Kingdom

One Liberty Plaza, 20th Floor, New York, NY 10006, USA

477 Williamstown Road, Port Melbourne, VIC 3207, Australia

314–321, 3rd Floor, Plot 3, Splendor Forum, Jasola District Centre, New Delhi – 110025, India

103 Penang Road, #05–06/07, Visioncrest Commercial, Singapore 238467

Cambridge University Press is part of Cambridge University Press & Assessment, a department of the University of Cambridge.

We share the University's mission to contribute to society through the pursuit of education, learning and research at the highest international levels of excellence.

www.cambridge.org
Information on this title: www.cambridge.org/9781009286046

DOI: 10.1017/9781009286022

First published 2023

A catalogue record for this publication is available from the British Library

Library of Congress Cataloging-in-Publication Data
NAMES: Ginsburg, Tom, editor. | Schonthal, Benjamin, 1976– editor.
TITLE: Buddhism and comparative constitutional law / edited by Tom Ginsburg, University of Chicago; Ben Schonthal, University of Otago, New Zealand.
DESCRIPTION: Cambridge, United Kingdom ; New York, NY : Cambridge University Press, 2022. | SERIES: Comparative constitutional law and policy | Includes bibliographical references and index.
IDENTIFIERS: LCCN 2022028560 (print) | LCCN 2022028561 (ebook) | ISBN 9781009286046 (hardback) | ISBN 9781009286053 (paperback) | ISBN 9781009286022 (epub)
SUBJECTS: LCSH: Constitutional law–Southeast Asia. | Constitutional law–East Asia. | Law–Southeast Asia–Buddhist influences. | Law–East Asia–Buddhist influences.
CLASSIFICATION: LCC KNC524 .B83 2022 (print) | LCC KNC524 (ebook) | DDC 342.59–dc23/eng/20220831
LC record available at https://lccn.loc.gov/2022028560
LC ebook record available at https://lccn.loc.gov/2022028561

ISBN 978-1-009-28604-6 Hardback

Contents

List of Contributors *page* xi
Preface xiii
by Rebecca Redwood French
Acknowledgments xvii
Notes on Transliteration and Language xix

1 **Introduction: Mapping the Buddhist–Constitutional Complex in Asia** 1
Tom Ginsburg and Benjamin Schonthal

PART I RELIGIOUS AND POLITICAL UNDERPINNINGS

2 **Buddhism and Constitutionalism in Precolonial Southeast Asia** 35
D. Christian Lammerts

3 **Theorising Constitutionalism in Buddhist-Dominant Asian Polities** 57
Asanga Welikala

PART II HIMALAYAN ASIA

4 **The Zhabdrung's Legacy: Buddhism and Constitutional Transformation in Bhutan** 73
Richard W. Whitecross

5 **The "Trick of Law": The Hermeneutics of Early Buddhist Law in Tibet** 99
Martin A. Mills

6 **Tibetan Buddhist Monastic Constitutional Law and Governmental Constitutional Law: Mutual Influences?** 124
Berthe Jansen

PART III SOUTHERN ASIA

7 Guardians of the Law: Sinhala Language and Buddhist Reformation in Postwar Sri Lanka 143
Krishantha Fedricks

8 Thai Constitutions as a Battle Ground for Political Authority: Barami versus Vox Populi 161
Khemthong Tonsakulrungruang

9 Establishing the King as the Source of the Constitution: Shifting 'Bricolaged' Narratives of Buddhist Kingship from Siam to Thailand 181
Eugénie Mérieau

10 Buddhist Constitutionalism beyond Constitutional Law: Buddhist Statecraft and Military Ideology in Myanmar 198
Iselin Frydenlund

11 Reconstituting the Divided Sangha: Buddhist Authority in Post-Conflict Cambodia 220
Benjamin Lawrence

PART IV NORTHERN AND NORTHEASTERN ASIA

12 Constitutional Buddhism: Japanese Buddhists and Constitutional Law 241
Levi McLaughlin

13 Governing Buddhism in Vietnam 272
Ngoc Son Bui

14 The Buddhist Association of China and Constitutional Law in Buddhist Majority Nations: The International Channels of Influence 285
André Laliberté

15 Governing "Lamaism" on the "Frontier": Buddhism and Law in Early Twentieth-Century Inner Mongolia 305
Daigengna Duoer

16 Buddhist Constitutional Battlegrounds: Using the Courts to Litigate Monastic Celibacy in South Korea (1955–1970) 325
Mark A. Nathan

PART V COMPARATIVE PERSPECTIVES

17 **On the Familiar Pleasures of Estrangement** 345
Deepa Das Acevedo

18 **Buddhism and Constitutionalism: A Comparison with the Canon Law** 354
Richard H. Helmholz

19 **Islam and Constitutional Law: Insights for the Emerging Field of Buddhist Constitutional Law** 360
Clark B. Lombardi

Contributors

Deepa Das Acevedo is Assistant Professor of Law at the University of Alabama School of Law.

Ngoc Son Bui is Associate Professor of Asian Laws at the Faculty of Law, University of Oxford, and a fellow of St. Hugh's College, Oxford.

Daigengna Duoer is a PhD Candidate in religion at the University of California, Santa Barbara.

Krishantha Fedricks is a PhD Candidate and a graduate teaching assistant in anthropology at the University of Texas–Austin as well as a Senior Lecturer in the Department of Sinhala at the University of Colombo.

Iselin Frydenlund is Professor of Religion at MF Norwegian School of Theology, Religion, and Society.

Tom Ginsburg is Professor of Law at the University of Chicago.

Richard H. Helmholz is Professor of Law at the University of Chicago Law School.

Berthe Jansen is Junior Professor of Tibetan Studies in Leipzig University.

André Laliberté is Professor of Comparative Politics at the School of Political Studies and Co-director of the Research Chair in Taiwan Studies at the University of Ottawa, Canada.

D. Christian Lammerts is Associate Professor of Religion at Rutgers University.

Benjamin Lawrence is a Research Fellow at the Centre for Asian Legal Studies, National University of Singapore.

Clark B. Lombardi is Professor of Law at the University of Washington School of Law and serves as the Director of Islamic Legal Studies.

Levi McLaughlin is Associate Professor in the Department of Philosophy and Religious Studies at North Carolina State University.

Eugénie Mérieau is Associate Professor of Public Law at the University of Paris 1 Panthéon-Sorbonne.

Martin A. Mills is Senior Lecturer in Anthropology at the University of Aberdeen, Scotland, and Director of the Scottish Centre for Himalayan Research.

Mark A. Nathan is Associate Professor in the Department of History and Director of the Asian Studies Program at the University at Buffalo, State University of New York.

Benjamin Schonthal is Professor of Buddhist Studies and Head of the Religion Programme at the University of Otago, where he also co-directs the Otago Centre for Law and Society.

Khemthong Tonsakulrungruang is Lecturer in constitutional law at Chulalongkorn University in Bangkok, Thailand.

Asanga Welikala is Senior Lecturer in Public Law, and the Director of the Edinburgh Centre for Constitutional Law, at the School of Law, University of Edinburgh.

Richard W. Whitecross is Head and Professor of Law at Edinburgh Napier University.

Preface

Rebecca Redwood French
State University of New York, School of Law

To understand the context of the current volume, it is necessary to return to the early discussions of Buddhism and Law. It began at the Bellagio Center on Lake Como, a sixteenth-century convent restored with exquisite taste in modern Italian design, where a group of scholars came together in the summer of 2006 for the first International Conference on Buddhism and Law. I arrived early in Italy to help set things up. Soon, the participants began to arrive from all around the globe: Leslie Gunawardena from Peradeniya University in Sri Lanka appeared, as did Bernard Faure from New York City. Ryuji Okudaira came in from Japan; José Cabezón and Vesna Wallace took long flights from Santa Barbara, as did Tim Brooks from Vancouver, and Frank Reynolds from the University of Chicago. Winni Sullivan, a theorist in religious studies, now at Indiana University, arrived, as did Richard Whitecross, a specialist on Bhutan. Andrew Huxley came from SOAS in London, Justin McDaniel, who worked in Laos, and Michael Thamtai came from Thailand. To round the conference off, Peter Skilling and Petra Kiefer-Pülz, two famous Pāli scholars, arrived from Thailand and Germany, respectively. For a week, in these beautiful halls filled with up-to-date electronics and technology, an ever-ready staff, and plentiful workspaces, the group engaged in intense and enjoyable discussions about the role of the Buddha, the different variants of the Vinaya, the problems with translation, the environment of law schools, the intersection of Buddhism and politics in different nations, and the place of Buddhism in different academic contexts. And slowly, they began discussing a possible roadmap for the new discipline of Buddhism and Law within the purview of Religion and Law, Religious Studies, Comparative Law, International Law, Asian Studies, and Buddhist Studies.

Throughout the conference, the participants were aware of misconceptions in the scholarly community about the nature of Buddhism and Law. The first was the misunderstanding in Western scholarship that Buddhism as a religion had not been a significant legal or political influence in any Asian country in which it predominated historically or presently. A second common misunderstanding was that the

Vinaya had been translated as "the book of discipline" in Western languages, which resulted in legal scholars assuming that it was not "law." Andrew Huxley, who worked in Myanmar, spoke of the colonial powers in Asia that had discarded and "disappeared" most secular Buddhist and Buddhist-influenced law codes. A fourth misconception was what constituted "religious influence on a legal system." While scholars well understand the Christian roots of legal policies in most Western states, the influence of Buddhism on Buddhist states in Asia over the past two millennia is often seen as "cultural" and not religious.

The most interesting day of that initial meeting was the last, when the group finally turned to what was needed to develop the field. The group spoke about the possibility of this project, and the obvious difficulties with it. Winni Sullivan started out by saying provocatively that, maybe, there was "no hole to fill."[1] She argued that the academic discipline of Religion and Law simply disregarded most religions outside of Christianity or, at times, Judaism, so perhaps it was no different for Buddhism. Andrew Huxley, with his sonorous, booming voice, interrupted to contradict, stating: "Arguing there is *no hole* is not right! There surely is a hole. Just look at the growth of Hindu Legal Studies, Islamic Legal Studies. The first professorship of Islamic, Hindu, and Jewish Law began in 1840 at Oxford University." The group then launched into a lively discussion on what Buddhist law was. Several points become clear. Participants agreed that if one can say that the United States, for example, is a Christian nation, then we can say that many of the current and historic societies of Asia are Buddhist-influenced societies and nations. The role of karma in legal decisions was "a way of justifying things," Bernard Faure said. Michael Thamtai added that "there is no difference between going to litigate and a karmic explanation. They act together, karma is also used in the sense of 'let's be compassionate to him.'"

One scholar cautioned that "Law in the West" was not a good contrast, because there is no unitary generalization available for what "the West" means, and then others presented a series of basic questions about the relationship between religion and law. Native American religions came up as did Muslims in Myanmar; the *adat* legal system of Southeast Asia; the situation of stateless persons; "the rule of law" in China, whether or not the notion of the "rule of law" is fundamentally hostile to Buddhism; and many other topics. While wide-ranging, exciting, and difficult at times, the conversation was always based on deep personal experience, as well as scholarly insight. As for the idea of justice, Peter Skilling provoked a lot of laughter with his example of Aṅgulimāla, a famous disciple of the Buddha, who began his life as a criminal with a necklace of fingers from his victims. Peter asked, "Was he just beyond justice?" Frank Reynolds summed up the week of conversations with a list of what was needed to establish the new discipline. He outlined the following components: a basic, introductory text explaining the field; a source volume with short

[1] All quotations come from the author's notes from the 2006 conference.

translations of the important texts; a scholarly network of excellent academics and scholars; a journal for the development of articles on the topic; a bibliography divided into appropriate categories with annotations of every entry; and a series of books on the topic of Buddhism and Law.

The present volume, *Buddhism and Comparative Constitutional Law*, skillfully edited by Tom Ginsburg and Benjamin Schonthal, is just what Frank Reynolds ordered. Engaging the scholars who have gathered together to form a Buddhism and Law network over the last sixteen years, then adding several comparative lawyers and scholars from other fields, they have assembled one of the first edited volumes on a specific and compelling topic in Buddhism and Law. Some large themes emerge as one reads the chapters, which have been central problematics of this field since the Bellagio Center conference years ago, and remain important issues for further research, such as the nature of Buddhist legal cosmologies. For cultures that precede modern constitutional law, developing a legal cosmology means presenting the rules, categories, and practical building blocks that structure legal reasoning and actions in a particular society or government as well as their interrelations, historical locations, and creative use. In this way, Buddhist concepts of law, legality, legal consciousness, legal history, and legal theory fit into ideas of government and citizenship. In each of these essays, the reader can detect the dynamic way in which Buddhism sits as a foundational backdrop for the legal cosmology of the society. This is the first time in which ideas of constitutionality, both modern and historical, have been seriously approached by Buddhist and Asian experts, and this volume will be a cornerstone in the development of the field for many years to come.

Acknowledgments

Our sincere gratitude to the National Science Foundation (NSF), Award No. 1921184, which originally funded a conference to present the papers that appear in this volume. We thank Reginald Sheehan, the NSF Program Officer, for his flexibility in allowing us to turn the workshop into a series of events that were both open to the interested public and also the basis for a seminar class held at the University of Chicago Law School. We thank Dean Thomas Miles and Deputy Dean Anthony Casey for their support. We also thank Ajay Mehrotra of the American Bar Foundation. A special debt of gratitude goes to Paride Stortini who has been an incredible research assistant and overall champion of this project over the course of nearly eighteen months. This volume benefited enormously from his efforts. We also thank Arunima Bhattacharjee for the important early assistance she provided on the project.

In addition to the authors, we had superb engagement from colleagues who attended the series and generously offered comments. We thank David Engel, Rebecca French, Ran Hirschl, Cuilan Liu, Clark Lombardi, Jessica Main, Mark McClish, Fernanda Pirie, Winnifred Sullivan, Vesna Wallace, Matthew Walton, and Roshan de Silva Wijeyeratne. Scholarship is always a collective endeavor and this volume especially so. Finally, the extraordinary students at the University of Chicago Law School seminar in early 2021 enriched this project tremendously.

Notes on Transliteration and Language

Buddhist texts are preserved in multiple languages, and even common Buddhist terms enter Asian vernaculars by way of multiple linguistic transformations. This means that a particular Buddhist phrase can appear in multiple forms and spellings across time and space, making it difficult to standardize terms for a volume such as this. In what follows, we employ the following conventions:

Where a Buddhist term is included in the Oxford English Dictionary (*OED*), we used the OED spelling unitalicized (e.g., dharma, sangha, nirvana).

Where a term did not appear in the OED, we used the following rules:

1. In chapters dealing with Theravāda Buddhist contexts, we opted for the Pāli forms of words (e.g., dhammarāja instead of dharmarāja).
2. In all other chapters we maintained the transliteration conventions specific to the languages in question, with the exception of favoring the Sanskrit form of common Buddhist terms.

1

Introduction

Mapping the Buddhist–Constitutional Complex in Asia

Tom Ginsburg and Benjamin Schonthal[*]

In 2011, the 14th Dalai Lama Tenzin Gyatso announced his intention to complete a major legal transformation that would redefine the government of the Tibetan community-in-exile. In a speech given from his headquarters in Dharamshala, the world's most well-known Buddhist monk confirmed that he would be retiring as the political leader of the Tibetan people. That event would catalyze a dramatic constitutional change: from a system based on the "rule by kings and religious figures," the Tibetan Government-in-Exile was to follow a new Charter that provided for democratically elected leaders, whose authority would be constrained by law (Mills 2018, 155 and passim; see also Brox 2016).[1] The preamble to the new 2011 constitutional text explained that, in spite of the Tibetan people's willingness to accept the continuation of theocracy, "His Holiness the Dalai Lama decided that the time had now come to complete the process of full democratization and that the Tibetan people should no longer remain dependent on a single individual" (Tibetan Parliament-in-Exile 2011, 2). The chapters of the Charter that followed laid out this vision. The "Tibetan People" would continue to promote "the noble Buddhist faith" and respect the Dalai Lama as "the manifestation of [the bodhisattva] Avalokiteshwara in human form . . . the master of all Buddhist teachings" (Article 17(11); Article 1).[2] But they would also uphold fundamental rights and hold elections, maintain a judiciary and bureaucracy, limit executive power, and follow standardized procedures for promulgating laws. Theocracy, in short, would give way to constitutional democracy.

This episode – which attracted more attention among Tibetologists than among scholars of comparative constitutional law – provides one tantalizing example of the

* The authors are particularly appreciative of D. Christian Lammerts and Levi McLaughlin for their comments on a draft of this chapter.

[1] A "Constitution for a Future Tibet" had appeared as early as 1963, with another major iteration coming in 1991.

[2] We use the spelling of the original. The more common spelling is the Sanskrit, Avalokiteshvara.

many ways in which Buddhism and constitutional thought have become entangled and interfused in Asian polities, both now and in the past. On the one hand, the event appears to be a clash of categorical opposites: something old and something new, a form of religion and political ordering, a system purportedly designed for ultimate release from the world, and one intent on structuring power within it. On the other hand, the very of idea of having a Tibetan Charter – one that is imaginatively descended from and modeled on a centuries-old system of rule by "the manifestation of Avalokiteshwara in human form" – implies that Buddhist and constitutional thought may in fact share certain things, among them symmetrical commitments to sovereignty, legitimacy, order, and continuity.

This volume examines the interactions of constitutional and Buddhist traditions in historical and contemporary Asia. This introduction makes the case for why this topic is important, and argues that despite surface incongruities, constitutionalism and Buddhism share certain values, even if they differ in their typical institutional forms. We consider Buddhist idioms that speak to constitutional ideals, arguing that the two discourses address common problems of legitimation and constraint that arise in human polities. Further, we demonstrate that the influence of Buddhism on the constitutional politics of contemporary Asia has been substantial. We then situate the various case studies examined in this book in terms of the interaction and intertwining between Buddhism and various examples of constitutions. We conclude with thoughts on how scholars can extend the findings presented here.

1.1 WHY BUDDHISM AND CONSTITUTIONAL LAW? EXAMINING THE BUDDHIST–CONSTITUTIONAL COMPLEX

As a collective project, this volume takes a twofold approach to the study of Buddhism and constitutions. It examines their nexus as a coming together of disparate traditions and as the integration of complementary ones. It considers the effects of constitutional discourse, institutions, and ideas on the practice of Buddhism and it examines the influence of Buddhist principles, actors, and rationales on the conception and practice of constitutional law. At the same time, the contributors to this volume also reveal that the spaces, discourses, and authorities associated with Buddhism are not always as foreign to those of constitutional thought as one might expect. Although we speak of Buddhism *and* constitutional law, in many ways, it is more accurate to talk about our object of investigation as the *Buddhist–constitutional complex*, an object that can connote both a singular amalgamation as well as a hybrid of distinct components. This play of commonality and difference, integration and separation, is echoed by the volume's authors, who come from a diverse variety of scholarly disciplines including law, Buddhist studies, political science, anthropology, and history.

The contributions that follow examine the Buddhist–constitutional complex in almost all jurisdictions in Asia that have a large Buddhist population.[3] While accurate estimates are difficult to come by, one can say that there are nearly 500 million Buddhists in Asia belonging to a variety of groups.[4] A majority of citizens in Sri Lanka, Myanmar, Thailand, Laos, and Cambodia follow the Theravāda ("the Doctrine of Elders") tradition of Buddhism, which they consider to be the oldest and purest form of the religion. Vietnam, China, Japan, Taiwan, and South Korea also have large numbers of Buddhists, although not enough to constitute an absolute majority.[5] Most Buddhists in these countries observe a version of the Mahāyāna ("the Great Vehicle") tradition of Buddhism, a broad and diverse collection of movements that, unlike the Theravāda tradition, differ widely in their key texts and doctrines. A majority of the population in Bhutan, Mongolia, and Tibet (including the Tibetan diaspora) identify as Buddhists and, for the most part, practice a version of the religion referred to as "the Thunderbolt Vehicle" (Vajrayāna), which originated in India before rising to particular prominence on the Tibetan plateau. Among other things, Vajrayāna Buddhists underscore the importance of esoteric knowledge and the institution of reincarnated monks, known as *tulku* in Tibet.[6]

Although it is difficult to generalize about law, society, or religion across all of these places, we believe these jurisdictions constitute an important and coherent set for comparative consideration. That is because these countries are all settings in which Buddhist communities, doctrines, and institutions have had a formative influence on social and political life, both historically and in the present. To understand the full range of constitutional politics and practice in these places requires familiarity with what Matthew Walton (2016, 4–9) calls the "moral universe" of Buddhism. This universe is grounded in ideas about transmigration and rebirth (*saṃsāra*), intentional action and its consequences (karma), cosmic truth and righteous teachings (dharma), spiritual awakening and those who have achieved it (buddhas and bodhisattvas). In the same way that Christian theological ideas and legal forms have had a major impact on the development and conception of constitutional law in Europe (Berman 1983; Tierney 1982), Buddhist concepts like these – and others discussed in the chapters that follow – have had an important influence on the development and application of national constitutions in Asia.

3 Our chapters directly examine all of the countries identified in this paragraph, except for Laos. Taiwan is discussed by Laliberté in Chapter 14.

4 On these difficulties, see Laliberté in Chapter 14. Our estimates come from www.pewforum.org/2012/12/18/global-religious-landscape-buddhist/.

5 According to the Pew Research Center, China is home to roughly half of the world's Buddhists: www.pewforum.org/2012/12/18/global-religious-landscape-buddhist/.

6 Vajrayāna is also understood to be a branch of the Mahāyāna. For those who would like more information about Buddhism and its major divisions, there are a number of good general introductions to Buddhism, among them: Gethin 1998; Harvey 2013; Lopez and Miles 2017; Prebish and Keown 2006; Strong 2002.

These jurisdictions have also given rise to a variety of genres and ideologies of legality that one might call "Buddhist law," about which more will be said below.

While we do not assert that discussions of constitutional law ought to be shaped by a strong bifurcation between "Asian values" and "Western" ones (Bauer and Bell 1999), we do argue that a full and complete understanding of constitutional law in many parts of Asia demands a fuller understanding of Buddhism. This includes the ways in which declaredly Buddhist rationales, narratives, and textual forms, along with Buddhist clerics and organizations, have shaped how governments, judiciaries, and everyday people understand the nature and purpose of constitutional projects. Moreover, we further insist that a rigorous understanding of Buddhism, particularly since the mid-twentieth century, requires an awareness of how the rise of constitution-based national polities – the most common form of legal–political governance in the world – have affected and often altered how Buddhists conceive their own structures and practices of self-administration. We thus see a conversation between two large historical "normative social practices" (Wallace 2014, 332) that shapes both.

1.2 BUDDHISM AND CONSTITUTIONAL LAW TODAY

To date, the kind of two-way conversation our authors present here has been relatively rare, among both scholars of Buddhism and scholars of constitutional law. With some important exceptions, scholars of Buddhism have not engaged with the literature on comparative constitutional law, and vice versa. This lack of scholarly engagement is all the more obvious when one considers the abundance of important scholarship examining the interactions of religion and constitutional law in other jurisdictions, most notably those with majority Christian or Muslim populations.[7]

One should not mistake this academic neglect for a lack of importance. As the chapters in this volume demonstrate, Buddhism plays a major role in Asia's constitutional cultures. Buddhist monks and lay activists have been central agents of constitutional change, engaging in "Buddhist legal activism" and "Buddhist-interest litigation" throughout the continent (Schonthal and Ginsburg 2016). Monk-led groups like the Bodu Bala Sena (BBS) in Sri Lanka or the Association for the Protection of Race and Religion (Ma Ba Tha)[8] in Myanmar have made legal activism and constitutional politics a key feature of their nationalist agendas (Frydenlund 2017; Walton and Aung Tun 2017–2018; Schonthal 2016b). Political regimes in China, Thailand, Myanmar, Vietnam, and South Korea have mandated

[7] Since 1970, at least thirty-four books have been written looking explicitly at the interactions of Islam and constitutional law, and at least nineteen books that focus primarily on constitutions and Christianity. An even greater body of work has thought to theorize the links between liberal constitutionalism and religion more generally.

[8] In 2018, the group renamed itself the Buddha Dhamma Charity Foundation.

the creation of constitution-like charters for Buddhist groups, in large part as ways to preempt any political and legal activism on the part of would-be Buddhist activists (Borchert 2020; Kyaw 2019; Larsson 2020; Liu 2020; Nathan 2018). Even in Japan, where strong expressions of religious identity are generally frowned upon in politics, the Buddhist organization Soka Gakkai has exerted a disproportionate influence on constitutional negotiations, largely through its affiliated political party Komeito (McLaughlin 2021).

Today, six of the seven Buddhist-majority countries in Asia (Myanmar, Sri Lanka, Thailand, Cambodia, Laos, and Bhutan) grant Buddhism special status or recognition in their constitutions, using a wide variety of formulae.[9] Article 9 of Sri Lanka's Constitution, for example, gives to Buddhism the "foremost place" and obliges the government to "protect and foster the Buddha Sāsana." The Constitution of Cambodia makes Buddhism the "religion of the state" and includes the country's two chief monks in its "Royal Council of the Throne," charged with choosing the monarch.[10] Bhutan's Constitution describes Buddhism as the "spiritual heritage of Bhutan" and makes it a matter of state policy to promote a society "rooted in a Buddhist ethos and universal human values."[11] Even socialist Laos revised its constitution in 2003 to provide that "the State respects and protects all lawful activities of Buddhists and of followers of other religions, [and] mobilizes and encourages Buddhist monks and novices as well as the priests of other religions to participate in activities that are beneficial to the country and people."[12] The 2017 Thai Constitution remains one of the most verbose on the topic, declaring not only that the king must be a Buddhist (sect. 7) but that the state should "support and protect Buddhism and other religions," which it glosses in the following way:

> In supporting and protecting Buddhism, which is the religion observed by the majority of Thai people for a long period of time, the State should promote and support education and dissemination of *dharmic* principles of Theravada Buddhism for the development of mind and wisdom development, and shall have measures and mechanisms to prevent Buddhism from being undermined in any form. The State should also encourage Buddhists to participate in implementing such measures or mechanisms. (sect. 67)

Visible in this paragraph are references to Buddhist history, soteriology, and political philosophy which have fed into Thailand's political culture and continue to define

[9] Of majority-Buddhist countries, only Mongolia does not mention Buddhism in its Constitution, perhaps because it was drafted in 1991 immediately following seventy years of Soviet domination.

[10] Art. 43. and Art. 13, respectively. Cambodia's constitution also obligates the state to "promote and develop Pali schools and Buddhist institutes," Art. 68.

[11] Art. 3.1 and Art. 9.20, respectively. In addition, Art. 2.1 provides that the King must be a Buddhist and Schedule 1 provides for Buddhist symbols in the national insignia and flag.

[12] Const. Lao People's Democratic Republic (1991, rev. 2003), Art. 9. See Bui (2021).

it in the present. In Thailand, as in other places, Buddhism remains closely bound up in the design, interpretation, and politics of constitutional law and practice.

1.3 MAPPING THIS VOLUME

The chapters that follow present the landscape of the Buddhist–constitutional complex in Asia. Given the relative absence of such mapping to date, the areas and topics we identify ought to be considered, for the most part, initial forays; broad areas of study that invite further exploration by scholars. The intellectual cartography undertaken here was conducted collaboratively between January and May 2021, in the midst of the Covid-19 pandemic, as part of an online workshop series in which all of the contributing authors participated, along with other scholars who generously contributed as discussants and commentators.

As a group, we explored a broad range of questions: what have been the roles of Buddhist monks, activist groups, and other religious actors in influencing constitutional changes? In what ways might constitution-making processes transform the practice and institutions of Buddhism in Asia? Do existing models in the study of religion and constitutional law adequately explain the dynamics of Buddhism and constitutional law in this region? How do Buddhist-inspired interpretations of public law differ from those of other interpretative traditions? Are there links across borders in the region, either in terms of borrowed concepts or religious networks, that shape constitutional thought and action? What historical antecedents and Buddhist doctrinal principles help us predict or understand these trends? Although the workshop series was, to the best of our knowledge, the first one dedicated to the topic of Buddhism and constitutional law, this intellectual endeavor would not have been possible were it not for the important foundations in the study of Buddhism and law laid down by other scholars, many of whom participated in the workshop and others who crowd the texts and bibliographies of the pages to follow.[13]

In the remainder of this introduction, we present a preliminary conceptual framework for the broader mapping of the Buddhist–constitutional complex. In the next section, we look to the orienting terms of our inquiry, Buddhism and constitutional law, which are themselves the subjects of perpetual definitional contestation. While we do not claim to resolve these contests, we nevertheless hope to give some sense of how these terms are used and inflected by the authors of this volume, and by Buddhist actors on the ground. Doing so requires that we disaggregate our binary into four, including two "-isms" and two forms of law: Buddhism and Buddhist law, and constitutionalism and constitutional law. After developing this framework, we next situate the various contributions in terms of this broad matrix.

[13] In addition to the authors whose names appear in this volume, other contributors and commentators are mentioned in the acknowledgements.

1.4 BUDDHISM AND CONSTITUTIONAL LAW: SETTING THE TERMS

At first glance, the conjunctive phrase "Buddhism and constitutional law" seems to suggest the coming together of two different sets of institutions, persons, ideas, and practices: some associated prima facie with Buddhism (such as monasteries, monks, meditation, and merit-making) and others with national constitutions (such as laws, legislators, and litigation). The field of view is, of course, more complicated than this, given the many definitions and referents associated with each of the terms as well as their inconsistent and variable use in different contexts.

Things get even messier when one projects the topic back into history. Somewhat confoundingly, premodern "Buddhist" texts do not speak about "Buddhism," but about a variety of other topics, including the dispensation (*sāsana*), the teaching (dharma), the words of the Buddha (*buddhavacana*), and other matters. "Constitution" does not fare much better. Even granting that "constitution" is a modern legal category, D. Christian Lammerts points out in his chapter that the types of Buddhist law that we would instinctively want to call constitutional *avant la lettre* do not appear to have been conceived as a distinct, separate domain of law in the same way that constitutional law is in the Western legal tradition. The laws that pronounce on institutions, processes, and offices of governance are not elevated as a separate body of "higher law" but are rather integrated with a miscellany of other matters: rules about witchcraft, tolls, taxes, rituals, bathing, animals, ordeals, and many others. The mass of "law-stuff" (Llewelyn and Hoebel 1941) in the premodern polities of Asia is far more variegated than that found in any modern rational–legal code.

The categorical challenges we struggle with here are similar to those that French and Nathan (2014) struggled with in their path-breaking volume *Introduction to Buddhism and Law*, where they also noted instability and dissensus around the categories contained in their title. An original intellectual sin – for some anyway – inheres in their volume as it does in ours: to speak of "Buddhism" or "law" as though they were coherent objects spanning regions and epochs is to imply a misleading consistency encompassing what can be highly disparate textual, ritual, and philosophical traditions.

What gives us some comfort, however, is that we scholars are not the only ones generalizing. As the subsequent chapters reveal, the legal and discursive fiction of a singular dispensation is one shared by most of the actors described in this volume. The protagonists in these chapters speak about a coherent community, lineage, and scriptural tradition associated with the Buddha, even if they mean very different things. To examine the Buddhist–constitutional complex is, therefore, both to rely on and transgress designations: to look for constitutions within fields designated as Buddhist; to look for Buddhism in fields designated as constitutional; and to attend carefully to how such acts of designation affect the lives of persons in particular places and times.

For those unfamiliar with Buddhism, we offer some preliminary details, concededly as generalizations, which might help frame the chapters to come. For those unfamiliar with constitutional law, we undertake an equally cursory overview.

1.5 BUDDHISM

As noted above, Buddhism constitutes one of the largest religions in Asia, and roughly 7 percent of the global population identifies with it. As with all religious traditions, Buddhism entails a range of different practices, some of which bear little similarity to each other. Nevertheless, a set of core ideas can be found in most manifestations. As the name suggests, all forms of Buddhism aver the existence of a special set of beings who discover the laws of the cosmos and, through so doing, become buddhas (literally, "awakened ones"). Some versions of Buddhism, particularly the Vajrayāna, identify many different buddhas who are thought to populate the universe at any one time. Other versions, such as Theravāda, underscore the extreme rarity of buddhahood and focus primarily on the central importance of a single historical buddha, an ancient South Asian prince named Siddhartha Gautama, who is credited with teaching the truths he discovered to humankind. This is the figure to whom we refer when we use the definite article and a capital B, *the* Buddha.

Although Buddhists venerate a variety of buddhas and other advanced beings on the path to buddhahood (called bodhisattvas), they will also affirm the importance of *the* Buddha as the awakened teacher who is closest to us in space-time, having lived "only" 2,500 years ago in the vicinity of what is today the Indian state of Bihar and Southern Nepal.[14] During his eighty years of life, the Buddha delivered a series of sermons explaining how the universe worked and how humans ought to behave. Those teachings – collectively referred to as the dharma – are thought to contain, in an abbreviated form cognizable by humans, the key truths of the cosmos (also referred to as the dharma), which might be (inadequately) summarised as follows:

> The cosmos, and all things in it, are guided by cycles of creation and destruction. Sentient beings similarly undergo countless cycles of birth, life, and death in an ongoing process called *saṃsāra* (literally "wandering"). One's journey through *saṃsāra* is not random but determined by volitional actions (karma) that one undertakes. Those who undertake meritorious actions will gain benefits including rewards in this and/or future lifetimes, while those who act immorally will suffer more. These cycles of rebirth and re-death, while they contain many pleasurable things, must in the final analysis be understood to be painful or stressful because even the greatest pleasures are ultimately temporary and impermanent. Therefore

[14] This is true for most, but not all, traditions of Buddhism. In particular, Pure Land Buddhism, a form of Mahāyāna, tends to focus its devotions on a different Buddha named Amitābha, who is imagined to be "close" in other ways. On Pure Land Buddhism generally, see Yu (2014).

one's ultimate goal should be to exit the cycle of *saṃsāra*. By following the teachings of the Buddha one can move toward nirvana, the ultimate "extinguishing" of one's rebirth in *saṃsāra*, in this lifetime or in a future life.

Beyond these core principles, tremendous variation exists. In the Theravāda tradition, for example, the goals of Buddhist practice tend to be the achievement of a better rebirth through meritorious actions (which include everyday moral conduct as well as acts of donation to build Buddhist monuments or support monastics). The progressive improvement of one's rebirths and strict adherence to the dharma, it is thought, will lead ultimately to nirvana. Mahāyāna traditions of Buddhism, by contrast, often emphasize the nearer-term achievement of bodhisattva-hood, a process of awakening in which one vows to defer individual nirvana in order to help other sentient beings attain salvation.

In all schools of Buddhism, the journey toward a better rebirth or awakening requires a combination of moral practices and techniques of mental cultivation. In many, but not all, traditions, these are thought to be most fully embodied in the community of monks and nuns (the sangha) who "go forth" from the normal life of a layperson and are ritually reborn as "sons and daughters of the Buddha."[15] In Southern and Himalayan Asia, Buddhist monks tend to be celibate; practices vary in Northeast Asia in this regard. On entry into the sangha, monastics are, at least in theory, expected to follow special rules which tend be based on the code of monastic law called the Vinaya Piṭaka ("the Basket of Discipline"), which contains rules of monastic conduct and organization that are considered to have been originally enunciated by the Buddha.[16] In most traditions of Buddhism, fully-ordained monks (*bhikkhus*) and nuns (*bhikkhunīs*) are charged with preserving the Buddha's entire dispensation of teachings, practices, and material artifacts such as relics and temples. They are therefore regarded as embodiments of and authorities on the Buddha's legacy.

1.6 BUDDHIST LAW

Although notions of law and legality appear throughout Buddhist traditions, there is no single phrase in premodern Buddhist texts that perfectly approximates the

[15] While there is a long and vibrant history of Buddhist nuns in Asia, the status of Buddhist nuns (*bhikkhunī*) today differs according to the schools of Buddhism, national policies, and local communities. There is a large literature on Buddhist nuns in modern Asia, including (Arai 1999; Cheng 2006; Heirman 2011; Kawanami 2013; Mrozik 2009; Salgado 2013; Seeger 2018).

[16] Although often referred to in the singular, the Vinaya Piṭaka has survived from the ancient period in six relatively complete versions, preserved in the languages of Pali, Sanskrit, Chinese, and Tibetan. Three of these versions are used by Buddhist monastics today: the Dharmaguptaka Vinaya predominates in China and Taiwan; the Mūlasarvāstivāda Vinaya recensions are used by monastics following Tibetan and Mongolian traditions, and the Pali Vinaya is used in the Theravāda sanghas that predominate in Southern Asia. It is worth noting that the practical importance and/or presumed centrality of the Vinaya differs among forms of Buddhism and monastic groups. On the history and variety of Vinaya texts see (Clarke 2015; Liu and Andrews 2017; Heirman 2007; Kieffer-Pülz 2021–2022).

English collocation "Buddhist law." The absence of such a phrase in emic discourse does not mean, however, that Buddhists failed to produce written codes and institutions that claimed to uphold and implement the teachings of the Buddha. The very idea of dharma – a term that encompasses both the law of the cosmos and the instructions of the Buddha – suggests the possibility of pairing transcendent and human injunctions in ways similar to those observed in European legal history. In the same way that lawmakers in early-modern Europe claimed to align the law of God and the law of man, or natural law and temporal law, so too did lawmakers in Asia claim to align dharma and temporal law.

How law actually worked to influence behaviour in historical Asia, dharmically or otherwise, is a vast topic for which we have little reliable evidence. What we have are various types of prescriptive texts. In his chapter, Lammerts identifies three interlacing "environments of 'Buddhist law'" operative in pre-colonial Southeast Asia. The first is *vinaya*, a term that, as used by monastics, refers not only to the rules of the Vinaya Piṭaka, but to the larger corpus of monastic regulations that sits around it, including so-called monastic constitutions that have served as guiding legal charters for monastics living in Sri Lanka, Tibet, and South Korea (Jansen 2018; Kaplan 2016; Schonthal 2021a; B. Sullivan 2020). The second environment is *dhammsattha*, a genre of legal treatises apparent in mainland Southeast Asia from the second millennium, which provided rules and jurisprudential principles for kings, judges, and other "good persons" responsible for resolving disputes (Baker and Phongpaichit 2016; Ishii 1986; Lammerts 2018). The third environment is *rājasattha*, royal orders that claimed to align worldly rule with Buddhist principles (Huxley 1997; Prasert Na Nagara and Griswold 1992; Zan 2000).

For Lammerts, all three environments are forms of Buddhist law because

> [e]ach entails a distinct relation between what may be called "Buddhism" and "law." Certain general features common to these environments include: 1) (usually) a form of material embodiment and circulation in writing; 2) an orientation toward the authority of a foundational, preternatural, text (the speech of a buddha, a cosmic treatise, or the speech of a king); and 3) a rationale or jurisprudential logic whereby the normative program of such legalism is imagined to have the capacity to enable or perpetuate, via different mechanics, the religion of Buddhism itself.

Although Lammerts applies this analysis only to the premodern polities of Southeast Asia, the framework could be extended further to encompass other genres of law in the contemporary period and other parts of Asia. By the terms of Lammerts' definitions, many of the national constitutions described earlier in this introduction would also qualify as "Buddhist law," as would the many types of statutes and administrative ordinances used in contemporary Asia to regulate Buddhist monks or protect Buddhist pilgrimage sites (Schonthal 2017–2018).

It is important to note that, in many contexts, the question of whether a given law qualifies as "Buddhist" is itself contested. One of the most striking examples of this can be seen in debates about the Buddhist character of the laws issued by the seventh-century Tibetan king Songtsen Gampo. Scholars disagree as to whether or not the body of laws promulgated by the putative founder of Tibet were originally conceived as embodying Buddhist principles. Some, such as Fernanda Pirie (2017, 406), insist that the earliest laws of Tibet were "not linked in any significant way with Buddhist principles" at their inception, but were retrospectively understood as such as part of an ideological project in the tenth and eleventh centuries to provide moral certainty in an era of political chaos. Others, such as French (1995), along with a variety of Tibetan jurists and scribes, prefer to read the legal archives of Tibet in a strongly Buddhist light.

Two chapters in this volume reflect on this debate and its implications. Martin Mills, whose perspective leans toward that of Pirie, characterizes the post-hoc Buddhicizing of Tibet's founding laws as a kind of "constitutional mythology" underwritten by hidden Buddhist virtues. According to this mythology, even those forms of royal law that seem to contradict the dharma are actually "skilful means" for governance, virtuous "tricks" that embody a deeper dharmic quality which is invisible to untrained individuals.

In her chapter, Berthe Jansen comes at the question of Tibetan law's Buddhist quality from another angle. Writing about monastic constitutions (*bca'yig*), she demonstrates that even this ostensibly most religious form of law cannot be understood in the absence of royal law. The texts reflect clear mutual influences. Monastic law always existed in the shadow of royal law, and temporal authorities frequently asserted jurisdiction in cases of serious crimes. She notes that "the very fact that various Indic Buddhist normative sources emphasize the sangha's legal autonomy is exactly because it was regularly being challenged." At the same time, monks did enjoy a good deal of both legal and practical autonomy, far more than did ordinary Tibetans.

1.7 CONSTITUTION, CONSTITUTIONAL LAW, CONSTITUTIONALISM

In the same way that Buddhism and Buddhist law implicate an unruly collection of referents, so too does the constitution have its own sets of semantically generative terms. The core term, *constitution*, itself is subject to multiple definitions. Modern usage emphasizes the importance of writing, focusing on a document or set of documents that declares the identity of a given community, organizes its structures of governing power, defines foundational norms, and authorizes further acts of rulemaking. Understood in this way, constitutions may be said to exist across a broad sweep of times and places. More narrowly understood, the term constitution ought to be reserved for the basic laws of nation-states that developed from the late eighteenth century onward. In this volume we keep both denotations in play: holding the definitional door ajar such that the term constitution refers both to the various types of foundational law used to regulate premodern polities and Buddhist monasteries, as well as to modern national constitutions, depending on usage (e.g., Schonthal 2021b).

We take a similarly accommodative stance toward the status of writing and the long-standing question of whether the term constitution ought to apply only to written codes or whether it might refer more generally to the broader congeries of written and unwritten rules and durable norms that exert strong influences on polities over time. Scholars frequently distinguish between the "large-C" constitution, which is the formal text that is now a feature of most countries, and the "small-c" body of broader norms and practices that actually structure political and legal behaviour. The latter might include formal rules, embodied in statutes and rules of legislative procedure, but also unwritten norms. We find all these usages implicated in the chapters that follow. While a written code, such as that which governs the Chogye monastic order in Korea, might exemplify a form of constitutional writing, our authors also analyze formative and perennial ideals that shape political culture, such as the ideal of *barami* in Thailand, which links political power to moral perfection and karmic consequences.

Linked to the idea of constitutions is the idea of *constitutionalism*. Constitutionalism, most agree, denotes the normative ideal that rulers should be constrained by a consistent set of norms, embodying commitment across time. Such commitments and limitations, scholars have argued, make political life possible by providing structures for joint action (Holmes 1995). Limited government is, in the modern conception, good government. The particular values associated with constitutionalism vary with the analyst, but generally involve some notion of human dignity or liberty.

Constitutional law is central to the practice of modern constitutionalism, reflecting the importance of legal constraint of government. The famous British jurist Albert Venn Dicey (1907) had a capacious definition of constitutional law as "all rules which directly or indirectly affect the distribution or the exercise of the sovereign power of the state." This definition seems to allow for informal or unwritten rules, of the kind embodied in every religious tradition. More narrowly, one might define constitutional law as the understanding of a constitution generated by lawyers and judges in the course of practices of adjudication and interpretation. So understood, many premodern Buddhist polities did not have constitutional law, but others may have had some analogs. After all, the idea that rulers should be limited by law may appear in many other cultural artifacts: philosophy and storytelling, ritual and art.

As this discussion suggests, we deploy a range of terms that specify the phenomena classified as constitutional. For our purposes, constitution refers to the fundamental norms of society, whether embodied in writing or other unwritten norms. Constitutionalism refers to the idea that these norms constrain the exercise of power. And constitutional law is the use of legal forms to express either of these concepts.

We use the adjective constitutional in purposefully broad ways, to suggest a link with one or more of these phenomena.

As should now be apparent, our approach is squarely within the tradition of what Hirschl (2014) calls comparative constitutional studies. That is, we do not focus strictly on the domains of the written constitution, or the disciplinary perspective of law. Rather, we understand constitutions broadly as a set of social practices that are best approached through interdisciplinary inquiry. At the same time, we distinguish constitutionalism as a value-imbued theory of normative constraint, that has powerful resonance in our era.

1.8 BUDDHISM AND CONSTITUTIONS, PAST AND PRESENT

Although this volume invokes the terms constitution and constitutionalism in deliberately broad ways, we are also cautious about reading contemporary categories back into history. That is because the terms Buddhism and constitutional law, even interpreted in the broadest sense, also seem to implicate a variety of other terms which do not travel very well when applied to the past, especially across geographical contexts. These categories include things like "religion," "state," and "secular" (Asad 2003; Day 2002).

The reverse direction of chronological travel should also be treated with care: what does it mean to invoke ancient Buddhist motifs, imagery, and ideals – such as the notion of *dharmarāja* or righteous kingship – in a contemporary context? Can we assume that these terms carry with them their older connotations, or should we think of them as rhetorical shells whose meanings owe more to the present than to their glossing in earlier manuscripts? As our workshop discussions revealed, thinking across the modern–premodern divide is always a delicate dance of difference and identity. Indeed, as David Engel reminded the workshop in his comments, the story is even more complex than that, given that there are many variants of the premodern just as there are "multiple modernities" (Eisenstadt 2000).

As with the Buddhist–constitutional complex, the inquiries into past also evoke complex patterns of similarity and difference. Consider for example one of the most basic binaries that inhere in many of the chapters that follow: the binary between something like religion and something like politics. Given recent critiques of secularism and the category of religion (Agrama 2012; Hurd 2015; W. F. Sullivan et al. 2015), as well as a recognition that the modern state has deeply theological origins (Bourdin 2010; Nelson 2010), one might be justified in feeling sceptical of inquiries that look for conjunctions between something like a religious and political domain prior to modernity. And yet, one does find a variety of terms and discourses within the premodern world that appear to carve similar discursive divisions in their imagination of society. Premodern Buddhist polities did not have a doctrine of secularism per se, but they drew on other logics of separation that, in various places and times, could be used to cleave apart domains of authority associated with the Buddha's commands and those associated with monarchs.

Ideas of virtuous kingship are important in this regard because they frequently implicate a distinction between two kinds of activities: those necessary for ensuring social order and justice in a given polity and those necessary for protecting and upholding the Buddha's teachings. In the Pali sources that influenced Theravāda Buddhist thought, for example, one finds a distinction between the "wheel of the dharma" (*dhamma-cakka*) and the "wheel of power" (*āṇā-cakka*), both of which were necessary for a well-functioning society, but which monks and kings were imagined to embody respectively (Gokhale 1969; Reynolds 1972).[17] Similar distinctions – for example, between the "orders of the king" and the "orders of the Buddha" – were also taken up throughout Southern Asian polities over time, often in the context of discussions about righteous rulers (Ladwig and Kourilsky 2017–2018; Larsson 2016; Schonthal 2021a). Two of the most common terms of praise ascribed to rulers – "wheel turner" (*cakravartin*) and "righteous king" (*dharmarāja*) – only make sense because they fuse otherwise juxtaposed notions of temporal and otherworldly authority, royal power, and moral restraint. In this sense they appear to incorporate, if only implicitly, quasi-constitutionalist ideas of normative limitation on the actions of the monarch in the service of cosmic law.

On the Tibetan plateau, one finds a similar contrast between *chos* and *srid*. *Chos* implicated the timeless laws of dharma, while *srid* referred to the rules issued by kings and other powerful elites, which governed relations in this lifetime (Cüppers et al. 2004; Reugg 2014). The system of religio-political control by lamas came to be known as the *chos srid gdan* or "dual system" that united *chos* and *srid*, in a manner not dissimilar to the ideal *dharmarāja* (a title also used to praise Tibetan monarchs).

While these kinds of arrangements do not conform to modern categories of the religious and the secular, they nevertheless suggest some awareness that monastic and monarchical authority come from different and analytically separable sources. Moreover, twentieth-century lawmakers and politicians have used these terms to justify polices that aim to separate those activities thought to be proper to Buddhism from those which are thought to be proper to statecraft. In mainland Southeast Asia, for example, the distinction between *dhamma-* and *ānā-cakkas* has been used to rationalize monks' denial of the right to vote or to hold public office (Larsson 2016), about which more will be said below. Similarly, Tibetan lawmakers drew heavily on the binary of *chos* and *srid* to translate the idea of secularism in the context of recent debates about the Charter of Tibetans-in-Exile (Brox 2010 and 2012).

In at least one case, the dharmic principle of *anicca* or impermanence has been used as a resource to undermine temporal law. Perhaps rationalizing his country's continuous constitutional turnover since 1932, the late King Rama IX of Thailand characterized constitutions as impermanent human creations, subject to replacement as conditions demand (Harding 2007). This illustrates another kind of

[17] See also Collins' (1998, 473–4) important remarks on the relative rareness of this pairing in Pali literature.

common rhetorical move, which is to characterize the formal constitution as a foreign, Western form, to be distinguished from the true and eternal dharma.

1.9 BUDDHIST CONSTITUTIONALISM?

Given that Buddhism and constitutional thought both draw upon categories that distinguish more-than-worldly authority from merely-worldly authority, idealised systems of order (dharma, rule of law) from practical acts of governing, the question then becomes how are these things brought together in particular forms of governance and legal texts? Put another way, what does it mean to both accommodate and align the wheels of dharma and power, or *chos* and *srid*, in a *constitutional* mode?

One way to talk about this merger in the context of national constitutions is to use the language of *Buddhist constitutionalism*, a formula that implies a purposeful comparison with other variants, such as secular or Islamic constitutionalism. The phrase also implies that there is something distinctive, vis-à-vis other constitutional variants, about the history and orientation of such a project. In an initial definition, Schonthal described Buddhist constitutionalism as

> attempts to use written constitutions and other basic laws to organize power in ways that protect and preserve Buddhist teachings and institutions, especially the institution of Buddhist monasticism, the *saṅgha*. (2017, 707)

According to this definition, what links together the various contemporary constitutional projects in Buddhist-majority states is two things: an impulse to safeguard Buddhism in general, and a concern with the sangha in particular. Schonthal argues that a defining feature of this kind of constitutional project is the question of "properly structuring the relationship between governing elites and Buddhist monks – each of whom have, historically, claimed special responsibilities and authority for the protection of the religion" (2017, 708).

An advantage of this formulation of Buddhist constitutionalism is that it acknowledges the kinds of entanglements that emerge between what we moderns would call religion and public law (Hirschl 2010). It defines the project in active terms, as a set of undertakings designed to generate, implement, or expand the promotion of Buddhism through, in this case, national constitutions. Such a definition admits, even normalizes, the possibility of monks engaged in law-making, or reincarnated *tulku* (such as the Dalai Lama) serving as heads of state. Yet, for some, it directs attention too strongly toward certain Buddhist authorities, namely the sangha, rather than others, such as lay elites or Buddhist political theory more generally.

Khemthong Tonsakulrungruang (2020) has argued that the study of "Buddhist constitutionalism" ought to take more seriously the profound influence and strategic deployment of Buddhist notions of karma and dharmic kingship on political behaviour in Thailand. He argues that one should view the constitutional history of Thailand as reflecting a contest between *two* forms of constitutionalism, a

Buddhist constitutionalism that has roots going back to the thirteenth century, and a liberal democratic version that emerges with the 1932 revolution (see also McCargo 2004). From this perspective, a modern project of Buddhist constitutionalism might mean imbuing the constitution with normative values associated with the dharma and trying to secure a righteous ruler who will act in accordance with internalized norms of appropriate restraint. Empowering a wise ruler rather than constraining a bad one thus serves as the focal point for Buddhist constitutionalism.

In her chapter, Eugénie Mérieau also notes the amalgamated structure of Buddhist constitutionalism in Thailand, albeit from a different angle. Examining the history of constitution-making in Siam/Thailand from 1932, Mérieau demonstrates the deep interfusion of Buddhist and European ideas of sovereignty, kingship, law, and constitution that make up the country's constitutional monarchy. This "bricolage" of legal authority (see also, Mérieau 2021) did not so much evolve naturally as through careful design. As Mérieau shows, Thailand's early constitutionalists, such as Pridi Banomyong, purposefully merged evolving theories of Thai constitutionalism with traditional notions of Buddhist kingship and ritual authority. Indeed, they went so far as to encourage the ritual, symbolic interpretation of the physical constitution as a sacred text akin to the Buddhist canon. Read through this history, the notion of Buddhist constitutionalism takes on an entirely new valence, in which the union of the two terms suggests not so much the support of Buddhism through constitutional measures, as the acts of grounding, rationalizing, and legitimating the entire edifice of the modern constitution itself within the framework of Buddhist cosmology and morality.

Yet another example of the way in which conjoined Buddhist and liberal logics can animate constitutional practice can be seen in the chapter by Richard W. Whitecross, who examines the relationship of Buddhism and national constitution-making in Bhutan. According to Whitecross, the "dual system of governance" established by Bhutan's theocratic founder, Zhabdrung Ngawang Namgyal, established a conceptual separation between religious and temporal power. When Bhutan produced its first written constitution in 2008, constitutionalizing the monarchy and introducing elections for the first time, the drafters reached back to the Zhabdrung's ideas to imbue the Himalayan kingdom with a Buddhist mantle. At the same time, they removed monks from having a direct role in governance, leading to a number of unintended consequences and a degree of popular unease about the constitutional status of Buddhism in this deeply religious country.

Iselin Frydenlund further expands the semantic range of Buddhist constitutionalism. Examining the evolution of constitutional law in post-independence Myanmar, she calls attention to the broader ambit of Buddhist constitutionalism beyond explicit concessions given in the constitutional text. In Frydenlund's view, state support for Buddhism can also be entrenched constitutionally through statutes, unwritten norms, and more subtle rhetorical genuflexions to the preeminence of

Buddhism, such as the calendrical conventions used in Myanmar's laws, which record the dates of legislation with reference to the birth of the Buddha. More provocatively, Frydenlund finds the presence of Buddhist constitutionalism in legal language and practices that purport to separate religion from politics in impartial ways. The very forms of secularism enacted by Myanmar's constitution, she argues, give preferential treatment to Buddhism by carving up "secular" and "religious" issues in ways that indirectly advantage Buddhist groups or adopt Buddhist perspectives on the proper role of religious clergy in voting, campaigning, and holding public office, and other political processes. Even attempts at separation cannot escape the deeply Buddhist political idiom of the majority population. As she notes, though, these practices of Buddhist statecraft have been challenged by ethnic and religious minority communities in Myanmar. The 2021 military coup ushered in a new period of contestation in this regard, as the democratic opposition adopted a new "Federal Democracy Charter" that declared an end to Buddhist constitutional privileges, while the military junta has positioned itself as the protector of Buddhism.

1.10 DIRECTIONS OF INFLUENCE: BUDDHIST CONSTITUTIONALISM AND CONSTITUTIONAL BUDDHISM

There is little question that Buddhist texts, institutions, and ideals have influenced the design, interpretation, and practice of constitutional law in contemporary Asia. As noted, similar arguments have long been made about Christianity in the European context by scholars such as Harold Berman and Brian Tierney. They and others argued even more explicitly that constitutional thought in the West, and the liberal constitutional tradition more generally, grew out of Christian theological principles and acts of ecclesiastical reformation in medieval Europe. Less well studied, both in Europe and in Asia, are the effects of "constitutional practice" (Schonthal 2016a, 11) – by which we mean the various, often high-profile, acts of drafting, implementing, and interpreting contemporary constitutional law – on the practice and institutional organization of Buddhism.

One example can be found in Krishantha Fedricks' chapter on Sri Lanka, which highlights how features of constitutional law – its histories, principles, and "linguistic ideologies" – influence the ways in which Buddhism is practiced and understood within a new Buddhist movement on the island. Drawing on his expertise in linguistic anthropology, Fedricks identifies both a conceptual symmetry and a historical continuity between two linguistic ideologies. The first is a "Sinhala-only" ideology that gained momentum in the decades following independence and which led to making Sinhala (rather than English or Tamil) the dominant language in Sri Lanka's 1972 and 1978 constitutions. The second is a "vernacularising" ideology that has been championed by a popular new Buddhist movement in Sri Lanka called Mahamevnāva and which led to Sinhala (rather than Pali) being the preferred language for Buddhist religiosity by that group. This reformist movement,

Fedricks insists, takes inspiration from provisions in Sri Lanka's constitution when creating its own manifestos, which underscore the ultimate goal of creating a transnational *gautama buddha rājya*, or Buddhist state.

Similar vectors of influence, running from national constitutions to Buddhist groups, can also be observed in Japan. Though the country has a long and rich history of engagement with Buddhism (dating back to the "Constitution" of Prince Shotoku of 604 CE), Buddhists in modern and contemporary Japan have operated under two constitutional regimes that marginalized their activities (Thomas 2016). The Meiji Constitution of 1889 enabled the wartime government to prioritize Shintō, while the postwar constitution reacted to that by institutionalizing a very strong separation of church and state. In his chapter on the topic, Levi McLaughlin demonstrates the strong social and cultural impacts that Japan's 1947 Constitution has had on the self-presentation and institutional organization of Buddhist groups. Using two case studies – one looking at the activities of Buddhist clerical training and humanitarian aid programs and the other tracking the development of the highly influential lay Buddhist group Soka Gakkai – McLaughlin stresses the strong social and legal impacts that Japan's modern constitutions have had on the activities of Buddhist organizations. Attention to the nation's constitutions has caused Japan's Buddhists to reorient, revise, and even reconceive their activities in ways that demonstrably conform to constitutional prohibitions against mixing religion with state.

So influential has Japan's Constitution been, that McLaughlin even proposes an alternative pairing of Buddhism and constitutional law from the forms described above: rather than a form of *Buddhist constitutionalism*, which seeks to align state law with Buddhist goals, Japan constitutes a case of *constitutional Buddhism*, the deliberate aligning of Buddhist organizations and activities with a national constitution. Religious organizations have themselves become constitutionalized, as institutional imaginaries flow from state to society (McLaughlin 2019). This illustrates powerfully our theme of mutual interdependence and construction.

1.11 FURTHER ENTANGLEMENTS IN THE BUDDHIST–CONSTITUTIONAL COMPLEX

We do not wish to give the mistaken impression that the only way to conceive of the relationships within the Buddhist–constitutional complex is as vectors of influence running one way or the other, with either Buddhist elements influencing the practice of constitutional law or constitutional prototypes shaping the practice of Buddhism. In many cases the dynamics of influence and integration are more complicated than this, as our designation of the Buddhist–constitutional complex implies. Rather than one domain defining the other, Buddhism and constitutional cultures codevelop and coconstitute each other. For example, in his chapter on Cambodia, Ben Lawrence examines the intermeshed histories of the country's two major Buddhist monastic bodies, the Thammayut and Mahanikay, through the various ways in which those divisions were recognized or occluded in constitutional texts from 1947 onwards. The 1947 Constitution, which appointed the patriarchs of each sect to the Council of the Throne, suggested a balance between the elite and royally affiliated lineage of the Thammayut sect (which had been imported from Siam) and the more populous, home-grown Mahanikay, to which more than 95 percent of monks claimed affiliation – a balance that seemed consequential in the waning days of French influence. When the same arrangement reemerged in the 1993 constitution following periods of control by the military, Khmer Rouge, and Vietnamese, it did not signal equality between the two sects, but rather, competition. By recognizing the two patriarchs in the constitution, lawmakers contributed to hardening sectarian identities, while at the same time obscuring the de facto dominance of the larger and politically connected Mahanikay. In this way, the effects of constitutional provisions were, as Lawrence tells us, "contingent" on complex histories of politics, alliances, elections, and occupation.

A different version of the intermeshing of national and monastic constitution-making can be seen in Mark Nathan's chapter, in the form of what might be called a double clash of constitutional orders: a clash, on the one hand, between the constitutions of South Korea's secular state and those of the country's Buddhist monastic orders; and a clash, on the other hand, between the monastic constitutions of celibate and non-celibate monks within the Chogye order. It is notable that all of these texts were classified using the same word for law, *hon*. The clashes may be more apparent than direct, yielding an impression of disharmony or incompatibility that was mobilized by different parties at different times. Nevertheless, the story Nathan tells – which culminates in an attempted ritual disembowelling on the grounds of the Supreme Court – reminds readers of the overlapping and nested lines of tension that can develop *between and among* forms of state law *and* Buddhist law, national constitutions, and monastic constitutions.

In his chapter on Thailand, Khemthong Tonsakulrungruang reminds readers that, while monks often play important roles in South and Southeast Asian politics, the influence of Buddhism on constitutional politics extends well beyond the impacts of the sangha. Remarking on the sudden rise and influence of unelected "watchdog agencies" in Thai political culture, Khemthong asks why these elitist, conservative, and anti-democratic institutions have been allowed to flourish and, for many, appear to be legitimate. His answer points to a particular concept that has been underlying Thai Buddhism for centuries and which has been usefully appropriated in modern Thai politics. The notion of *barami*, or moral perfection, Khemthong argues, undergirds popular culture in Thailand and feeds into a conservative political mentality that aligns tradition, morality, hierarchy, elitism, and Buddhism with good governance and Thai-ness. At the same time, the doctrine also seems to align democracy, popular sovereignty and free debate with foreignness, Western imperialism, and political chaos. In Khemthong's estimation, Thai-style democracy is *dhammacracy*, a philosophy of governance rooted in the idea that, by virtue of their past karmic merit, a small group of powerful elites has the moral authority to rule over a broader population of less meritorious, less virtuous, less capable people. It is this "*barami*-based" political philosophy, he argues, that explains the elite-centric shape of Thai constitutional culture from 1997 onward.

These analytical and descriptive accounts also have normative implications. Acknowledging a contrast, even an incommensurability, between models of liberal constitutionalism which emanate from "the West" and forms of Buddhist normativity and legality endemic to Asia, Asanga Welikala calls for the creation of alternative models of constitutionalism that might have more global purchase (see also, de Silva Wijeyeratne 2013). These new models, argues Welikala, would have more fidelity to normative and descriptive dimensions of constitutional practice in Asia. They would have to draw both from the fields of "Buddhism and law" and comparative constitutional law to think of alternative paradigms that "could make the constraining function of constitutionalism in its normative dimension more consistent with, and less jarring to, the Buddhist–Asian ethos."

1.12 THE CONSTITUTIONAL REGULATION OF SĀSANA AND SANGHA

Looking at these diverse case studies, it is clear that the Buddhist–constitutional complex in Asia is both similar to and different from the intermeshing of religion and constitutions in other parts of the world. One point of distinction is the understanding of precisely what is being protected when constitution drafters obligate the state to protect "Buddhism," or, as it is commonly referred to in South and Southeast Asia, the Buddha *sāsana* (the "instructions of the Buddha").[18] One legal commission in Sri Lanka, for example, glossed the term *sāsana* as referring to the following:

> the Buddha, the nine other-worldly truths (*dhamma*-s) discovered by the Buddha, the complete teaching of the Buddha (*dhamma*), the jewel of the monks, the limb of Buddhist temples together with forest hermitages and meditation centres, bodhi trees, stupas, image houses, relic palaces, monastic preaching books and [other] books, meeting houses for monks, fields and properties that belong to temples, Buddhist education, the shrines to important deities endowed by Buddhist kings (*devalaya*), female renunciants (*silmātā-s*) and their sanctuaries, the lay persons who have gone to the triple gem for refuge, Buddhist literature, culture and civilisation, Buddhist festivals, processions (*perahæra*), offerings and customs, Buddhist principles (*pratipatti*) and ethics (*ācāra dharma*), as well as those things like this that are basic to [the Sāsana's] cultivation. (Government of Sri Lanka 2002, 15)

[18] On the complexity of the term *sāsana* see Carter (1993).

As one can see in this example, those who draft and interpret laws designed to protect Buddhism, *qua sāsana*, often understand it in different terms than US Supreme Court justices would understand "religion." More than a set of beliefs and practices held by individuals congregating voluntarily as a "church,"[19] the *sāsana* explicitly denotes a broad range of ideas, texts, objects, institutions, properties, and practices. In short, it is a capacious term interpreted, in many cases, as covering the entire ideal and material legacy of the Buddha and his followers.

In addition to being regarded as an abstract and collective noun, Theravāda Buddhists also understand the *sāsana* in a more personalistic and concrete sense: like all things in *saṃsāra*, the *sāsana* is also finite, subject to degeneration and decline and predicted to vanish within the next 2,500 years (Nattier 1991; Turner 2014). In this frame of reference, constitutional mandates to protect the *sāsana* are not simply attempts to prevent damage to an otherwise stable dispensation, but calls to extend Buddhism's existence over time, by actively defending the Buddha's fragile legacy against anything that might hasten the decline that is already underway.

Another point of distinction is the tendency to use constitutional mandates to promote Buddhism as a pretence for inhibiting Buddhist monks from intervening in politics. As mentioned above, the Constitutions of Myanmar, Thailand, Laos, and Bhutan prohibit Buddhist monks from voting or holding public office, in order to protect them from the supposedly profaning impact of politics on what should be a purely "religious" vocation circumscribed by the rules of *vinaya* (Larsson 2015). Although similar restrictions were abandoned in Cambodia, Buddhist monks there have launched pressure campaigns encouraging the government to reintroduce such measures (Lawrence 2022). Analogous dynamics can be found throughout colonial and postcolonial Asia (Streicher 2021a; Brac de la Perrière 2021). This kind of logic, which urges separation of religion and politics in the name of protecting the former against the latter, is, of course, familiar to historians of American constitutional law: similar rationales appear in Madison's "Letter to the Danbury Baptists." The universe of Buddhist constitutionalism, however, gives the separation of sangha and state its own kind of virtuous patina (Frydenlund 2016; Streicher 2021b).

Claims of separation notwithstanding, projects of statecraft in Asia, both old and new, have often engaged in reforming and regulating Buddhist monks. The records left by kings who ruled in premodern Sri Lanka, Myanmar, and Thailand celebrate the monarchs' role in "cleansing" the sangha of impious monks and restructuring the remaining clerics as an orderly, centralized hierarchy (Bechert 1970; Tambiah 1976). As Daigengna Duoer's chapter on early twentieth-century Inner Mongolia reminds us, Japan's imperial government undertook similar projects of monastic manipulation under the sign of purification, using lama education programmes and clerical organizations to reshape the Tibetan and Mongolian clergy in ways that

[19] On "church" as a legal category in US jurisprudence as well as debates over the corporate imagination of religion, see W. F. Sullivan (2020).

cohered with reformist understandings of Buddhism popular in Japan at the time.[20] The region of Inner Mongolia was the site of contested political authority, exposing monasteries to the regulatory approaches of Japan, the Republic of China and, less directly, theocratic government and subsequently communism that took hold in Outer Mongolia.

Leninist governments by definition seek to penetrate all social institutions, but they vary in their particular approaches to doing so. As Ngoc Son Bui demonstrates, the Leninist government of Vietnam has sought to draw legitimacy from Buddhism, while of course coopting and regulating its institutions. The Charter of the Buddhist Sangha of Vietnam mimics constitutional forms while providing a structure for governance of Buddhist institutions. It is, in this sense, an instrument producing constitutional Buddhism of a particular type. As compared with other Leninist regimes, the Vietnamese government has a softer regulatory approach (in part because of the important role of Buddhist institutions in resisting the government of South Vietnam during the Vietnam war), as well as a generally reformist orientation of the government within a one-party framework. But there is no doubt that Buddhist institutions play a subservient role to state-building needs.

The apogee of such attempts might be seen in the various regulations for Buddhist monks promulgated by the People's Republic of China (PRC). With Buddhism the dominant faith among the country's Tibetan and Mongolian minority populations, it was perhaps inevitable that the Chinese Communist Party (CCP) would seek to control and coopt it. But the CCP has been particularly aggressive in recent years, as it has tightened controls over every aspect of Chinese society. One of the mechanisms directed at Buddhist institutions has been the establishment of the Buddhist Association of China, described in detail in the chapter by André Laliberté (see also, Liu 2020). He notes that the Buddhist Association plays both an internal regulatory role as well as one involving external representation. As China has been stymied in acquiring a leadership role in global Buddhist organizations, it has launched its own World Buddhist Forum, in part to accomplish diplomatic goals of bringing Taiwan back into the national fold. This Buddhist diplomacy reflects the seemingly complete subservience of Buddhist institutions to national goals as defined by the Leninist Party-State. Viewed through the prism of contemporary Vietnamese and Chinese laws, then, the modern Buddhist–constitutional complex can be seen not only as touching discourses and imagery that moralise state power, but also those that seemed to routinize, regularize, and reform monastic power.[21]

[20] A similar drive to reform monastic education and forms of knowledge are visible in early modern efforts by kings to edit and compile the collection of texts that can be considered "the word of the buddha," *buddhavacana* (Lammerts 2018, 137–78).

[21] Understood this way, the political-*cum*-religious institution of the reincarnate lama, popular throughout Tibet and Mongolia, might be seen as a perfect synthesis of both inclinations: the spiritualizing of statecraft and the etatization of monasticism.

1.13 IDEALS AND ACTUALITIES IN CONSTITUTIONAL HISTORIES

As is always the case in comparative constitutional studies more generally, investigations of Buddhism and constitutional law must reckon with the distance between what texts say and what humans do, between the ideals of constitutionalism written down and the actual realities about which those ideals claim to speak. In his workshop comments, Mark McClish pointed out that we have no evidence that the pious duties of the king listed in ancient Indian *dharmaśāstra* texts actually functioned as limitations on royal power. Despite a long history of scholars underscoring the moral limits placed on rulers by "sacred" norms and brahmins, the actual behaviour of rulers in premodern India remains an open question. Similar questions were raised by Lammerts, who cautioned scholars against assuming that ideologies of virtuous kingship that appear in early Buddhist texts – notions of *dharmarāja*, *cakravartin*, or bodhisattva – necessarily constrained the behaviour of kings in practice. We simply do not know. Those who are interested in finding premodern forms of Buddhist constitutionalism, Lammerts suggests, should not be spellbound by the images of dharmic kingship that appear throughout Buddhist studies and contemporary politics in Southern Asia, but look for more direct evidence about how law-making actually worked on the ground.

Of course, many legal historians find themselves wrestling with similar dilemmas. Generally speaking, legal archives provide an abundance of normative sources such as codes, court records, and juristic writing that explain what *ought* to happen, but comparatively few sources that help scholars evaluate whether people actually do what the texts demand. Therefore, it is impossible to know whether the various ideals of limited rule laid out in Buddhist texts ever translated into actual constraints on the powerful. Here, methodological concerns found in legal history, in Buddhist studies, and in constitutional studies converge. In recent years, the field of comparative constitutional studies has become increasingly attentive to the deviations between rule-of-law ideals and political actualities (Hirschl 2014). Ideas of illiberal or autocratic constitutions – which have become increasingly relevant to constitutional studies and the current world order – evince a similar scepticism about the relationships between rules and outcomes (Ginsburg and Simpser 2014). They highlight the ways in which textual norms not only deviate from human actions but may in fact serve as ideological cover for the very opposite types of behaviour. This methodological parallax between Buddhist and constitutional studies casts important light on our attempts to locate Buddhist constitutionalism in history. The textual ideals on which scholars rely may serve more as propaganda than guardrails on power.

Among the various benefits of interdisciplinary inquiries into the Buddhist–constitutional complex are the potential sharing of approaches and techniques for thinking about the work of normative texts in the world, beyond the question of whether textual ideals are accurate or reliable indicia of human behaviour. As several scholars in this volume and at the workshop pointed out, the study of constitutions across cultures, geographies, and histories can sensitize scholars of both Buddhism and law to manifold ways in which the rhetoric of normative texts may be interpreted or used: to hide acts of domination, or justify rebellion, or to elevate the importance of one group (e.g., monks or judges) above others (e.g., kings or presidents). At the same time, these kinds of studies should also remind legal historians that, even as pure ideals, legal codes and concepts also influence actors on the ground, even if not in the injunctive way suggested by texts themselves. As Fernanda Pirie urged in her comments, premodern forms of law were not always meant to be practical and enforceable, in the way we understand today. Legal texts are also cosmologies, narratives, ideologies – all which are, themselves, actors in history.[22]

1.14 COMPARATIVE REFLECTIONS

In what ways is the nexus of Buddhism and constitutional law distinctive vis-à-vis other religio–constitutional arrangements, beyond the particularities of *sāsana* and sangha mentioned above? Mills, in his chapter on Tibet, identifies a "core soteriological distinction" between Buddhism and Abrahamic traditions which he sees as essential to legal thinking. In Buddhist traditions, the personal morality of lawmakers, mostly kings, is integral to the legitimacy of law. This is different, he insists, from the monotheistic faiths, which underscore the divine origin of proper law that exists apart from the individual.

Of course, Buddhist polities also had a theory of transcendent law, dharma, that would ideally constrain the behaviour of humans. As with notions of divine law in Christian or Islamic traditions, the consequences for transgressing dharmic principles were, in the first instance, soteriological. Those who flouted dharma risked a variety of unpleasant outcomes: the prolonging of *saṃsāra*, an inferior rebirth (as an animal or hungry ghost), even a reincarnation in hell. While some readers might want to dismiss these threats as imaginary, one can nevertheless assume that for many Buddhists the cosmic laws of dharma are understood to be no less "real," and perhaps more reliable, than the laws of kings or countries (Engel and Engel 2010).

Buddhism has likely shaped the expression and exercise of power in other ways as well. Whether or not premodern kings or contemporary politicians actually altered their behaviour out of concern for dharma's laws, the idea that rulers should govern in dharmic ways has undoubtedly provided ideological parameters for the normalization and presentation of political authority. As with other religious traditions, rulers in Buddhist-majority polities take pains to advertise their fidelity to local expectations about the nature of moral rule (Blackburn 2017; Holt 1996; Schober 2011).

[22] On the "legal cosmology" of Tibetan Buddhists, see French (1995).

Critics and reformers may also appeal to the laws of dharma to call for political change (Bowie 2014; Ladwig 2014). Sulak Sivaraksa (2007), for example, has invoked dharma as a source of principles of justice to guide judges and as a grounding for substantive freedoms of thought, speech, and action, as well as the notion of equality before the law. Similarly, the Dalai Lama (Gyatso 1999) draws on dharmic principles of liberality, forbearance, and non-violence to support arguments of complementarity between Buddhism and liberal democracy. These programmatic efforts are important, especially as they inform political projects like that of the Tibetan exiles laid out at the beginning of this introduction. In all of this, the Buddhist–constitutional complex looks very much like the Islamic– or Christian–constitutional complex. It contains a set of resources (discourses, texts, ideals, ritual scripts) that might be used to express or contest power using a Buddhist grammar, and that can be deployed in conversations about governance.

What other distinctions might one make? The final section of this volume offers comparative reflections from scholars of religious legal traditions outside Buddhism. Deepa Das Acevedo points to a number of instructive similarities and differences in the ways that constitutional law and religion interact in Buddhist-majority settings and the Hindu-majority jurisdiction of India. Despite certain dissimilarities between Buddhism and Hinduism as religious traditions, Das Acevedo finds in Bhutan, Korea, and Sri Lanka points of profound resonance with India. Like that of Bhutan, India's Constitution also encodes ambiguity, even inconsistency, into its treatment of the majority religion, suggesting both separation and integration of religion and state. As in Korea, India's judiciary both avows and violates the autonomy of religious communities and encourages (rather than resolves) religious disputes. And, much as in Sri Lanka, state-legal idioms and ideals in India work to shape religious institutions and practices. The Indian judiciary's willingness to wade into intra-religious disputes is instructive for the relationships among state and religion uncovered in this volume.

At the same time, one finds strong similarities with religio-legal histories in other parts of the world, including Europe and the Middle East. Richard Helmholz, one of the foremost experts on medieval canon law, offers a number of reflections on the similarities between Christian law, Buddhist law, and constitutional law. Pointing to the distinct legal status of clerics in canon law, for example, he suggests a striking complementarity between "the benefit of clergy" in medieval Europe and the distinct status and various prerogatives accorded to Buddhist monks and nuns in premodern and modern Asia. Helmholz also identifies several principles of canon law that seem consonant with constitutionalism in the sense of limits on governing power and protections of individual rights. These incipient constitutional principles include the (partial) freedom of conscience for believers, protections against self-incrimination, and biblically derived notions of common welfare rights. The juxtaposition with Buddhism is illuminating, for one does not see the same obvious incorporation of substantive norms into constitutional law in the modern period.

Instead, one might conclude that Buddhism's influence has been at the level of the unwritten small-c constitutional norms that structure the exercise of power. The medieval Church in Europe promoted and benefited from the development of its own legal personality, which had powerful spill-over effects in Western legal development. We do not know about the same process in Asia. We do know, however, that Buddhist monasteries could hold property and had internal jurisdiction over at least some crimes committed by the members of the sangha (Gunawardana 1979; Jansen 2018; B. Sullivan 2020). This raises the question of the limits of state power in dealing with monastic institutions, as well as what the conceptions of proper temporal authority were.

In a similar vein, Clark Lombardi explores the chapters from the perspective of Islamic law. In contrast with both Christianity and Buddhism, the Muslim world lacks a separate class of people who follow their own legal code. The *ulama*, or community of scholars, plays an important role in articulating the law and staffing positions in the legal system, but it is not subject to a distinct set of rules. The moral code and the law itself is, in principle, the same for everyone, but its source in revealed scripture means that human beings only have partial access to it. The tools developed for elaboration of the law in the Islamic tradition led, in practice, to diverse and multiple human interpretations through legal institutions. This pluralism, which is a defining feature of Islamic law, raises similar questions to those observed in Buddhist legal settings: Whose voices are considered probative on correct practice? How does one distinguish questions that are open to plural interpretations from those for which uniformity is required? Lombardi speculates on myriad cross-religious comparisons and divergences that may emerge as the field of Buddhism and comparative constitutional law evolves.

1.15 CONCLUSION

Rather than concluding inquiry into the Buddhist–constitutional complex, the contributions in this volume only begin to open up the field. The comparative reflections in the final section of the book perhaps confirm the point made by French and Nathan (2014) that the Buddhist legal tradition is less consolidated as an object of study than are those of other religious traditions. The internal pluralism of the Islamic legal tradition, for example, was ultimately constrained by the legal character of the Qu'ran, and the consolidation of the legal tradition by the jurists operating in subsequent centuries. As Hallaq (2004) has argued, these jurists formed the essential connecting tissue between state and society.

Buddhist polities, by contrast, routinely demonstrate the impact of the transcendent law on human governance, constitutional and otherwise, even if they do not attribute to the Buddha himself positive legislation binding upon all humans. Dharma could inform the laws made by rulers and the decisions made by judges. In certain times and places (though not universally), dharma itself was even imagined as a cosmic legal system (*dhammasattha*) readymade for implementation by the virtuous (Lammerts 2018). Nevertheless, in all cases dharma required mediation and modulation in its application to the sociopolitical sphere; and these modes of application, although they often drew on common repertoires (the *dharmarāja* ideal, the dual system, and so on), also included creative elaborations particular to a given place and time. The Buddhist–constitutional complex has, in this way, been as creative as it has been influential. To be sure, some scholars have noted inherent tensions between aspects of the Buddha's teachings (e.g., on non-violence), on the one hand, and statecraft (e.g., warfare), on the other, implying that dharmic kingship was equal parts ideal and impossibility (Collins 1998, 414–96; Zimmerman 2006). This might have meant that, compared with Christianity and Islam, the "law" of dharma might be less convincing as a rationale for social ordering, given that rulers had to claim not only that they upheld the dharma but that they themselves were the embodiments (karmically and otherwise) of its virtue. But viewed from the broad socio-legal perspective offered in this volume, the "law" of dharma has clearly had an impact on social ordering as great as the laws of *shari`a* or Torah.

More can be said about the Buddhist–constitutional complex, and much more will be illuminated in the chapters that follow. Whether or not the terrain of Buddhism and constitutional law has similar contours to other areas of comparative constitutional studies we cannot yet say. As a field-in-the-making, we only hope that this rough guide will encourage and enable others to go further.

REFERENCES

Agrama, Hussein Ali. 2012. *Questioning Secularism: Islam, Sovereignty, and the Rule of Law in Modern Egypt*. Chicago: University of Chicago Press.

Arai, Paula Kane Robinson. 1999. *Women Living Zen: Japanese Sōtō Buddhist Nuns*. New York: Oxford University Press.

Asad, Talal. 2003. *Formations of the Secular: Christianity, Islam, Modernity*. Palo Alto: Stanford University Press.

Baker, Chris and Phongpaichit, Pasuk. 2016. *The Palace Law of Ayutthaya and the Thammasat: Law and Kingship in Siam*. Ithaca: Cornell University Press.

Bauer, Joanne and Bell, Daniel. 1999. *The East Asian Challenge for Human Rights*. New York: Cambridge University Press.

Bechert, Heinz. 1970. "Theravada Buddhist Sangha: Some General Observations on Historical and Political Factors in Its Development." *The Journal of Asian Studies* 29 (August): 761–78. https://doi.org/10.2307/2943086.

Berman, Harold J. 1983. *Law and Revolution, the Formation of the Western Legal Tradition*. Cambridge: Harvard University Press.

Blackburn, Anne M. 2017. "Buddhist Technologies of Statecraft and Millennial Moments." *History and Theory* 56 (1): 71–9. https://doi.org/10.1111/hith.12004.

Borchert, Thomas. 2020. "Belt-and-Road Buddhists: Religion-Making and the Rebuilding of Minority Buddhism in the Reform Era." *Review of Religion and Chinese Society* 7 (1): 92–119. https://doi.org/10.1163/22143955-00701005.

Bourdin, Bernard. 2010. *The Theological–Political Origins of the Modern State*. Tr. Susan Pickford. Washington: Catholic University Press.

Bowie, Katherine. 2014. "The Saint with Indra's Sword: Khruubaa Srivichai and Buddhist Millenarianism in Northern Thailand." *Comparative Studies in Society and History* 56 (July): 681–713. https://doi.org/10.1017/s0010417514000292.

Brac de la Perrière, Bénédicte. 2021. "'Religion' as an Issue in Political Transition. Two Competing Secularities in Buddhist Burma (Myanmar)." HAL: Open Science. https://hal.archives-ouvertes.fr/hal-03500666.

Brox, Trine. 2010. "Changing the Tibetan Way? Contesting Secularisms in the Tibetan Diaspora." In *Tibetan Studies. An Anthology*, edited by Peter Schweiger and Saadet Arslan, 117–42. Halle: IITBS.

2012. "Unyoking the Religious from the Secular." In *Varieties of Secularism in Asia: Anthropological Explorations of Religion, Politics, and the Spiritual*, edited by Nils Bubandt and Martijn van Beek, 55–74. New York: Routledge.

2016. *Tibetan Democracy: Governance, Leadership and Conflict in Exile*. London: I.B. Tauris.

Bui, Ngoc Son. 2021. "Constitutional Amendment in Laos." *International Journal of Constitutional Law* 17: 756–86.

Carter, John Ross. 1993. "The Origin and Development of 'Buddhism' and 'Religion' in the Study of Theravada Buddhism." In *On Understanding Buddhists. Essays on the Theravāda Tradition in Sri Lanka*, 9–26. Albany: SUNY Press.

Cheng, Wei-Yi. 2006. *Buddhist Nuns in Taiwan and Sri Lanka: A Critique of the Feminist Perspective*. London: Routledge. https://doi.org/10.4324/9780203966518.

Clarke, Shayne. 2015. "Vinayas." In *Brill's Encyclopedia of Buddhism*, edited by Jonathan A. Silk, I: Literature and Languages: 60–87. Leiden: Brill.

Collins, Steven. 1998. *Nirvana and Other Buddhist Felicities: Utopias of the Pali Imaginaire*. Cambridge: Cambridge University Press.

Cüppers, Christoph, Ruegg, David Seyfort, Ardussi, John, Stoddard, Heather, Vitali, Roberto, Walters, Michael, Sperling, Elliot, et al., eds. 2004. *The Relationship between Religion and State (chos srid zung 'brel) in Traditional Tibet: Proceedings of a Seminar held in Lumbini, Nepal, March 2000*. Lumbini: Lumbini International Research Institute.

Day, Tony. 2002. *Fluid Iron: State Formation in Southeast Asia*. Honolulu: University of Hawai'i Press.

de Silva Wijeyeratne, Roshan. 2013. *Nation, Constitutionalism and Buddhism in Sri Lanka*. London: Routledge.

Eisenstadt, S. N. 2000. "Multiple Modernities." *Daedalus* 129: 1–29.

Engel, David and Engel, Jaruwan. 2010. *Tort, Custom and Karma: Globalization and Legal Consciousness in Thailand*. Palo Alto: Stanford University Press.

French, Rebecca Redwood. 1995. *The Golden Yoke: The Legal Cosmology of Buddhist Tibet*. Ithaca: Cornell University Press.

French, Rebecca and Nathan, Mark, eds. 2014. *Buddhism and Law: An Introduction*. New York: Cambridge University Press.

Frydenlund, Iselin. 2016. "Particularist Goals through Universalist Means: The Political Paradoxes of Buddhist Revivalism in Sri Lanka." In *Buddhism and the Political Process*, edited by Hiroko Kawakami, 97–120. London: Palgrave Macmillan.

2017. "Religious Liberty for Whom? The Buddhist Politics of Religious Freedom during Myanmar's Transition to Democracy." *Nordic Journal of Human Rights* 35 (January): 55–73. https://doi.org/10.1080/18918131.2017.1288950.

Gethin, Rupert. 1998. *The Foundations of Buddhism*. Oxford: Oxford University Press.

Ginsburg, Tom and Simpser, Alberto, eds. 2014. *Constitutions in Authoritarian Regimes*. New York: Cambridge University Press.
Gokhale, Balkrishna Govind. 1969. "The Early Buddhist View of the State." *Journal of the American Oriental Society* 89 (4): 731–8.
Government of Sri Lanka. 2002. *Report of the Buddha Sasana Presidential Commission: Summary of Conclusions and Recommendations*. Colombo: Ministry of Buddha Sasana.
Gunawardana, R. A. L. H. 1979. *Robe and Plough: Monasticism and Economic Interest in Early Medieval Sri Lanka*. The Association for Asian Studies: Monographs and Papers, No. XXXV. Tucson: University of Arizona Press.
Gyatso, Tenzin (14th Dalai Lama). 1999. "Buddhism, Asian Values, and Democracy." *Journal of Democracy* 10 (1): 1–7.
Hallaq, Wael. 2004. *The Origins and Evolution of Islamic Law*. New York: Cambridge University Press.
Harding, Andrew. 2007. "Buddhism, Human Rights and Constitutional Reform in Thailand." *Asian Journal of Comparative Law* 2: 1–25.
Harvey, Peter. 2013. *An Introduction to Buddhism*. New York: Cambridge University Press.
Heirman, Ann. 2007. "Vinaya: From India to China." In *The Spread of Buddhism*, edited by Ann Heirman and Stephan Peter Bumbacher, 167–202. Leiden: Brill. https://brill.com/view/book/edcoll/9789047420064/Bej.9789004158306.i-474_007.xml.
2011. "Buddhist Nuns: Between Past and Present." *Numen* 58: 603–31.
Hirschl, Ran. 2010. *Constitutional Theocracy*. New York: Oxford University Press.
2014. *Comparative Matters*. New York: Oxford University Press.
Holmes, Stephen. 1995. *Passions and Constraint: On the Theory of Liberal Democracy*. Chicago: University of Chicago Press.
Holt, John. 1996. *The Religious World of Kīrti Śrī: Buddhism, Art, and Politics in Late Medieval Sri Lanka*. London: Oxford University Press.
Hurd, Elizabeth Shakman. 2015. *Beyond Religious Freedom: The New Global Politics of Religion*. Princeton: Princeton University Press.
Huxley, Andrew. 1997. "Studying Theravada Legal Literature." *Journal of the International Association of Buddhist Studies* 20: 63–92.
Ishii, Yoneo. 1986. "The Thai Thammasat (with a Note on the Lao Thammasat)." In *The Laws of South-East Asia*, edited by M. D. Hooker, 143–203. NUS: ISEAS.
Jansen, Berthe. 2018. *The Monastery Rules: Buddhist Monastic Organization in Pre-Modern Tibet*. Berkeley: University of California Press.
Kaplan, Uri. 2016. "Updating the Vinaya: Formulating Buddhist Monastic Laws and Pure Rules in Contemporary Korea." *Contemporary Buddhism* 17 (2): 252–74.
Kawanami, Hiroko. 2013. *Renunciation and Empowerment of Buddhist Nuns in Myanmar–Burma: Building a Community of Female Faithful*. Social Sciences in Asia, 33. Leiden: Brill.
Kieffer-Pülz, Petra. 2021–2022. "Brief Summary of the Development of Buddhist Monastic Law Codes and Institutions." *Buddhism, Law & Society* 6: 147–84.
Kyaw, Nyi Nyi. 2019. "Regulating Buddhism in Myanmar: The Case of Deviant Buddhist Sects." In *Regulating Religion in Asia*, edited by Jaclyn L. Neo, Arif A. Jamal, and Daniel P. S. Goh, 169–86. Cambridge: Cambridge University Press. https://doi.org/10.1017/9781108235983.009.
Ladwig, Patrice. 2014. "Millennialism, Charisma and Utopia: Revolutionary Potentialities in Pre-Modern Lao and Thai Theravāda Buddhism." *Politics, Religion & Ideology* 15 (2): 308–29. https://doi.org/10.1080/21567689.2014.899067.

Ladwig, Patrice, and Gregory Kourilsky. 2017–2018. "Governing the Monastic Order in Laos: Pre-Modern Buddhist Legal Traditions and Their Transformation under French Colonialism." *Buddhism, Law & Society* 3: 191–242.

Lammerts, D. Christian. 2018. *Buddhist Law in Burma: A History of Dhammasattha Texts and Jurisprudence, 1250–1850*. Honolulu: University of Hawai'i Press.

Larsson, Tomas. 2015. "Monkish Politics in Southeast Asia: Religious Disenfranchisement in Comparative and Theoretical Perspective." *Modern Asian Studies* 49: 40–82.

2016. "Keeping Monks in Their Place?" *Asian Journal of Law and Society* 3 (1): 17–28.

2020. "Royal Succession and the Politics of Religious Purification in Contemporary Thailand." *Journal of Contemporary Asia* 19 (2): 1–21. https://doi.org/10.1080/00472336.2020.1849775.

Lawrence, Benjamin. 2022. "Monkish Constitutionalism: Contesting the Enfranchisement of Cambodia's Buddhist Sangha." *Journal of Law and Religion* 37 (2): 1–25.

Liu, Cuilan. 2020. "The Fall of a Chinese Buddhist Monk: Law and State Governance of Buddhism in Post-Imperial China." *Journal of Law and Religion* 35 (3): 432–49. https://doi.org/10.1017/jlr.2020.34.

Liu, Cuilan, and Susan Andrews. 2017. "Introduction." In *Rules of Engagement: Medieval Traditions of Buddhist Monastic Regulation*, edited by Susan Andrews, Jinhua Chen, and Cuilian Liu, 9–24. Hamburg Buddhist Studies 9. Bochum; Freiburg: Projektverlag.

Llewelyn, Karl and E. Adamson Hoebel. 1941. *The Cheyenne Way*. Norman: University of Oklahoma Press.

Lopez, Donald S. Jr., and Jack Miles. 2017. *The Norton Anthology of World Religions: Buddhism*. New York and London: W.W. Norton.

McCargo, Duncan. 2004. "Buddhism, Democracy and Identity in Thailand." *Democratization* 11 (4): 155–70.

McLaughlin, Levi. 2019. *Soka Gakkai's Human Revolution: The Rise of a Mimetic Nation in Modern Japan*. Honolulu: University of Hawai'i Press.

2021. "Soka Gakkai's Impact on Constitutional Revision Attempts." In *Japanese Constitutional Revisionism and Civic Activism*, edited by Helen Hardacre, Timothy S. George, Keigo Komamura, and Franziska Seraphim, 161–74. Lanham: Lexington Books.

Mérieau, Eugénie. 2021. *Constitutional Bricolage: Thailand's Sacred Monarchy vs. The Rule of Law*. London: Bloomsbury Publishing.

2018. "Buddhist Constitutionalism in Thailand: When Rājadhammā Supersedes the Constitution." *Asian Journal of Comparative Law* 13 (2): 283–305.

Mills, Martin A. 2018. "Last Gift of the God-King." In *Tibetan Subjectivities on the Global Stage: Negotiating Dispossession*, edited by Shelly Bhoil and Enrique Galvan-Alvarez, 155–75. London: Rowman & Littlefield.

Mrozik, Susanne. 2009. "A Robed Revolution: The Contemporary Buddhist Nun's (Bhikṣuṇī) Movement." *Religion Compass* 3 (3): 360–78.

Nathan, Mark A. 2018. *From the Mountains to the Cities: A History of Buddhist Propagation in Modern Korea*. Honolulu: University of Hawai'i Press.

Nattier, Jan. 1991. *Once Upon a Future Time: Studies in a Buddhist Prophecy of Decline*. Berkeley: Asian Humanities Press.

Nelson, Eric. 2010. *The Hebrew Republic: Jewish Sources and the Transformation of European Political Thought*. Cambridge: Harvard University Press.

Pirie, Fernanda. 2017. "Buddhist Law in Early Tibet: The Emergence of an Ideology." *Journal of Law and Religion* 32 (3): 406–22.

Prasert Na Nagara, and Alexander B. Griswold. 1992. *Epigraphic and Historical Studies*. Bangkok: Historical Society.

Prebish, Charles S., and Damien Keown. 2006. *Introducing Buddhism*. New York: Routledge.
Reugg, D. Seyfort. 2014. "The Temporal and the Spiritual, and the So-Called Patron–Client Relation in the Governance of Inner Asia and Tibet." In *Patronage as Politics in South Asia*, edited by Anastasia Piliavsky, 67–79. New York: Cambridge University Press.
Reynolds, Frank. 1972. "The Two Wheels of Dhamma: A Study of Early Buddhism." In *The Two Wheels of Dhamma*, edited by Gananath Obeyesekere, Frank Reynolds, and Bardwell Smith, 6–30. Boston: American Academy of Religion.
Salgado, Nirmala S. 2013. *Buddhist Nuns and Gendered Practice: In Search of the Female Renunciant*. New York: Oxford University Press.
Schober, Juliane. 2011. *Modern Buddhist Conjunctures in Myanmar*. Honolulu: University of Hawai'i Press.
Schonthal, Benjamin. 2016a. *Buddhism, Politics and Limits of Law: The Pyrrhic Constitutionalism of Sri Lanka*. New York: Cambridge University Press.
2016b. "Making the 'Muslim Other' in Myanmar and Sri Lanka." In *Islam, State, and Society in Myanmar*, edited by M. Crouch, 234–57. Delhi: Oxford University Press.
2017. "Formations of Buddhist Constitutionalism in South and Southeast Asia." *International Journal of Constitutional Law* 15 (3): 705–33.
2017–2018. "Buddhist Legal Pluralism? Looking Again at Monastic Governance in Modern South and Southeast Asia." *Buddhism, Law & Society* 3: vii–xxxvii.
2021a. "Buddhist Law Beyond the Vinaya: Monastic Constitutions (*Katikāvatas*) and Their Transformations in Colonial Sri Lanka." *History of Religions* 60 (4): 1–38.
2021b. "The Case for Religious Constitutions: Comparative Constitutional Law among Buddhists and Other Religious Groups." *Law & Social Inquiry* 47(2): 391–419.
Schonthal, Benjamin, and Tom Ginsburg. 2016. "Setting an Agenda for the Socio-Legal Study of Contemporary Buddhism." *Asian Journal of Law and Society* 3 (February): 1–15.
Seeger, Martin. 2018. *Gender and the Path to Awakening: Hidden Histories of Nuns in Modern Thai Buddhism*. Chiang Mai: Silkworm Books.
Sivaraksa, Sulak. 2007 "Buddhist Concept of Law." *LAW Magazine* 1: 12–16.
Streicher, Ruth. 2021a. "Imperialism, Buddhism and Islam in Siam: Exploring the Buddhist Secular in the Nangsue Sadaeng Kitchanukit, 1867." *Journal of Southeast Asian Studies* 52 (1): 7–25. https://doi.org/10.1017/S0022463421000126.
2021b. "Introduction: Towards an Analysis of Buddhist Secular Grammars." *Journal of Southeast Asian Studies* 52 (1): 2–6. https://doi.org/10.1017/S0022463421000096.
Strong, John. 2002. *The Experience of Buddhism: Sources and Interpretations*. Belmont: Wadsworth Pub. Co.
Sullivan, Brenton. 2020. *Building a Religious Empire: Tibetan Buddhism, Bureaucracy, and the Rise of the Gelukpa*. Philadelphia: University of Pennsylvania Press.
Sullivan, Winnifred Fallers. 2020. *Church State Corporation: Construing Religion in US Law*. Chicago: University of Chicago Press.
Sullivan, Winnifred Fallers, Elizabeth Shakman Hurd, Saba Mahmood, and Peter G. Danchin, eds. 2015. *Politics of Religious Freedom*. Chicago: University of Chicago Press.
Tambiah, Stanley J. 1976. *World Conqueror and World Renouncer: A Study of Buddhism and Polity in Thailand against a Historical Background*. Cambridge: Cambridge University Press.
Thomas, Jolyon. 2016. "Varieties of Religious Freedom in Japanese Buddhist Responses to the 1899 Religions Bill." *Asian Journal of Law and Society* 3 (1): 49–70.
Tibetan Parliament-in-Exile. 2011. *The Charter of Tibetans-in-Exile*. https://tibet.net/wp-content/uploads/2021/04/English-Charter-final.doc.pdf.

Tierney, Brian. 1982. *Religion, Law, and the Growth of Constitutional Thought, 1150–1650*. New York: Cambridge University Press.

Tonsakulrungruang, Khemthong. 2020. *Toward a New Buddhist Constitutionalism: Law and Religion in the Kingdom of Thailand*. PhD dissertation, Bristol University, UK.

Turner, Alicia Marie. 2014. *Saving Buddhism: The Impermanence of Religion in Colonial Burma*. Honolulu: University of Hawai'i Press.

Wallace, Vesna. 2014. "Buddhist Laws in Mongolia." In *Buddhism and Law: An Introduction*, edited by Rebecca Redwood French and Mark A. Nathan, 319–33. New York: Cambridge University Press.

Walton, Matthew J. 2016. *Buddhism, Politics and Political Thought in Myanmar*. New York: Cambridge University Press.

Walton, Matthew J. and Aung Tun. 2017–2018. "Monks and the Ambiguities of Law in Myanmar." *Buddhism, Law & Society* 3: 1–38.

Yu, Jimmy. 2014. "Pure Land Devotion in East Asia." In *The Wiley Blackwell Companion to East and Inner Asian Buddhism*, edited by Mario Poceski, 201–20. Chichester: Wiley Blackwell.

Zan, Myint. 2000. "Woe unto Ye Lawyers: Three Royal Orders Concerning Pleaders in Early Seventeenth-Century Burma." *American Journal of Legal History* 44 (1): 40–72.

Zimmerman, Michael. 2006. "Only a Fool Becomes a King: Buddhist Stances on Punishment." In *Buddhism and Violence*, edited by Michael Zimmermann, Chiew Hui Ho and Philip Pierce. LIRI Seimar Proceedings Series, vol. 2. 213–42. Lumbini: Lumbini International Research Institute.

PART I

Religious and Political Underpinnings

2

Buddhism and Constitutionalism in Precolonial Southeast Asia

*D. Christian Lammerts**

In Siam and, it seems, in all the Indianized kingdoms, one finds, alongside custom, another source of law, which is none other than *dharmaśāstra*, a specific contribution of Hindu civilization. The king does not legislate. His essential mission is to assure and maintain peace among his subjects. As such, he must ensure the proper administration of justice and fulfill the role of supreme judge in disputes that arise among his subjects. In this capacity, also, he can and must enact punishments against those who disturb the order. He may still lay down the rules for the organization of courts and the procedure to be followed before them; in sum, to take all measures so that his subjects live in peace. But all this constitutes only, so to speak, the outer casing of the law. As for the substance of law, that is, as for the rules for which it is a question of ensuring compliance, the king does not create them, because the law is entirely contained in immemorial custom and *dharmaśāstra*. The king is simply the defender and protector of custom and *dharmaśāstra*. This does not prevent the king from being an absolute sovereign and being able to do whatever he wants. He is therefore at liberty to make decisions contrary to *dharmaśāstra* and established custom. But such decisions have only the force of royal authority, they are not law. On the contrary, when the decisions of the king conform to equity, as understood by *dharmaśāstra*, they merge with it and are invested with the same authority.

(Lingat 1937, 21–22)

2.1 THE PROBLEM

The king does not make law. His sovereignty is absolute. Law, as dhamma, originates outside the king, who merely acts as the judge and enforcer of law. The commands of the king are not legal enactments. They form the "outer casing of the law" as "mere orders … personal and accidental injunctions" (Lingat 1950, 9).

* For their comments and criticisms on this chapter the author is grateful to Fernanda Pirie, Benjamin Schonthal, Tom Ginsburg, and the participants of the Buddhism and Comparative Constitutional Law workshop.

The authority of royal command is proportionate to the degree that it conforms to dhamma as an exogenous standard of justice.

This thesis on precolonial Southeast Asian law by Robert Lingat reflects a particularly entrenched perspective in the history of scholarship on Buddhist (and more broadly Indic) constitutionalism – even if scholars themselves have not always employed the phrase. It highlights a certain antinomy, if not an antinomianism, at the heart of reflection on Buddhist "law." On the one hand, the political function and legal authority of the king is thoroughly restrained, if not eclipsed, by dhamma (Sanskrit, dharma), envisaged as a sort of natural law. The pragmatics of this dhamma, seen to be embodied either in Tai, Mon, Khmer, or Burmese *dhammasattha*[1] texts, or in classical Pali sutras manifesting a buddha's speech, therefore furnish the skeleton of a constitutionalist doctrine purportedly realized in the historical practice of Buddhist communities.

The influence of this position, which locates law, as dhamma, outside kingship, is pervasive in Buddhist and Asian legal studies, but not always in the way our sources might anticipate, for the claim is not, simply, that there are forms of "natural" or "non-state" law. Indeed, to the extent that constitutional features have been considered at all by scholars of precolonial Buddhisms, we have hardly advanced beyond this perspective. It is brought to bear in nearly every analysis of Buddhist law or politics; for example, when the normative dimensions of Buddhist kingship are analyzed in relation to the *dasarājadhammā* ("ten laws for kings") and the related *dhammarājā* motif (Gokhale 1953; 1966; 1969; Collins 2006, 460ff.), the career of the primordial Buddhist king Mahāsammata (Tambiah 1989), or the beleaguered figure of the *cakravartin* ("'wheel-turner' king;" Tambiah 1976, 39ff.). It is there, also, in devaluations of royal authority that elevate the status, in dhamma/law, of monasticism (Collins 2006, 420). Such are the so-called ideologies of Buddhist kingship, Collins posits, which are "exemplified from any period and place in Southern Asia, across which Pali texts spread as the Theravāda form of Buddhism was adopted by monarchs, many of them would-be Wheel-turning Kings (*cakkavatti*-s) seeking what they hoped would be a universal empire, emblazoned with the universal truths of Buddhism" (Collins 2006, 415). Frank Reynolds, commenting upon the tropes of *dhammarājā*, *cakravartin*, and Mahāsammata as found in the early strata of Pali texts, remarks that "these elements are of crucial importance because they provided a commonly accepted, orthodox basis for the richer and

[1] I advise against Lingat's occasional habit of employing the Sanskrit term *dharmaśāstra* to name a corpus of texts that was never written in Sanskrit. In references to this genre of Buddhist legal literature, on which more below, I employ the usual Pali term *dhammasattha*. Some examples of attested vernacular forms across the region include: *dhammasāt* (Mon), *dhammasat* (Burmese), *thaṃmasat* (Shan), *dhammasatr* (Tai Khoen), *dharrmaśāstr* (central Thai), *dhammasātr* (Khmer). For a consideration of *dhammasattha*'s connection with what Lingat calls a "specific contribution of Hindu civilization," see Lammerts 2018, 13–17.

more complex patterns of royal symbolism and political involvement which were developed during the subsequent periods of Buddhist history" (Reynolds 1972, 23).

Accordingly, as Balkrishna Gokhale claimed, Buddhism would seem to offer many resources to scholars of constitutionalism. Dhamma, "a constitutional concept of great significance" (Gokhale 1953, 161), operates as the framework that enables and constrains the king and the organs of royal power. Dhamma, as the "king of the king who is a *cakravartin*, a righteous king who rules by dhamma"[2] serves as a check on tyranny. As William Koenig restates the formula in relation to eighteenth- and nineteenth-century Burma, "the ruler became but the servant and agency of dhamma and his righteous conduct or sinful behavior infected the whole universe" (Koenig 1990, 68). On this reading, political and legal institutions find their justification in dhamma (in its representative texts), and it is dhamma (its representative texts) that places limits upon them in the name of supreme justice.

Lingat's corollary however belies the puzzle. He adds that the king's sovereignty is absolute; an absolutism circumscribed by law. It is my suspicion that Lingat, who among all authors to have contributed to the debate on constitutionalism – again, without naming it as such – in precolonial Theravāda Buddhism was surely the most well acquainted with a relevant archive (viz., local legal texts produced by the historical contexts in question) is here hedging his bets. He wants to have it both ways. An absolutism, but a righteous, or dhamma-constrained, absolutism – an aporia.

In what follows I aim, firstly, to raise criticisms of this now standard presupposition. The analysis of precolonial Buddhist constitutionalism developed by the likes of Lingat, Gokhale, Tambiah, Reynolds, Collins, and many others – and still very much current in the scholarly literature – is rooted in a speculative theorization of Buddhist constitutionalist law-as-exogenous-dhamma. This theory resists, with remarkable tenacity, most actual domains of law or legislation themselves, if by these terms we signify those forms of historical evidence that pertain to formal dispute resolution by courts and judges, juristic institutions and processes, or the normative, enforceable distribution and organization of social, economic, and political power. The rhetoric of kingship encountered in classical Pali Buddhist texts, despite its occasional (likewise rhetorical) redeployment even in legal discourse,[3] is in tension with precolonial Southeast Asian laws, jurisprudence, and juridical practices, and, moreover, with what is knowable about the operation, transformation, and effect of classical Pali Buddhist discourses of kingship and politics in history. This is so in the first instance empirically because the rhetoric of kingship advanced in local Southeast Asian law texts is rarely, if ever, closely

2 *rañño cakkavattissa dhammikassa dhammarañño rājā* (AN III, 149); referenced in Gokhale 1953, 162.

3 See Lammerts 2018, 184–89 for examples of how the *dasarājadhamma* and *cakravartin* motifs have been deployed in Burmese legal texts.

parallel to classical figurations. Local Buddhist narratives of Mahāsammata and Manu, which I have written about at length elsewhere, are a perfect example: the jurisprudential significations of Thai and Burmese variants of *their* biographies bear only a "similar dissimilitude" to representations in the Pali sutras and commentaries (Lammerts 2013; Lammerts 2018, 48, 66–71). We have been misled, in my view, by work that has, by and large, taken a misplaced rhetoric of royal dhamma as proxy for law.[4]

This argument is not intended to diminish the significance of classical Pali figurations of dhamma (those related to kingship or otherwise), via their local translations and transformations, for the general history of Buddhism or law in precolonial Southeast Asia. The salience of these figurations is to be established on a case-by-case basis.[5] Here my aim is to demonstrate that standard scholarly conceits about precolonial or "traditional" Buddhist constitutionalism – conceits concerning "righteous" and "wheel-turning" monarchs, or the exogenous, abstract dhamma that, as a higher principle of justice, somehow itself "reigns" sovereign and thereby exerts a regulatory function – are not, in fact, operative *constitutional* or even *legal* concepts according to the attested vocabularies of the legal history itself. There are many thousands of extant legal manuscripts and inscriptions, in many languages, from across precolonial Southeast Asia. Fewer than 1 percent have received any competent hermeneutical scrutiny. If we want to understand the changing historical expressions of Buddhist constitutional thought and practice, we must learn to read them. In doing so, it quickly becomes apparent that the construction of Buddhist constitutionalism according to the academic field is woefully at odds with, and does not do justice to, the richness and nuance of the archive.

By turning to more prevalent, effective, and historically situated legal discourses, this essay confirms that constitutionalism is indeed a pervasive feature of Buddhist lawmaking in precolonial Southeast Asia, yet its form bears little resemblance to classical tropes of dhamma. It may even be broader than any narrow focus on kingship and politics would suggest. The surviving testimony readily shows that the constitution of political power was *not* a separate or higher sphere of law with a singular genesis or formal instantiation. This is to say, constitutional discourse, including the ordering of the offices of the king (*rājā*), and of the monastic community (sangha), was part of an all-embracing process of *constitutionalizing* that encompassed other social, economic, and familial arenas. Thus, attempts to characterize or criticize constitutionalism in precolonial Buddhist law require that

4 Baker and Pasuk (2021) have recently voiced a similar criticism of claims by Lingat and Prince Dhani Nivat regarding the supposed legal restraints imposed by dhamma upon Siamese kings. Their analysis is additionally valuable for its engagement with Thai-language sources and scholarship, including Lingat's *Prawatisat kotmai thai* ("History of Thai Law").

5 A highly effective example of such an approach is Patrick Jory's book (2016) examining the intellectual history of Thai kingship in light of the concept of Buddhist perfection (*pāramī*).

we respond to this more capacious scope of law-writing. It demands that we reimagine that thing we call "law," and to see the constitution of *rājā* or lordship in immediate relation to other, constituted, legal phenomena. This undoubtedly betrays a certain friction with modern conceptions of constitutionalism that envision it as a singular type of legal creature narrowly concerned with regulating the exercise of executive power.

2.2 THREE ENVIRONMENTS

There are three principal, occasionally intersecting or conflicting, environments[6] of "Buddhist law" in precolonial Southeast Asia: *vinaya*, *dhammasattha*, and *rājasattha* ("royal legislation" or "royal edict/command").[7] Each entails a distinct relation between what may be called "Buddhism" and "law." Certain general features common to these environments include: (1) (usually) a form of material embodiment and circulation in writing, (2) an orientation toward the authority of a foundational, preternatural, text (the speech of a buddha, a cosmic treatise, or the speech of a king), and (3) a rationale or jurisprudential logic whereby the normative program of such legalism is imagined to have the capacity to enable or perpetuate, via different mechanics, the religion of Buddhism itself.

2.2.1 *Vinaya*

Broadly speaking, and eventually from such a distant perspective that the analysis begins to lose utility, the monastic *vinaya* – the paradigmatic though non-exhaustive subset of the broad category of monastic law (laws governing monks) – is the only environment of precolonial Southeast Asian law that is somewhat shared, in terms of a general repertoire and jurisprudence, among diverse Buddhist traditions across Asia. This apparent unity is also deceptive. There are multiple, more or less partial or complete, variant *vinayas* transmitted in several different languages (Clarke 2015),

6 I am indebted to Benjamin Schonthal for the image of "legal environments." The phrase calls attention to the "overlapping and nonexclusive nature of . . . legal contexts" that "interlace and impinge upon each other" and "cannot be viewed in isolation and are not always imagined as mutually compatible" (Schonthal 2016, 138).

7 This way of drawing the picture excludes various genres of records of local legal practice, including judicial rulings, stone inscriptions, land and population registers, contracts, and so on, which often summon influences from multiple environments. On Burmese inscriptions as legal texts, see Lammerts (2022); for debt contracts, see Saito 2019, Htun Yee 1999a; for judicial rulings, see Htun Yee 2006. These documents are set aside here since they generally serve procedural, not legislative, ends as forms of written evidence. Scholars have unanimously mischaracterized the corpus of judicial rulings (*vinicchaya*), for example, as judicial "precedent." Nevertheless, the *vinicchaya* genre begins to shade into the domain of jurisprudence when it comes to certain compendia that served as exemplars of judicial reasoning to be emulated by judges. The *Decisions of Sudhammacārī* is a key text of the latter sort (see Latter 1850, 1–29; Sparks 1851).

whose employment and application by monastic communities in history is highly uneven across time and space. Nevertheless, the influence of this law in Southeast Asia is hardly slight: a lengthy excerpt of the Pali *vinaya*, the *bodhikathā* of *Vinaya-mahāvagga*, is attested in Pyu epigraphy (discovered in Kunzeik, modern-day Burma), from around the sixth to seventh centuries CE, making this legal treatise, or a section thereof, possibly the earliest documented transmission of Buddhist literature in the region (Skilling 1997, 95 n. 7).[8]

While *vinaya* texts were widely transmitted, copied, glossed, and kept in monastic libraries across Asia, perhaps unsurprisingly there is rather little direct evidence that *vinaya* law was in fact routinely observed in the everyday life of monks, and indeed in some cases, including in fairly recent times, there is considerable evidence that *vinaya* was wittingly transgressed or ignored. In many contexts, the classical *vinaya* texts and their commentaries are supplanted in practice by a preference for manuals, pamphlets, summaries, and rulebooks on monastic law and administration that comment upon, or occasionally depart from, that corpus (Blackburn 1999). In certain areas – though not prominently in Southeast Asia – what we tend to think of as *vinaya* "properly speaking" was supplemented, or displaced, through the issuance of local documents that may be classified as monastic "constitutions," "guidelines," or "charters" (Jansen 2015) – e.g., *katikāvata* in Sri Lanka (Ratnapala 1971; Schonthal 2021a), or *chayik* in the Tibetan sphere (Ellingson 1990; Jansen 2018; Sullivan 2021) – which established norms for the operation of one or more monastic communities and, sometimes, those laypersons who happened to interact with them (Jansen 2018, 19, 153–57). In Burma, moreover, certain dimensions of monastic law were, in the seventeenth century and perhaps earlier, at least partly imagined to fall under the jurisdiction of *dhammasattha*, which presented norms decidedly at odds with the Pali *vinaya* and its commentaries – a feature of the legal history that stimulated considerable debate among eighteenth- and nineteenth-century jurists (Lammerts 2018, 112–15, 164–68). And nearly everywhere throughout Buddhist Asia, kings regularly legislated rules for monks that often had no relationship whatsoever to *vinaya*.

Despite differences internal to, and in the application of, the various Buddhist *vinaya* literatures, this massive corpus tends toward a rather uniform jurisprudence concerning the sources and aims of law. Authoritative *vinaya* rules are understood to derive ultimately from the lawmaking efforts of a singular type of legislator: a buddha.[9] Gautama Buddha's first legislative act, some two decades after he attained

[8] For a recent edition of this inscription by Arlo Griffiths and D. Christian Lammerts, see http://hisoma.huma-num.fr/exist/apps/pyu/works/PYU040.xml.

[9] A basic interpretive framework of *vinaya* jurisprudence, the four "great standards" (*mahā-ā padesa*), stipulates that when a legal question is not explicitly answered by the preserved legislation of a buddha (*sutta*; i.e., the *vinaya* rules), its resolution must conform to that legislation by analogy (*suttānuloma*). If an answer remains elusive, only then is it permissible to defer to the teachings of the 500 *arahants* involved in the First Buddhist Council

omniscience, was the declaration of the first *pārājika* (an offense leading to loss of clerical status) forbidding sex, including with animals or nonhumans (*amanussa*), among his male monastic disciples. The *vinaya* presupposes that other buddhas also promulgated laws for monks and some of Gautama's own rules are attributed to them. The rationale of *vinaya* is routinely advocated in language that stresses its essential role in maintaining a functioning monastic system of lineage and discipleship, creating the possibility for rituals such as ordination, ensuring the survival of the Buddhist teachings, and even promoting the achievement of nirvana.[10]

Until very recently the category of "Buddhist law" has been understood, entirely incorrectly, yet more or less exclusively, in terms of *vinaya*. But *vinaya* is not, at least not according to its founding vision,[11] a universal body of norms regulating the entire Buddhist community including the laity. This circumscription around the monastic population thus insinuates the existence of a plural legal environment, as scholars such as Robert Lingat (1951, 164) and Andrew Huxley (1999, 325) have observed. While the overtly "religious" character of *vinaya* law is uncontroversial – the rules are attributed to an omniscient superhuman legislator and exist to facilitate the advancement of ritual and soteriological imperatives – the corpus is largely comprised of what we might call administrative law; much of its content pertains to the mundane organization and business of monastic institutions and the everyday comportment of monks and nuns. Nevertheless, *vinaya* was, and remains, a major body of law and litigation in Southeast Asia as elsewhere, and proceedings of *vinaya* courts, tried by monastic judges, survive from the early seventeenth century (Lammerts 2018, 37–43) and continue into the present across the Theravāda world (Schonthal 2017–2018; Schonthal 2021b; Janaka and Crosby 2017).

The constitutional dimensions of *vinaya*, as well as those genres of monastic regulations and guidelines mentioned above, are immediately suggestive. Yet these have been hardly explored, perhaps due partly to the relative absence of considerations of kingship and politics in much of monastic legal discourse, though perhaps more so due to bias and a lack of appetite on behalf of comparative constitutional law scholars (Mérieau 2020). Nevertheless, as Benjamin Schonthal (2021c) has recently argued, there are strong grounds to characterize *vinaya* and local genres of monastic law as manifesting constitutions, inasmuch as these documents aim not

(*ācariyavāda*), or, failing that, the legal opinions of later monastic jurists (*attanomāti*). See Kieffer-Pülz, 2016–2017, 111–15. On the *mahāpadesa* framework applied beyond the monastic context in *dhammasattha*, see Lammerts 2018, 161.

10 Compare for example the summary treatment at Sp, 104–5; translated in Jayawickrama 1986, 92–93.

11 *Vinaya* rules have moved beyond the monastery in various times and places, exerting a significant influence on aspects of lay jurisprudence. One among many examples of this phenomenon is the widespread adoption of the *vinaya* motif of the "twenty-five types of theft" (Kieffer-Pülz 2011) that is elaborated in Southeast Asian *dhammasattha* texts (Lammerts 2018, 72–73).

only to legislate rules for monks, but also to organize the institution, offices, and judicial processes of the monastic community.

2.2.2 *Dhammasattha*

Dhammasattha ("treatise on dhamma" or "instructions of dhamma") is the Pali name of a regional Southeast Asian genre of legal literature that has a documented history of transmission in Burma beginning in the mid-thirteenth century (Lammerts 2018, Ch. 2). Later references to and manuscript witnesses of the genre are attested in what is today Thailand, Laos, Yunnan, Cambodia, and Bangladesh. In Burma alone there are well over one hundred individual *dhammasattha* treatises surviving in thousands of palm-leaf and paper manuscripts. By the phrase *legal literature*, I mean firstly the generic sense of texts that present rules and sanctions related to matters such as inheritance, marriage, contract, theft, assault, etc., and also prescribe norms and procedures for adjudicating disputes (courts, ordeals, witnesses, evidence, judges, etc.). More specifically, however, I refer to the fact that these texts (like so many embodiments of law) are *literary* expressions. Some are written as poetry, and all *dhammasatthas* – quite unlike their Sanskrit *dharmaśāstra* cousins – repeatedly, even excessively, employ narrative (i.e., stories), such as the example from *The Responsa of Manurājā* discussed below, somewhat akin to the model of the Buddhist *vinayas*, in the characterization of a rule.

There are considerable limitations to our knowledge of *dhammsattha*. The scope and substantive content of any text called *dhammasattha* (or cognate vernacular terms) during the earliest historical phase – before the seventeenth century – are uncertain, since the textual traditions are difficult to date. There is also a question whether the word "*dhammasattha*" during this early phase indexed a perception of a legal genre or corpus, or if it simply referred to a single text. Nevertheless, some general contours of *dhammasattha* as a source of law are evident from the thirteenth to fifteenth centuries onward.

The first Burmese inscription to invoke *dhammasattha* does so in the context of a retelling of a trial pertaining to a complex dispute within the extended royal family over the inheritance of land and slaves to be donated to a monastery (Lammerts 2018, 21–22). During the trial, the king orders his officials to consult *dhammasāt* (= *dhammasattha*) to determine the legitimate line of succession. The officials carry out the king's command, and the inheritance is consequently awarded to the heir perceived to be sanctioned by the text. This heir then proceeds to donate the inherited property to a monastery in the year 1232.

In Thailand, the vernacular word *dharrmaśāstra* first appears in an inscription dated to around 1400 as part of a compound with the term *rājaśāstra*.[12] According to

[12] On the problematic date of this inscription, see Baker and Pasuk 2021, 28 n. 27. I add that the history and transmission of the genre in Siam (central Thailand) between c. 1400, the

this inscription, a king, presumably Rāmarājādhirāja, the ruler of Ayutthaya,[13] announces, "in the center of the city of Sukhothai," a series of royal pronouncements (*oṅkāra*)[14] dealing mainly with slavery and theft. Punishment (e.g., for stealing slaves) or reward (e.g., for facilitating the return of stolen property), the king says repeatedly, shall be "in accordance with the rule [or "measure"[15]] of *dharrmaśāstra* and *rājaśāstra*."[16]

In the Burmese inheritance dispute, we see that royal judgment defers to the authority of the text to determine the rule. The judgment of the king is to let the *dhammasāt* establish the verdict. His judgment is simply a deferral of judgment to the letter of the law text. The Thai evidence, by contrast, is not a trial context, but an account of lawmaking by the king. The inscription represents law as established by royal command. Rāmarājādhirāja refers to *dharrmaśāstra*, and also royal edicts (*rājaśāstra*), only as a source for determining legitimate fines and compensation.

In his discussion of Rāmarājādhirāja's inscription, Lingat (1951, 182–83) writes:

> "[The inscription] contains, a rare thing, if not unique in Asia, a series of legislative provisions. However, these provisions are placed under the double authority of *dhammasattham-rājasattham*. [...] So we have there, in a relatively early period, and in any case close to the foundation of Ayutthaya, evidence for the existence, in Tai country, of a *dhammasattham* already generally employed as a legal principle, which suggests its introduction dates back to an even earlier era."

A year earlier, Lingat (1950, 24) elaborated what is meant by this "double authority":

> "The Royal prescriptions engraved on [Rāmarājādhirāja's inscription] are said to have been enacted according to *dharmasāt-rājasat,* i.e. according to the system which derives authority of royal orders from the authority of a supreme Dharma."

Lingat appears to recognize the royal legislative features of the text as an exception, a "rare thing, if not unique in Asia," for sovereigns influenced by the Indic religions are, according to him, always dutiful servants of dhamma. Lingat could no doubt read the original inscription as well as anyone. Yet he fails to adequately explain, perhaps because it troubles his conception of the "supreme Dharma" governing all Buddhist law, that the laws for slavery and theft mentioned in the inscription are nowhere characterized, in fact, as deriving from the authority of *dharmaśāstra*. The force of the king's speech (*oṅkāra*) does not emanate from any source outside the king himself. While it is facile to argue that the legislative prerogative of the king

approximate date of this inscription, and 1805, the date of the recension of the *dhammasattha* in the *Three Seals Code* (Baker and Pasuk 2016), remains something of a mystery. See Baker and Pasuk 2021, 28–29 for an overview of the evidence.

[13] For the historical context see Griswold and Prasert 1975.

[14] On this term see Lammerts 2019–2020, 52 n. 61.

[15] The Thai/Khmer term *khanāt/knāt* implies the sense of measure, scale, rule, or model.

[16] For an edition and English translation of this inscription see Griswold and Prasert 1969; reprinted in Griswold and Prasert 1992, 109–44.

results, to some degree, from his capacious merit (*puñña*), and is thus not entirely disconnected from cosmological or ritual considerations,[17] this is rather different from claiming that dhamma *qua* dhamma is the only legitimate source of law, or that all law was necessarily derivative of an exogenous source, whether dhamma, *dhammasattha*, or custom.

The *Dhammavilāsa dhammasat* is the earliest surviving *dhammasattha* text from Burma, written in vernacular Burmese, including some scattered Pali verses and citations, sometime before 1638 (Lammerts 2018, 56). It was shortly followed by the vernacular *Responsa of Manurājā* (*Manurājā lhyok thuṃḥ*),[18] a series of jurisprudential questions and answers (*pucchā-vissajjanā*) between a legist and king, compiled sometime between 1638 and 1648. In 1651 or 1652 the *Manusāra dhammasattha* was composed by the monk Tipiṭakālaṅkāra and a lay jurist styled Manurājā, the "eater" of taxes of Kaing Village. *Manusāra* is a Pali verse legal text that was probably compiled on the basis of earlier, now apparently lost, vernacular law treatises, to which was appended an interphrasal Burmese gloss commentary (*nissaya*). The *Manusāra* verses were eventually reedited and glossed anew in a recension by Vaṇṇadhamma Kyaw Htin, also titled *Manusāra dhammasattha*, in 1769. Judging from surviving manuscript copies as well as citations and references in other legal texts, Vaṇṇadhamma's *Manusāra* was among the most popular and widely circulated law books in late precolonial Burma.

The *dhammasattha* corpus – which, in Burma, expands by more than a hundred additional treatises during the eighteenth to nineteenth centuries – is definable as a species of "Buddhist law" in at least three different senses, each of which are quite dissimilar from *vinaya* jurisprudence, since only very rarely are its rules directly attributed to any buddha (and when they are so-attributed, the buddha is usually Dīpaṅkara). In the earliest surviving texts, including those mentioned above, dhammasattha law is represented as an earthly instantiation of a cosmic treatise. The original text of the law is inscribed – in "letters as big as a cow" – on the boundary-wall of the universe, from which it is transcribed and transmitted to the human realm by the variously-named seer Manu, Manusāra, or Manosāra, who magically retrieves the alien text during the reign of the first king Mahāsammata.[19] In addition

[17] See, for example, the description of the king's merit in the epigraph's "preamble" delineating his majesty (Griswold and Prasert 1969, 116–17, 124–28).

[18] While this text is not strictly a *dhammasattha* treatise in terms of form and content, it is presented as a commentary on certain *dhammasattha* laws, often categorized by precolonial bibliographers as a *dhammasattha*, and remained influential in the development of the genre in the eighteenth to nineteenth centuries, for example by serving as the basis of Vaṇṇadhamma's *Vinicchayapakāsanī* of 1771. The *Responsa*, which circulated under several different titles, is conventionally attributed to the authors of the 1651/2 *Manusāra* (viz., Kaingza Manurājā and Tipiṭakālaṅkāra), although not unproblematically (Lammerts 2018, 130–31).

[19] For a translation of the origin story in *Dhammavilāsa*, see Lammerts 2005. A draft edition of the *nissaya* version of the tale in the 1651/2 *Manusāra* may be found in Lammerts 2010, 502–8, 554–95. For an analysis of the Burmese narratives and their relation to accounts of Mahāsammata and Manu in transregional Pali literature, see Lammerts 2018, 66–71, 107–10.

to its origins in outer space, accessible only to superhuman cosmonauts, *dhammasattha* texts are engaged in a complex relationship with Buddhist *vinaya* and sutra texts, which are frequently redeployed, although sometimes with substantial changes, to justify or illuminate certain laws. Finally, *dhammasattha* texts repeatedly remind their audience that the norms they prescribe are intended to preserve and perpetuate the *sāsana* ("teachings") of Gautama Buddha, and that observing *dhammasattha* law offers a range of worldly (*lokiya*) and supermundane (*lokuttara*) benefits for judges and litigants, not least including nirvana.[20]

Dhammasattha is neither a form of positive law nor "state" law – at least not prior to the mid-nineteenth century when functionaries of the British colonial state began to transfigure and redeploy the genre for use by the imperial judiciary. The laws are not attributed to any legislator; like stars they are a natural feature of the cosmos and will ultimately perish along with it. Over the course of the development of *dhammasattha* jurisprudence it is however certain that legists increasingly sought to align laws of the corpus with the provisions of *vinaya* and sutra. This entailed a self-conscious project of "purifying" aspects of the legal tradition and bringing them into putative alignment with a buddha's speech. This involved, among other things, attributing rules to various buddhas or to ancient kings and bodhisattvas depicted in the *jātaka* corpus. A certain trend in the direction of emergent positivity is clearly evident. These complex reformulations, still too poorly understood, were discrete projects by laymen and monks who focused their efforts on different legal treatises and topics, not an organized or centralized movement of religio-legal reform under the explicit banner of the palace (Lammerts 2018, 172–78). Nevertheless, during the full history of its transmission in precolonial Burma, *dhammasattha* texts were repeatedly justified in terms of their ability to extend the longevity of Buddhism in the world by establishing social, political, and economic norms that would, it was argued, increase human material wealth and thereby generate ever more resources for the support and expansion of Buddhist institutions.

Despite the circumscribed role of the *rājā* in the production or purification of *dhammasattha* law, if we are to understand constitutionalist norms in the "thin sense,"[21] as laws that regulate kingship or politics, *dhammasattha* provides no shortage of examples. Akin to Brāhmaṇical *dharmaśāstra*, there are laws about how a king should judge legal disputes, how he should urinate and brush his teeth, how he should worship the triple gem, about his prerogatives in assigning fines and punishment, about taxation, about royal property and insignia, about demarcating the extent of the realm's territorial boundaries, about transgressions against the throne (rebellion, treason), about the king's duties to investigate crimes, about the

For a central Thai example dated 1805 that is closely parallel with *Manusāra*, see Baker and Pasuk 2016, 33–39.

20 For a fuller explication of these features, see Lammerts 2018, particularly Ch. 6.

21 Raz 1998, 153.

qualifications and appointment of ministers, officers, and judges, and so forth. There are even laws that govern the exemption of royal animals from criminal prosecution for trespass, causing destruction, or committing murder. The history and variation of these or similar rules could easily be mined to furnish examples of constitutionalist dimensions of *dhammasattha* law.

2.2.2.1 An Example of a Plausibly Constitutional Provision

Dhammasattha treatises are usually organized around eighteen major "titles of law" (typically called "roots;" *mūla* in Pali or *amrac* in Burmese – a category clearly related to the *vyavahārapada* framework of Brāhmaṇical *dharmaśāstra*): debt, inheritance, assault, theft, slavery, gifts, gambling, marriage, and so on. Provisions dealing with procedure are sometimes grouped together in a prefatory section, or sometimes scattered throughout relevant discussions of substantive law. One of the more interesting procedural clauses in the corpus, which has bearing on the question of regulating the king, concerns what we shall refer to as the "statute of limitations" on bringing legal suits. Toward the end of its introductory section, after enumerating the eighteen "titles of law," *Dhammavilāsa* states:

> Among the eighteen foundational titles of law in the *dhammasat*, the following four titles of law may be litigated when the king, lord of water and earth, has changed: the law of taking loans, the law of inheritance,[22] the law of *saṅghika* monastic lands, and the law of hereditary slaves (*mi lā pha lā kyvan*). But the following four titles of law shall not be litigated when the king, lord of water and earth, has changed: the law of murder, the law of intentional physical assault and verbal abuse, the law of rape,[23] and the law of theft of property, gold, or silver. Thus has the seer Manu declared.[24]

The *Manusāra* of 1651/2 puts the same law this way:

> I cite these verses (*gāthā*) regarding the nine types of legal disputes (*amhu*) that should be dismissed upon the change of king:
>
> *Pasayhanaṃ abbhūtañ ca paradārañ ca vadhakaṃ* |
> *Vañcanaṃ gūhanaṃ lumpaṃ corakaṃ ghātakan ti 'me* ||
> *Aṭṭā nava viparito rājā*[25] *vinā vinicchayā* |
> *Na pana iṇakadāsaṃ pacchā passaṃ palāyanaṃ* ||

[22] Omitted, presumably by scribal error, in UCL 9926.

[23] *mayāḥ khuiḥ*, literally, "wife-stealing." This phrase is often best translated as "rape," although it also covers adulterous sexual relationships in which a married woman is a consensual accomplice.

[24] NL Kaṅḥ 18, kaṃ.r; UCL 9926, khī.r; BL 12248, khū.v; UBhS 163–582, khā.r.

[25] A majority of witnesses read *viparite rājā*, although with *viparite* (loc. sg.) we would expect *raññe* (loc. sg.), as emended by Vaṇṇadhamma in his later recension of the text. A minority of manuscripts have *viparito rājā* (nom. sg.). The Burmese gloss clearly indicates that the clause was taken as an absolute construction. For present purposes, therefore, I analyze *viparito rājā* as an elusive "nominative absolute," while noting that it is hardly beyond suspicion. On the

> Suppression [of uprisings/rebellion], gambling, [transgressions against] another's wife, murder,
>
> fraud, concealment [of another's property], armed robbery, theft, destruction. These nine legal suits (*aṭṭa*) are without a ruling (*vinicchaya*) when the king changes.
>
> But not suits [involving] a runaway debtor or runaway slave who is apprehended after [the change of reign].[26]

Provisions along similar lines are repeated, with minor variation, in most subsequent *dhammasattha* treatises compiled up to the colonial era. Their implication is that the period for initiating a legal proceeding in what we might call "criminal" cases – including murder, assault, rape, and theft – is limited to the reign of the king on the throne at the time the crime was committed. Following a change of reign, the ability to bring a suit lapses. This is not the case, however, when it comes to other titles of law, such as inheritance or monastic property. The window for litigating these domains does not expire.

As far as I am aware, this curious provision is unique to Burma, or minimally is not something echoed by Sanskrit *dharmaśāstra* rules or those of Thai or Cambodian *dhammasattha*. The only scholar to have commented upon it, the legal historian Shwe Baw, surmised that the logic underlying the formulation and persistence of the rule is uncertain, as is the question of whether it was ever observed in practice (1955, 538–39). Nevertheless, the law suggests that the reigning king has a special relationship to crimes committed during his tenure. Judges or kings themselves do not have legal authority (in *dhammasattha*'s field of view) to pass judgment over crimes perpetrated during the reign of former kings.

This, it seems to me, is one among many examples of a constitutionalist provision furnished by the *dhammasattha* corpus. The rule simultaneously enables and constrains the operation of courts in relation to certain categories of substantive law. Moreover, it imposes a limitation upon not only judges, but upon the king's judicial power, for he is unable to adjudicate crimes committed prior to his coronation. A likely explanation for the law may be found in the fact that personal status was a determining factor in deciding "criminal" cases such as murder, assault, rape, and theft. The appropriate punishment for such crimes is assigned as a function of the socioeconomic "class" (Burmese, *amyuiḥ*; Pali, *vaṇṇa*) of both victim and perpetrator. In cases of murder and rape, for example, penalties often involved fines linked to the variable "body-price" (*kuiy bhuiḥ*) of the victim, sometimes in addition to corporal punishment such as mutilation, the value of which was determined by socioeconomic status, such as being a poor person, rich

doubtfulness of the nominative absolute in Pali, see von Hinüber 1968, 28–31. I thank Petra Kieffer-Pülz and Aleix Ruiz-Falqés for a stimulating discussion about the syntax of these verses.

26 UCL 105682, ññu.v; BL 12241, ṭū.r; NL Taṅ 10 jhī.r; UCL 5440, jau.r.

person, "Good Person," military officer, minister, relative of the king, and so on. Status identities were highly fluid, inasmuch as they were bestowed by or in light of a dependent relationship with the reigning king, his kinspeople, and clients. They were not fixed in perpetuity across reigns in the same way as certain other social identities – such as, for example, father and daughter, husband and wife, monk, or hereditary slave status – which were of essential concern in other domains of law.

It is worth reiterating that this brief example of one among very many constitutional provisions in *dhammasattha* has absolutely nothing to do with a representation of the king as a *dhammarājā*, *cakravartin*, or bodhisattva. Nor does it relate to conceptions of exogenous dhamma as higher justice. The law, or if you prefer, the "dhamma" (Burmese, *tarāḥ*), of the text is no doubt authorized by a justificatory narrative (like all law), which at times invokes certain complex figurations of cosmology and kingship, such as the story of Mahāsammata and Manu, but these figurations alone are woefully inadequate to the task of elucidating the substance and mechanics of individual constitutionalist rules such as this. This is to say, again, that if we want to understand the operation of Buddhist constitutionalism in precolonial Southeast Asia, there is simply no substitute for direct engagement with the evidence of the legal texts themselves.

2.2.3 *Royal Legislation*

The legal ecosystem inhabited by *dhammasattha* recognized multiple sites of authoritative law. *Dhammasattha* was not a purely self-referential normative environment, but one that sanctioned forms of legal-textual alterity that could, and sometimes did, conflict with its own norms, including both *vinaya* and royal legislation (*rājasattha*). These other environments or genres of legislation did not necessarily differ on cosmological or ritual grounds – for example, in the sense that one was "religious" and the other "secular" – but were nonetheless deferred to on certain occasions. Indeed, *dhammasattha* texts not only recognize a hierarchy of law but yield to royal command as legislation of the highest authority superseding all other legal rules.

For example, in the final section of its seventh chapter, *Responsa of Manurājā* states:

> Regarding the point that *rājasattha* has authority over *dhammasattha*, and an agreement (*gati*) annuls *rājasattha*: Despite whatever *dhammasattha* may authorize, the three spheres of life, wealth, and body shall be regulated by the command of the sovereign (*rājasattha*) prescribed by kings of great merit. Yet, despite whatever royal edicts might authorize, an agreement annuls royal legislation when the two litigants have reached mutual consensus. The following [tale] is evidence (*sakse*, lit. "a witness") for this norm (*thuṃḥ caṃ*):
>
> Once upon a time, two men entered into the service of the king. One day, the king asked them, "in what do you place your trust (*yuṃ*)?" One man replied, "only karma." The other replied, "only my lord the king." To the man who said that he

trusted only karma, the king gave a bunch of bananas. To the man who said that he trusted only his lord, the king gave a coconut that had been filled with gold.

When the two men departed the palace and were out on the road, the one with the coconut said, "I have many children and grandchildren at home, whereas you have none, therefore let us exchange the coconut for the bananas."

When he reached his house, the man who trusted only the king distributed the bananas among his children and grandchildren. The man who trusted only karma, when he arrived home, split open the coconut, found it filled with gold, and became rich.

Later, when they returned to the palace, the king inquired, "which of you has become rich?" The man who had said he trusted only the king replied, "your servant is still poor." But the man who said he trusted only karma replied, "your servant is now rich."

The king then asked what they had done with the bananas and coconut he had given them.

"Because I have many children and grandchildren, I exchanged the coconut my lord had presented to me."

The king said, "I wanted *you* to have the gold-filled coconut. Because you exchanged it for the bananas, your colleague has received the gold and is now rich."

The man responded, "Before I exchanged the coconut, I did not know that it was filled with gold intended for me. If this is true, a legal ruling (*acī raṅ*) resolving this case should be issued in accordance with the original intention of your gift."

The king ruled that his original intention was irrelevant to the case. Since the two men mutually agreed to the exchange, their agreement must stand.

From that time onward, even when kings or other men may judge or command that someone receive something, the legal decision (*cī raṅ thuṃḥ*) has conformed to the mutual agreement of litigants. Thus, *rājasattha* has authority over *dhammasattha*, and an agreement annuls *rājasattha*.[27]

In this rule and its accompanying narrative, *dhammasattha* subordinates itself to the legislation of the sovereign, nullifying its own jurisdiction over all legal questions on which the king himself might wish to issue an edict. However, *rājasattha* is also limited by mutual consensus or contractual agreement as a higher standard that even *dhammasattha* or royal law cannot abrogate. This provision echoes a maxim frequently encountered in Burmese legal documents, according to which *dhammasattha* law and formal tribunals become necessary only when disputes cannot be settled through other, non-legal means. That is, when parties to a dispute reach consensus in the resolution of conflict, there is no cause to invoke the law, even if the terms of the agreement do not conform to established legal norms. Even when the law is invoked, a trial held, and a judge has issued a ruling, transcripts of precolonial Burmese trial

[27] UCL 4645, gū.r; UCL 8270, gau.r; UCL 105690, ṭha.v.

proceedings often conclude by stating that the litigants faced each other and together ate pickled tea (*lak phak*), symbolizing their mutual acceptance of and submission to the decision.[28] This ultimate goal of conflict resolution, outstripping any formal "legal" remedies, is not limited to the *dhammasattha* corpus, but is frequently promoted in surviving texts of royal edicts themselves.

The sovereign power of the king to determine and inflict corporal punishment according to royal legislation is also something routinely granted by dhammasattha law. For example, *Dhammavilāsa* states, in relation to oath breakers:

> In fortified towns and large and small villages of the realm and in districts of the royal dominion that have been described [in the foregoing], whosoever makes an oath of truth in front of Good People, such as bhikkhus and *brāhmaṇas*, or others, saying that they will not break the oath, and then at a later time breaks that oath, they should be mercilessly beaten with the cane so that in the future they do not do it again. If the oath breaker is a person of high social status, they should be dragged down from their residence, their head covering or face cloth removed, and with their head bent down in shame they must leave their relatives behind and go to work as a gravedigger (*dvanḥ caṇḍāla*). They should be confined in the elephant or horse stable under the house. Let them collect the elephant and horse shit for two days, or four or five days, or six or seven days, or eight days, nine days, ten days, or a fortnight. Such is the punishment they should receive. This type of punishment is known as *maṅḥ daṇ* ("punishment of the king," *rājadaṇḍa*). If they will not accept this sort of punishment once it has been given, let them pay a fine of 5 gold pieces or 100 silver coins. They should never again be trusted. They should suffer defeat in all legal affairs. However, if such a man is executed, or if his feet or hands are cut off, one should not invoke *dhammasattha*. In such cases one has invoked royal legislation (*rājasattha*). The judge who does this [i.e. invokes the *dhammasattha* as justification for corporal punishment] shall suffer punishment in the Four Hells.[29]

A representative (though inexhaustive) collection of hundreds of Burmese royal edicts (Pali *rājasattha*; Burmese, *amin. tau*, "royal speech") dated (not always unproblematically) between the late sixteenth and late nineteenth centuries has been edited by the historian Than Tun and published along with English-language summaries of each edict.[30] A cursory perusal of this remarkable corpus immediately reveals the legislative imperatives of Burmese kingship, a sort of paradigmatically Austinian archive of law as sovereign command, in which the king takes center stage in legislating the realm through the regulation of political institutions and identities. While the edicts are usually presented in the king's first-person voice, they were

[28] Such features obviously invite comparison with other contexts of dispute resolution, for example in medieval Europe or modern Tibet, which have preferred to avoid recourse to formal law, on which see Pirie 2013, 33–38; Keyser 2012.

[29] UCL 7490, gai.r; UCL 9926, go.v; DhV Kaṅḥ 18, khau.v; BL 12248, ga.v; UBhS 163–582, gī.r.

[30] Than Tun 1983–1990 (available online: https://repository.kulib.kyoto-u.ac.jp/dspace/handle/2433/173188). A related late precolonial genre of royal law is the *upade* legislation issued during the reigns of King Mindon and King Thibaw (1853–85), on which see Htun Yee 1999b.

often executed and proclaimed by his ministerial advisors at the palace. In one of the earliest such documents, for example, issued 29 April 1597, King Nyaungyan-min declares a lengthy list of dozens of duties for newly appointed ministers at the rank of *senapati*, including that they:

> ... Ceaselessly work to regulate the affairs of the realm; ... render legal judgments that diligently strive to diminish theft, murder, and arson; render legal judgments for all beings that are proportionate to the offense; investigate and record in writing for the palace archive the qualifications of all subordinate royal officers (*amhu thamḥ*); ... support and exhibit *saṅgaha*[31] to the four social classes; ... advise the king when disputes arise, presenting him with the legal norm (*thumḥ caṃ*), so he may properly adjudicate the case; ... do not judge cases under the sway of anger, ignorance, or greed for money;[32]... do not maltreat or oppress the people; ... observe the five precepts (*sīla*) every day; observe the *uposatha* [i.e., observe the eight precepts] four times a month; strive to perform meritorious deeds; send *mettā* to the lord who holds authority [= the reigning king]; for the sake of all beings, meditate '*sabbe sattā averā hontu*' [may all beings be free from evil];[33] ... do not allow the royal finances in the palace treasury to become depleted; do not follow the desires of women; avoid the three kinds of judicial bribes (*uccā taṃ cuiḥ*);[34] ... in the first watch of the night, confer with those who know the *dhammasattha* and tales of judicial decisions, those who know legal norms, those who know how to judge and understand how to investigate, those who know trading and buying and selling, those who know the scriptures (*kyamḥ gan*), and those who know about astrology.[35] ...[36]

Many other edicts seek to regulate the conduct of tax officials, military servicemen, traders, monks, and slaves, and particularly the comportment of judges and the operation and fees of legal courts. Numerous examples demonstrate that the edicts of former kings may be regarded as settled law or established "precedent," or they

31 *saṅgaha pru*. This suggests that the ministers should demonstrate the four *saṅgahavatthu* – *dāna, peyyavajja, atthacariyā, samānattatā* (generosity, kind speech, beneficial conduct, and impartiality) – frequently mentioned in Pali and Burmese literature.

32 This is parallel with the provision frequently encountered in *dhammasattha* treatises that judges must avoid the four "bad courses" (*agati*) of desire, fear, anger, and ignorance, on which see Lammerts 2018, 35, 83–86, 189–90.

33 Compare Jā II, 61, etc. This is a standard verbal formula offering protection (*anugganha*). *Avera* is often translated as "without hatred," although this tends to miss the sense here, wherein *vera* is essentially synonymous with *pāpa, akusala, apuñña*, and so on.

34 The precise referent is unspecified, and there are at least two different formulations of threefold bribery. The most common in Burmese judicial contexts refers to a fraudulent decision made by a judge out of consideration for: (1) personal enrichment (*dhanaggāha*), (2) love or affection (*pīyamitta*) for one of the litigants, or (3) a blood relative (*ñātilohita*) who is of one of the litigants.

35 This clause reflects those sections in *dhammasattha* and *dharmaśāstra* texts where the nightly "routine" of a king is detailed.

36 This order is reproduced in Than Tun 1983–1990, Vol. 2, although it is drawn by him from U Htun Yee n.d., 2–3. Htun Yee takes the order from a manuscript in the private collection of historian Toe Hla. There are some complexities relating to this text, not least that it appears to have been issued prior to Nyaungyan-min's formal consecration.

might be seen to be in conflict, nullified by the dictate of the reigning monarch. The orders also reveal the integration of *dhammasattha* law into royal law, in a sort of reversal of *dhammasattha*'s pluralist deference to *rājasattha* mentioned above: for example, an edict dated June 23, 1607, states that judges should follow *dhammasattha* norms in the conduct of trials and determination of punitive fines, or another dated August 11, 1692, that prescribes that the division of heritable property for military officers shall follow *dhammasattha* rules of succession.

Lingat would surely contend that "such decisions have only the force of royal authority, they do not make law" (Lingat 1937, 22). While such commands are not, in most cases, grounded in *dhammasattha*, nor in any "supreme Dharma," nor in the words of a buddha, it is rather difficult to conceptualize a definition of "law" with which the *rājā*'s edict, as lavishly depicted in these documents, is incongruous, especially given that the transgression of such edicts was met with "severe punishment," including bodily mutilation and execution (September 6, 1573). Likewise, Chris Baker and Pasuk Phongpaichit have recently demonstrated *contra* Lingat that in the neighboring context of precolonial Thailand "the evidence for kings making laws is very strong" (Baker and Pasuk 2021, 29).

2.3 THE OUTER CASING OF THE LAW

The study of constitutional aspects of Buddhist law is beleaguered by the faithfully monogamous marriage of constitution and "state" in theoretical discussions, as well as, relatedly, the dissociation of constitutional law from other types of law. Aristotle popularized the distinct status of constitutions in *Politics*. Yet this persistent decoupling, so influential in modern Europe and contemporary constitutionalist scholarship, fails to account for the fact that in many terrains of history, including precolonial Southeast Asia, the regulation of the action of the political sphere has not been conceived of as at all distinct from other forms of law and lawmaking. Here all law is "constitutive" or "constituting," and the *rājā*, for example, is merely another staged character in the legal performance.

If we are to try to engage constitutional aspects of precolonial Buddhist law, it is therefore necessary to expand the inherited parameters of the governing analysis, since a significant quantum of such law, until quite recently, has not been legislated under the aegis of a *rājā* (or "state"), much less by a *demos*, or "We the People," even if it occasionally sought to regulate the throne. It is an anthropological commonplace that all formations of community, including the most acephalous, entail a regulatory or normative dimension that seeks to negotiate or manage relations of power, and thus evince constitutionalist aspects or strategies (Amborn 2009). Recognizing such features of Buddhist legal discourse, however, at least those *actually* circulating in precolonial Southeast Asia, asks us to think about constitutionalism from a somewhat different angle, one more aligned with the contours of our archive.

If we would like to discover Buddhist constitutionalist norms, if by this we mean the "thin," non-Aristotelian sense of laws that order spheres of politics or institutional power (*the palace, the monastery*), we need not search very far at all. These are abundant across the several Southeast Asian legal environments discussed above, and I have offered only a handful of illustrative specimens, mostly from Burmese *dhammasattha*. There are extensive, readily accessible, examples elsewhere, too. Among these are the recently translated *Kot Monthianban* ("Palace Law of Ayutthaya;" Baker and Pasuk 2016), the long-ago translated "*lois constitutionnelles*" of precolonial Cambodia (Leclère 1898, I, 37–232), as well as the local varieties of monastic law treated in the work of Berthe Jansen (2018), Benjamin Schonthal (2021a; 2021c), and Brenton Sullivan (2021). It is nevertheless evident from the examples given above that the heretofore standard approach, fixated on the rhetorical tropes of Buddhist kingship spellbound by dhamma, fails to nominate even approximately viable candidates.

As Chris Baker and Pasuk Phongpaichit have recently observed, "the basis of kingship in Siam and neighboring states is often described solely in relation to sacredness and religious power through terms such as *devaraja* (god king), *thammaraja* (dhamma king), and *cakravartin* (wheel-turning emperor)" (Baker and Pasuk 2016, ix). This indefensible predicament needs to change. There is, in short, no sparsity of rich legal documentation from precolonial Buddhist Southeast Asia that offers scholars access to distinctive local forms of constitutionalist thought and practice. Classical Pali repertoires are no doubt variously relevant to the discussion, but often in oblique and surprising ways. Indeed, the foregoing analysis argues for precisely an inversion of Lingat's influential thesis. The integument or "outer casing of the law" is neither the king's command nor the complex historical substance of lawmaking in whichever of our three environments, but rather the conceit of dhamma as the "king of kings," which has received far too much attention in scholarship, at the expense of legal history itself.

ABBREVIATIONS

BL	British Library
NL	National Library of Myanmar, Yangon
UBhS	U Bho Thi Manuscript Library, Thaton
UCL	Universities' Central Library, Yangon

REFERENCES

Amborn, Hermann. 2009. *Law as Refuge of Anarchy: Societies without Hegemony or State.* Cambridge: MIT Press.

[AN] Morris, Richard, and E. Hardy. 1883–1900. *The Aṅguttara-nikāya*. 5 vols. London: Pali Text Society.

Baker, Chris and Pasuk Phongpaichit. 2016. *The Palace Law of Ayutthaya and the Thammasat*. Ithaca: Southeast Asia Program Publications, Cornell University.

2021. "Thammasat, Custom, and Royal Authority in Siam's Legal History." In *Thai Legal History: From Traditional to Modern Law*, edited by Andrew Harding and Munin Pongsapan, 23–40. Cambridge: Cambridge University Press.

Blackburn, Anne. 1999. "Looking for the *Vinaya*: Monastic Discipline in the Practical Canons of the Theravāda." *Journal of the International Association of Buddhist Studies* 22 (2): 281–309.

Clarke, Shayne. 2015. "Vinayas." In *Brill's Encyclopedia of Buddhism*, Vol. 1, edited by Jonathan A. Silk, et al., 60–87. Leiden: Brill.

Collins, Steven. 2006. *Nirvāna and Other Buddhist Felicities*. New York: Cambridge.

Dhammavilāsa dhammasat. NL Kaṅḥ 18; UCL 7490; UCL 9926; BL 12248; UBhS 163–582.

Ellingson, Ter. 1990. "Tibetan Monastic Constitutions: The bCa' yig." In *Reflections on Tibetan Culture: Essays in Memory of Turrell V. Wylie*, edited by L. Epstein and R. F. Sherburne, 205–29. Lewiston: Edward Mellen.

Gokhale, Balkrishna. 1953. "Dhammiko Dhammarāja: A Study in Buddhist Constitutional Concepts." In *Indica: The Indian Historical Research Institute Silver Jubilee Commemoration Volume*, 161–65. Bombay: St. Xavier's College.

1966. "Early Buddhist Kingship." *Journal of Asian Studies* 26 (1): 15–22.

1969. "The Early Buddhist View of the State." *Journal of the American Oriental Society*, 89 (4): 731–38.

Griswold, A. B. and Prasert Na Nagara. 1969. "A Law Promulgated by the King of Ayudhyā in 1397 A.D." *Journal of the Siam Society* 57 (1): 109–48.

1975. "Kingship and Society at Sukhodaya." In *Change and Persistence in Thai Society: Essays in Honor of Lauriston Sharp*, edited by G. William Skinner and A. Thomas Kirsch, 29–92. Ithaca: Cornell University Press.

1992. *Epigraphical and Historical Studies*. Bangkok: The Historical Society.

von Hinüber, Oskar. 1968. *Studien zur Kausussyntax des Pāli, Besonders des Vinaya-Piṭaka*. München: Kitzinger.

Htun Yee [Thvanḥ Rī]. n.d. *Ññoṅ ramḥ khet amin. tau myāḥ*, vol. 1. Yangon: Mran mā mhu bimān.

1999a. *Kunḥ bhoṅ khet ṅve khyeḥ sakkarāj cā khyup myāḥ: Collection of Thet-kayit (Moneylending Contracts of Myanmar Rural Area in Kon-baung Period)*. 3 Vols. Toyohashi: Aichi University.

1999b. *Ratanā puṃ khet upade myāḥ: Collection of Upade (Laws and Regulations of Myanmar Last Two Kings)*. Toyohashi: Aichi University.

2006. *Kunḥ bhoṅ khet phrat cā poṅḥ khyup: Collection of Hpyat-sa (Legal Cases and Court Decisions of Myanmar in the Kon-baung Period, A.D. 1752–1885)*. 4 vols. Yangon: Mran mā mhu bimān cā pe bhaṇ.

Huxley, Andrew. 1999. "Buddhist Case Law on Theft: The Vinītavatthu on the Second Pārājika." *Journal of Buddhist Ethics*, 6: 313–30.

Janaka, Ashin and Crosby, Kate. 2017. "Heresy and Monastic Malpractice in the Buddhist Court Cases (Vinicchaya) of Modern Burma (Myanmar)." *Contemporary Buddhism* 18: 199–261.

Jansen, Berthe. 2015. "Monastic Organizational Guidelines." In *Brill's Encyclopedia of Buddhism*, Vol. 1, edited by Jonathan A. Silk, et al., 442–49. Leiden: Brill.

2018. *The Monastery Rules: Buddhist Monastic Organization in Pre-Modern Tibet*. Berkeley: University of California Press.

[Jā] Fausbøll, V. 1877–1896. *The Jātaka, together with Its Commentary, Being Tales of the Anterior Births of Gotama Buddha*. 6 vols. London: Trübner.

Jayawickrama, N. A. 1986. *The Inception of Discipline and the Vinaya Nidāna*. London: Pali Text Society.

Jory, Patrick. 2016. *Thailand's Theory of Monarchy: The Vessantara Jātaka and the Idea of the Perfect Man*. Albany: State University of New York Press.

Keyser, Richard L. 2012. "'Agreement Supersedes Law, and Love Judgement:' Legal Flexibility and Amicable Settlement in Anglo-Norman England." *Law and History Review* 30 (1): 37–88.

Kieffer-Pülz, Petra. 2011. "The Law of Theft: Regulations in the Theravāda Vinaya and the Law Commentaries." *Journal of the Pali Text Society* 31: 1–54.

2016–2017. "Translocal Debates and Legal Hermeneutics: Early Pāli Vinaya Texts in the Adjudication of Sīmā Procedures, c. 1200–1900 C.E." *Journal of Buddhism, Law & Society* 2: 103–58.

Koenig, William J. 1990. *The Burmese Polity, 1752–1819: Politics, Administration, and Social Organization in the Early Kon-baung Period*. Ann Arbor: Center for South and Southeast Asian Studies, University of Michigan.

Lammerts, D. Christian. 2005. *The Dhammavilāsa Dhammathat: A Critical Historiography, Analysis, and Translation of the Text*. M.A. thesis, Cornell University.

2010. *Buddhism and Written Law: Dhammasattha Manuscripts and Texts in Premodern Burma*. PhD thesis, Cornell University.

2013. "Narratives of Buddhist Legislation: Textual Authority and Legal Heterodoxy in Seventeenth through Nineteenth-Century Burma." *Journal of Southeast Asian Studies* 44, (1): 118–44.

2018. *Buddhist Law in Burma: A History of Dhammasattha Texts and Jurisprudence, 1250–1850*. Honolulu: University of Hawai'i Press.

2019–2020. "Judicial Ordeals in Premodern Thailand: Robert Lingat's 'Les ordalies au siam' (1949), An Annotated Translation and Commentary." *Journal of Buddhism, Law & Society* 5: 31–60.

2022. "Burmese Inscriptions as Buddhist Legal Texts." *Journal of Buddhism, Law & Society*.

Latter, Thomas. 1850. *Selections from the Vernacular Boodhist Literature of Burmah*. Maulmain: American Baptist Missionary Press.

Leclère, Adhémard. 1898. *Les Codes Cambodgiens*. 2 Vols. Paris: Ernest Leroux.

Lingat, Robert. 1937. "L'influence indoue dans l'ancien droit siamois." In *Institut de droit comparé, conférences 1936*, edited by Robert Lingat and Denise Paulme, 1–29. Paris: Domat-Montchrestien.

1950. "Evolution of the Concept of Law in Burma and Siam." *Journal of the Siam Society* 38 (1): 9–31.

1951. "La conception du droit dans l'indochine hînayâniste." *Bulletin de l'École Française d'Extrême-Orient*, 44 (1): 163–87.

Manurājā lhyok thuṃḥ (Responsa of Manurājā). UCL 4645; UCL 8270; UCL 105690.

Manusāra dhammasattha. UCL 105682; BL 12241; NL Taṅ 10; UCL 5440.

Mérieau, Eugénie. 2020. "Area Studies and the Decolonisation of Comparative Law: Insights from Alternative Southeast Asian Constitutional Modernities." *International Quarterly for Asian Studies* 51 (3–4): 67–84.

Pirie, Fernanda. 2013. *The Anthropology of Law*. Oxford: Oxford University Press.

Ratnapala, Nandasena. 1971. *The Katikāvatas: Laws of the Buddhist Order of Ceylon from the 12th Century to the 18th Century*. München: Kitzinger.

Raz, Joseph. 1998. "On the Authority and Interpretation of Constitutions: Some Preliminaries." In *Constitutionalism: Philosophical Foundations*, edited by Larry Alexander, 152–93. New York: Cambridge University Press.

Reynolds, Frank. 1972. "Two Wheels of the Dhamma: A Study of Early Buddhism." In *The Two Wheels of the Dharma*, edited by Frank Reynolds and Bardwell Smith, 6–30. Chambersburg: American Academy of Religion.

Saito, Teruko. 2019. *18–19 seiki Biruma shakkin shōmon no kenkyū: Tōnan Ajia no hitotsu no kinsei* [A Study of Debt Contracts in 18–19th century Burma: A Southeast Asian Early Modernity]. Kyoto: Kyoto Daigaku Gakujutsu Shuppankai.

Schonthal, Benjamin. 2016. "Environments of Law: Islam, Buddhism, and the State in Contemporary Sri Lanka." *Journal of Asian Studies* 75 (1): 137–56.

2017–2018. "Litigating Vinaya: Buddhist Law and Public Law in Contemporary Sri Lanka." *Journal of Buddhism, Law & Society* 3: 69–111

2021a. "Buddhist Law Beyond the Vinaya: Monastic Constitutions (*Katikāvatas*) and their Transformations in Colonial Sri Lanka." *History of Religions* 60 (4): 287–324.

2021b. "Judging in the Buddha's Court: A Buddhist Judicial System in Contemporary Asia." *Asian Journal of Law and Society* 8 (2): 206–25.

2021c. "The Case for Religious Constitutions: Comparative Constitutional Law among Buddhists, and Other Religious Groups." *Law and Social Inquiry* 47 (2): 391–419.

Shwe Baw. 1955. *Origin and Development of Burmese Legal Literature*. PhD thesis, University of London.

Skilling, Peter. 1997. "The Advent of Theravāda Buddhism to Mainland South-East Asia." *Journal of the International Association of Buddhist Studies* 20 (1): 93–107.

[Sp] Takakusu, Junjiro, and Makoto Nagai. 1924–1947. *Samantapāsādikā: Buddhaghosa's Commentary on the Vinaya Piṭaka*. 7 vols. London: Pali Text Society.

Sparks, T. P. 1851. *Decisions of Princess Thoo-Dhamma Tsari: Translated from the Burmese, According to the Text of Lieut. T. Latter*. Maulmain: American Mission Press.

Sullivan, Brenton. 2021. *Building a Religious Empire: Tibetan Buddhism, Bureaucracy, and the Rise of the Gelukpa*. Philadelphia: University of Pennsylvania Press.

Tambiah, Stanley. 1976. *World Conqueror & World Renouncer*. New York: Cambridge University Press.

1989. "King Mahāsammata: The First King in the Buddhist Story of Creation, and his Persisting Relevance." *Journal of the Anthropological Society of Oxford* 20 (2): 101–22.

Than Tun. 1983–1990. *The Royal Orders of Burma*. 10 vols. Kyoto: Center for Southeast Asian Studies, Kyoto University.

3

Theorising Constitutionalism in Buddhist-Dominant Asian Polities

*Asanga Welikala**

3.1 INTRODUCTION

One of the main research questions of this volume is: Do existing models in the study of religion and constitutional law adequately explain the dynamics of Buddhism and constitutional law in Asia? This might be broken down into two further and somewhat more specific questions, namely, what are the elements of a theory of constitutionalism that have the capacity to explain existing constitutional practice, and on that basis, prescribe certain general norms of constitutional order, in Buddhist-dominant Asian polities?

In giving some preliminary answers to these two questions within the scope of a short chapter, I rely on the following assumptions. I define the empirical context of study as "Buddhist-dominant Asian polities," meaning contemporary states in Asia where Buddhism is a material and salient influence on the law and politics of constitutionalism. This group of countries is both geographically widespread and extremely diverse in terms of its socioeconomic structures, societal and political cultures, and, importantly, its traditions of Buddhism. Notwithstanding those differences, we possess sufficient comparative knowledge in the field of "Buddhism and Law" studies to be plausibly able to work with a set of general propositions about how Buddhism influences constitutionalism. Buddhist-dominant Asian polities are also highly varied in terms of constitutional democracy, representing everything from non-democracies to consolidated democracies, meaning that there is no common concept of analytical constitutionalism through which we can understand their governance and politics. The normative assumptions underpinning the

* Thanks to Rohan Edrisinha, Tom Ginsburg, Andrew Harding, Dinesha Samararatne, and most of all, Benjamin Schonthal, for their penetrating and helpful comments on a previous draft. Many of those comments raise complex and difficult points that require addressing in future work. However, and subject to the customary caveat, I am grateful to these friends for helping make this initial statement of my views more coherent than they were in the original draft.

dominant contemporary discourse of comparative constitutional law, chiefly the assumptions concerning the autonomy and normative superiority of legal norms over other norms, are either inadequate or inappropriate for analysing the constitutional cultures of these countries. As a consequence, mainstream comparative constitutional law has found it difficult to find purchase in these countries as an explanatory framework, a normative philosophy of good government, and as a technology of constitutional design.

Existing accounts therefore do not adequately deal with the key relationships between politics, law, and culture, which produce, legitimate, structure, and limit governing power – in a word, constitutionalism – in Buddhist-dominant Asian polities. These relationships are between, on the one hand, the constitutional forms of legal authority that more or less originate in some version of a Western model, and on the other hand, the formal or informal modes of the exercise of political or public power that more or less derive from Buddhist-infused cultural norms. The first step in the construction of a meaningful theory of constitutionalism for and in this category of polity, therefore, is to be able to provide a descriptive account of this relationship between authority and power, form and function, state and society, institutions and culture.[1] This account must not be distorted by either external substantive normative assumptions (e.g., derived from liberalism) or by a "normativist style" of theorising.[2] In particular, it must not be assumed from the facile resemblance of constitutional forms to Western models that Western values can be used to understand and evaluate their operation. The methodology of theory-building in this first phase thus ought to be descriptive and interpretative, as opposed to normative and prescriptive, so as to achieve two important preliminary aims. The first is to capture, as accurately as possible, the reality of constitutionalism as it is actually practiced in these polities. The second is to provide plausible and explicit explanations of the various dialectic or syncretic ways in which the interaction between Western forms and Buddhist norms gives shape to the practice of constitutionalism. Only once such a satisfactory descriptive account has been developed should we turn our attention to the normative dimensions of a theory of constitutionalism, that is, questions about the nature of power-constraining principles, and the reasons by which they are justified.

This two-step theory-building exercise engages the two distinct bodies of scholarship already mentioned – "Buddhism and Law" studies and mainstream comparative constitutional law – which have hitherto developed along parallel trajectories. Driven mostly by the methodological frames and substantive concerns of religious

1 I use the term "descriptive theory" here in the same sense and a similar context as John Griffiths (Griffiths 1986).

2 Loughlin defines the "normativist style" as "rooted in the belief in the ideal of the separation of powers and in the need to subordinate government to law. This style highlights law's adjudicative and control functions and therefore its rule orientation and conceptual nature. Normativism essentially reflects an ideal of the autonomy of law" (Loughlin 1992, 60).

studies, anthropology, sociology, and history, "Buddhism and Law" studies aspire to an emic approach to understanding Buddhist conceptions of law and legal order. Comparative constitutional law, typifying an etic approach, is driven by lawyers and political scientists, with the formalist methodologies characteristic of those disciplines and concerned mostly with structures, institutions, and procedures of political power and legal authority. Even when comparative constitutional law concerns itself with agentic and cultural questions, it usually looks at local specificities from the perspective of certain ideal-typical normative frameworks, which are Western in origin, but are projected now as values of universal application.[3] These two bodies of knowledge, in terms of both methodology and substance, have their strengths and weaknesses as partial accounts of constitutionalism in Buddhist societies, but as noted, they have largely developed without much engagement with each other. In theorising a model of constitutionalism that could have the best potential explanatory and prescriptive value in Buddhist-dominant Asian polities, "Buddhism and Law" studies and comparative constitutional law should therefore be brought into a dialogic conversation.

Such a conversation would have two dimensions. One the one hand, it would draw from the contextual insights of "Buddhism and Law" to answer general questions of constitutionalism posed by comparative constitutional law, and thus contribute to the broadening and deepening of the potential contribution of "Buddhism and Law." On the other hand – and this is what this chapter is mostly concerned with – it would be the beginning of a process of refining the conceptual equipment of comparative constitutional law in two related ways. One would consist of modest and incremental ways of improving current methods of "doing" constitutional comparativism, while the other involves a more fundamental and even radical revaluation of the foundations of the discipline. The more modest challenge would be that, through its incorporation of "Buddhism and Law" insights, comparative constitutional law could become more methodologically and analytically responsive to the normative and institutional specificities of the constitutional cultures of Buddhist-dominant Asian polities. The more radical possibility is that it could be an opportunity to reappraise the prevailing liberal normativity of mainstream comparative constitutional law in a novel way.

This new pathway to reappraisal is presented by a consideration of the dynamic, as opposed to an either/or, relationship between tradition and modernity in Buddhist-Asian societies. Serving as an analogy for revisiting comparative constitutional law's origins in the European Enlightenment, this enables multiple meanings of that intellectual watershed to be rediscovered, in particular, alternatives to the dominant liberal narrative of the Enlightenment as (liberal) modernity's triumph over (illiberal) tradition. Such alternative meanings of constitutional

3 For this general point being made from the perspective of the case of Buddhism and constitutional law in Sri Lanka, see Schonthal 2016, Chapter 8.

modernity have the potential to pluralise the normative foundations of comparative constitutional law, and to curb liberalism's dominance within its discourse and practice. Some of these alternative meanings of constitutional modernity could make the constraining function of constitutionalism in its normative dimension more consistent with, and less jarring to, the Buddhist-Asian ethos than individualist liberal precepts, without at the same time undermining their constraining function. It would also make the necessary reappraisal of the normative core of comparative constitutional law an inclusive and iterative process between different world cultures.[4]

3.2 BUDDHISM AND LAW STUDIES AND CONSTITUTIONAL LAW

There are a number of insights relevant to constitutional theory-building that might be gleaned from the emergent literature on "Buddhism and Law." Extensively discussed in this literature, albeit not always in ways that directly help the constitutional theorist, are Buddhist ideas of law and dharma, personhood, sovereignty, statehood, political order, collective identity and nationalism, political and territorial space, political ethics, and the relationships between the sangha and laity in general and rulers in particular.

One of the first lessons is that understanding constitutionalism in the Buddhist world demands a comparative methodology that is contextual, which is to say, an approach that looks at the interplay of positive law and other informal types of law in the context of history, politics, culture, and society (French and Nathan 2014, 17–24). For this reason, it is also necessarily a multidisciplinary endeavour. A comparative methodology that focuses only on formal law or institutions, or one that looks at constitutional structures that resemble Western models through Western normative values or animating conventions alone, is likely to result in heavily misleading conclusions. Of course, even in fully modern constitutional systems of positive law, scholars understand that there is more to constitutionalism than the formal laws of the system (Ferejohn, Rakove, and Riley 2010, 10–11). But the difference here is that constitutionalism involves an interplay between laws, rules, norms, practices, and modes of behaviour that emanate from at least two fundamentally different cultural sources – the Western and Buddhist traditions – and often more than two sources depending on the "cultural packages" accompanying legal transplantation through which the given Buddhist-dominant legal system has historically taken shape (French and Nathan 2014, 22 n. 6).

In terms of traditional comparative law methods, the approach that perhaps has the greatest relevance for constitutional law is the idea of legal transplants,

[4] For similar observations from the perspective of the related field of comparative political theory, see Walton 2017, 20–21. See also Moore 2016.

because this permits study not only of how legal concepts are transmitted between different polities, but also examines "the role of power, legitimacy, and authority in their transmission" (French and Nathan 2014, 21). French and Nathan note the prevalence of studies concerning what appear to be "private law" in the Buddhist world, but they underscore a caution that is especially important for constitutional law: " ... a subject for investigation is the degree to which the public-private dichotomy enshrined in Comparative Law discourse is of heuristic value in Buddhism, and also whether or not these putatively universal constructs are too culturally and historically determined to be useful" (French and Nathan 2014, 19–20). This is a point that holds true across a much broader set of issues in constitutional law than simply the public/private divide. Similarly, legal history is a field that contributes much to our understanding of constitutional law by helping us gain a better understanding of law in the past, explaining the role of law in history, and in these ways giving us a more complete understanding of the present (Harding 2021, 1–3).

In terms of substance, Buddhism is directly and extensively concerned with questions of social, political, economic, and legal order; its concerns and its regulatory ambitions are not just otherworldly (French and Nathan 2014, 14 n. 6). In "Buddhism and Law" studies, the idea of law includes the modern conception of a legal system as the body of binding rules governing a polity, conceptions of justice underpinning those rules, and the institutions and procedures for its creation and execution as well as adjudication under those rules. However, as French and Nathan pertinently add, " ... law also includes other practices, such as ... the social customs, practices, and rules that constitute a form of social control for the maintenance of the group; and ... social manners, customary practices, etiquette, and general behaviours regulating silence, speech, and interaction" (French and Nathan 2014, 13–14). This clearly underscores the expansive notion of "law" in Buddhist societies, and this is salient for determining the province of constitutionalism in both the descriptive and normative sense.

Buddhist law operates in a diffuse, fragmented, pluralistic, overlapping, and syncretic way, which must be understood on its own terms. Comparison with other systems of religious law in world history may help in appropriate cases (e.g., law within the Ottoman empire, which functioned in similarly plural and dialectical ways over a large and heterogenous territory). But other comparisons (e.g., with the canon law of medieval Europe) may lead to misleading conclusions, such as the equation of the strength and coherence of the legal system with qualities such as centralisation, codification, and institutionalisation. As French and Nathan argue, "The Buddhist tradition has always been known for its wide diversity in terms of its vast store of sacred texts and different canons, multiple buddhas and bodhisattvas, and accommodation to local beliefs and worldviews" (French and Nathan 2014, 14). This pluralistic, open-ended, and adaptable character of Buddhist law is not a weakness or a marker of incoherence but the very source of its vitality. It is one reason why Buddhism has been both able to form the basis of historic state-formation in so many societies in such a geographically vast and culturally diverse expanse across Asia, and continue to influence the legal systems and political processes of these countries today (French and Nathan 2014, 15). Yet at the same time, this fundamental pluralism is what also explains why there has never been a unified object called "Buddhist law" in the same sense as Islamic law, Jewish law, or canon law.

One of the most important lessons for constitutional theorising that emerges from this brief survey is thus the theme of pluralism. Within Buddhism's unity is a rich pluralism of contextualised expressions. The theme of inherent pluralism is salient in both analytical and normative terms. In the analytical sense, it tells us that constitutionalism in Buddhist societies ought not be constructed on overdetermined positivist categories. Similarly, strong analytical regimes of separation – between domains such as law, politics, culture, and society, or state and religion, or state and society, or the public and the private, or the individual and the collective – would also be inadvisable in building descriptive theory in these contexts. Likewise, the distinctive nature of legal authority, political power, and the forms of their interactions in Buddhist Asia raise questions about how theoretical frameworks on law and religion built with primarily the Abrahamic monotheistic religions in mind might work in this region.[5]

In the normative sense, the inherent diversity of both the Buddhist world and Buddhist traditions appears to offer a rich empirical and ideational basis for developing metaconstitutional theories (or foundational political theories) for constitutional order and constitutional design. Given the centrality of the themes of pluralism and syncretism to the formation of these theories, they moreover promise to take shape in ways that are very different to the Western European and North American historical and cultural contexts from which monistic and centralist theories that currently serve comparative constitutional law have emerged.[6] In particular, we should note that the sociological pluralism of the type we must account for in the Buddhist world has little to do with the value pluralism of Western liberalism, and likewise, the syncretic character of its various constitutionalisms is both a cause and consequence of a historical experience with modern state-formation that is fundamentally different to that of the West. Put another way, plausible constitutional theory for Buddhist-dominant polities cannot be constructed through the prism of Enlightenment liberalism, and its principles of individualism, voluntary choice, and its various regimes of separation.

5 See e.g., Hirschl and Shachar 2018. The authors persistently refer to Hindu and Buddhist *nationalisms*, that is, a modernist form of political mobilisation, in order to fit these two Asian religions into their framework of competing orders.

6 For recent explorations of these themes of pluralism and syncretism in relation to African and Confucian constitutionalisms, see Gebeye 2021 and Bui 2017.

3.3 COMPARATIVE CONSTITUTIONAL LAW AND BUDDHIST-DOMINANT ASIAN POLITIES

As is well-established, comparative constitutional law developed in a succession of waves as a result of major global events, such as the response to the horrors of World War II, decolonisation, and the third wave of democratisation beginning with the collapse of Latin American dictatorships in the 1970s through to the fall of the Soviet bloc in the 1990s. It has now become a self-sustaining interdisciplinary academic field as well as a community of practice, through the linkages between international development policy and constitution-building as an instrument of democratisation and conflict resolution in the global south. In the post-Cold War period, when comparative constitutional law saw its greatest expansion, it has also undergone several phases of rapid discursive evolution, with new challenges superseding older concerns and new information technologies assisting comparativism in multiple ways. For example, a major shift has been from the comparative study of specific subjects within municipal constitutions to the comparative study of general themes of constitutionalism (Tushnet 2018, 1–11). More recently, scholars have noted a "global south turn" in the field, to which we will return in a moment.

One thing about comparative constitutional law that has remained stable and constant throughout this period of exponential growth is its core set of normative precepts, and an institutional design heuristic that is intended to realise those goals. The latter includes democratic elections, constitutional bills of justiciable rights, strong-form judicial review, the separation of powers, fourth pillar institutions, and other institutional devices for constraining power and protecting the rule of law. This normative-institutional core has been defined by the values of liberal constitutionalism, also theorised as "liberal constitutional democracy" (Ginsburg and Huq 2018, 9–15), "the postwar paradigm" (Weinrib 2006, Chapter 4), and "structural-liberalism" (Dowdle and Wilkinson 2017, 17–20). Heavily influenced by the American and French encounters with Enlightenment thought, the normative dimension of the core can be said to encapsulate the following theses. I present these theses here in a highly abstracted and stylised form, with some sacrifice of historical complexity and nuance for the sake of analytical clarity.

The American and French revolutions and consequent constitutional foundings represented the historical paradigm shift of social and political organisation from tradition to modernity (or as the shift is sometimes described, from hierarchy to equality, status to contract, religion to reason). Premodern society was a source of human misery. By the application of human reason and human will, however, society and indeed human nature was radically reconstructed so as to ensure liberty, equality, and fraternity for all. Human beings possess the vast power to destroy and recreate society on a total scale. The constitutional modernity so created is underpinned by two key principles. First, constituted authority is legitimate only to the extent that it is based on the general will of the people. Second, the moral basis of any obligation of obedience to authority, which necessarily involves some restriction on individual freedom, is that it is self-imposed. Only the individual can decide what these self-imposed limits are, based on the individual's own exercise of reason. Any other restraint emanating from existing legal, political, social, and especially religious structures of the community in which the individual lives, lacks the legitimacy required by constitutional modernity.

The philosophy of liberal constitutionalism therefore is based on a historical mindset that sharply and favourably distinguishes modernity from whatever form of order that was present before. It reproduces a sociological worldview of individualism, a normative commitment to individual choice based on the voluntary will, a rejection or at least a subordination of any conception of natural or cosmological order as a legitimate basis of constitutional order, and a set of institutional commitments geared to the protection of individual liberty rights as the main end of constitutionalism. Moreover, constitutional liberalism, as a variant of Enlightenment thought, casts its normative principles as universal precepts applicable to the whole of humanity. This represented a rejection of the premodern notion of the constitution as the expression of the identity of specific politico-cultural communities, or broadly, the concept of the "body politic" (Collingwood 1942, Chapter XXIV) in classical Western political theory, or the synecdochical polities bound by ritual idioms in premodern Buddhist states (Nissan and Stirrat 1990, Chapter 2).

The success of liberal constitutionalism within the American experience, together with the global geopolitical position of the United States in the post-World War II and post-Cold War era, made it possible for a theory otherwise contingent on time, place, and culture, to be projected as the basis of a universal theory of constitutionalism.[7] Liberal constitutionalism's universality, of course, has always been a contested claim within and without the Western tradition (Dowdle and Wilkinson 2017, n. 21). The unevenness of democratisation in Buddhist-dominant Asian polities immediately demonstrates at least one of the sources of contestation, namely, that the universalist blueprint struggles to gain traction in societies where there is a powerful existing source of values and ideas of selfhood. Indeed, it would have been surprising if liberalism's individualist principles had gained more traction in Buddhist societies, where constitutional ordering is cosmological and karmic rather than rationalist and secular. Bluntly put, on the Buddhist view of the nature of social life and of political obligation, the legitimacy and acceptance of constitutional arrangements are not dependent on individual reason and will (although in the Buddhist democracies these will have a place in constitutional politics and law), but on other fundamental concepts of the moral universe, and on the Buddha's teachings on the human

7 The migration of Western constitutional ideas to the non-Western world of course began in the earlier colonial era, but the transmission of constitutional liberalism through the expansion of comparative constitutional law is the unique product of the formally non-imperial era of American global dominance after 1945.

nature and the nature of political authority (Schonthal 2016, n. 4; Walton 2017, n. 5; de Silva-Wijeyeratne 2013).

Constitutional forms may be imposed, borrowed, or imported from the West, but this does not mean either that these societies have also collectively converted to the liberal normativity that liberalism assumes to be the essential condition of constitutional modernity, or that the adoption of Western constitutional forms denotes a clean rupture between traditional and modern constitutionalism. Rather, the more accurate depiction would be that tradition and modernity in relation to constitutionalism are not two counterposed elements separated by time and distinctive normative conceptions of legitimate order, but are coeval, coterminous, and coexisting elements of a longer and continuing story of historical evolution (Welikala 2017). Buddhist-dominant Asian polities had different encounters with the West in the age of Western imperialism; some were, and some were not, colonies. But while the Western influence did transform the legal forms of constitutionalism in virtually all of them, it did not create or fundamentally reconstitute the modern *culture* of constitutionalism.

Of course, this experience has not been unique to Buddhist Asia, and the challenge posed by the clear dissonance between the normative assumptions of the current paradigm of comparative constitutional law and the realities of democratisation in the global south has led to a "Southern turn" in the scholarship (Dann, Riegner, and Bönnemann 2020, 3). This work is still developing, but recent contributions broadly fall into either rejectionist or accommodationist attitudes about liberal constitutionalism, with a number of different types of argument within each category. Rejectionist views are of three types (Dann, Riegner, and Bönnemann 2020, chapters 2–5). The two strongest forms of rejectionism are the arguments that hold that liberal constitutionalism's association with either colonialism, or colonialism's successor paradigm of "classical modernist" (Smith 1998, Chapter 1) post-colonial nation-state building, makes it inappropriate wholesale for the post-colonial world. The key objection here is to the assumed superiority of the Enlightenment conception of modernity and progress that underpinned both paternalist colonial constitutional development and post-colonial classical modernism. The somewhat softer form of rejectionist arguments are those that question if the Western cultural and historical particularities, which are the inseparable context of liberal constitutionalism's successful operation, render it inapplicable to non-Western conditions. This is a type of amendatory critique that may blend into accomodationism, provided its analytical concerns are satisfactorily met. Accommodationist accounts argue for the relevance and retention of liberal constitutionalism in the global south, either through a "re-imagining" of substantive liberal values from a global south perspective (Roux 2021), or through a "self-reflexive" style of constitutionalism (Dowdle and Wilkinson 2017, n. 21). Accommodationist accounts, as Dowdle and Wilkinson put it, are about constitutionalism " . . . *beyond* liberalism, not *against* liberalism" (Dowdle and Wilkinson 2017, 1).

All these views have their explanatory and normative value, although perhaps the rejectionist accounts are less persuasive overall than the accommodationist ones.

Despite being based on valid considerations of justice and dignity of former colonial peoples, the rejectionist approach can nevertheless be seen as too binary to form the basis of a satisfactory account of constitutional contexts in which the reality is not, and ought not to be, defined by an either/or choice between democratic and some other form of constitutionalism, but as a dialectical or syncretic relationship between the two. As noted before, both the descriptive and prescriptive tasks of constitutional theory are defined by this reality in Buddhist Asia. Thus, while the accommodationists offer more to this undertaking, a characteristic feature of their work is the acceptance of the dominant Franco–American interpretation of the Enlightenment and the consequential substantive model of modern liberal constitutionalism that is the legacy of their revolutions. This interpretation reifies liberty and reason, as outlined above, but it ignores a central dimension of the intellectual debates of the Enlightenment, namely, social and political virtue.

Himmelfarb characterises this body of Enlightenment thought as the "sociology of virtue," counterposed to the two other strands she labels the "ideology of reason" and the "politics of liberty" (Himmelfarb 2008, 3–22). This strain of Enlightenment thought focuses empirically on sociological and historical traits of societies, and normatively on social virtue and political morality, for its account of modern constitutionalism. Less preoccupied with the evils of religion as well as less enamoured with the potency of human reason, this style of constitutionalism foregrounds the innate human capacities for moral conduct as the basis of a statecraft of limited politics, scepticism, prudence, and accommodation, and values tradition and organicism alongside reason and liberty. It opposes revolution and holds that constitutional statecraft was primarily about the management of human imperfection.

What can we extrapolate from this for the present? Himmelfarb gives us a descriptive and empiricist model of constitutionalism that tracks the descent of certain aspects of the present's constitutional arrangements to alternative, more primordial, sources of human nature. She also suggests an underlying concept of social consent to constitutional arrangements, but this is organic rather than rationalist. The longevity of the constitution (*qua* body politic) and its deep social acceptance exist in a symbiosis; and it is this symbiosis that invests the constitution with legitimacy. The constitution, in this reading, is the whole body of legal and political rules and moral principles that authorise the institutions of government and regulate the relationship between government and society. No sharp distinctions are drawn in this conception between the political, social, and cultural spheres of life.

If this should raise understandable concerns that the model favours established patterns of hierarchical social, economic, and political power that are inimical to the interests of individuals, minorities, and vulnerable social groups, it would be important to emphasise that this model of constitutionalism as an ideal type also, crucially, integrates the function of principles derived from reason and the common good in its normative dimension. The role of objective reason and a notion of the common good are critical here, as this is what distinguishes this model from one based solely on the ascriptive demands of the dominant religion or ethnicity – as one might find in the context of the ethnic and religious pluralism of Buddhist-dominant Asian polities, or in the latent traditions of the pre-democratic past that have mutated into modern forms of authoritarianism, or in the other hierarchical structures that adversely affect non-dominant groups and individuals. A model of constitutional modernity of this type, it can be argued, is more consistent with the empirical realities that constitutionalism encounters in Buddhist-dominant Asian polities than a model based on reason and revolution. Its organicism can readily embrace the cosmological ordering of the Buddhist world. Its traditionalism enables ancient traditions of Buddhist societies to be treated with respect, rather than with the derision of tradition that often accompanies liberalism's reification of individualism and rationalism.

But how does it function as a constitutionalism of limitation on power and authority? Buddhist political ideas are primarily about enabling virtuous rule, and its principles of limitation rely primarily on moral suasion (the *dasa-rājadhamma* being the exemplary device). These techniques are more often than not inadequate for the purposes of disciplining the vast power of the modern state. While therefore it is clear that law must have a meaningful role in disciplining politics, and the institutional means of operationalising this function can look very similar to those of liberal constitutionalism, the crucial difference is the way in which the principle of limitations is normatively justified. Unlike liberal constitutionalism, the organic conception of constitutionalism Himmelfarb foregrounds is not concerned with remoulding state and society in the image of its ideal conception of the good. The idea of limits here serves *not* a transformative, *but* a preservative purpose, although preservation may require prudent and proportionate reformation. Concerned primarily with maintaining peace, order, and good government, this model of constitutionalism strives to ensure that the constitution is not instrumentalised in favour of this or that substantive conception of the good, whether that is liberal constitutionalism, or monistic ideologies (such as nationalism and authoritarianism) in plural societies, which may be contrary both to modern democratic values and the inherent pluralism of the Buddhist tradition. The constitution, rather, remains fundamentally a procedural framework that enables the peaceful co-existence of multiple and competing conceptions of the good, albeit within the "moeurs"[8] of the particular Buddhist society to which it gives political and legal expression.

3.4 CONCLUSION

This brief outline of the makings of a theory of constitutionalism in and for Buddhist-dominant Asian polities of course leaves many questions yet unanswered.

8 Ibid. 5. By 'moeurs' de Tocqueville meant the "habits of the mind" and the "habits of the heart" that make up "the whole moral and intellectual state of a people."

Further research would be needed to more fully theorise the foundational, normative, and institutional aspects of this model. However, what I hope I have achieved through these brief reflections is to underscore the point that liberal constitutionalism is neither the sole nor even an essential basis for constitutional democracy. If that premise is accepted, then complementary pathways for constructive scholarship open up, which may give us a better model of constitutionalism for Buddhist Asia, and via greater epistemological self-awareness, the regeneration of comparative constitutional law on more plural and inclusive foundations.

REFERENCES

Bui, Ngoc Son. 2017. *Confucian Constitutionalism in East Asia*. New York: Routledge 2017.

Collingwood, Robin George. 1942. *The New Leviathan or Man, Society, Civilization and Barbarism*. Oxford: Clarendon Press.

Dann, Philipp, Riegner, Michael and Bönnemann, Maxim eds. 2020. *The Global South and Comparative Constitutional Law*. Oxford: Oxford University Press.

de Silva Wijeyeratne, Roshan. 2013. *Nation, Constitutionalism and Buddhism in Sri Lanka*. New York: Routledge.

Dowdle, Michael W., and Wilkinson, Michael A. 2017. "On the Limits of Constitutional Liberalism: In Search of Constitutional Reflexivity." In *Constitutionalism Beyond Liberalism*, edited by Michael W. Dowdle and Michael A. Wilkinson. Cambridge: Cambridge University Press.

Ferejohn, John, Rakove, Jack N., and Riley, Jonathan, eds. 2010. *Constitutional Culture and Democratic Rule*. Cambridge: Cambridge University Press.

French, Rebecca Redwood and Nathan, Mark A., eds. 2014. *Buddhism and Law: An Introduction*. Cambridge: Cambridge University Press.

Gebeye, Berihun. 2021. *A Theory of African Constitutionalism*. Oxford: Oxford University Press.

Ginsburg, Tom, and Huq, Aziz Z. 2018. *How to Save a Constitutional Democracy*. Chicago: The University of Chicago Press.

Griffiths, John. 1986. "What Is Legal Pluralism?" *The Journal of Legal Pluralism and Unofficial Law* 18 (24): 1–55.

Harding, Andrew. 2021. "Introduction." In *Thai Legal History: From Traditional to Modern Law*, edited by Andrew Harding and Munin Pongsapan. Cambridge: Cambridge University Press.

Himmelfarb, Gertrude. 2008. *The Roads to Modernity: The British, French and American Enlightenments*. New York: Vintage Books.

Hirschl, Ran, and Shachar, Ayelet. 2018. "Competing Orders? The Challenge of Religion to Modern Constitutionalism." *The University of Chicago Law Review* 85 (2): 425–56.

Loughlin, Martin. 1992. *Public Law and Political Theory*. Oxford: Oxford University Press.

Nissan, Elizabeth, and Stirrat, Roderick L. 1990. "The Generation of Communal Identities." In *Sri Lanka: History and Roots of Conflict*, edited by Jonathan Spencer. New York: Routledge.

Roux, Theunis. 2021. "The Global South and Liberal Constitutionalism: Incommensurable Opposites?" *Australian Public Law*, July 2, 2021. Accessed on December 15, 2021. https://auspublaw.org/2021/07/the-global-south-and-liberal-constitutionalism-incommensurable-opposites/

Schonthal, Benjamin. 2016. *Buddhism, Politics and the Limits of Law: The Pyrrhic Constitutionalism of Sri Lanka*. Cambridge: Cambridge University Press.

Smith, Anthony D. 1998. *Nationalism and Modernism: A Critical Survey of Recent Theories of Nations and Nationalism*. New York: Routledge.

Tushnet, Mark. (2014) 2018. *Advanced Introduction to Comparative Constitutional Law*. Cheltenham: Edward Elgar.

Walton, Matthew J. 2017. *Buddhism, Politics and Political Thought in Myanmar* Cambridge: Cambridge University Press.

Weinrib, Lorraine E. 2006. "The Postwar Paradigm and American Exceptionalism." In *The Migration of Constitutional Ideas*, edited by Sujit Choudhry. Cambridge: Cambridge University Press.

Welikala, Asanga. 2017. "The Idea of Constitutional Incrementalism." *CPA Working Papers on Constitutional Reform* 14. Accessed on December 15, 2021. http://constitutionalreforms.org/wp-content/uploads/2016/06/Working Paper-14.pdf

PART II

Himalayan Asia

4

The Zhabdrung's Legacy

Buddhism and Constitutional Transformation in Bhutan

Richard W. Whitecross

4.1 INTRODUCTION

Constitutional democracy emerged in Bhutan, the last surviving independent Buddhist state located in the eastern Himalaya, in an unusual way. It arrived neither as the result of colonialism, as in Malaysia, nor from popular democratic movements, as in Nepal in the early 1990s. Rather, limited monarchy was introduced by royal command (*kasho*). The monarchy circumscribed its own power, without any overt pressure to do so.

Buddhism and governance were intertwined in the Bhutanese system of government created in the early seventeenth century by Zhabdrung Ngawang Namgyal,[1] the Tibetan religious leader who unified the country and conceived it as a "religious" estate. This intertwining of religion and government ended on July 18, 2008, when the first written Constitution of Bhutan was enacted, seven years after the royal command to prepare its drafting. The new Constitution declared Buddhism "the spiritual heritage" of Bhutan, whilst removing representatives of the Central Monk Body from the National Assembly. This separation of religion and politics was underscored by the Electoral Commission's ban on public religious events in the six months leading up to elections (Election Commission of Bhutan 2012).

Buddhism and Bhutanese social and cultural life are difficult to separate. Elizabeth Allison has observed the role of Tibetan, or Vajrayāna Buddhism, in shaping the "attitudes, practices and beliefs" of the eastern Himalaya (2015). The above-mentioned definition of Buddhism as the spiritual heritage of the kingdom can be found in Article 3 of the Constitution. Yet, as Matthew Moore notes, "there is very little discussion in the [constitutional] document" about Buddhism (2016, 51). Although the Constitution does not declare Buddhism to be the "state

[1] The title Zhabdrung (*zhabs drung*) means "at the feet of/ in the presence of" and is an honorific title. It is used, unless indicated otherwise, to refer to Zhabdrung Ngawang Namgyal (1594–1651).

religion," scholars interpret Article 3, and the Constitution in general, as promoting Buddhism as the state religion.[2] Indeed, during the drafting and finalizing of the Constitution, the Fourth King, the then-Crown Prince, the chairman of the drafting committee, and other officials asserted that the Constitution and its new form of government were consistent with Buddhism. Therefore, on what basis is the Constitution consistent with Buddhism and what are the post-enactment implications of such claims?

Leo Rose has observed that Bhutan posed a "novel methodological problem," for it was, in his opinion, "data-free" (1977, 10). Much has changed since Rose's research in the 1970s, though it is still true that the "early history of this remarkable country is enveloped in great obscurity" (White 1999, 99). But some aspects of governance are becoming more legible. In this regard, this chapter focuses on the recent process of constitution making and Buddhism following the enactment of the Constitution in 2008. The first section contextualizes the interrelationship between religion and government in the Bhutanese polity between the early and mid-seventeenth century, as well as the establishment of the hereditary monarchy in 1907. The twentieth century saw the consolidation of the monarchy along with major political reforms in the mid- to late twentieth century that informed the preparation of the 2008 Constitution. The second section focuses on how the constitutional drafting committee navigated the debates and sensitivities over whether to declare Buddhism the state religion and the roles of the two main schools of Vajrayāna Buddhism found in Bhutan, the Drukpa Kagyu and the Nyingma.

The third and final section draws on interviews with Bhutanese about their changing perspectives on Buddhism and politics in Bhutan following the enactment of the 2008 Constitution. These interviews enable us to understand some of the consequences that are only gradually emerging over a decade after the ratification and enactment of the Constitution. Two principal themes emerge: the unexpected outcome of the separation of religion and politics, as reflected in lay monk/practitioners[3] choosing to put aside their religious role so that they can enter village-level politics; and the role of the monarch as Buddhist king and royal *kidu* (royal prerogative to grant aid).[4] The chapter concludes by arguing that whilst there is a minority that wishes to amend the Constitution to make Buddhism the state religion, there is a growing concern about the unintended consequences of the Constitution and, more specifically, the exclusion of religious practitioners from engaging in local-level politics as part of a more general ambivalence between the legitimizing power of "continuity" and the demands of "modernity."

[2] For example, Givel (2015), in reference to Art. 4(1) of the Constitution, says that it is "[a] mandate to preserve and promote Mahāyāna Buddhism as a state religion and policy," 23.

[3] Tib/Dzo: *sgom chen*.

[4] Tib/Dzo: *skyid sdug*.

4.2 THE ZHABDRUNG NGAWANG NAMGYAL: THE DRUKPA STATE AND DUAL SYSTEM

The first half of the seventeenth century saw the creation of the three "great theocracies of the greater Tibetan cultural world" (Smith 2001, 119): the Ganden Phodrang in Lhasa, the Jetsun Dampa lineage among the Khalkha Mongols, and the Drukpa state established by the Zhabdrung, Ngawang Namgyal, in Bhutan.[5] The Zhabdrung fled Tibet in 1616 following a dispute over his recognition as the reincarnation of Padma Karpo, the Fourth Drukpa Kagyu hierarch. From his arrival in Bhutan, the Zhabdrung began the process of unifying those leading families affiliated with the Drukpa Kagyu school, such as the 'Ob mtsho family, whilst dealing with the internal opposition and the external threats from Tibet (Phuntsho 2013).

According to a biography of the Zhabdrung, after entering a three-year-long retreat in 1623/24, he experienced a series of visions, including one where he saw the founder of the Drukpa Kagyu school, Tsangpa Gyare, and his protector deity, Mahakala, both encouraging him to establish a Drukpa state "by securing both spiritual and political power over the southern lands" (Phuntsho 2013, 223). In 1624, news of the death of the Tsangpa ruler in 1621, which had been kept secret, emerged. His death was attributed by Tibetans and Bhutanese to the Zhabdrung's use of magic. Shortly afterwards, the Zhabdrung, assuming the title "Great Magician," composed the "Sixteen I-s."[6] As in any iconic document of this form, the first three I-s are significant:

1. I turn the Wheel of the Dual System
2. I am a good refuge for all
3. I hold the teachings of the Glorious Drukpa (Phuntsho 2013, 220).

It is interesting that the first I does not refer – as might be expected in the Buddhist context – to "a good refuge." Instead, it is based on the Zhabdrung's role as the embodiment of a system of government in which he combines religious (*chos*) and secular authority (*srid*). It is in this role that he is the "good refuge for all."

In 1625/26, the Zhabdrung sent out edicts stamped with the seal of the "Sixteen I-s" to be placed at strategic locations on mountain passes, cliffs, and other sites, declaring that "all gods, humans and spirits of the Lhomonkazhi, from this day, fall under the dominion of the great magician Ngawang Namgyal and everyone must heed his words."[7] The construction of fortified monasteries (*dzongs*) in the major

5 We should not overlook Sikkim, for the seventeenth century saw the establishment of an absolute monarchy under a Buddhist king, *chosgyal*.

6 Tib/Dzo: *mthu chen* and *Nga bcu drug ma*.

7 Lhomonkhazhi – Southern Land with Four Approaches – one of the historical names for Bhutan (Phuntsho 2013, 233; Sangay Dorji 1999, 188).

valleys of western Bhutan enabled him to establish control over the region. In time, further *dzongs* were built across central and eastern Bhutan, helping combat the ongoing threat from Mongol and Tibetan forces.[8] Unlike the administrative fortresses of Tibet, the *dzongs* of Bhutan were, and remain, both administrative centers and monasteries.

The organization of the Drukpa administration took its definitive form during the 1630s and 1640s, shortly before the Zhabdrung's death in 1651. The Zhabdrung embodied both religious and secular authority, as witnessed by the Portuguese missionary Father Cacella: "He was the King and at the same time the Chief Lama" (Aris 1986, 173). The Zhabdrung created two positions: a regent, called the "Druk Desi," was appointed to exercise political power,[9] and a Chief Abbot, the "Druk Je Khenpo," was entrusted with the spiritual and administrative leadership of the Drukpa Kagyu religious institutions.[10] The introduction of these two positions created the Dual System (*chhoe-sid-nyi*),[11] a term still used in contemporary Bhutan, including in Article 2(2) of the Constitution, referring to the "religious and secular" branches of the state.[12]

Whilst the concept of the Dual System was not new, the Bhutanese version can be distinguished from the one used in Tibet. Unlike in Tibet, where lay officials dealt with secular matters, and monks dealt with religious affairs, in Bhutan, government officials were ordained. Whilst it is tempting to understand the concept of the Dual System as separating religion and politics or secular matters, Georgios Halkias points out an ambiguity in the concept. According to his view of the concept of "dual sovereignty":

> While there are clear lines of demarcation between the role of the Buddha and his sangha and the function of the king, there is often a blurring of these lines in the literary, practical, and cultural manifestations of Buddhism across Asia. Ambiguity is nowhere more evident than in the promotion and application of notions of "dual sovereignty" combined in a single person capable of arbitrating secular and spiritual power in this world and the world beyond. (2013, 493)

This ambiguity is particularly relevant to Bhutan. The Desi and Je Khenpo were below the Zhabdrung, who embodied both secular and spiritual power in his

8 Tib/Dzo: r*dzong*.

9 Tib/Dzo:'*druk sde srid*.

10 Tib/Dzo: '*drug rje mkhan po*. The dispute over his recognition served to split the Drukpa Kagyu school further. Prior to the dispute, the Drukpa Kagyu school was divided into three main branches: upper, middle, and lower. The middle school split into two: the northern lineage continued in Tibet and in Bhutan, and the southern lineage continued under the Chief Abbot, the Druk Je Khenpo (Aris 1979, 172–81).

11 Tib/Dzo *chos srid gnyis*. I use the Romanized Dzongkha that appears in the English version of the Constitution for consistency.

12 For an interesting analysis and summary of the term "Dual System" in Tibetan and Bhutanese sources, see Schwerk 2019.

function as "the Wheel of the Dual System." It may have been his hope that he would be succeeded by his only son, but the son's early death prevented the position of Zhabdrung from becoming hereditary. As a result, in time, the Zhabdrung passed to a series of incarnations, below whom the Desi and Je Khenpo oversaw the running of the Drukpa state.

The theocratic basis of the Zhabdrung system of government is outlined in two available law codes. The early eighteenth-century law code – the *Bka 'khrims* – and the Black Stone Edict set out detailed rules for government officials. Notably, both draw parallels between the system of government instituted by the Zhabdrung and that of the Tibetan empire under Srong-btsan Gampo.[13] Each text emphasizes that the purpose of Drukpa Kagyu theocracy established by the Zhabdrung was to bring happiness to the populace, for "if there is no law, happiness for the beings does not arise. The beings are not happy, there is no sense that the Dharma masters of the Drukpa uphold the two teachings [Dual System]" (Windischgratz and Wangdi 2019, 15). Bhutan itself was divided into three large regions: Paro, Dagana, and Trongsar. Each region was placed under a "universal lama" who was also the governor.[14] The Zhabdrung system of government was to remain in place until the establishment of the monarchy in 1907.

4.3 CIVIL WAR AND THE DECLINE OF THE DUAL SYSTEM: EIGHTEENTH AND NINETEENTH CENTURIES

The Dual System functioned reasonably well until the last quarter of the eighteenth century, when a rivalry emerged between regional governors who vied for the post of Desi. Similarly, rival candidates as reincarnations of the Zhabdrung were promoted by individual governors (Aris 1979). Despite its central government being weak and fragmented, Bhutan retained its independence. The weakened central government eventually lost its authority to the Trongsa governor, Jigme Namgyel, in the mid-nineteenth century (Pommaret 1997). A major figure in the 1864 Duar War with the British, Jigme Namgyel defeated various political rivals, such as the governor of Paro, to claim power in 1870. Building on his success, his son Ugyen Wangchuk further consolidated power after his father's death in 1881 and developed closer ties with the British, notably through his role as a mediator during the Younghusband expedition to Tibet in 1904. Sir Frances Younghusband described Ugyen Wangchuk's role in the treaty with the Tibetan authorities as "highly instrumental in effecting a settlement" (Kohli 1982, 164). With the death of the Zhabdrung, Jigme Chogyel, in 1904 and the retirement of the fifty-seventh Desi, Yeshe Ngodrup, in

[13] Tib: srong brtsan sgam po (Aris 1986; Windischgratz and Wangdi 2019). For a discussion of Srongtsen Gampo, please see Chapter 5 by Martin Mills in this volume.

[14] Tib/Dzo: *spyi bla ma* and *dpon slob*.

1905, a political vacuum appeared in Bhutan.[15] The absence of both a religious and a secular head of state threatened the recent stability of the country and provided the basis for the creation of the Wangchuck monarchy.

4.4 THE CONTRACT OF MONARCHY: PRESERVING THE ZHABDRUNG'S LEGACY

In late 1906, Ugyen Dorji, the drungpa (local official) of Haa, submitted a letter to the State Council proposing that Ugyen Wangchuk be elected King of Bhutan. Furthermore, Ugyen Dorji proposed that the position should be hereditary. The letter was addressed to the Desi, the Je Khenpo, the four monastic masters, the regional governors of Punakha, Thimphu, and Wangdi, the three governors of Paro, Trongsa, and Dagana, plus various officials. Whilst it is usually presented that there was unanimous agreement that Ugyen Wangchuck be elected king, Phuntsho notes there are no records of the reactions of the clergy and state administrators to the petition (2013, 520). The coronation was held at Punakha on December 17, 1907. A British mission attended under John Claude White, the British political officer for Sikkim and Darjeeling. The ceremony took place in the main assembly hall in Punakha Dzong. Two important features of the ceremony need to be highlighted. The first is that a contract (*genja*) establishing the monarchy was signed during the ceremony.[16] The contract states:

> To the lotus feet of the Precious Judge, the Exalted one of the Dual System.
>
> It is submitted that while from former times in our kingdom of Bhutan, the Great Regent took office from among any that came forth from the lamas and teachers of the monastic college or from the council of ministers and the regional governors, there was otherwise no hereditary monarch … the purport of this contract expressing the deliberations and common desire of all those mentioned above … Sir Ugyen Wangchuck is empowered as *hereditary* monarch … has been installed on the Golden Throne … and to the succession of his royal heirs. (Aris 1994, 96)

The clear statement that the monarchy would be hereditary is central to the contract. It was a simple formula, yet one that made an important point: the system of rule by reincarnations was ended.

[15] It should be noted here that the Zhabdrung Jigme Chogyel was the Mind Incarnation of the original Zhabdrung Ngawang Namgyal (Thugtrul). The fifty-seventh Desi Yeshe Ngodrup was himself an incarnation of the Zhabdrung known as the Sungtrul, or Speech Incarnation. Following the death of the Zhabdrung Ngawang Namgyal, three lineages of Zhabdrung were to emerge in the eighteenth century: Body (sku sprul), Speech (gsung sprul), and Mind (thugs sprul). The Body lineage was born in Sikkim and did not continue. However, the Speech incarnation was born in southern Bhutan (Dagana) and the Mind incarnation in Tibet. According to Phuntsho, a "convenient accommodation" was arrived at to recognize each rival incarnate: "Both lines became legitimate but the Thugtrul incarnates assumed a slightly superior position" (2013, 335).

[16] Tib/Dzo: *rgan rgya*.

The second aspect worth our attention is that, after reading out the oath of allegiance to the new king, the Je Khenpo fixed the *Ngachudrukma* seal to the top of the document in vermillion. State officials, governors, representatives of the people, and other lamas then affixed their own seals. The application of the *Ngachudrukma* seal underscored that the new monarchy was not replacing the Zhabdrung; rather the new monarchy and its dynasty were a continuation of the Zhabdrung's vision. The ritual used at the coronation in 1907 underlined – indeed continues to underline – the hereditary nature of the monarchy and the continuity of the Zhabdrung's vision. The key moment in the coronation of each Bhutanese king is not the public ceremony. Rather, the high point of each coronation is the receipt by the new king of the five colored scarves from the Je Khenpo in front of the Zhabdrung's shrine in the Machen Temple in Punakha Dzong. This private moment marks, for the Bhutanese, the legitimacy and recognition of the monarch by the Zhabdrung. It is unclear if the intention was for the monarch to replace the Desi (secular ruler); however, the last Desi, Yeshe Ngodup, was also a Speech reincarnation of the founding Zhabdrung. Tensions arose as the new king assumed power, as Yeshe Ngodrup, the former Desi and incarnate felt sidelined. In 1915, he became the fifty-third Je Khenpo, until his death in 1917. The king died in 1926 and was succeeded by his son, Jigme Wangchuk.

In 1908–1909, the sixth reincarnation of the Zhabdrung Thugtrul (Mind Incarnation) lineage was identified in Arunachal Pradesh, his parents having migrated there from Bhutan.[17] The young reincarnate, Jigme Dorji returned eventually to Bhutan. After the death of the First King, moves by his supporters to recover the temporal powers of the Zhabdrung led to conflict between the Second King and the reincarnate Zhabdrung. Matters reached a head in 1931, when the brothers of the Zhabdrung sought political support from Gandhi. Shortly afterwards, the Zhabdrung was murdered at Talo, near Punakha (Aris 1994, 119–25; Wangchuck 1998). These events were perceived at the time as presenting a serious threat to the institution of hereditary monarchy.

From the 1930s onwards, the Second King, Jigme Wangchuk concentrated his efforts on reforming and centralizing the administrative system. The structure of Dual System established by the Zhabdrung Ngawang Namgyal remained in place; however, it was recognized by the Bhutanese elite, as well as by the British, that the strife of the nineteenth century was due to the lack of effective control. To address this, the king created a central cabinet to assist him: the state minister, the chief of protocol, the chamberlain, and, depending on the season, the Thimphu or Punakha

[17] Several lineages, representing the Body, Speech, and Mind of the Zhabdrung emerged in Bhutan after the death of Zhabdrung Ngawang Namgyal in 1651 was eventually announced in 1705. The Thugtrul refers to the Mind lineage. See Aris for a discussion of the concept of multiple reincarnation (Aris 1979, 258–62).

governor. It is important to note that the Central Monk Body did not have any direct role in government.

4.5 REFORM AND RENEWAL: DRUKPA KAGYU REPRESENTATION IN GOVERNMENT

The first two kings consolidated royal authority and control in Bhutan. The transition to the monarchy perpetuated the structures of the Zhabdrung government, and as Michael Aris has noted, "the state is still today [in the early 1990s] presented as the church triumphant under the motto 'the Glorious Drukpa Victorious in All Directions'" (1994, 24). The succession of the Third King, Jigme Dorji Wangchuk, in 1952, saw the breadth and pace of economic, political, and social change, supported by India, accelerate. From the royal edict creating the National Assembly in 1953, a series of reforms sought to restructure the Bhutanese administrative system.[18] A notable aspect of the creation of the National Assembly was the provision for representation by the state-sponsored Central Monk Body of the Drukpa Kagyu school headed by the Je Khenpo.[19] The National Assembly primarily performed an advisory role until 1965, when a new Royal Advisory Council was established which included a representative of the Central Monk Body.[20] The Royal Advisory Council took over the advisory role from the National Assembly, which in turn focused on developing its legislative functions.

The Third King refined the changes made to the central bureaucracy, which oversaw the wider structural changes in government toward creating a distinct separation of powers. New ministries and governmental departments were established, and a regular centralized bureaucracy emerged, offering positions for the emerging numbers of formally educated Bhutanese. The personal, charismatic aspects of the former system remained, but with the separation of the judiciary under the High Court in 1968, the district officers relinquished their roles as dispensers of justice. Local government continued to draw on preexisting forms, although the villages were reorganized into *gewog* under the supervision of a *gup* (village headman) and eventually, once membership of the National Assembly was reformed in the 1960s, the *gewog* were represented by *chimi* (representatives).

Starting in 1961, a series of Five Year Plans took shape, with each plan emphasizing various goals and policies. Until the late 1980s all of these plans can be characterized as secular and outward-looking. Central to the changes was the introduction of formal state education. Until the 1950s, the only education available in Bhutan was provided in monasteries and *dzongs* and focused on the monastic curriculum (Kinga 2002, 19–21; Phuntsho 2000). The introduction of secular

18 Dzo: *tshogs 'du chen mo.*

19 Dzo: *gzhung drwa tshang.*

20 Dzo: *blo gro tshogs sde.*

education broke this connection and depended initially on Indian schoolteachers. Kinga describes the new education system as "creating administrative and technical personnel . . . required for development programmes" (Kinga 2002, 20).

The sudden death of the Third King in 1972 led to the ascension of his son, the Fourth King, Jigme Sengye Wangchuk. In a public declaration following his succession to the throne, he recognized the religious authority of the Je Khenpo and stated that he had no intention of "making any competing claims" in terms of religious authority (Kinga 2002, 20).

The main emphasis of royal government continued to focus on the infrastructure of Bhutan. The Sixth Five Year Plan issued in 1987 saw a shift in emphasis:

> The wellbeing and security of the country depends on the strength of its *culture, traditions, and value systems*. Therefore, every effort must be made to foster the unfailing faith, love and respect for the country's traditional values and institutions that have provided the basis and ensured the security and sovereignty of the nation while giving it a *distinct national identity*.[21]

In 1989, a royal decree stressed the importance of a shared culture uniting the Bhutanese, irrespective of religion or ethnic group. At this point, relations between the government and the political leaders of the ethnic Nepali communities, who had settled in Bhutan in the early part of the twentieth century, deteriorated. The implementation of the new "One Nation, One People" policies and the new Citizenship Act escalated tension on both sides.

The period between the late 1980s and 1990s was a troubled one for Bhutan. The widely reported exodus of approximately 100,000 Nepali speakers, primarily from southern Bhutan, to refugee camps in eastern Nepal brought Bhutan under the scrutiny of a range of international organizations, notably Amnesty International, the International Red Cross, and the United Nations High Commission for Refugees (UNHCR). To address the criticisms made by these organizations, the royal government began a series of legal reforms. The reforms of the legal system were instigated under the supervision of Chief Justice Lyonpo Sonam Tobgye. These included improving the training of judges and restructuring the criminal justice system. At the same time, the government introduced the first formal legal education course, the National Legal Course, which included classes on Bhutanese and international law, Buddhist literature, and religion (Royal Court of Justice 1999, Appendix C. iv–viii).

4.6 THE END TO DIRECT ROYAL RULE: CABINET GOVERNMENT

"[The] Bhutanese monarchy," it has been said "has always been very flexible in its attitude towards political structures" (Mathou 1999, 120). On June 10, 1998, the

[21] National Assembly 65th Session, June 1987, Resolution No. 18. Emphasis added.

Fourth King announced the devolution of his full executive power to an elected cabinet of ministers. In retrospect, the *kasho* (royal command) transferring royal power to the cabinet of ministers was the first step toward a written constitution and the introduction of parliamentary democracy. In the *kasho*, the Fourth King states that "having observed the political systems of other countries, it is important that Bhutan should have a system of government that is best suited for the needs and requirements of a small nation ... to ensure its continued wellbeing and security and safeguard its status as a sovereign independent country" (Wangchuck 1998, 5). This suggests that the Fourth King was actively seeking to reform the system of government.

During the ten-year period of cabinet government, the role and prestige of the monarchy remained unchanged. Responsibility for governing the country rested with the cabinet ministers. The National Assembly elected the cabinet ministers, with the king playing an important role in indicating his support for the cabinet. The ministers were accountable to the National Assembly, and the Central Monk Body continued to be represented among the members. The role of the king, even after the *de jure* transfer of powers to the cabinet, remained central.

4.7 DRAFTING THE CONSTITUTION: RE-IMAGINING THE POLITY

The move toward democratization continued to be led by the Fourth King. Although the June 1998 edict transferred royal power to a cabinet elected by the National Assembly, the Fourth King retained considerable charismatic power. Therefore, when the king issued a royal edict on September 4, 2001, that Bhutan should have a written constitution, his command was acted on. In December 2001, a committee was established to prepare a draft constitution. A drafting committee of thirty-nine delegates under the chairmanship of Chief Justice Sonam Tobgye, was appointed. Among the thirty-nine delegates were two monastic representatives nominated by the Je Khenpo. The drafting committee held a series of meetings in different locations in Bhutan and prepared a draft which was first submitted to the king and then to the cabinet.[22]

After the completion of the draft Constitution, the chief justice commented that the most difficult sections to draft related to local government, whilst the most sensitive discussions revolved around Buddhism and the role of the Central Monk Body. Underlying the discussions on Buddhism were concerns expressed by one delegate that "ethnic and religious differences are the main causes of problems in

[22] The drafting committee held its first meeting in Thimphu between November 30 and December 14, 2001. A further series of eight sessions of varying duration were held in Punakha, Bumthang, and Thimphu. The first draft was submitted to the Fourth King on December 9, 2002, and a second draft on June 11, 2003. It was not until late 2005 that a draft version was publicly circulated, and series of public events held across the country.

this world."[23] The same delegate referenced the problems caused by vying religious factions when the Zhabdrung, Ngawang Namgyal, arrived in the seventeenth century. More significantly, he noted, "we have experienced it ourselves . . . in recent years in Dramitse. Tibet lost its independence because of politicization of religion."[24] The observation drew the drafting committee's attention to a brief challenge to the central government that had arisen in the 1990s in eastern Bhutan.

Three recurring themes emerge from the available notes of the drafting committee deliberations. The first is that the Dual System established by the Zhabdrung should be consolidated in the monarch. The second is a concern about the potential for religion to cause social division. The third is an emphasis on the similarity between the two main Buddhist schools in Bhutan, the Drukpa Kagyu and the Nyingma. The Punakha *chimi* argued that Kagyu and Nyingma "are just like different paths leading to the same destination."[25] The comment is accurate for, although each school can be distinguished by its particular ritual practices and teachings, both draw on texts translated from Sanskrit into Classical Tibetan and on philosophical treatises and commentaries by masters of each school (Mynak Trulku 1997).

Prior to the publication of the draft Constitution in March 2005, rumors of the uncertainty about its contents circulated through Thimphu. When the draft was published, the king, cabinet ministers, the chief justice, and other officials began a series of meetings in each of the twenty *dzongkhags* (districts). The meetings, as reported by the media, appear to reveal a deep unease among the people who attended them toward both the draft Constitution and the proposed new form of government. Among the key concerns reported during these public meetings were provisions for the removal of the monarch and, at least during the first meetings, the fact that Buddhism was not declared the state religion. The king and the ministers addressed the concerns expressed during these meetings, with the king noting that the language used in the Dzongkha text presented difficulties for many ordinary people. As a result of the meetings and later debates, the draft Constitution underwent at least two further phases of revision with a third version of the Constitution released in August 2006. Finally, it is worth noting that the draft Constitution was published on the Internet, stimulating wide-ranging discussions and drawing critical comments from anonymous Bhutanese bloggers. The Internet has provided the Bhutanese with a range of platforms on which they are able, anonymously, to comment and critique a range of policies, including the draft Constitution. However, it is unclear to what extent, if any, the views expressed in chat rooms or other platforms influenced the revision and final version of the Constitution.

[23] Dasho Ugen Dorji, Hon. Speaker of the National Assembly (Drafting Committee n.d., 4.61).

[24] Dorji (Drafting Committee n.d., 4.61). Dramitse is a Nyingma monastery located in Mongar district, eastern Bhutan.

[25] Namgyal Phuntsho, Punakha chimi (Drafting Committee n.d., 4.62).

The final Constitution came into force on July 18, 2008. In a televised event, the occasion was marked with a simple ceremony held in the main temple of Thimphu Dzong. A special version of the Constitution, written in gold Dzongkha script, was placed before the images of the Buddha, Guru Rinpoche, and the Zhabdrung Ngawang Namgyal. Beside it was a copy of the Zhabdrung's own law code underscoring the continuity between the government established by him in the early seventeenth century and the new system of government established by the Constitution. The ceremony was marked by prayers "for the prosperity of the nation and the fulfilment of the aspirations of the Bhutanese people" (Dorji, Penjore and Wangchuk 2008). The Fifth King, in an act reminiscent of the 1907 coronation, added his seal to the Constitution. After the ceremony, the Constitution text was escorted to the National Assembly "where it was placed before the Golden Throne."

Before turning to consider the Constitution, it is worth commenting on the transition from the Fourth to the Fifth King. On December 9, 2006, the Fourth King announced in a *kasho* that he was abdicating and transferring his power to the Fifth King. The *kasho* ends with a "religious homage and a prayer for the nation" that emphasizes Bhutan as a Buddhist country and the legacy of the Zhabdrung:

> May the blessing of Ugyen Guru Rinpoche, the father of our nation, Zhabdrung Ngawang Namgyal, and our guardian deities continue to guide the destiny of our country and protect the future of the Glorious Palden Drukpa. (Pommaret 2015, 258)

The *kasho* shocked the Bhutanese; the draft Constitution provided for the monarch to step down once they reached the age of sixty-five. The Fourth King was only fifty-one. When I spoke with the Bhutanese about the Fourth King's abdication and the *kasho*, they described the Fourth King as being a religious monarch, succinctly expressed in this final statement. The sacral element of the Bhutanese monarch is a theme to which we will return later in the chapter.

4.8 THE CONSTITUTION: SEPARATION OF RELIGION AND POLITICS

According to the chairman of the constitutional drafting committee, Lyonpo Sonam Tobgye, the "Constitution is . . . the Supreme Law of the nation and throws light on the structure of the polity" (Tobgye 2015, 1). Lyonpo Sonam Tobgye's exposition on the new Constitution emphasized the role of the monarch as a "Buddhist" monarch, but the new government structure removed the Central Monk Body from the executive and legislature. Buddhism is mentioned as "ideology and precepts" or as the "ethics" that underpin the "tradition, culture, [and] philosophy" of Bhutan (Tobgye 2015, 1–2). To understand the Constitution's underlying reconfiguration of the Bhutanese polity, this section analyzes select articles that highlight the intention of the constitutional drafters to separate religion and politics in Bhutan.

4.8.1 *An Invocation: Three Jewels and the Protectors*

Before turning to consider the Constitution proper, it is worth noting the preamble. Set out on a separate page in both the Dzongkha and English versions, the preamble is contained within a circular representation of a mandala.[26] In the four corners of the page and surrounding the mandala are four white conch shells (reminiscent of those on the Zhabdrung's *Ngachudrukma* seal),[27] each with a flowing ribbon. The outer circle of flames protects an inner circle or fence of gold *vajras*.[28] Inside the circle of *vajras* are eight dharma wheels, each separated by eight mantras written in Lantsa script with the actual text of the preamble in the center.[29] The precise symbolism of the preamble's mandala may not be fully understood by ordinary Bhutanese: for example, the white conch shells are associated with, among other things, the proclamation of the *buddhadharma*. But the idiom of the text is familiar and recognizable.

Preamble

WE, the people of Bhutan:

BLESSED by the Triple Gem, the protection of our guardian deities, the wisdom of our leaders, the everlasting fortunes of the Pelden Drukpa and the guidance of His Majesty the Druk Gyalpo Jigme Khesar Namgyel Wangchuck;

SOLEMNLY pledging ourselves to strengthen the sovereignty of Bhutan, to secure the blessings of liberty, to ensure justice and tranquility and to enhance the unity, happiness and well-being of the people for all time;

DO HEREBY ordain and adopt this Constitution for the Kingdom of Bhutan on the Fifteenth Day of the Fifth Month of the Male Earth Rat Year corresponding to the Eighteenth Day of July, Two Thousand and Eight.

The opening line in English mirrors other written constitutions. In the Dzongkha version, the term "*nga bcas*" or "we" is used to emphasis the "people as a collective body" (Tobgye 2015, 22). However, the English translation glosses references to a range of deities. The complete Dzongkha invocation to the "guardian deities" refers to "dharma protectors" (*chos skyong*) and guardian deities (*srung ma*).[30] The preamble succinctly merges the range of worldly deities that still play an important role in religious practices at the local and national level. The opening section of the preamble mirrors the language found in the preamble to the Supreme Law Code

26 Tib/Dzo: *dkyil 'khor*.

27 Tib/Dzo: *Dung dkar*.

28 The "mountain of fire" (Tib: *me ri*) follows the traditional sequence of yellow, blue, red, and green. Vajra–Tib: *rdo rje*.

29 Tib/Dzo: *'khor lo*. Lantsa is an Indian Buddhist script used for mantra based on Sanskrit.

30 The Dzongkha reads: *rang re'i chos skyong srung ma'i mgon skyabs*.

1959 and other statutes.[31] In his discussion of the preamble, Lyonpo Sonam Tobgye simply states, "this invocation denotes the records of historical and religious beliefs and its derivative values" (Tobgye 2015, 22–23). Whilst acknowledging Bhutan's religious beliefs and values, this comment glosses over for the non-Dzongkha reader the richer, fuller meaning given in the Dzongkha version, which is firmly rooted in the ritual practices of the Drukpa state.[32] It serves as a reminder that we should not overlook or undervalue the implicit underlying cultural and religious values of the drafters, including the chairman of the drafting committee.

4.8.2 *Article 1: The Kingdom of Bhutan*

Broad and wide-ranging, Article 1 contains provisions on territory and international borders, as well as on the national flag, national anthem, national day, and national language (Article 1(5), 1(6), 1(7) and 1(8)). These provisions underscore the importance to the Bhutanese state of recognition, both internally and externally, of its independence and distinct identity. Of significance, Article 1 of the Constitution defines the sovereignty of Bhutan and the new structure of the Bhutanese state. Declared by Article 1(2) to be a "democratic constitutional monarchy," the Bhutanese state "shall be a separation of the Executive, Legislative and Judiciary" (Article 1(13)). It is worth noting that according to Lyonpo Sonam Tobgye this separation of powers has deep roots in premodern Bhutan. According to him "[the] Zhabdrung's *Kathrim* and the *Thimzhung Chhenmo* [also] have a provision on separation of powers" (Tobgye 2015, 26). According to Article 1 (11), the Supreme Court "shall be the guardian of this Constitution and the final authority on its interpretation." Here too one finds a hidden Buddhist element, given that the new Supreme Court complex in Thimphu was designed as a mandala with each of the five court buildings dedicated to one of the five *dhyāna* buddhas (Whitecross 2018).

4.8.3 *Article 2: The Monarch*

In the process of developing the Constitution, the role and position of the monarch was a key consideration. The Fourth King instigated the shift from direct royal rule to cabinet government and, with the 2008 Constitution, to an elected parliament and national government for the first time in Bhutanese political history. In discussions with the Bhutanese during the years between the royal *kasho* and the finalization of the Constitution, the future role of the monarch was one about which they

[31] *Khrims Gzhung Chennmo* 1959. A more recent example is the Water Act 2011, which has a foreword that opens with references to Padmasambhava and to Zhabdrung Ngawang Namgyal.

[32] As with all Bhutanese legislation or legal texts, the Dzongkha version is the definitive text rather than the English version. Following the public consultation in 2004, the Dzongkha version underwent further work to ensure it would be easily understood.

expressed deep concern. These Bhutanese interlocutors identified the monarch with their sense of national identity and implicitly, the wellbeing of the country.[33] Article 2 is one of the longest in the Constitution, running to twenty-six subsections, two of which will be analyzed. Article 2(1) states that "His Majesty the Druk Gyalpo is the Head of State and the symbol of unity of the Kingdom and of the people of Bhutan." This simple statement captures and addresses Bhutanese concerns about and views of the monarch. As with the Zhabdrung, the monarch is the apex of the political system.

The sacral, religious dimension of the monarch is expressed specifically in Article 2(2). The article does two key things. Firstly, it proclaims that the Dual System (*Chhoe-sid-nyi*) remains in place "unified in the person of the Druk Gyalpo" (Article 2(2)). Secondly, it declares that the Druk Gyalpo, "as a Buddhist, shall be the upholder of the *Chhoe-sid*." This goes further than the 1907 contract for the monarchy because it sets out, for the first time, that religious (*chos*) and secular (*srid*) authority are combined in one person: the monarch. This is very reminiscent of the previously mentioned Zhabdrung declaration "I turn the Wheel of the Dual System." Where it was unclear whether Ugyen Wangchuk, when elected in 1907 as king, was replacing the Desi or both the Desi and the Zhabdrung lineages, this matter has been implicitly addressed by Article 2(2).[34] The monarch continues Zhabdrung Ngawang Namgyal's legacy of merging temporal and religious authority. This is further underscored by the provision in Article 10 requiring that each session of the parliament open with the king present and accompanied by rituals introduced by the Zhabdrung. These include the opening and closing of each session with Buddhist prayers.[35] The monarch, as the Zhabdrung's legitimate heir, embodies the Dual System and is explicitly a Buddhist.

4.8.4 *Article 3: Spiritual Heritage*

The Constitution states in Article 3(1) that "Buddhism is the spiritual heritage of Bhutan, which promotes the principles and values of peace, non-violence, compassion, and tolerance." The intention of the drafters was, after debate, not to declare Buddhism, or a particular Vajrayāna school of Buddhism, to be the state religion. Rather, its centrality to Bhutanese culture, society, and history should be acknowledged. As suggested in the introduction, the separation of Bhutanese culture and

33 This was noticeable after the Fourth King led a short military action in southwest Bhutan to remove various Indian insurgent groups from Bhutanese territory (November/December 2003).

34 Implicitly, it addresses any concerns that had previously arisen from subsequent incarnations of the Zhabdrung during the twentieth century.

35 Art. 10(6). At the commencement of each session of parliament, the Druk Gyalpo shall be received in a joint sitting of parliament with Chibdrel Ceremony. Each session shall be opened with a *Zhugdrel-phunsum tshog-pai ten-drel* and each session shall conclude with the *Tashi-mon-lam*.

society from the pervasive presence of Buddhism is a difficult challenge with which drafters grappled.

Under the Dual System established by Zhabdrung Ngawang Namgyal, monks and religious figures played a key role in the administration of the Drukpa state. The political reforms of the Third King ensured that the Drukpa Kagyu order were represented in government and on the Royal Advisory Council. However, Article 3(3) of the 2008 Constitution states:

> It shall be the responsibility of religious institutions and personalities to promote the spiritual heritage of the country while also ensuring that religion remains separate from politics in Bhutan. *Religious institutions and personalities shall remain above politics* [emphasis added].

For the first time since the foundation of the Drukpa state in the 1620s, religious figures from the Drukpa Kagyu order are excluded from participating in politics at any level. Of course, this exclusion applies across all religious practitioners, not only those in the Central Monk Body, and includes non-Buddhist "institutions and personalities."[36] The decision to break with the tradition of including representatives and advisors from the Central Monk Body (Zhung Dratshang) was not taken lightly.[37] However, it was probably recognized by those involved in drafting the Constitution that its terms could not exempt the Central Monk Body from this exclusion from political activities if it was to achieve the envisaged separation of politics and religion.

Article 3(4)–(6) briefly addresses the appointment of the Je Khenpo and the five *lopons* (spiritual masters), as well as the membership of the Dratshang Committee.[38] These provisions solely concern the Central Monk Body. Other Buddhist organizations must comply with the requirements set out in the Religious Organizations Act 2007. It is important to note that the majority of temples, monasteries, and other religious institutions are privately owned, or community based.

Of course, it would be difficult, after 400 years, to remove state support for the Central Monk Body. After all, the declaration of the "glorious Drukpa victorious in every direction" implicitly refers to the Drukpa Kagyu school. The Central Monk Body continues to perform the rituals for the wellbeing of the kingdom and, accordingly, the Constitution states in Article 3(7) that "the Zhung Dratshang and Rabdeys shall continue to receive adequate funds and other facilities from the State." Therefore, whilst no longer represented in the reformed National Assembly or National Council, the Drukpa Kagyu retains the official endorsement of the Bhutanese state.

[36] In this way, it is similar to the disenfranchisement of religious clergy in Myanmar, which Iselin Frydenlund describes in Chapter 10.

[37] Dzo: *gzhung grwa tshang* literally means the State Monk Body and is usually referred to as the Central Monk Body.

[38] The Dratshang Committee (*grwa tshang lhan tshog*) has oversight of the Central Monk Body.

The state is given further responsibilities under Article 4. This article focuses on the role of culture and heritage. Article 4(1) states that:

> The State shall endeavor to preserve, protect, and promote the cultural heritage of the country, including monuments, places, and objects of artistic or historic interest, *Dzongs*, *Lhakhangs*, *Goendeys*, *Ten-sum*, *Nyes*, language, literature, music, visual arts, and religion to enrich society and the cultural life of the citizens.

Whereas Buddhism is defined as the "spiritual heritage" of the kingdom, Article 4(1) classes religious sites and buildings, as well as "religion," as part of Bhutan's "cultural heritage." There is an interesting merging of tangible and intangible culture encompassed by Article 4(1). The Bhutanese state has in recent years recognized the importance of its national culture, as well as the vulnerability of religious sites and their contents to natural disasters, fire, theft, and vandalism. What is unclear from the wording is to what extent the Bhutanese state is obliged to "promote" religion. The clause is arguably heavily focused on Buddhist cultural heritage, and by extension "religion" refers to Buddhism, rather than Hinduism, which is practiced by Nepali speakers. The state has supported the construction of a major new Hindu temple in the capital, Thimphu, but there have been claims by Hindu organizations that their other planning applications are less likely to be given approval than those submitted by Buddhist organizations (U.S. Department of State, Office of International Religious Freedom 2019, 1).

4.8.5 *Religion: State Policy and Fundamental Rights*

References to religion and to Buddhism appear in several other articles of the Constitution. Under Article 7(4) on Fundamental Rights, Bhutanese citizens enjoy the freedom of religion, subject to the state being able to reasonably restrict this freedom to avoid "incitement to an offence on the grounds of race, sex, language, religion or region" (Article 7(22)(d)). This provision is further developed in Article 15 on political parties, which explicitly prohibits parties organizing on a regional, ethnic, or religious basis. The Election Act 2008 builds on these restrictions, suggesting that the state is concerned with the potential of religion, as well as other markers of difference, to undermine "national cohesion and stability."

Whilst political parties and candidates must not use religion as the basis for membership, the principles underlying state policy set out in Article 9 include a clear statement reminiscent of those contained in earlier law codes that emphasized the "happiness" of the populace. Article 9(2) declares that "the State shall strive to promote those conditions that will enable the pursuit of Gross National Happiness [GNH]."[39] In the period following the enactment of the Constitution, the concept

[39] Art. 9 contains twenty-four sections ranging from Gross National Happiness to the right to a fair trial, and broader principles reflecting its international obligations, for example in relation to the rights of children and women, as well as around employment, health, and education.

of Gross National Happiness was secular, and focused on four pillars: sustainable and equitable socio-economic development; environmental conservation; the preservation and promotion of culture; and good governance (Royal Government of Bhutan 2009). In turn, these four pillars were incorporated into nine domains of GNH set out in the 2010 "GNH Index of Bhutan."[40] Whilst acknowledging that "socially engaged Buddhism and Buddhist moral and ethical engagement with happiness influences GNH," Ritu Verma describes GNH as "a secular concept" (2017). In the 2015 GNH survey, questions on spiritual practice and belief (for example, around compassion, karma, and meditation practice) were refined and extended, allowing for a more nuanced presentation of the underlying Buddhist ethics that informs GNH (Ura et al. 2015).

Finally, Article 9(20) builds on the idea of Buddhism as a "spiritual" and "cultural heritage," by promising that the state will "strive to create conditions that will enable the true and sustainable development of a good and compassionate society rooted in Buddhist ethos and universal human values." This is the most explicit reference in the Constitution to Buddhism and its values. For his part, the chief justice who helped design this clause has suggested that "Buddhist ethos" refers to the six perfections of Buddhist morality, or *pāramitās* (Tobgye 2015, 137).

If Buddhism is not the official state religion and the Central Monk Body is not part of the government, how can the constitutional scheme be described as "Buddhist" in any strong sense? The answer lies in its embodiment of the Dual System explicitly by the monarch himself – a novel situation in Bhutanese history. The coronation rituals created for enthronement symbolically present the monarch as the legitimate successor of the Zhabdrung. The monarch, as a Buddhist king, takes the role of the Zhabdrung, supported by the prime minister and government (secular) and by the Je Khenpo and Central Monk Body (religious). The status of the monarch as a Buddhist king, however, sits alongside other constitutional principles that claim to separate religion and politics.

4.9 WHAT DO THE BHUTANESE THINK OF THE CONSTITUTION?

The previous sections considered the nature of the theocracy established by Zhabdrung Ngawang Namgyal and its development up to the enactment of the 2008 Constitution, focusing particularly on the legal texts themselves. This section considers how Bhutanese citizens have interpreted those texts, drawing on recent interviews with the Bhutanese about their views of the Constitution.[41] Two principal themes emerged

[40] The nine domains are: living standards, health, education, ecological diversity and resilience, cultural diversity and resilience, community vitality, time use, psychological wellbeing, and good governance (Ura, Alkire, Zangmo, and Wangdi 2012).

[41] Interviews were conducted via Zoom and Facetime. In total, ten interviews were conducted with seven men and three women. All of the interviewees are from farming families, three hold

during these interviews. The first theme relates to the separation of religion and politics. The second returns to the conceptualization of the Buddhist monarch in light of the recent role of the Fifth King in leading the country's efforts to contain the COVID-19 pandemic, as well as in responding to associated economic challenges. The interviews focused on ordinary Bhutanese citizens, rather than lawyers, judges, or state officials. This approach was chosen to redress the discussion of the Constitution as a legal document by acknowledging its value as a living document.

4.10 FROM GOMCHEN TO GUP: AN UNEXPECTED CONSEQUENCE

Aku Sengge rises early every morning. In a small room off the main living space, in front of an altar made from tubular shelving, he begins his daily ritual practice. Once the morning prayers and mantra recitations are completed, accompanied with the occasional ringing of a small hand bell and, on certain days, the rattle of a small hand drum, he prepares breakfast for his family. Now that he is retired, he devotes his days to religious practice. Born and raised in northeastern Bhutan adjacent to the Tibetan border, Aku Sengge was sent to become a monk when he was twelve. He remained in the local monastery in Kurtoe where he learned to read Classical Tibetan, and to perform a range of rituals, as well as to carry out a range of tailoring tasks, including making appliqué thangkas. In his late twenties he met his wife, and when she fell pregnant, he decided to leave the monastery to raise a family. Since settling in his wife's village, Aku Sengge has become an indispensable part of local life, conducting rituals for his neighbors.

A devout practitioner, Aku Sengge, became close to the village lay monk/ practitioner. The elderly *gomchen* appreciated Aku Sengge's knowledge of rituals and his ability to read Classical Tibetan.[42] It was through his participation in and conduct of the annual rituals for his neighbors that Aku Sengge eventually became the village *gomchen*. Outside the formal state-sponsored monastic body, the *gomchen* is an important feature of local, everyday religious practice in villages and rural communities. They are called on to perform rituals and prayers at times of childbirth, marriage, and death, to remove sickness, and for "other social and religious functions" (Kinga 2002, 27). Aku Sengge's own teacher taught him about the local deities and spirits that are a prominent feature of popular religious practice throughout Bhutan.

Despite his fulfilling life, Aku Sengge is worried. His son died young, and his daughter moved away from her natal village to teach Dzongkha in another district. Education and a desire for a life removed from agriculture has led many young

university-level degrees, three hold college-level degrees, and four have no formal educational qualifications. Two were aged 60+, four were 50+, and the remaining four were 40+. They were located in the following districts: Phuentsholing (1), Paro (1), Thimphu (3), Jakar (2), Tashigang (1), Kanglung (2).

[42] Tib: *chos skad*.

people, particularly, though not exclusively, men, to leave the village. Few of the young people want to train to become *gomchen*, and Aku Sengge worries that there will be no new *gomchen* to continue the practices taught to him. His concerns touch on a wider social challenge: the migration from rural to urban settings that has escalated over the last decade.

A younger Bhutanese informant has different concerns. Karma Tshering asked to join a monastery when he was sixteen. Originally from the eastern district of Tashigang, he was educated and raised at the military base at Tencholing, in Wangduephodrang. After eight years of study, he decided to return to lay life and moved back to his mother's home village in Tashigang district. His maternal aunt's husband was the village *gomchen* and his uncle welcomed him as his assistant *gomchen*. Through Karma's family ties and his attendance at ceremonies hosted by village households and the annual rituals for the community, he established a good reputation. However, Karma, who had attended high school until he was sixteen, explained he wanted to help his neighbors in more practical ways. Acknowledging the important spiritual role of being a *gomchen*, Karma decided after discussion with his family, in particular his mother, aunt, and uncle, to stop being a *gomchen* in order to be able to vote and, more importantly for Karma, to stand for election at the village level. These activities were forbidden to *gomchen* by Bhutanese law.

In interpreting the aim of the Constitution to separate politics and religion, Section 184 of the Election Act 2008 states that:

> A *tulku* [reincarnate], lam [religious person], any influential religious personality or ordained member of any religion or religious institutions excluding the laity, as determined/registered as religious organizations or religious personalities under the provisions of the Religious Organizations Act 2007, shall neither join a political party nor participate in the electoral process as they must remain above politics and cannot use their influence for the benefit of any party or candidate.

Gomchen, as locally "influential religious personalities," may not stand for election nor vote. Aku Sengge is equivocal about his lack of voting rights. He views politics as a worldly activity that distracts from religious practice, specifically meditation and merit making. During the various elections held since 2008, he has avoided all meetings and chosen not to take part in discussions, even with family members of the candidates put forward. Aku Sengge's attitude contrasts with that of Karma.

Karma lacks the necessary educational requirements to stand for the National Assembly or the National Council. Both require "a formal university degree" (Election Act, Sections 176(d), 177(d)). However, he is "functionally literate and possesses skills adequate to discharge his duties" as a member of the local government (Election Act, Section 178(d)). Karma explained: "It was my mother who first suggested it. I was surprised because she wanted me to be a monk … Now she feels that if she can't stand, I should." However, Karma's surprise at his mother's change of attitude and her preference that he take on a local political role was echoed by other Bhutanese. A former monk from eastern Bhutan, Tenzin, commented that women in his home village were increasingly looking to learn about business, and less inclined to attend to the annual rituals. Although the comment was made in passing, it is one that others have observed in recent years.

Concerns over the decline of religious practice are not new in Bhutan. Nor can these observations be taken to suggest that Buddhism is waning in the country. They do suggest that the formal separation of politics and religion, inaugurated by the 2008 Constitution, may be having unexpected consequences. These include the declining numbers of *gomchen* and the number who are choosing to set aside their lay monk/practitioner status. Karma's decision was made because of the legal prohibitions set out in the Election Act. Yet, his mother was a key factor in his decision. Her preference that her son give up his status as a *gomchen* echoes Tenzin's own observations about changes taking place at the local level. This was highlighted in 2016, when both candidates for the local government position of *gup* (village chief) in Bartsham were former *gomchen* (Zangmo 2016).

Echoing the separation between religion and politics that appears in the 2008 Constitution, the Religious Organizations Act of 2007 applies a similar rubric to all organizations except for the Central Monk Body.[43] At present, the register of religious organizations shows 127 entries, all Buddhist, except 2 Hindu organizations. The legal body created to oversee the implementation of the Act, the Chhodey Lhentshog,[44] has six duties set out in Section 13. These include, in addition to promoting "the principles and values of peace, non-violence, compassion, and tolerance" echoing the phrasing of Article 3(1), working to "create the conditions that will enable the true and sustainable developments of a good and compassionate society rooted in Buddhist ethos" (The Religious Organizations Act 2007, Section 13 (a) and (b)). The fourth duty is to "ensure that religion remains separate from politics in the country" (Section 13(d)).

Based on the provisions of the Religious Organizations Act 2007 and the Elections Act 2008, there have been bans on public religious activities ahead of upcoming elections. For example, the Election Commission of Bhutan issued a notification that it expected religious institutions and clergy "shall not hold, conduct, organize or host any public activities from January 1 until the election." The Election Commissioner, Chogyel Dago Rigdzin, described the ban as a "preventative measure" to avoid the mixing of politics and religion. Guidelines published by the Election Commission remind readers that under the Constitution, religious institutions and personalities "shall be responsible ... to promote the spiritual heritage of the country while also ensuring that religion remains separate from politics in Bhutan" (Election Commission of Bhutan 2012, 1). The Guidelines go on to define a "religious personality" as a Bhutanese "citizen who is a monk, *gomchen*, nun, priest, *sādhu*, pundit, an

[43] Dzo: *dGe 'dun grwa tshang*, an alternative term for the Central Monk Body.

[44] Dzo: *Chos sde lhan tshogs*, Religious Council.

ordained, or a robed person of any religion" (3). The Guidelines then prohibit "performing or sponsoring any activity of religious nature for or by a political party, candidate or supporter . . . that could be exploited for political gains" (2).

Aku Senge and Karma both commented that the ban included important practices that they, as *gomchen*, regularly performed, such as rituals dedicated to the local deities that form a major part of religious practice at the village level.[45] Do they feel that the current laws should be amended? Aku Senge worries about the longer-term impact of the prohibitions. For him, failing to perform the rituals regularly is serious. His concerns range from the immediate spiritual and welfare concerns of not performing the rituals for individuals and communities, to the necessity of rituals for building and representing communities. Karma hopes that by encouraging a public discussion over the prohibitions on rituals before elections and the impact on *gomchen* that the current laws will be repealed. Karma's comments reflected concerns expressed by Tshering Dorji, an elected member of the National Council for whom "Buddhism has played [a] significant role in the life of an individual citizen and leaders, which in turn has shaped Bhutanese polity, culture, and society. That is why I appreciate the merit in the need for the religion to stay above (not separate from) politics in our context" (2012).

4.11 THE BUDDHIST MONARCH: GRANTING KIDU IN A PANDEMIC

> Throughout my reign, I will never rule you as a King. I will protect you as a parent, care for you as a brother and serve you as a son. I shall give you everything and keep nothing; I shall live such a life as a good human being that you may find it worthy to serve as an example for your children; I have no personal goals other than to fulfil your hopes and aspirations. I shall always serve, day and night, in the spirit of kindness, justice and equality.
>
> His Majesty's Coronation Address, Punakha Dzong, November 6, 2008

Conducting any interviews at present means that interviewer and interviewee share one problem: the COVID-19 pandemic. A recurring theme across the interviews was the role of the Fifth King in supporting the Bhutanese government's control of the pandemic. The handling of the pandemic by the Bhutanese authorities has been remarkable: national lockdowns were successfully rolled out and enforced, citizens flown home by the state, and infection rates were kept low, with only one death (Drexler 2021). In his public speeches and messages throughout 2020, the Fifth King regularly supported the Bhutanese government in its work to contain the virus and to reassure the population.

[45] The Guidelines specify the following rituals: *kelha-yuellha-neydhag-zhidhag soelkha*, *dralha soelni* (various forms of local deity), *tordog phangni* (torma rituals), *jangkri*, *pawo pamo soelni* (shaman/medium), *gegtrey phangni* (expulsion rituals), witchcraft, exorcism . . . *wang*, *lung thri* (forms of empowerment) (Election Commission of Bhutan 2012, 2).

The discussion of the king's words and, more importantly, his actions, highlighted one key feature: the granting of *kidu* (royal relief). The above-discussed Article 2 of the Constitution of Bhutan sets out the right of the monarch to give *kidu* to those in need. An established feature associated with the monarch – the right to ask for and be awarded *kidu* – was described by one interviewee as "going for shelter to the king." Awarding *kidu* is for many a demonstration of the king's fulfilment of his Buddhist duties as king. *Kidu* has featured in several speeches by the Fifth King, notably in 2012, when he linked the granting of *kidu* to sacred duty: "a King's sacred duty is in looking after the wellbeing and *kidu* of our people" (Wangchuk 2012). In 2020, as a result of the closing of the borders and the cessation of tourism, it is estimated that up to 50,000 Bhutanese have either lost their main source of income or employment.

In April 2020, the Druk Gyalpo's Relief Kidu fund was launched by the Fifth King.[46] The fund was established to support those whose incomes have been affected by the pandemic. Originally set to run for three months, the relief fund was extended until July 2022. Between April 2020 and March 2022, the fund has provided financial support to over 54,783 applicants.[47] The practical and symbolic significance of the relief fund was emphasized in interviews. The sacral element of the monarch, though not expressed in such terms, was noticeable to observers and Bhutanese alike, and suggests that for many Bhutanese, Article 2 encapsulates their views on the Fifth King as a Buddhist king. Admittedly, for some who grew up and remember tales of their grandparents living under the Second King there appears to have been a shift in the perception or character of the monarch. This shift appears linked to the increased focus on the Fourth King and, more recently, on the Fifth King, as Buddhist monarchs.

The Fourth King, Jigme Sengye Wangchuk was (and is) revered by the Bhutanese in a way that other earlier kings do not appear to have been.[48] In a longevity prayer written for the Fourth King in about 1967 when he was crown prince, Dilgo Khyentse, a prominent Tibetan Nyingma teacher, appealed to the Bodhisattva Padmasambhava on behalf of the king,

> With your power of blessing and pervasive charisma,
> In the southern great land of Dharma,
> May the crown prince reign supreme in great fame,
> During his noble reign as Dharma king,
> And may his service toward all people.
>
> (Palmo 2008, 246–48)[49]

[46] Dzo: *'brug rgyal po'i rgud gso'i skyid sdug*.

[47] https://royalkidu.bt/ (last accessed July 11, 2022).

[48] A similar point is made by Khemthong Tonsakulrungruang in Chapter 8 in relation to the late Thai king, Bhumibol.

[49] Chapter 16, "Blessing Bhutan," is by the Queen Mother Kesang Chodron Wangchuck (mother of the Fourth King) and Lopon Pemala.

The emphasis on the Fourth King as a dharma king appears to foreshadow how he became viewed by the Bhutanese. During earlier fieldwork and more recent discussions with the Bhutanese, several commented on the family descent of the Fourth King and Fifth King from the Buddhist teacher Pema Linga (1450–1521). More recently, in a publication marking his sixtieth birthday, the Fourth King is explicitly described as a bodhisattva and *cakravartin* king, a common theme that is discussed in other chapters in this volume. In the recent pandemic, we see a similar portrayal of the current king, the fifth Druk Gyalpo, Jigme Khesar Namgyal Wangchuk. In one conversation, the *cakravartin* king was described as appearing during difficult times and that the Fourth King demonstrated this throughout his reign, particularly through his vision to transform the government of Bhutan. The religious dimensions of the monarch have been cultivated and serve to elevate him above the political fray, associating him and his successor with the wellbeing of the kingdom. As discussed above, the separation of religion from politics was aimed at placing religion – or specifically Buddhism – above politics. In a similar way, the reconfiguration of the political system of government allows the expressly Buddhist monarch to be on the one hand supportive of governments and on the other, above "politics."

4.12 CONCLUSION

Four hundred years after his arrival in Bhutan, Zhabdrung Ngawang Namgyal's legacy remains. The election as king of Ugyen Wangchuck in 1907 shifted political power and control to the monarch. The move to cabinet government was the first step of a trajectory raising the monarch above everyday politics and government, and towards the unifying role of the Zhabdrung. The removal of the Central Monk Body from government marked a shift in the relationship between state and religion, but not one that undermined or removed the centrality of Buddhism in Bhutanese life. Rather, the Constitution recast the Dual System through its embodiment in the person of the monarch. As argued above, the Constitution transformed the role of the monarch as a Buddhist king, a dimension that was not promoted by the first two Bhutanese kings. The Fourth King, as prophesized by Drudra Dorje (Pommaret 2015, 258), ordered the preparation of the Constitution, marking a shift toward the explicit sacralization of the monarch, as bodhisattva, *dharmarāja*, and *cakravartin*. However, as illustrated above, there are concerns about the unintended consequences on religious practices and practitioners of the desire by the drafters of the Constitution to separate politics and religion. Running through the discussions of the drafting committee, and in more recent public discussions about the separation of Buddhism and politics, is a tension between continuity with the past – real or imagined – and modernity. Perhaps, as some informants suggested, the current restrictions will be removed as Bhutan matures as a democracy. Yet there are strong forces that other Bhutanese view as marking a decline in religion – Buddhism – in

Bhutan. As Aku Senge wistfully noted, each generation "must work out what the dharma – Buddhism – means to them."

REFERENCES

Allison, Elizabeth. 2015. "Religion Inscribed in the Landscape: Sacred Sites, Local Deities and Natural Resources." In *The Changing World Religion Map*, edited by Stanley D. Brunn, 439–59. Dordrecht: Springer.

Aris, Michael. 1979. *Bhutan: The Early History of a Himalayan Kingdom*. Warminster: Aris & Phillips.

1986. *Sources for the History of Bhutan*. Vienna: Arbeitskries fur Tibetische und Buddhistische Studien Universitat Wien.

1994. *The Raven Crown: The Origins of Buddhist Monarchy in Bhutan*. London: Serindia Publications.

Dorji, Kinley, Penjore, Ugyen, and Wangchuk, Rinzin. 2008. "The Constitution of the Kingdom of Bhutan Has Been Adopted." *RAO Online*, July 19, www.raonline.ch/pages/bt/pol/bt_polconst01i.html

Dorji, Sangay. 1999. *dpal 'brug pa rin po che zhabs drung nga dbang rnam rgyal gyi rnam*. Thimphu: Dzongkha Development Commission.

Dorji, Tshering. 2012. "Religion and Politics. What Is the Right Mix?" *Tshering Dorji's Blog*, July 30. https://tsheringbhutan.wordpress.com/2012/07/30/religion-and-politics-what-is-the-right-mix/. Accessed February 7, 2021.

Drafting Committee. n.d. *Minutes of the Drafting Committee* (English). High Court of Judiciary (no longer available).

Drexler, Madeline. 2021. "The Unlikeliest Pandemic Success Story." *The Atlantic*. February 10.

Druk Gyalpo's Relief Kidu. 2021. https://royalkidu.bt/. Accessed July 11, 2022.

Election Commission of Bhutan. 2012. *Guidelines for Interpretation of Section 184 of the Election Act of the Kingdom of Bhutan, 2008, Concerning Religion and Elections*. Thimphu: Election Commission.

Givel, Michael. 2015. "Mahayana Buddhism and Gross National Happiness in Bhutan." *International Journal of Wellbeing* 5 (2): 14–27.

Halkias, Georgios T. 2013. "The Enlightened Sovereign: Kingship and Buddhism in Indo-Tibetan Tradition." In *A Companion to Buddhist Philosophy*, edited by Steven Emmanuel, 491–511. Chichester: Wiley-Blackwell.

Kinga, Sonam. 2002. *Changes in Bhutanese Social Structure. Impacts of Fifty Years of Reforms: 1952–2002*. Chiba: Institute of Developing Economies, Japan External Trade Organisation.

Kohli, Manorama. 1982. *India and Bhutan. A Study in Interrelations 1772–1910*. New Delhi: Munshiram Manoharlal Publishers.

Mathou, Thierry. 1999. "Bhutan: Political Reform in a Buddhist Monarchy." *Journal of Bhutan Studies* 1 (1): 114–45.

Moore, Matthew J. 2016. *Buddhism and Political Theory*. New York: Oxford University Press.

Mynak Tulku. 1997. "Religion and Ritual." In *Bhutan: Mountain Fortress of the Gods*, edited by Christian Schicklgruber and Françoise Pommaret, 137–57. London: Serindia Publications.

Palmo, Ani Jinba (trans.). 2008. *Brilliant Moon: The Autobiography of Dilgo Khyentse*. Boston: Shambhala Press.

Phuntsho, Karma. 2000. "On the Two Ways of Learning in Bhutan." *Journal of Bhutan Studies* 2(2): 96–126.

2013. *The History of Bhutan*. Noida: Random House India.

Pommaret, Françoise. 1997. "The Birth of a Nation." In *Bhutan: Mountain Fortress of the Gods*, edited by Christian Schicklgruber and Françoise Pommaret, 179–207. London: Serindia Publications.

2015. "The Cakravartin King." In *The Bodhisattva King: His Majesty Jigme Singye Wangchuck*, edited by Thierry Mathou, 253–67. Bangkok: Bhutan Publishing House.

Rose, Leo E. 1977. *The Politics of Bhutan*. Ithaca: Cornell University Press.

Royal Court of Justice. 1999. *The Bhutanese Legal System*. Thimphu: Royal Court of Justice.

Royal Government of Bhutan. 2009. *Tenth Five Year Plan (2008–2013), vol. 1*. Thimphu: Gross National Happiness Commission.

Schwerk, Dagmar. 2019. "Drawing Lines in a Mandala: A Sketch of Boundaries between Religion and Politics in Bhutan." Working Paper Series of the HCAS "Multiple Secularities – Beyond the West, Beyond Modernities" 12. Leipzig: Leipzig University.

Smith, E. Gene. 2001. *Among Tibetan Texts: History and Literature of the Himalayan Plateau*. Boston: Wisdom Publications.

Tobgye, Sonam. 2015. *The Constitution of Bhutan: Principles and Philosophies*.Thimphu: Royal Court of Justice.

Ura, Karma, Alkire, Sabina, Zangmo, Tshoki and Wangdi, Karma. 2012. *A Short Guide to Gross National Happiness Index*. Thimphu: Centre for Bhutan Studies.

2015. *Provisional Findings of the 2015 GNH Survey*. Thimphu: Center for Bhutan Studies and Gross National Happiness Research.

US Department of State, Office of International Religious Freedom. 2019. *Bhutan 2019 International Religious Freedom Report*. www.state.gov/reports/2019-report-on-international-religious-freedom/bhutan/.

Verma, Ritu. 2017. "Gross National Happiness: Meaning, Measure and Degrowth in a Living Development Alternative." *Journal of Political Ecology* 24: 476–90.

Wangchuck, Ashi Dorji Wangmo (HM the Queen of Bhutan). 1999. *Of Rainbows and Clouds: The Life of Yab Ugyen Dorji as Told to His Daughter*. London: Serindia.

Wangchuck, Jigme Khesar Namgyel (HM the Fifth Druk Gyalpo). 2012. "About His Majesty the King of Bhutan." July 26. http://kidufoundation.org/about-his-majesty-the-king-of-bhutan/

Wangchuck, Jigme Singye (HM the Fourth Druk Gyalpo). 1998. "Kasho Issued to the Speaker of the National Assembly." June 10. www.nab.gov.bt/assets/uploads/docs/resolution/2014/76th_Session.pdf

White, J. Claude. 1999 (1909). *Sikkim and Bhutan: Twenty-One Years on the North-East Frontier, 1887–1908*. Delhi: DK Fine Art Press.

Whitecross, Richard W. 2018. "*Thrimskhang* and the Spatial Evolution of the Courthouse in Bhutan." In *Buddhism, Culture and Society in Bhutan*, edited by Seiji Kumagai, 97–115. Kathmandu: Vajra Press.

Windischgratz, Michaela and Wangdi, Rinzin. 2019. *The Black-Slate Edict of Punakha Dzong*. Thimphu: JSW Law Publishing Series.

Zangmo, Tanden. 2016. "Two Ex-Gomchens Vying for Bartsham Gup Post." *The Bhutanese*, August 13. https://thebhutanese.bt/two-ex-gomchens-vying-for-bartsham-gup-post/

5

The "Trick of Law"

The Hermeneutics of Early Buddhist Law in Tibet

*Martin A. Mills**

5.1 INTRODUCTION

Constitutionalism – the principle that government should be limited in its powers, and those limits enshrined within laws that stand above the individuals and institutions that govern – is generally regarded as a good thing. As a good thing, it might seem obvious that everyone, or at least as many people as possible, should have it. Here, of course, things get trickier: after all, the very concept of whether something is a good idea depends on an underlying moral (and ultimately religious) culture, one that may not be shared universally or organized in a comparable way. For present purposes, one of the most salient questions facing any study of Buddhism and constitutional law is whether constitutionalism as a legal ideal might be consonant with Buddhism at all. That it might not be does not, of course, imply that Buddhist culture must be in some sense deficient, or indeed a 'bad thing.' Instead, we must actively consider the possibility that it is a *different* thing. In what follows, I will examine how, in Tibetan constitutional history, one of those major differences lies in the perceived role of the personal morality and ethical insight of Buddhist rulers and lawmakers.

Before addressing that question, however, it is worth rendering explicit how Western constitutional thinking depends upon its own Christian (or more broadly, Abrahamic) history of 'Higher Law,' or foundational constitutional principle. As Richard Helmholz (2010) has pointed out with great clarity elsewhere, Western constitutionalism is generally underlaid by three facets of Christian ecclesiastical thinking, all of which are in some sense either negated by, or have no direct equivalent in, many Buddhist traditions.

* For help in preparing this paper and the ideas behind it, my profuse thanks go to Jill Sudbury, Benjamin Schonthal, Tom Ginsburg, Daniel Wojahn, Sam Van Schaik, Fernanda Pirie, Rebecca French, Matthew Kapstein, Ron Davidson, Robert Mayer, Cathy Cantwell, and of course the many sharp-eyed and -eared attendees of the Constitutional Buddhism conference.

The first principle is that the fundamental rules of Biblical law "stand outside our own volition, indeed our own full understanding," largely as a consequence of having been bequeathed by God, rather than men. This is most obvious in the case of the Hebrew foundations of Biblical law, wherein Moses received the Ten Commandments from God on tablets of stone at Mount Sinai, and the law in the direct verbal instructions from God in the revelations of Leviticus; it is also inscribed in the Gospel of John's opening proclamation that *In principio erat Verbum, et Verbum erat apud Deum, et Deus erat Verbum* ("In the beginning was the Word, and the Word was with God, and the Word was God." John 1:1). In this sense, the word of true law, in a Biblical sense, necessarily precedes its human adjudicants and disseminators, who thereby cannot stand above or prior to it. Even in the case of secular and royal law, the Christian tradition – following the writings of Paul and Peter – ascribes the authority of kings and emperors to the power vested in them by God, rather than as something that flows from them personally (Roman 13:1–7; 1 Peter 2:13).

The second principle is that human law – whether ecclesiastical, royal, or secular – could not infringe or adjudicate upon the realm of 'hidden things' (*De occultis non judicat ecclesia*). Neither the devices and desires of the heart nor the personal convictions of the soul can be judged by a public court of law, coming instead under the jurisdiction and judgement of God, through private prayer, confession, and repentance.

In combination, the upshot of these two principles has been to set aside private (or 'inner') morality and insight from the scope of formal law, which exists in the public realm *between* individuals. Law in a formal sense is received primarily in textual form and submitted to and interpreted by persons not as individuals, but as representatives of an office in the Weberian sense – that is, as contractees, citizens, subjects, soldiers, judges, or monarchs. This 'exclusion of the inner' in turn serves as the foundation of what we might call a 'constitutionalist disposition.' This is the view that human law is, *or at least should be*, a public matter in both principle and practice, the parameters of which lie outside the subjectivities of the individual human heart. In the study of legal history, this disposition is found most clearly in the assumption that if you are seeking the source of a legal code or doctrine you will find it in one of two places: either in a previous legal codex, or in the hand of the divine. The one place you would not, or at least should not, find its source is within the heart of the lawgiver.

This disposition is not universally shared within the history of Christendom. Ideas, after all, do not hold sway by themselves. The two principles above found their place within constitutional history largely as a consequence of the birth-pangs of the Protestant Reformation in Europe, which often pitted private conviction against royal law. This struggle framed the formation of American constitutionalism. As Edwin Corwin pithily summarized in 1955:

> The Reformation superseded the infallible Pope with an infallible Bible; the American Revolution replaced the sway of a king with that of a document. (1955, 1)

Indeed, this rejection of the personal authority of rulers in making and applying law has motivated the penning of most of the world's great constitutions. If the king himself (that is, in his 'body natural' as English law would term it – see Kantorowicz 1957) cannot be the source of law, then he must be constrained by it. This is the essence of what Richard Helmholz rightly identifies as the third main aspect of constitutionalism: its role in providing "structured and substantive limitations on government," restrictions that apply either to (i) the boundaries between private rights (such as personal religious convictions) and public law (such as nationally established religions) and (ii) claims by monarchs and legislators to exist 'above the law' – a possibility deemed not only illegitimate but impossible according to the first principle, above.

While appropriate to the 'Higher Law' ideas held by certain forms of Christian constitutionalism, this methodological exclusion of the personal moral qualities of the lawmaker sits far less easily with Buddhist conceptions of law. Here, the legitimate role of the *personal morality and sagacity* of emperors, kings, and judges in both producing, overseeing, and interpreting law remains vital to the general understanding of Buddhist constitutional thought.

In large part, this derives from one of the core distinctions between Buddhism and the Abrahamic faiths. Within Buddhism, the central soteriological framework does not lie in the gulf between sinful humanity and a lawmaking and judging Godhead, but rather in a combination of paths (Sanskrit. *mārga*; Tib. *lam*) and grounds (S. *bhūmi*; T. *sa*) that lead, through ethical realization, to liberation from *saṃsāra*.

While Buddhism certainly has ample place in its cosmologies for divine realms and deities, this overarching 'path and grounds' framework sees both the human and the divine as *subordinate* to its vision of suffering and liberation. Indeed, humans and deities are only seen as morally distinct from one another as a matter of degree, not kind – a property shared within Hinduism (Fuller 1992, 3–4).

As a consequence, law in any absolute sense is neither recognized as, nor legitimated by, being divine in origin: while gods may be called upon as witnesses or guarantors and may also be seen to make demands that bind particular communities to certain ritual practices and prohibitions, there is simply no Buddhist equivalent of the Ten Commandments.

However, this is not to say that the Buddhist doctrine regards law as a purely personal and subjective matter. Here, we need to recognize that the term dharma involves two distinct but related meanings, particularly in Mahāyāna Buddhist thought. The first meaning is dharma as a doctrine of reality: that phenomena are characterized by impermanence, non-self, and emptiness, and that clinging to those phenomena produces suffering. Dharma from this perspective is seen to exist eternally, whether a Buddha emerges in the world to reveal it or not (Williams et al 2000, 8) – it therefore precedes personal realization. The second meaning, however, refers to the paths that lead from ignorance of reality to knowledge and awakening, and from suffering to liberation. Travelling these paths involves different vehicles (S. *yāna*; T. *theg pa*) or traditions of teaching – most conventionally the *Śrāvakayāna* (T. *nyan thos kyi theg pa*, 'hearer vehicle'), the *Pratyekabuddhayāna* (T. *rang rgyal gyi theg pa*, 'solitary realizer vehicle'), and the *Bodhisattvayāna* (T. *byang chub sems dpa'i theg pa*, 'bodhisattva vehicle').

This last reference to the various 'vehicles' for teachings of the dharma is most famously illustrated in the parable of the burning house in the *Lotus Sūtra*, told by the Buddha to his disciple Śāriputra. In the parable, a wealthy man returns home to find his house on fire and his many children, unaware of the danger, engrossed in playing with their toys. Knowing that there is only one exit from the house and that trying to herd them out himself will take too long, the Buddha explains the solution devised by the wise father:

> At that time the rich man had this thought: the house is already in flames from this huge fire. If I and my sons do not get out at once, we are certain to be burned. I must now invent some expedient means that will make it possible for the children to escape harm. The father understood his sons and knew what various toys and curious objects each child customarily liked and what would delight them. And so he said to them, "The kind of playthings you like are rare and hard to find. If you do not take them when you can, you will surely regret it later. For example, things like these goat-carts, deer-carts and ox-carts. They are outside the gate now where you can play with them. So you must come out of this burning house at once. Then whatever ones you want, I will give them all to you!" At that time, when the sons heard their father telling them about these rare playthings, because such things were just what they had wanted, each felt emboldened in heart and, pushing and shoving one another, they all came wildly dashing out of the burning house. (Watson 1993, 56–57)

When the children emerge from the burning house, however, they discover only *one* vehicle: a large jewel-encrusted carriage drawn by a pure white ox. Challenging Śāriputra as to whether the rich man had lied to his children (and thereby whether it is deceitful to teach different *yānas*), the Buddha explains that while it was necessary to preach several vehicles "to attract and guide living beings," in truth there is only one ultimate vehicle (S. *ekayāna*; T. *theg pa gcig pa*) of Buddhahood, which becomes clear once beings have escaped from the burning house of *saṃsāra*. He concludes, "that rich man was not guilty of falsehood. The Tathagata does the same, and he is without falsehood."

The purpose of the burning house parable is explicitly to explain the Mahāyāna distinction between the transcendent wisdom that sees reality, and the conventional wisdom of 'skillful means' (S. *upāyakauśalya*; T. *thabs la mkhas pa*) that is historically imminent and sees what each individual disciple requires at a particular point of the path in order to be released from *saṃsāra*. While the latter wisdom is seen to arise out of the cultivation of the former, the latter does not *take the form* of the former: the goat cart and the jewel-encrusted carriage are different.

This Buddhist emphasis on the soteriology of *path* and *vehicle* means that, while there is a 'final reality' that exists prior to personal insight into it, any 'law' that is focused on Buddhist goals of liberation from *saṃsāra* depends upon a conventional and historically situated moment between teacher and disciple or, as we shall see, between a Buddhist ruler and subject, and most particularly upon the "wisdom of skillful means" possessed by the teacher and ruler. As a consequence, from the Mahāyāna perspective especially, the 'hidden' (in the sense of inner personal morality and ethical insight) cannot be excluded from the process of situated lawmaking. More than this, because the Buddhist path contains *ethical insight* at its heart, law is understood as being emphatically *within* personal volition and understanding.

Nevertheless, royal law in Buddhist kingdoms was generally understood to be distinct from Buddhist codes of lay and monastic discipline, thus separating out constitutional principle into two distinct spheres (Pirie 2017a, 406). In what follows, I will examine one of the few apparent exceptions to this split when it comes to Buddhist legal culture: the claim, widespread in Tibetan history, that its first Buddhist emperor, the seventh century Purgyal ruler, Songtsen Gampo, based the first written law codes of his new empire on the 'ten virtues' (T. *dge ba bcu*) of Mahāyāna Buddhism – something of an early test case of "Buddhist constitutionalism."

To do that, however, it is necessary to ask not simply whether Buddhist constitutional law is a contradiction in terms, but first and foremost to ask what Buddhist religious thinkers thought about public law in the first place. Here I will address the views of late Indian and Tibetan Mahāyāna writers. I will argue that they had much to say on this subject – in particular, regarding the origins, reality, and objectives of legal governance – much of which requires us to pay close attention both to legal texts and codes as well as to the rich philosophy and hermeneutics of governance within the Mahāyāna tradition.

Before moving on, a few words are necessary on the relationship between the terms constitutional and constitutionalism as used in this chapter. By 'constitutional,' I mean the very general sense of pertaining to understandings, however diverse, of the nature and form of legitimate governance, what Philip Abrams referred to as the "state-idea" (Abrams 1988). This is distinct from 'constitutionalism,' that far narrower idea that texts provide for formal limits on legitimate governance (generally in abstract, office-bearing terms). Thus, while the United Kingdom may lack a single written constitution, it certainly has deeply embedded constitutional and constitutionalist ideas. Constitutionalism thus argues that constitutional ideas should be rendered in a very specific way: one which, regardless of how secular it may claim to be, follows the principles of Christian ecclesiastical law in separating overarching law from the person of rulers, both in theory and in practice.

To these terms, however, I would add one further – that of "constitutional mythology," a phrase I have explored briefly elsewhere (Mills 2011 and 2018), but which is hugely pertinent to the general study of Tibetan historiography. Tibetan history-writers, rather than seeking to discuss their ideas of governance in abstract, legislative terms, tend to embed those ideas *within* the life-narratives of key historical figures. In doing so, and in rendering coherently those ideas within the narrative, they usually transform those narratives significantly, in effect turning source material into mythology.

Such constitutional mythologies are exceptional neither to Tibet, nor to Buddhist societies, nor indeed to non-Western legal cultures – they are simply to be found in those constitutional frameworks that have not yet been captured by the rationalized, rule-based format of modern constitutional texts. Space precludes a comparative review of this here, but a single example will suffice: that of the constitutional status of the English monarch. The political theology of early modern English kingship has been examined in depth in Ernst Kantorowicz's magisterial 1957 study, *The King's Two Bodies*. But to grasp the full strangeness of English constitutional mythology, there are few better places than the opening page of John Allen's *Inquiry into the Rise and Growth of the Royal Prerogative in England*:

> To unlearned persons desirous of understanding the constitution of England, the transcendent attributes ascribed to the King, in his high political capacity, must prove a stumbling block at the very commencement of their studies. They may have heard that the law of England attributes to the King absolute perfection, absolute immortality, and legal ubiquity. They will be told that the King of England is not only not capable of doing wrong, but of thinking wrong, that he cannot mean to do an improper thing, that in him there is no folly or weakness. They will be informed that he never dies, that he is invisible as well as immortal, and that in the eye of the law he is present at one and the same instant in every court of justice within his dominion. (1830, 1)

Such constitutional mythologies might offend our modern sensibilities, appearing as folklore-ish renditions of the supernatural, the products of irrational and uncritical piety. This, however, is mainly because, as moderns, we are used to our constitutional ideals of governance being enshrined within the pages of a document, rather than being hung upon the shoulders of a historical person. For the Tibetan tradition, such a person was Songtsen Gampo and, later, the ruling Dalai Lamas (Mills 2018).

5.2 THE FIRST WRITTEN TIBETAN LAW CODES

Tibet's Purgyal Empire Period – during which the Yarlung Dynasty of southern Tibet expanded to found one of the most powerful empires of first millennium Asia, bringing into being what we call Tibet today – is revealed to us only partially in scattered piles of historical fragments: monumental inscriptions, tattered imperial records hidden in the library cave of Dunhuang, and textual portions retranscribed by Tibetan historians across the intervening centuries.

In addition to these early fragments, however, later Tibetan tradition offers scholars a millennium worth of revealed prophecies, religious commentaries, and scholarly ethnohistories of the Tibetan Empire. Together these sources combine to create the received tradition prevalent from the medieval period onwards. These texts were generally composed from the late tenth century at the earliest, several hundred years after Songtsen Gampo's reign and in the wake of the fall of the Tibetan Empire. The accounts of Songtsen Gampo's life and rule can be found in some of Tibet's most famous post-imperial literature: from the 'hidden treasure' (*terma*) literature of the post-dynastic period such as the eleventh-century *Pillar Testament* and the twelfth century *Compendium of Maṇis*, to later histories such as Sonam Gyaltsen's fourteenth-century *Clear Mirror of Royal Genealogies* or Pawo Tsuglag Threngwa's sixteenth-century *Feast for the Wise*. All of these sources present an idealized portrait of his rule, with many elements that are simply absent for near-contemporary accounts, such as those found at Dunhuang.

These post-imperial texts narrate the lives of the great and pious 'religion kings' (*chögyel*) that brought about the 'First Diffusion' (*sngar dar*) of Buddhism to Tibet, and with it the foundations of Buddhist culture in Tibet. Foremost among these 'religion kings' was the thirty-third *tsenpo* (emperor) of the Yarlung Dynasty, Tri Songtsen or Songtsen Gampo (or 'Songtsen the Wise,' c. 569?–649?). He was heralded by subsequent Tibetan tradition as the human manifestation of the celestial bodhisattva Avalokiteśvara, Tibet's patron Buddhist tutelary deity; as having expanded the imperial borders massively, effectively founding Tibet, as we now understand it, out of a medley of surrounding polities; as having founded the city of Lhasa as his personal fief; as having constructed the famed Jokhang, Ramoché, and Trandruk temples; as having brought writing and Buddhist scriptures to Tibet; and most of all for our purposes, as having inscribed the first written legal codes (*bka' khrims*). To say, as some have, that Songtsen the Wise was to Tibetans as King Arthur was to the British is to understate the matter; a closer analogy would be King Solomon's role in the history of Israel.

5.3 THE RECEIVED TRADITION AND ITS CRITICS

In these post-imperial narratives, the codification of imperial written law under Songtsen Gampo went hand in hand with the emperor's initiation of a Tibetan written script and formal court literacy. Texts such as the eleventh-century *Pillar Testament* record how, during the reign of Songtsen Gampo's ancestor Lhatotori, Buddhist scriptures and a *stūpa* fell from the sky onto the roof of the dynastic palace at Yumbulagang in the Yarlung Valley. Among them was the *Karandavyūha*, a *sūtra* detailing the qualities and worship of the great Mahāyāna bodhisattva Avalokiteśvara, celestial protector of the Land of the Snows. However, Lhatotori and his court were illiterate and unable to read the newly revealed scriptures, and as a consequence he had this 'Powerful Secret' sealed in a casket, enshrined and left for future generations to unravel.

Five generations later, as Songtsen Gampo expanded the Purgyal Empire across the Tibetan Plateau, he sent emissaries to India to study writing and grammar. Among these emissaries, most of whom died from the rigors of the journey and the Indian climate, was the young Sambhota of the clan Thonmi, a ministerial scion reputed for his intelligence. Arriving in India, he studied for years under two scholars, Kamsadatta and Devavidyāsimha, transforming the fifty consonants of the Indian Gupta script into thirty consonants of the Tibetan spoken language.

After some years, Thonmi Sambhota and Kamsadatta returned to Tibet, bringing with them several Buddhist texts. The *Pillar Testament* describes how, on his arrival at Lhasa, Thonmi both translated the texts in Lhatotori's casket and aided the emperor in formulating Tibet's first written law codes:

> To the joy of the king, [Thonmi Sambhota] offered him the noble doctrine of the Mahāyāna, whereupon the king said: "Can you read the 'powerful secret' of my ancestor Lhatotori Nyenshel?" Lotsāwa Sambhoṭa studied them, reading *Vimalamitra's Glorious Mudras for Amending Breaches*, the *Karandavyūha Sūtra*, *Nāgā's Glorious Mudras for Amending Breaches* and *Reversing the Karma of the Ten Non-Virtues*.
>
> They established four legal codes of the laws of the ten virtues. Then, in studying the script, the king did not go out for four years. The ministers said, "In not coming out for four years, the king is a know-nothing idiot! The happiness of the Tibetan people is down to us, the ministers."
>
> The king overheard this, and thinking, "If they call me an idiot, it will not be possible to tame the people," spoke thus: "All you ministers and people, come and gather around me! When I, the king, remained in one palace and didn't move around from place to place, you were happy. Yet you ministers are saying that this very happiness of the Tibetan people is down to the ministers and that the people are under the command of the ministers." Having said this, he gave them an order: "It has become necessary for me to formulate the laws of the ten virtues. I wanted to make the law before. Previously, the lawless twelve minor border kingdoms of Tibet, lacking law, created manifold wickedness, harming my maternal lineage. All the people within my kingdom wanted blood price if a murder was committed and compensation if there was theft; wanted compensation for assault or robbery; for adultery, they desired the adultery price; and punishments to be enacted for lying, divisive speech, covetousness; harmful intent, wrong view and whatever actions were against the law. [The king] having declared this, the ministers thought: "this king is wise (*sgam po*) and will correctly hold and protect the practices of the holy doctrine." Being of profound mind, therefore, they named him King Songtsen the Wise." (*KKM*: 107–8)[1]

[1] See also Uray's rendition of this episode (Uray 1972, 25–26).

The *Pillar Testament* rendition of the founding of Buddhist law translated above does indeed closely approximate the classical ten virtues within wider Mahāyāna literature: the three virtues of body (avoiding killing, stealing, and sexual misconduct), speech (avoiding lying, gossip, harsh speech, and slander), and mind (avoiding avarice, ill-will, and wrong views).

This is the version of the narrative of Songtsen Gampo's founding of the law of the ten virtues that probably represents the *locus classicus* of the later medieval received tradition. Its generally understood implication, at least among modern scholars, is that the emperor, in collaboration with Thonmi Sambhota, formulated his royal law on the basis of its codification in a Sanskrit text on the ten virtues, variously rendered as *Reversing the Karma of the Ten Non-Virtues*, or more simply *The Ten Virtues*, and that this was some version of, or commentary on, the *Daśakuśalāni Sūtra*. The later (and more famous and widespread) *Compendium of Maṇis*, supports this general interpretation:

> Then the emanated king, in order to introduce the sentient beings of the snowy land to the dharma, applied the law based on the *Sūtra of the Ten Virtues*. (MKB, Vol. E: f. 375–76)

But if the *Pillar Testament* presents us with the *locus classicus* for the received tradition of Songtsen Gampo's relationship with "the ten virtues," other texts and sources present a far less clear picture, one that has made the received tradition the object of considerable scholarly criticism. The most common and substantial criticism focuses on the historical possibility of literary transmission: that Songtsen Gampo's laws were based on pre-existing Indian texts on the ten virtues such as the *Daśakuśalāni Sūtra*. The core criticisms here are, firstly, that there seem to be no mention of them in any contemporary or near-contemporary imperial sources related to Songtsen Gampo's rule. Indeed, nothing resembling the *Daśakuśalāni* seems to arrive in Tibet until at least one and a half centuries after Songtsen Gampo's death. Thus Rolf Stein, in his 1986 essay, "Tibetica Antiqua IV: La tradition relative au début du bouddhisme au Tibet," places the first Tibetan literary references to the ten virtues in and around the reign of Trisong Détsen, a century later: in Buddhaguhya's letter to emperor Trisong Détsen (Tanjur No 5693, vol. 129, 284, col. 5); in the translation of the *Ten Teachings of Kṣitigarbha, Great Summary of the Mahāyāna* into Tibetan by the Chan master Rnam par mi rtog pa in 800 (Kanjur No 905, Chapter 6); and, finally, in the imperial promulgation of the text in 822 (Stein 1986). Even then, as Fernanda Pirie has argued in detail, it was not associated with the practice of royal governance or administration (2017a). In other words, the assertion that Songtsen Gampo deployed the 'law of the ten virtues' *exclusively* on the basis of textual transmission from India is fairly clearly a *post hoc* fabrication.

The second criticism is that the legal code that is said to have emerged from this process – of both the 'ten virtues' and the appended 'sixteen norms of moral behavior' – is only barely recognizable as the classical ten virtues. Thus, for example, the fourteenth-century *Clear Mirror of Royal Genealogies* lists these as follows:

> Thonmi Sambhota, Gar Tongtsan Yulzung, Tiseru Gongton, Nyang Trizang Yangton, and one hundred ministers in all levelled differences and, in accordance with the king's behest, enacted the law of the ten virtues:
>
> (i) The good should be rewarded, and the wicked punished.
> (ii) The high should be suppressed by law, and the low skillfully protected.
> (iii) The bodyguard should be divided into four units.
> (iv) Highland water should be assembled into ponds, and lowland water conducted into channels.
> (v) Weights and measures should be organized, and fields divided into plots.
> (vi) People are to train in writing.
> (vii) Horses should be marked with ownership-colors.
> (viii) Exemplary customs should be established.
> (ix) Those making quarrels should be punished.
> (x) Murder should be fined variably.
> (xi) That which is stolen should be substituted eightfold, and with the thing itself, ninefold.
> (xii) Adulterers, having been castrated, should be banished to another country; liars/frauds should have their tongues cut off.
>
> Furthermore:
>
> (i) Go for refuge in the Three Jewels, showing them devotion and respect.
> (ii) Maintain gratitude to one's parents and honor them.
> (iii) Do not forget benefactors such as fathers, uncles, and elders, the three, and repay them in kindness.
> (iv) Do not quarrel with superior persons and noblemen, but have faith in them, and adapt one's manners and behavior to them.
> (v) Fix one's mind on the divine religion and writings and understand their meaning.
> (vi) Have trust in karmic causation and avoid perpetrating sins.
> (vii) Be of benefit to friends and neighbors, and do not enact mischievous thoughts.
> (viii) Acting from a straightforward foundation, rest in a mind of renunciation.
> (ix) Showing moderation in food and alcohol, act modestly.
> (x) Returning debts on time, do not act dishonestly with weights and measures.
> (xi) Do not think on matters to which one is neither promised nor commissioned.
> (xii) Among friends, remain independent of women's useless gossip.
> (xiii) When the truth or falsity [of a case] does not emerge, pledge [one's] oaths before the local gods and protectors of the teachings as witnesses.
>
> Taking the ten virtues as an exemplar, the twenty laws of Tibet were finalized at Shomara and affixed with the seal of the king and all the ministers, and so they were propagated [in Tibet] like the light of the sun and moon. (KKM, ff. 159–60)[2]

[2] See also Sørensen 1994: 180–84 for comparison.

Indeed, from this perspective, sources like the *Clear Mirror* themselves appear quite confused at times. For example, the enumeration of the king's new laws, as outlined above, is directly preceded by a section which states that Songtsen Gampo's imperial law was derived less from sacred India than from Tibet's northern neighbors:

> Having adopted accounting from the eastern kingdom [China] and the Mi-Nyag; translated the holy doctrine from India in the south; unlocked treasuries of food, wealth, and fineries from the Sogdians and Nepalese in the west; *and adopted law and work (practices) from the Tartars and Uyghurs in the north* – in short, having enacted dominion over the four directions, he became the helmsman king over half the world. (GSM, f. 158, emphasis added)[3]

Indeed, on the question of Songtsen Gampo's law codes, we find them variously presented as the 'law of the ten virtues,' the ten religious virtues and sixteen codes of moral behavior, the four religious laws and sixteen secular ones, and, often enough, as the six law books. Even these presentations are once again at odds with the complex sets of legal precedents and procedures found in partial fragments in the Dunhuang documents (Dotson 2006).

Possibly the most confusing source on this is the tenth-century *Considerations of Wa* which, as one of the earliest post-dynastic sources, seems to claim that Songtsen Gampo *both did and did not* base his laws on the ten virtues. Thus, it describes the arrival of Thonmi Sambhota, accompanied by an indecipherable copy of *The Ten Virtues* (*dGe ba bcu*; *Daśakuśalāni*):

> [Returning to Tibet, Thonmi Sambhota] was accompanied by [Kamsadatta], an Indian versed in reading and writing, and took with him some [texts of] the doctrine such as *Chos dkon mchog sprin* [*Ratnameghasfitra*], *Pad ma dkar po*, *Rin po che tog*, *gZugs grwa lnga* and *dGe ba bcu* [*Daśakuśalāni*]. As there was nobody to translate them, the [texts of the] doctrine received the royal seal and were placed in the treasury of Phying pa [castle]. Then [the emperor] announced: "In my lineage after five generations there will be a descendant who will spread the doctrine of Buddha, and at that time the casket should be opened." (dBZh, 27–28)

Whereupon the emperor entered retreat for four years, at the end of which he nonetheless produced laws "on the basis of the ten virtues":

> He therefore held a discussion with his four attendants who had been taught the alphabet and in four months, on the basis of the Ten Virtues, he made the law (*bka' khrims*) and put it into writing. [It included] the 'wergild' for the taking of human life, compensation (*rku 'jal*) for theft and robbery, the [cutting off of] the nose and the [removing of] eyes for sexual misbehavior, the taking of oaths for preventing lying, etc.). Wangdu and Diemberger 2000, 28)

[3] See also Sørensen 1994:180.

The picture here is therefore a confused one, and while, for example, the *Pillar Testament* is extremely explicit that the ten virtues as understood in the classical Indian formulation were proposed by Songtsen Gampo – specifically, in the text itself, putting them in his own reported speech – , the principal assertion by post-imperial writers appears to be that, whatever form the imperial law actually took, it was in essence the 'ten virtues' (see also Uray 1972, n. 53).

We can see this in the way the *Considerations of Wa* asserts – indeed, within the same passage – that despite the fact that the *dGe ba bcu* (*Daśakuśalāni*) text would not be translated for a further five generations, the king's law was nonetheless *based on* the ten virtues. This, at the very least, suggests that we need a wider frame of reference for understanding the post-dynastic claim that Songtsen Gampo's laws were 'based on the ten virtues' than pure textual transmission.

In trying to make sense of all this – and perhaps more pertinently trying to understand how Tibetan post-imperial writers themselves made sense of it – one of the most important questions to address is: What precise legal reality was implied by a term such as "law based on the ten virtues?" In many respects, and by extension, this question evokes a much larger question about whether later writers, working as they also were within the fragmented ruins of the old Tibetan Empire, regarded Songtsen Gampo's reign as institutionally 'Buddhist' in the first place.

For many modern historians of Tibet, the received tradition of Songtsen Gampo's founding of written law cannot be taken as reliably historical,[4] with Andreĭ Vostrikov famously lamenting the inability of Tibetan historians to "distinguish facts from myths – what is historical from what is legendary" (1970, 59). Toni Huber provides a somewhat more nuanced take on this frustratingly labile historical moment:

> A large amount of painstaking historical, philological, and archaeological research now supports the view that what Tibetans have held most dear about their purported early Buddhist past and its founding figures is more a creative product of later, Buddhist-inspired history writing than a reflection of contemporary circumstance during the dynastic period. (1996, 58)

In approaching this problem, modern scholarship has frequently taken a distinctly political approach. The core conclusion – that much of Songtsen Gampo's rule is a post hoc idealization – is either understood in terms of a bald political partisanship such as the 'progressive glorification of royal ancestors' (Aris, 1997, 9; Dotson, 2006, 11; Sørensen, 1994, 24; Tucci, 1962, 126) or some version of Hobsbawm and Ranger's 'invented tradition' (1983), in which events such as Songtsen Gampo's development of the 'law of the ten virtues' is a post hoc projection of textual ideas that actually came to Tibet centuries later (Stein 1986, 213–14, see also below). In many cases, this is treated as a pious elaboration. For others still, it is sufficient simply to discreetly

[4] See Alexander Macdonald's wonderful review of modern scholarly disappointment (2003, 129–31).

express doubt as to the historicity of such accounts and move on (Pirie 2017a, 2017b; van Schaik 2016).

5.4 LAW BEYOND THE TEXTS

It is worth being clear at this point: most of the criticisms, regarding *the integrity of the textual lineage* connecting the Indian corpus of Buddhist ideas about the ten virtues to Songtsen Gampo's laws, seem entirely sound. Setting aside the view that 'hidden treasure' revelations, discovered more than three hundred years after the events they describe, retain any privileged claim to historicity, there is effectively no evidence that the ten virtues as a textual tradition or codex existed in Tibet prior to Trisong Détsen's rule, more than a century after the death of Songtsen Gampo. In this regard, post-imperial claims that there was a *textual lineage* that bridged between the Indian tradition of Mahāyāna Buddhism and Songtsen Gampo's laws (such as in the *Compendium of Maṇis*) remain unsupported, at least according to our present records.

With that said, however, we should be careful not to allow the dubious historicity of such claims to distract us from two important considerations: firstly, the sheer difficulty in objectively assessing what exactly makes Songtsen Gampo's kingdom 'Buddhist'; and, secondly, the actual meaning and significance of such a post hoc fabrication, beyond merely whether it was true. It is possible, after all, to refuse to be taken in by an ideological claim *and* simultaneously to take it seriously as an influential artifact in its own right, which is itself worthy of further analysis.

While there are, so far, no known contemporary or near-contemporary written references to Buddhism during Songtsen Gampo's rule, we are reasonably certain that some of the great edifices of Tibetan Buddhism – in particular, the Jokhang, Ramoché, and Trandruk temples – seem almost certainly to have been built during that time. The significance of those building projects remains unknown to us, and the contemporary written records from that time are spartan at best. Upon what do we rely as criteria for such a designation as 'Buddhist': what people did, or what people said about what they did? Do we depend upon our own definitions of what counts as Buddhist, those of the time, those of later Buddhist writers, or indeed those of the nearby non-Tibetan courts? More specifically, when it comes to a phrase like "based on the ten virtues," are we sure we know what the writers of the *Pillar Testament* or the *Considerations of Wa* meant by this when they put pen to paper?

Such assessments are necessarily and inevitably interpretative: they depend not simply on a verifiable history of textual and monumental sources, but also on an identifiable hermeneutics of governance and history. As Paul Ricœur described in detail, the simple fact of 'writing afterwards' changes the significance of historical events precisely because one knows *what came after* (1983). England's King John signing the Magna Carta at Runnymede in 1215 was famously described by Stubbs' *Constitutional History of England* (1874–78) as the earliest spark of the spirit and growth of democracy, but we can be sure that neither King John nor the rebel barons he met with had any such idea in their heads.

In this regard, the historicity, intent, and Buddhist credentials of Songtsen Gampo's law codes raise three distinct kinds of question:

(i) *What can we understand of the Tibetan imperial period from contemporary and near-contemporary sources?* This is typically the subject of Old Tibetan Studies, and centers around the study of archaeological remains, such as the royal tombs, imperial inscriptions, and the vast textual collections unpacked from Dunhuang, such as the Old Tibetan Annals, the Tibetan Chronicle, and the many legal fragments and case law reports.

(ii) *What can we glean from later, post-imperial sources about the Tibetan imperial period?* This inquiry involves either filtering out accumulated additions and interpolations within post-imperial works or sourcing their references, thus mining them for the contents of putative original imperial material. The most famous of such endeavors is undoubtedly Géza Uray and Helga Uebach's analysis of textual sources to unpick the original imperial texts (Uebach 1992, Uray 1967 and 1972). In what follows, in order to create some continuity in this debate, I will revisit some of Uray's own examples in light of my own analysis.

(iii) *What can we glean from those later sources about how post-imperial Tibetan writers understood and thought about history-writing itself?* This question, which I will also attend to, relates to what Huber refers to as "Buddhist-inspired history writing." Here, it is not sufficient to simply argue that subsequent Buddhist historiography was 'pious' (a common cipher for 'simple' and 'uncritical') or indeed that historical figures were simply 'glorified' (a distinctly Christological term, along with words like 'majesty' and 'power,' all associated with Hebrew and Greek notions of the divine). Nor can we necessarily be taken in by too monolithic a notion of 'tradition' with regard to the early post-imperial sources. While a 'received tradition' may have emerged by the late medieval period, we know that texts such as the *Considerations of Wa*, the *Pillar Testament*, and the *Compendium of Maṇis* emerged during a remarkably fractured and fractious period of Tibetan history (indeed, the so-called post-imperial *silbu-dü*, or 'time of fragmentation'). Much like today's scholars, the medieval authors of these and many other works were themselves trying to make sense of a difficult and often confusing range of historical sources from the imperial period, some (most notably the likes of Pawo Tsuglag Threngwa) engaged in extensive and detailed textual reconstruction, and others (such as Lama Dampa Sonam Gyaltsen, author of the

> *Clear Mirror*) seeking to integrate their textual sources into a particular and sophisticated historical worldview and understanding of governance. Many were trained Buddhist chroniclers with significant philosophical training in the Mahāyāna. In other words, we can and should expect to find political, philosophical, and historiographic principles at work in their writings, just as Corwin could identify complex and sophisticated Christological ideas at work in the 'higher law' of American constitutional thought.

And indeed, this *is* what we find. The textual sources, both before and after the imperial period, consistently tell us that while texts are important, they are not the sole domain or object of constitutional thought and history.

5.5 THE HERMENEUTICS OF BUDDHIST KINGSHIP

Previously, I have argued that works such as the *Pillar Testament* and the *Compendium of Maṇis* are clearly influenced – both substantively and organizationally – by the hermeneutics of the *Avataṃsaka Sūtra*, a voluminous and influential Mahāyāna scripture from around the third or fourth century CE (Mills 2012).

The *Avataṃsaka* (also known as the *Mahāvaipulya Buddhāvataṃsaka Sūtra*) was translated into Chinese in two versions by Buddhabhadra in 418–20 and Śikṣānanda in 695–99 and rendered into Tibetan in the ninth century CE by the Indian *paṇḍita* Jinamitra at Samyé during the reign of Trisong Détsen (Ōtake 2007). Thematically, the *Avataṃsaka Sūtra* centers on the question of the cosmological reality of the historical Buddha as an object of devotion and discipleship, and the role of bodhisattvas within the world. Its most famous chapters – the *Daśabhūmika* ("Ten Grounds"; Tib: *'phags pa sa bcu pa'i mdo*) and the *Gaṇḍavyūha* ("Flower Array," T. Tib. *sdong po bkod pa'i mdo*) – have much to say on the subject of bodhisattva-kingship and the nature of history, and lengthy sections are given over to the precise status and role of the ten virtues and ten non-virtues in the path of the bodhisattva. There are three aspects of this that will be considered in this chapter, since they give us a doorway into understanding the post-imperial view of Songtsen Gampo's law: the *Avataṃsaka Sūtra*'s notions of the origins of law, the reality of law, and the objectives of law.

5.5.1 *The Origins of the Law*

The *Daśabhūmika*, or *Sutra of the Ten Grounds*, details the ten virtues and their relationship with kingly law: specifically, it explains in depth both the ten virtues and the three realms of lower rebirth (familiar to many from the 'wheel of life' motif painted at the entrance to Mahāyāna Buddhist temples and monasteries) to which the ten non-virtues lead. An important aspect of the *Ten Grounds*' explanation is that the ten virtues are not primarily understood as a code of personal discipline, but as the personal qualities of a bodhisattva who has attained the second ground (the 'stage of purity'). That is, the virtues emerge 'naturally' from their stage of realization. For example, on the question of virtues of body:

> Enlightening beings in the stage of Purity naturally become imbued with ten virtuous ways of acting: they avoid taking life, they abandon weapons and hostility, they have conscience and sympathy and are compassionate and kind to all living beings, wishing for their welfare. They do not harm living beings even in their fantasies, much less injure other beings by gross physical harm with the conception of beings as such. The enlightening beings also abandon taking what is not given. They are satisfied with what they have and do not desire others' possessions. Thinking of things that belong to others as belonging to others, they do not give rise to any intention to steal and do not take even so much as a blade of grass or a leaf that is not given to them, much less take the necessities of life from others. The enlightening beings also abandon sexual misconduct. They are satisfied with their own spouses and do not desire the spouses of others. They do not give rise to desire for others' spouses, much less have sexual intercourse with them. (Cleary 1993, 714)

The *Daśabhūmika Sūtra* clearly identifies this second bodhisattva ground as occupied by monarchs and emperors:

> This is a brief explanation of the second stage of enlightening beings, the stage of Purity. Many of the enlightening beings in this stage are sovereigns, lords of four continents, and masters of the law, competent, powerful, able to rid beings of the impurities of bad behavior, to set them on the ten paths of virtuous conduct … Here enlightening beings become monarchs, leading sentient beings by the ten virtues: by all the virtue they have amassed, they will become saviors of the world, rich in the ten powers. (Cleary 1993, 718–20)

In this sense, the *Avataṃsaka Sūtra* presents the virtuous king as inherently inclined toward the ten virtues, which spontaneously and karmically emerge, along with their royal status, from the stage of the path they have reached as a bodhisattva. Thus, lawmaking and the morality of the lawmaker are seen as naturally and logically intertwined. As with the narrative of Songtsen Gampo's formulation of the first written laws, these are seen as produced spontaneously from his wisdom (*sgam po*).

If we were to take such an understanding as our basis for the historical formulation of law – which I would argue that some medieval Tibetan writers certainly did – there is no necessary requirement for Songtsen Gampo to base his new written legal code on a specific pre-existing text or coding of the ten virtues. To say that his law was "emergent from the ten virtues" was to say that it emerged from his personal qualities as a regal bodhisattva.

This formulation, I would argue, can help explain the persistent conditional linguistic forms used by subsequent writers to relate the 'ten virtues' to the specific elements of Songtsen Gampo's law. Thus, the *Considerations of Wa* states:

> For four months, the *tsenpo* wrote the law codes, *drawn out from the foundation of the ten virtues*. (dBZh, 28)[5]

Here, "drawn out from the foundation" is *gzhi blangs*, in which *gzhi* is a basis, foundation or birthplace. Similarly, Orgyan Lingpa's *Five Books of Law* has:

> *Conjoined with the ten virtues*, a decree of law was composed. (KDNg, f. 20b.2)

And the *Treatise Known as Gateway to Engaging with the Dharma* by Sonam Tsémo (1142–82) has:

> *Taking the ten virtues as a basis/beginning*, the law was composed. (Uray 1972, 53)

In all cases, this implicit connection between the ten virtues and the law is regularly understood not as a transposition or replication, but rather as an inspiration or spontaneous production. As we shall see below, this implies a potential distinction between the moral intentions of the lawgiver and the laws they produce.

5.5.2 *The Reality of the Law*

The second aspect of the *Avataṃsaka Sūtra*'s treatment of governance is the manner in which rule, whether religious or political, is seen as perspectivally disparate. Quite literally, both buddhas and bodhisattvas are 'seen' differently by different people, depending on those people's spiritual inclinations and stage of realization.

In the opening verses of the *Gaṇḍavyūha* chapter, this perspectival standpoint is laid out in voluminous detail. The text, famous for its presentation of the Mahāyāna view of the hierarchical distinction between the Mahāyāna and Śrāvakayāna vehicles, describes the Buddha's teaching of the "coming forth of the lion" at Sravasti, in the garden of Anathapindada in the Jeta grove, to five thousand bodhisattvas, kings, and hearer-disciples (Cleary 1993, 1138). On entering meditative concentration, the Buddha reveals that he is not simply sitting in a grand kingly pavilion at Sravasti, but instead at the epicenter of an infinite buddha-field, its ground made of diamond and jewels, the pavilion a mighty palace the size of a city, all surrounded by and coextensive with an infinite number of buddha-fields, worlds and palaces, each inhabited with hosts of buddhas, bodhisattvas, and world-turning emperors. All of this vast cosmological drama was witnessed by the five thousand bodhisattvas attending upon the Buddha, but not his closest disciples, Śāriputra, Maudgalyāyana, Mahākāśyapa, Revata, Subhūti, Aniruddha, Nandika, Kapphiṇa, Kātyāyana, Pūrṇa Maitrāyaniputra, and so on, for whom little of note happened.

The *Gaṇḍavyūha* then renders in extensive detail the reasons for the different views of the bodhisattvas and the hearers which, it asserts, revolves around the fact

5 See Lewis Doney for a slightly different translation (Doney 2020, 105). Emphasis is added in all excerpts.

that the disciples, being *hearers* rather than *bodhisattvas*, seek only the personal peace of nirvana and are therefore incapable of the compassionate omniscience involved in the *bodhisattva* vehicle:

> Because they were emancipated by the *vehicle* of hearers, they had realized the path of hearers, they had fulfilled the sphere of practices of hearers, they were fixed in the fruit of hearers; they rested on the knowledge of the light of truth, they were fixed at the limit of reality, they had gone to the state of eternal peace, they had no thought of great compassion and had no pity for the beings of the world; they had accomplished what they had to do for themselves. (Cleary 1993, 1147)

There then follows a lengthy discourse elaborating this general perspectival principle in multiple examples. Thus,

> The situation was like that of hundreds of thousands of ghosts gathered on the bank of the great river Ganges, hungry and thirsty, naked, without shelter, emaciated, dehydrated by the wind and heat, attacked by flocks of crows, terrorized by wolves and jackals – they do not see the Ganges River, or they may see it as dry, without water, or full of ashes, because they are shrouded by actions that blind them. In the same way the old great disciples there in the Jeta grove did not see or penetrate the transfigurations of the Buddha, because they rejected omniscience and their eyes were veiled by ignorance. (Cleary 1993, 1148)

This same view is commonly enough expressed today. Thus, Dilgo Khyentse Rinpoche, in his recent commentary on the twelfth-century *Copper Mountain Testament*, which shares some authorship with the *Compendium of Maṇis*, argues:

> Try to understand this comparison: the Buddha's twelve deeds and so forth differ in the traditions of the Hīnayāna and Mahāyāna [forms of Buddhism]. We only take the Mahāyāna version to be truly authentic. The Hīnayāna version is what was perceived through the limited vision of Hīnayāna disciples. This is the same as the analogy of a white conch shell being seen to be yellow by someone who has jaundice . . . The inconsistencies and dissimilarities in the life stories of enlightened beings come about because those beings are perceived differently from different levels of people who are influenced . . . The buddhas appeared [in different ways] because of the different karmic perceptions of different followers. (Dilgo Khyentse Rinpoche 1993, 12)

This aspect of the *Avataṃsaka Sūtra* clearly influenced post-dynastic Tibetan writings on these subjects, both in substantive, narrative, and philosophical terms. The famous tale of Songtsen Gampo's meeting with the two monks of Khotan, found in almost all post-imperial Tibetan renditions and generally seen as the seminal portrayal of Songtsen Gampo as the bodhisattva Avalokiteśvara, is a classic example (Mills 2012). The two monks are described as receiving a vision in Khotan that Songtsen Gampo was Avalokiteśvara in person. Making the long pilgrimage to Central Tibet to meet the emperor, however, they witness a terrifying spectacle of torture and carnage in the name of the king's law, leading them to reject the idea that he could possibly be Avalokiteśvara. Summoned before the king, however, he explains to them that what they saw were not actual people being harmed, but illusory manifestations (*sprul pa*), magically produced each day by the ruler. This vignette demonstrates clear matches with the *Gaṇḍavyūha*'s account of the seeker Sudhana's meeting with the Indian king Anala (Mills 2012).

In the post-dynastic texts on Songtsen Gampo's life from the *Pillar Testament* onwards this moral perspectivism is formalized, not only in the story of the Khotanese monks, but also in a series of narrative tropes that appear episodically throughout his royal biography. Indeed, even the king's birth is presented in terms of levels of illusion and clarity:

> Three different ways of seeing this event arose: to the Buddhas of the Ten Directions, it appeared that the sublime Chenrésik, having planned the liberation of sentient beings in the snowy land of Tibet on the basis of the power of prayers in former times, shining like a brilliant lamp in the darkness of this wild region, had cast his gaze upon that precious place. In the perception of the Bodhisattvas of the Ten Grounds, it appeared that Chenrésik, with the intention of leading the sentient beings of this wild and snowy realm to the Dharma, manifested himself as a king who would strive to benefit beings by means appropriate to each. In the perception of the common black-headed people, it appeared that a son of unsurpassed wonder had been born to the king. (GSM, ff. 140–42)[6]

Likewise, as post-imperial texts such as the *Pillar Testament* and *Clear Mirror* regularly state, the essential relationship between the ten virtues of Buddhist doctrine and kingly law are, like the Buddha Śākyamuni's "coming forth of the lion," seen only by bodhisattvas and those others "who have eyes to see."

5.5.3 *The Objectives of the Law*

If, as mentioned above, there was potentially a difference between the spontaneous moral intentions of the bodhisattva-king and the laws he formulated, this was because such a formulation was understood to take into account the moral nature of the Tibetan people themselves. This is most obvious in the tale of the Khotanese monks mentioned above. Songtsen Gampo explains to the terrified monks:

> Those who are to be tamed by me are not clothed by peace. [Therefore], through the door of wrathful means, illusory people are punished. (KKM 1989, 304)

And, in the *Compendium of Maṇis* version of this tale:

> The Tibetan people, having a monkey-father and a rock demoness mother, were difficult to subdue [and thus] difficult to lead to religion. As a consequence, fearful religious law was protectively employed. (MKB, Vol. 1(E), ff. 407)

6 See also Sørensen 1994, 161–62.

This idea of the nature of a people as an object of law – as an intermediary function in the formation of legal codes and practice themselves – is similarly enshrined in the *Gaṇḍavyūha* chapter of the *Avataṃsaka Sūtra*. Thus, after the seeker Sudhana questions King Anala's apparently ruthless and bloody application of the law in his kingdom, Anala explains:

> I have attained enlightening beings' magical liberation. The people in my realm are given to all sorts of evildoing – murder, theft, rape, falsehood, slander, vilification, divisive talk, covetousness, malice, false views, villainy, violence, cruelty. I am unable to turn them away from evildoing by any other means, so in order to subdue them, mature them, guide them, and secure their welfare, out of compassion I have illusory executioners kill and maim illusory criminals, making a display of intense suffering and pain; seeing this, the people in my realm become afraid to do evil. Seeing the people alarmed by this device, I have them give up evildoing and conduct themselves virtuously; then I establish them in ultimate security, the end of all suffering, the bliss of omniscience. (Cleary 1993, 1245)

In Mahāyāna Buddhist terms, this is of course the principle of 'skillful means' discussed above, in some respects similar in logic to the Islamic concept of the "objectives of the law" (*maqasid al-shari'ah*). This is the jurisprudential principle that the law, however it is formed, must lead people toward a particular set of religious objectives (Kamali 1999), even if they do not completely understand their full religious significance. Within such a perspective, law is goal-oriented rather than simply normative. In the Islamic legal traditions, these are largely focused on the formation of mutual aid, compassion, and education within the Islamic community itself. In the post-dynastic Tibetan sources and the *Avataṃsaka*, the objectives of law are focused on avoidance of the lower realms of rebirth and, as we saw above, "ultimate security, the end of all suffering, the bliss of omniscience." Similarly, in the seventeenth century, Geluk scholar Sumpa Khenpo described how:

> At that time good laws were introduced by the king and the councilors, in order to lead the Tibetan subjects to the excellent religion, according to which (the laws) the men steady in the ten virtues and the so-called "sixteen pure human moral rules," (notably) . . . should be noblemen. (Uray 1972, 54)

In the tale of the Khotanese monks and also the *Gaṇḍavyūha*, such a goal required both the deployment of wrathful kingly means and the performance of 'illusory manifestation' (*sprul ba*): in the *Pillar Testament*, the *Compendium of Maṇis*, and the *Clear Mirror*, Songtsen Gampo is depicted as magically producing both victims and torturers and executioners, all with the objective of terrifying his subjects into observing the ten virtues. Put simply, in goal-oriented jurisprudence, codified law does not need to look like the "ten virtues" in order to lead Tibetans toward them.

Medieval Tibetan writers thus identified a disjuncture between the intentions of Songtsen Gampo as bodhisattva-king and the necessities of ruling non-virtuous and recalcitrant populations, a recurring theme in Tibetans' historical self-understanding. Similarly, in Müsépa's *Lineage of Sakya Succession* (1475),[7] the story is told of how the Sakya ruler Pakpa carried out harsh laws. When a monk grew concerned at this behavior by a Buddhist ruler, Pakpa – in a manner remarkably similar to Songtsen Gampo and the Khotanese monks – explained the skillful means behind his actions. The monk later exclaimed:

> Being truly amazed at [Pakpa] Lama's ability, he told everyone he saw about this incident. He realized that Pakpa's actions and behavior were performed to tame all beings, and that the animal slaughter, tax collection, and corvée labor pertained to the karma of the individuals. May I come to regard [all these actions] as the extraordinary [karmic consequences]! (Mus srad pa: *Sa skya gdung rabs*)

This obviously means that, from this Tibetan perspective, law as a form of royal and governmental regulation can and does often 'look' very different from more normatively identified Buddhist ethical principles. The relationship between the two is expressly understood as indirect, mediated by the nature of the people ruled over, and the wisdom and skillful means of the ruler as bodhisattva.

Indeed, in a sense the secular law (as opposed to the Buddhist *vinaya*) is understood as derivative and in a very real sense 'illusory.' Thus, in his *Naming of the Sources of Religious Sponsors* (StSby, ff. 14–15), the Geluk historian Longdöl Lama Ngawang Losang (1719–94/5), explained how this involved law as a 'trick' (T. *zol*):

> If (it is asked) so: What are the sixteen (points) of the law of the sixteen pure human moral rules composed by king Songtsen Gampo . . . As in this way the ten virtues of the excellent religion were completed by the trick (*zol*) of law, the gates of the three damnations were closed, the way of paradise and liberation was widened. So it is said. (Uray 1972, 54)

Here, Longdöl's use of the term *zol* is cognate with the notion of a magician's illusion, akin in many respects to the Mahāyāna idea of 'illusory manifestations.' In this respect, the post-dynastic texts are both explicit and repetitious on the point, following the philosophical view of the *Avataṃsaka Sūtra*: that the reality and mechanisms of law, and therefore of kingly rule itself, are illusory in nature, and certainly not clear to ordinary eyes.

5.6 CONCLUSION

In his monumental study of Buddhism in Tibetan societies, *Civilised Shamans*, Geoffrey Samuel commented extensively on the historical tensions between two modalities of Tibetan religious life: the clerical and the shamanic. The *shamanic*, Samuel argued, invoked "alternative modes of reality" that were fundamental to the

[7] Mus srad pa (1424–98): *Sa skya gdung rabs*. Text ref. S1550: Sakya Research Centre.

vicissitudes of everyday life and often ethically antinomian in application; while the *clerical* concentrated on the authority of scholarship, philosophical analysis, and adherence to more classical rule-bound notions of ethical behavior (1993, 9–10). Indeed, in line with Samuel's analysis, there are Tibetan clerical approaches that emphasize a clear lineage of textual sources that leads from Indian Buddhism to Tibetan law.

Nonetheless, most of what has been discussed above fits very neatly into Samuel's characterization of the 'shamanic modality': the idea of public law as a kind of 'trick', 'manifestation', or 'skillful means': the notion of reality, and in particular the reality of governance, as being perspectival and somewhat illusory; the idea that ethics is a hidden underlying or fundamental reality that shapes law, even laws that do not seem to follow ethical codes in any straightforward or obvious way.

In seeking to understand these things, we are forced to grapple with a Buddhist tradition that is different from Helmholz's portrait of European and American constitutional thought in three key ways. First and foremost, public law in this view was expressly understood as not *directly* embodying or representing Buddhist norms and rulings, but rather as moving toward the underlying objectives of those norms and rulings. This principle was not uniquely Tibetan but derived from long-established Mahāyāna logics about the nature of the spiritual path (*lam*) toward liberation, and the place of rulers and monarchs on that path. This meant that law was seen as Buddhist in a complex and perspectival way. Secondly, as with the Islamic traditions of jurisprudence, public law was understood as goal-focused rather than norm-focused. The form of law was seen as determined by larger moral objectives that, in turn, were derived from a wider picture of Buddhist striving toward liberation. Thirdly, and as a consequence of the above, the quality of public law was seen as dependent on the personal moral insight and sagacity of the lawmaker. While there is seen to be a clear distinction between royal law and the monastic code of discipline, both are seen to derive from the wisdom of the founding leader, whether that be the emperor or the Buddha.

In regard to its origins, reality, and objectives then, Buddhist law (within this Mahāyāna framework, at least) is quite unlike Helmholz's description of Christian constitutional thought, in that Buddhist law (in the Tibetan examples discussed in this chapter) *must* exist within the purview of the lawmaker's "own full understanding" because "hidden things" – namely, private conviction and morality – are seen to be essential elements in its formation.

Thus, the post-imperial narratives about Songtsen Gampo's founding of the law both emphasize a textual lineage (in particular, reference to a '*sūtra* of the ten virtues') as well as valorizing the wisdom of Songtsen Gampo in formulating the laws 'based on the ten virtues.' Like the wealthy father standing outside his burning house in the *Lotus Sūtra* parable then, medieval Tibetan histories of law present multiple legitimations to promote Tibetans' flight from non-virtue to law. And as with the parable, this may be seen as a 'trick,' but it is not seen to be a falsehood.

TIBETAN SOURCES

ANK 2000. ཨ་མེས་ཞབས་ངག་དབང་ཀུན་དགའ་བསོད་ནམས་ཀྱི་བཀའ་འབུམ། (*The Collected Works of A-mes-shab Ngag-dbang Kun-dgah bSod-nams*). TBRC: W29307.

dBZh དབའ་བཞེད། (*Considerations of Wa*). Wangdu, Pasang, and Hildegard Diemberger. 2000. *dBa' bzhed – The Royal Narrative Concerning the Bringing of the Buddha's Doctrine to Tibet.* Wien: Verlag der Otserreichischen Akademie der Wissenschaften.

CJsG བསོད་ནམས་རྩེ་མོ། (1142–1182) ཆོས་ལ་འཇུག་པའི་སྒོ་ཞེས་བྱ་བའི་བསྟན་བཅོས། (*Treatise Known as Gateway to Engaging with the Dharma*). TBRC: W2DB4568.

GSM བསོད་ནམས་རྒྱལ་མཚན། (1312–1375) རྒྱལ་རབས་གསལ་བའི་མེ་ལོང་ (*Clear Mirror of Royal Genealogies*) W23770.

KDNg ཨོ་རྒྱན་གླིང་པ། (b. 1323) བཀའ་ཐང་སྡེ་ལྔ། (*Five Books of Law*). TBRC: W17319.

KhGSt (*Feast for the Wise*) དཔའ་བོ་གཙུག་ལག་ཕྲེང་བ་ (1504–1566) ཆོས་འབྱུང་མཁས་པའི་དགའ་སྟོན་ TBRC: W1PD96069.

KKM rGya-mtsho, Smon-lam, ed. 1989. བཀའ་ཆེམས་ཀ་ཁོལ་མ་ (*Pillar Testament*) Lanzhou: Kan su'u mi rigs dpe skrun khang.

MKB 1975. མ་ཎི་བཀའ་འབུམ་ (*Compendium of Maṇis*). Bla brgyud gsol 'debs dan lo rgyus skor sgrub thabs kyi chos skor. New Delhi.

Mus srad pa མུས་སྲད་པ་ (1424–1498) ས་སྐྱ་གདུང་རབས། *Sa skya gdung rabs*. S1550: Sakya Research Centre.

StSby ཀློང་རྫོལ་བླ་མ་ངག་དབང་བློ་བཟང་། (1719–94/5) བསྟན་པའི་སྦྱིན་བདག་བྱུང་ཚུལ་གྱི་མིང་གི་གྲངས། (*Naming of the Sources of Religious Sponsors*) TBRC: W1NLM293.

REFERENCES

Abrams, Philip. 1988. "Notes on the Difficulty of Studying the State." *Journal of Historical Sociology* 1 (1): 58–89.

Allen, John. 1830. *Inquiry into the Rise and Growth of the Royal Prerogative in England.* London: Longman.

Aris, Michael. 1997. "Foreword." In *Tibetan Histories: A Bibliography of Tibetan-Language Historical Works*, edited by Dan Martin, 9–12. London: Serindia.

Cleary, Thomas. 1993. *The Flower Ornament Scripture. Translation of the Avatamsaka Sutra.* Boston: Shambhala.

Corwin, Edward S. 1955. *The 'Higher Law' Background of American Constitutional Law, vol.* 1. Ithaca: Cornell University Press.

Doney, Lewis. 2020. *Bringing Buddhism to Tibet: History and Narrative in the Dba' bzhed Manuscript.* Berlin/Boston: Walter de Gruyter GmbH.

Dotson, Brandon. 2006. *Administration and Law in the Tibetan Empire: The Section on Law and State and Its Old Tibetan Antecedents.* Unpublished PhD thesis, University of Oxford.

2009. *The Old Tibetan Annals: An Annotated Translation of Tibet's First History*. Vienna: Austrian Academy of Sciences Press.
Fuller, Christopher. 1992. *The Camphor Flame: Popular Hinduism and Society in India*. Princeton: Princeton University Press.
Helmholz, Richard H. 2010. "Human Rights in the Canon law." In *Christianity and Human Rights: An Introduction*, edited by John Witte, Jr. and Frank Alexander, 99–112. Cambridge: Cambridge University Press.
Hobsbawm, Eric, and Ranger, Terence. 1983. *The Invention of Tradition*. Cambridge: Cambridge University Press.
Huber, Toni. 1996. "Literal or Literary: Reflections on New Translations of History's Mirror." *Tibet Journal* 21 (4): 58–67.
Kamali, Mohammad Hashim. 1999. "'Maqāṣid Al-Sharī'ah': The Objectives of Islamic Law." *Islamic Studies* 38 (2): 193–208.
Kantorowicz, Ernst. 1957. *The King's Two Bodies: A Study in Medieval Political Thought*. Princeton: Princeton University Press.
Khyentse, Dilgo. 1993. "Foreword." In *The Lotus-Born: The Life Story of Padmasambhava*, by Yeshe Tsongyal, 3–7. Hong Kong: Rangjung Yeshe Publications.
Macdonald, Alexander W. 2003 (1982). "Religion in Tibet at the Time of Srong-Btsan Sgam-Po: Myth as History." In *History of Tibet*, edited by Alex McKay, 129–40. London: Routledge.
Mills, Martin A. 2011. "The Many Bodies of King Songtsen Gampo: Constitutional Mythology in Tibetan History." In *Exploring Tibet's History and Culture*, edited by Pabitrakumar Roy, 88–120. New Delhi: Central University of Tibetan Studies.
2012. "Ritual as History in Tibetan Divine Kingship: Notes on the Myth of the Khotanese Monks." *History of Religions* 51 (3): 219–38.
2018. "Last Gift of the God-King: Narrating the Dalai Lama's Resignation." In *Tibetan Subjectivities on the Global Stage*, edited by Shelley Bhoil and Enrique Galvan-Alvarez, 155–74. New York: Lexington Books.
Ōtake, Susumu. 2007. "On the origin and early development of the Buddhāvataṃsaka Sūtra." In *Reflecting Mirrors: Perspectives on Huayan Buddhism*, edited by Imre Hamar, 87–107. Wiesbaden: Harrassowitz.
Pirie, Fernanda. 2017a. "Buddhist Law in Early Tibet: The Emergence of an Ideology." *Journal of Law and Religion* 32 (3): 406–22.
2017b. "Which 'Two Laws'? The Concept of *trimnyi* (*khrims gnyis*) in Medieval Tibet." *Cahiers d'Extrême-Asie* 26 (1): 41–60.
Ricœur, Paul. 1983. *Time and Narrative, vol. 1*, trans. Kathleen McLaughlin and David Pellauer. Chicago: University of Chicago Press.
Samuel, Geoffrey. 1993. *Civilised Shamans: Buddhism in Tibetan Societies*. Princeton: Princeton University Press.
Sørensen, Per. 1994. *Tibetan Buddhist Historiography: The Mirror Illuminating the Royal Genealogies*. Wiesbaden: Harrassowitz Verlag.
Stein, Rolf. 1986. "Tibetica Antiqua IV: La tradition relative au début du bouddhisme au Tibet." *Bulletin de l'École Française d'Extrême Orient* LXXV: 169–96.
Tucci, Giuseppe. 1962. "The Two Wives of Srong-btsan sgam-po." *Oriens Extremus* 9: 161–66.
Uebach, Helga. 1992. "Notes on the Section of Law and State in the Chos-'byung of IDe'u." In *Tibetan Studies: Proceedings of the 5th Seminar of the International Association for Tibetan Studies Narita 1989*, edited by Ihara Shōren and Yamaguchi Zuihō, 823–32. Narita: Naritasan Shinshoji.

Uray, Géza. 1967. "Traces of a narrative of the Old Tibetan Chronicle in the Mkhas pa'i dga' ston." *Monumenta Serica* 26 (1): 498–505.

1972. "The Narrative of Legislation and Organization of the Mkhas-Pa'i Dga'- Ston: The Origins of the Traditions Concerning Sroṅ-Brcan Sgam-Po as First Legislator and Organizer of Tibet." *Acta Orientalia Academiae Scientiarum Hungaricae* 26 (1): 11–68.

van Schaik, Sam. 2016. *The Spirit of Tibetan Buddhism*. New Haven: Yale University Press.

Vostrikov, Andreĭ Ivanovich. 1970. *Tibetan Historical Literature*. Calcutta: R.D. Press.

Wangdu, Pasang and Diemberger, Hildegard. 2000. *dBa' bzhed - The Royal Narrative Concerning the Bringing of the Buddha's Doctrine to Tibet*. Vienna: Verlag der Österreichischen Akademie der Wissenschaften.

Watson, B. 1993. *The Lotus Sutra*. New York: Columbia University Press.

Williams, P. 2009. *Mahayana Buddhism: The Doctrinal Foundations* (2nd ed.). Oxon: Routledge.

6

Tibetan Buddhist Monastic Constitutional Law and Governmental Constitutional Law

Mutual Influences?

*Berthe Jansen**

6.1 INTRODUCTION

Did constitutional law exist in Tibet? According to one popular source, the *Encyclopedia Britannica*, constitutional law denotes "the body of rules, doctrines, and practices that govern the operation of political communities." The entry continues: "In modern times, the most important political community has been the state."[1] Lending a broad interpretation to the phrase "political communities," I hypothesize that, in the context of pre-1950s Tibet, Buddhist monasteries could be constituted as communities that not only governed themselves but also exercised political and judicial power far beyond the monasteries' boundary markers. The relative autonomy of the monasteries, their power, and unique legal status mean that a study of Tibet's legal system would be incomplete without considering monastic "constitutional law." Furthermore, there are a number of indications that monastic concepts of the law influenced the Tibetan state's legal procedures.

This chapter explores a number of these influences. Regarding the so-called monastic ideologies of law, one has to be aware that these are hardly ever found explicitly in legal literature. This is significant since "despite the many remarkable achievements of Tibet's religious leadership in areas of culture including literature and the arts, philosophy, and spiritual discipline, *sustained reflection on the basis of political organization* itself was *never part of traditional learning*"(Kapstein 2006, 138).[2] Similarly, Ruegg states: "The search for theoretical models and ancient Indian historical precedents which might have served Tibetan thinkers is, however, no straightforward matter, for our Tibetan sources are not as explicit on the subject as

* This investigation is part of my research project on Buddhism and Law in early modern Tibet, which is funded by the Dutch Research Council (NWO).

[1] *Encyclopedia Britannica*, available at www.britannica.com/topic/constitutional-law.

[2] Italics added.

we would wish" (2013 [1997], 220).[3] More specifically, with regard to Tibetan law, Tucci writes: "There is no profane literature to speak of, because culture belonged entirely to the monks; even the laws which ruled Tibet for several centuries, although bearing the names of the kings who enforced them, were almost certainly written down by lamas"(1949, 94).

By extension, primary sources available today do not contain much reflection by Tibetan authors on how religion and the law were to be reconciled. To get a glimpse of Tibetan Buddhist legal thinking, one has to read between the lines of prescriptive legal texts as well as works that describe the juridical process.

In recent decades, a number of compilations of older Tibetan legal texts have been published in the Tibetan Autonomous Region as well as in China proper. Some of these volumes contain a classification of "religious" legal texts (*chos khrims*) and secular legal texts (*srid khrims*).[4] The religious legal texts tend to be monastic guidelines (*bca' yig*), a genre of texts that deals with the rules within monastic institutions (see Jansen 2015, 2016, and 2018). This distinction between Tibetan religious rules and secular rules is by no means a modern one; it is not uncommon that monastic guidelines written between the twelfth century and the 1950s refer to the secular law, and that secular law books from similar periods refer to monastic guidelines. My interest lies in the connections between these so-called religious and secular legal texts, between laws for monks and laws for lay people. Aside from contents and vocabulary use, authorship connects these two types of legal texts. This is obvious when the legal texts are written by – for example – the fifth Dalai Lama (1617–82), but less clear when the author is unknown. By reading these works closely and noting the quotations drawn from other types of literature contained in them, we get a better understanding of the ways in which the author was educated and inspired.

6.2 TIBET'S LEGAL CODES

Generally speaking, in the Indian classical model, the relationship between the king and Buddhist monastics is modeled on that of the advice-giving monk – the *kalyāṇamitra*, if you will – and the well-meaning king, who is occasionally prone to violence. This relationship between ruler and "spiritual friend," between "donor" and "priest," which is particularly prevalent in the Mahāyāna tradition, has been extensively studied and commented upon by scholars of Buddhism (most notably by Ruegg 1991; 2013 [1997], but also see Deeg 2016). While there are instances in which

[3] See also Ruegg 1991.

[4] e.g., *Bod kyi khrims srol skor gyi lo rgyus yig tshags phyogs sgrig zhal lce phyogs sgrig* 2016; *Snga rabs bod kyi srid khrims gsal ba'i me long* 2014; *Gzhung dga' ldan pho brang skabs kyi khrims srol bca' chings bdams bsgrigs*. 2008; *Snga rabs bod kyi srid khrims* 2004; *Bod kyi snga rabs khrims srol yig cha bdams bsgrigs* 1989; *Zhal lce phyogs bsdus: Bod kyi dus rabs rims byung gi khrims yig phyogs bsdus dwangs byed ke ta ka zhe bya ba bzhugs so* 1987.

this Buddhist relationship between religion and politics became a historical reality, it appears that more often than not, the two domains – secular rule and the Dharma – were not easily distinguishable categories. This is to say that the lines between them were often blurry, if they existed at all.

The presence of a prosperous and powerful sangha meant that there was less need for the sponsorship and protection of a secular ruler. In premodern Tibet, where monks and monasteries were, at times, particularly influential, the harmonious merging of the "secular" and the religious domains even became an explicit desideratum (Tib. *Chos srid zung 'brel*). Even so, the monks in their monasteries were meant to keep to their own "constitutional" laws – "the body of rules, doctrines, and practices" that governed their communities – while lay Tibetans were expected to abide by local "secular" laws. The former consisted of *praṭimokṣa* vows, the *vinaya* more generally, other religious vows, more universal Buddhist ethics, and last but not least, the more localized and often highly pragmatic "monastic guidelines" (*bca' yig*). These guidelines were often written by religious figures of high standing. A fair number of surviving sets of guidelines were authored by monks who also had significant political power.[5] Therefore, the same monks who wrote the texts that regulated monasteries were also responsible for issuing official decrees, judicial decisions, and possibly legal codes. One would thus expect there to be considerable similarities between these genres of literature, something upon which I will further elaborate below.

That monks had their own "laws" meant that they were – again in theory – not subject to the laws of the local ruler. In serious cases such as murder, however, this also meant that monastics could get punished twice. First the monk would be beaten, forcibly disrobed, and expelled. Next, he would be tried as a lay person in a secular court (Jansen 2018, 171). Minor legal cases that involved both monks and lay people were often solved through mediation or through adjudication at the monastery in whose territory the case had taken place. Among historians of Tibet there is a general consensus that in such cases, the monks had a greater advantage.

While the Tibetan tradition claims that law emerged on the basis of Buddhist notions, in fact when Buddhism was first adopted as the royal religion in the eighth century, legal works preserved in Dunhuang roughly datable to that time did not directly reflect Buddhist sentiments. It seems that a juridical system was already in place during the height of the Tibetan empire (Pirie 2017, 409–10).[6] According to Uray, the introduction of Buddhism did indeed promote the development (and possible adaptation) of (new) legal codes, which suggests that the imperial legal codes from the seventh and eighth centuries reflected the new religion's influence (Uray 1972, 11–68; also see Jansen 2020a). In those codes, four fundamental laws are

5 e.g., the fifth, seventh and thirteenth Dalai Lamas; various Panchen lamas; the crown-prince of Sikkim. On the latter see Jansen 2014.

6 Also see van der Kuijp 1999. For an exploration of those laws see Dotson 2006.

given, prohibiting murder, thievery, lechery, and the bearing of false witness. These works also refer to the ten non-virtuous acts (*mi dge ba bcu*), which appear to be an obvious reference to the basic Buddhist ethical framework. In other words, "Buddhism contributed to the substance of Tibetan laws, as well as providing their formal framework" (Dreyfus 1995, 120).

There is no universal agreement on these points, however. Schuh claims that the legal texts that were subsequently produced (the *Zhal lce*) were *not* based on these non-virtuous acts, nor on the sixteen pure human rules (*mi chos gtsang ma bcu drug*).[7] Schuh argues that the influence of Buddhism was a "retrospective, purely fictitious, ideological construct" (1984, 299–300). Van der Kuijp has also noted "the total absence of anything that might remotely be construed as Buddhist, except for their propagandistic introductions written for the purposes of legitimation and authority"(1999, 288).[8] My contention is that while the legal codes in their earliest beginnings, for example, those dateable to the early seventh century, may not have been Buddhist, they most certainly came to integrate Buddhist values as time passed and as legal texts were further edited, elaborated, and "modernized" to accommodate the sentiments of the day. As a result, Tibetan legal codes contain a mix of notions, ideas, and vocabulary – often difficult to understand even for highly educated readers of Tibetan.

Perhaps the most well-known and widespread Tibetan legal code is "The Sixteen Pronouncements" (*Zhal lce bcu drug*). Although nothing of the contents suggests as much, the origin of this code is traditionally attributed to King Songtsen Gampo (Srong btsan sgam po, seventh century CE), who is credited with igniting the flame of Buddhism in Tibet (see Chapter 5, this volume). Some see the genre of *zhal lce* texts as being Tibet's constitution, and indeed at certain times in the history of Tibet certain *zhal lce* codes did actually function as something referred to as an authoritative "body of rules" used to govern the operation of political communities. At the same time, we also know that informal socio-legal practices formed, and still form, a large part of the social reality in Tibetan regions (see Pirie 2006). The fact remains that Tibet's literary and oral tradition – now and in the past – points to these texts as foundational when discussing Tibetan law.[9]

We have always assumed that the various *zhal lce* works are individual and distinct texts, which borrow heavily from each other. Upon closer examination, it appears that any given *zhal lce* text bases itself on previous works, ultimately referring back to the presumed original version by the *dharmarāja* Songtsen Gampo. This is reminiscent of the Buddhist genre of commentarial literature (e.g., *śāstras*) that try to clarify, apprise, and make relevant the authoritative source, namely the words of the

7 While these sets are nowadays seen as unproblematically Buddhist, it appears that they were closer to being codes of morality, containing considerable overlap with Chinese Confucian principles. See Uray 1972; Yamaguchi 1987; Roesler 2015.

8 Also see Pirie 2013a, 170.

9 For an overview of these texts as a genre see French 1996.

Buddha, the sutras. In a similar way, the deified ruler Songtsen Gampo's legal visions – whatever those may have been – have not been and can never be changed or contradicted.[10] However, they can be *adapted* to certain times and circumstances. A number of variations and adaptations exist, resulting in not only various numbers of pronouncements but also different contents among the recensions.[11] While the relatively early legal code (fourteenth century CE) studied by Pirie maintains the framework of a list of a set number of laws, "[i]t seems as if the writer has carried out, or commissioned, a survey of contemporary customs and recorded different practices" (Pirie 2020, 605). Not coincidentally, this is similar to how the monastery's rulebooks were – and are still – composed (Jansen 2018, 21–22).

Confusingly, legal codes (*zhal lce*) that look like different editions of the same work (as they both have the same number of articles) may also be distinct works altogether. It is therefore better to speak of a genre of *zhal lce* texts, rather than of textual variations, which suggests that there was one *Ur*-text on which all others are based (despite what the Tibetan tradition itself may claim). To improve our understanding of this genre then, scholars should stop viewing and treating individual *zhal lce* texts as existing independently and start looking at the works as *a corpus*. In this way, we can see how the legal texts interact with each other. This philological approach to legal texts has been a desideratum for decades now.[12] Obviously, the format of the *zhal lce* genre is more or less fixed: there are to be a number (twelve, thirteen, fifteen, or sixteen) of "laws" on which the author then comments. Frequently, the works have long introductions, sometimes relating the "history" or origins of law in Tibet (see Jansen 2020a).

It appears that these pronouncements had a mainly symbolic function, nonetheless they were deeply engrained in what has been called the "legal consciousness" of the Tibetans (see Pirie 2013b, 239–41). The purpose of the main Tibetan legal codes, the *zhal lce* – in particular after the Ganden Phodrang government (headed by the fifth Dalai Lama) was established in 1642 – is seen by some to be pro forma, mere symbolic representations of juridical power (Pirie 2016, 241; Cassinelli and Ekvall 1969, 153). As Pirie has rightly remarked, "there is little evidence that the provisions of rules and agreements . . . were applied in any detail" (Pirie 2016, 232). Still, I have found that the different *zhal lce* texts draw upon each other: they cite, rework, and

[10] This is perhaps similar to how the Christian Ten Commandments are not subject to appeal or amendment on account of their sacred nature. See Chapter 18 by Helmholz in this volume.

[11] These texts were reproduced and circulated widely throughout Tibet, well into the twentieth century.

[12] i.e., Schuh 1984, 297: "Ohne eine Edition der inzwischen bekannt gewordenen Gesetzbücher und ohne eine erfolrgreiche Suche nach weitern Rechtsbüchern des tibetischen Mittelalters werden viele Fragen zur Rechtsgeschichte in Tibet nur hypothetisch oder überhaupt nicht beantwort bleiben."; Cüppers, 2011b: "Obwohl in neuerer Zeit Wissenschaftler sich mit dem traditionellen Recht in Tibet beschäftigen, gibt es jedoch bisher keine philologische Bearbeitung dieser Werke." (www.tibet-encyclopaedia.de/gesetzbuecher.html) This philological groundwork is part of an ongoing research project in which I am involved.

reinterpret earlier versions. Much like the way in which a Tibetan scholar would attempt to make an old Buddhist text from India fit the sensibilities of a much later audience, there appear to be instances in which authors seem to "update" and maintain the relevance of the previously existing *zhal lce* by explaining them in the terms of that day. While this is not evidence that they were applied in a court of law, the regular updating of these texts does suggest they were far from obsolete to those who dealt with legal matters.

6.3 MONASTIC CONSTITUTIONAL LAW?

I have mentioned that monks and monasteries generally were not subject to "secular" laws. Stein argues that this is one of the reasons why monasteries should be seen as "independent overlords," since "monasteries are exempt from tax and services, they can be regarded as independent overlords, for they own land and serfs yielding them taxes and services, and discharge all the functions of authority (justice, etc.)"(Stein 1972 [1962], 141). What is unknown, however, is exactly how this legal unit functioned. The question also arises: To what extent were monasteries autonomous in terms of jurisdiction? When considering Buddhist monasticism as an Asian phenomenon, in general terms and without relation to a particular cultural setting, some scholars have suggested that monks are only ever answerable to themselves (Carrasco 1959, 121): in other words, by taking his ordination vows, the monk is no longer subject to the secular authority and answers only to the Buddhist code of discipline, the *vinaya* (e.g., Vermeersch 2008, 151). The monastic legal code, the *Mūlasarvastivādavinaya*, that Tibetan monks adhere to makes it clear that the king must acknowledge that lay law does not apply to the monks and monastic law does not apply to the laymen (Schopen 1995, 117). Buddhist sutras, such as the *Ākāśagarbha Sūtra*, also reflect this notion. In this particular sutra the Buddha names five transgressions for a member of the *kṣatriya* caste who is due to become a ruler. One of these transgressions is the forcibly disrobing or punishing of Buddhist monks – regardless of whether they are innocent of their crimes and transgressions:

> Taking by force the saffron robes of those who have shaved their heads and beards for my sake and donned the saffron robes – whether they uphold the precepts or not, whether they observe the discipline or not – thus making them householders; inflicting corporal punishment on them, imprisoning, or killing them: all of these constitute the third root transgression.[13]

[13] This translation is by the Sakya Pandita Translation Group (International Buddhist Academy Division) on behalf of 84000: Translating the Words of the Buddha (https://read.84000.co/translation/UT22084-066-018.html). D66, 273a: *gang yang nga'i phyir skra dang kha spu bregs nas | gos ngur smrig bgos pa bslab pa 'dzin kyang rung | bslab pa mi 'dzin kyang rung | tshul khrims 'chal kyang rung | tshul khrims dang ldan yang rung ste de'i gos ngur smrig dag 'phrog cing khyim par byed dam | lus la chad pas gcod par byed dam | btson rar 'jug par byed | srog dang 'bral bar byed pa 'di ni ltung ba'i rtsa ba gsum pa'o|*.

Later on, this sutra prophesizes that monks will, in a future time, resort to plundering and stealing (even from temples) in order to pay the fines the ruler has imposed on them (D66, 277b), displaying an awareness of what a ruler's strong juridical hold on monastics could lead to. From this, and other historically better attested instances, we can gather that the notion of the legally independent renunciant represents a mere ideal – one that in and of itself has value – but which is thoroughly ahistorical.

The very fact that various Indic Buddhist normative sources emphasize the Sangha's legal autonomy is exactly because it was regularly being challenged. Throughout history, mass forced disrobements of monks, or "sangha purifications," initiated by secular rulers were a regular occurrence in countries such as China, Mongolia, Burma, Thailand, and Sri Lanka. Naturally, this was more often than not a pretext for political gain and not necessarily done out of concern for the purity of the monkhood. It is perhaps significant that for the case of Tibet, the only time that Tibetan sources attest to such a thing happening is during the reign of Glang Dar ma (r. ?838 to ?841), an "anti-Buddhist" king who, as Tibetan historiographers report, forced monks out of their monasteries and made them wear lay clothes. Later historians suppose that the Glang Dar ma was not the villain he was made out to be and that he even restored Buddhist monuments during his lifetime (e.g., Karmay 2003; Yamaguchi 1996). The decline in monastic Buddhism in Central Tibet that followed Glang Dar ma's reign was more likely due to the economic drain posed by the still relatively new phenomena of monks and monasteries during a time when the region was hit by multiple natural disasters. Clear parallels can be drawn with the large-scale laicization of monks under Emperor Wuzong (武宗 814–46; r. 840–46) in Tang dynasty China that took place around the same time (Gernet 1995, 14–25; Weinstein 1987). Perhaps the more pertinent question is how monks saw themselves, and the vows and monastic rules that they were bound to, in relation to secular laws, rules, and rulers. To put this in more abstract terms: What is the relationship between religious ideals and the secular space?

According to Ellingson, who was the first Western scholar to investigate the genre, monastic guidelines were based on "secular" law codes (Ellingson 1990, 205). A preliminary comparison of the *bca' yig* and the extant legal codes of Tibet indeed indicates that – in particular, terminologically and linguistically – there are striking similarities between the two genres. One of the possible reasons for these similarities is the fact that the authors of the two types of texts were often one and the same. This is because the educated few were almost always heavily influenced by monastic training, in one way or the other. As mentioned above, there are even instances of law codes that were *explicitly* based on monastic guidelines, of which the code of conduct issued by the Bhutanese state (*Sgrig lam rnam gzhag*), which is in current use, is a case in point (Penjore 2011, 23).[14] While the question as to

[14] For the constitutions of Bhutan see Aris 1979; Whitecross 2014.

how exactly monastic guidelines and legal documents are related requires further investigation,[15] my research suggests that the one genre was not necessarily based on the other but that they were still strongly related and made use of each other. Answering this question involves a more in-depth philological study of legal texts and their "Buddhist and monastic" heritage, details of which are beyond the scope of this chapter.[16]

My research into legal texts from the mid-seventeenth century and later has so far revealed that the judicial independence enjoyed by many monasteries was not simply asserted by the monastic authorities themselves but was also deliberately awarded to them by the government or local ruler (or the authors of these texts). This notion is indeed clearly stated in many sets of monastic guidelines, as well as in legal texts. Both of these subsets of legal constitutional literature refer to each other. The monastic guidelines tend to stress that monks' behavior should be in accordance with the "royal laws" (*rgyal khrims*), while legal texts issued by rulers emphasize that monastics are to live by their own rules. My research has shown that the latter works often display an acute awareness of the internal contents of the monastic guidelines, suggesting that the authors either were informed by monastic agents, or had a monastic background themselves. A legal edict issued in 1643 – possibly one of the very first to have been issued by the young Ganden Phodrang government – addresses all Tibetans, of high or low status, monk or layperson. Its authorship is contested, but there are indications that the fifth Dalai Lama was involved in composing it. The edict addresses the monk community separately, while at the same time also exerting authority over the monasteries (and other religious institutions) by stating the following:

> People who have committed grave offenses such as murder may not be given refuge in the religious institutions. From now on, one is to be wise and successful [by] remaining in accordance with the Dharma, without disregarding the instructions established by the general monkhood (*spyi mchod*)[17] who are [to behave] in accordance with their own monastic guidelines (*bca' yig*). Whether one is high or low, no one is to go carelessly into the financial accounts[18] of what is definitely the general monkhood's.[19]

15 In terms of chronology, naturally "Tibetan secular law preceded ecclesiastic law," which only began with the first ordinations at Samye in the middle of the second half of the eighth century. See Van der Kuijp 1999, 289.

16 This is part of my current research project.

17 This gloss is suggested by Cüppers (2011, 172). It can also refer to specific kinds of festivals or other religious ceremonies.

18 *mtho khongs* or *mtho khong* (version C) is here read as *tho khungs*, which means (bank-) account.

19 *mi bsad sogs khrims 'gal nyes byas che ba byas pa'i rigs rnams chos sde khag rnams su rten skyabs ma byed / de phyin rang rang gi bca' yig dang mthun pa'i / spyi mchod tshugs kha ma bor ba'i chos mthun gzhugs mkhas byas rjes / drag zhan sus kyang spyi mchod yin nges kyi mtho khongs nang la rtsis med du 'gro ba ma byed/*. See Jansen 2023.

On the one hand, the decree forbids monasteries from taking in wanted criminals;[20] on the other it simply reminds the monks that they have their own laws to abide to. It is furthermore interesting that the language used in the text is very similar to monastic guidelines written around the same time.[21]

Another legal text, apparently written during the Tsangpa (Gtsang pa) dynasty (1565–1642), similarly views the monastery as a separate legal entity: it states how people guilty of thieving should be punished (by, for example, chopping off of the hand), but it also describes how monasteries generally dealt with their own monk-thieves: they were to be expelled under the sound of the *gaṇḍi* and be treated in accordance with the monastery's own set of guidelines.[22] It thus appears that monastic legal independence was not just condoned but also encouraged by the legal codes. If the periodization of the aforementioned legal text is indeed correct, this interdependence of monastic and secular law was not necessarily a result of the "unification of Church and State" that took place under the fifth Dalai Lama but existed prior to it. In other legal texts, the genre of *bca' yig*, and by extension monastic law, are referred to numerous times. My previous research on this genre did not properly touch upon the political usage of the genre of monastic guidelines, but here we find that lawmakers read them, referred to them, and invoked their (religious) authority.

6.4 CONSTITUTIONAL LAW AND THE SANGHA

The liberties that monasteries and monks were meant to have had clearly existed in theory, as evidenced by Tibetan legal texts. By extension then, one would presume that monks and monasteries were not expected to pay taxes. A number of edicts, issued by various rulers, reinforce the exemptions monastics tended to enjoy. An edict issued by the fifth Dalai Lama in 1648 for the holy place La stod (also spelled Las stod) that forbids hunting in the region along with hindering monks from collecting alms, also explicitly warns that monastics living in the region were not to be harassed.[23] Another edict written for the abbot of Bsam grub dgon in 'Bar rta (situated in Ldan ma, Kham, currently part of Sichuan province) on behalf of the seventh Dalai Lama in 1748, similarly reminds the local rulers and inhabitants to

[20] That this in fact happened is attested by Duncan's eyewitness account of eastern Tibet before 1959: "The monastery is the haven of refuge for the criminal. A hundred feet from the Batang Monastery is a place called Jaoo-Gyatse-Pung 'the life hell of a hundred steps' which once reached by the breaker of a law secures for him the protection of the lamas until his case is settled by mediators of the parties involved. As wealth can settle for any deed, even murder, this right of refuge is more valuable for the rich than the poor." (Duncan 1998, 172).

[21] For an examination, critical edition, and annotated translation of this work see Jansen 2022.

[22] *Gtsang stod rgyal blon gyi mdzad pa zhal lce bcu drug pa*: 198–9: *dge 'dun nang khul nas rkun ma byas tshe* (198) *'gan dung btang ba'i gnas nas dbyung ba sogs so so'i bca' yig dang mthun ba gyis/*. This exact procedure of casting out monastic criminals is described in various *bca' yig*, see Jansen 2018, 168.

[23] See Schuh 1981, vol. 5, document XXXIII: 316–22.

allow monks of said monastery to move around freely; not to rob them; not to hinder their access to water and grass; and for the guardians of the roads, paths, and bridges not to harass them. The audience of the edict is furthermore reminded that the monastery should not be taxed in any way.[24] A much earlier but similar legal text written in 1267 by the famous Sakya (Sa skya) monk Phakpa ('Phags pa 1235–80) for all those "people included among the Sakyapa, big or small" requests them to exempt the monks of Chos sding monastery from military duty, taxes, and labor (*dmag khral las gsum*); from land and commercial taxes (*sho dam kha*);[25] and from giving foods and corvée labor (*za ma 'u lag*). Significantly, Phakpa writes this at the behest of the king (*rgyal po lung gis*) – presumably Kublai Khan.[26] It appears that since this legal note mostly concerns religious matters – that is to say, the sangha's concerns – the authority lay with the "preceptor" rather than with the "donor," in other words with the religious leader and not with the king.[27]

These documents, of which there are many more, confirm the notion that monks and monasteries had their own legal systems, but also that they were perhaps better protected than their lay fellow countrymen by the laws that were upheld outside of their monastic boundaries. Scholars should, however, be cautious in how they interpret such texts. If indeed all monks and monasteries were and had always been "untaxable" and not to be harassed in any way, why would there be a need to confirm this in multiple legal documents? The presence of these prohibitions suggests that monasteries and their inhabitants were indeed occasionally subjected to taxes levied by local rulers – be it legally or illegally. This is further attested by the famous Mahāsiddha Tangtong Gyalpo (Thang stong rgyal po ?1361–1485), who in his biography, written by his disciple Mönpo Dewa Zangpo (Mon pa Bde ba bzang po, fifteenth century), is recorded to have addressed and criticized all the leaders of Tibet for their poor leadership, since kings in this "degenerate age":

> ... monger for war, disallowing *tantrikas* and monastics to practice the Dharma
> They pursue monasteries for inflated[28] taxes and corvée labor
> They take delight in sinners and cheaters, saying they are "tough guys"
> They accuse those who are innocent of breaking the law
> When they are not eloquent enough[29]

24 See Schuh 1981, vol. 5, document XXXV: 329–30.

25 According to Schuh *sho* is a loanword from "sino-mongolian" indicating land taxes (Schuh 1981, vol. 5: 343).

26 See Schuh 1981 vol. 5, document XXXVII: 341–5.

27 cf. Ruegg 2013 [1997], 220: "Moreover, in view of the many demands doubtless made on their time and energy and of their numberless practical day-to-day concerns and responsibilities, it is likely that neither Pakpa in his relation with Qubilai Khaghan nor his uncle Sakya Paṇḍita in his relation with Prince Köden was ever in a position to compose a full theoretical treatise on the 'constitutional' relation between the two orders represented by the officiant/spiritual preceptor and the donor-ruler."

28 Tib: *'gol*, this translation is tentative.

29 Mon pa bde ba bzang po: 460: *sngags btsun rnams chos byed mi 'jug par dmag la 'deg | dgon pa rnams la khral'gol'u lag'ded | sdig can g.yo rgyu can la pho rgod po zer bya dga' byed | khog skyon med kyang gtam lab ma mkhas na | khrims la'gel zer |.*

The protagonist of this biography is critical of local rulers of Tibet whom he calls self-centered. Clearly, Tangtong Gyalpo, who was *not* a monk, merely makes an appeal to the rulers' conscience, since he had not much political clout beyond his charisma and immense popularity among the people of Tibet (and beyond). Significant here is the notion that raising taxes among the monks is presented as morally abject – nonetheless it is implied that these taxes were indeed levied. The issue of taxes directly addresses the tension between monastic juridical independence and the concerns of local rulers seeking to control the monks, possibly by limiting their income.

Along with the liberties and exemptions that monastic institutions enjoyed also came responsibilities. For monasteries, to remain legal sub-units was contingent on them remaining diligent with respect to specific religious matters. A legal decree issued by the fifth Dalai Lama, for example, states that the monastery of Bsam gtan gling (in Skyid grong, in southwestern Tibet) was to be left alone by local rulers, to be allowed to make use of the fields in the surroundings, and to be exempt from taxation – but only for as long as the monks would continue to perform rituals for the living and the dead, uphold the *vinaya* [ritual] cycle, make offerings at the temples, and take responsibility for repairs and leaks (of the monastic compound) in a proper manner.[30] This same document also warns that no one can hunt on the monastic grounds.[31] Elsewhere, I have demonstrated that monks were often also burdened with the responsibility of policing their own monastery's territory to prevent hunting and other untoward activities (Jansen 2018, 154–5). Indeed, when monasteries defaulted on their basic responsibilities, the local rulers or the government were allowed to intervene, which they did do not infrequently.[32]

The monk-polymath 'Jam mgon Mi pham (1846–1912) confirms to the king of Derge that the secular ruler is entirely justified to put monks in their place, *despite the fact that Buddhist sutras advise against it*:

> In like fashion,
> sutras such as the *Ākāśagarbha* and so forth,
> state that our teacher, the Buddha,
> prohibits the punishment of monks.
> They state that if the followers of the Buddha
> are subjected to legal punishments,
> the power of the kingdom's merit diminishes
> and becomes the reason for its destruction.

[30] See Schuh 1981, vol. 5, document XL: 369: *grwa ris | gson gshin dge rgyun | 'dul la lkhor las | gtsug lag khang la dkar bsnon mchod pa | zhig gsos thig cha[g] kyi las khur rnams tshul ldan sgrub cing* . . ..

[31] For a fascinating study on hunting regulations in Tibet see Huber 2004.

[32] A number of these occasions will be treated as case studies in my forthcoming monograph on Buddhism and Law in early modern Tibet.

> However, in this degenerate age,
> there are many monks who are exceedingly unruly,
> When they cannot be disciplined
> through the sangha council's religious procedures,
> then the king needs to do this.
>
> (trans. by Cabezón 2016, 192)

This advice to the king of Derge (Bde dge, in Kham, current-day Sichuan province), which is self-consciously modeled upon Indic *nītiśāstras* (Cabezón 2016, 247), continues with the procedure of how the king needs to relate himself to the sangha in those instances. The prerogative of the king to purge the sangha of unwanted elements – occurring often in other Buddhist countries – may have been justified by Buddhist monastic scholars, but in practice there are very few historical instances that a ruler (even when a monk himself) actually managed to bring about large-scale changes among the sangha in greater Tibet. This is something attempted by the thirteenth Dalai Lama (1876–1933), with limited success: many reforms aimed at the monkhood were reversed after his demise (Bell 1998 [1946]; Goldstein 1989).

By contrast, we see that the power relations among monks and their rulers in Mongolia, for example, were very different. There, the rulers, who of course also claimed to uphold the dual system of "Church and State" (*lugs gnyis*), regularly "defrocked" and punished monks for minor transgressions (Wallace 2010). A Mongolian post-Qing era law code ("Laws and Regulations to Actually Follow," M. *Jinkhene Yavakh Dagaj Khuuly Dürem*), which covers monastic, criminal, and civil law, in place between 1913 and 1918, states that monks caught gambling were to be punished with up to a hundred strikes of the whip – not dissimilar from the proscribed punishment for laypeople (Wallace 2014, 331). The difference between the legal privileges of Mongolian and Tibetan monks here is remarkable, more so since all monastics involved historically follow Tibetan Buddhism, but it may well lie in the fact that many Buddhist monasteries in Tibetan areas, especially from the seventeenth century onwards, were both politically and economically powerful on a local and translocal level.

In Tibet, when monks and monasteries were subjected to government intervention, it was more often than not for political or sectarian reasons – no large-scale sangha-purifications ever took place.[33] One famous instance of this is the incident that occurred in 1921 when monk managers of Drepung Loseling ('Bras spungs Blo sel gling), a monastic college of the largest monastery in central Tibet, tried to repossess certain estates by force. Drepung Loseling had previously invoked the thirteenth Dalai Lama's ire by siding with the Chinese during their brief takeover of Lhasa in 1911–12. The monks involved were caught hiding in the mountains behind

[33] The thirteenth Dalai Lama did try–albeit unsuccessfully–to do exactly this, but it failed also because the large Dge lugs monasteries in Central Tibet opposed his attempts at modernization. See Bell 1998 [1946] and Goldstein 1989.

Drepung monastery (Goldstein 1989, 104–5); they were beaten, and then officially expelled. According to a Tibetan minister Charles Bell spoke with about the matter, the ringleaders were then "made over to different officials with iron fetters on their legs and cangues (square wooden boards, each side three feet long) round their necks." They were subsequently set to work in the stables (Bell 1998 [1946], 332). The government's harsh treatment of these men resulted in violent protests by the Drepung Loseling monks, who marched to the summer palace to purposefully disturb the Dalai Lama's retreat. In the end, 3,000 Tibetan soldiers had to be deployed to restore calm in the Tibetan capital (Goldstein 1989, 106–7). The relatively powerful political position the thirteenth Dalai Lama found himself in at the time – evidenced by his triumph over thousands of rebellious monks – was, however, something of a historical anomaly: throughout the roughly 300 years of the Dalai Lamas being the official heads of state, only the fifth, the thirteenth, and the fourteenth Dalai Lama held any significant power.

The monastic antipathy toward government intervention has become even more distinct in the last seventy years, during which Tibetan monasteries have had to deal with the highly repressive People's Republic of China. When, in the 1980s, monasteries were rebuilt and monastic education was reestablished, the tendency toward monastic (legal) autonomy was also rekindled. Many of the current-day protests initiated by monks and laity alike arise fundamentally from structural repression but are initially set off by the government's interference in monastic affairs. An example of this is the large-scale protest that resulted from the attempts by the Chinese communist government to reinstate the Great Prayer Festival (*smon lam chen mo*) in Lhasa in 1986.

This age-old festival had been traditionally used by the Tibetan government to strengthen its bond with the Buddhist clergy. During this three-week period, monks from the three large Geluk monasteries in and near Lhasa would flock toward the city to conduct prayers for the success of the Tibetan government. Monks, refusing to pray on behalf of a repressive communist government, protested the mandate to attend, which resulted in large-scale arrests. Subsequent boycotts and further arrests eventually sparked the riots that took place on March 5, 1988. Attempts to quell the riots with violence resulted in an unknown number of deaths (for the historical context of this see Jansen 2020b). Similar protests, in many cases relating to religious self-determination, crop up time and again in Chinese-ruled Tibetan areas. Understanding the historical precedent for these protests to be based in the long tradition of monastic legal autonomy is helpful in comprehending the regularity and vehemence with which they occur.

6.5 CONCLUDING REMARKS

The very basic function of monastic law as understood by monastic authors themselves is rather similar, if not identical, to law outside of the Tibetan monastery.

Laws–and by extension justice–essentially serve to secure social order in both milieus. In Tibetan societies, where the government has traditionally been symbolically prominent yet functionally absent, the distinctions between law and custom (Ramble 2008, 41) – or for that matter law and morality – are less easily made. The same may be said for other Buddhist traditions in Asia.[34] Buddhist morality and secular law ultimately are both "normative social practices" and also "symbolic expressions of social values" (Wallace 2014, 332). Religion – and by extension Buddhism – is often viewed by scholars as providing a means of social control, which implies, to cite Gombrich, "a system of rewards and punishments, either internalized during socialization or externally supplied by institutions, or both" (1975, 218). The two kinds of legal codes thus existed symbiotically in order to support this social order.

What this chapter emphasizes is that monks – or to be more specific, monastic members of a monastery – had a special legal status that awarded them significantly more liberties than lay Tibetans. At the same time, monastic institutions were supposed to "pay" for those liberties by carrying out duties that were seen as essentially the responsibility of monks. When a monastery neglected these religious, ritual, and social duties, its special legal status was nullified, which could potentially have severe consequences. The bodies of rules that governed the monastery and its inhabitants, as well as those which governed the rest of the Tibetans, display an awareness and an acceptance of the status of the monastic institutions. These two sub-genres of legal works clearly influenced each other, not just because their authors were often one and the same but also because the inherently Buddhist value of putting the sangha first was shared among all legal actors.

REFERENCES

Tibetan Language Materials

Ākāśagarbhasūtra (*Nam mkha' snying po'i mdo*). *Degé Kangyur, vol.* 66 (mdo sde, za), folios 264.a–283.b.

Bod kyi khrims srol skor gyi lo rgyus yig tshags phyogs sgrig zhal lce phyogs sgrig. 2016. Rdo sbis Tshe ring rgyal & Rdo sbis Tshe ring rdo rje eds. Lhasa: Bod ljongs mi dmangs dpe skrun khang.

Bod kyi snga rabs khrims srol yig cha bdams bsgrigs. 1989. Lhasa: Bod ljongs mi dmangs dpe skrun khang.

Gzhung dga' ldan pho brang skabs kyi khrims srol bca' chings bdams bsgrigs. 2008. Nor bu bsam 'phel (ed.). Beijing: Mi rigs dpe skrun khang.

Mon pa bDe ba bzang po. 1984–85. *Bla ma thang stong rgyal po'i rnam thar gsal ba'i sgron me*. In *Thang stong rgyal po gsung 'bum, vol.* 2. National Library of Bhutan, 3–591.

Snga rabs bod kyi srid khrims. 2004. Bsod nams tshe ring (ed.). Beijing: Mi rigs dpe skrun khang.

[34] A similar remark can be made with regard to Burma, for example. See Huxley 1995, 81.

Snga rabs bod kyi srid khrims gsal ba'i me long. 2014. Bsod nams tshe ring (ed.). Beijing: Mi rigs, dpe skrun khang.

Zhal lce phyogs bsdus: Bod kyi dus rabs rims byung gi khrims yig phyogs bsdus dwangs byed ke ta ka zhe bya ba bzhugs so. 1987. Tshe ring bde skyid (ed.). Xinhua: Bod ljongs mi dmangs dpe skrun khang.

Other Sources

Aris, Michael. 1979. *Bhutan: The Early History of a Himalayan Kingdom*. Warminster: Aris & Phillips.

Bell, Charles. 1998 [1946]. *Portrait of a Dalai Lama: The Life and Times of the Great Thirteenth*. Delhi: Book Faith India.

Carrasco, Pedro. 1959. *Land and Polity in Tibet*. Seattle: University of Washington Press.

Cassinelli, Charles William, and Ekvall, Robert B. 1969. *A Tibetan Principality: The Political System of Sakya*. Ithaca: Cornell University Press.

Cüppers, Christoph. 2011a. "Ein Erlaß des Königs Gushri Khan aus dem Jahr 1643." *Zentralasiatische Studien des Seminars für Sprach und Kulturwissenschaft Zentralasiens* 40: 164–77.

2011b. www.tibet-encyclopaedia.de/gesetzbuecher.html. Accessed on November 15, 2021.

Deeg, Max. 2016. "The Order of the dharma and the order of rulership: On the relationship between monastic community and worldly power in the history of Buddhism." *Fruehmittelalteriche Studien - Jahrbuch des Instituts für Fruehmittelalterforschug der Universität Münster* 50 (1): 297–314.

Dotson, Brandon. 2006. *Administration and Law in the Tibetan Empire: The Section on Law and State and its Old Tibetan Antecedents*. DPhil dissertation, Oxford University.

Dreyfus, Georges. 1995. "Law, State and Political Ideology in Tibet." *Journal of International Association of Buddhist Studies* 18 (1): 117–38.

Duncan, Marion H. 1998 [1964]. *Customs and Superstitions of Tibet*. Delhi: Book Faith India.

Ellingson, Ter. 1990. "Tibetan Monastic Constitutions: The bCa' yig." In *Reflections on Tibetan Culture: Essays in Memory of Turrell V. Wylie*, edited by Lawrence Epstein and Richard F. Sherburne, 205–29. Lewiston: Edward Mellen Press.

French, Rebecca Redwood. 1996. "Tibetan Legal Literature: The Law Codes of the Dga' Ldan Pho Brang." In *Tibetan Literature: Studies in Genre*, edited by Sopa Lhundup, José I. Cabezón and Roger R. Jackson, 438–57. Ithaca: Snow Lion.

Gernet, Jacques. 1995. *Buddhism in Chinese Society: An Economic History from the Fifth to the Tenth Centuries*, trans. Franciscus Verellen. New York: Columbia University Press.

Goldstein, Melvyn C. 1989. *A History of Modern Tibet, 1913-1951: The Demise of the Lamaist State*. Berkeley: University of California Press.

Gombrich, Richard F. 1975. "Buddhist Karma and Social Control." *Comparative Studies in Society and History* 17 (2): 212–20.

Huber, Toni. 2004. "Territorial Control by 'Sealing': A Religio-Political Practice in Tibet." *Zentralasiatischen Studien* 33: 127–52.

Huxley, Andrew. 1995. "Studying Theravāda Legal Literature." *Journal of the International Association of Buddhist Studies* 20 (1): 63–91.

Jansen, Berthe. 2014. "The Monastic Guidelines (bCa' yig) by Sidkeong Tulku: Monasteries, Sex and Reform in Sikkim." *Journal of the Royal Asiatic Society* 24 (4): 597–622.

2015. "Monastic Organizational Guidelines." In *Brill's Encyclopedia of Buddhism, vol. 1*, edited by Jonathan Silk et al., 442–49. Leiden: Brill.

2016. "Monastic Guidelines (*bCa' yig*): Tibetan Social History from a Buddhist Studies Perspective." In *Social Regulation: Case Studies from Tibetan History* (Proceedings of the International Association of Tibetan Studies Conference, Ulan Baatar, 2013), edited by Jeannine Bischoff and Saul Mullard, 64–98. Leiden: Brill.
2018. *The Monastery Rules: Buddhist Monastic Organization in Pre-modern Tibet*. Oakland: University of California Press.
2020a. "The Origins of Tibetan Law: Some Notes on Intertextuality and the Reception History of Tibetan Legal Texts." *Revue d'Etudes Tibétaines* 55: 221–44.
2020b. "Law and Order during the Lhasa Great Prayer Festival." In *On a Day of a Month of the Fire Bird Year: Festschrift for Peter Schwieger on the Occasion of His 65th Birthday*, edited by Jeannine Bischoff, Petra Maurer, and Charles Ramble, 415–35. Lumbini: Lumbini International Research Institute.
2022. "Visualising Tibetan Social History through Philology: A Case-Study of a Legal Decree in Eight Versions." CRCAO.
Kapstein, Matthew. 2006. *The Tibetans*. Oxford: Blackwell.
Karmay, Samten. 2003. "King Langdarma and His Rule." In *Tibet and Her Neighbors*, edited by Alex McKay, 57–68. London: Edition Hansjörg.
Mipham, Jamgön and José I. Cabezón (trans.) 2017. *The Just King: The Tibetan Buddhist Classic on Leading an Ethical Life*. Boulder: Shambhala Publications.
Penjore, Dorji. 2011. "Rows of Auspicious Seats: The Role of *bzhugs gral phun sum tshogs pa'i rten 'brel* Ritual in the Founding of the First Bhutanese State in the 17th Century." *Journal of Bhutan Studies* 24: 1–42.
Pirie, Fernanda. 2006. "Secular Morality, Village Law, and Buddhism in Tibetan Societies." *Journal of the Royal Anthropological Institute* 12 (1): 173–90.
2013a. "Who Were the Tibetan lawmakers?" In *Tibetans Who Escaped the Historian's Net: Studies in the Social History of Tibetan Societies*, edited by Charles Ramble, Peter Schwieger and Alice Travers, 161–78. Kathmandu: Vajra Publications.
2013b. "Law and Religion in Historic Tibet." In *Religion in Disputes: Pervasiveness of Religious Normativity in Disputing Processes*, edited by Franz von Benda-Beckmann, Keebet von Benda-Beckmann, Martin Ramstedt and Bertram Turner, 231–47. New York: Palgrave Macmillan.
2016. "State, Law, and Morality in Traditional Tibet." In *Social Regulation: Case Studies from Tibetan History*, edited by Jeannine Bischoff and Saul Mullard, 231–49. Leiden: Brill.
2017. "Buddhist Law in Early Tibet: The Emergence of an Ideology." *Journal of Law and Religion* 32 (3): 406–22.
2020. "The Making of Tibetan Law: The *Khrims gnyis lta ba'i me long*." In *On a Day of a Month of a Fire Bird Year: Festschrift for Peter Schwieger*, edited by Jeanine Bisschoff, Petra Maurer and Charles Ramble, 599–618. Lumbini: Lumbini International Research Institute.
Ramble, Charles. 2008. *The Navel of the Demoness: Tibetan Buddhism and Civil Religion in Highland Nepal*. New York: Oxford University Press.
Roesler, Ulrike. 2015. "'16 Human Norms' (mi chos bcu drug) – Indian, Chinese, and Tibetan." In *The Illuminating Mirror: Tibetan Studies in Honour of Per K. Sørensen on the Occasion of his 65th Birthday*, edited by Olaf Czaja and Guntram Hazod, 389–409. Wiesbaden: Dr. Ludwig Reichert Verlag.
Ruegg, D. Seyfort. 1991. "*Mchod yon / yon mchod* and *mchod gnas / yon gnas*: On the Historiography and Semantics of a Tibetan Religio-Social and Religio-Political Concept." In *Tibetan History and Language: Studies Dedicated to Uray Geza on His*

Seventieth Birthday, edited by Ernst Steinkellner, 441–53. Vienna: Arbeitskreis für tibetische und buddhistische Studien.

2013 [1997]. "The Preceptor-Donor Relation in Thirteenth Century Tibetan Society and Polity: Its Inner Asian Precursors and Indian Models." In *The Tibet History Reader*, edited by Gray Tuttle and Kurtis Schaeffer, 211–32. New York: Columbia University Press.

Schopen, Gregory. 1995. "Monastic Law Meets the Real World: A Monk's Continuing Right to Inherit Family Property in Classical India." *History of Religions* 35 (2): 101–23.

Schuh, Dieter. 1981. *Grundlagen tibetischer Siegelkunde: Eine Untersuchung über tibetische Siegelaufschriften in 'Phags-pa-Schrift*. Monumenta Tibetica Historica, *vol.* 5. Sankt Augustin: VGH Wissenschaftsverlag.

1984. "Recht und Gesetz in Tibet." In *Tibetan and Buddhist Studies: Commemorating the 200th Anniversary of Alexander Csoma de Kőrös*, edited by Louis Ligeti, 291–311. Budapest: Akadémiai kiadó.

Schwieger, Peter. 2021. *Conflict in a Buddhist Society: Tibet under the Dalai Lamas*. Honolulu: University of Hawai'i Press.

Stein, Rolf A. [1962] 1972. *Tibetan Civilization*. Stanford: Stanford University Press.

Tucci, Giuseppe. 1949. *Tibetan Painted Scrolls, vol.* 1. Rome: Libreria dello Stato.

Uray, Geza. 1972. "The Narrative of the Legislation and Organization of the Mkhas pa'i dga' ston: The Origins of the Traditions Concerning Sroṅ-brcan Sgam-po as the First Legislator and Organizer of Tibet." *Acta Orientalia Academiae Scientiarum Hungaricae* 26: 11–68.

Van der Kuijp, Leonard. 1999. "The Yoke Is on the Reader: A Recent Study of Tibetan Jurisprudence." *Central Asiatic Journal* 43: 266–92.

Vermeersch, Sem. 2008. *The Power of the Buddhas: The Politics of Buddhism during the Koryŏ Dynasty (918–1392)*. Cambridge: Harvard University Press.

Wallace, Vesna. 2014. "Buddhist Laws in Mongolia." In *Buddhism and Law: An Introduction*, edited by Rebecca Redwood French and Mark A. Nathan, 319–33. New York: Cambridge University Press.

2010. "Legalized Violence: Punitive Measures of Buddhist Khans in Mongolia." In *Buddhist Warfare*, edited by Michael Jerryson and Mark Juergensmeyer, 91–103. Oxford: Oxford University Press.

Weinstein, Stanley. 1987. *Buddhism under the T'ang*. Cambridge: Cambridge University Press.

Whitecross, Richard W. 2014. "Buddhism and Constitutions in Bhutan." In *Buddhism and Law: An Introduction*, edited by Rebecca Redwood French and Mark A. Nathan, 350–67. New York: Cambridge University Press.

Yamaguchi, Zuihō. 1987. *Chibetto, vol.* 1. Tokyo: Tokyo daigaku shuppankai.

1996 "The Fiction of King Dar ma's Persecution of Buddhism." In *Du Dunhuang au Japon: études chinoises et bouddhiques offertes à Michel Soymié*, edited by Jean-Pierre Drège, 231–58. Geneva: Droz.

Websites

www.britannica.com/topic/constitutional-law. Accessed on November 15, 2021.

https://read.84000.co/translation/UT22084-066-018.html. Accessed on July 26, 2022.

PART III

Southern Asia

7

Guardians of the Law

Sinhala Language and Buddhist Reformation in Postwar Sri Lanka

Krishantha Fedricks

7.1 INTRODUCTION

Discussions of Buddhism and constitutional law frequently focus on one direction of influence: the influence of Buddhist principles on the guiding law of the state. But what about the other direction? In what ways do notions of constitutional law find their way into Buddhist institutions? Are there notions within Buddhist communities, both traditional and emergent, that seem similar to the notion of constitutional law?

This chapter builds on previous work that examines Buddhism and constitutional law in Sri Lanka and other Theravāda contexts.[1] While it considers the broader dynamics of politics, nationalism, and Buddhist groups that helped shape Sri Lanka's 1972 and 1978 Constitutions – which officially give to Buddhism "the foremost place" and oblige the state to "protect and foster" it – this chapter directs its major questions about Buddhism and constitutional law elsewhere. It investigates a Buddhist group that claims to commit itself to nonviolence and scriptural Buddhist reform, and it examines the ways in which this group blends religious practice with linguistic and nationalist ideologies drawn from secular constitutionalism.

More specifically, this chapter looks closely at a new transnational movement of televangelist Buddhist monks, who form part of the "Mahamevnāva Monastery" in Sri Lanka. These monks publicly proclaim their support for a state of Gautama Buddha (*gautama buddha rājya*) that is governed by the authentic doctrine (*saebae dahama*). They also encourage their followers to liberate themselves from all suffering (*siyalu dukin*) by attaining nirvana in this life. This Mahamevnāva group believes that most everyday Buddhists fail to live up to the Buddha's teaching and the Noble Eightfold Path to nirvana because they do not fully understand the language in which the teaching has been preserved.

[1] See among others: de Silva-Wijeyeratne 2014; Schonthal 2016 Frydenlund 2017; Harris 2018; Kyaw 2019; , Tonsakulrungruang 2020.

Mahamevnāva believes, not unlike constitutional draftspersons, that the correct language – in the form of accurate vernacular translations of the Buddha's teaching – might solve the problem. Although the monks of this group claim to maintain a separation of religion and political life and actively cultivate an air of other-worldliness, they actually use the status and prestige that Sinhala acquires through the Constitution to argue for its use in sacred contexts. In their case, Mahamevnāva insists that a reform of Buddhism ought to involve a reform of the language used in rituals and textual practices. More specifically, they believe that Buddhist practices ought to shift from Pāli, the Buddhist canonical and ritual language to Sinhala (Harvey 2012), the majority language of the Sinhalese Buddhists which is one of the two official languages in the country (Dharmadasa 2000).

As a linguistic anthropologist, I draw upon tools of linguistic analysis and ethnography to offer a unique viewpoint on the interrelations of Buddhism and constitutional law. More specifically, I use the concept of linguistic ideologies, by which I mean "the ideas with which participants and observers frame their understanding of linguistic varieties and map those understandings onto people, events, and activities that are significant to them," (Irvine and Gal 2000) in order to explain the influence of constitutional law on Buddhist practices. This chapter shows how Mahamevnāva has taken the linguistic ideology of Sinhala nationalism, the ideology which was absolutely central to constitutional practice in Sri Lanka and made it a central tenet of Buddhist practice. The group has also taken a core idea of Sri Lankan constitutionalism – that the law of the land should be accessible to and representative of the "nation," and turned it into a soteriological principle of direct access to nirvana. By making these points, I suggest that both the Constitution and Mahamevnāva's Buddhist reforms embody similar forms of linguistic ideology in which the ideal state – for example either the Republic of Sri Lanka or the ideal Buddhist state – can be realized by creating "public" texts for the uplift of the "nation."

In what follows, I will first sketch the histories of constitutional debates on the Sinhala language in colonial and postcolonial Sri Lanka and their nationalist underpinnings. I will then consider the emergence of the Mahamevnāva monastic group and their interpretation of Buddhism, language, and state. In contrast to the popular idea that Buddhism influences public law in many South and Southeast Asian societies, I demonstrate that constitutional design and interpretation have also come to influence Buddhism.

7.2 LANGUAGE POLICY AND MONASTIC POLITICS IN POST-INDEPENDENCE SRI LANKA

In postcolonial constitutional debates in Sri Lanka, the issue of the "national language" became one of the major themes of both religious and political spheres.[2]

[2] Regarding the need to establish a national language, D. B. Jayatilaka, an active member of the Buddhist revival, stated: "It is impossible for a people to grow to their full manhood, to their

A number of lay and monastic groups have been concerned with protecting the linguistic preeminence of the ethnic majority Sinhalese while at the same time ensuring the safeguarding of Buddhism, the main religion of the ethnic Sinhalese.[3] Buddhist monks allied with politicians and political parties which promised to secure the authority of the Sinhala language and Buddhism. According to some scholars, the development of this relationship between politically engaged monks and Sinhalese nationalist politicians was an opposition to the secular, Western-style government that was implemented during colonialism and continued to be used in the newly sovereign nation (Kapferer 1998).

Religio-linguistic politics based on ethnic outbidding gained pace, especially in the early 1950s in post-independence Sri Lanka, with the formation of the Sri Lanka Freedom Party (SLFP) under the leadership of S. W. R. D. Bandaranaike.[4] During the general election in 1956, Bandaranaike promised to safeguard the interests of the Sinhalese Buddhists by offering populist social reforms such as the introduction of the Sinhala-only official language policy. His attempts to reform the status of official language/s echoed the dominant "one nation–one language" ideology which grew during the colonial period as a reaction against the dominance of English. Sinhala-only politics came to be seen as a tool of decolonization. This fed a growing culture of linguistic nationalism which was, as K. M. De Silva points out, a form of "populist nationalism, in contrast to the elitist constitutionalism of the early years after independence" (De Silva 1986, 164).

In the decade following independence in 1948, Buddhist pressure groups – mainly monastic organizations – campaigned for the adoption of a Sinhala-only policy, and for the restoration of the "rightful status" of Buddhism (Phadnis 1976, 65). The newly

fullest stature, unless the individuals that compose that people have a language of their own, in which they give expression to their highest and best thoughts" (*Debates, LC* 1928: 367). Jayatilaka emphasizes the necessity of replacing English with a language that appropriately reflects an authentic Sri Lankan identity. He also supports the cause for making Sinhala the national language and recognizes the Sinhalese people as the founders of the island, and the perceived need for them to reclaim authority over their country.

3 The Sinhalese people who are predominantly Buddhist are the major ethnic group in Sri Lanka. They constitute, according to government statistics from 2012, 74.9 percent of the population. The Sinhala–Buddhist identity in Sri Lanka derives from two factors: (1) the Sinhala language and (2) the Buddhist religion. These factors have been enthusiastically promoted in the development of a Sinhalese Buddhist ethno-religious nationalism in post-colonial politics as part of the larger discourse on nation building. They have also been at the core of the discourse on constitutional reform and legislature.

4 Bandaranaike relied upon socially and politically influential groups, albeit non-elite, popularly known as *panchamaha balavegaya* (five great forces), which included the Buddhist clergy, indigenous physicians, teachers, farmers, and workers to carry his political message to his major vote base in Sinhalese villages. To win the general elections of 1956, Bandaranaike also formed an electoral alliance with the pro-Sinhala nationalist parties. The election coalition manifesto declared "Sinhala only within 24 hours" with "reasonable use of Tamil." The 'Sinhala-only' movement had developed and, under the influence of the monks, had become linked to the issue of state support for Buddhism (Tambiah 1992: 42–44).

formed Eksath Bhikku Peramuna (EBP) or the United Monks Front, for example, played a critical role in the 1956 general election as a major political pressure group. They presented a ten-point agenda (the Dasa Panatha) to Bandaranaike which included making Sinhala the only official language and giving Buddhism its "rightful" place (Tambiah 1992, 42–44).

Shortly after Bandaranaike was elected as the prime minister in 1956, the parliament passed the Sinhala Only Act,[5] which made the majority language the sole official language of the country. Government institutions such as the Department of Official Language Affairs and the Department of Swabhasha were brought under the purview of the Prime Minister from October 1, 1956. A separate Ministry of Cultural Affairs, which was largely mandated with preserving Sinhalese culture and Buddhism, was also established in that year. In accordance with the Sinhala Only Act, a number of activities were carried out by the Official Languages Department. This included publishing the Government Gazette in Sinhala, franking official letters in Sinhala, issuing important government circulars in Sinhala, printing official publications in Sinhala, compiling glossaries of technical terms, and implementing language training classes for government servants. In addition, two major *pirivenas*, or "oriental study centers," the Vidyalankara and Vidyodaya, were transformed into universities, further encouraging the study of Sinhala and Buddhism with the benefit of added government funding. These attempts led to a cultural revolution in the following years, popularly known as "the Revolution of 1956" (*panas haye peraliya*).

Predictably, the Sinhala-only language policy marginalized non-Sinhala speaking minorities in the multilingual country. It not only promoted religio-ethno-linguistic nationalism on both sides of the ethnic divide, but became a key source of frustration and anger among Tamil nationalist groups, including a variety of militant movements (most notably the Liberation Tigers of Tamil Eelam) that gained influence beginning in the 1980s (Wilson 1975). Ethnic riots against Tamils erupted in July 1983 in the Sinhala-dominant south, and the subsequent civil war conditions further complicated the problems related to linguistic rights of the minority Tamils.[6]

During this time, the notion of Tamil as a minority language had been used as a justification for separatist aspirations among Tamils. Even the Indo-Sri Lanka Accord signed by Sri Lankan President J. R. Jayewardene and Indian Prime

[5] The Sinhala Only bill was introduced by Bandaranaike in the House of Representatives, supported by the main opposition UNP voting with the government and was opposed by the Tamil parties (Federal Party and All Ceylon Tamil Congress) and leftist parties (Lanka Sama Samaja Party and Communist Party). Because Tamil was not given the same official language status as Sinhala, minority Tamils actively tendered their support to the Federal Party's nonviolence campaigns.

[6] Discussing this period of 'linguistic nationalism of civil war,' DeVotta (2004) says: "while economic rivalry and ethnic jealousies partly lay behind the 1983 riots, the major reasons were the Sinhala-only policy and the culture of ethnic outbidding and institutional decay that the language issue initiated, enculturated, and legitimated" (157).

Minister Rajiv Gandhi in July 1987, which declared that Sri Lanka is "a multi-ethnic and multilingual plural society," could not ameliorate the situation. The country was unsettled by mass protests organized by monks, political parties, and lay Buddhist associations under the powerful umbrella organization *Mavbima Sirakeeme Wiyaparaya*, or "The movement for safeguarding the motherland" (Amunugama 1991). Tamil and English were, in the end, proclaimed to be official languages, along with Sinhala in 1988, as a part of the 13th amendment to the Constitution. Tamil was raised to the status of an official language, while English was assigned the position of a "link language."[7] Nevertheless, linguistic nationalism and Sinhala-only attitudes still endure among many parts of the population.

7.3 RESURGENCE OF SINHALA-BUDDHIST NATIONALISM IN POSTWAR SRI LANKA

Sri Lanka saw a resurgence of Sinhalese Buddhist nationalism after the end of its three-decade-long civil war in 2009, with the emergence of numerous extremist groups of Buddhist monks.[8] Yet, the driving ideological force that fueled postwar ethnonationalism has shifted from Sinhalese ethno-linguistic nationalism to the global rhetoric of war on terror. For instance, in 2012, an extreme Sinhalese Buddhist organization called the Bodu Bala Sena (Buddhist Power Force or BBS) was created under the leadership of Ven. Galagodaththe Gnānasara and Ven. Kirama Wimalajothi.[9] One of the key objectives of this organization was to draw attention to the threats of minority ethnic and religious groups, especially extremist Islamic groups, faced by the Sinhalese Buddhists (Zuhair 2016, 20). The BBS claimed that their major goal was to protect the rights of Sinhalese Buddhists who have no international links, in the face of both internal and external threats. Along with other less prominent organizations such as Sinhala Ravaya, Sinha-le and Mahasohon Balakaya, the BBS launched a virulent anti-Muslim campaign and finally led violent actions against the Muslims in various parts of the island. These movements draw upon this post-independence history of Sinhala-only politics, blending it further with Buddhist nationalism.

7 This part of the 13th amendment to the constitution stated, "Tamil shall also be an official language." However, the legality of the word "also" was not explained in the relevant constitutional provision. As K. M. De Silva (1993) observed, "[a]lthough there is some ambiguity about the position of English, its legal position appears to be almost equal to Sinhalese and Tamil in many areas" (299). The provisions of the 13th amendment were clarified and indeed consolidated by the 16th amendment. The benefits of the 13th amendment to the Constitution have not, in fact, percolated down to the Tamil-speaking population in the country due to the lack of policy implementation. The Tamil language was afforded parity status only after Tamil youths mobilized militarily, seeking a separate state, Eelam.

8 For a comparative discussion on the rise of Buddhist Power Force (BBS) and militant Buddhist groups in Myanmar see Schonthal and Walton (2016).

9 Ven. Kirama Vimalajothi subsequently disavowed the group.

7.4 EMERGENCE OF THE MAHAMEVNĀVA MONASTERY

During this time, a nonviolent movement of televangelist Buddhist monks, collectively part of the Mahamevnāva Monastery (Pāli: Mahāmeghavana), named after the legendary monastery founded by Mahinda when Buddhism was introduced into the island in the third century BCE, has emerged under the guidance of Ven. Kiribathgoda Gnānānanda.[10] Gnānānanda's movement has challenged mainstream Buddhist nationalistic politics by criticizing common linguistic and ritual practices with the aim of rediscovering *saebae dahama*, or the authentic teaching of the Buddha. Defining its religious mission and the Mahamevnāva's objectives, the website states: "Mahamevnāva Buddhist Monastery was established to benefit the spiritual development of human beings through the teachings of Buddha. Founded in 1999 in Sri Lanka by Ven. Kiribathgoda Gnānānanda Thero, its sole purpose is to spread the original teachings of the Buddha. The monastery is a warm and welcoming place for everyone to investigate true happiness through Dhamma and meditation."[11] Several key messages are embedded in this seemingly banal welcome. First, Mahamevnāva identifies with the *original* teachings of the Buddha, which they believe are found in the sutras of the Pali canon. Mahamevnāva's stress on the sutras is part of a more general textual orientation for the community, which claims to base its practices not simply on the authority of the Pali texts themselves, but on a particular, authorized Sinhala translation of those texts that the group has produced. Using these texts, they consider the doctrine (dharma) and the monastic code (*vinaya*) as the twin pillars of *Buddha Nītiya* (the law of the Buddha), which functions as their religious constitution. According to Ven. Gnānānanda, Mahamevnāva's mission consists of three major aims, namely, helping the *buddha sāsana* (teaching of the Buddha)[12] to endure, ending the suffering of *saṃsāra* in this life, and preserving the teaching of the Buddha for future generations. He is critical of the current state of Buddhist practice: "What we are doing now is just visiting monks at the temple and talking nonsense with them till evening. We do not discuss anything related to the teaching of the Buddha. Even monks show no enthusiasm to teach anything. We should change this" (Gnānānanda 2010, 36).

[10] Ven. Gnānānanda was originally born into a Catholic family, but he claims that his birth inspired his parents to become Buddhist and to raise him as a Buddhist. After becoming a monk in his teens, he entered the traditional monastic educational system, but soon left the university in search of a more direct path to realizing the True Dharma in the exact way that the Buddha had taught it. After spending time as an ascetic in the Himalayas – in imitation of the Buddha – Gnānānanda returned to Sri Lanka and began studying the sutras of the Buddha directly. Having gained a realization of the Dharma, he founded the Mahamevnāwa monastery as a forest hermitage in Polgahawela (Berkwitz 2016, 112).

[11] Mahamevnāwa, "Starting of the monastery," https://mahamevnawa.lk/en/about-us/(Accessed May 2, 2021).

[12] Generally, the term *sāsana* designates everything that is related to the Buddha's teaching: Buddhist doctrine, its propagation, study, and putting into practice.

Gnānānanda's reformist stance seeks to replace common forms of Buddhism, which he claims have been politicized and influenced by non-Buddhist practices. In its place, he advocates for a fully 'spiritual' form of the tradition, which might end the suffering of all. The implication here is that there are other types of so-called Buddhist practices that revolve around false views, not taught by the Buddha. Mahamevnāva ridicules monastic political activism and popular rituals, such as tying banners around Bodhi trees (which are thought to dispel the negative fruits of karma) or reciting protective verses in Pāli by rote memory. These, Mahamevnāva's monks claim, are ineffective for true spiritual development, and secondary to the practice of the path to liberation that the Buddha has outlined. They lament that the traditional Buddhists (*sāmpradaika bauddhayo*) who do not follow the noble path to nirvana are Buddhists only by name (*namata bauddayo*) and are misled by the opportunist monks and politicians who emphasize this-worldly benefits and material wealth. According to Mahamevnāva, the correct path that should be followed by "True Buddhists" (*saebae bauddhayo*) includes developing an understanding and practicing of the Four Noble Truths, the Noble Eightfold Path, and the system of Dependent Co-origination (*paṭicca-samuppāda*).

Ven. Gnānānanda has argued that mere knowledge of the religious ideals that were revealed by the Buddha is not enough to be a True Buddhist. Rather, those ideals must be enacted to become free from suffering in this world. He claims that the doctrine of dependent origination, *paṭicca-samuppāda*, is the real dharma, and should be investigated by people to develop their insight and to become virtuous persons (*satpuruṣa*): "The Buddha's teaching is for the wise person. This wise person can belong to any caste, clan, race, or ethnic group. The Buddha's teaching is not limited to a single nation, it is for the wise man. If there is no wise man in one clan, no one is able to reach out the teaching" (Gnānānanda 2016, 95–96). Ven. Gnānānanda often states that the major threat to Buddhism is the majority Buddhists themselves, who do not follow the teaching of the Buddha; therefore, they are responsible for the declining of the Buddha's dispensation, the *buddha sāsana*, in contemporary society. Even though politicized Buddhist monks and their followers fought for the political status of the Sinhala language and Buddhist religion, Mahamevnāva posits that they have neither taught their followers to pursue the correct path of the doctrine, nor hastened the ideal "kingdom/state of the Buddha" (*gautama buddha rājya*).

7.5 *ME GAUTAMA BUDDHA RĀJYAYAY*: "THIS IS THE STATE OF GAUTAMA BUDDHA"

The desired *gautama buddha rājya* is not a specific polity defined by a set of secular laws, geographical boundaries, or specific political authority, but a more general climate in which the Buddhist doctrine reigns supreme. Consider, for example, the following statement in their official print magazine, *Mahamēgha*:

> If there is an undefeatable supreme state in the entire human history, that is the State of Gautama Buddha (*gautama buddha rājya*) and neither humans nor superhuman forces can overthrow the powerful rule of the supreme lord Buddha. In this supreme state of Gautama Buddha there are no territorial boundaries, ethnic disparities, or any other divisions such as clergy-laity, gender. Hence the unity of this state cannot be broken. Anyone who believes in the supreme power of the Buddha and accepts him as the only king and his doctrine as the supreme rule, establishes strong connections with the other noble citizens. They are protected by the unity of the state. True guardians of the state of Gautama Buddha are the ones who follow the Buddha and his doctrine ("Gautama Buddha Rājyaye Maha Rajun Sarana Yamu" 2015).

What is notable here is that Mahamevnāva's definition of the Buddhist state appears to draw inspiration from Sri Lanka's secular Constitution. Similar to protecting Buddhism's "foremost place" in the Sri Lankan Constitution, which also protects the rights and freedoms of all citizens, the *buddha rājya* of Mahamevnāva's celebrates the "true Buddhist" which anyone can be.

A secular-legal mentality also appears to apply to the Mahamevnāva's criticisms of the activities of politically active Buddhist monks who, in their estimation, attempted to rule the country rather than practice the doctrine or guide their lay followers on the path of nirvana. For Mahamevnāva, the disappearance of true dharma is caused mostly by the decline of the *vinaya* (monastic discipline) with the emergence of such politized Buddhist monks. Ven. Gnānānanda posits:

> We should clearly understand the [real] followers of [the Buddha]. We follow the *maharath* (monks who attained nirvana), who followed the noble teaching of the Buddha to achieve different levels of spiritual liberation. Monks in the Buddha's time dedicated themselves to cultivate *sīla* (virtuous conduct), *samādhi* (concentration) and *prajñā* (wisdom). We can also develop *śraddhā* (faith) when we think about these noble followers of the Buddha. Can you build *śraddhā* when you see a Buddhist monk making a political speech on a stage? Or by seeing a misbehaving monk in a protest?. . . We should have the ability to differentiate the followers of the Buddha from the others. Who is on the path of doctrine? Who is not? Then, you will realize who is truthful and who is not. (Gnānānanda 2010, 31–32)

Mahamevnāva laments that the decline of the "true teaching" in the island occurred from time to time due to both internal and external forces. For instance, Ven. Gnānānanda posits that the historical decline of Gautama Buddha's *sāsana* happened in the late medieval period of Sri Lankan history, when "Mahāyāna influences" arrived from India and led people to aspire to become Buddhas and to see the future Buddha Maitreya (Gnānānanda 2004, 42). In contemporary society, such decline is caused by the ignorance of the lay people misguided by politicized and opportunist monks.

Also apparent among Mahamevnāva Buddhists is an attitude towards the Buddha's teaching, or dharma, that treats it as a constitution for everyday life, a set of rules applicable to everyone in the world. In their rendering, Buddhism is not merely a religion of blind followers, but contains the true principles of the world itself, the *loka dharmaya*. Due to influences of other religious rituals and misinterpretation of the dharma, the philosophical value of the dharma has been covered with false faith. During an interview I conducted with Ven. Bandarawela Saddhasheela, a young Mahamevnāva monk who was residing in Mahamevnāva Monastery in California, he said that the terms Buddhist or Buddhism themselves emerged very much later, when the idea of religion became prominent. For him, there was no religion called Buddhism during the Buddha's time and the followers did not identify themselves as Buddhists. What Siddhartha Gautama did, according to Ven. Saddhasheela, was to preach *loka darmaya*, and the people who had the wisdom and accumulated good karma could realize it through listening to him.[13]

Mahamevnāva's focus on the *gautama buddha rājya*, which is governed by these dharmic ideals, serves to orient the group's reformist project towards a transnational Buddhist citizenship. Explaining who is a "True Buddhist citizen" (*saebae bauddha puravaesiya*), Ven. Gnānānanda explains:

> We all are blessed because we have the opportunity to listen to the teachings of the Buddha. There are no divisions based on ethnicity, caste, religion or clan in it ... Nobody is superior because of the language he speaks. No matter whether he speaks English, Tamil, or Sinhala, it does not make anyone superior. Even the skin color does not make anyone superior ... Anyone can be superior depending on the good or bad karma he commits. (Gnānānanda 2016, 119)

This broadly inclusive stance has assisted Mahamevnāva in expanding their movement across multiple continents and creating a single ethical community. Since the establishment of the first branch of the temple at Polgahawela, Sri Lanka, in August 1999, the organization has expanded to seventy branches in Sri Lanka and worldwide including the United States, Australia, India, Canada, Germany, England, and Dubai. This network is instrumental in establishing their imagined state of Gautama Buddha across geographical, ethnic, caste, and class boundaries.

Mahamevnāva has also adopted modern media and technology to disseminate their interpretation of Buddhism among the members of this transnational Buddhist state. It is the first organized Sri Lankan Buddhist group to adopt multimedia technologies – including TV, radio, print media, and internet – as part of their religious mission. They also use modern televisual technologies such as drones, camera-equipped helicopters, and other audio-visual techniques to create new ritual spectacles, meaningful for media modalities such as TV, radio, DVD, and the internet, and to make these rituals accessible to their wider transnational audience.

[13] Bandarawela Saddhasheela, interview with the author, December 2012.

7.6 LINGUISTIC REFORMATION IN THE BUDDHIST STATE

While Mahamevnāva's reformation poses challenges to mainstream Buddhist monastic politics and rituals, it holds different ideologies about the religious language of their imagined Buddhist state. On the one hand, they stress that the authentic teachings of the Buddha can be found in the Pāli canon. On the other hand, they argue that the doctrine should be rendered in a simple, vernacular language so that Buddhists may understand it. In this way, Mahamevnāva downgrades the authoritative status of Pāli in traditional Buddhist practice, while also questioning the language's inherent sacredness and disavowing the idea that simply chanting Pāli verses produces supernatural powers.

This attitude towards Pāli is an innovation. Although monastic politics during the colonial and postcolonial period has been anchored in the status of Sinhala, Pāli central importance in Sri Lankan Buddhism was never in dispute. Pāli is an Indo-Aryan language, and its origins go back to the ancient Indian language called Māgadhi, spoken in the state of Magadha where the Buddha spent the greater part of his life. Theravāda Buddhists believe that the truest and most authentic versions of the earliest and most important scriptures, such as the "The Three Baskets," were preserved in Pāli.[14] The *Dīpavaṃsa* and *Mahāvaṃsa*, the two major chronicles in Sri Lanka, relate the writing down of the scriptures in Pāli during the reign of the Sri Lankan King Vattagāmani Abhaya (89–77 BCE). In some cases, Pāli was even used as a medium of communication between kingdoms in the premodern Buddhist world (Blackburn 2010).

In fact, a second language ideology runs alongside the Sinhala-only attitude described above. This ideology, which is held among many Buddhists in Sri Lanka, maintains that Sinhala is a "low" and colloquialized language derived from the "high" language of Pāli, in which Buddhist texts and rituals are preserved (Ferguson 1959, Gair 1986, Paolillo 1997). Moreover, given that Pāli is imagined to be the language of the Buddha himself, its sound and appearance are thought to be inherently efficacious, capable of generating karmic merit and having a protective effect (Hackett 2011). Deegalle Mahinda documents a number of verbal rituals

[14] In Theravāda Buddhism, Pali scripture is treated as the sacred medium, as it enshrines the word of the Buddha – particularly the dhamma and *vinaya*. It is generally known as the Pali canon, or Buddhist canon, because it contains the fundamental principles of Buddhism. The Pali term for the Pali canon is Tipiṭaka, from *ti* 'three' + *Piṭaka* 'text, scripture, or basket (where things are collected)', which literally designates its three major divisions of teachings: The Vinaya Piṭaka is the collection of monastic rules laid down by the Buddha for monks and nuns. The Sutta Piṭaka is the collection of discourses, or specific teachings that were adaptively expounded by the Buddha to suit the individual, place, and event or situation in question, together with supplemental material. The Abhidhamma Piṭaka is the collection of the teachings that are purely substantive or academic, without reference to any individuals or events, and without any supplemental material. The Pali canon is not a single-volume scripture, but an enormous set of scriptures containing as many as 84,000 textual units.

and preaching styles prevalent in traditional Sri Lankan Buddhism that exemplify the place of Pāli acoustics in those rituals (2006). Among these are the modern poetic genre of preaching called *kavi bana*, devotional hymns or *gāthā*, and protective verses (*paritta*), that form a central part of many Buddhist rituals. For devotees, the sacredness of these verbal rituals is derived from the acoustics of Pāli language and unique verbal styles.

For Mahamevnāva, Pāli is an unintelligible language for their followers, which makes them ignorant of true dhamma. Therefore, Mahamevnāva argue that colloquial Sinhala should be used for religious activities, as it is for other modern activities including public law. Highlighting the importance of comprehensible language in achieving their religious mission, the official website of Mahamevnāva states:

> Here the Buddha's teachings are presented in modern language that is easy to understand. What makes Mahamevnāva unique is the effort to bring the Supreme Dhamma to listeners in its original form. Because of this, both young and old listen to the Dhamma and practice virtue, concentration, mindfulness and wisdom to realize the Four Noble Truths revealed by the Supreme Buddha. Presently there are more than 650 monks, more than 100 Anagarika nuns, and thousands of lay disciples practicing Dhamma at Mahamevnāva Monasteries around the world. (Mahamevnāva 2021)

The program of Mahamevnāva is in large part directed toward bringing Sinhalese Buddhists toward an authentic understanding and practice of the Buddha's dhamma through simplified language. Their emphasis on simple Sinhala in disseminating dhamma serves to orient their teachings to a transnational Buddhist audience affiliated to their branch temples around the world. Ven. Gnānānanda maintains that he was able to learn the true dhamma by studying the Pāli canon directly in Pāli, which required years of study. By translating these texts into vernacular, he hopes people will arrive at a similar knowledge of the truth discovered and taught by the Buddha.

Ven. Gnānānanda's linguistic ideology also aims to 'disenchant' Pāli by clearing from some of its magical associations. For example, he posits in one of his sermons that most Buddhist monks do not know the meaning of many of the protective verses they chant in Pāli. According to him, these monks utter aspirated sounds in these Pāli verses expecting those sounds to extinguish the non-human evil forces and that there is no logic behind this other than ignorance. These misbeliefs, he points out, are caused by ignorance of the true dhamma, one which has existed among Buddhists for centuries. In a statement that resembles the interpretive attitude of many public law jurists, Ven. Gnānānanda insists that protection from the spiritual law (the dhamma) can be expected only when one fully and accurately understands it.

The parallels between Sri Lankan constitutional law and 'true' Buddhist practice were even more pronounced in a discussion I conducted with a Mahamevnāva monk, who argued that:

> even though the Constitution of Sri Lanka favors Sinhala and Buddhism as this is a Sinhala-Buddhist country, our monks have failed to disseminate the Buddha's word in intelligible language so that the entire Buddhist state is at risk. Real followers of the Buddha are not the Buddhists by birth who blindly follow the religious rituals or recite hymns and protective verses (*paritta*) in Pāli by heart, but the ones who understand the doctrine and practice meditation.[15]

In other words, in order to fully realize the guarantees of Sri Lanka's Constitution and to safeguard Buddhism, Buddhists had to fully understand the teachings of the Buddha. According to this monk and Mahamevnāva more generally, the proper enactment of Sri Lanka's constitutional language depended on the proper recognition of the Buddha's religious language.

7.7 POPULARIZING RELIGIOUS TEXTS AND RITUALS IN SINHALA

In order to make colloquial Sinhala the medium of the true doctrine, Mahamevnāva has translated the threefold Buddhist canon and protective verses from Pāli to simple Sinhala, and they are developing novel forms of chanting and devotional rituals. In the book series of Mahamevnāva Tipiṭaka translation entitled *Mahamevnāve Bodhi Gnāna Tripitaka Granta Mālā*, there is a Sinhala verse translated from Pāli highlighted in the title page. The verse explains that "the dhamma (doctrine) and *vinaya* (monastic code) are shining only when they are exposed, not when they are hidden" (Mahamevnāve Bodhignāna Tripitaka Granta Mālā 2004), indicating that the teachings of the Buddha should be in a comprehensible language in order for the followers to easily understand them.

In addition to translating the Tipiṭaka and protective verses from Pāli to Sinhala, Mahamevnāva has published more than 100 books in simple Sinhala, including books of Buddhist stories aimed at children. Their *Mahamēgha* monthly magazine attracts thousands of Sinhalese readers while the Shraddha television channel, Damviru radio channel, and YouTube video channel are popularizing among the Sinhalese around the world a vernacular version of Buddhism through innovative televised rituals.

These activities of vernacularization of religious texts can be understood in the larger discourse of religious language planning. As Sinnemäki and Saarikivi suggest, there are two competing processes at work in language planning in many religious communities: the preservation of doctrinal purity and the unity of the community, on the one hand, and the need to understand the sacred texts and doctrine, on the other (2019). They argue that translations that alter the understanding and expression of a religion may prove harmful for unity and continuity, because languages never have identical semantics and the metaphors typical of each language are

[15] A Mahamevnāva monk in discussion with the author, January 2020.

culture-bound. The same conflict arose when the Mahamevnāva Tipiṭaka translations provoked a backlash from mainstream Buddhist monks. For instance, the late Ven. Bellanwila Wimalaratana, a well-known and outspoken Buddhist monk, at a public gathering in Colombo in 2013 criticized Mahamevnāva's use of "vulgar Sinhala" (*hadu Sinhala*) for the Tipiṭaka translations because, according to him, it challenges the purity of the dhamma in Pāli language and that of the Buddhist tradition. When I asked Ven. Saddhasheela of the Mahamevnāva to comment on these allegations during my encounters with him, he claimed that the purity or impurity of dhamma relies not upon the vehicle in which it is transported, but the accuracy of the content.

Most recently, Mahamevnāva translated the *Mahāvaṃsa* (Great Chronicle), the most celebrated literary work in Sinhalese Buddhist nationalism, into simple Sinhala from Pāli. Originally written during the sixth century CE in the Anuradhapura period and attributed to a Buddhist monk named Mahānāma, the *Mahāvaṃsa* consists of thirty-seven chapters describing the founding of the Sinhala kingdom by Vijaya, who migrated from India during the sixth century BCE, as well as the history of Buddhism up to king Mahāsena, who lived during the third century CE.[16] More importantly, the chronicle legitimates the relationship between Sri Lanka and Buddhism by claiming that Buddha chose the island to preserve and promote his teachings. Sinhalese Buddhists thus ardently hold that Sri Lanka is *sinhaladipa* (the island of the Sinhalese) and *dhammadipa* (the island containing Buddha's teachings).

The *Mahāvaṃsa* was first translated into literary Sinhala between 1877 and 1883, during the British colonial period by Ven. Hikkaduwe Sri Sumangala and Don Andris de Silva. Ven. Gnānānanda translated the chronicle again into colloquial Sinhala and the final volume of the series of the translation was launched in 2019 during a ceremony named *Mahāwanshabimāni* held in the Mahamevnāva temple in Kaduwela. The president of Sri Lanka (2019–2022), Gotabhaya Rajapakse, who was then a presidential candidate, attended the ceremony as the chief guest, and the first copy of the translation was handed over to him by Ven. Gnānānanda.

At the launch ceremony, Ven. Gnānānanda made a speech where he stated that all Sri Lankans, including Buddhist monks, are ignorant of history. Therefore, according to him, these Buddhist monks shamelessly propagate ideas against both Buddhism and the history of the Sinhalese people. The only way that the nation can be protected is by making the *Mahāvaṃsa* available for a broad readership. In

[16] The *Mahāvaṃsa* played a decisive role in shaping the modern ideologies of Sinhalese Buddhist nationalism, with its depiction of the Sinhalese king Dutugemunu (who reigned between 161 and 137 BCE) as the chronicle's supreme hero. According to the chronicle, King Dutugemunu vanquished the foreign non-Buddhist Tamil king Elara and unified the country as a centralised Sinhalese Buddhist kingdom, with the blessings and staunch support of the sangha, the Buddhist clergy. Thus, King Dutugemunu became the historical figure of Sinhalese Buddhist nationalism and revival in the nineteenth and twentieth centuries.

addition, Gnānānanda said that he translated the chronicle into simple Sinhala in order to make it easier for the public to read and learn about the Sinhalese nation, *buddha sāsana*, and the role of the Buddhist clergy. Strongly apparent in this speech, then, was the linkage between linguistic purity and religio-national flourishing. As with the decades of legal discussions that had occurred over the twentieth century, prioritizing Sinhala was cast as the key to ensuring the future of Sri Lanka.

Yet, Mahamevnāva has gone further to link Sinhala language with Buddhism and the idea of a Buddhist state, using the appeal of popular culture. Consider, as one example, the creation of a mega-ritual called *arahantaka vandanāva*, or "the veneration of enlightened monks," organized in 2017 in Polonnaruwa, which included music and songs. The ritual was a massive public celebration broadcast over all Mahmevnāva's media outlets. The opening of the ritual was a recorded song in Sinhala performed by professional singers while the attendees were engaged in the act of *arahant* veneration. The lyrics of the song describe the Buddha's path as the only way of liberation, and with the merits people gain from *arahant* veneration, they accumulate merit toward achieving nirvana in this life. The melody of the song makes it closer to secular songs rather than to the rhythm and style of stereotypical Mahamevnāva hymns.

The incorporation of these popular aesthetic forms in religious rituals set them apart from the dominant religious public, while it appeals to the interests of a wider audience. In an interview I conducted with a woman in her mid-twenties who attended the ritual with a group of friends, she revealed that these innovative aesthetic practices are important means to distract them from popular music, which attach them to this-worldly suffering. Further, she asserted that these recorded songs can be enjoyed over and over again whenever she wants to motivate herself to practice dhamma.

Scholars recognize that the consumption of popular culture in religious or political traditions creates new forms of publics across the world. For instance, Charles Hirschkind's work analyzes the production of Islamic recorded sermons vis-à-vis a recalibration of politics in Islamic countries (Hirschkind 2006). Junxi Qian proposes that the public singing of nationalist songs can constitute an alternative community through the agentive reinterpretation of lyrics (Qian 2014). As Shoemaker (2017) posits, the recognized characteristic of these productions is that they offer a dialogical space that resists normative tropes and complicates the ways in which audience understands marginalized groups, religious or political positions, social issues, or social life differently from the way mainstream consumers do.

In Mahamevnāva's case, Sinhalized styles in rituals and texts allow them to constitute new religious identities within the same religion and pose challenges to the linguistic ideologies of mainstream Buddhism, establishing alternative religio-linguistic nationalism. Through the use of constitutional language for religious rituals and religious texts, Mahamevnāva attempt to democratize Buddhist practice, allowing the public to access what they believe is "true" doctrine.

Similarly, Sinhalized ritual forms and texts created by Mahamevnāva constitute a language community which is part of their imagined *gautama buddha rājya*. These rituals function as boundary markers for their group, which, like a constitutional public, binds both monks and laypeople in a single imagined collective. These textual and ritual practices confirm Michael Warner's idea that publics rely on archived and indexed records of their texts and discourses to establish "style" that allow "participants in its discourse to understand themselves as directly and actively belonging to a social entity that exists historically in secular time and has consciousness of itself, though it has no existence apart from the activity of its own discursive circulation" (2002).

7.8 CONCLUSION

The relation between Buddhism and constitutional law is not just a one-way story of Buddhist influences on public law. It is also a story of how concepts and ideas that are prominent in constitutional design and interpretation come to influence Buddhism. Mahamevnāva is a perfect example of this for two reasons. First, they have taken the linguistic ideology of Sinhalese nationalism, which was central to constitutional practice in post-independence Sri Lanka and made it the language of Buddhism. Ven. Gnānānanda has reshaped the "official" language of public Buddhism in much the same way that constitutional experts have reshaped the official public language of Sri Lanka. In both cases, a Sinhalization program has taken place. Although these Sinhalization projects did not overlap in time, they can be seen as emerging from similar and connected historical trajectories, running from colonialism to anticolonial movements, to projects of populist nationalism. In its own programs of religious reform, the Mahamevnāva group has creatively borrowed the prestige of Sinhala language – acquired through the Constitution and nationalist politics – and deployed it in religious reforms to constitute an ideal religious state. In other words, debates over constitutional law have, today, found their way into debates over Buddhism.

Second, Mahamevnāva has in its own way taken up the very concept of constitutional law: it has transformed the constitutional principle that the law of the land should be accessible to and representative of the nation and turned it into a soteriological principle – that the Buddha's dharma should be available and interpretable to all. The constitution of a country is a set of rules regulating the powers of its government and the rights and duties of its citizens. A codified constitution is one in which key provisions are collected together in a single legal document; it should be accessible and representative of its citizens. Mahamevnāva monks have borrowed this principle to make Buddhist doctrine transparent and accessible to its followers. Vernacularizing religious and historical texts, rebuilding religious rituals, and circulating them among a transnational audience through modern media technologies are key strategies in a broader mission of democratizing Buddhist doctrine – and with it, the pursuit of nirvana. Both of these interactions between the Constitution and the Mahamevnāva reforms embody similar forms of linguistic ideology in which the ideal state can be realized by creating "public" texts for the uplift of the "nation."

ACKNOWLEDGMENT

The author would like to thank the Wenner-Gren Foundation for Anthropological Research for the generous support of his dissertation research, without which this chapter would not have been possible. He would also like to thank Benjamin Schonthal and Courtney Handman for substantive comments on this chapter. Finally, thanks to Tom Ginsburg and Roshan de Silva Wijeratne for a very productive conversation and their comments on the early version of this chapter at the workshop.

REFERENCES

Amunugama, Sarath. 1991. "Buddhaputra and Bhumiputra? Dilemmas of Modern Sinhala Buddhist Monks in Relation to Ethnic and Political Conflict." *Religion* 21 (2): 115–39.

Berkwitz, Stephen. 2016. "A Buddhist Media Pioneer: Ven. Kiribathgoda Gnānānanda." In *Figures of Buddhist Modernity in Asia*, edited by J. Samuels, J. McDaniel, and M. Rowe, 30–33. Honolulu: University of Hawai'i Press.

Blackburn, Anne M. 2010. *Locations of Buddhism: Colonialism and Modernity in Sri Lanka*. Chicago: The University of Chicago Press.

De Silva, K. M. 1986. *Managing Ethnic Tensions in Multi-ethnic societies: Sri Lanka 1880–1985*. Lanham: University Press of America.

1993. "The Making of the Indo-Sri Lanka Accord: The Final Phase, June–July 1987." In *Peace Accords and Ethnic Conflict*, edited by K. M. de Silva and S. W. R. de A. Samarasinghe, 112–55. London: Pinter Publishers.

de Silva-Wijeyeratne, Roshan. 2014. *Nation, Constitutionalism and Buddhism in Sri Lanka*. New York: Routledge.

Deegalle, Mahinda. 2006. *Popularizing Buddhism: Preaching as Performance in Sri Lanka*. New York: University of New York Press.

DeVotta, Neil. 2004. *Blowback: Linguistic Nationalism, Institutional Decay, and Ethnic Conflict in Sri Lanka*. Stanford: Stanford University Press.

Dharmadasa, K. N. O. 2000. *Bhashawa Ha Samajaya*. Colombo: Godage and Brothers.

Ferguson, Charles A. 1959. "Diglossia." *Word* 15 (2): 325–40.

Frydenlund, Iselin. 2017. "Religious Liberty for Whom? The Buddhist Politics of Religious Freedom during Myanmar's Transition to Democracy." *Nordic Journal of Human Rights* 35 (1): 55–73.

Gair, James W. 1986. "Sinhala Diglossia Revisited, or Diglossia Dies Hard." In *South Asian Languages, Structure Convergence and diaglossia*, edited by Colin P. Masica Krishnamurti and Anjani Sinha, 147–64. Delhi: Motilal Basarsidas.

"Gautama Buddha Rājyaye Maha Rajun Sarana Yamu." 2015. *Mahamēgha*, February 4, 2015. https://mahamegha.lk/2015/02/04/maharajun-sarana-yamu/. Accessed August 22, 2021.

Gnānānanda, Kiribathgoda. 2004. *Andura Viniwida Eliya Dakinnata*. Colombo: Dayawansa Jayakodi.

2010. *Ape Nawa Wasara Buddha Warshayay*. Polgahawela: Mahamegha Publishers.
2016. *Lokayen Nidahasweema*. Polgahawela: Mahamegha Publishers.
Hackett, Rosalind. 2011. "Auditory Materials." In *Engler Handbook of Research Methods in Religious Studies*, edited by Michael Stausberg and Steven Engler, 447–58. New York: Routledge.
Harris, Ian. 2018. "Buddhist Republicanism in Cambodia: A Colonialist Legacy?" In *Theravada Buddhism in Colonial Context*, edited by Thomas Borchert, 206–19. Abingdon: Routledge.
Harvey, Peter. 2012. *An Introduction to Buddhism*. 2nd ed. Cambridge: Cambridge University Press.
Hirschkind, Charles. 2006. *The Ethical Soundscape: Cassette Sermons and Islamic Counterpublics*. Columbia: Columbia University Press.
Irvine, Judith and Gal, Susan. 2000. "Language Ideology and Linguistic Differentiation." In *Regimes of Language: Ideologies, Polities and Identities*, edited by Paul V. Kroskrity, 35–84. Santa Fe: School of American Research Press.
Kapferer, Bruce. 1998. *Legends of People, Myths of State: Violence, Intolerance and Political Culture in Sri Lanka and Australia*. Washington: Smithsonian Institution Press.
Kyaw, Nyi. 2019. "Regulating Buddhism in Myanmar." In *Regulating Religion in Asia*, edited by Jaclyn L. Neo, Arif A. Jamal and Daniel P. S. Goh, 169–86. Cambridge: Cambridge University Press.
Mahamegha. 2015. "Gautama Budda Rajjaye Maha Rajun Sarana Yamu." February 04, https://mahamegha.lk/2015/02/04/maharajun-sarana-yamu/. Accessed May 2, 2021.
Mahamevanwa. 2021. "About us." https://mahamevnawa.lk/en/about-us/. Accessed May 2, 2021.
Mahamevnāve Bodhignāna Tripitaka Granta Mālā. 2004. Polgahawela: Bodhi Gnana Sabhawa.
Paolillo, John C. 1997. "Sinhala Diglossia: Discrete or Continuous Variation?" *Language in Society* 26 (2): 269–96.
Phadnis, Urmila. 1976. *Religion and Politics in Sri Lanka*. London: C. Hurst & Co Publishers Ltd.
Qian, Junxi. 2014. "From Performance to Politics? Constructing Public and Counterpublic in the Singing of Red Songs." *European Journal of Cultural Studies* 17 (5): 602–28.
Schonthal, Benjamin. 2016. *Buddhism, Politics and the Limits of Law: The Pyrrhic Constitutionalism of Sri Lanka*. Cambridge: Cambridge University Press.
Schonthal, Benjamin and Walton, Matthew J. 2016. "The (New) Buddhist Nationalisms? Sumetries and Specificitis in Sri Lanka and Myanmar." *Contemporary Buddhism* 17 (1): 81–115.
Shoemaker, Terry. 2017. "Escaping Our Shitty Reality: Counterpublics, *Orange Is the New Black*, and Religion." *Journal of Religion and Popular Culture* 29 (3): 217–29.
Sinnemäki, Kaisu Tatu-Kustaa and Saarikivi, Janne. 2019. "Sacred Language: Reformation, Nationalism, and Linguistic Culture." In *On the Legacy of Lutheranism in Finland: Societal Perspectives 2, Studia Fennica Historica*, no. 25, edited by Kaius Sinnemäki, Anneli Portman, Jouni Tilli and Robert H. Nelson, 39–68. Helsinki: Suomalaisen kirjallisuuden seura.
Sri Dhammananda Thero, K. 2021. "The Significance of Paritta Chanting." What Buddhists Believe: The Significance of Paritta Chanting, www.budsas.org.. Accessed July 21, 2022.
1992. *Buddhism Betrayed? Religion, Politics, and Violence in Sri Lanka*. Chicago: The University of Chicago Press.

Tonsakulrungruang, Khemthong. 2020. *Toward A New Buddhist Constitutionalism: Law and Religion in the Kingdom of Thailand*. Unpublished PhD Dissertation.

Warner, Michael. 2002. "Publics and Counterpublics." *Public Culture* 14: 49–90.

Wilson, A. J. 1975. *Electoral Politics in An Emergent State*. Cambridge: Cambridge University Press.

Zuhair, Ayesha. 2016. *Dynamics of Sinhala-Buddhist Nationalism in Post-War Sri Lanka*. Colombo: Center for Policy Alternatives.

8

Thai Constitutions as a Battle Ground for Political Authority

Barami versus Vox Populi

Khemthong Tonsakulrungruang

8.1 BEYOND SANGHA AND RELIGIOUS FREEDOM

Discussions of Buddhism and constitutional law tend to focus on a relatively limited set of topics, usually freedom of religion (Khemthong 2021) and the administration of sangha (Larsson 2018; Katewadee 2019). While important, such narrow coverage implies that the modern legal system of Thailand has already broken away from the past because it insinuates that Buddhism's influence on law is presently confined to only a few aspects of law that explicitly deal with religion. Often, these studies treat law as a set of positive rules, adopted from the European and Anglo-Saxon cultures, to replace the traditional code of Buddhist-inspired *dhammasattha*. Law, especially a constitution, is taken to represent modernity.

Recently this view has been facing growing challenges. While it is true that the contemporary Thai legal system is a Western import, a growing body of literature is beginning to suggest that certain ancient elements are still active and vibrant, shaping the conscience of legislators, law enforcers, lawyers, and judges alike (Harding & Munin 2021; Thongchai 2021; Mérieau 2018; Dressel 2018; Streckfuss 2011). Thai legal scholars in particular are often criticized for a lack of awareness of these issues (Thongchai 2021, 114) given that they focus on comparative work, looking for the right model to be adapted into the local context – without realizing that it is the local context that makes these transplants problematic.

This chapter seeks to challenge these trends. It argues that Thai constitutional law, in particular in the last decade, is heavily influenced not only by the Western idea of liberal democratic constitutionalism but also traditional ideas of power derived from Thai Buddhism. Notions of *dhammarāja* are clearly important in this regard (Mérieau 2018). Yet there are other notions, relating to the king's role in political and constitutional crises and to the overall structure of the supreme law of the land. Particularly important are the ways in which constitutional design has become the battleground for ideological contestation between liberal democracy, which relies on the popular mandate as the source of political legitimacy, and the Buddhist concept of *barami*, the perfect man. The contest has become particularly acute in recent years when Thailand has taken an undemocratic path.

This chapter examines how previously existing Buddhist notions, such as *barami*, have enabled the phenomenal rise of the judiciary and other elite agencies, which have lately become the imposing forces that steer Thailand's constitutional regime further away from liberal democracy. Even the high point of democratic constitutionalism, the adoption of the 1997 People's Constitution, turns out to have also provided resources for *barami*-type notions of public authority. The chapter begins with recent history and then turns to explicate the notion of *barami* and its continued relevance.

8.2 THE RISE OF UNELECTED ELITES

Thailand's constitutional history is a turbulent one. In 1932, Siam ended absolute monarchy and introduced the concept of constitutional democracy, but an alliance of royalist conservatives and military dictators interrupted the democratization process. Coups occurred regularly whenever the military felt that electoral politics had reached a deadlock. Still, liberal democracy clung on and occasionally emerged, first among university students and, later, the middle class (Hewison 2015). Sometimes crises arose when the two factions – military and democratic reformers – clashed. The king would intervene as a *deus ex machina* to preserve the fragile political equilibrium (McCargo 2005). Thailand's turbulent political history reflects this ongoing struggle, which resulted in a high constitutional turnover. The sixteen years since the 2006 coup have witnessed a continuation of these general trends in contemporary Thai constitutional law.

Since 2006, constitutional development has been characterized by the rise of the judiciary in politics, a phenomenon known as "judicial activism" (Dressel & Khemthong 2019, 6; Khemthong 2018; Dressel 2010). This phenomenon is characterized by the fact that judges feel empowered to assert their preference on political decisions (Barroso 2019). This activism began in 2006, together with the coup and the beginning of democratic decline. Mass protests and two coups in 2006 and 2014 undermined the democratization that had been achieved under the 1997 Constitution. Right-wing conservatives occupied key public offices, including constitution-drafting bodies, while nationalism, royalism, and moralism were offered as antidotes to the Western imports of democracy and liberalism (Hewison 2015, 57–60; Ukrist 2008). Inevitably, the last two constitutions of 2007 and 2017 tilted Thailand further toward authoritarianism.

However, attributing all of this to judicial activism is misleading. These activities involved not only the judiciary but also other unelected bodies. Judicial activism that took place in 2006 is only one symptom of a constitutional design that had reshaped politics since its beginning a decade earlier. In 1997, Thailand carried out a major reform to consolidate its democracy and permanently end military intervention. On the one hand, the 1997 Constitution promoted the idea of popular sovereignty with a progressive bill of rights, a new electoral system that favored national-level parties, and several mechanisms to assist a prime minister to boost his leadership (Borwornsak 2010, 41). On the other hand, the charter also introduced new constitutional bodies that could serve as final arbiters, outside the usual group of army generals and the king (McCargo 1998). The 1997 drafters further identified corruption as a key threat to the democratically elected government (and key justification for previous military intervention). Therefore, the drafters suggested stronger checks and balances and better monitoring procedures by introducing a new set of watchdog agencies that were autonomous and more powerful (Thailand Research Fund 2017).

As a result, the 1997 Constitution established a number of new actors: the Constitutional Court, the Administrative Court, the Criminal Division for Political Office Holders of the Supreme Court, the National Anti-Corruption Commission (NACC), the Election Commission (EC), the National Human Rights Commission (NHRC), the Ombudsman, and the Auditor General Office (AGO). Their mission was to uphold the sense of accountability of elected politicians without external help from the military. The NACC acted as a prosecutor for high-profile corruption cases. The EC was an election organizer. The Ombudsman heard general complaints, while the NHRC focused on human rights cases. The AGO audited the government's finance. The judicialization of Thai politics occurred also because some important cases would be referred to the abovementioned three courts.

Whereas independent regulatory agencies were already part of the Thai administrative branch, these independent accountability agencies – the watchdogs – were novel and were not categorized into the same group. The 1997 Constitution intended these watchdog agencies to be non-partisan independent bodies (Dissatat 2011) and placed them under neither the parliament nor the cabinet. Procedures for appointment and removal were prescribed in the constitution: a panel of professionals, representatives of political parties, as well as civic societies, would convene to nominate a candidate, who had to meet very high standards of expertise and ethics, before the non-partisan senate approved the list. Once appointed, their terms in office outlasted those of the government. They enjoyed autonomy in managing their own budget and personnel. Overall, these watchdog agencies gave an impression similar to that of the judiciary: they acted as guardians of democracy against short-sighted and self-interested elected politicians. Yet, there was no effective mechanism to watch the watchdogs. They were not subject to political oversight. Theoretically, they were still liable for criminal offences and impeachment for high crimes.[1] But their decisions would not be judicially reviewable.

[1] Constitution of Thailand, B.E. 2540 (1997), sec 303.

The first few years were promising. The Constitutional Court handed five-year bans to those politicians who failed to disclose their assets (Harding & Leyland 2010, 180). One minister was convicted for corruption, an unprecedented event.[2] Elections were mostly free and fair. Inquiry by NACC and AGO instilled a greater sense of transparency and accountability in the civil service. However, in late 2005 a constitutional crisis emerged. The highly popular Thaksin Shinawatra, who came into power in 2001, had skillfully dominated the parliament as well as watchdog agencies, effectively rendering the new check-and-balance mechanisms useless. His regime was tainted by human rights violations, harassment of his political enemies, and corruption (Kasian 2006). Unfortunately, through lobbying and manipulation, Thaksin was able to coopt the Constitutional Court, NACC, and EC, so that they all refused to investigate allegations of his corruption (Kasian 2006, 28–29). Their inertia led to a growing sense of distrust among the public.

The prime minister's ambitious rise alarmed many Thais who formed an opposition movement (Hewison 2010, 27) which eventually grew more radical. The anti-Thaksin movement blamed the constitution and liberal democracy for being the root of these recent political evils. A key strategy of the movement was to turn legal and political issues into moral ones. Thaksin was portrayed as a greedy, disloyal, and immoral representative of 'imported' electoral democracy. Thaksin's opponents, by contrast, were associated with patriotism, Buddhism, and, most importantly, royalism as preferable choices for Thailand (Connors 2008, 154–155; Ukrist 2008). In this way, their campaign resonated deliberately with the traditional three pillars of "Thainess": namely, the nation, the religion, and the king. Opponents of Thaksin even asked the king to take over control from Thaksin (Connors 2008, 155–156). This was the beginning of Thailand's moralistic politics, known as *khon dee* politics (politics of the righteous people), which emphasizes appointing righteous persons to public office to rule over an ignorant populace.

The first round of conflict culminated in the 2006 coup, led by radical conservatives, and fueled by animosity towards democracy. The coup leaders invited the return of the military and of several of the temporarily disbanded watchdog agencies. Members of the EC were even sentenced to imprisonment. But the 2006 coup was also a turning point in the conception and deployment of the watchdog agencies. The right-wing conservatives appreciated the role and capacity of the judiciary and agencies in imposing constraints on elected politicians. They appreciated especially the Constitutional Court's invalidation of the 2006 election (Khemthong 2018, 200–202). Thus, in designing the 2007 Constitution, conservative politicians restored and further empowered these watchdog agencies. Thailand's judiciary had long been a passive accomplice of coup makers, endorsing the legality of every coup since

[2] See the case of Rakkiat Sukthana at www.abc.net.au/news/2003-10-28/thai-ex-minister-found-guilty-of-corruption/1500788.

1947 (Piyabutr 2017). However, the anti-democracy camp in 2006 enlisted the judiciary as an active player in punishing its political enemies.

The 2007 Constitution hinted at the new understanding of these agencies. Firstly, Section 3 of the constitution makes the legislative, executive, judiciary, and constitutional agencies, as well as other state agencies, subject to the rule of law.[3] The clause implicitly acknowledged watchdog agencies, which the new constitution referred to as the constitutional agencies, to be detached from the threefold separation of power. Secondly, the new constitution amended the rule on nominations of the watchdogs, making the process more politically isolated and homogenous. The numbers of political representatives in the nomination commission were reduced, and the commission was to be dominated by representatives of the judiciary and of other watchdog agencies.[4] This homogeneity, together with absence of political oversight, allowed conservatives to capture the nomination process and recruit only from a pool of right-wing candidates (Dressel & Khemthong 2019). Watchdog agencies were still unaccountable, but they would now work in the interest of the antidemocratic faction. The third and most crucial change applied to the legal authority of the watchdog agencies. The constitution gave more bite to weaker bodies. Most interesting was the Ombudsman's new duty of preparing the code of ethics for other agencies, hence acting as the moral policeman for the entire group.[5] This office gained tremendous power to oversee the other branches of the government with virtual impunity.

Post-2006 politics was characterized by the growing role of these unelected bodies in toppling democratic governments linked to Thaksin, and the endorsement of Thaksin's enemies. The EC filed a petition to dissolve Thaksin's proxy, the People's Power Party, but spared his rival, the Democrat Party, by failing to submit the complaint in time (Khemthong 2016, 180–182). The NACC relentlessly investigated Thaksin's men for failing to follow a constitutional protocol on treaty-making, as well as the rice subsidy scheme. But the NACC never pursued a case against the Democrat Party. The agency dragged its feet in investigating the Democrat Party and the Royal Thai Army's role in a deadly 2010 crackdown on Thaksin's supporters (Haberkorn 2018, 194–201). The NHRC, for its part, refused to acknowledge any human rights abuses related to that crackdown. Most importantly, the Constitutional Court disqualified many of Thaksin's allies from office and blocked key policies (Khemthong 2018 and 2019). The Constitutional Court was accused of corruption, but no action was taken (Khemthong 2018, 189). In its decisions, the court often showed distrust toward politicians while emphasizing morality as a pretense for overriding the majority's choice (Khemthong 2017). A volley of lawsuits

3 The Constitution of Thailand, B.E. 2550 (2007), sec. 3.

4 2007 Constitution, sec. 206.

5 2007 Constitution, sec. 280.

badly jeopardized the legitimacy of the democratic government, leading ultimately to another coup d'état.

When it became clear that the conservatives could never defeat Thaksin in normal electoral politics, another mass protest shut down Bangkok for months. On 22 May 2014, a junta calling itself the National Council of Peace and Order (NCPO) overthrew the government in a coup. Even compared with many earlier coups, it deployed excessive force by incarcerating, detaining, torturing, and even murdering thousands of people – many of whom later fled abroad (Amnesty International 2014). The unelected watchdog agencies kept silent about such abuses. The NACC and NHRC refused to investigate corruption scandals and human rights violations of the junta. The Constitutional Court raised no objection to the junta's legitimacy. Meanwhile, the EC helped intimidate dissidents in the 2016 constitutional referendum (Desatova & Alexander 2021) and the NACC charged Yingluck Shinawatra and her ministers of corruption.

Watchdog agencies continued to gain influence under the 2014 junta. The 2017 Constitution modified the nomination process by further streamlining the nomination panel for these agencies to a small group from the judiciary and fellow watchdog bodies.[6] Given that the junta-appointed National Legislative Assembly acted as the new senate, the junta was effectively able to nominate its sympathizers and cronies into the watchdog agencies. Under the 2017 Constitution, the NACC can now investigate not only criminal cases but even cases of 'unethical conduct.'[7] With the 2017 charter, the EC can order a new election in case of possible fraud,[8] while the Ombudsman has powers to report directly to the cabinet if the agency fails to address its recommendation.[9] In fact, the NHRC is the only body that has had its power diminished. It can no longer file a case of human rights violation against a state agency and is now in charge of defending the Thai government in cases of human rights reports that wrongly or inaccurately accuse the state.[10]

8.3 *BARAMI* AS POLITICAL AUTHORITY

The rise of unelected bodies, like those in Thailand, has been well documented worldwide. The phenomenon is generally associated with democratic deficits: when the existing political mechanism fails to make sound public policies, a novel institution replaces the old one, bringing with it impartial scientific or economic expertise (Vibert 2007; Veerayooth 2016). However, Thailand's empowerment of independent constitutional agencies is different. Watchdog agencies are concerned with accountability, not with regulation. They are not a response to democratic

6 The Constitution of Thailand B.E. 2560 (2017), sec. 203 and 217.
7 The Constitution of Thailand B.E. 2560 (2017), sec. 234 (1).
8 The Constitution of Thailand B.E. 2560 (2017), sec. 224.
9 The Constitution of Thailand B.E. 2560 (2017), sec. 230.
10 The Constitution of Thailand B.E. 2560 (2017), sec. 247.

shortfalls in decision-making but to perceived moral deficiencies. Therefore, Thailand's constitutionally created watchdog agencies act not as regulatory experts, but as moral authorities designed to restrain immoral politicians.

How could the few govern the many? While *vox populi* is often regarded as the source of legitimacy in a democratic regime, not all regimes or institutions reflect this. Unelected regulatory agencies may claim impartial knowledge as justification (Vibert 2007, 116), yet watchdog agencies in Thailand can claim no such expertise. Their source of legitimacy is linked instead to Buddhism, and the ancient concept of moral perfection, or *barami*.

8.3.1 *Understanding* Barami

A belief in karma (in Pali, *kamma*) – moral laws of cause and effect – forms the basis of Thai Buddhism. Simply put, a person reaps what he or she sows. Good deeds result in merit (*bunna*), while evil deeds generate their own negative results (Ishii 1986, 14–16; Jackson 1989, 40–41). Merit that is acquired through good deeds in this life insures a better situation in the next life. The system is not supposed to be deterministic, however, people commonly believe that they are born in their current condition because of the amount of merit and demerit accumulated in past lives. Buddhism encourages a person to constantly improve one's fortune by making new merit and avoiding committing further evil. Ultimately, a person with high merit will obtain true understanding of the Buddha's teaching and gain release from the cycle of rebirths by attaining nirvana, at which point all of one's sufferings will come to an end.

For most people nirvana is a distant prospect. Monks might be interested in this spiritual goal, but ordinary folks are generally not ready to follow such practices of renouncing the mundane world. Their goals tend to be more practical and materialistic, such as improving their worldly situation. A person of high merit is said to enjoy wealth, wisdom, or good family fortune, for example (Terwiel 2012, Chapter 9), whereas demerit produces undesirable consequences, including poverty, ailment, or demotion at work.

Thai Buddhists believe that some forms of good karma produce not ordinary *bunna*, but a quality known as *barami*. The relationship between the two, *bunna* and *barami*, is not always clear but *barami* is used principally in a political sense. Although there is no perfect translation, *barami* is understood as perfection or virtues (Jory 2016, 15–18). It can be used as 'power,' and a person with a high level of *barami* is fit to rule.

Examples of *barami* appear in stories about the Buddha's various rebirths, which treat him as a personification of dhamma (Nidhi 2012, 329–330). The stories often emphasize that, to become a buddha, a person must accumulate the ultimate level of *barami*, which could only be achieved through countless rebirths. It is a journey spanning eons and involving rebirth as various life forms, for example, an elephant, a quail, a deer, or a prince. In each life, the buddha-to-be is described as undergoing adventures that demonstrate certain kinds of virtues. In Thai versions of these stories, many incarnations are similar to quests that the Buddha must overcome to gain more *barami*. Gradually, he perfects himself, therefore reaching the status of Buddha. These stories, known as *jātaka*, are weaved into a larger tapestry of time, connecting the previous buddhas with the coming Maitreya Buddha of the future (Nidhi 2012, 331–340).

Accounts of *jātaka* are scattered throughout Buddhist texts, both in the canon (the Tipiṭaka) and outside of it (Baker & Pasuk 2019, xix–xxi). *Jātaka*s often begin with a framing story explaining how a previous rebirth is linked to the present one: an incident, *cause célèbre*, or a dispute among monks. The story often ends with some moral guidance in which characters in the story are linked to particular people in the Buddha's life, as previous incarnations, or the Buddha's close associates or enemies.

*Jātaka*s are a major source of Buddhism through which many Thais learn about religion. Particularly in premodern times, few people read the canon, which was written in Pali on a palm leaf. Sacred books were to be worshipped, in many cases, not studied. The canonical approach to Buddhist studies would not begin until the turn of the twentieth century, when King Chulalongkorn ordered his half-brother Sangha Raja to reform monastic education (Phibul 2015, Ishii 1986, 85–88). *Jātaka*s by contrast were treated as entertainment because they entailed life and death and other drama and were easy to tell orally to illiterate locals through performance (Jory 2016; Baker & Pasuk 2019, xii). Later generations 'borrowed' the religious credibility of the stories and added their local lore into the *jātaka* genre, expanding the local *jātaka* universe (Baker & Pasuk 2019, xvii–xix).

In this worldview, the Buddha stands as the most meritorious, most perfect person of our time. But there are several other individuals endeavoring to reach such exalted status. They are known as bodhisattvas (Pali: *bodhisatta*), those on the path to becoming the future buddha (Jory 2016, 17–19). Many Thai kings were identified as bodhisattva, associating their political power with moral superiority (Jory 2016, 50–54; Skilling 2007; Sweaerer 2010, 105). In this way, the concept of *barami* came to explain the king's authority over his subjects. As the most perfect man (next to the Buddha), he was portrayed as being morally entitled to the throne as well as empowered to wage wars against other less perfect monarchs. Some scholars have even described premodern Thai statecraft as a space of several smaller tributary kingdoms united by one man's charisma (Tambiah 1976, 102; Sunait 1990; Prapod 2010, 18–19).

According to some sources, the well-being of a Buddhist kingdom depended on the *barami* of this single person, which was not static, but in danger of being eroded. Barami could be depleted, requiring the king to practice dhamma. If the king behaved, the kingdom was supposed to prosper. Those rulers who ignored dhamma brought disasters, draughts, floods, or fires to their subjects. Folklore from northern

Thai kingdoms tells a story of a kingdom that sank overnight as a punishment for the behavior of an evil king (Chai-anan & Sombat 1980, 46–51).

One of the most important works of literature on *barami* is *Trai Phum Phra Ruang*, the "Three Worlds of King Ruang." Composed by King Lithai in the fourteenth century as a reading on Buddhism for his mother, *Trai Phum Phra Ruang* is also a great work of political literature (Reynolds 1976; Cholthira 1974). The text describes vividly a cosmology consisting of many worlds of deities, men, demons, and other creatures covering four continents, and their people and fauna. It tells the story of the creation of the universe at the start of the last eon, drawing from many other important Buddhist texts.[11]

The underlying message of the *Trai Phum* is clear: a sentient being's fate is determined by its karma (Jackson 1993, 70–74). The book begins with a description of the lowest realm of hell, gradually working its way up through different realms of animals, ghosts, and demons. Lower realms are full of creatures of disgusting birth and lowly livelihood, feeding on mud and waste, and of ugly unsightly aspect. The later chapters deal with the realm of humans and gods of varying qualities. The lower heavens are full of worldly pleasures, while the higher realms enjoy more sublime ones. Within the present world, the three continents hold people of perfect appearance and longevity. They know no sadness. Their lands have food aplenty and no hardship will ever befall them. All this is because the residents of the three continents practice dhamma.[12]

The *Trai Phum* describes the political system as dominated by kings who have accumulated *barami* over their past lives (Chontira 1974, 116). According to this view, they are entitled to their throne and prestige as well as loyalty from their subjects. Such kings speak in words that are always just and fair. They dispense with wealth without reservation and, as a result of their moral character, ensure that the kingdom's wealth grows even wider. The kings are described as *cakravartin* (Pali: *cakkavattin*), 'wheel turners' who have the power to defeat all others and who guide their citizens and protect dhamma (Chai-anan & Sombat 1980, 61–67). *Barami* brings kings power and wisdom as well as a fair appearance, perfect for a ruler. Other members of society are born or assigned into their places, high and low, according to their karma too.

In the fifteenth century, the Kingdom of Ayutthaya implemented its own hierarchical scheme called the *sakdina* system, in order to regulate its workforce (Akin 2017). All men and women, from a beggar to the viceroy, were assigned certain rankings, from 5 *rai* to 100,000 *rai*. All benefits and duties are conferred based on the ranking. The *sakdina* system created a social and political organization similar to the *Trai Phum*'s karma-based cosmology. On this sociopolitical pyramid, the king sits at

[11] This article relies principally on a modernized version prepared by the Department of Fine Arts in 2012 at Vajirayana Digital Library, https://vajirayana.org/.

[12] Chapter 5: The realm of human at Vajirayana Digital Library, https://vajirayana.org/.

the zenith as the most perfect man. Below him are courtiers, commoners, and other persons. As with the *Trai Phum*, men with higher *barami* were imagined to rule over those with lower *barami*.

These notions of *barami* came under immense pressure by the end of the nineteenth century. Newly arrived Christian missionaries challenged Buddhism, criticizing it as a mythical barbaric religion. Siamese aristocrats responded by redefining Buddhism (Thongchai 2015; Jackson 1993, 43–47). They emphasized the 'rational' features of the Pali canon and tried to discredit elements such as miracles as later corruptions of an essentially logical religion. *Trai Phum* and *jātakas* were downgraded from the status of sacred texts to fables (Jory 2002).

These changes to Buddhism fit with the construction of the new Thai nation-state, which emphasized the Western concept of sovereignty. King Chulalongkorn was the first Thai king to claim this kind of sovereignty, which, unlike *barami*, was absolute, static, and, most importantly, inheritable by his son. Where ancient kingdoms were loosely constructed, consisting of greater and lesser kings along with dominant and tributary states, under the new political philosophy the king's power was imagined to reach every corner of the new Thai "geo-body" without ever waning (Thongchai 1994). Chulalongkorn relied less on *barami* and more on written legal codes.

One might assume that the era of *barami*-based Buddhist kingship was over in the nineteenth century. But is that the case? King Chulalongkorn was the first modern king, but he was also revered as a demi-god. The worshipping of Chulalongkorn suggests that the king was still viewed with high *barami*. Even those aristocrats who were pressured to undertake the reforms of modern Thai Buddhism might not have abandoned the *barami* concept entirely. For example, King Vajiravuth, Chulalongkorn's son and successor, ordered a royal anthem called *san-sern-phra-barami*, which praises His Majesty's *barami*. A Thai reference to a man of high power is still *phu mi barami*, meaning 'one who has barami.' When a man falls from his grace, some will say that he has depleted his *barami*, *mod barami*. Buddhism as a religious philosophy may have been rationalized and modernized, but Buddhism as a political ideology remained unchanged (Gray 1986). Many Thais seem to adopt a rationalistic version of Buddhism for their personal life philosophy and guidance, while advocating for traditional *barami*-based sociopolitical hierarchy (Nidhi 2012, 311–325). How could *barami* be preserved and popularized in the modern age?

8.3.2 *Popularizing* Barami

Seven hundred years are enough for belief in *barami* to seep into Thais' deepest conscience. Few have heard of *Trai Phum* and fewer still read it. But for most Thais, men are not equal. As one Thai proverb goes, one can compete in a boat race, but one could not compete in *bun* (merit) and *wasana* (luck). The taboo of someone whose lifestyle is not compatible with his or her social status always draws criticism.

This kind of thinking is still prevalent among conservatives. As Thai politics turn more moralistic, conservative voices often chant the mantra that men are not equal. They justify the authoritarian regime by labelling ordinary people as stupid and not worthy of the right to self-governance (Apichat & Anusorn 2017, 97–116). Only good people can acquire an office of political power (Aim 2020, 151). *Barami*, I would argue, is still one of the most important sources of political authority in twenty-first-century Thailand.

Some might argue that, as evidenced by declining attendance at temples, along with a declining number of monks and temples (Channarong 2011), Thais are becoming less religious and therefore *barami* is not important. Yet, the majority of Thais learn about *barami* through contemporary and vernacular sources. For example, the story of Phra Malai is a popular narrative that also emphasizes the importance of karma (Igunma 2013). The story focuses on an *arahant* called Malai who visits heaven and hell. In hell, he documents the types of punishment related to a given action. A drinker is fed red-hot molten copper. An adulterer is forced to climb a *Bombax* tree with sharp iron thorns while being preyed on by crows. Those who insult an *arahant* would have mouths as narrow as a needle hole, and therefore, be forever hungry. Beliefs like these are deeply entangled in the Thai conscience, even among those who do not regularly attend temples. Most Thais could probably recite an evil deed and its matching punishment even without having read the tale of Phra Malai. Some monks and nuns even offer a service where disciples are told which type of bad behavior results in which type of mishap. By matching certain types of merit to a specific blessing, these monks and nuns recommend merit-making according to one's goal. It is common to find a book or a TV show that discusses a participant's past lives and the consequence of his or her karma.[13]

Several *jātaka*s were turned into plays, and later, literature of prose and verse, making them popular moral tales as much as Buddhist stories. *Rathasenajātaka* became *Phra Rot-Meri*, the story of Prince Rathasena's adventure into the land of a monster queen, Meri, ending in romantic tragedy (Baker & Pasuk 2019, 57). *Suthanajātaka* was adapted into *Suthana-Manohara*, another adventure of Prince Suthana in pursuit of a mythical half-woman, half-bird princess, Manohara (Baker & Pasuk 2019, 1). *Suvannasankhajātaka* is retold as the story of Sank Tong, a prince who was born with a golden conch (Baker & Pasuk 2019, 27). *Samuddaghosajātaka* is *Samuddhaghosa*, another adventure of Prince Samuddhaghosa who was kidnapped by a playful god and introduced, for a night, to a princess (Baker & Pasuk 2019, 75). All these stories depict a protagonist of a noble class, with beautiful aspect and exceptional courage. They were given a difficult task but received aid from gods and goddesses who believed that a man of high merit deserved better treatment and

[13] One of the best-known figures is Mae Chi Tossapon, or Nun Tossapon, who has run the program called *Scan Kamma* (Scanning your karma) since early 2000. Nun Tossapon scans a person's karma and suggests a sometimes very controversial solution.

should not suffer. These stories are still being made into dances, cartoons, and TV series to this day.

The best-known of the *jātaka* stories is that of the Buddha's penultimate rebirth before his final incarnation, in which he is born as a king named Vessantara. The story of Prince Vessantara emphasizes the importance of generosity or giving, *dāna*. Vessantara inspires the exceedingly popular performance of *Mahachat*, "the Great Birth," where monks recite the entire beautiful prose of Prince Vessantara's adventure within a single day. The importance of this story and this celebration have been analyzed by Patrick Jory, who argues that it forms the foundation of Thailand's theory of divine kingship (2016).

Even King Bhumibol was involved in popularizing *jātaka* stories, rewriting *Mahajanakajātaka* to teach the virtue of perseverance (Bhumibol 1996). The story tells of Prince Mahachanok, who had to swim in the ocean for seven days straight before the Goddess Mekhala rescued him. It became a big hit in Thailand, and a best-selling book. Later, it was simplified and illustrated by a famous cartoonist, Chai Ratchawat (1999). It was also adapted into an opera by Somtow Sucharitkul.[14] A new breed of mango was grown to honor the story in which the prince learned to resurrect a delicious mango tree which had been ravished by ignorant greedy men: the king named it "Mahajanaka mango."

These stories of *barami* and *bunna* are included in the national educational curriculum. For most Thais, the primary contact point with Buddhism is in public education, of which the first twelve years are compulsory, and where Buddhism-inspired stories constitute a significant part of the reading list. These readings reflect Buddhist thinking about karma and its effects. It does not include *Trai Phum*, but it does include the tale of Phra Malai and the *Vessantara Jātaka*.

Moreover, notions of *barami* have been a big part of the modern idealizations of kingship in Thailand. King Bhumibol himself is said to be the living example of the perfect man filled with *barami*. In the last thirty years of his reign, Thailand witnessed the rise of hyper-royalism, an excessive worship of the monarch as the morally absolute ruler (Thongchai 2016). Through this process, Bhumibol has been elevated from a hard-working developer of the nation into a semi-divine figure. Some prominent royalists, such as a public scholar, Kukrit Pramoj, told accounts of King Bhumibol's *barami*, for example, that His Majesty seemed to be able to command animals and weather patterns. Other stories tell that when the king was presiding over a ceremony, his presence stopped the drizzling rain or, in the case of a hot sunny day, brought light showers, equivalent to spraying holy water. Bhumibol was revered for possessing an innate spiritual power. These accounts are openly published in newspapers (Siamrath 2016).

During the peak of the Cold War, when Thailand was struggling against a communist insurgency, the king's *barami* became the basis to produce a powerful

[14] See <www.youtube.com/watch?v=7BSvgOAVSMg>.

amulet, "Phra Somdej Chitrlada," named after the king's palace. The amulet needed no further ceremony of sacralization because the presence of the king was deemed sufficient to ensure it. It was distributed to security personnel, soldiers, border-patrol police, local militias, and other government employees who were fighting against communism (Art & Culture Magazine 2021; Kom Chad Luek 2012). Many military personnel confirmed that the sacred amulet saved their lives. Several senior monks confirmed that Bhumibol had great interest and knowledge in dhamma and had even attained various levels of enlightenment – implying that he was one genuine bodhisattva (MGR Online 2016). At his funeral, Thais were amazed by the news that a flock of white birds were circling his crematorium as a sign of *barami* (Matichon 2016). All of these accounts, some well documented, others anecdotal, provide the public with an image of a mythical king.

8.3.3 Barami *and "Dhammacracy"*

The Buddhist notion of *barami* evolved to justify absolute monarchy in premodern times, but can it become part of Thailand's democracy today? Unfortunately, recent developments suggest that there is a problem with its use in a modern democratic system. The idea of *barami* suggests that only a meritorious and morally upright individual will rise to power. In other words, it allows only *khon dee* (good persons) into public office while excluding *khon mai dee* (bad persons). The core idea of democracy, by contrast, is basically to give the most popular person power, regardless of his or her personal moral quality. However, this risk is compensated with the limited duration of one's political office. When Buddhist intelligentsia compares Buddhism and democracy, the conclusion is always that Western-imported ideology is inferior to the finer, and more nuanced, traditional one.

Thailand has come too far to return to absolute monarchy, which was abolished in 1932. The best the conservatives can offer is to forge a new ideology that suppresses democracy while justifying an undemocratic regime. The result of this process is "dhammacracy," the governance of dhamma.[15]

The famous monk Buddhadasa is regarded as the leading scholar of modernist Buddhism in Thailand. He advocates dhammic socialist dictatorship against liberal democracy (Buddhadasa 1975; Jackson 2003, 239–242). Buddhadasa imagines a Platonic-style philosopher-king whose objective and behavior are constrained by his own inner dhammic morality. Thus, his goal could only be to serve the whole and never be corrupt. According to Buddhadasa, dhammic socialist dictatorships are more efficient than capitalist democracies, which are too individualistic. In his estimation, MPs in a democratic government will waste precious time arguing, not for the public interest, but for their own wealth.

[15] The term was used, with a slightly different meaning, by Schalk to describe a Sinhalese-Buddhist concept of governance in the Sri Lankan context (1991).

This view is supported by other scholars of the conservative spectrum (Pinyapan 2019, 329–330). Chamlong Srimuang, the leader of the People's Alliance for Democracy (PAD), which toppled Thaksin and incited a coup, was himself an admirer of the righteous dictatorial style of governance (Nelson 2010). The remark is undoubtedly controversial, leading to criticism that Buddhadasa's ideas were used to support authoritarianism (Wanpat 2017; Gabaude 1990; Jackson 2003, 243–244).

Perhaps, the most important articulation of *barami*-based political authority came from King Bhumibol, himself the embodiment of a hierarchical moral order. His 1969 speech delivered at the Vajiravuth boy scout camp in Chon buri succinctly encapsulated the essence of what the ideal Buddhist constitutionalism should be like. In the speech, the king admitted that there were good and bad people. While bad people could not always be converted, Thais could exclude those people from politics while supporting the rule of good people.[16] The speech was hugely popular, and it has become a mandate for the conservatives, appalled by the democratic idea that an evil yet popular man could win office. It is often recited to justify antidemocratic protests and coups. Bhumibol was himself a proof of his own theory when he intervened to settle political disputes.

The concepts of karma and *barami* form important building blocks of "dhammacracy," the ultimate goal of which is to impose dhamma over any form of political regime (Jackson 1993, 77–80). In its application, "dhammacracy" forms the foundation of Thai-style democracy but can simply be a euphemism for authoritarianism (Hewison & Kengkij 2010; Connors 2008). The king's *barami* radiates to those who have close proximity to him: politically, his *barami* is extended to army generals, who are portrayed as guardians of the throne and of the nation (Chambers & Napisa 2016, 425). Thai-style democracy thus places the king at the top of the political system. Below are his loyal senior bureaucrats, especially army generals, above corrupt and selfish civilian politicians. The lowest ranking is that of the populace, who are deemed to always vote for the wrong politicians. Thai-style democracy therefore permits military coup intervention in the name of His Majesty (Thongchai 2018). The system of Thai-style democracy was formed during the military dictatorship in the Cold War period, but it began to crumble with the political and economic liberalization of the 1990s. That was when the majority demanded the 1997 political reform.

With the benefit of hindsight, the efforts of Thai-style democracy and the *barami*-based political authority can be detected even in the 1997 Constitution, questioning its name of the People's Constitution. The 1997 Charter is called the People's Constitution due to its empowerment of the people through a very progressive list of rights and liberties, and because it was produced as a result of a popular

[16] Royal speech at the opening ceremony for the 6th National Boy Scout Assembly on 11 December 1969.

movement. But the initial agenda resulted in the introduction of the new judicial and independent watchdog bodies (Connors 2002).

The judicialization of politics often makes authoritarians' control of politics appear to conform more to the international norm of democracy than an outright military junta (Landau & Dixon 2020, 1335–1338). Yet, in Thailand these judicial and independent agencies replaced the military as the new actor of high *barami*. Their goal was, in this sense, also to impose control over elected politicians and to prevent a political crisis. They are elite not only because they enjoy superior power, but also because these offices are limited to a few people of extraordinary qualification. The discrepancy is obvious in comparison to qualification for MP candidates. While any person aged twenty-five and above is eligible to run for parliament, a candidate for the watchdog agencies must be forty-five years old and have acquired higher education and a certain bureaucratic rank – for example, director-general of a government department, chief of a court, or professor – and display exemplary behavior and morality. All of these could arguably be considered modern signifiers of one's *barami*. It should be no surprise therefore that Borwornsak Uwanno, the constitutional law scholar and key advocate of the 1997 Constitution drafting, later advocated "dhammacracy" (2016).

Independent agencies are not a new feature in Thai public administration, the Bank of Thailand being one fine example of an independent body under the cabinet's arm-length control. The Court of Justice has undoubtedly been independent from the political branches since 1901. Nevertheless, these new judicial and watchdog agencies are particularly significant because they are more independent than ever, with the constitution guaranteeing virtually no meaningful political oversight. Moreover, unlike the Court of Justice, these agencies are not bound by any tradition that serves as an implicit constraint. They are basically the fourth, fifth, sixth, and many other branches of government. The constitutions recognize them as separate from the conventional trinity of powers. There is therefore no guidance or constitutional convention to provide advice on how the legislative, executive, or judiciary should scrutinize them. The independence of these agencies, together with their expansive jurisdiction, may be necessary for scrutinizing politicians. But they are also a tangible display of *barami*, according to which a meritorious elite is set above the political actors. In fact, it might be argued that candidates are selected not because of their unique professional qualifications, but because of their moral quality. The Constitutional Court judges are the best example of this: no judge serving on that body can be described as an expert in public law (Somchai 2018); and the better-known ones have a reputation for notable ascetic style, such as Jaran Pakdithanakul, whose interest in Buddhism is well known.

Why did the constitution drafters not install mechanisms to hold these elite bodies accountable? In a way, the political ideals of the *Trai Phum* have become self-fulfilling prophecies in modern Thailand: *barami* is considered to enhance political authority and so political authority comes to stand in for *barami*. More often than not, Thais accept that political authority indicates *barami* and that *barami* entails morality. All of this upends the Western concept of power and the famous maxim that power tends to corrupt. In Thailand, absolute power can never be corrupt because absolute power is granted only to a person of *barami*, which in itself guarantees righteousness.

8.4 *BARAMI* VERSUS *VOX POPULI*

The first sign of trouble for Thaksin has been associated with his remark on June 29, 2006, that *phu mi barami nok ratthathammanoon*, "the one with *barami* outside the constitution, was manipulating the constitutional politics." (Chai-anan 2006). In a way, the remark also encapsulated well the tension between *barami* and Thai constitutional politics. Thaksin was becoming so popular that he had the potential to overshadow the country's already incumbent perfect man, the king (Jory 2016, 184–88). In a view based on *Trai Phum*, such a dislocation could not stand, as it threatened to upend an entire scheme of moral authority and karmic merit that, even if not explicit, upheld the legitimacy of Thailand's system of social and political inequality. As Thaksin sought to eclipse King Bhumibol, the king's close aide and the head of privy council, General Prem Tinnasulanonda, called for the military to stage a coup and restore the proper order of things, placing the king (the epitome of *barami*) back in the center of power.

The military alone could not carry out a coup successfully. It was the king's criticism of Thaksin and the Constitutional Court – and its group of *khon dee* – that invalidated the 2006 election and justified Thaksin's ousting (Ukrist 2008; Khemthong 2016, 79–177). The event symbolizes the mixture of Buddhism and constitutional politics in post-2006 Thailand: the rise of unelected elite agencies, legitimated by notions of *barami*, and the decline of popular ideals of democracy.

But how long can *barami* suppress the voice of the people? The judiciary and watchdog agencies are under massive pressure: every time they punish democratically elected politicians, more people question whether they are legitimized to do so. Their supposedly high morality fails to prevent them from exercising power arbitrarily. *Barami* as a source of political legitimacy is today sounding somewhat less convincing to angry ears.

REFERENCES

Aim Sinpeng. 2020. "From the Yellow Shirts to the Whistle Rebels: Comparative Analysis of the People's Alliance for Democracy (PAD) and the People's Democratic Reform Committee (PDRC)." In *Routledge Handbook of Contemporary Thailand*, edited by Pavin Chachavalpongpun, 145–55. New York: Routledge.

Akin Rabibadhana. 2017. พระมหากษัตริย์-ขุนนาง: นาย-ไพร่ในโครงสร้างสังคมไทยยุคต้นกรุงรัตนโกสินทร์ [The Organization of Thai Society in the Early Bangkok Period 1782–1873]. Bangkok: Kob Fai Foundation.

Amnesty International. 2014. Thailand: Attitude Adjustment: 100 Days Under Martial Law. www.amnesty.org/en/documents/ASA39/011/2014/en/ (accessed June 5, 2021).

Apichat Satitniramai and Unno Anusorn. 2017. *“การเมืองคนดี”: ความคิดปฏิบัติการและอัตลักษณ์ทางการเมืองของผู้สนับสนุน “ขบวนการเปลี่ยนแปลงประเทศไทย”* [“Good Man’s Politics”: Political Thoughts, Practices, and Identities of the “Change Thailand Movement” Supporters]. Research Report, National Policies and International Relations Division, The Thailand Research Fund.

Art & Culture Magazine. 2021. พระสมเด็จจิตรลดา พระเครื่องทรงสร้างของในหลวงรัชกาลที่ 9 [Phra Somdej Chitrlada, the Amulet of the Ninth King]. Last modified April 9, 2021. www.silpa-mag.com/history/article_50863.

Baker, Chris and Pasuk Phongpaichit. 2019. *The Palace Law of Ayuttaha and the Thammasat: Law and Kingship in Siam*, 166. Ithaca: Cornell University Press.

Barroso, Luís Roberto. 2019. “Countermajoritarian, Representative, and Enlightened: The Roles of Constitutional Courts in Democracies.” *The American Journal of Comparative Law* 67 (1): 109–43.

Bhumibol Adulyadej. 1996. *พระมหาชนก* [The story of Mahajanaka]. Bangkok: Amarin Printing & Publishing.

1999. ‘พระมหาชนก: ฉบับการ์ตูน’ [The story of Mahajanaka: cartoon edition]. Illustrated by Chai Ratchawat, 119. Bangkok: Amarin Printing & Publishing.

Borwornsak Uwanno. 2010. *คำอธิบายวิชากฎหมายรัฐธรรมนูญ* [On Constitutional Law]. Bangkok: Institute of Legal Education of the Thai Bar.

2016. *หลักนิติธรรม ประชาธิปไตย และธรรมาธิปไตย* [Rule of Law, Democracy, and Dhammacracy]. Individual Study Paper, The Rule of Law and Democracy Course, The Constitutional Court.

Buddhadasa Bhikkhu. 1975. *ธัมมิกสังคมนิยมแบบเผด็จการ* [Dictatorial Dhammic Socialism]. Bangkok: Cremation Memorial of Montha Meunnikorn.

Chai-anan Samudavanija. 2006. ผู้มีบารมีนอกรัฐธรรมนูญ [*Barami* Person of Extra-Constitutional]. MGR Online. https://mgronline.com/daily/detail/9490000091103 (accessed June 5, 2021).

Chai-anan Samudavanija and Sombat Thamrongthanyawong. 1980. *ความคิดทางการเมืองและสังคมไทย* [Thai Political and Social Ideas]. Bangkok: Bannakij.

Chambers, Paul and Napisa Waitoolkiat. 2016. “The Resilience of Monarchised Military in Thailand.” *Journal of Contemporary Asia* 46 (3): 425–44.

Channarong Boonnoon. 2011. การลดจำนวนของพระสงฆ์และผลกระทบต่อพระพุทธศาสนาในอนาคต [Reducing the Number of Monks and Their Impact on Buddhism in the Future]. *Journal of Buddhist Studies Chulalongkorn University* 18 (3): 7–30.

Cholthira Klud-U. 1974. ไตรภูมิพระร่วง รากฐานของอุดมการณ์การเมืองไทย [Trai Phum Phra Ruang: The Foundation of Thai Political Ideology]. *Thammasart Journal* 4 (1): 106–21.

Connors, Michael. 2002. “Framing the People’s Constitution.” In *Reforming Thai Politics*, edited by Duncan McCargo, 37–55. Copenhagen: NIAS Press.

2008. “Article of Faith: The Failure of Royal Liberalism in Thailand.” *Journal of Contemporary Asia* 38 (1): 143–65.

Desatova, Petra and Alexander, Saowanee T. 2021. *Election Commissions and Non-democratic Outcomes: Thailand’s Contentious 2019 Election*. Thousand Oaks: Politics. https://doi.org/10.1177/02633957211000978.

Dissatat Hotrakit. 2011. องค์กรของรัฐที่เป็นอิสระในระบบกฎหมายไทย [Independent State Entity in Thai Legal System]. In *แทนดอกไม้ไหว้ครู* [Gratitude to Professor Wisanu Krue-ngam], edited by Narongdech Srukhosit, 39–52. Bangkok: S Charoen Printing Co., Ltd.

Dressel, Björn. 2010. “Judicialization of Politics or Politicization of the Judiciary? Considerations from Recent Events in Thailand.” *Pacific Review* 23 (5): 671–91.

2018. "Thailand's Traditional Trinity and the Rule of Law: Can They Coexist?" *Asian Studies Review* 42 (2): 268–85.

Dressel, Björn and Khemthong Tonsakulrungruang. 2019. "Coloured Judgements? The Work of the Thai Constitutional Court, 1998–2016." *Journal of Contemporary Asia* 19 (1): 1–23.

Gabaude, Louis. 1990. "Thai Society and Buddhadasa: Structural Difficulties." In *Radical Conservativism Buddhism in the Contemporary World*, edited by Sulak Sivaraksa, 211–29. Bangkok: International Network of Engaged Buddhism.

Gray, Christine. 1986. *Thailand: The Soteriological State in the 1970s*. PhD dissertation, Anthropology: The Faculty of The Division of Social Sciences, University of Chicago.

Haberkorn, Tyrell. 2018. *In Plain Sight: Impunity and Human Rights in Thailand*. Wisconsin: The University of Wisconsin Press.

Harding, Andrew and Leyland, Peter. 2010. *The Constitutional System of Thailand: A Contextual Analysis*. Oxford and Portland: Hart.

Harding, Andrew and Munin Pongsapan, eds. 2021. *Thai Legal History: From Traditional to Modern Law*. Cambridge: Cambridge University Press.

Hewison, Kevin. 2010. "Thaksin Shinawatra and the Reshaping of Thai Politics." *Contemporary Politics* 16 (2): 119–33.

2015. "Thailand: Contestation Over Elections, Sovereignty and Representation." *Journal of Representative Democracy* 51 (1): 51–62.

Hewison, Kevin and Kengkij Kitirianglarp. 2010. "Thai-Style Democracy: The Royalist Struggle for Thailand's Politics." In *Saying the Unsayable: Monarchy and Democracy in Thailand*, edited by Søren Ivarsson and Lotte Isager, 179–202. Copenhagen: NIAS Press.

Igunma, Jana. 2013. "A Buddhist Monk's Journeys to Heaven and Hell." *The Journal of the International Association of Buddhist Universities* 6 (3): 65–82.

Ishii, Yoneo. 1986. *Sangha, State, and Society: Thai Buddhism in History*. Kyoto: Central for Southeast Asian Studies, Kyoto University.

Jackson, Peter A. 1989. *Buddhism, Legitimation, and Conflict: The Political Functions of Urban Thai Buddhism*. Singapore: Institute of Southeast Asian Studies.

1993. "Re-interpreting the *Traiphuum Phra Ruang*: Political Functions of Buddhist Symbolism in Contemporary Thailand." In *Buddhist Trends in Southeast Asia*, edited by Trevor Ling, 64–100. Singapore: Institute of Southeast Asian Studies.

2002. "Thai and Western Buddhist Scholarship in the Age of Colonization: King Chulalongkorn Redefines the Jatakas." *The Journal of Asian Studies* 61 (3): 891–918.

2003. *Buddhadasa: Theravada Buddhism and Modernist Reform in Thailand*. Chiang Mai: Silkworms.

Jory, Patrick. 2016. *Thailand's Theory of Monarchy: The Vessantara Jātaka and the Idea of the Perfect Man*. New York: SUNY Press.

Kasian Tejapira. 2006. "Toppling Thaksin." *New Left Review* 39 (May–June): 5–37

Katewadee Kularbkeaw. 2019. *The Politics of Thai Buddhism under the NCPO Junta*. Singapore: ISEAS-Yusof Ishak Institute.

Khemthong Tonsakulrungruang. 2016. 'Thailand: An Abuse of Judicial Review.' In *The Judicial Review of Elections in Asia*, edited by Yap Po Jen. Routledge.

2017. "Entrenching the Minority: The Constitutional Court in Thailand's Political Conflict." *Washington International Law Journal* 26 (2): 247–68.

2018. "The Constitutional Court of Thailand: From Activism to Arbitrariness." In *Constitutional Courts in Asia: A Comparative Perspective*, edited by Albert H. Y. Chen and Andrew Harding, 184–213. New York: Cambridge University Press.

2019. "Constitutional Amendment in Thailand: Amending in the Spectre of Parliamentary Dictatorship." *Journal of Comparative Law* 14 (1): 173–87.

2021. "The Revival of Buddhist Nationalism in Thailand and Its Adverse Impact on Religious Freedom." *Asian Journal of Law and Society*. https://doi.org/10.1017/als.2020.48.

Kom Chad Luek. 2012. พระกำลังแผ่นดินกำลังแรง!'ทั้งพุทธคุณและค่านิยม' [The Sacred and Popular Amulet of the Land]. Last modified December 4, 2012. www.komchadluek.net/news/lifestyle/146362.

Landau, David and Dixon, Rosalind. 2020. "Abusive Judicial Review: Court against Democracy." *U.C. Davis Law Review* 53 (3): 1313–87.

Larsson, Thomas. 2018. "Buddhist Bureaucracy and Religious Freedom in Thailand." *Journal of Law and Religion* 33 (2): 197–211.

MGR Online. 2016. พระอริยสงฆ์ กับ "ในหลวง รัชกาลที่ 9" [Enlightened Monks and Rama IX King]. Last modified November 1, 2016. https://mgronline.com/dhamma/detail/9590000109033.

Matichon. 2016. เผย 'หมอกขุมเกตุ' ปกคลุมกรุง อาลัยพระบาทสมเด็จพระเจ้าอยู่หัวในพระบรมโกศ [Fog Mourning the Late King]. Last modified October 1, 2016. www.matichon.co.th/local/news_320906.

McCargo, Duncan. 1998. "Alternative Meanings of Political Reform in Contemporary Thailand." *The Copenhagen Journal of Asian Studies* 13 (5): 5–30.

2005. "Network Monarchy and Legitimacy Crises in Thailand." *The Pacific Review* 18 (4): 499–519.

Mérieau, Eugenie. 2018. "Buddhist Constitutionalism in Thailand: When Rājadhammā Supersedes the Constitution." *Asian Journal of Comparative Law* 13 (2): 283–305. doi:10.1017/asjcl.2018.16.

Nelson, Michael H. 2010. "People's Alliance for Democracy: From 'New Politics' to a 'Real' Political Party?" In *Legitimacy Crisis and Political Conflict in Thailand*, edited by Marc Askew, 119–59. Chiang Mai: Silkworm Books.

Nidhi Eowsriwong. 2012. *ปากไก่และใบเรือ* [Pen and Sail]. 4th ed. Nonthaburi: Same Sky Book.

Phibul Choompolpaisal. 2015. "Political Buddhism and the Modernisation of Thai Monastic Education: From Wachirayan to Phimonlatham (1880s–1960s)." *Contemporary Buddhism* 16 (2): 428–50.

Pinyapan Potjanalawan. 2019. *ไทยปิฎก* [Thai-pitaka]. Bangkok: Illuminations Editions.

Piyabutr Saengkanokkul. 2017. *ศาลรัฐประหาร: ตุลาการ ระบอบเผด็จการ และนิติรัฐประหาร* [The Court of Coup: Judiciary, Dictatorial Regime, and Legal Coup]. Nonthaburi: Same Sky Book.

Prapod Assavavirulhakarn. 2010. *The Ascendancy of Theravada Buddhism in Southeast Asia*. Chiang Mai: Silkworm.

Reynolds, Craig J. 1976. "Buddhist Cosmography in Thai History, with Special Reference to Nineteenth-Century Culture Change." *The Journal of Asian Studies* 35 (2): 203–20.

Schalk, Peter. 1991. "The Sinhala Concept of 'Dharmacracy' as an Obstacle to Peace in a Crisis of the State." In *Asian Societies in Comparative Perspective: Nordic Proceedings in Asian Studies* 2, 929–54. Denmark: Nordic Institute of Asian Studies and Scandinavian South and East Asian Researchers.

Siamrath. 2016. กฤษดาภินิหารของ ในหลวงฯที่ "คึกฤทธิ์" เห็น [The King's Miracle as Kukrit Pramoj Had Seen]. Last modified October 1, 2016. https://siamrath.co.th/n/5229.

Skilling, Peter. 2007. "King, Sangha, and Brahmans." In *Buddhism, Power, and Political Order*, edited by Ian Harris, 182–215. New York: Routledge.

Somchai Preechasinlapakul. 2018. "ศาลรัฐธรรมนูญ ที่ไร้ผู้เชี่ยวชาญรัฐธรรมนูญ" [The Constitutional Court without Constitutional Experts]. Last modified July 11, 2018. The 101 World. www.the101.world/constitutional-court-without-constitution-expert/.

Streckfuss, David. 2011. *Truth on Trial in Thailand: Defamation, Treason, and Lese Majeste*. London: Routledge.

Sunait Chutintaranond. 1990. "'Mandala,' 'Segmentary State' and Politics of Centralization in Medieval Ayudhaya." *Journal of Siam Society* 78 (1): 88–100.

Sweaerer, Donald. 2010. *The Buddhist World of Southeast Asia*. 2nd ed. Albany: State University of New York Press.

Tambiah, Stanley J. 1976. *World Conqueror and World Renouncer*. Cambridge: Cambridge University Press.

Terwiel, Barrend Jan. *Monks and Magic: Revisiting a Classic Study of Religious Ceremonies in Thailand*. Copenhagen: NIAS Press.

Thailand Research Fund. 2017. *การปฏิรูปการเมืองไทย ฐานคิดและข้อเสนอว่าด้วยการออกแบบรัฐธรรมนูญฉบับประชาชน ปี 2540* [Thai Political Reform: Conceptual Basis and Proposal on Constitutional Design for the People's Constitution B.E. 2540]. Bangkok: Thailand Research Fund.

Thongchai Winichakul 1994. *Siam Mapped: A History of the Geo-Body of a Nation*. Honolulu: The University of Hawai'i Press.

2015. "Buddhist Apologetics and a Genealogy of Comparative Religion in Siam." *Numen* 62 (1): 75–99.

2016. *Thailand's Hyper-Royalism: Its Past Success and Present Predicament*. Singapore: ISEAS–Yusof Ishak Institute.

2018. "Toppling Democracy." *Journal of Contemporary Asia* 38 (1): 11–37.

2021. นิติรัฐอภิสิทธิ์และราชนิติธรรม: ประวัติศาสตร์ภูมิปัญญาของ Rule by Law แบบไทย [Thai-style Rule of Law and Legal State]. In *รัฐราชาชาติ ว่าด้วยรัฐไทยในปัจจุบัน* [The Royalist Nationalist State: On Contemporary Thai State], edited by Thongchai Winichakul, 135–232. Nonthaburi: Same Sky Book.

Ukrist Pathmanand. 2008. "Nation, Religion and Monarchy in the Fight against Thaksin." Last modified August 13, 2008. New Mandala. www.newmandala.org/nation-religion-and-monarchy-in-the-fight-against-thaksin/

Veerayooth Kanchoochat. 2016. "Reign-Seeking and the Rise of the Unelected in Thailand." *Journal of Contemporary Asia* 46 (3): 486–503.

Vibert, Frank. 2007. *The Rise of the Unelected: Democracy and the New Separation of Power*. Cambridge: Cambridge University Press.

Wanpat Youngmevittaya. 2017. พุทธทาสกับการให้ความชอบธรรมต่ออุดมการณ์แห่งรัฐไทย [Buddhadasa and the Legitimation for the Ideology of the Thai State]. *Journal of Social Science Naresuan University* 13 (1): 181–224.

9

Establishing the King as the Source of the Constitution

Shifting 'Bricolaged' Narratives of Buddhist Kingship from Siam to Thailand

Eugénie Mérieau

9.1 INTRODUCTION

Thailand's constitutional order, as defined and redefined constantly by courts, scholars, and kings from the late nineteenth century until present, is a bricolage of constitutional monarchy and Buddhist kingship (Mérieau 2021b). In the mid-nineteenth century, doctrines of law and kingship still relied mostly on concepts derived from Hinduism and Buddhism. These doctrines were expressed in religious texts, treatises, and tales as well as in the *Phrathammasat* portion of the Three Seals Code, dating back from the Chakri Reformation of the early nineteenth century. From the late nineteenth century, in its quest to become "civilized" (*siwilai*) and to escape colonization, Siam engaged in a process of legal "modernisation" (Thongchai 2000). Thai modern legal categories, concepts, rules, and doctrines were creatively invented, based on borrowings from Western countries (from both common law and civil law traditions), then hybridised with "re-invented" indigenous categories, often rooted in Buddhism.

In particular, Thai scholars and jurists indigenised European legal categories by creating neologisms based on Pali, the sacred language of Theravāda Buddhist scriptures, and by fusing European doctrines with similar Buddhist narratives. Besides the well-known history of the lèse-majesté law (Streckfuss 2011, Mérieau 2021a), one of these foundational "mergers" includes the hybridisation of the European, monarchist, myth of the royal constitutional "octroy" (the king as the source of law, who benevolently grants the Constitution to his subjects) with the Thai Hindu-Buddhist myth of the *dhammarāja* king (the king is the upholder of the dharma/natural law, who turns the wheel of the law). As a result, the king became, in Thai doctrine, both the granter and "turner" of the country's foundational law, the source of the Thai constitutional order. This ideal was enshrined in the preambles of the successive Thai constitutions from 1932 until this day, embodied in state institutions and reenacted in various state ceremonies, themselves "bricolaged" using Buddhist and Western symbolism, such as the ceremony of royal "constitution-granting." The narrative of the king as the source of the Constitution is one of the key aspects of Thailand's "Buddhist constitutionalism" (Mérieau 2018).

The current Constitution, the 2017 Constitution, was "granted" (de jure: promulgated) by King Vajiralongkorn on 6 April 2017 – the date of the anniversary of the Chakri dynasty's foundation. The ritual depicted the king, seated on a golden throne, signing the book of the Constitution in three copies to a kneeling then-leader of the military junta, General Prayuth Chan-ocha (now "elected" Prime Minister). The Constitution, in the form of a folded golden book called *samutthai*, was handed back and forth between the king and the leader of the military junta on a golden tray used to pass sacred objects and/or to pass objects from/to sacred people, called a *phanwenfa*. The ceremony presented the Constitution as rooted in an ancient tradition of Thai law drawing on Hindu and Buddhist ideas and images. Echoing the tripartite nature of the Buddhist canon (Pali: Tipiṭaka, literally three baskets), the *samutthai* was kept in three thrice-folded copies. The golden tray symbolised the royal gift of a sacred constitution: the king was here performing the ritual of "constitutional octroy" according to which the Constitution is a sacred grant of the king onto his people.

Yet, the imagery was a bricolage of the European idea of law as a gift from the king with the Hindu-Buddhist idea of the king as the upholder and turner of the sacred law, the dhamma. In this construction, the king is not only the source of the positive legal order, but also the upholder of the natural (cosmic) legal order. This doctrinal bricolage, as performed in the "constitution-granting" ritual, undoubtedly aims to consolidate the king's authority and legitimacy. Yet, it is not without its challenges, as a bitter competition for legal supremacy plays out between the king and the Constitution (or rather, between their respective defenders), a conflict which still remains at the heart of the current Thai political crisis. This chapter will trace this process of doctrinal bricolage from the nineteenth century until present and reflect on some of its implications.

9.2 THE KING-*DHAMMARĀJA* AS UPHOLDER OF THE 'ANCIENT CONSTITUTION' IN THE *PHRATHAMMASAT* OF THE THREE SEALS CODE (1805)

In the mid-nineteenth century, the laws governing the Siamese monarchy were part of a wider body of legal prescriptions assembled in a code called the "Three Seals Code" (*kotmai tra sam duang*). The Three Seals Code had been compiled on the order of Phraputtayotfachulalok (r. 1782–1809), later known as Rama I, the founder of the Chakri dynasty, by a commission of royal scribes, pundits, and *brāhmaṇas* (Lingat 1929; Wales 1934). It was named after the three seals of the north (mythological lion), south (mythological elephant), and centre (crystal lotus) corresponding respectively to the Ministry of the Interior, the Ministry of Defence, and the Ministry of Finance, a testimony to the territorial rather than functional organisation of the ancient administration of Siam. Three official copies of the Code were kept: one was deposited at the Royal Library, another in the king's apartment, and a third in the Court of Justice.

9.2.1 *The King According to the* Phrathammasat

The Three Seals Code contained a reconstructed version of the old laws of Siam, dating back to the Ayutthaya, Thonburi, and early Bangkok periods. It had three components: the *Phrathammasat* exposing the various sources of disputes (*mula-khadi*) as derived, it claimed, from the Hindu Code of Manu; the *Phrarachasat* detailing the various "ramifications of disputes" – namely, laws/rulings claimed to be made by kings based on the principles of the *Phrathammasat*; and other pieces of royal legislation not claimed to be derived from the *Phrathammasat*, called the *Phrarachanitisat*, which were concerned mostly with administrative matters, such as key royal edicts on legal procedures and civil and military administration, but also to some extent with constitutional matters, such as the palace Law (*kot montien ban*) regulating the exercise of royal power.

The *Phrathammasat* opens with a mention of the Three Jewels: the Buddha, "discoverer of the Four Noble Truths," the dhamma, or "nine transcendental practices, to which must be added knowledge," and finally the sangha, "the noble community of the eight perfect disciples of the monk community." The text glorifies the ideal of kingship as practiced by past kings as *dhammarāja* or Buddhist righteous rulers, who governed according to the Ten Virtues of a Righteous King (*totsapit-rajadharma*) (Saichon 2003; Thianpanya 2008). In its normative components, the *Phrathammasat* also states that the king ought to subject his rule to the "Ten Virtues of a Righteous King" as well as the *thammasat* at all times. Therefore, according to the *Phrathammasat*, the Siamese king ought not to have legislative power, as the king was only to have adjudicating powers: namely, his role was to apply the *thammasat*, not to modify it (Lingat 1941, 26–31).[1] The *Phrathammasat* also established kings as bodhisattva, or Buddha-to-be, as *cakravartin*, or universal sovereign rulers, and finally as *mahāsammata* or great elected kings.

9.2.2 *The King*-Mahāsammata *Doctrine*

Besides being a *cakravartin* and a bodhisattva, the *dhammarāja* is also referred to in the *Phrathammasat* as a *mahāsammata*. The *Phrathammasat* opens with the following tale of origin: "A Lord bodhisattva was born as a great man at the start of this era. After a time, disputes arose, and nobody could be found to control them. Everyone came together in a meeting and appointed this great man to be the ruler

[1] On the actual practice of royal law-making during the Ayuthaya Kingdom and early Rattanakosin kingdoms, see Baker and Phongpaichit 2021.

with the name King Mahāsammata, equipped with the seven gem attributes [referring to the *cakravartin*][2], and accepted by all four continents." (translation in Baker and Pongpaichit 2016, 106). In the *Phrathammasat*, the *mahāsammata* king is elected by popular acclamation for his qualities, as the "most capable" person to end chaos through the implementation of the dhamma. The *mahāsammata* theory thus posits a contractual basis of kingship, but without discarding the religious origin of kingship.[3] Indeed, the *Phrathammasat* states that the king was chosen by the people based on his previously accumulated merit, which allowed him to claim sovereignty and rule over the people:

> All the branch matters described here [were created by] past kings [who] had miraculous wisdom and accumulated merit (*barami*) to be rulers over the populace, to have fought with enemies, and to be powerful under the splendid white umbrella, upholding moral truth, honesty, good conduct with wisdom, insight and reason, with the intention to make the city and territory within the realm prosper in happiness and joy. (Baker and Phongpaichit 2016, 100)

According to the *Phrathammasat*, kingship is acquired through the principle of karmic retribution: the king reigns "thanks to the power of his merits" and this is the basis of his "popular" election. As Stanley Tambiah puts it:

> [The] elective theory of kingship is counterbalanced by asserting at the same time that Mahāsammata was a virtuous man, an embodiment of dharma and destined to become a Buddha; and that it was as his minister that the sage Manu discovered the perfect law. Thus we see how a contractual theory of government is yoked to the charismatic properties of kingship, thereby constantly compelling the pragmatics of politics to measure itself against an enduring standard. (1976, 13)

9.2.3 *Secularisation of the King-*dhammarāja *Doctrine*

The beliefs or religious-legal doctrines of kingship listed above, as written in the *Phrathammasat*, have their origins in the Pali Canon, most notably in the *Aggañña Sutta* and the *jātaka* or tales of the past lives of Buddha, as well as in various treatises and epics, most notably the *Three Worlds*, a book about heavens and hells that contains the first systematic description of the world according to the Buddhist cosmology, and the *Ramakien*, a Siamese version of the Ramayana. These were rewritten in the early nineteenth century, prior to the launch of the legal

[2] The seven gem attributes are those of a *cakravartin* or universal ruler, as described in the cosmogony of the Three Worlds: the gem wheel, the gem elephant, the gem horse, the gem woman, the gem treasurer, the gem son, and the gem jewel (Reynolds and Reynolds 1982, 125–72).

[3] On the idea of contract, see Huxley 1996 and Collins 1996.

codification process, on the order of Rama I as part of his project of the restoration of royal authority relying on Buddhism (Wenk 1968; Wyatt 1982).

Among the *jātaka* tales, Rama I placed particular emphasis on the tale of the very last incarnation of the Buddha as Prince Vessantara (Wales 1931, 31; Jory 2016). In the tale, the prince gives away everything he possesses, including his wife and children, to attain enlightenment, and this is precisely how he succeeds in becoming the Buddha. In his version of the *Three Worlds*, Rama I placed particular emphasis on the story of the King-*dhammarāja* (*cakravartin*-bodhisattva), which he put at the very centre of the story.[4] Lastly, his version of the *Ramakien* tells the story of a prince, Phra Ram, said to exhibit the practice of the "Ten Virtues of a Righteous King." He is also of divine nature as an avatar of the god Vishnu (Phra Narai in Thai). Thanks to his royal virtues, his fights with demons to save his abducted wife Sita are ultimately victorious. These three stories, as rewritten in the early nineteenth century on the order of Rama I, included powerful allegories of the Siamese concept of royalty, which underscored the ideals of Buddhist royal virtue mentioned above. In the end, both the *Three Worlds* and the Tipiṭaka were referred to in the preface to the *Phrathammasat* (Baker and Pasuk 2016, 104), but the *Ramakien* was not.

From the mid-nineteenth century, the tale of Vessantara, the *Three Worlds*, and the *Ramakien* began to be progressively reduced to the status of non-historical, non-scientific "tales," while the Hindu gods were downgraded to make way for the worship owed to the Buddha. The Siamese kings were nonetheless considered *sommuthithep* or "supposed gods," avatars of Vishnu or Shiva, an idea that was reenacted in state ceremonies (Riggs 1966, 99). Yet, the entire scientific and historical character of Buddhist literature was discarded. The *jātakas* and stories of

[4] Chapter 1 deals with the realm of hell beings, Chapter 2 with the realm of animals, Chapter 3 with the realm of the suffering ghosts, Chapter 4 with the realm of the Asura, Chapter 5 with the realm of men, Chapter 6 with the realm of the *devata*, Chapter 7 with the world with only a remnant of material factors, Chapter 8 with the world without material form, Chapter 9 with the Cakkavaka and the Jambu continent, Chapter 10 with the destruction and renewal of the Mahakappa, and Chapter 11 with *nibbana* and the path. Originally written in the times of Ayuthaya and rewritten at the time of the Chakri Reformation, it describes a world composed of thirty-one levels of birth and rebirth governed by the laws of karma and *dharma*. According to the *Three Worlds* cosmogony, the highest levels of the cosmos are the realm of the *brahma* (*phrom*), whereas *thevada* or *thep* inhabit inferior levels. Dusit, the fourth level of paradise, is the house of the *bodhisatva* before he returns as Buddha. The *sommuthithep* Buddhist King finds himself at the summit of the terrestrial hierarchy, acting as an interface between hell and paradise. In the fourteenth-century version, the character of the Universal Monarch, called *chakravatin*, appears halfway through the book, between hell and paradise. He is described as resting in his Palace when the Wheel of the Law, the Dharmachak, rises out of the Ocean to reward his practice of the ten Buddhist Virtues. Then, turning the Wheel of the Law, the Universal Monarch conquers the four continents of the Universe, before returning to the Palace. His triumphant return is welcomed by the apparition of celestial attributes: woman, elephant, horse etc. See Reynolds and Reynolds 1982. In the Rama I version of the *Three Worlds*, the Book opens on the very figure of the Dharmaraja.

the life of the Buddhas, which until then had been considered historical facts, as well as the *Three Worlds*, which until then had been considered somewhat of a treatise on geography (Thongchai 1994) were reassessed and rebranded as "folk tales": they became part of the Western category of literature. The theories of the bodhisattva and *cakravartin* as well as the *mahāsammata* were likewise dismissed as old superstitions (Jory 2016, 21).

The general movement towards rationalisation and secularisation that had been born out of the encounter with the West was bringing about new challenges to the monarchy. The monarch could no longer derive his authority simply from a supposed lineage linking him to the Buddha, nor from his status as Buddha-to-be or universal sovereign. Instead, the monarchy would have to base its legitimacy on the dynastic principle pertaining to a specific territory and population. The *mahāsammata* doctrine of the elected king would have to be secularised and "legalised" to make it acceptable by Western standards. At the same time, based on European understandings of law and kingship, new tools and doctrines of sovereignty could be devised to enable Siamese kings to acquire effective legislative power and then use the law to consolidate their authority. Among these tools, the principle of a modern constitution soon appealed to Siamese kings.

9.3 THE KING-*DHAMMARĀJA* IN THE 1932 "GRANTED" CONSTITUTION

From the end of the nineteenth century to the first decades of the twentieth century, successive Thai kings Chulalongkorn (r. 1868–1910), Vajiravudh (r. 1910–25) and Prajadhipok (r. 1925–35) engaged in various constitution-drafting projects. In order to establish absolutism, King Chulalongkorn had a Bonapartist Constitution (but without a parliament) drafted by an advisor in 1889.[5] His successors, King Vajiravudh and King Prajadhipok, likewise engaged in constitution-drafting experiments, in 1918,[6] 1926,[7] and 1932,[8] drawing from various models derived from the unwritten British Constitution, but all nonetheless articulated around the project of securing royal sovereignty.

These constitutional drafts all attempted to consolidate royal authority by establishing the king as the source of the Constitution and increasing his legislative powers, drawing on the nineteenth-century European model of so-called limited monarchy, especially in its Bonapartist version, as well as on the newly imported tenets of legal positivism, which vested legal authority in the dicta of sovereigns

5 พระราชกฤษฎีกาฉบับ ๑ ว่าด้วยราชประเพณีกรุงสยาม [1889 First Law on Royal Custom in Siam].

6 ธรรมนูญ ดุสิตธานี ลักษณปกครองคณะนนาคาภิบาล [1918 Constitution of the Administration of the Municipality], 7 November 1918.

7 'An Outline of Preliminary Draft' [Francis B. Sayre's draft Constitution], 27 July 1926.

8 'An Outline of Changes in the Form of Government' [Phraya Sriwisanwacha – Raymond B. Stevens draft Constitution], March 1932.

rather than cosmic principles. In particular, kings and their legal advisors looked to the doctrine of "granted constitutionalism," which established the king as the sovereign source of the Constitution, a modern construct from continental European monarchies, which could easily be hybridised with traditional theories of Buddhist kingship.

9.3.1 *The Bricolage of the Word "Constitution"* ("Rattathammanun")

These endeavours, however, were hijacked by the 1932 Revolution, which abolished the absolute monarchy in Siam. In June 1932, the People's Party, under the leadership of French-educated jurist Pridi Banomyong, imposed a constitution on King Prajadhipok. As the concept of "constitution" was imported, Pridi and his group needed to create a Thai term for it. To translate the foreign word "constitution," they could either build a secularised term, or a term rooted in the Buddhist idea of law, dhamma, *thamma* in Thai. The People's Party chose to rely on terms found in the Three Seals Code and called its first constitution the "Fundamental Rule of Procedure for the Administration of Siam" (*phrarachabanyat thammanun kan pokkrong phaendin*). *Phrarachabanyat* referred at the time to royal legislation, while *thammanun* referred to dhamma: in the Three Seals Code, the title containing the cosmic law discovered by Manu was called *laksana phrathammanun*. Finally, *phaendin* was the traditional term for territory, which was strongly associated with traditional conceptions of kingship. The term was thus entirely rooted in Thai traditional concepts of law and kingship.

The term however did not survive long. An influential prince who was sympathetic to the revolution, Oxford-educated Wan Waithayakon, proposed a new word: *rattathammanun*, based on a new, secularist, Western-oriented word *rat* for state and on the traditional, Buddhist-derived word *thammanun*. To him, a constitution was "sacred" (*saksith*) and the word used to refer to it should denote this sacredness. At the same time, a constitution was also a modern construct based on Western political concepts, such as the idea of a nation-state. In accordance with Prince Wan's proposal, the following Constitution, adopted in December of the same year, was called *rattathammanun*, mixing Buddhist and Western conceptions of law and kingship.

9.3.2 *Merging the King-*dhammarāja *Doctrine and Doctrine of "Granted Constitutionalism"*

The preamble of the December 1932 Constitution enshrined Hindu-Buddhist doctrines of kingship. It stated that the Constitution, on the one hand, had been "granted" (*phrarachathan*) *by* the king and, on the other hand, bestowed *upon* the king the duty "to preserve the country eternally". The preamble delved into the "150 years of absolute monarchy under the principle of the Ten Virtues of a Righteous

King." The king's full name with titles, added to the preamble of the Constitution, occupied the whole of the first page of the Constitution in thirteen lines. He bore the titles of bodhisattva, *mahāsammata*, Great Elect, *cakravartin*, divine angel, reincarnation of Vishnu, and, last but not least, *dhammarāja*. In the first title of the Constitution, dealing with kingship, the traditional conceptions of kingship and the law were twisted and secularised: as the supreme commander of the army, the king was associated with the traditional function of *cakravartin*, as the patron of Buddhism, with that of bodhisattva, and as the sovereign exercising legislative, executive, and judicial power in the name of the people, with the *dhammarāja–mahāsammata*.

The December 1932 Constitution stated that sovereignty did not *belong to* Siamese subjects but "*emanate[d] from* the people," being "exercised by the king in accordance with the dispositions of this Constitution" (Article 2). Sovereignty was referred to by a new term, *amnatipatai*, formed from a Pali suffix. According to Phraya Sriwisanwacha, one of the key drafters of the December Constitution:

> When we say that sovereignty comes from the people, it means that the king ascends the throne upon *invitation by* the people, what is in conformity with our old precept which stated in the name of the king that he had been elected. (Nattapol 2013, 16)

Likewise, Prime Minister Phraya Manopakorn Nithithada explained that this article on sovereignty and the doctrine it relied on in fact derived from the *mahāsammata* doctrine:

> In reality, the first part of the article [on sovereignty] is simply a reaffirmation of our ancient traditions (*phrapheni boran*). Indeed, if we open ancient books, it is said in the very name of the king that he has been elected; in the coronation ceremony, there are brahmins and high civil servants who give the crown jewels, representing the fact that the king ascends the throne at the invitation of the people and not by Heaven's Will, what some foreign countries cannot understand. (Noranit 2009, 19)

In the parliamentary debates of 1932, Phraya Manopakorn Nithithada also explained that the Constitution was "granted" by the king, therefore the king always retained sovereignty, as he pre-existed the Constitution. But, because he was "elected," he did so "in the name of the people." This rationale justified why the Constitution did not mandate that the king swear an oath of allegiance to uphold it. As a member of the Constitution-drafting committee explained: "We know well that the king must swear an oath before the representatives of the Theravāda gods, as well as Buddha, etc. Consequently, [the text] can remain silent [on the issue of the royal oath to the Constitution]" (Noranit 2009, 48).

The result is that, in the Siamese constitutional imaginary of that time, the king was accountable to Theravāda gods and dhamma, but not to the Constitution he "gave"; he must uphold dhamma but does not need to submit himself to "his own"

Constitution. Therefore, the 1932 Constitution, which by all accounts resembled a Western parliamentary monarchy constitution, was nevertheless very much influenced by the king-*dhammarāja* doctrine. The king remained, albeit in a modernised and more symbolic form, the law-giver or, rather, the constitution-giver.

9.3.3 *The Cult of the Sacred Constitution (as a Royal Gift)*

It must be noted that during this time, religious discourse increasingly permeated the way the Constitution was understood: members of the People's Party framed the Constitution as "sacred" (*rattathammanun saksith*) (Nattapol 2013, 18–19; Suthachai 2008, 33–34; Bandit 2007, 13) precisely because it had been a "king's octroy" (*rattathammanun phrarachathan*). In 1933, as a royalist counterrevolution was looming large, revolutionaries including Pridi Banomyong used the idea of the "royally granted constitution" to mobilise people throughout the country in its defence, despite the fact that they had fought for the recognition of parliamentary sovereignty at the expense of royal sovereignty. Symbolically, constitutional supremacy was replacing royal supremacy, even while drawing its legitimacy from the monarchy and borrowing its modes of legitimation, many of which had their roots in Buddhism. Eventually, the royalist counterrevolution was defeated, and its leaders went into exile.

From 1934, as a way to consolidate the revolution, the government, led by Pridi as minister of the interior, continued to work hard to shift the locus of sacredness from the monarchy to the Constitution. The Constitution became the object of a truly official cult. An "Association for the Constitution" (*samakhom khana rattathammanoon*), with branches all over the country, organised celebrations and marches in the honour of the Constitution, mimicking past ceremonies for the king (Puli 2018). The Constitution was worshipped as a "royal gift," angering then-King Prajadhipok. In his last words before abdication, as he hopelessly pleaded with the government to get back some of his old, customary royal prerogatives, he wrote to the members of the People's Party: "The Constitution should not be sacred, it should be revisable. It is not right to venerate it with scented candles as you do, venerating the Constitution is a joke!" (Mérieau 2021, 99). Following Prajadhipok's abdication in March 1935, the People's Party aimed to fill the void left by the disappearance of the figure of the king by relying even more on the cult of the Constitution. Firmly in power, and without a king, the People's Party commissioned two monuments to honour the new cult of the Constitution.

The first edifice, called "Safeguarding the Constitution" was built in 1936 to commemorate the victory of the People's Party over the attempted royalist counterrevolution led by Prince Boworadet in 1933. It is the burial site of the remains of those who "fought and died for the Constitution" (Thanavi 2018, 235). A second monument, the "Democracy Monument," was commissioned in 1939 to commemorate the 1932 abolition of the absolute monarchy. It portrays Thai democracy as being composed of five elements: the four branches of the Thai security forces (Army, Navy, Air Force, and Thai police) at the periphery, and the Constitution, at its core. The Constitution is represented in a Buddhist-scripture-like longitudinal book made of golden palm leaves, the *samutthai*, placed on top of two royal golden trays used for sacred objects – the *phanwenfa* – in effect, displaying the Constitution as a sacred object. The security forces are represented by three erect, obelisk-like, 24-metre-high wings surrounding and overlooking the Constitution. The monument embodies the following narrative: that democracy takes the form of a sacred "granted" Constitution, whose guardian is the military (Nidhi 2004, 106). In both these monuments, it is the Constitution, rather than the king, that becomes the sacred centre of the nation: the Democracy Monument also marks Thailand's "kilometre zero" – the central location from which all distances are measured (Thanavi 2016). As such, it is the Constitution that becomes the rallying symbol of the nation.

9.4 THE KING-*DHAMMARĀJA* IN CONTEMPORARY CONSTITUTIONAL DOCTRINE

Following King Prajadhipok's abdication in 1935, his nephew, Ananda Mahidol, was proclaimed king by the Assembly. As he was then a young student in Switzerland, a council of regents was appointed, giving the People's Party free rein to design Thai political institutions and eradicate any traces of royal sovereignty. From Ananda's return to the kingdom in 1946 onwards, the monarchy started to reclaim Buddhism at the expense of the People's Party and reaffirm its role as *dhammarāja*-source of the Constitution.

9.4.1 *Duties of a King: Performing Constitution-Granting Ceremonies*

In 1946, King Ananda Mahidol agreed to return to the kingdom at the request of then-prime minister Pridi Banomyong in order to promulgate the 1946 Constitution: for Pridi, it was important to have the king ritually re-enact the myth of the "royal octroy" in order to make the 1946 Constitution as "sacred" as its predecessor, the December 1932 Constitution. The ceremony was grandiose and seemed to mark the reconciliation between the monarchy and the People's Party. However, a few days later, King Ananda died from a bullet wound in the head in his palace bedchamber. Amidst the state of general shock and confusion, his younger brother, Bhumibol Adulyadej was named king as Rama IX. He was crowned in May 1950 in a traditional Hindu-Buddhist ceremony in which he made clear that he was mobilising Buddhist narratives on kingship to establish his authority as a *dhammarāja*. He pronounced the following, very short Accession Speech: "I shall reign by dharma, for the benefit and happiness of all the Thai people."

The return of Bhumibol to the kingdom coincided with the rise of military dictatorship. In 1957, US-backed General Sarit Thanarat seized power in a coup, with the support of the king. General Sarit had nothing but contempt for the constitutional project, which he considered alien to Thai culture. Yet he appointed a constitution-drafting assembly, which doubled as acting legislative assembly, and whose work continued until after his death in 1963. In 1968, the Assembly had finally a complete text: it was promulgated in great pomp by King Bhumibol in a ceremony of "royal octroy" (Darling 1977, 117). The king, seated on his throne, signed the three copies of the Constitution on a *phanwenfa* tray, given to his people. The ceremony was televised and photographed, with copies distributed all over the kingdom for people to worship. Bhumibol had presided over his first "constitution-granting ceremony," just as Prajadhipok had done in 1932 and Ananda in 1946. Even though the 1968 Constitution did not last long – it would be abolished by a coup in 1971 – this ceremony marked a turning point: from this moment, King Bhumibol would increasingly act as a modern *dhammarāja*, or at least his actions would increasingly be interpreted as such by the legal profession. The concept of *dhammarāja* would invite itself back into law handbooks, articles, and essays.

Bhumibol had a first occasion to project an image of true *dhammarāja* in 1973. That year, students demanded that the military, which had come to power in the 1971 coup, resign and let them draft a new, democratic constitution. On 14 October 1973, they organised mass protests all over Bangkok. The king offered shelter and protection in his palace to the students who were fleeing the police. These moments were photographed, and the photographs distributed throughout the kingdom. Thanks to the king's intervention, the protests were successful: the military government resigned, and Bhumibol "granted" the students a prime minister of his own choice but to their liking, Sanya Dharmasakti, the rector of Thammasat University. Rama IX also proposed the convening of a "National Convention" of nearly 2,500 members who would be tasked with the selection of new members of the parliament. He then dissolved the Assembly and directly appointed the members of the National Convention through a Royal Command. The National Convention was headed by Prince Wan Waithayakorn, the author of the Buddhist-inspired Thai neologism for "Constitution." The National Convention selected the members of the new parliament in December 1973. Finally, a new constitution-drafting committee was appointed. The drafting started in early 1974 and the Constitution was first presented to the cabinet in February, before sailing through the Assembly.

9.4.2 *The Concept of* Rachaprachasamai *Constitution (King-People "Joint" Constitution)*

The 1974 Constitution had literally been granted by the king through direct royal appointment of both the prime minister, called "the royally-granted prime minister" (*nayok phrarachathan*) and the legislature, called the "royally-granted house" (*sapha phrarachathan*). Its preamble reaffirmed the myth of Prajadhipok's initial royal octroy:

> King Prajadhipok granted the constitution of Siam to the Siamese people on December 10, 1932 – which established democracy in Siam, in accordance with the royal wish to grant royal power to the Siamese people in its entirety, not to a person or a group in particular; [a democracy] in which the Head of State exercises sovereignty of the people in accordance with the provisions of the Constitution.[9]

In line with the principle of royal sovereignty inherent in the doctrine of royal octroy, the king could veto, as well as order, the holding of a referendum on any proposition of constitutional revision (Article 220). This Constitution, which was highly royalist – as the Senate was initially fully and directly appointed by the king (Article 107) – was referred to as the "King-People Joint Constitution" (*rattathamanun chabap rachaphrachasamasai*), owing to the role played by the king in its engineering, together with the amount of public participation involved (Kobkua 1981, 58). *Rachaphrachasamasai* (joint King-people) was actually a transformation of the old doctrine of *anekchonnikon samosonsammut* according to which the king and the people are one united body, a complementarity between "Heaven" and "Earth," itself echoing the *mahāsammata* doctrine:

> According to the mode of governance of *rachaphrachasamasai*, the Monarchy and the people govern together. The Monarchy has more prerogative to govern than in a democracy and the people also have more power to govern than in the past experience of Thai Democracy. The Monarchy and the People in such a system are not dangers to one another. They love each other and help each other always. If the Monarchy and the People unite to govern the country together, and help each other out, as has always been the case, I have the hope that our land will turn into the land of peace and development in all dimensions according to the wishes of the people. (Kukrit 1971)

In the same period, a new doctrinal theory, named "Democracy with the King as Head of State" (*prachatipatai seung mi phramahakasat pen pramuk*), emerged, building on the idea of *rachaprachasamasai* and mixing elements of constitutional monarchy, notably Walter Bagehot's tripartite convention (the king has "the right to be consulted, to warn and to encourage") and elements of Buddhist kingship. This theory referred to kingship as being defined by the Ten Virtues of a Righteous King, and by the king's election – in other words, the modern king was still both a *dhammarāja* and a *mahāsammata*. In "the Democratic System with the King as Head of State," there were two sources of law. The positive law (*khotmai*) gave the king the power to exercise sovereignty in the executive, legislative, and judicial domains through the cabinet, the parliament and the judiciary, as well as grant royal pardons and receive petitions from the people, following Bagehot's tripartite

[9] 1974 Constitution of the Kingdom of Thailand, preamble. Translation by the author.

convention. The royal customary law (*rachaphrapheni*) was composed of the 26 Royal Virtues. These were the Ten Virtues of a Righteous King (generosity, morals, sacrifice, honesty, gentleness, diligence, compassion, non-violence and non-harm, patience, and righteousness); the Twelve Virtues of the *cakravartin* (*chakravativat*) (to love and be compassionate to his subjects, to adhere and maintain dhamma, to judge cases with justice, equity and rapidity, to listen to the advice of philosophers and act accordingly, to abstain from committing the five major sins – killing, stealing, committing adultery, lying, and drinking alcohol – to feel compassion and not envy the wealth or the work of the people, to collect taxes but not to increase them, to give to the poor, to distribute wealth to civil servants, to judge cases meticulously, to honour and look after *brāhmaṇas* and philosophers, and to distribute rewards and honours to those who are deserving); and the additional Four Virtues of a bodhisattva (*sangkhahawatu*) (a sense of sacrifice, carefulness in speech, social usefulness in action, consistency and appropriateness of action) (Thanin 1976, 32–33).

The aim of a *dhammarāja* king is to attain the status of *cakravartin* and bodhisattva by demonstrating the perfect practice of these twenty-six cumulative virtues (Sawaeng 2000, 90–93). As presented in this formula, then, modern Buddhist kingship still relied on the ideals of bodhisattva, *cakravartin*, *mahāsammata*, and *dhammarāja*, and royal customary law still pre-existed positive law. In his authoritative handbook on the subject, Thanin Kraivichien gives, as an example of a key kingly duty, that of giving (*than*) a constitution to his subjects (1976, 33).

9.4.3 *The Concept of "Shared Sovereignty" between the King and the People*

In developing the theory of "Democracy with the King as Head of State," Thanin suggested that "Thai-Style Democracy" did not require a constitution nor elections held periodically. Since the king was, in a mythical sense, elected, and thereby represented the people, there was democracy, even in times of military dictatorship. In addition, the king always retained his sovereignty: being the army chief, the king was, during coups or when there was no constitution under military dictatorship, still fully sovereign (Thanin 1976, 26–29). Regarding the king's role in times of crisis, Thanin stated: "when the country enters into a crisis, one can no longer rely on the constitution at all. One must rely on the wisdom (*phrapricha*) of the king" (1976, 58). Thanin's legal theory established the king as commander of the army and source of political legitimacy. He linked it with the legality of military coups through the royal prerogative of declaring and revoking martial law:

> In military terms, the monarchy (*phramahakasat*) means "great warrior." This is because in ancient times, the king was the one leading in the battlefield, fighting courageously against the enemy . . . The legacy has continued until today, and that is why the king is the army chief according to the constitution . . . The title of general (*chompon*) is the highest in the military hierarchy, it is true, but the king has an even higher status, which is army chief. It is not a military rank, but it is a title for

> the monarchy specially, which is based on royal constitutional customs (*nittira-chaphrapheni*) since ancient times … That is why this constitution gives the king the title of army chief and the power to declare and revoke Martial Law. (1976, 26)

Finally, building on both the theory of *rachaprachasamasai* and the theory of "Democracy with the King as Head of State," prominent Thai jurists later developed the "doctrine of King-people's shared sovereignty," according to which the king and the people hold joint or shared sovereignty, something which bears practical consequences in times of military coups:

> In the Thai democratic system, sovereignty is held by the king and the people. It thus differs from other countries in which the people are the only bearer of sovereignty. There are two reasons for this. The first reason relates to traditions (*phrapheni*). The Thai Monarchy is identified with the Thai people, and this has become a tradition. The second reason relates to law. Sovereignty has at all times belonged to the king. When the People's Party changed the system of government, the royalty, holder of sovereignty, granted it to the people by giving a constitution. The king accepted to be placed under the authority of the constitution but would still have the sovereign power in the name of the people. Whenever a coup abolishes the constitution, one must consider that the power given with the constitution goes back to the monarch, being the sovereign before June 24, 1932. (Bowornsak 2007, 143)

According to this doctrine – which was never explicitly accepted by the court (Mérieau 2021, 241) – whenever the king signs the interim constitution after a coup, the act is considered legal, and sovereignty becomes "shared" with the people. The coup then is legalised whenever it bears the king's signature. This all derived from the fact that the king is the source of the Constitution. In *The Monarchy in the System of Democracy*, a book commissioned by the National Legislative Assembly appointed by the military in 2007, prominent Thai jurist Meechai Reechupan explained how Thailand's luck, "a luck unique in comparison to other countries," was that all Thai kings, whether absolute or constitutional monarchs, had always ruled according to doctrines of Buddhist kingship, and because – since Prajadhipok had unilaterally granted the 1932 Constitution to the people (the Interim Constitution bearing the sole signature of the king) – the monarchy remains to date the source (*thi ma*) of the Constitution and constitutionalism in the country (Meechai 2007, 5). Even though this doctrine was never explicitly recognised by the courts, implicit references and traces of the doctrine can be found in several landmark rulings of the Constitutional Court.

9.5 CONCLUSION

The *dhammarāja* (*cakravartin*/bodhisattva) and *mahāsammata* theories of royal power – what can be called "the four images of Buddhist kingship" – were progressively secularised throughout the late nineteenth and early twentieth centuries, then Westernised and articulated with legal and constitutional theories in the 1930s. The Siamese term for dhamma, based on the Pali word, was used to Buddhicise the Western borrowings so as to "indigenise" them. The nineteenth-century European model of limited monarchy, relying on the idea of the royally granted constitution, was imported and hybridised with the doctrine of the elected king and the Hindu-Buddhist conceptions of kingship and the law. By the 1930s, all references to the dhamma, the *thammasat* or the *rajasat* had seemingly been removed from the law and the doctrines of kingship, but in fact, they had been re-invested in a new sacred object: the Constitution. The fiction of the Constitution as a royal octroy was enshrined in the preamble to the 1932 Constitution and since then, a reference to the royal octroy appeared in almost all permanent constitutions. In law handbooks, various doctrines on royal sovereignty (such as *rachaprachamasai*) married the doctrine of "granted constitutionalism" with that of the *dhammarāja* doctrine. Altogether, the doctrine of royal constitutional octroy, according to which the Constitution is a royal gift, established the king as the source of the Thai constitutional order, therefore endowed with powers to grant, suspend, and abolish the Constitution.

These various theories, derived from the bricolage of Western and Buddhist concepts of the Constitution as the king's gift to his people, still have much salience today. The 2017 Constitution states in its preamble that it has been graciously "granted" by King Vajiralongkorn, following the initial "royal octroy" of a constitution by King Prajadhipok in 1932. Additionally, the document refers to the Buddhist-kingship-infused narrative of "Democracy with the King as Head of State" almost fifteen times in the body of its text: "Democracy with the King as Head of State" is defined as Thailand's constitutional identity, protected by the Constitutional Court from both amendment (through an eternity clause prohibiting amendment) and from "threats" by political parties and individuals (by a clause allowing the court to order the cessation of such "threat" including the dissolution of the political party in question). Like former Thai constitutions, the 2017 Constitution gives the king a constitutional veto over all constitutional, legislative, and executive matters – in fact, the title on the monarchy in successive Thai constitutions has been the most stable of all titles since 1932. In the words of Thanin, "the reason why the status of the monarchy was never changed in any epoch, no matter how many times the constitution was abrogated, is because this institution has ultimate stability and has inherent perfection so that there has never been any need to alter it" (1976, 30).

REFERENCES

Baker, Chris and Pasuk Phongpaichit. 2016. *The Palace Law of Ayutthaya and the Thammasat: Law and Kingship in Siam*. Ithaca: Cornell University Press.

2021. "Thammasat, Custom, and Royal Authority in Siam's Legal History." In *Thai Legal History: From Traditional to Modern Law*, edited by Andrew Harding and Munin Pongsapan, 23–40. Cambridge: Cambridge University Press.

Bandit Chanrochanakit. 2007. *ชีวประวัติธรรมนูญการปกครองและรัฐธรรมนูญแห่งราชอาณาจักรไทย พ.ศ.* 2475–2520 [*A Biography of the Interim Constitutions and the Constitutions of the Kingdom of Thailand* 1932–1977]. Bangkok: Research Development Fund.

Bowornsak Uwanno. 2007. *กฎหมายมหาชน เล่ม 2: การแบ่งแยกกฎหมายมหาชน-เอกชน และพัฒนาการกฎหมายมหาชนในประเทศไทย* [*Public Law Vol. 2: The Separation of Public Law and Private Law and the Development of Public Law in Thailand*]. Bangkok: Chulalongkorn University Press.

Collins, Steven. 1996. "The Lion's Roar on the Wheel-Turning King: A Response to Andrew Huxley's 'The Buddha and the Social Contract.'" *Journal of Indian Philosophy* 24: 421–46.

Darling, Frank C. 1977. "Thailand in 1976: Another Defeat for Constitutional Democracy." *Asian Survey* 17: 116–32.

Huxley, Andrew. 1996. "The Buddha and the Social Contract." *Journal of Indian Philosophy* 24: 407–20.

Jory, Patrick. 2016. *Thailand's Theory of Monarchy: The Vessantara Jataka and the Idea of the Perfect Man*. New York: State University of New York Press.

Kobkua Suwannathat-Pian. 1981. "The Monarchy and Constitutional Change since 1972." In *Reforming Thai Politics*, edited by Duncan McCargo, 57–71. Copenhagen: NIAS.

Kukrit Pramoj. 1971. Column in *Siam Rath*, 11 December.

Lingat, Robert. 1929. "Note sur la révision des lois siamoises en 1805." *Journal of the Siam Society* 23: 19–27.

1941. "Evolution of the Conception of Law in Burma and Siam." *Journal of the Siam Society* 38: 9–31.

Meechai Reechupan. 2007. "The King According to the Constitution." In *พระมหากษัตริย์ในระบอบประชาธิปไตย* [*The Monarchy in the System of Democracy*], edited by National Legislative Assembly, 4–9. Bangkok: Office of the National Legislative Assembly.

Mérieau Eugénie. 2018. "Buddhist Constitutionalism in Thailand: When Rājadhammā Supersedes the Constitution." *Asian Journal of Comparative Law* 13: 283–305.

2021. *Constitutional Bricolage: Thailand's Sacred Monarchy vs. The Rule of Law*. Oxford: Hart.

Nattapol Chaiching. 2013. *ขอฝันใฝ่ในฝัน อันเหลือเชื่อ.* [*Dreaming the Impossible Dream: The Counter-Revolutionary Movement in Siam*]. Nonthaburi: Same Sky Books.

Nidhi Eoseewong. 2004. ชาติไทย, เมืองไทย, แบบเรียนและอนุสาวรีย์ ว่าด้วยวัฒนธรรม, รัฐ และรูปการจิตสำนึก. [*The Thai Nation, Thai Politics, Textbook and Monuments: About Culture, the State, and Consciousness*]. Bangkok: Matichon.

Noranit Settabutr (ed). 2009. *เอกสารการพิจารณาร่างรัฐธรรมนูญ ๑๐ ธันวาคม ๒๔๗๕.* [*Documents Related to the Examination of the Draft 10 December 1932 Constitution*]. Bangkok: Thammasat University Press.

Puli Fuwongcharoen. 2018. "Long live the Rattathammanun." *Modern Asian Studies* 52 (2): 609–44.

Reynolds, Frank and Mani Reynolds. 1982. *Three Worlds According to King Ruang: A Thai Buddhist Cosmology*. Berkeley: University of California Press.

Riggs, Fred. 1966. *Thailand: The Modernization of the Bureaucratic Polity*. Honolulu: East-West Center.

Saichon Sattayanurak. 2003. *พุทธศาสนากับแนวคิดทางการเมืองใน รัชสมัยพระบาทสมเด็จพระพุทธยอดฟ้าจุฬาโลก (พ.ศ. 2325–2352)* [*Buddhism and Political Ideologies in the Times of Phraphuttayotfachulalok (1782–1809)*]. Bangkok: Matichon.

Sawaeng Bunchalemphiwat. 2000. *ประวัติศาสตร์กฎหมายไทย*. [Thai Legal History]. Bangkok: Winyuchon.

Suthachai Yimprasert. 2008. *สายธารประวัติศาสตร์ประชาธิปไตยไทย*. [A View of the History of Thai Democracy]. Bangkok: Democracy Foundation.

Tambiah, Stanley Jeyaraja. 1976. *World Conqueror and World Renouncer: A Study of Buddhism and Polity in Thailand against a Historical Background*. Cambridge: Cambridge University Press.

Thanavi Chotpradit. 2016. *Revolution versus Counter-Revolution: The People's Party and the Royalist(s) in Visual Dialogue*. PhD dissertation, University of London.

2018. "Countering Royalism with Constitutionalism: The People's Party's Visual Culture after the Boworadet Rebellion." *South East Asia Research* 26: 235–55.

Thanin Kraivichien. 1976. *พระมหากษัตริย์ไทยในระบอบประชาธิปไตย*. [The Thai Monarchy in the Democratic System]. Bangkok: Ministry of Education.

Thianpanya Paphatsaun. 2008. *จักรวาลวิทยาสยาม: การศึกษาที่มาของอำนาจทางการเมืองและกฎหมายในกฎหมายตราสามดวง*. [*Siamese Cosmology: A Study of the Sources of Political and Legal Authorities in the Three Seals Law*]. Bangkok: Thammasat University Press.

Thongchai Winichakul. 1994. *Siam Mapped: A History of the Geo-body of a Nation*. Honolulu: University of Hawai'i Press.

2000. "The Quest for 'Siwilai': A Geographical Discourse of Civilizational Thinking in the Late Nineteenth and Early Twentieth-Century Siam." *The Journal of Asian Studies* 59: 528–49.

Wales, H. G. Quaritch. 1931. *Siamese State Ceremonies: Their History and Function*. London: Bernard Quaritch Ltd.

1934. *Ancient Siamese Government and Administration*. London: Bernard Quaritch Ltd.

Wenk, Klaus. 1968. *The Restoration of Thailand under Rama I, 1782–1809*. Tucson: University of Arizona Press.

Wyatt, David K. 1982. "The Subtle Revolution of King Rama I of Siam." In *Moral Order and the Question of Change: Essays on Southeast Asian Thought*, edited by David K. Wyatt and Alexander Woodside, 9–52. New Haven: Yale University Southeast Asia Studies.

10

Buddhist Constitutionalism beyond Constitutional Law

Buddhist Statecraft and Military Ideology in Myanmar

*Iselin Frydenlund**

10.1 INTRODUCTION: BUDDHIST CONSTITUTIONALISM UNDER MILITARY RULE

In Burma/Myanmar, the constitutional regulation of religion has undergone major shifts following the country's successive political transformations from democratic multi-party system to one-party (one man) socialist military rule, to military "law and order" rule, to hybrid regime and "post-dictatorship," and as of February 1, 2021, direct military rule. The constitutional management of religion in Burma/Myanmar has relied upon democratic procedures or been the object of public discussion only for very short periods of time (1948–58, 1960–62, 2011–21). Moreover, due to military rule and the illiberal 1974 and 2008 Constitutions, legal claims and litigation have rarely been a way for politically disempowered actors, such as non-Buddhist religious minorities or Buddhist "deviant" groups, to gain state recognition or support.

With the 2011 political reforms, however, legal debates about religion surfaced again in parliament, as well as in the public sphere. This paper looks at various forms of constitutional practice with regards to religion in Burma/Myanmar, by which I mean "the acts of drafting, debating, implementing and invoking constitutional law" (Schonthal 2016, 11). It should be underlined from the onset that such activism as a form of public practice has – even during the years of political liberalization – been scarce on account of authoritarian, military rule. Exactly how the February 1, 2021, military coup will affect constitutional law in Myanmar remains to be seen, but Buddhist protectionist associations such as the Buddha Dhamma Parahita (formerly known as MaBaTha) issued statements showing strong support for the 2008 Constitution, just hours before the coup. This indicates support to the Tatmadaw (the military) at least among certain leading monks, and more importantly for the

* I wish to thank Benjamin Schonthal, Matt Walton, D. Christian Lammerts, and Tom Ginsburg for their insightful comments on this chapter.

purpose of this paper, support for the ways in which Buddhism is protected in the Constitution.

"Buddhist constitutionalism" is defined by Benjamin Schonthal (2017, 707) as "attempts to use written constitutions and other basic laws to organize power in ways that protect and preserve Buddhist teachings and institutions, especially the institution of Buddhist monasticism, the sangha." Central to Buddhist constitutionalism are questions about how to balance royal/political authority and ecclesiastical authority. This, Schonthal points out, is in contrast to Islamic constitutionalism (which concerns the application of transcendent laws in a man-made legal order), as well as secular-liberal constitutionalism and questions regarding the balance between religious privileges and general religious rights. As this chapter will show, the case of Burma/Myanmar clearly confirms the centrality of questions pertaining to the balance between political and ecclesiastical authority. However, the paper also argues for a broader understanding of Buddhist constitutionalism, which expands the concept beyond the conundrum of political versus ecclesiastical authority, to include a wider range of policies and laws that seek to enact constitutional preferences for Buddhism. This expanded set of pro-Buddhist policies include prima facie "secular" civil law and the Penal Code as well. Thus, the key regulatory issue at stake is not only sangha affairs, but also the privileging of Buddhism vis-à-vis other religions in a wide array of policies and state law. Broadening the concept of Buddhist constitutionalism in this way helps scholars to acknowledge the unwritten or "living" forms of Buddhist constitutionalism that also influence social and political life.

This chapter proceeds in five parts. The first section analyses Buddhist constitutionalism in postcolonial Burma/Myanmar from a historical perspective. The second section analyses Buddhist constitutionalism and its return in the 2008 Constitution. The third section discusses current regulatory contestations between political and ecclesiastical authorities, making the argument that secularism in postcolonial Burma/Myanmar is a function of Buddhist constitutionalism, rather than the result of British colonial policies. The fourth section discusses what I suggest is the protection of Buddhism through "secular" law, focusing on the 2015 "race and religion" laws and religious offense legislation. The fifth and last section analyzes Buddhist constitutionalism as a form of alterity vis-à-vis Myanmar's religious minority communities.

10.2 HISTORICAL BACKGROUND: THE RETURN OF BUDDHIST CONSTITUTIONALISM IN MYANMAR

Inspired by clauses in the Irish Constitution at that time, Burma's 1947 Constitution included two articles of consequence as it relates to Buddhism: Article 21(1) held that "The State recognizes the special position of Buddhism as the faith professed by the great majority of the citizens of the Union;" Article 21 (4) prohibited the "abuse of religion for political purposes." This ambiguity between state protection for Buddhism, on the one hand, and strict separation of religion and politics on the other came to mark Burmese democratic politics in the years to follow.

Independent Burma's first prime minister, U Nu, had a strong Buddhist revivalist agenda, and the initial few years of democracy witnessed vibrant constitutional debates and activism to promote state protection of Buddhism. The Buddhist constitutional policies of the U Nu era included the Vinasaya Act of 1949 (registration of monks and sangha courts), the Buddha Sasana Council Act (1949), the Pali University and Dhammacariya Act (1950), and the Pali Education Board Act (1952). Monastic associations at the time suggested that Buddhism should be the state religion and opposed freedom of religion. In his 1960 campaign, U Nu called for Buddhism to become the state religion and managed, in August 1961, against strong opposition from Burma's non-Buddhist minorities, to make Buddhism the state religion (Kyaw Win, Mya Han & Thein Hlaing 2011, 96–102). However, this constitutional amendment was soon to be abolished by General Ne Win, who came to power during the military coup of March 2, 1962.

The first period of military rule (1962–88) represents a radical shift in the constitutional regulation of religion and secularism (as ideology) in Burma. In contrast to U Nu, the Ne Win regime hardly referred to Buddhism, and the 1974 Constitution does not mention any state preference for Buddhism. Furthermore, the 1974 Constitution is strictly secularist in that it states that "Religion and religious organizations shall not be used for political purposes" (Article 156c). It grants equality before the law and religious freedom, but limits those rights with reference to "national solidarity and the socialist social order" (Article 153b, The Constitution of the Socialist Republic of Burma 1974). The 1974 Constitution did not offer any form of legislative representation for ethnic groups, but introduced new forms of recognition of ethnic claims, such as "Seven States" and "Seven Divisions" (Crouch 2019).

Ne Win generally turned a blind eye to the issue of regulating the sangha throughout the 1960s and 1970s. However, Buddhism – particularly the sangha – was subject to increased legal regulation from 1980 onwards, in order to control so-called "unruly" monks and subsequently to curb monastic resistance to the regime. In May 1980, General Ne Win's government convened the Sangha Convention of All Buddhist Gaing for the Purification, Perpetuation, and Propagation of Theravāda Buddhism, and, in the name of "purification," streamlined the sangha and imposed direct control over its monastic members. Only nine *gaings* (Buddhist sects) have since become officially recognized by the state. Ne Win also formed the State Sangha Maha Nayaka Committee, which oversees the sangha.

Attempts to effectively act on the Vinasaya Act from 1949 had failed during the early years of Ne Win's rule as part of its secularist orientations (Tin Maung Maung Than 1988). *Vinaya* transgressions were only to be dealt with within each monastic lineage, or *gaing*. Without a state-backed supra-*gaing* structure in place, no rulings regarding heresy (*adhamma*) could be made. It was not until 1980 that a specific legal system to deal with *vinaya* cases came into place at the national level, as will be discussed in detail later.

The 1988 democratic uprising eventually led to the collapse of the socialist regime, only to be replaced by direct military rule (1988–2011): first through the State Law and Order Restoration Council (SLORC) and later by the State Peace and Development Council (SPDC). The new junta abandoned a socialist ideology altogether, and the SLORC/SPDC made "law and order" its new slogan, which did not imply the rule of law, but rather subsuming law *into* order. In this period, a new hierarchy of judges, comprised of bureaucrats and administrators, resurrected a system marked by non-independence and "unrule" of law. As Cheesman (2015) points out, in contrast to the Ne Win years, soldiers were no longer necessary in the courtroom as the civilian judiciary was fully subordinated to military interests.

From 1988 to 2008 the country was ruled without a constitution, but in the same period the military was preoccupied with drafting a new constitution, making the drafting process of the 2008 Constitution one of the longest constitution-making exercises in the world (Crouch 2019, 27). The drafting of a new constitution was part of General Khin Nyunt's 2003 document, "Roadmap to a Discipline-Flourishing Democracy."[1] The constitution-making process was isolated from public debates, and submissions from ethnic groups regarding language rights and customary laws were ignored (Crouch 2019). To what extent Buddhist monks and laypeople outside of the military were active in pushing the constitution-makers for constitutional protection of Buddhism remains unclear. What is clear, however, is that the Buddhist protection clause (Article 361, 2008 Constitution) is taken verbatim from the 1947 Constitution. One explanation for the return of Buddhist constitutionalism relates to military reorientation after the 1988 violent crackdown on the student movement and pro-democracy monks. The regime needed to repair its relations to the sangha through its so-called *saya-dayaka* (monk-donor) program, which eventually resulted in a state-sponsored Buddhist nationalist ideology (Schober 2011). However, reducing monastic-military relations to pure strategy would be to ignore the fact that the military is largely comprised of Buddhists and that monks serve as "military chaplains," consoling soldiers and boosting their morale, for example during the 2017 massive violence against the Rohingya population in Rakhine. Thus, understanding the importance of Buddhism to the military needs to move beyond mere instrumentalism.

10.3 SECULARISM AS A FUNCTION OF BUDDHIST CONSTITUTIONALISM

The highly controversial 2008 Constitution institutionalized a military state in Myanmar, enabling the role of the military in governance. It contains three

[1] Matthew Walton (2017, 167–74) has argued that the concept of discipline-flourishing democracy is connected to Buddhist principles of unity and discipline, but also fears of anarchy.

meta-principles: non-disintegration of the Union, non-disintegration of national solidarity, and the perpetuation of sovereignty (*Basic Principles*, 2008 Constitution). The military treats the 2008 Constitution as a sacred object – insisting on faithfulness to the Constitution itself – and resists all attempts at constitutional reform. This raises some interesting questions about ideology, rituals, and materiality with regard to the 2008 Constitution. First, in saying that it is sacred, I refer to the fact that it is treated as a self-referencing text, the authority of which lies within its status as a foundational charter for military rule – a document that, for the military, ought not to be changed. Second, members of parliament are obliged to make an oath (which is outlined in Schedule Four of the Constitution itself) to "uphold and abide by the Constitution," and by that, pressurizing MPs to be loyal to military ideology as enshrined in the Constitution. The material book is used in this oath-making ritual in parliament (for military and civilian MPs alike), as a way for the military to ensure loyalty to its ideology. This explains Aung San Suu Kyi and the initial refusal by her party, the National League for Democracy (NLD), to partake in the Oath ritual in 2012.

As a political document that enshrines the authoritarian ideology of the military state, it would be an understatement to say that the 2008 Constitution has received strong criticism. The 2008 Constitution is the site of contestation between the military, the ethnic minority parties, and the NLD, and constitutional reform has been first priority for the NLD. Not surprisingly, therefore, after the February 1, 2021, military coup, protesters have been tearing apart or burning the material book in public, and later posting images of such events on social media, as a sign of their commitment to end military rule.

Put simply, the principle of non-secession and self-determination is controversial for the ethnic minorities and their political parties and Ethnic Armed Organizations (EAOs), while the role of the military in politics has been the main issue of contestation for democracy activists in majority population areas. Importantly, however, the question of Buddhist constitutionalism is, as we shall see, one that has been avoided in public debate, but simmers under the surface.

The 2008 Constitution is a mix of ideas from the 1947 Constitution, the 1974 Constitution and the post-1988 military ideology. Put another way, it draws on colonial legality, socialist legality, and military legality. Importantly, it focuses on duties rather than rights, which affects the ways in which religion is regulated. In the following, I will identify what can be regarded as "Buddhist" in the 2008 Constitution, identifying four sites of Buddhist constitutionalism in the text: religious privilege, morality, temporality, and, counterintuitively, secularism.

First, there is the privileged, but not necessarily preeminent, status given to Buddhism as a religion. Article 361 grants Buddhism a special position as the majority religion, which is taken almost verbatim from the 1947 Constitution (Article 21 [1]). Article 362 "recognizes Christianity, Islam, Hinduism and Animism as the religions existing in the Union at the day of the coming into operation of this Constitution."[2] In this way, the Constitution balances Buddhist constitutionalism on the one hand, and the recognition of Christianity, Islam, Hinduism, and Animism and, as discussed below, secularist orientations on the other.

Second, Chapter 1, "Basic Principles of the Union," lists as a state responsibility that "The Union shall strive for youth to have strong and dynamic patriotic spirit, the correct way of thinking and to develop the five noble strengths" (Article 33). This is a reference to the Buddhist principle of *pañcabalāni* ("five strengths"): faith (*saddhā*), energy (*viriya*), mindfulness (*sati*), concentration (*samādhi*), and wisdom (*paññā*). This is, in fact, the only explicit reference to Buddhist principles in the entire Constitution. It is an article that cannot be missed as it not only imbues the text with a certain Buddhist quality, but even more importantly, explicitly makes it a state obligation to foster new generations of Buddhist citizens. This emphasis on Buddhist virtues is not present in the 1947 and 1974 Constitutions.[3]

Third, as in the Thai and the Sri Lankan constitutions, Buddhist constitutional privilege in Myanmar is also shown in the preference of the Buddhist calendar. Referring to the approval date of the Constitution – the tenth waxing day of Kasone 1370 M.E. ("May 29, 2008, CE" in the official English translation) – the text situates the political community with reference to Buddhist historiography. The Burmese Buddhist calendar is used in all legislation, in addition to a range of other social settings, including the press statement announcing the 2021 military coup. Burmese Buddhist temporality is also present in the 1947 and the 1974 Constitutions, and for the latter, it is the only reference to Buddhism.

Fourth, parallel to the constitutional privileges discussed above, the 2008 Constitution expresses a specific secularist orientation by referring to a remarkably strong separation between "religion" and "politics." Some of these articles are similar to the two previous constitutions, while other articles are new to the 2008 Constitution, expanding on existing principles of institutional differentiation between "religion" and "politics." Chapter 4, the "Legislature," Article 121, specifies who is disqualified for election to the Legislature, listing (among many others) persons who receive support from foreign religious organizations (Article 121g), persons who convince others to vote or not vote based on "religion for political purpose" (Article 121h) and members of religious orders (Article 121i). In addition to banning parliamentarians from using religion for electoral purposes, Chapter 8, "Citizen, Fundamental Rights and Duties of the Citizens," bans the abuse of "religion" (however defined) for political purposes among citizens *generally*

[2] The 1947 clause includes an important "some": "The State also recognizes Islam, Christianity, Hinduism and Animism as *some* of the religions existing in the Union at the date of the coming into operation of this Constitution" (italics added), opening up for the existence of other religions not mentioned in the text.

[3] In the 1947 Constitution, the focus is on health and working capacity "to strengthen the defensive capacity of the State" (Article 39). Cultivating citizens' morality is not mentioned here.

(Article 364). Any action that sows enmity between religions and races is considered unlawful (Article 364).

On elections and voting rights, Chapter 9 (Article 392a) states "members of religious orders" do not have the right to vote, which is primarily interpreted as Buddhist monks and nuns, as well as Catholic fathers and nuns, but in practice this is a field open for negotiation, and one might add, corruption. Ordained members of the Catholic Church are disenfranchised, the Muslim ulema are granted voting rights, and Protestant, Evangelical, and Baptist ministers are, depending on local context, sometimes entitled to vote and sometimes not. The rationale behind these distinctions is less than clear, but as the Constitution specifically states "members of religious orders" it is reasonable to argue that the distinctions in voting rights depend, at least in part, on officials' perceptions about how organized a group is – and perhaps how closely it resembles sangha organizational structures. As such, this can be read as an example of a Buddhist formatting process of non-Buddhist institutionalized religion.

The principle of separation between "religion" and "politics" is further elaborated in Chapter 10, "Political Parties," which specifically prohibits political parties from directly or indirectly receiving funding from a religious association (Article 407c), and furthermore, that a political party is not allowed continued existence if it is found guilty of "abusing religion for political purpose" (Article 407d). In case of violation, the party's registration shall be revoked. This provision is further developed in the Political Parties Registration Law No. 2/2012, 6(d) which prohibits political parties from writing, speaking, and campaigning in a manner that will instigate conflict or violence among religious and ethnic groups or individuals. Articles 121 and 407 are new to the 2008 Constitution, indicating how the Tatmadaw military foresaw how religion could be a mobilizing factor in parliamentary elections.

How are we to understand this particular conceptual division between the "religious," the "secular," and the "political" expressed in Myanmar's three constitutions? It is my contention that in the case of postcolonial Burma/Myanmar, secularism was not separate from Buddhist constitutionalism, but rather a function of it. This likely echoed British legal distinctions between the "religious" and the "secular" that undergirded colonial policies. However, this path dependency might also predate British colonial policies of secularism: a key point in Theravāda Buddhist political ideology is a formal divide between the state and the monastic order.[4] With the introduction of modern political systems, this has been interpreted in different ways. Sri Lanka introduced universal suffrage as early as 1931, and

[4] For example, as expressed in the *Samantapasadika*, Buddhagosa's famous *vinaya* commentary, about monks not serving in royal office. Such boundary-making between monastic and political spheres does of course not imply that monks have *not* served as close advisors to kings, but, noticeably, that authoritative sources in *vinaya* jurisprudence have valued institutional differentiation and considered it to be an issue of regulatory importance. I thank Jens Borgland for this reference.

accordingly the monks gained civil and political rights on a par with all other citizens (Schonthal 2016). This is completely different from the situation in Myanmar (and Thailand), where Buddhist monks and nuns are deprived of their political rights. The ostensible reason is to cohere with a Theravāda Buddhist political paradigm, namely that there should be a formal separation between the monastic order and political power. Translated into modern democratic language, lawmakers have justified these provisions as *protecting* the order from political participation. This kind of logic goes back to 1946 when monks in Burma were formally disenfranchised, after strong pressure from the monks themselves (Larsson 2015).

The 2008 Constitution reads "members of religious orders," which means that monks and nuns do not have the right to vote, form political parties, stand for election, or sit in parliament. Melissa Crouch (2019, 62) argues that this reflects "the Tatmadaw's concern that Buddhist monastic authority is a rival center of power that needs to be constrained in the military-state." Myanmar's half-million monks and nuns comprise a significant base of would-be voters, and it is easy to jump to the conclusion that this rule was introduced either by British colonial powers due to their secularist preferences, or by the later military regime in order to restrict monastic "political activities" and hence curb regime resistance. In this way, the question of monastic disenfranchisement represents a political paradox. One the one hand, it points to the privileged status of Buddhism within the Myanmar state. On the other hand, it represents a very strict form of secularism, with certain obvious illiberal consequences of depriving particular groups of their basic social and political rights. Importantly – and this is a point to which I shall return in more detail later – this particular form of secularism or even the use of "secular" law is not inimical to Buddhist constitutionalism. It can rather be seen as a function of it.

Leaving the question of secularism aside for a moment, what exactly does the preferential treatment of Buddhism mean in the Burmese context? It should be noted that the Constitution does not grant Buddhism the status of state religion, but as I argue in an earlier article (Frydenlund 2017), Article 361 as well as post-1988 reorientations toward Buddhist symbols and institutions indicate that the state has become a de facto Buddhist state. State policies in support of religion have their support in Article 363, which says that "[t]he Union may assist and protect the religions [*bathathathanamyar*] it recognizes to its utmost." Clearly, this implies state support for all recognized religions, but as shown below, what it means in reality is heavy state support for specific forms of Theravāda Buddhism.

For example, the Department for the Promotion and Propagation of the Sasana, under the Ministry of Religious Affairs and Culture (MoRAC) reaffirms the constitutionally protected right of religious freedom but gives economic and administrative priority to Buddhism as the majority religion. The Ministry also appears to favor Buddhism over other religions in the higher education sector, as seen in state funding of the State Pariyatti University and the International Theravāda Buddhist

Missionary University. In addition, the Ministry coordinates Buddhist missionary activities in the name of *thathana-pyu* or "the dissemination of *sāsana*," which has been an essential political project of the Myanmar state since the 1990s (Kawanami 2021). The most controversial aspects of the missionary politics relate to missionary activities in ethnic minority areas dominated by non-Buddhist religions and has been a long-standing concern for Christians in the Chin and Kachin States.

MoRAC is also responsible for dealing with sangha matters, in consultation with the State Sangha Maha Nayaka Committee often referred to as the MaHaNa – a state-sponsored monastic body that oversees the sangha. Despite its focus on Buddhist affairs, the MoRAC also oversees affairs relating to religious minorities. However, a mapping of attitudes toward the nature of the state and its regulation of religion in Myanmar found that representatives from religious minority communities felt marginalized in relation to the Ministry in terms of protection in territorial disputes with Buddhist monks, access to information, and, above all, with regards to financial support (United Institute of Peace 2021). Such minority grievances raise questions of Buddhist constitutionalism as a form of exclusionary politics that has effects on majority–minority relations. This point will be discussed toward the end of this chapter.

10.4 "PURIFYING" THE SANGHA THROUGH "HYBRID" LAW

Similar to Thailand, but different from Sri Lanka, Buddhist constitutionalism in Myanmar implies heavy regulation of the monastic order. In Thailand, Schonthal (2017, 715) notes "crises relate to the integration or expulsion of Buddhist groups from an official national monkhood," while in Sri Lanka they relate to "deep disagreements over the proper sources of Buddhist authority." Comparing Burma/Myanmar to Thailand and Sri Lanka, it becomes clear that in spite of instances of monastic resistance to the military regime (e.g., 1988 and 2007) – or as in specific cases of contestation discussed below – a combination of the military state, laws regulating the sangha and the centralized organization of monks in Myanmar inhibit large conflicts *within* Buddhism, or between the state and the sangha. There are important exceptions to this general trend, however, and questions persist about the integration or expulsion of groups from the state-sanctioned sangha. Disagreements over Buddhist authority also occasionally arise.

As discussed below, with state patronage of Buddhism comes heavy regulation of the sangha. In the following, I analyze two recent examples of contestation over what is considered "proper" monastic behavior: the first case shows how the Penal Code is used to enforce monastic judgments in cases of non-acceptance of the monastic court's ruling; the second case illustrates the friction between state monastic authorities and certain monks with regard to definitions of the "political." Such cases sometimes imply a principled resistance to heavy sangha regulation per se, but they can also point to political difference, or specific issues of contestation.

10.4.1 *The* Vinicchaya *Court System*

Under British colonial rule, the monastic community retained a relative degree of autonomy in overseeing its internal affairs. It was not until 1980, under the rule of General Ne Win, that a state-level judiciary would oversee monastic affairs. With the establishment of the Buddhist state court system (called *Vinicchaya*), the state has acquired a highly effective means to uphold specific notions of Theravāda Buddhist orthodoxy and orthopraxy. The court has absolute authority in doctrinal matters and constitutes a particular Buddhist legal culture that shapes and formats Buddhist thought and practice in decisive ways. In these courts, monks may be charged with heresy (*adhamma*) and malpractice (*avinaya*) under the jurisdiction of the MaHaNa. Between 1981 and 2017, twenty-one cases were brought before the state Vinicchaya committee, of which three concerned monastic misconduct, and the rest hinged on the degree of misrepresentation or false understanding of Buddhist doctrine. All of the accused have been found guilty (Janaka and Crosby 2017, Kawanami 2021).

With few exceptions, those convicted have accepted the court's decisions. In the two cases where the accused have refused to accept the verdict, the 1990 Law Relating to the Sangha Organization has also been at the regime's disposal. This law states that anyone disobeying the Vinicchaya Court can be sentenced with up to three years imprisonment. Another legal instrument at hand to ensure compliance is the Penal Code, especially Sections 295–298, on "religious offense." So far, this has only been applied in the most recent Vinicchaya Court case, namely the Mopyar case. The monk, U Nyana (often referred to as U Mopyar, a reference to his sky-blue outfit), had been found guilty in 1983 of making false superhuman claims – a charge which, according to the *vinaya*, requires expulsion from the order. Later, he was accused of having established a new *gaing*, based on his particular "doctrine of present action." Based on a ruling from 2011, the Mopyar *gaing* was officially outlawed by the state on the grounds that U Mopyar taught *adhamma*, or "wrong teachings" (Kawanami 2021). His teaching, which appeared to negate karmic logics of reward and retribution, seems to have been of particular concern to the monastic guardians of Theravādin orthodoxy. When U Mopyar did not comply with the rulings of the Vinicchaya Court, a recommendation was sent from the court to the Ministry of Religious Affairs, and he was charged under Sections 295 and 295-A of the Penal Code for acts "intended to offend religious feelings," in this case insulting Buddhism. Critics even claimed his activities were an attempt to destroy Theravāda Buddhism. U Nyana was also charged under Section 5(e) and 5(j) of the 1950 Emergency Provisions Act for behavior deemed to be a threat to national security, under which he was sentenced to a further twenty years imprisonment (Kawanami 2021, 21). In 2016 MaHaNa reconfirmed its stand on the Mopyar group as being an illegal sect and both MaHaNa and MaBaTha stated that U Nyana was an internal enemy (*thathana atwin yanthu*) of Myanmar Buddhism (Kawanami 2021, 22).

As shown by the Mopyar case, secular state law can function as a "back-up" resource when specific Vinicchaya Court regulations fail to regulate "deviant" behavior. The Buddhist court system in Myanmar is mostly a legal mechanism for the conservative and largely "apolitical" sangha hierarchy to uphold specific notions of purity and orthodoxy, within a defined sphere of elite textual specialists (*pariyatti* monks). The driver of this system is the wish to protect the *sāsana* from impurity and corruption, based on a specific form of Buddhist scriptural fundamentalism unique to Myanmar. Furthermore, state mechanisms for the legal regulation of religion, both religious and secular, are potential tools for the exercise of political power.

All of this seems to have intensified after the 2011 political liberalization, when the term *adhamma* replaced the term *micchaa ditthi* ("wrong views"). Kawanami (2021, 19) observes that compared to *micchaa ditthi*, *adhamma* is a broader and more politically loaded term, and that "any particular religious viewpoints that are regarded as threatening to law and order have been called *adhamma* as a means of de-authenticating and discrediting them." In this way accusations of and prosecutions for heresy remain tools of the state policy of *ngyeinwut pibya-ye* (law and order). Thus, Vinicchaya court cases (as well as religious offense cases discussed below) show how the legal regulation of religious offense, blasphemy and heresy have served both religious and political interests.

10.4.2 *MaBaTha: Testing the Limits for "Political" Engagement*

Given the specific, legally inflected distinction between religion and politics in Myanmar, Buddhist associations such as MaBaTha – which since the 2011 political liberalization have been particularly active in the public sphere – need to avoid possible allegations of "doing politics." As discussed above, the task of overseeing and deciding on appropriate monastic behavior lies with the MaHaNa, including to what extent monastics are involved in "politics."[5] While constitutional articles that prohibit monastic engagement in *formal* politics (such as monastic disenfranchisement, non-eligibility for parliament, or being members of political parties) are clear-cut, other aspects of constitutional secularism (such as Article 364) are polysemantic fields open for contestation and negotiation. As the MaBaTha case discussed below indicates, what is deemed by MaHaNa as *adhamma*, or political activity largely depends upon the views of the current government. The case began with the 2013 MaHaNa ruling against a loosely organized monastic network called "969,"[6] which can be seen as a forerunner to MaBaTha. Or to be precise, MaHaNa banned

[5] The 1990 Law does not specifically consider what constitutes "politics," and it remains unclear if monks have been convicted for "doing politics," and if so under what provisions. Rather, activist monks can be charged with allegations of state defamation, religious offense, or under emergency laws.

[6] The 969 refers to the nine qualities of the Buddha, the six of the Dhamma, and the nine of the Sangha, which together constitute the "three Jewels of Buddhism."

the *political* use of the 969 symbol, as well as the creation of formal organizations associated with the symbol, but did not ban the 969 symbol itself, nor did it judge the teachings of 969 as *adhamma*.

With the entry of the NLD into office in 2016, the ties between the government and MaBaTha loosened. Likely responding to the preferences of the newly elected political leaders, MaHaNa reduced its previous support for MaBaTha by denying them formal recognition as a lawful monastic organization (Walton & Tun 2016). In 2017, after allegations of anti-Muslim hate speech, MaHaNa banned Ashin Wirathu from public speaking and preaching for one year. The decision was made a few days after Ashin Wirathu had publicly expressed support for the assassination of Myanmar's leading constitutional lawyer, U Ko Ni, a Muslim. A few months later, MaHaNa ruled that the "MaBaTha" name was not in compliance with the 1990 Sangha Law and ordered all MaBaTha signs and symbols be removed (while stopping short of condemning the organization or its activities). While most MaBaTha groups accepted the enforced rebrand and simply continued their activities, the chapters in Mandalay and the Karen State refused, arguing that MaBaTha was not an official sangha organization, and thus did not breach the 1990 Sangha Law. Read one way, the MaBaTha–MaHaNa disputes in 2016–17 might suggest that monks are less regulated compared to those in, say, Thailand. Yet it is important to note that this semi-independence is more contingent upon political context than on legal flexibility: under USDP rule the MaHaNa supported MaBaTha and its campaign for the so-called race and religion laws, while it limited MaBaTha once the NLD came into power. As previously noted, MaBaTha monks supported MaHaNa in banning the Mopyar sect. Clearly, then, the contestation between MaHaNa and MaBaTha is more about manoeuvring shifting political landscapes than resistance to high levels of state regulation per se.

10.5 DEFENDING BUDDHISM THROUGH CIVIL LAW AND THE PENAL CODE

So far, I have analyzed some of the ways in which state obligations to protect Buddhism have resulted in heavy sangha regulation. In the following sections, I move to other areas of state law such as civil law and the Penal Code, which appear to be based on principles of secularism and equality between ethnic and religious groups (a kind of de jure egalitarianism). However, as I will argue below, even these forms of "secular" law have increasingly been used as legal tools for Buddhist protectionist actors, which can be seen as attempts at legally locking in Buddhist claims to the state. Or put differently, they can be seen as acts of Buddhist statecraft.

Understanding how nominally secular law can be used to enact Buddhist constitutionalism is particularly important given the restricted space for constitutional practice in Myanmar: the Constitution's provisions have not been the subject of constitutional adjudication; there are very few Constitutional Tribunal decisions; access to the tribunal is highly restricted; and the protection of rights via petition in the Supreme Court is highly circumscribed (Crouch 2019). Therefore, there is very limited space for taking Buddhist grievances to the higher judiciary. Under military rule, public law is weak and the possibilities for Buddhist interest litigation or legal activism curbed. Certainly, the Vinicchaya Court is important for sangha regulation and doctrinal issues, but it was not until the years following the 2011 political reforms, that Buddhist activists could engage in public legal activism to secure the *sāsana* beyond Vinicchaya courts. In the following, I analyze two forms of Buddhist legal activism in secular state law, which aim at securing the *sāsana* in lay Buddhist society.

10.5.1 *The 2015 Race and Religion Laws*

The early years of political liberalization (2011–15) witnessed a marked rise in Buddhist nationalism. In 2015 this resulted in the passing of a package of four laws, referred to as the "race and religion laws," which sought to regulate marriages between Buddhist women and non-Buddhist men, to prevent forced conversion, to abolish polygamy and extra-marital affairs, and to promote birth control and family planning in certain regions of the country.[7] Mobilization of MaBaTha was key to passing the legislation, and their declared motivation for legal activism was the protection of Buddhism, particularly against the alleged "Islamization" of Myanmar and claims of violations of religious freedom for Buddhists, predominantly Buddhist women (Frydenlund 2017).

Among these laws, the Religious Conversion Law is of particular interest because it makes explicit reference to the Constitution. The final version of the Conversion Law does not have a preamble, but a preamble contained in its second draft version gives a clue of the rationale behind the law. That draft preamble repeats the language of Article 34 of the Constitution on freedom of religion, but states that there is a need for transparency and a system in place to ensure the right to freedom of religion and the freedom to choose and convert to another religion. A repeated aim is to ensure that change of religion is according to the individual's "own free will."[8] A set of formal procedures and an application process supposedly guarantees converts free will, including an interview with a committee to ensure that the applicant has a free conscience. Compared to the first draft, the final law contains a more developed religious freedom discourse, in which the stated aim is not to ban conversion, but to secure freedom from coercion. This is also evident in the fact that

7 Control of Population and Health Care Law No 28/2015; the Religious Conversion Law (Conversion Law) No 48/2015; the Myanmar Buddhist Women Special Marriage Law No 50/2015 (Marriage Law); the Monogamy Law No 54/2015.

8 "Religious Conversion Law (draft)." On file with author.

the law allows for persons to declare allegiance to atheism, or no-religion (*batha-me*), thereby explicitly stating for the first time one's right *not* to have a religion (Frydenlund 2018).

With the exception of the Marriage Law (which distinguishes between "Buddhist" and "non-Buddhist"), the language of the "race and religion laws" refers to "religion" (*batha*) in the neutral, which means that the laws apply to all Myanmar citizens, regardless of the religious identity given in one's National Identity Card. Given the political-legal context and the rationale given by MaBaTha itself, the laws were clearly made to protect Buddhism, but their generic language makes them seem applicable to all citizens. As with the monastic disenfranchisement discussed above, supposedly secular laws do not always ensure impartiality and neutrality with regard to state regulation of religion. They can also be effective means for protecting religious privilege.

10.5.2 *Protecting Buddhism from "Offense"*

Compared to the monastic courts discussed above, cases involving lay people – Buddhist or non-Buddhist – with regard to "religious offence" fall under the Penal Code and are usually dealt with in general state courts (as the Mopyar case illustrates, however, a case can also move from the monastic court to the general court.) Such "religious offense" legislation was introduced by the colonial state to ensure interreligious harmony between its subjects as it sought to protect the religious feelings of *all* citizens.[9]

Since 2011, charges of religious offense against lay people have become another important form of *sāsana* protection (Frydenlund 2019). In particular, two cases of religious offense have made national headlines in recent years, both passed after strong mobilization by MaBaTha.[10] The first case involved a dual British/New Zealand citizen, Phil Blackwood, and two Burmese citizens, Tun Thurein and Htut Ko Ko Lwin. All were found guilty in 2015 of "insulting religion" for a psychedelic bar advertisement depicting the Buddha wearing headphones and accompanied by the text "Bottomless Frozen Mararita [sic] K 15000." On the eve of December 9, 2014, Blackwood posted the ad on Facebook to promote cheap drinks at the V Gastro Bar in Yangon. The ad went viral, and after having received several complaints, he removed the image and posted an apology. Following

9 The Penal Code contains five sections pertaining to "religious offence": 295. Injuring or defiling place of worship, with intent to insult the religion of any class; 295-A. Deliberate and malicious acts intended to outrage religious feelings of any class by insulting its religion or religious beliefs; 296. Disturbing religious assembly; 297. Trespassing on burial places etc.; 298. Uttering words etc. with deliberate intent to wound religious feelings.

10 Only weeks after the Htin Lin Oo verdict in June 2015, the MaBaTha at its annual conference in Insein published a twelve-point statement in which they demanded blasphemous (*pyit mhar saw kar thaw*) attacks against monks to be stopped (Fuller 2016).

complaints made by MaBaTha, the police took action. Only hours later the three were arrested and sent to prison, charged under the Penal Code, Sections 295 and 295-A. According to the judge, who heard the case in the Bahan Township Court, Blackwood's apologies in court did not remove his guilt of having "intentionally plotted to insult religious belief" (Kyaw Phyo Tha 2014). The judge deemed, moreover, that Blackwood should have known that this would hurt Buddhist feelings and sentenced the three men to two and a half years in prison with hard labor.

The second case was against the writer and NLD activist, Htin Lin Oo, who gave a speech at a literary festival in Chaung-U Township in Sagaing Division in 2014. In this speech, he criticized the use of Buddhism to promote discrimination. Shortly afterwards, a ten-minute edited video appeared on social media, causing outrage among MaBaTha monks. He was charged by the Chaung-U Township Court, after a complaint was filed against him by township officials, under Sections 295-A and 298. In his speech Htin Lin Oo pointed out that the Buddha was not Burmese, not Shan, not Karen, nor did he belong to any of Myanmar's national races. He stated, "if you want to be an extreme nationalist and if you love to maintain your race that much, don't believe in Buddhism." The speech concluded by stating that "Our Buddhism is being destroyed by these people wearing robes".[11] He was acquitted of the charge of "wounding religious feelings," but found guilty of the charge of "insulting religion." He was sentenced to two years in prison, then released, but was among the first to be sentenced again after the 2021 military coup.

In both cases, MaBaTha monks attended the public spectacles outside the respective courtrooms – something that would have been unthinkable just a few years before. During military rule, judicial proceedings were held in secret. There were closed trials and no coverage of cases in public media, particularly from the 1980s onwards. Yet the conjuncture of economic and political liberalization, as well as a new media reality, created new spaces for monastic engagement in public life, including legal activism. Although press freedom was still under heavy pressure, court cases were again reported in the media. From the MaBaTha point of view, race and religion legislation and blasphemy cases were tools that could be used to protect the *sāsana* and ensure that the state acted as a guardian of Buddhism.

10.6 CONTESTING BUDDHIST CONSTITUTIONALISM

So far, I have made the argument that Buddhist constitutionalism in Myanmar has produced a specific form of secularism through the process of legally defining religion in particular ways. I have also argued for the need to address Buddhist constitutionalism beyond the constitutional text in order to capture how a wide range of policies and

[11] You Tube clip, www.youtube.com/watch?v=opiWM3c_5sg.

legal practices promote Buddhism in particular ways. This calls for a differentiation between explicit and implicit forms of Buddhist constitutionalism. In the following section, I will analyze the practice of Buddhist constitutionalism in the context of massive humanitarian crisis, ethnic cleansing, and civil war. Again, as discussed above in regard to the prima facie secular and egalitarian quality of the Penal Code and the "race and religion laws," I would like to emphasize the need for the study of Buddhist constitutionalism to go beyond sangha-political controversies and systematically analyze the effects of Buddhist constitutional practices upon interreligious relations and ethnic minorities.

Historically, several of Burma's insurgencies are related to the question of Buddhist constitutionalism. Both the formation of the Kachin Independence Army and the Chin rebellion can be seen as direct responses to the 1961 amendment to make Buddhism the state religion (a move that was overturned by the military following its 1962 coup). Even among non-Bamar ethnic groups that are majority Buddhist, such as the Shan, the 1961 efforts to make Buddhism the state religion were seen as counter to the Panglong Agreement and so resisted. Therefore, peace negotiations and religious constitutionalism are two closely related questions, at least as seen from an ethnic and religious minority point of view.

As previously discussed, the military is concerned with presenting itself as the protector of the *sāsana*. For example, at the third Advisory Forum on National Reconciliation and Peace in Myanmar in NayPyiTaw on November 14, 2019, the Commander-in-Chief of Defense Services, Senior General Min Aung Hlaing, explicitly reminded the multireligious audience of the fact that Buddhism has a special position in Myanmar. General Hlaing said:

> Despite the fact that every country around the world has citizens of different religions, all of them pay heed to the religion which is practiced by the majority in the country. Cultural evidence suggests that religious beliefs in Myanmar date back to Pyu Period, the most ancient period of the country. Pagodas in Bagan are testimony to the fact that Theravāda Buddhism has been practiced by the majority since Bagan Period, the first Myanmar Empire in AD 11. And there are also comprehensive historical records that the majority of Myanmar citizens have wholeheartedly embraced Buddhism in successive periods. Only after Myanmar fell under colonial rule, followers of Christ and other religions have increased. (Global New Light of Myanmar 2019, 59)

In this speech Hlaing clearly privileges Buddhism over other religions, while at the same time degrading other religions as non-indigenous, colonial newcomers. Simultaneously, the military is building up its Buddhist networks, through sangha donations and ritual celebrations. As MaBaTha experienced restrictions under NLD rule, the military has reinvigorated organizations like the Young Men's Buddhist Association (YMBA) in order to expand the fields of Buddhist-military interaction. For example, at one YMBA event only two months prior to the coup, the leading

MaBaTha monk, Insein Sayadaw, participated in Buddhist functions together with Hlaing. Hlaing also made large donations to Insein Sayadaw in the same period.

For decades, the need for decentralization and a federal structure has been claimed by democracy activists, EAOs, and international actors as the way to peace and democracy. As discussed in detail below, from the EAOs' perspectives, this new federal state is to be secular, thereby respecting the principles of the 1947 Panglong Agreement. This is also in line with Christian (political) theologies among Christian ethnic minority communities such as the Chin, Kachin, and Karen, which hold a secular state as a prerequisite and a *sine qua non* in a future federal and democratic state. Rooted in the Christian (often Baptist) theological notion of the separation between religious and political powers, Myanmar's proponents of Christian political theology dismiss calls for a Buddhist state as extreme, even if they show limited understanding of the historical background and colonial grievances of Buddhists who make such calls.[12]

Demands for a secular state were in fact granted in the 2015 National Ceasefire Agreement (NCA). Given the strong support among Myanmar's religious majority for Buddhist constitutionalism, it is rather surprising that the NCA did not attract much attention, as it offered a totally new vision on the relationship between religion and state. Section 1(e) of the NCA, which was first signed by the Thein Sein government and eight EAOs on October 15, 2015 (with two more joining on February 13, 2018) sought to "establish a secular state based on the principle of the separation of religion and state in order to avoid abuse of religion for political interests."[13] The explicit mention of "separation of religion and state" was novel and went against Article 361 of the Constitution. In 2016, the newly formed NLD government took a new initiative to end decades of armed conflict. This process, called the Union Peace Conference, was mostly known as the "Twenty-first Century Panglong," an explicit reference to the famous 1947 agreement between the Burmese government under Aung San and the Shan, Kachin, and Chin peoples. While building on the 2015 NCA, the Union Peace Conference was intended to be more inclusive and to transform the military state into a democratic federal state. Again, the question of state regulation of religion resurfaced, if not in public debate, then at least among those involved in the peace process. The "secular state" clause in the 2015 NCA was, however, changed in the Union Accord Part III which was signed on August 21, 2020. Here, clause three reads the purpose as: "To establish a nation where there is no misuse of religion for political purpose and where politics and religion are separated from each other" (Global New Light of Myanmar 2020, 10). This is more in line with the 2008 Constitution, but the reasons behind this semantic shift remain unclear. It will also be a point for new negotiation if a peace process recommences if – or when – the civil war-like situation across the country

[12] Frydenlund, fieldnotes, 2018.
[13] https://peacemaker.un.org/sites/peacemaker.un.org/files/MM_151510_NCAAgreement.pdf.

since 2021 ends. If it does, one of the challenging issues is state regulation of religion at the sub-national level. One proposal that appears to have been accepted as part of the peace process is for states/regions to draft their own constitutions, which has been a key demand since the 1960s (Crouch 2019). How religion will be dealt with at the sub-national level needs to be discussed as demands for religious privileges at regional level are likely.

As previously noted, religious minority communities have, since the late 1940s, worked for a secular constitution. Due to military rule, the political space for debates on the constitutional regulation of religion have been almost non-existent. However, under the NLD government (2016–21) the 2019 constitutional amendment process provided new opportunities for political parties to discuss the issue. "The Union of Myanmar Constitution (2008) Amendment Joint Committee" comprised representatives from the ruling NLD, the military, the USDP, and ethnic minority parties, and by July 2019 they had received thousands of recommendations. However, the NLD, which chaired the committee, confirmed the constitutional recognition of the five religions (Buddhism, Christianity, Islam, Hinduism, and Animism), but did not discuss other religion clauses at all.

By contrast, members from ethnic minority parties suggested changes. For example, the Shan National League for Democracy (SNLD) and the Mon National Party (MNP) suggested deleting conditions of public order, morality, health, and other provisions of the Constitution that limit the right to freedom of religion. They suggested that freedom of religion should be absolute, and no conditions be imposed on it. The Ta'ang (Palaung) National Party called for the inclusion of a subsection to declare that the Union of Myanmar would be a secular state. The SNLD also suggested entirely removing Article 360, which restricts the right to religious freedom as granted in Article 34. The SNLD, together with the Zomi Congress for Democracy (ZCD), proposed to remove Article 361 (granting Buddhism a special position). The ZCD further advocated for deleting Article 362 which names Christianity, Islam, Hinduism, and Animism religions recognized by the state and replacing it with this: "Every citizen has the right to profess any religion of his or her faith." The SNLD and the Pa'O National Organization (PNO) wanted to oblige the state to assist and protect the religions it recognizes by suggesting removing the phrase "to its utmost" from Section 363, which seems to enable the state to give an excuse in cases of inability to protect and assist the religions.[14]

However, the NLD, the USDP, and the military bloc in parliament did not touch these constitutional sections relating to religion in their recommendations made to the committee, or in draft bills separately submitted. Therefore, questions about the

[14] "Proposals by Political Parties, Groups and Independent Representatives for (Constitutional) Amendment, Deletion, and Additions," circulated by the Office of the Pyidaungsu Hluttaw to members of parliament on July 15, 2019, 15. Quoted in United Institute of Peace (USIP) report 2021, unpublished.

constitutional regulation of religion did not arise when the bills were debated in parliament. Except those few ethnic parties that suggested changes, questions concerning constitutional regulation of religion did not reach the broader public. A notable fact is that the NLD claimed no official stance on religion, although there has been widespread support among NLD members for Buddhist constitutional privileges (Laird 2020). The lack of interest shown by the military MPs, the USDP, and the NLD in discussing Buddhist constitutional privileges in parliament, demonstrates the broad consensus at the time among the Bamar Buddhist majority about Buddhist constitutionalism. When minorities have worked to raise this question in formal politics, the Bamar Buddhist political elites – including both the military and the NLD – have chosen to lay the issue to rest.

10.7 CONCLUSION: BUDDHIST CONSTITUTIONALISM IN A MILITARY STATE

Secularism as an ideology of the military state (1962–2011) lost its ground as the military sought to legitimize its rule through Buddhist symbols and structures. This process had already begun in the post-1988 period, but was amplified, I suggest, with the 2008 Constitution and during the years of political liberalization and semi-civilian rule (2011–16, 2016–21). The first period under the rule of the USDP allowed for Buddhist legal activism in the public sphere. In alliance with the USDP and the military, Buddhist pressure groups engaged in Buddhist lawmaking, not with the aim of having religious laws govern the state (as a form of constitutional theocracy), but to protect Buddhism from internal and external threats. This, I contend, is a form of Buddhist statecraft, anchored in constitutional preference for Buddhism. But could the claim be made that Myanmar is a Buddhist state? Seen from a strictly legal perspective, the answer is no. The Constitution neither holds Buddhism as the religion of the state (as in Cambodia), nor does it say anywhere that the head of state must be Buddhist (as in Thailand). Nonetheless, *in practice* the head of state must be Buddhist, and as the military has refashioned itself as the protector of Buddhism, spreading its protective wings over Buddhist legal activism, it can be argued that Myanmar is a de facto Buddhist state.

Perhaps the most salient and under-appreciated feature of Buddhist constitutionalism in Myanmar is its distinct form of secularism, which I suggest, also privileges Buddhism in ways that are not always acknowledged. In fact, to understand how the military state has shaped Buddhist constitutionalism, one must start with two important observations: first, what might be called "Buddhist secularism" (focused on a strict separation between religion and politics rooted in Buddhist political ideology) has served military interests. This is testified by the amplification of such distinctions in the 2008 Constitution compared to the 1947 and the 1974 Constitutions. Second, the military state has granted limited space for constitutional jurisprudence, for example to clarify what Buddhist constitutionalism might imply.

The 2015 "race and religion laws," which caused massive protests among religious minority communities and human rights groups alike, were never heard at the Constitutional Tribunal (a constitutionally recognized forum for all constitutional disputes[15]), to assess their coherence with rights to religious freedom. Even the Myanmar Commission of Human Rights avoided assessing the case as it was considered too politically sensitive (Frydenlund 2017). In both ways, this supposed absence of religion from law and politics has, in fact, advantaged Buddhism.

The practice of limited constitutional jurisprudence in an authoritarian state also suggests that we need to expand the study of Buddhist constitutionalism beyond constitutional law, to include its implicit or unwritten forms. Conceptionally, this bears some affinity with the notion of a "living constitution" like we find in China (Xin He 2014), indicating the importance of context and practice beyond the written text. Such implicit forms point to a larger constitutional complex of policies, laws, courts, and legal practices aimed at acting out the constitutional preference for Buddhism. For example, the Vinicchaya courts are not mentioned in the Constitution, but can be seen as "constitutional statues," that is, as "sets of foundational, basic laws that structure the relationship between monks and rulers" (Schonthal 2018, 6). If we broaden the notion of constitutional statues beyond monastic regulatory concerns to include state Buddhist missionary policies, Buddhist civil laws, religious offense legislation, and Buddhist interest litigation, we will be able to capture Buddhist constitutionalism as an extensive form of Buddhist statecraft.

The 2021 military coup brought about a new twist to the state–religion nexus in Myanmar. After the coup, elected members of parliament formed the Committee Representing Pyidaugsu Hluttaw (CRPH), which on April 16, 2021, formed the National Union Government (NUG). The NUG claims to be the only legitimate government of Myanmar and includes representatives from the NLD and ethnic minority parties. It represents a new cross-ethnic and multireligious political force against the military. The military, through its State Administration Council (SAC), declared the shadow government illegal.

Just prior to the formation of the NUG, the CRPH "annulled" the 2008 Constitution and declared a "Federal Democracy Charter." In relation to the historically contentious position of Buddhist constitutionalism, the charter states that the Federal Union shall practice a political system that has separation between politics and religion. In the English version of the document, the word "secular" is used, while in the Burmese version it reads "a political system not based on religion." Although not explicitly expressing that the state should be religion-neutral, both the Burmese and the English versions of the text indicate the end of

[15] From 2011 to 2018 the Tribunal only published decisions in thirteen cases, none on religious matters.

constitutional preferential treatment of Buddhism.[16] The military for its part declared in May 2021 – through its new puppet organization the YMBA – General Hlaing to be a bodhisattva, thereby confirming the aim of creating a Buddhist-military state. In a televised speech on August 1, 2021, General Hlaing extended emergency rule to August 2023 and declared himself the thirteenth prime minister of Myanmar. In that speech, he explicitly presented SAC rule as pro-Buddhist (in contrast to the previous NLD rule), and importantly, as being in line with the religious clauses of the 2008 Constitution (Global New Light of Myanmar, 2021). Thus, while democratic forces work toward a more inclusive Myanmar, the military will stand as the protector of Buddhist constitutionalism, making it an integral part of military ideology as enshrined in the 2008 Constitution.

REFERENCES

Cheesman, Nick. 2015. *Opposing the Rule of Law: How Myanmar's Courts Make Law and Order*. Cambridge: Cambridge University Press.

Constitution of the Republic of the Union of Myanmar. 2008. Official bilingual version. Ministry of Information.

Constitution of the Socialist Republic of Burma. 1974. Avaivlable at https://www.burmalibrary.org/sites/burmalibrary.org/files/obl/docs07/1974Constitution.pdf

Constitution of the Union of Burma, 1947. Available at https://www.burmalibrary.org/sites/burmalibrary.org/files/obl/docs07/1947Constitution-facsimile-red.pdf)

Crouch, Melissa. 2019. *The Constitution of Myanmar. A Contextual Analysis*. Oxford: Hart Publishing.

Frydenlund, Iselin. 2017. "Religious Liberty for Whom? The Buddhist Politics of Religious Freedom During Myanmar's Transition to Democracy." *Nordic Journal of Human Rights* 35 (1): 55–73.

2018. "The Birth of Buddhist Politics of Religious Freedom in Myanmar." *Journal of Religious and Political Practice* 4 (1): 107–21.

2019. "The Rise of Religious Offence in Transitional Myanmar." In *Outrage: The Rise of Religious Offence in Contemporary South Asia*, edited by Paul Rollier, Kathinka Frøystad and Arild Engelsen Ruud, 77–102. London: UCL Press.

Frydenlund, Iselin, Pum Za Mang, Phyo Wai and Hayward, Susan. 2021. "Religious Responses to the Military Coup in Myanmar." *Review of Faith and International Affairs* 19 (3): 77–88.

Fuller, Paul. 2016. "The Idea of 'Blasphemy' in the Pāli Canon and Modern Myanmar." *Journal of Religion and Violence* 4 (2): 159–81.

Global New Light of Myanmar. 2019. "Interfaith Body Holds 3rd Advisory Forum on National Reconciliation, Peace in Myanmar." November 5.

2020. "Myanmar signs Union Accord Part III for establishing Democratic Federal Union." August 22.

[16] "Federal Democracy Charter Part I," *Declaration of Federal Democracy Union*, 2021, 5. Available at https://crphmyanmar.org/wp-content/uploads/2021/04/Federal-Democracy-Charter-English.pdf. For more on religious responses to the coup, see Frydenlund et al., 2021.

2021. "The Speech Made by State Administration Council Chairman Senior General Min Aung Hlaing on the Occasion of Six Months on 1 August 2021 since the State Administration Council has taken the State's Responsibilities." August 2.

Janaka, Ashin and Crosby, Kate. 2017. "Heresy and Monastic Malpractice in the Buddhist Court Cases (Vinicchaya) of Modern Burma (Myanmar)." *Contemporary Buddhism* 18 (1): 199–261.

Kawanami, Hiroko. 2021. "The Making of a Buddhist Heretic: A Case Study of Sky-Blue Sect." *Journal of Buddhism, Law & Society* 6: 1–25.

Kyaw Phyo Tha. 2014. 'Police Arrest New Zealander, 2 Burmese for Promotion Insulting Buddhism', December 11. www.irrawaddy.com/news/burma/police-arrest-new-zealand-er-2-burmese-promotion-insulting-buddhism.html, currently unavailable.

Kyaw Win, Mya Han, and Thein Hlaing. 2011. *Myanmar Politics: 1958–1962: Volume III*. Yangon: Department of Historical Research.

Laird, Hanna. 2020. *Sāsana Over Secularity. A Discourse Analysis of the Role of Religion for the National League for Democracy in Transitional Myanmar*. MA thesis.

Larsson, Tomas. 2015. "Monkish Politics in Southeast Asia: Religious Disenfranchisement in Comparative and Theoretical Perspective." *Modern Asian Studies* 49: 40–82.

Penal Code. 1861. Available at Burma Library, www.burmalibrary.org/show.php?cat=1860.

Samantapasadika, Sp 996, 997, 7, vol. V. Oxford: Pali Text Society.

Schober, Juliane. 2011. *Modern Buddhist Conjunctures in Myanmar: Cultural Narratives, Colonial Legacies, and Civil Society*. Honolulu: University of Hawai'i Press.

Schonthal, Ben. 2016. *Buddhism, Politics and the Limits of Law, The Pyrrhic Constitutionalism of Sri Lanka*. New York: Cambridge University Press.

2017. "Formations of Buddhist Constitutionalism in South and Southeast Asia." *International Journal of Constitutional Law* 15: 705–15.

2018. "Buddhism and Constitutional Practice." *Asian Journal of Comparative Law*: 245–54.

Tin Maung Maung Than. 1988. "The "Sangha" and "Sasana" in Socialist Burma." *Sojourn: Journal of Social Issues in Southeast Asia* 3(1): 26–61

United Institute of Peace. 2021. *The State-Religion Nexus in Myanmar State-Religion Relations in Peace-Making, Constitutional Reform, and Elections*. Unpublished report.

Walton, Matthew J. 2017. *Buddhism, Politics and Political Thought in Myanmar*. Cambridge: Cambridge University Press.

Walton, Matthew J. and Aung Tun. 2016. "What the State Sangha Committee Actually Said about Ma Ba Tha." *Tea Circle*, July 29.

Xin He. 2014. "The Party's Leadership as a Living Constitution in China." In *Constitutions in Authoritarian Regimes*, edited by Tom Ginsburg and Alberto Simpser: 245–64. New York: Cambridge University Press.

11

Reconstituting the Divided Sangha

Buddhist Authority in Post-Conflict Cambodia

Benjamin Lawrence

11.1 INTRODUCTION

The Cambodian Constitution was the product of an internationalized peace process that saw the United Nations Transitional Authority in Cambodia (UNTAC) supervise a short-lived nationwide ceasefire, assume responsibility for state administration, and facilitate the election of a Constituent Assembly. The subsequent promulgation of the Constitution was meant to introduce a triple transition: from war to peace, from Marx to market, and from dictatorship to democracy. The 1993 Constitution also returned Cambodia to a system of constitutional monarchy, largely based on that which had been overthrown in a military-led coup d'état of 1970. The Constitution also reaffirmed the status of Buddhism as the state religion (a status which had already been reintroduced by constitutional reforms in 1989). Beyond this, Cambodia's new constitutional document also recognized a transition that had already taken place within Cambodia's Buddhist institutions: namely, the move from what had been a unified sangha to one in which authority was again divided between two major monastic sects, the Mahanikay and the Thammayut. Alongside several other articles that clearly related to Buddhism – the Article 4 reintroduction of the national motto, "Nation Religion King," the Article 43 assertion that "Buddhism shall be the religion of the State," and the Article 68 provision of a mandate for the state to "help promote and develop Pāli schools and Buddhist institutes" – another article, Article 13, had major implications for the religion it was ostensibly discussing, relating to the rarefied issue of how to structure the "Council of the Throne." The article specified that, upon the death of one king, a new king should be declared within seven days by a council that included the Supreme Patriarchs (*sanghareach*[1]) of the

[1] *Sanghareach* (Khmer) is, like *Sangharaja*, literally translated as "Sangha King." The title Supreme Patriarch will be used herein.

Mahanikay and of the Thammayut, along with seven other members (all elected to offices in the civilian government).[2]

Although the present version differs slightly in its composition, the Council of the Throne established in 1993 can effectively be understood as a reincarnation of an institution that had been formalized in Cambodia's first formal constitution, initially the product of a joint Franco–Khmer Commission while Cambodia was still under French colonial rule, and eventually promulgated in 1947. In both instances, the Constitution provided for an elected monarchy of sorts, with the mechanism of royal succession being placed primarily under the control of the government rather than the royal family, albeit initially at the behest of King Norodom Sihanouk (Jennar 1995, 35). This chapter traces the contours of Buddhist authority in Cambodia since 1947, as that authority changed, disappeared, and reemerged. It also links these changes to Cambodia's changing constitutional orders in those years. It argues that the bifurcation of Buddhist authority recognized in the current Constitution is the result of historical and political contingencies that continue to affect the interaction of Buddhism and public law in Cambodia. This account begins from a recognition that while the inclusion of the two Supreme Patriarchs on the reconstituted Council of the Throne was a predictable outcome of the constitution-making process of 1993, it was in fact only possible because of a wholesale restructuring of the architecture of sangha authority that had been initiated less than two years earlier. The presence of *two* Supreme Patriarchs, representing separately the Mahanikay and Thammayut sects, was made possible by the fact that Cambodia's Buddhist authorities had themselves effectively been reconstituted and divided into two over the course of 1991 and 1992, shortly after the negotiation of the Paris Peace Accords, which in turn formed the basis of Cambodia's 1993 Constitution.

While the distinctions between Mahanikay and Thammayut sects are relatively slight in doctrinal terms, the division between the two is both politically and symbolically significant, as this chapter will explain. The arrival of the Thammayut sect in the mid-nineteenth century was historically controversial precisely because it introduced divisions in religious authority between a traditional Mahanikay sect, which remained broadly popular, and a newer lineage that had been imported from Siam and was almost exclusively associated with urban elites and aristocracy. These divisions remained latent throughout the colonial and immediate post-independence eras, and only threatened to surface after the fall of the monarchy in 1970. After the tragedies of the Democratic Kampuchea period, in which the Khmer Rouge entirely deconstructed and destroyed Cambodia's religious institutions, the country's Buddhist sangha reemerged slowly, in a hobbled and

2 Art. 14 states that: 'The King of Cambodia shall be a member of the Royal family, be at least 30 years old and descend from the bloodline of King Ang Duong, King Norodom or King Sisowath.' The Constitution of the Kingdom of Cambodia 1993, Art. 14. The other seven members of the Throne Council include the President and first and second Vice Presidents of both the Senate and the National Assembly, and the Prime Minister.

homogenized form. During the 1980s, the sangha's membership was tightly restricted, and its structures unified and centralized under the auspices of the historically more prominent Mahanikay sect. Only after the reinstatement of Buddhism as the state religion in 1989, and the return of King Norodom Sihanouk during the negotiation of the Paris Accords, was the Thammayut sect reestablished. The Mahanikay and Thammayut sects, then, continued to be represented separately by their respective Supreme Patriarchs, who have occasionally adopted different stances on social and political issues. However, an additional ambivalence has been introduced since 2006, with the creation of the superordinate position of Great Supreme Patriarch, not to mention the immediate elevation of Samdech Tep Vong – the former head of the unified sangha of the 1980s and the Supreme Patriarch of the Mahanikay sect from 1991 to 2006 – to that position.

As this chapter will demonstrate, the existence of a division within the sangha's authority in Cambodia, let alone the constitutional recognition of this division, is far from inevitable. Instead, it can be understood as part of a political settlement that sought to end Cambodia's decades-old civil war, and which has subsequently been superseded to some degree by changes in the political landscape, particularly the declining influence of royalism as a political force in Cambodia (Norén-Nilsson 2016b). To convey the historical significance of this configuration of Buddhist authority in Cambodia, and its constitutional recognition, this chapter will start by providing a brief account of the arrival of the Thammayut sect into Cambodia's religious and political milieu, and its gradual consolidation in Cambodia over the course of the French colonial rule. The following section will then sketch the contours of the relationship between sangha and state authority after independence from France, following the overthrow of the monarchy, under Khmer Rouge rule, and during the protracted period of civil war thereafter, noting how the postures of these various regimes were reflected in the corresponding Constitutions of 1947, 1972, 1976, and 1979. The short-lived period under the Constitution of the State of Cambodia provided an opening for the reconstitution of sangha institutions which has in turn shaped the current constitutional order. The remainder of the chapter considers these legacies, examining the design of the new constitutional text and highlighting the ways in which the sangha has manifested its (newly redivided) authority in Cambodia since 1993. It ends with a discussion of the creation of the position of Great Supreme Patriarch in 2006, noting its symbolic implications and placing those implications in the broader sociopolitical context of contemporary Cambodia. This chapter will ultimately demonstrate that the structure of sangha authority in Cambodia continues to be the subject of political influence and intervention.

11.2 OF ROYAL IMPORT: THE THAMMAYUT SECT AND IN ITS HISTORICAL CONTEXT

The Mahanikay sect, which remains the largest monastic order in Cambodia, traces its roots back to the arrival of Theravāda Buddhism in the Angkorian empire

(Kent 2016, 378). Initially influencing only the ruling elite, as reflected in the fact that many princes are said to have ordained as monks as part of their training for effective leadership, Theravāda Buddhism was increasingly widespread in the general Khmer population by the fourteenth century (Yang Sam 1987, 1, 7). As Alexandra Kent explains, "[w]hile Hinduism seems to have been ... fairly irrelevant to daily life in the villages, Theravāda Buddhism became woven into the fabric of rural life." The fact that "young village men could now acquire religious credentials by ordaining as Buddhist monks" allowed for a "socially diverse" sangha to develop in a decentralised manner across the Kingdom (Kent 2016, 379). Whether as a result of this shift in social and political ordering, of infighting within the ruling elite, or of external factors, the newly Theravāda Buddhist kingdom soon went into a prolonged decline (known as the "middle period" in Cambodian historiography). This was catalyzed by the sacking first of Angkor, and then of the short lived alternative capital in Longvek. As a result, while the center of the Kingdom's (diminishing) political authority moved southeast to Udong (near the current capital of Phnom Penh), the center of its Buddhist influence moved to Ayutthaya, and eventually to Bangkok. In the words of the historian, Alain Forest, "[m]onks destined to become the most respected Venerables of the Cambodian sangha came to the monasteries of these two capitals," while from a religious perspective Udong became "little more than an extension of its Siamese counterparts" (2008, 23). Nevertheless, historical accounts of the early nineteenth century court in Phnom Penh speak of "a fairly rigid hierarchy" in which the Buddhist patriarchs sat just below the royal family (Harris 2005, 51).

It is in this context that the teachings, practices, and order of the Thammayut sect were established in Cambodia in 1853. Arriving "through the importation of courtly Buddhist practice and thought from Thailand," Cambodia's Thammayut fraternity was derived from that established by Mongkut (later, King Rama IV) two decades earlier (Kent 2008, 84). Concerned primarily with monastic practice, which Mongkut perceived to have erred from the word of the Vinaya, the Thammayut movement can be understood as an attempt to purify Buddhist practice by returning to a more direct and strict reading of Pāli scripture. Thammayut texts and teachings, to which much of the more mystical Buddhist practices in Cambodia at the time would have been antithetical, were initially introduced to Cambodia under King Ang Duong, who acquired eighty bundles of texts, and also sent both of his sons (Norodom and Sisowath) to ordain with the fraternity (Peng, Kong & Menzel 2016, 395). However, the commitment of the Cambodian crown to Thammayut teaching was made explicit when Ang Duong's successor – King Norodom – sponsored the construction of a Thammayut temple next to the royal palace as the Cambodian capital moved to Phnom Penh in 1867 (Edwards 2007, 103–9). That temple, Wat Botum Vadey, remains the center of Thammayut practice in Cambodia today.

Yet, Thammayut teachings appear to have remained the preserve of the aristocracy and urban elite in Cambodia, while the unreformed majority – which came to be known as the Mahanikay – prevailed across the rest of Cambodian society. While royal patronage was central to its ability to gain a foothold in Phnom Penh, the Thammayut initially also benefited from the support of colonial authorities. As Penny Edwards explains, French "manipulation of strategic alliances with the Thammayut and Mahanikay would fundamentally alter the balance of power between the two sects" (Edwards 2007, 110). Initially sympathetic to the rationalism and modernist ambitions of the reformist movement, colonial authorities later became suspicious of the extent to which Thammayut leaders continued to be influenced by developments, and allied to institutions, in Siam. As the colonial administration's engagement with Buddhism developed, therefore, French allegiances shifted towards the Mahanikay. By giving preferential opportunities for further religious study abroad, Edwards notes, "French scholars and colonial institutes stymied the monopolization of Cambodge's 'national' religion, Buddhism, by a sect they identified as Siamese in origin and orientation" (Edwards 2007, 112).[3] Ultimately, the Thammayut would establish itself in Cambodia, but only in a limited way: a reality which is underlined by the fact that, by the turn of the twentieth century, the Mahanikay made up 97 percent of all temples nationwide, although this number dropped as low as 85 percent in areas around the capital (Harris 2005, 111). The Thammayut sect represented only a small fraction of Cambodia's monastic community at this time, but it had a concentrated influence close to the center of political power.

The Thammayut's consolidation in Cambodia occurred contemporaneously with the formalization of Buddhist authority through an attempt at state-led centralization. This process began in 1880, when King Norodom – apparently inspired by Mongkut's creation of a national sangha in Thailand – ordered the restructuring of the sangha, resulting in the appointment of the most senior Mahanikay monk – Venerable Nil Tieng – to the apex position of Supreme Patriarch, and the elevation of the most senior Thammayut monk – *Samdech Preah Maha* Sokhoun Pan – to the second highest position (Harris 2005, 109). These appointments occurred within a broader milieu that, according to French colonial functionary and author of the 1899 book *Le Buddhisme au Cambodge*, Adhémard Leclère, contained "a multitude of sanghas" (Leclère 1899).

While recognizing Mahanikay ascendency, this formalized hierarchy nonetheless recognized the coexistence within it of two distinct monastic orders, each with their own hierarchies and leadership. This new status quo was soon refined by French colonial authorities, as they began just two decades later to formalize sangha authority in secular law. Specifically, the authorities of the French Protectorate in Cambodia introduced procedures for the state administration's registration of temples in 1904, and for its registration of monks and novices in 1916, before

[3] Also, note that the shift in the attention of colonial authorities also appears to have precipitated a reformist movement within the Mahanikay, which rose in prominence under French rule over the first half of the twentieth century.

restructuring the sangha nationwide and bringing it under state authority in 1919. In February and September of 1943, meanwhile, the complete restructuring of the sangha hierarchy was ordered by royal decrees that gave the Supreme Patriarchs of the Mahanikay and Thammayut greater independence to appoint chief monks at the provincial level, but still made these appointments subject to approval by the king and the Ministry of Cults and Religious Affairs. Ultimately, however, this formal recognition of two distinct monastic fraternities within a single, unified sangha authority belied a social undercurrent of increasing tension, in which both Mahanikay and Thammayut authorities had sought to obstruct one another's activities.[4] The divisiveness of this situation was most forcefully articulated in the anti-colonial publication *Nagaravatta*, which cited the division as a potential cause for the decline of Buddhism in the country and called for the eradication of divisions within the sangha (albeit without success) under the slogan of "One Nation, One Religion" (Edwards 2007, 208). This phrase would reemerge in the 1980s, as will be discussed shortly.

Cambodia's first formal Constitution was promulgated by King Norodom Sihanouk in 1947, after a drafting process initially led by a joint Franco–Khmer Commission but then taken up by an elected Constituent Assembly. The process eventually produced a draft which largely followed the contours of that of the French Fourth Republic (Jennar 1995, 35–36). One notable change from the first Franco–Khmer Commission draft, which was introduced at the request of King Sihanouk, however, was the introduction of a system of elected (rather than hereditary) monarchy (Jennar 1995, 35–36). This, in turn, demanded the creation of a Crown Council which would lead the selection process; a Council that was chaired by the President of the Family Council of the Royal Family, but also included the President of the National Assembly, the President of the Council of the Kingdom, the President of the Council of Ministers, and the Supreme Patriarchs of both the Mahanikay and Thammayut monastic orders (Article 28). Beyond the inclusion of the two Supreme Patriarchs on the Crown Council, reference to Buddhism, or religion more generally, can be found in Article 8, guaranteeing freedom of religion, and recognizing Buddhism as "the religion of the state," and Article 49, which explicitly excludes members of the sangha from the principle of universal suffrage. The 1947 Constitution also refers to the King as *dhammika mahareach* ("great

[4] For example, Harris notes that "The hostility is illustrated by the fate of the *Vinayavaṇṇanà*, the foundation document of the Thammayut, which tells how King Mongkut came to see the need for reform of monastic Buddhism in Siam. It was first translated from Thai into Khmer in 1912, but this first edition is now quite rare because traditionalist members of the Mahanikay were successful in ensuring its systematic destruction" (2005, 108). Meanwhile, Edwards suggests that "[m]any Thammayut monks were actively obstructing the diffusion of the Royal Library's 'works of popularization' in their key zones of influence, namely Battambang, Siem Reap, and Sisophon" (2007, 205).

righteous king"), implying that he was the protector and patron of Buddhism, and the embodiment of rightful rule according to Buddhist principles.

The period which followed full independence from France – which was finally negotiated by Sihanouk in 1953 – is frequently referred to in glowing terms. In his book, *Khmer Buddhism and Politics from 1954 to 1984*, for example, Yang Sam claims that "this time was probably the peak period of modern Khmer Buddhism" (1987, 2). The Buddhist credentials of Sihanouk's post-independence rule (first as king, then as president, and later in a hybrid prince-and-head-of-state role) are discussed at length elsewhere (Harris 2005, 144–56). However, it is worth noting that, in the context of general growth in the size of the Buddhist sangha, this period actually saw a relative decline in the size and influence of the Thammayut sect. From a total of 202 monasteries at the moment of independence, there were only 139 still operating by 1970, while the number of Mahanikay temples increased from 2,461 to 3,369 in the same period (Yang Sam 1987, 17). This decline in the Thammayut sect is attributed by Yang Sam to a generalized unwillingness to abandon ritual practices (typically associated with Brahmanical and animist traditions), a reluctance amongst rural Cambodians to send their children to ordain in Thammayut temples which tended to be concentrated around the capital of Phnom Penh, and the emergence of a dynamic reformist movement within the Mahanikay. As a result, there appears to have been an increasingly widely felt sentiment that the Thammayut order enhanced division and disharmony in Cambodia's monastic and lay community, because it "emphasized the division of social classes between the royalty, the rich and the poor" (Yang Sam 1987, 17). While this divisiveness is frequently remarked upon by historical accounts of the period, it did not manifest in open confrontations within the sangha.

Serious divisions within the sangha became increasingly evident as, in 1970, Cambodia descended into civil war. The fall of the Kingdom of Cambodia, courtesy of parliament's dismissal of Sihanouk as Head of State, and the seizing of power by military General Lon Nol, had the support of many notable figures within the sangha, particularly reformist elements within the Mahanikay sect. Venerable Khieu Chum, for example, gained notoriety for his critique of the sangha's dependence on monarchy, which he argued the Buddha himself had rejected, and after the coup became a prominent supporter of republicanism. Khieu Chum's vision of a republican but nonetheless Buddhist Cambodia – which he articulated with increasing clarity after 1970 (Harris 2008, 98) – would also inspire later political leaders, such as Heng Samrin during the early 1980s (Yang Sam 1987, 83). Meanwhile, only private appeals from then Mahanikay Supreme Patriarch, Huot Tat, prevented a significant number of Thammayut monks from embarking on a march to protest the overthrow of Sihanouk and the imminent dissolution of the monarchy.

The Khmer Republic – which was eventually formalized in the 1972 Constitution – was far from secular, let alone anticlerical. Lon Nol himself described the ongoing civil war, against the communist insurrection led by the Khmer Rouge, as "a religious war" against a "*thmil*" (devil/atheist) enemy (Harris 2005, 174). Article 2 of the Constitution of the Khmer Republic also recognized Buddhism as the state religion. The removal of the monarchy meant that the Crown Council had been dispensed with, thereby removing previous references to the leaders of the Thammayut and Mahanikay sects in the new charter. Nevertheless, Lon Nol had already reassured both leaders in the months after the coup that: "the present radical change of political rule is not meant to be prejudicial to Buddhism, which remains the state religion as it has up till now" (Harris 2012, 16).

The subsequent rise of the Khmer Rouge was a disaster for Buddhism. Though a number of Buddhist monks appear to have been involved in the Indochinese Communist Party and then the Communist Party of Kampuchea in earlier years, the Khmer Rouge's four years of rule under the Democratic Kampuchea regime were characterized by the complete destruction of religious institutions, the systematic elimination of Buddhist leadership, and the generalized defrocking and mistreatment of monks from urban centers. Inevitably, the Constitution of Democratic Kampuchea, promulgated in 1975, did not recognize a state religion, and although it did purport to recognize the right to worship in Article 20, it simultaneously forbade the worship of any "reactionary religion which is detrimental to Democratic Cambodia and the Cambodian people." This latter prohibition appears to have been interpreted so broadly as to prohibit the practice of any religion, other than the animism of highland communities. Whether as a result of an intentional policy of eradication or not, less than 100 – and by some estimates only 12 – Cambodian monks survived the Democratic Kampuchea period, meaning that some 80,000 monks had been lost over the course of a period in which almost a quarter of the population died from either exhaustion, starvation, disease, torture or execution (Yang Sam 1987, 81; Kent 2016, 383).

11.3 RECONSTRUCTING THE SANGHA

The fall of Democratic Kampuchea, then, might have provided an opportunity to rebuild Buddhist institutions in the wake of the destruction wrought by Khmer Rouge rule. Though the Vietnamese-installed People's Republic of Kampuchea (PRK) was ideologically opposed to the promotion of Buddhism, it nevertheless "allowed the restoration of temples and a restricted revival of the sangha" in order to accrue some much-needed legitimacy (Kent 2008, 383). Strict limits were introduced on the expansion of the sangha, preventing anyone under the age of fifty from ordaining, and limiting to four the number of monks residing at any particular temple (Marston 2009). Meanwhile, historical accounts of the period describe a situation in which Buddhism was made wholly subservient to the authority of the party (the National United Front Salvation of Kampuchea, herein the Front) and the PRK state. As John Marston explains, the restored sangha "was considered a mass organization structurally parallel to labor unions and the women's association," such that newly appointed Buddhist leaders (officially ordained at a ceremony in 1975) were nonetheless "under the administrative direction of Front officials." Temple (*wat*) committees that were primarily constituted by laypeople exercised "great power over the direction of the *wat*," ensuring some portion of donations would be directed to broader community initiatives (Marston 2009, 225–26). As such, Buddhist monks were treated as "state employees" and were expected to sustain themselves by growing vegetables on temple land. The unique reality of this status is similarly reflected in the fact that monks were formally enfranchised and allowed to run for public office for the first time by way of Article 31 of the 1979 Constitution of the People's Republic of Kampuchea.[5]

Meanwhile, Buddhist authority was reconstituted in the form a single, unified sangha (the "Front order," or *braḥ saṅgh raṇasirsa*). After being one of seven people to take part in the first official ordination ceremony, which was overseen by a group of Theravāda monks brought in from Vietnam, Tep Vong was soon selected to sit at the apex of the new monastic order, as well as to sit as the vice president of the National Assembly. Although this privileged political position could be perceived as a recognition of the status of Buddhist authority, it is better understood – particularly from a historical perspective that recognizes the conventional separation between Buddhist and state authority – as an attempt to ensure the subservience of the sangha hierarchy to the state. From his position in the National Assembly, for example, Tep Vong is reported to have offered justifications for state-led political violence against domestic political dissent, which he sought to base in Buddhist doctrine.

Meanwhile, the sangha over which Tep Vong now presided as President (*pradhān*) – rather than Supreme Patriarch (*saṅghareach*), with its royal connotations – was officially one without sects or divisions. "Now we make no difference between the two orders; there is at present only one sangha," Tep Vong is reported to have told a Vietnamese reporter. Another senior monk – Oum Soum – later remarked that "our monks are neither Mahanikay nor Thammayut but are Nationalist monks" (Yang Sam 1987, 86). However, some accounts indicate that in reality the teaching and practice of the sangha at the time leaned heavily towards Mahanikay rather than Thammayut conventions in all relevant respects. Writing in 1987, for example, Yang Sam explains that the "overall practices [of the unified *braḥ saṅgh raṇasirsa*] are those of the Mahanikay order" (1987, 87). In response, there appear to have been some attempts to reestablish a Thammayut monastic order, which were suppressed on the basis that any Buddhist institutions outside of the officially recognized order were illegal. That these initiatives appear to have been so swiftly and categorically dealt with by Front or PRK authorities suggests that there was a particular sensitivity to any potential for an alternative locus of Buddhist

[5] As Tomas Larsson explains, the (re)enfranchisement of Buddhist monks was typically the preserve of the "most virulently anti-religious and anti-clerical regimes" (2015, 71).

authority to develop, given that this could provide a challenge to the legitimacy of the *braḥ saṅgh raṇasirsa*. By contrast, the establishment of unofficial *wats*, which circumvented the rigid registration restrictions imposed by the state, were relatively commonplace at this time (Bektimirova 2002).

11.4 THE RETURN OF A DIVIDED SANGHA

The most recent reconstitution of Buddhist authority in Cambodia was ultimately precipitated by global events. The Soviet policy of *perestroika*, which saw the reduction of aid to Vietnam as part of the gradual winding-down of the Cold War, ultimately forced Hanoi to reconsider its support for the PRK regime. Plans for the first withdrawal of Vietnamese troops from Cambodia were announced in May 1988 (Cima 1989). This, in turn, prompted Hun Sen, who had become prime minister of the PRK three years prior, to undertake a series of fundamental reforms, starting with the almost immediate lifting of limits on ordination to the sangha and culminating in the promulgation of the Constitution of the State of Cambodia (SoC) in 1989. While the Constitution of the SoC bore many similarities to that which had preceded it, it also contained a number of significant changes. Alongside the reintroduction of private property and the shift away from a planned economy, for instance, the SoC Constitution in Article 6 reinstated Buddhism as the state religion and removed provisions of Article 31 which had previously enfranchised Buddhist monks. The new constitutional recognition of Buddhism's special status was accompanied by a public apology from Hun Sen for the "mistakes" made toward religion over the previous decade of the Front's rule (Harris 2005, 200).

While significant in themselves, the reforms of the State of Cambodia era must also be understood as symbolic moves designed to further open up the opportunity for a comprehensive peace agreement to end the country's ongoing civil war.[6] Negotiations toward this settlement had begun by the middle of 1988, at the First Jakarta Informal Meeting, and culminated in the signing of the Paris Peace Agreements on October 23, 1991. In this context, steps such as the constitutional recognition in 1989 of Buddhism as the state religion must be understood as attempts to reassure other warring parties and the international community. As John Marston explains: "the reforms represented the country as amenable to basic changes of the kind that would make a settlement with resistance factions feasible" (2009, 226).

Significant structural changes to the sangha, meanwhile, began apace toward the end of 1991, after the signing of the Paris Peace Accords enabled the return of Norordom Sihanouk in November of that year. The *braḥ saṅgh raṇasirsa* was

6 Since the fall of Democratic Kampuchea, the civil war had pitted the Front and its Vietnamese patrons against a coalition made up of the royalist FUNCINPEC (*Front uni national pour un Cambodge indépendant, neutre, pacifique et coopératif*), the anti-communist Khmer People's National Liberation Front (KPNLF), and remnants of the Khmer Rouge, which still controlled significant portions of the country's western and southwestern provinces.

promptly dissolved, and the returning former king appears to have immediately (and unofficially) resumed a role as patron of the sangha. As such, Sihanouk awarded Tep Vong the royally imbued title of *Sanghareach*, and concurrently applied the same title to the prominent, Paris-based Thammayut monk, Bou Kry, whose temple had accommodated Sihanouk's son (Prince Sihamoni) when he ordained as a monk almost a decade earlier. By February 1992, the separate monastic orders of Mahanikay and Thammayut sects had been fully reconstituted. The two Supreme Patriarchs, Tep Vong and Bou Kry, respectively, sat at the apex of the two newly reconstituted hierarchies, with power to appoint Chief Monks at province, municipality, district, and village level via *preah sangha prakas* (sangha decrees), with the cosignature of the Minister for Cults and Religious Affairs (Peng, Kong & Menzel 2016, 411). Though there is no reference to the sangha or to Buddhism in the Accords,[7] it seems likely that this reconstitution of the sangha, along lines closely resembling that which had existed prior to the fall of the Kingdom of Cambodia in 1970, was at least an implicit – if not explicitly agreed but unwritten – aspect of the broader political settlement.

Cambodia's peace-time state authority, then, was reconstituted after that of its religious authorities. In an eighteen-month process beginning in March 1992, the United Nations Transitional Authority in Cambodia assumed responsibility for the functions of the Cambodian state, sought to oversee the disarmament of the warring factions, and administered elections in May 1993. Ahead of that election, both *samdech* Tep Vong and *samdech* Bou Kry unsuccessfully sought to secure an exception to the universal franchise, so as to prevent monks from both monastic orders being allowed to vote for what would be the first time in the country's history (Larsson 2015). The denial of this request by the head of the UNTAC mission, Yasushi Akashi, ultimately set a precedent whereby monks have been formally included in the franchise ever since, much to the chagrin of the two patriarchs. Nevertheless, the Constituent Assembly formed by the 1993 elections, in which the royalist FUNCINPEC won a narrow majority, went on to draft a constitution (promulgated on September 24, 1993) which restored Cambodia to the status of constitutional monarchy, and otherwise synthesized key features of the amended 1947 Constitution of the Kingdom of Cambodia and the 1989 Constitution of the State of Cambodia: Article 4 of the Constitution restored the national motto of "Nation, Religion, King"; Article 43 reaffirmed the special status of Buddhism as the state religion; and Article 68 provided the state with a duty to "develop Pāli schools and Buddhist institutes." Along with the reinstatement of the monarchy, meanwhile, in Article 13 came the reforming of the Council of the Throne, wherein the

7 There is also virtually no mention of religion more broadly, other than the general commitment to human rights in Part 3 of the Accords and a guarantee provided in Annex 5 that the Constitution due to be drafted pursuant to UN-administered elections would include the right to freedom of religion and a prohibition against religious discrimination.

Supreme Patriarchs of the Mahanikay and Thammayut were joined by the president and first and second vice presidents of the National Assembly, the prime minister, and (after the formation of the Upper House in 1999) by the president and first and second vice presidents of the Senate.

Most scholars view the UNTAC experiment and its legacies as having been a heavily qualified success, particularly with regard to its purported democracy-building mandate. A major reason for this was that Cambodia's multi-party political settlement could not be reconciled with an institutional context that otherwise remained overwhelmingly dominated by the Cambodian People's Party (herein, CPP).[8] Many of these dynamics were paralleled in the reconstituted sangha. This is most clearly embodied by Tep Vong, who remained at the top of the sangha hierarchy (as Supreme Patriarch of the Mahanikay sect) after 1993, despite his close association with the PRK regime. This continuity has, according to Alexandra Kent, meant that Tep Vong – and much of the hierarchy of the post-1993 Cambodian sangha more generally – "continues to be popularly viewed as the religious mouthpiece of a Vietnamese-friendly [CPP] government," in spite of the formal independence that has been afforded to Buddhist institutions (Kent 2008, 85). In the newly reestablished Thammayut order, meanwhile, positions of significant influence were actually held by other CPP-affiliated, Mahanikay-educated monks. The position immediately below Bou Kry, Ian Harris notes, was filled by the Oum Soum, who had himself been a prominent figure in the *braḥ saṅgh raṇasirsa* of the 1980s (Harris 2005, 214–15). Similarly, the lay chairman of the Pagoda Council at Wat Botum Vadey – the temple built by King Norodom as the center of the Thammayut sect and, after 1992, the home of Bou Kry[9] – was none other than the father of Hun Sen (Harris 2005, 215). According to Harris, the positioning of such figures can be understood as an attempt to surveil the Thammayut order, which was likely to have been viewed with suspicion by the CPP even after the uneasy and fragile peace had been established. In fact, Harris states that "it could be argued that they are well placed to feed intelligence to the relevant authorities" (Harris 2005, 214–15). While appointments within each order were ostensibly the prerogative of their respective *Sanghareach*, there are indications that these decisions were subject to political influence and intervention at the local level. Alexandra Kent, for example, reports data showing that "head monks are not always elected by the monks but may instead be instated through the support of local politically supported officials" (Kent 2008, 89). Though formally reconstituted as two distinct orders, and to a large extent formally independent from the state, the order of the Thammayut

8 The CPP was the new name given in 1991 to the National United Front Salvation of Kampuchea, which had ruled Cambodia with Vietnamese support since the overthrow of the Khmer Rouge in 1979.

9 Although historically the center of the Thammayut monastic order, and still of central importance to the sect, the majority of monks at Wat Botum Vadey are also now Mahanikay.

was – from 1992 – largely in a process of transition which reflected the broader political change that was ongoing in Cambodia.

11.5 POST-1993 PRACTICE

Despite their new configuration and the relative autonomy it appeared to confer, the Thammayut and Mahanikay sects were largely unified in the public positions on significant social and political questions. One issue where daylight was visible between the two, however, was in response to the HIV/AIDS epidemic that gathered momentum after the departure of UNTAC (Ledgerwood 1994). The difference in posture between the Supreme Patriarchs of the two orders came to a head in 2000, around a conference organized for Buddhist monks by the National AIDS Authority, with significant support from international donors. Specifically, Tep Vong made only a brief appearance at the conference, and later explained that his reticence reflected a more fundamental skepticism about the involvement of monks in HIV/AIDS education or support to people with HIV/AIDS. Suggesting that the extent of the epidemic had been inflated by the CPP's political opponents in order to discredit the ruling party, Tep Vong argued that the official figure of 170,000 was incorrect and that only around 30,000 people had contracted HIV (Post Staff 2000). Meanwhile, the Supreme Patriarch argued, the holding of workshops brought unwanted attention, since "the more people who attend the meeting, the more people will tell the world Cambodia is not good" (Post Staff 2000). Rather, Tep Vong appears to have advocated a more hardline approach, suggesting the government should first crack down on vice in the country before involving monks in awareness-raising activities, and ultimately suggested the sangha's stance should be to withhold support, since those who were suffering were only being punished for their immorality: a kind of karmic justice. "If we help sick people, then we will only encourage them not to be afraid of catching the virus," Tep Vong also explained "[i]f you support the people with AIDS then we openly broadcast to the world we support AIDS" (Post Staff 2000).

The Supreme Patriarch's stance was not shared throughout the Mahanikay sect, of which he was the premier authority, however, as many monks were profoundly involved in the fight against HIV/AIDS across the country, and in offering care to people with AIDS. Neither was the stance shared by the Thammayut Supreme Patriarch. In contrast to Tep Vong, Bou Kry was more conciliatory towards those suffering from the disease and largely supportive of monks' engagement with the HIV/AIDS issue. "The subject should be mixed with Buddhist sermons – and every monk has to do that," the Thammayut Supreme Patriarch told the English-language *Phnom Penh Post* newspaper, before explicitly dismissing the idea of suppression as a strategy and advocating education as "the best way." Finally, Bou Kry called on monks "to give moral support to the sick [with AIDS] so they can die peacefully – even though they have committed a bad thing" (Post Staff 2000). On what was an increasingly politicized societal issue, in other words, the division of the sangha between Mahanikay and Thammayut orders – as well as the heterogeneity of practice that was possible within the former – allowed for Cambodia's Buddhist monks to be prominently involved in the dissemination of information about HIV/AIDS, and in the provision of important services to its sufferers at a time when state capacity was still profoundly limited.

Simultaneously, tensions between the two orders threatened to surface over a more overtly political issue: the deaths of sixteen supporters of the opposition politician Sam Rainsy, who were killed by a grenade attack in the public park immediately outside of Wat Botum Vadey in March 1997. Sam Rainsy, it seems, had already established a relationship with the Thammayut Supreme Patriarch, who resided at the Wat Botum Vadey temple at the time: both had been part of the Cambodian diaspora in France during the 1980s, at which point Bou Kry is rumored to have told worshipers to donate to the FUNCINPEC party, with whom Sam Rainsy was affiliated at the time (Harris 2005, 214). Meanwhile, Sam Rainsy had himself spent three weeks ordained as a monk at the temple just a year prior to the attack. Although Bou Kry steered clear of any comment at the time of the killings, he provided some measured remarks to journalists three years later, as supporters of Sam Rainsy sought to erect a stupa in the park to memorialize the dead. Aware that three previous such memorials had been removed or destroyed by authorities, Bou Kry told journalists that he was "very concerned" about the fate of the fourth iteration, noting that the stupa contained a Buddha statue and that any damage done to the statue "would be like they were attacking the Buddhist religion" (O'Connell and Saroeun 2000). The Supreme Patriarch's sympathy, however, may have been made clearer when the stupa was temporarily rehoused within the walls of Wat Botum Vadey. In the context of a profoundly polarized political context, and in light of Bou Kry's general opposition to Buddhist figures engaging in politics, such support (muted though it was) can be understood as a politically symbolic gesture.

The two Supreme Patriarchs have also been engaged in political matters when called upon to participate in the deliberations of the Council of the Throne, confirming King Sihamoni's ascension in 2004. This process was complicated by the fact that Sihamoni was to be selected as king in the wake of his father's abdication of the throne, an event for which there was no provision made in the constitutional articles relating to royal succession. Sihanouk's abdication came in the midst of a post-election political crisis (Peou 2006). As with the elections five years earlier (Khuy 1998), the 2003 elections had seen the CPP win a majority of seats in the National Assembly but fall short of the super-majority needed to form a government. Initially the CPP failed in attempts to form a coalition with opposition parties who disputed the results of the election. Provided a "supreme role as arbitrator to ensure the regular execution of public powers" by Article 9 of the Constitution, Sihanouk's frustrations with the dysfunction of Cambodia's political system and the inability of the parties to reach a compromise, which he described as a "dishonorable deadlock" (Yun 2003), came to the fore as he repeatedly threatened to abdicate the throne (Yun 2004). By contrast, Bou Kry appears not to have intervened to stop Sihanouk from abdicating. Instead, shortly after King Sihanouk had formally issued his notice of abdication, Bou Kry publicly stated his support for Norodom Sihamoni to assume the throne. "Prince Sihamoni deserves the position because it belongs to him," the Thammayut Supreme Patriarch explained, noting that the prince – who had previously ordained as a Thammayut monk at a temple in France in 1981, where he came under Bou Kry's personal guidance – had immediately sought his personal advice after hearing of the abdication (Lor & Leung 2021). The contrast between these two positions – Tep Vong's attempt to persuade Sihanouk to remain on the throne and Bou Kry's close involvement in preparing Sihamoni to succeed his father, which he did in October 2004 – hint at the ongoing closeness between the royal family and the Thammayut sect, if not also the Mahanikay Patriarch's view of the throne as a symbol of political stability, compromise and, ultimately, legitimacy for the ruling party (Lawrence 2020).

A significant alteration to the configuration of the sangha hierarchies was made in 2006, though this was not reflected in any change in the composition of the Council of the Throne, let alone the text of the Constitution more generally. Specifically, a new position of Great Supreme Patriarch was established by royal decree (No. NS/RKT/0506/207, 2006), with Tep Vong being appointed, and his previous position as Supreme Patriarch of the Mahanikay being filled by his former deputy, Nuon Nget (Royal Decree No. PS/RKT/0406/200, 2006). As such, a figure who had until that point been the Supreme Patriarch of the Mahanikay, and who had himself presided over the unified *braḥ saṅgh raṇasirsa* of the 1980s, became the ultimate authority within the Cambodian sangha once again. Tep Vong became the first Supreme Patriarch to represent both the Mahanikay and Thammayut orders of the Cambodian sangha since Nil Teang was appointed to a similar position in 1859. The move, which was signed by the recently crowned King Sihamoni, was immediately criticized by opponents and dissidents. One former monk, Chin Channa, who himself claimed to have been "hounded out" of the sangha due to his interest in politics, described the change at the time as "politically made only to undermine and downgrade the Dhammayuth [sic] and put it under the influence of the CPP," and noted that the move had been made possible by a political context in which "royalists are declining." Striking a similar tone to that of Chin Channa, opposition political leader Sam Rainsy similarly argued that "[t]he best way to maintain peace as it is today, is to please keep it [the structure of sangha authority] the same." This call went unheeded, however, and a year later a royalist-affiliated newspaper,[10]

[10] *Khmer Amatak News* was informally associated with Prince Norodom Ranariddh, the former leader of FUNCINPEC who had – at this point – formed his own eponymous political party, the NRP.

Khmer Amatak News, was threatened with closure after it published a story praising Thammayut Supreme Patriarch Bou Kry for his ability to rise above politics and accusing Tep Vong of using his position to act as "the CPP's spokesman" (Yun 2007).[11]

Despite having won enough seats in the National Assembly in the 2003 elections to avert a super-majority for the CPP, the royalist political movement was clearly on the wane. This decline was not helped by the abdication (and withdrawal from political life) of Sihanouk, with whom the vast majority of royalist political prestige continued to adhere (Norén-Nilsson 2016a, 2016b). Ultimately, the reality of this decline was borne out two years later, when the royalist opposition parties (namely, FUNCINPEC and the Norodom Ranariddh Party that splintered from it) were resoundingly defeated in the 2008 elections.[12] The return, recognition, and then relative relegation of the Thammayut vis-à-vis the more popular Mahanikay sect can be understood to reflect the plight of royalism as a political force, and even the direction of Cambodia's post-conflict political settlement more generally. In other words, both the reintroduction in 1992 of the Thammayut order to Cambodia and the subsequent elevation of a Mahanikay Supreme Patriarch (and particularly Tep Vong) to a position of ascendency over his Thammayut counterpart less than fifteen years later are symptomatic of changes in the post-conflict political settlement in Cambodia. Just as the former development reflected the progress of a peace process in which the ruling CPP was compelled to compromise with royalist political and military opponents led by Sihanouk, so the latter can be understood as a consequence of the extent to which that compromise had subsequently been superseded by political developments, and thus abandoned.

11.6 CONCLUSION

The constitution of Buddhist authority, and of the two monastic orders that make up contemporary Cambodia's sangha, then, has historically been subject to broader political shifts in Cambodian society. That trend continues to hold into the present day. Since its royally sanctioned introduction to Cambodia in 1853, members of the Thammayut sect have remained a minority within Cambodia's sangha community. Initially encouraged by colonial authorities who identified with the order's commitment to rationalization, the Thammayut fell out of favor with the French as suspicion grew around its connection to Thailand. Royal patronage of the Thammayut remained a constant, however. As such, from Cambodia's first written constitution,

[11] Within the year, the outlet had seen its license suspended as it became embroiled in another dispute, this time with another figure from within the now fractious and fragmented royalist movement (Lor 2007).

[12] In fact, aside from the 2018 elections (the results of which were foreclosed by the dissolution of the opposition Cambodian National Rescue Party less than a year prior), the 2008 elections stand as an anomaly in Cambodia's post-1993 electoral history, as the only elections in which the CPP was able to muster more than 50 percent of the popular vote.

promulgated in 1947, the place of the Thammayut has largely run alongside the place of the monarchy. After being accorded equivalent status from 1947, and through the immediate post-independence era dominated by Norodom Sihanouk, the division of authority within the sangha was maintained by the Khmer Republic, albeit without the constitutional recognition that came with the existence of a Crown Council. While the Cambodian sangha then suffered almost universally at the hands of the Khmer Rouge, it was Thammayut authority that was most notably sidelined during the initial (limited) rebirth of Buddhist institutions in the 1980s, as the People's Republic of Kampuchea recognized only a homogenous, unified sangha that officially knew no sectarian difference but, in reality, largely favored Mahanikay practice. The return of a divided sangha, intriguingly, was a religious representation of what was supposed to be a moment of increasing unity thereafter, as the peace negotiations of 1988–91 were paralleled by increased religious freedom and, eventually, the reconstitution of separate Mahanikay and Thammayut orders.

From one vantage point, Cambodia's contemporary configuration of Buddhist authority appears quite similar to that which existed at the turn of the twentieth century. At that time, a Great Supreme Patriarch sat alone at the apex of the hierarchy of sangha authority, with separate sect-specific Supreme Patriarchs for the Mahanikay and Thammayut immediately beneath him. In this role, Tep Vong appears able to exert a palpable influence over questions of monastic discipline and practice, as well as to claim a singular symbolic significance as the primary representative of Cambodia's state religion. Yet, the text of the Constitution, and particularly the provisions of Article 13 on the Council of the Throne, continue to evoke a relative equivalence between the two sects by including only the two Supreme Patriarchs. This ambivalence may reflect the particular significance of the Thammayut to the institution of the monarchy, meaning that the Thammayut leadership is permitted greater prominence in questions relating to the crown than in other matters. Alternatively, it may simply be the result of a reluctance to change the constitutional text to acknowledge what may yet turn out to be a temporary status quo. It is not clear, in other words, whether the position of Great Supreme Patriarch will be a permanent feature in the configuration of Cambodia's sangha hierarchy, or whether it is considered to inhere with the particular person of Tep Vong. What is clear, however, is that Tep Vong's current preeminence, and his ascendency to the position of Great Supreme Patriarch, along with any attempt to maintain that position whenever Tep Vong's occupancy to it comes to an end, is a reflection of political contingencies in Cambodian society, particularly the place of royalism as a political movement and the monarchy as a social institution in Cambodia.

REFERENCES

Bektimirova, Nadezhda. 2002. "The Religious Situation in Cambodia in the 1990s." *Religion, State & Society* 30 (1): 63–72. https://doi.org/10.1080/09637490220127639.

Cima, Ronald J. 1989. "Vietnam in 1988: The Brink of Renewal." *Asian Survey* 29 (1): 64–72. https://doi.org/10.2307/2644517.

Croissant, Aurel and Beate Martín. 2006. *Between Consolidation and Crisis: Elections and Democracy in Five Nations in Southeast Asia, vol. 3*. Southeast Asian Modernities. Münster: LIT.

Edwards, Penny. 2007.*Cambodge: The Cultivation of a Nation, 1860–1945*. Southeast Asia – Politics, Meaning, and Memory. Honolulu: University of Hawai'i Press.

Forest, Alain. 2008. 'Modernism and Morality in the Colonial Era.' In *People of Virtue: Reconfiguring Religion, Power and Moral Order in Cambodia Today*, edited by Alexandra Kent and David P. Chandler, 16–34. Copenhagen: NIAS Press.

Harris, Ian. 2005. *Cambodian Buddhism: History and Practice*. Honolulu: University of Hawai'i Press.

2008. "The Monk and the King: Khieu Chum and Regime Change in Cambodia." *Udaya: Journal of Khmer Studies* 9: 81–112.

2012. *Buddhism in a Dark Age: Cambodian Monks under Pol Pot*. University of Hawai'i Press. https://muse.jhu.edu/book/19862.

Jennar, Raoul Marc. 1995. *The Cambodian Constitutions, 1953–1993*. Bangkok: White Lotus.

Kent, Alexandra. 2008. "Peace, Power and Pagodas in Present-Day Cambodia." *Contemporary Buddhism* 9 (1): 77–97.

2016. "A Shifting Universe: Religion and Moral Order in Cambodia." In *The Handbook of Contemporary Cambodia*. London: Routledge.

Kent, Alexandra and David P. Chandler. 2008. *People of Virtue*. NIAS Press.

Khuy, Sokhoeun. 1998. 'Talks Fruitless; King Hints at Abdication.' *The Cambodia Daily*, September 7. https://english.cambodiadaily.com/news/talks-fruitless-king-hints-at-abdication-10598/.

Larsson, Tomas. 2015. "Monkish Politics in Southeast Asia: Religious Disenfranchisement in Comparative and Theoretical Perspective." *Modern Asian Studies* 49 (1): 40–82. https://doi.org/10.1017/S0026749X14000419.

Lawrence, Benjamin. 2020. "Outlawing Opposition, Imposing Rule of Law: Authoritarian Constitutionalism in Cambodia." *Asian Journal of Comparative Law* 15 (2): 225–49.

Leclère, Adhémard. 1899. *Le Buddhisme au Cambodge*. Paris: E. Leroux.

Ledgerwood, Judy L. 1994. "UN Peacekeeping Missions: The Lessons from Cambodia." *Asia-Pacific Issues* 11 (1):1–10

Leung, Wency. 2004. "King Appeals to Top Monk to Let Him Abdicate." *The Cambodia Daily*, August 3. https://english.cambodiadaily.com/news/king-appeals-to-top-monk-to-let-him-abdicate-42105/.

Lor, Chandara. 2007. "Khmer Amatak Newspaper License Suspended." *The Cambodia Daily*, October 9. https://english.cambodiadaily.com/news/khmer-amatak-newspaper-license-suspended-78596/.

Lor, Chandara and Leung, Wency. 2021. "Mentor Says the Throne Belongs to Sihamoni." *The Cambodia Daily*, October 13, 2004. https://english.cambodiadaily.com/news/mentor-says-the-throne-belongs-to-sihamoni-43247/.

Marston, John. 2009. 'Cambodian Religion Since 1989.' In *Beyond Democracy in Cambodia, vol. 12*, edited by Joakim Öjendal and Mona Lilja. Democracy in Asia Series. Copenhagen: NIAS Press.

Norén-Nilsson, Astrid. 2016a. *Cambodia's Second Kingdom: Nation, Imagination, and Democracy*. Ithaca: Southeast Asia Program, Cornell University.

2016b. "The Demise of Cambodian Royalism and the Legacy of Sihanouk." *Sojourn: Journal of Social Issues in Southeast Asia* 31 (1): 1–36.

O'connell, Stephen and Bou Saroeun. 2000. "Stupa Standoff Simmers after Fourth Round." *Phnom Penh Post*, May 26. www.phnompenhpost.com/national/stupa-standoff-simmers-after-fourth-round.

Öjendal, Joakim and Lilja, Mona. 2009. *Beyond Democracy in Cambodia, vol. 12*. Democracy in Asia Series. Copenhagen: NIAS Press.

Peng, H. O. R., Kong Phallack and Menzel, Jörg. 2016. *Cambodian Constitutional Law*. Singapore: Konrad Adenauer Stiftung.

Post Staff. 2000. "Top Monks Disagree on Role in Fighting AIDS." *Phnom Penh Post*, June 9. www.phnompenhpost.com/national/top-monks-disagree-role-fighting-aids.

Samean, Yun. 2003. "King Might Turn to Ballot to End Crisis." *The Cambodia Daily*, December 15. https://english.cambodiadaily.com/news/king-might-turn-to-ballot-to-end-crisis-70476/.

2004a. "King Says He Won't Return." *The Cambodia Daily*, March 26. https://english.cambodiadaily.com/news/king-says-he-wont-return-39413/.

2004b. "Hun Sen Ignores King's Threat to Abdicate." *The Cambodia Daily*, August 5. https://english.cambodiadaily.com/news/hun-sen-ignores-kings-threat-to-abdicate-42152/.

2007. "Gov't Accuses Paper of Stoking Religious Tensions." *The Cambodia Daily*, February 5. https://english.cambodiadaily.com/news/govt-accuses-paper-of-stoking-religious-tensions-2-72895/.

Peou, Sorpong. 2006. 'Consolidation or Crisis of Democracy? Cambodia's Parliamentary Elections in 2003 & Beyond.' In *Between Consolidation and Crisis: Elections and Democracy in Five Nations in Southeast Asia*, edited by Aurel Croissant and Beate Martin. Berlin: Lit Verlag.

Yang, Sam. 1987. *Khmer Buddhism and Politics from 1954 to 1984*. Newington: Khmer Studies Institute.

PART IV

Northern and Northeastern Asia

12

Constitutional Buddhism

Japanese Buddhists and Constitutional Law

Levi McLaughlin

12.1 INTRODUCTION: FINDING BUDDHISM IN JAPAN'S POSTWAR CONSTITUTIONAL ORDER

When it comes to constitutional law, Japan contrasts starkly with most other nominally Buddhist-majority polities. In spite of the fact that Japan conventionally numbers among countries with a population that is mostly Buddhist, Buddhism appears to have exerted a marginal influence on the composition and legal application of Japan's modern constitutions (enacted in 1890 and 1947). This chapter considers historical causes and effects of Buddhism's scant presence in the Supreme Court of Japan's deliberations on constitutional religion/state divides, and it considers the impact of the 1947 Constitution's strong separations between religion and state on the actions and attitudes of Japanese Buddhist actors. It discusses reasons why Japan's identity as a Buddhist nation should be reconsidered in light of Buddhism's low profile in its legal record, and it provides two case studies – of Buddhists' post-disaster aid mobilization and lay Buddhist engagement in electoral politics – to illustrate how Japan's postwar constitutional separations guide Japanese Buddhists as they mitigate legal challenges and confront concerns about violating constitutional norms. By highlighting ways Japanese Buddhist individuals and institutions have been shaped by concern for constitutional law, in spite of appearing rarely in court deliberations on religious freedom, I propose that Japanese Buddhism exhibits an inversion of tendencies found in many other Buddhist-majority regions. It thus serves as a necessary counterexample to include in a global overview of Buddhism and comparative constitutional law. In contrast to what Benjamin Schonthal terms a "Buddhist constitutionalism" evident in countries whose national constitutions have been drafted in keeping with forms of governance maintained by monastic lineages, Japanese Buddhist individuals and organizations represent what might be conceived as Buddhist constitutionalism's mirror opposite, that of "constitutional Buddhism" (Schonthal 2017).[1] The institutional makeup of Japanese Buddhist organizations and the dispositions and tactics cultivated by their clerical and lay adherents indicate that explicitly non-religious constitutional law serves Japan's Buddhists as an operative framework. It is one they continually adapt in order to establish their legitimacy in the face of potential legal challenges, a leery public, and a need to preserve their increasingly precarious traditions.

Let us explore how a distinctive relationship between Buddhism and constitutionalism emerged in Japan. Today, Japan distinguishes itself by having the world's longest-ever unamended national constitution. Put into effect on May 3, 1947, the postwar Japanese Constitution is also notable for its multiple articles that lay out how religion is to be separated from the state.[2] This emphatic demarcation is a product of reforms carried out by the US Occupation (1945–1952) after Japan's surrender to the Allied powers on August 15, 1945.[3] As its advisors deliberated on how to articulate rights guaranteeing freedom of religion, the Occupation sought to forestall any possibility that Japan would return to its wartime-era regime requirement that the people of Japan foster loyalty as imperial subjects by taking part in Shintō shrine-based rituals.[4] These requirements were sanctioned by Japan's 1890 Constitution, in which Article 28 stipulated that "Japanese subjects shall, within limits not prejudicial to peace and order, and not antagonistic to their duties as subjects, enjoy freedom of religious belief."[5] Until 1945, Japan's imperial subjects were promised the legal right to maintain private belief in Buddhism, Christianity, or other religions, but were nonetheless required to take part in ritual veneration of Shintō deities, including the Emperor, as civic obligations.[6] General Douglas MacArthur, Supreme Commander for the Allied Powers, and his advisors on religion characterized the wartime

[1] For discussions of monastic regulations as viable comparisons to national constitutions, see Schonthal 2021.

[2] For the text of the 1947 Constitution (in English), which is reproduced throughout this chapter, see Prime Minister of Japan and His Cabinet 1946.

[3] For analyses of the Occupation, the drafting and promulgation of the 1947 Constitution, and related developments in the immediate postwar years, see Dower 1999; Gordon 1993; Ruoff 2020; Thomas 2019.

[4] In this chapter, I follow Thomas in adding the macron to Shintō (save in Occupation-era uses of "State Shinto") to indicate the long vowel in Japanese, even though "Shinto" is recognized as an English-language term, to emphasize it as an entity distinguished from religion in pre-1945 Japan and one that remains distinctive in the present constitutional order (2019). I do not add macrons to "Soka Gakkai" or "Komeito" because these organizations do not use them in their own English-language publications.

[5] The English-language text of the 1890 Constitution (promulgated in 1889) is available at National Diet Library 2021.

[6] While the 1890 Constitution did not stipulate veneration at Shintō shrines as a legal requirement, Article 28 supported executive orders that required schools and other institutions to organize visits to shrines and other ritual practices. These requirements were enforced with increasing severity by Japan's wartime government. See Nakai 2017 for examples of how Christians contended with these mandates.

requirement to uphold what they termed "State Shinto" as evidence that post-imperial Japan needed guidance to establish "true" religious freedom.[7] Jolyon Thomas demonstrates, however, that Japan's 1890 Constitution was on par with international norms for qualified forms of religious freedom, as embodied in the constitutions of the imperial powers that served as models for Japan's expansion into its own empire (2019). As a polity that installed requirements for civic engagement in ritual veneration of its deified sovereign, Japan's contingent prewar and wartime religious freedoms were those of a normal constitutional government of the late nineteenth to the early twentieth centuries.

In contrast to its 1890 predecessor, the 1947 Constitution declares that sovereignty resides in the people of Japan and that the Emperor is relegated to "the symbol of the State and of the unity of the people." Article 20 ensures that religious freedom is no longer limited by obligations for Japan's citizens (no longer imperial subjects) to accommodate civic dedication to a non- or supra-religious Shintō, and that Shintō is demoted to a religion that is to no longer enjoy state support.[8] Article 89 prevents the Japanese state from subsidizing Shintō shrines, as it did during the imperial era, and Shintō instead now ranks alongside Buddhism and other religions that are guaranteed freedom but whose institutions must comply with the 1951 Religious Juridical Persons Law (revised significantly in 1996 and multiple times since) in order to enjoy privileges as *shūkyō hōjin*, or "religious juridical persons," not least of which is relief from paying tax on revenue-producing property and faith-related activities.[9]

Much of the scholarship on religion and constitutional law in postwar Japan thus focuses on Articles 20 and 89 to identify issues related to religion/state separations. Some studies also investigate religious concerns with Article 9, Japan's famed postwar "peace clause." Commitments by religion-affiliated actors to defending, amending, or doing away with Article 9 have animated much activism and debate, while Articles 20 and 89 set religious activities, institutions, and objectives apart from state enterprises.[10] It is worth presenting the text of these three articles in full, given that their contents pertain to challenges Buddhists have faced continually in postwar Japan, and to specific instances in this chapter:

[7] Analyses of "State Shinto," its construction by the Allied forces, and how the category has been elaborated upon in political and religious discourses, have developed in recent years. Valuable studies in English include Hardacre 2017; Josephson 2012; Mullins 2021; Rots 2017; Thomas 2019; Zhong 2016.

[8] For an analysis of legal and other ramifications of the shift from imperial subject to democratically enfranchised citizen, see Avenell 2010.

[9] The 1951 law was enacted as a corrective for a December 28, 1945, directive intended to eliminate "State Shinto" that made it excessively easy to register as a religious juridical person. For a clause-by-clause analysis of 1996 amendments to the 1951 Religious Juridical Persons Law, see LoBreglio 1997.

[10] See Larsson 2020 for extensive citations and discussions of research on religion and constitutional law in Japan. See also Hardacre et al. 2021; O'Brien and Ohkoshi 1996.

Article 9

(1) *Aspiring sincerely to an international peace based on justice and order, the Japanese people forever renounce war as a sovereign right of the nation and the threat or use of force as a means of settling international disputes.*
(2) *In order to accomplish the aim of the preceding paragraph, land, sea, and air forces, as well as other war potential, will never be maintained. The right of belligerency of the state will not be recognized.*

Article 20

(1) *Freedom of religion is guaranteed to all. No religious organization shall receive any privileges from the State, nor exercise any political authority.*
(2) *No person shall be compelled to take part in any religious act, celebration, rite or practice.*
(3) *The State and its organs shall refrain from religious education or any other religious activity.*

Article 89

No public money or other property shall be expended or appropriated for the use, benefit or maintenance of any religious institution or association, or for any charitable, educational or benevolent enterprises not under the control of public authority.

Despite the importance of the religion-related clauses to Japan's Constitution, their application in Supreme Court cases has been sparing, and uneven. Cases brought before the Supreme Court of Japan that have involved rulings that interpret Articles 20 and 89 have almost exclusively concerned Shintō shrines and rituals (Hardacre 1989, 2017; Larsson 2017; 2020). The only religious freedom case in Japan's highest court that has involved a Buddhist defendant was *Nishida* v. *Japan* (1963), in which a faith healer ordained in Shingon Buddhism was convicted for inflicting a head injury on a young woman in the course of exorcizing her of a *tanuki* (raccoon dog) spirit. The court rejected the practitioner Nishida's claim that injuries resulting from her ritual practice did not qualify as a criminal act, even though her right to carry out exorcisms was protected by Article 20, stipulating in the decision that the Constitution's Article 12 confirms that people must refrain from abusing their freedoms and rights and must utilize them for public welfare.[11] The only other non-Shintō religious freedom case was decided on February 24, 2021, when the Supreme Court justices announced in a 14–1 ruling that a Confucian temple in a public park in Naha (Okinawa prefecture) operates as a religious facility,

[11] For details on *Nishida* v. *Japan*, see Larsson, 2020, 203; Takahata 2007. For accounts of female Buddhist exorcists practicing around the time of *Nishida* v. *Japan*, see Blacker 1975.

in spite of its registration as a "general incorporated association" (*ippan shadan hōjin*), and that a waiver of land usage fees it received from the city government violated the constitutional divide (Abe 2021; Kyodo 2021).

Some of the most high-profile cases concerning Shintō have involved suits by affiliates of other religions who have charged that their constitutional rights were violated by rituals carried out at shrines with the agreement or support of governmental representatives. The most heated controversy has tended to surround disputes related to Yasukuni Shrine, where spirits of Japan's war dead, including Class A war criminals executed following the Tokyo Trials, are enshrined.[12] These cases also involve the network of prefecture-level "nation-protecting shrines" (*gokoku jinja*) at which the spirits of local residents who died in service to the Japanese nation are revered. Helen Hardacre chronicles the travails of the widow of an active-duty Japan Self Defense Forces (the postwar Japanese armed services) member who was killed in a traffic accident in 1968. She sued the Yamaguchi Prefecture Veterans' Association for deifying her husband via an apotheosizing rite (called *gōshi*) at the prefectural-level nation-protecting shrine, claiming that this violated her Christian beliefs. The Supreme Court ultimately decided against her, ruling that the shrine was also protected by the Constitution's guarantee of freedom of belief and possessed the right to "seek the tranquility of that person's soul through the religion that expresses one's faith" (Hardacre 2017, 420–422; see also Field 1991).

Concern about transgressing the postwar constitutional religion/state divide has encouraged a disposition on the part of Japan's religious professionals to proceed with extreme caution so as not to be accused of inappropriately pushing religion into public life. As I will discuss through attention to the chapter's two case studies, a type of separation anxiety is especially apparent in the personal conduct and institutional undertakings of Japanese Buddhist clergy and lay activists. Buddhist practitioners in Japan typically foster an extreme aversion for entanglement with constitutional matters. The early postwar case of a practitioner who invoked freedoms guaranteed by Article 20 is exceptional. The defendant Nishida was marginalized on multiple fronts: by virtue of not being a temple priest, because she engaged in the stigma-laden practice of exorcism (which tends to be downplayed by temple-based clergy), and because she was an ordained woman in a clerical hierarchy dominated by men.[13]

Another Buddhist cleric made a notable appearance in Japan's highest court, as a plaintiff in a case that involved a ruling on constitutional issues. Ernils Larsson details the activities of Anzai Kenjō, a Jōdo Shinshū (True Pure Land) Buddhist priest who distinguished himself as the organizational head of twenty-four plaintiffs

[12] For discussions of Yasukuni Shrine and post-1947 efforts on the part of the Association of Shinto Shrines to regain state support for it, see Mullins 2021.

[13] For discussions of women clergy and their quotidian engagements with local-level parishioners, see Rowe 2017; Starling 2019. For accounts of exorcism in Japanese Buddhism and its renewal in the wake of the March 2011 disasters in northeast Japan, see Takahashi 2016.

in a well-documented and long-lasting case called the Ehime Tamagushiryō lawsuit that culminated in the 1997 *Anzai* v. *Shiraishi* decision. Anzai and his fellow plaintiffs, with support from the Japan Buddhist Federation, were pitted against Shiraishi Haruki, governor of Ehime prefecture, who commissioned a *tamagushiryō* shrine offering ritual with public funds. Anzai and his allies decried this act as state patronage of Shintō that violated constitutional guarantees (Larsson 2017, chapter 7).[14] This instance of a Buddhist activist bringing a religious freedom case to the Japanese courts is extremely rare, and while there are numerous legal challenges pertaining to contracts, property, taxation, and other matters that involve Buddhist temples, their clergy, and their parishioners, Japan's Buddhists have generally avoided litigation over constitutional issues.[15] It is likely that this absence in the court record is an important reason why legal scholars tend not to scrutinize Japanese Buddhism in studies of constitutional law.[16]

12.2 CHALLENGES JAPAN PRESENTS TO TREATING BUDDHISM AS A FRAMEWORK FOR COMPARATIVE CONSTITUTIONAL LAW

How should we make sense of contrasts between Japan and other countries with large Buddhist populations in comparative constitutional law? Specifically, how shall we account for Japanese Buddhism's low profile in cases pertaining to religious

[14] A majority of ten Supreme Court justices found that the Ehime governor had violated the terms of Article 20. See also Abe 2011.

[15] Buddhists in Japan have been consistently embroiled in lawsuits that involve matters other than constitutionally guaranteed religious freedoms. One high-profile example that is relevant to this chapter's case studies are suits by and against Soka Gakkai. The largely negative public image of the lay Nichiren Buddhist organization Soka Gakkai has been profoundly impacted by the early tendency of the group to go after its religious and political rivals through threatened or real legal action, and the group has weathered a large number of legal challenges. Many of these conflicts surround defamation suits, particularly in matters that pertain to Soka Gakkai's leadership, as well as suits pertaining to its registry as a religious juridical person, often in connection to its object of worship. Numerous challenges have concerned the Gakkai's 1991 schism with its erstwhile temple Buddhist parent denomination Nichiren Shōshū, some of which involve efforts by Gakkai parishioners to move family graves away from the auspices of the Shōshū head temple Taisekiji and other denominational properties to Soka Gakkai "memorial parks" (cemeteries). None of these many legal disputes have led to constitutional challenges in the Supreme Court of Japan. For information on Soka Gakkai's grave matters, see Shimada Hiromi et al. 2007; Tōyō Tetsugaku Kenkyūjo, 1993; 2006. Representative examples of the large volume of publications on Soka Gakkai-related defamation suits and connected legal challenges include Genron Shuppan no Jiyū o Mamoru Kai, 2012; Kurata Takuji et al. 2002; Matsumoto 1973; and Okkotsu 2003.

[16] Attention to cases below the Supreme Court level yields a limited number of lawsuits brought by Buddhists on religious freedom grounds. Mark Mullins details the lead-up to a February 26, 2009 decision in the Osaka District Court that struck down an attempt by an ecumenical group of plaintiffs (Buddhist and Christian) to sue Yasukuni Shrine for carrying out ritual enshrinements without permission (2021, 137–143).

freedom? A detailed history exceeds the capacity of this chapter, but a cursory overview is necessary to clarify reasons for Japanese Buddhism's all but complete absence from religious freedom-related court proceedings.

In the centuries immediately preceding Japan's rapid transformation into an imperial power following the 1868 Meiji Restoration, Buddhist temples enjoyed governmental support from the Tokugawa (1603–1867) regime. Clergy were responsible for maintaining a "temple registration system" (*terauke seido*) that functioned as a census, family registry, basis for taxation, and a means for officials to root out social undesirables, such as outcastes (*hinin*) and Christians.[17] From the beginning of the Meiji era (1868–1912), the new regime began to promote Shintō. A new policy of *shinbutsu bunri*, or "separation of the *kami* (Shintō deities) and buddhas," contributed to violent uprisings led by nativists as part of the *haibutsu kishaku* (abolish the Buddha, destroy Śākyamuṇi) movement that saw the destruction of numerous Buddhist temples and their material holdings, the defrocking of priests or their transformation into Shintō clergy, and the seizure of Buddhist lands and other wealth.[18] Thereafter, throughout the Meiji, Taishō (1912–1926), and early Shōwa (1926–1989) eras, Shintō was designated by the nation's powerholders as Japan's primordial faith and was routinely contrasted to the "foreign" tradition of Buddhism.[19] Buddhists sought to demonstrate the relevance of their teachings and traditions by undertaking reforms to suit state priorities, pledging fealty to the nation, and taking part enthusiastically in imperialist exploits, including war and violence against civilian populations.[20]

Following World War II, Japanese Buddhism continued to experience upheaval. As religions were subjected to a new constitutional regime, parishioner bases shifted dramatically as millions emigrated from rural areas into Japan's cities, driving the country's postwar "economic miracle." Even as numerous so-called new religions (many based in Buddhism), such as Reiyūkai, Risshō Kōseikai, Shinnyo-en, Soka Gakkai, and others attracted millions of converts in the postwar decades, these years saw a steady decline in denominational Buddhist patronage due to a reduction in temples' regional communities and a growing tendency in Japan toward disavowal of religious identity.[21] Aversion to self-identifying as religious was

17 Leading scholarship on Buddhist temples during the Tokugawa era includes Hardacre 2002; Hur 2007; Tamamuro 2001; and Williams 2004.

18 For investigations of *haibutsu kishaku* events and their effects, see Ketelaar 1989; Thal 2005; Yasumaru 1979.

19 For origins of this ideological movement and its Meiji-era developments, see Sawada 2004.

20 The consequences of Buddhists' support for the Japanese imperial project have inspired intense scholarly engagement. See Klautau 2014; Klautau and Krämer 2021; Victoria 2006. For counter-examples of Buddhists who at times opposed governmental authorities and promoted progressive ideals, see Shields 2017.

21 For analyses of shifts in postwar Japanese temple-based Buddhism, including attention to rural depopulation and other demographic changes, see Covell 2005; Rowe 2011; Sakurai and Kawamata 2016. For discussions of the category "new religions" and its development in postwar Japan, see Baffelli and Reader 2019; McLaughlin 2019a.

exacerbated dramatically by events in the mid-1990s, most crucially the January 1995 Kobe-area earthquake and the sarin gas attacks by the apocalyptic new religion Aum Shinrikyō.[22] While religion's public image was salvaged somewhat by positive impressions of aid mobilization by Buddhists and other religious activists after the March 11, 2011 compound disasters in northeast Japan, the generations that came of age after Aum have retained what many refer to as a "religion allergy."[23] People in Japan today rarely describe themselves as religious, partly out of fear of triggering lingering associations with violence and social marginality.

The Japanese government's statistics on religion, and some measurements by well-known pollsters, tend to mask the Japanese public's distaste for explicit religious avowals. According to the 2020 *Shūkyō nenkan* [religion almanac], an annual report issued by Japan's Agency for Cultural Affairs, there were 84,329 Buddhist-based organizations in Japan, including temples and other entities registered as religious juridical persons. As a proportion of the total number of legally designated religious bodies in the country, this amounts to 42.7 percent. Moreover, these organizations claimed 84,835,110 parishioners, or just over 67 percent of the Japanese population. A decade earlier, Japan ranked as the third-largest Buddhist nation in the world, in terms of adherent numbers, according to measures provided by the Pew Research Center's 2010 Global Religious Landscape survey.[24] Going by these figures alone, it would seem appropriate to place Japan alongside Myanmar, Sri Lanka, Thailand, Tibet, and other identifiably Buddhist-majority countries and regions in a comparative framework.

However, popular Japanese nervousness about religion, including Buddhism, and prevaricating attitudes expressed both by those who deny religious affiliation and by self-described Buddhists, requires that we call this comparison into question. Most recent surveys cast Japan's identity as a Buddhist country into doubt. The Pew-Templeton Global Religious Futures Project calculates that self-identified Buddhists in Japan comprised 36.2 percent in 2010 and projected a drop to 33.2 percent in 2020; in 2050, only 25.1 percent of a rapidly aging, and shrinking, Japanese population is predicted to identify as Buddhist, and 67.7 percent will be religiously unaffiliated (Global Religious Futures Project 2016). A survey undertaken by the NHK Broadcasting Culture Research Institute in 2018 found that 38 percent of respondents affirmed belief in the buddhas, while 31 percent professed belief in the *kami* of Shintō. Ambiguity surrounds these NHK figures, given that respondents were mostly unwilling to firmly reject religion: only 32 percent confirmed that they "did not believe" in divine powers, 71 percent carried out ritual visits to (predominantly Buddhist) family graves, and only 12 percent did not perform religious activities

[22] For accounts of the impact of the Aum attacks on the category "religion," see Baffelli and Reader 2012.

[23] For discussions of aversion to the category "religion," as well as critiques of the statistical measures of Japanese religious identity I cite here, see Horii 2018.

[24] See Agency for Cultural Affairs 2020; Pew Forum on Religion & Public Life 2012.

of any type. The 2018 belief rates nonetheless conform to a broader trend of steady decline in reported religious activity observable in figures recorded from 1898, when close to 90 percent of the population claimed faith in the buddhas and *kami*.[25]

The other chapters in this volume speak to the significant legal and political influence of Buddhist clergy and lay proponents in other parts of Asia. In most cases, these chapters indicate a level of Buddhist influence on public life that differs markedly from that found in Japan today. Contrasts between Japan and Theravāda-dominant polities in Southeast Asia are perhaps most glaring. Khemthong Tonsakulrungruang points to the persistence underlining all of the Thai constitutions from 1932 to 2017 of presumptions about the *dhammarāja*, the Buddhism-based notion of kingly power, and *barami* (karmic bonds and consequences) as means to perpetuate non-democratic command by an authoritarian elite as morally justifiable. Krishantha Fedricks highlights conflicts in post-civil war Sri Lanka between rival Sinhalese Buddhists, including monastics elected to parliament, who engage in intra-Buddhist disputes to produce competing visions of Buddhism-based ethnonationalist ideals they propose for constitutional enshrinement. Iselin Frydenlund identifies a comparable imperative in Myanmar to protect Buddhism against perceived enemies of the dharma by enacting laws that establish the country as a de facto Buddhist nation. Frydenlund expands upon Schonthal's notion of "Buddhist constitutionalism" to outline how Burmese legal, military, and ecclesiastical forces have combined to privilege Buddhism as the state's foundation. These examples make clear that, at least in Southeast Asia, Buddhism endures as a non-negotiable, taken-for-granted starting point from which to create and interpret constitutional law.

Postwar Japan, formulated as a constitutional polity based in an unamended constitution written by an occupying government that rejected specific religious commitments in favor of commitment to universal values, could be characterized as the inverse of these Southeast Asian examples.[26] The Japanese situation contrasts also with Buddhism's legal profile in neighboring countries in Northeast Asia, which share Japan's Mahāyāna Buddhist heritage. Mark Nathan, for instance, chronicles appeals by monks to the Supreme Court of Korea to arbitrate in disputes over interpretation of monastic rules of conduct (*vinaya*) and emphasizes the importance of court battles in determining South Korea's contemporary system of Buddhist lay and monastic orders. And the legal profile of Buddhism in the People's Republic of China differs from its status in contemporary Japan, as Cuilan Liu details in her research on the potentially surprising extent to which Chinese courts lean toward benefiting Buddhist claimants in inheritance disputes and otherwise avoid

[25] See NHK Broadcasting Culture Research Institute 2020. For analyses of trends in data on postwar religious affiliation and participation, see Ishii 2008.

[26] See Thomas 2019 for more on the Occupation authorities' emphasis on universal values and the process by which its drafters came to reject specific religious priorities.

diminishing the legal authority of Buddhist institutions and lineages associated with the Buddhist Association of China, in spite of constitutional divisions between religion and state and the absolute dominance of the officially atheist Chinese Communist Party (Liu 2020).

Comparisons that take into account premodern Japanese regimes would position Japan closer to polities defined by Buddhist epistemologies. This volume's studies of pre-1950 Tibetan monastic political rule, the pre-2008 Drukpa State in Bhutan, and Mongolian precedents provided by Berthe Jansen, Richard W. Whitecross, and Daigengna Duoer suggest exciting potential for expanding the comparative constitutional law framework to include a comparison of premodern Japan with Tibetan and other non-Japanese premodern Buddhist political orders. Regulatory norms within northern Asian antecedents could be compared productively with those of Japan after the establishment of Buddhism in the archipelago from the sixth century. This comparison would require that we follow these scholars in broadening our understanding of "constitution" to accommodate regulations that contrast with jurisprudence modeled on European standards.[27] Japan, as it coalesced in antiquity as a polity controlled by the Yamato court, began as a bureaucracy that promoted Buddhist ideals of kingship. The early Japanese court supported a network of government-sponsored monasteries and nunneries dedicated to protecting the country from disease, invasion, and social upheaval, and it included administration of the monastic community as a foundational component of governance.[28] An expanded interpretive purview would accommodate Japan's Seventeen-Article Constitution of 604 and the Taihō Code of 703; while neither necessarily qualify as "proper" constitutions, both centralize monastic Buddhism as a foundational component of government, as do numerous edicts in the centuries that followed. Buddhist norms that informed early Japanese governmental structures, however, are not apparent in the country's contemporary constitutional order. Including Japan in a comparative constitutional law exercise thus requires clear historical specificity.

Despite contemporary Japanese Buddhism's comparative distance from law and government, and in spite of the fact that Buddhist priests and lay activists have appeared rarely in cases heard by Japanese courts, they and their organizations deserve attention in regard to present-day constitutional concerns. While Shintō has taken precedence in the courts, Buddhists have been forced to contend with constitutionally guaranteed divides in order to carry out individual and collective activities, formulate their institutions, and overcome popular suspicion propelled by

[27] For analysis of what this expansion of the category "constitution" into the *vinaya* entails, see Schonthal 2021.

[28] There is an extensive literature on inextricable connections between Buddhism and government that persisted throughout Japanese history prior to the Meiji and postwar constitutional orders. Representative examples include Kuroda 1996; Ooms 2008; Piggott 1997; and Sango 2015. See also Japan-relevant sources in the 2021 entry on "Buddhist Statecraft" (Benn and Balkwill 2021).

postwar expectations that religious activists will steer clear of government in all its forms. This has meant that Buddhism, and Buddhists, in Japan have been defined by constitutional wording and interpretation. Additionally, Japanese Buddhist contentions with the 1947 Constitution contrast in crucial ways with examples found in other nominally Buddhism-majority countries. They thus provide valuable nuance to a comprehensive comparative constitutional law inquiry.

Here, I present two contrasting examples of Japanese Buddhist activists whose efforts have been constitutionally defined. The first is aid mobilization and training for religious professionals by Buddhist priests and other denominationally affiliated volunteers in the wake of the January 17, 1995, Great Hanshin Earthquake disaster and the March 11, 2011, compound disasters in northeast Japan. Because of restrictions enshrined in Articles 20 and 89, Buddhist aid providers have faced steep challenges negotiating access to state or state-affiliated facilities that would allow them to distribute material aid to the living and perform rituals to pacify the deceased. Having learned harsh lessons from difficult experiences in 1995, most notably with damage to the category "religion" wreaked by Aum Shinrikyō, activists in northeast Japan were able to navigate constitutional divides to the extent that they transformed emergency measures implemented following the 2011 earthquake, tsunami, and nuclear cataclysms into training programs for religious social welfare providers, the most prominent of which is now housed at a prestigious public university. This section outlines how constitutional concerns shaped the direction of these post-disaster initiatives. In particular, it demonstrates how uneasiness about direct religious engagement in public social welfare provision led, ironically, to use of sectarian resources to train Buddhist priests to "overcome religion" in order to secure positions in hospitals, hospices, and other caregiving settings. It also highlights uncertainty about the future of Buddhist-led care provider training programs and places for clergy in care provision teams, due in large part to persistent concerns about Japan's constitutional religion/state divide.

The second example is the most well-known instance of sustained political engagement on a mass scale by a Japanese Buddhist organization, namely the actions of the lay Nichiren Buddhist organization, Soka Gakkai, and its affiliated political party, Komeito. This section considers the transformative impact of constitutional law on shifts undertaken by the religion and the party by chronicling a dramatic transformation that began with Soka Gakkai's initial electoral forays in pursuit of an eschatological Nichiren Buddhist objective and led to Komeito's rise to the position of casting vote in the National Diet. It also surveys politics surrounding constitutional law that are strongly affected by Komeito's pivotal role in guiding successive governmental reinterpretations of Article 9. As the junior partner in the national-level governing coalition and a significant force in subnational politics, Komeito certainly represents the most prominent, and controversial, intersection of Japanese Buddhism and constitutional law. The case of Komeito also stands out as a promising example of Buddhist groups' entanglements with constitutional law and party politics that is ripe for transnational comparison. Finally, this section considers another aspect of Soka Gakkai and Komeito that invites comparisons between legal contexts, namely how Japanese Buddhist practitioners' mimesis of the constitutional form, the legal structures that gird it, and practices of commemorating and promoting the national constitution produces forms of "constitutional Buddhism." In the chapter's conclusion, I suggest ways Soka Gakkai and Komeito serve as a counterpoint to a pattern of "Buddhist constitutionalism" in order to productively complicate this volume's comparative project.

12.3 NAVIGATING CONSTITUTIONAL RELIGION/STATE DIVIDES BY "OVERCOMING RELIGION": POST-DISASTER INITIATIVES BY JAPANESE BUDDHIST AID PROVIDERS

Covid-19 was hard on training initiatives for Japanese Buddhists of all stripes, including those for Buddhist clergy and laity who provide clinical care. In a January 2021 email to the author, Taniyama Yōzō, Jōdo Shinshū priest and professor at Tōhoku University's Department of Practical Religious Studies in Sendai, lamented that training programs for *rinshō shūkyōshi*, or "Interfaith Chaplains," only went forward in 2021 at his department and at Ryūkoku University, a Jōdo Shinshū institution in Kyoto. Interfaith Chaplain training programs modeled on modules created in large part by him were on hold at the Jesuit institution Sophia University in Tokyo and at the headquarters of the Buddhism-based new religion Risshō Kōseikai. Declining enrolment in these certification programs can be blamed on an abrupt shift to online learning and difficulties finding clinical placements under pandemic conditions. But these initiatives faced challenges even before the onset of Covid-19, on account of uneasiness in Japan about religion in public spaces.

It is thus all the more notable that the care provider certification program founded by Taniyama and his colleagues found a place in a public university. Tōhoku University's Department of Practical Religious Studies serves as a principal coordinator for the Society for Interfaith Chaplaincy in Japan (Nihon Rinshō Shūkyōshikai), which Taniyama founded in 2016 in cooperation with fellow priests from temple-based Japanese Buddhist denominations, Christian clergy, and representatives from a number of new religions, notably Konkōkyō, Risshō Kōseikai, and Tenrikyō. They have collaborated with psychologists, grief care specialists, hospice care workers, and other clinical experts to provide services for the dead and the bereaved after the March 11, 2011 disasters.[29] Mostly referred to as "3.11," the Great East Japan Earthquake disasters left upwards of 24,600 people dead, injured, or missing, and

[29] For analyses of Interfaith Chaplaincy and its related initiatives, see Berman 2018; Graf 2016; Horie and Takahashi 2021; Kasai 2016; McLaughlin 2016a.

dealt a severe psychic blow to Japan. They also inspired Japan's largest mobilization of religious actors and their resources since the Pacific War.[30]

Interfaith Chaplaincy can be characterized as a constructive response to negative attitudes that Buddhist aid providers have confronted after disasters. This new class of post-disaster chaplains learned harsh lessons after the January 17, 1995, Great Hanshin earthquake, which devastated the city of Kobe and its surrounding area in western Japan. Approximately 6,400 people were killed in and around Kobe and many thousands were displaced. The national government failed to coordinate effectively, and the suffering of residents, which stretched into the months after January 17, underscored a woeful lack of state preparation.[31] Failure by state agencies to deliver reliable assistance inspired people from across Japan to contribute to an upsurge in volunteering. Organizations of many different types mark the Hanshin earthquake anniversary as Hōsai no Hi, or "Disaster Prevention and Volunteerism Day," by engaging in volunteer activities across the country. Religious volunteerism emerged as a significant component of this post-Hanshin response.

Following the January 1995 earthquake, hundreds of volunteer groups from temple Buddhist sects, new religions, Christian organizations, and Shintō shrines, including many that lost their own affiliates and facilities, mobilized to rescue disaster victims. Religious organizations housed numerous displaced residents in homes, temples, churches, and other institutions, raised funds for relief, and otherwise cared for survivors and the deceased. However, Buddhist clerics described running up against an "allergy to religion" when it came to dealing with state agencies (*Chūgai Nippō*, 1996). Their testimony makes clear that negative sentiments about religion in Japanese public life find purchase in the language of the 1947 Constitution, which sets the standard for how to condemn religious influence in the public sphere. Japanese religious aid launched in January 1995 faced opposition from a public that suspected aid groups might be hiding covert proselytization agendas and from government agencies that were nervous about transgressing constitutional principles. Priests interviewed about their 1995 aid activism described receiving requests from representatives of government agencies to not display any overt signs of their religious affiliation, even as these clergy sought to perform sutra recitations over bodies of the deceased. This is a memorial act that is their vocational specialty, and Buddhist invocations over the dead remain conventional in Japan. One Jōdoshū (Pure Land Sect) representative emphasized the hostility religious organizations faced in dealing with governmental restrictions, recounting how he and fellow clerical aid providers were denied permission to carry out

[30] For a summary of statistical measures of the religious response to 3.11, see McLaughlin 2016b. Comprehensive figures on 3.11 casualties and reconstruction efforts in Fukushima, Miyagi, and Iwate prefectures are updated by Japan's Reconstruction Agency at www.reconstruction.go.jp/. See also Kingston 2012; Gill, Steger, and Slater 2013.

[31] For overviews of the Hanshin disaster, its aftermath, and details on religious responses, see Kuroda and Tsuganesawa 1999; Miki 2001.

funerary activities in public facilities while wearing their vestments. As a result, bodies that were lying in repose did not receive memorial rites.[32]

Negative sentiments about religious aid provision prevented news about salutary efforts from making it into widespread media coverage. One notable example from Jōdo Shinshū, Japan's largest temple-based Buddhist denomination, received only scant public notice. The Japan Buddhist Federation (Zen Nihon Bukkyōkai) calculated that 536 Jōdo Shinshū Hongwanji-ha (Hongwanji lineage) temples were damaged or destroyed in the Hanshin earthquake, and that it lost twelve priests and clerical family members, the most of any denomination.[33] These deaths number among the 1,200 parishioners it lost, accounting for 19 percent of the total number of dead. In the absence of reliable government assistance, temple priests in the disaster area set about aiding local residents. Hongwanji-ha's single largest aid activity was initiated by its Hokkaido Parish Young Priest's Association. This group of volunteer clerics traveled more than 1500 km from the northern island of Hokkaido to Kobe, where they constructed twenty prefab housing units for refugees on the premises of the temple Kōenji, a facility that they called the Rokkō Hermitage (Rokkōan), named for the Kobe landmark Mount Rokkō. A total of 3,600 volunteers, including Jōdo Shinshū priests but also lay affiliates and other participants, cooperated to care for the material and psychological needs of victims housed in the prefab units. The Hermitage served as a base for the sect's volunteers, who delivered material goods and counseling to Kobe residents struggling to carry on in the most devastated regions of the city.

Though public distaste for news about religious activism rendered this initiative largely invisible, the Rokkō Hermitage created an important precedent upon which Japan's Buddhist denominations have built in responding to subsequent disasters. Importantly, especially in terms of attention to constitutional law, in spite of the fact that the complex stood on temple grounds, its Shinshū organizers intentionally designated it as a non-religious facility open to all in need. Secondly, resources at the Hermitage focused on the emotional and psychological needs of refugees rather than temple-based ritual responses. Hermitage residents were cared for by careful attention to a category that gained popularity in the broader context of the Hanshin disaster: *kokoro no kea*, or "care for the heart/mind/spirit," a catch-all term referring to counseling and related measures taken to aid bereaved survivors. To raise funds for the Rokkō Hermitage, Hongwanji-ha appealed to the emotional bonds between disaster survivors and empathetic fellow citizens by enjoining activists from across Japan to sacrifice part of their daily expenses to feed the large budget the Rokkō

[32] *Chūgai Nippō* 1996. See also McLaughlin, 2016a.

[33] These details and those that follow regarding Jōdo Shinshū aid initiatives following the Hanshin disaster are discussed in Miki 2012; Nishihonganji Hanshin/Awaji Daishinsai Fukkō Shien Renraku Kyōgikai 1998.

Hermitage required. Volunteer work thus rose to the fore as a means by which the True Pure Land sect could demonstrate its relevance to the Japanese public.

Religious responses to the March 11, 2011, disasters indicate that many religious organizations in Japan internalized the hard lessons of 1995 and put in place plans to dispatch aid in ways that mitigated public fears about violating constitutional prohibitions. Upon hearing news of the earthquake, tsunami, and nuclear disaster, the headquarters of every imaginable sort of Japanese religious organization immediately suspended ordinary operations to mobilize relief. Measurements of aid mobilization after 3.11 indicate that relief and reconstruction initiatives launched by religious organizations made up a significant portion of the humanitarian response (McLaughlin 2016b; Okamoto 2014). Japanese religious activists were among the first on the scene after the tsunami hit, opening their temples, shrines, churches, and other facilities to refugees as they dispatched volunteers to search mountains of wreckage for bodies and provide survivors with crucial emergency supplies. Long after most government agencies and other aid providers wrapped up their operations in northeastern Japan, religious practitioners continue to serve afflicted communities.

As they devised care initiatives, affiliates of Japan's Buddhist denominations understood the need to conform with the expectation that they limit obvious religious displays. This concern was evident in the immediate tsunami aftermath. For example, priests associated with the Sendai Buddhist Association who volunteered to perform sutras over bodies gathered at municipally-administered disaster response centers composed an ad hoc manual that called for clerics to limit their recitations to no more than ten minutes in order to avoid triggering accusations that they were violating constitutional provisions (Fujiyama 2020, 130–131). These same priests would contribute to the publication of a comprehensive disaster response guidebook for religious practitioners that includes attention to difficulties temples encounter being recognized as "designated evacuation shelters" (*shitei hinanjo*) by municipal and prefectural authorities (Buddhist NGO Network 2013, 33).

From March 2011, Japanese religion engaged in a double mobilization: while transporting personnel and emergency supplies to disaster-afflicted regions, religious groups and their advocates also mounted an elaborate print and electronic media campaign intended to disseminate images of aid work that would forestall the negative impressions that dominated coverage seventeen years earlier. In contrast to post-Hanshin prevarications over clerical involvement in first-phase relief work, accounts curated from 2011 by media-savvy religious activists and sympathetic academics cast Buddhist priests in ways that skilfully affirmed constitutional priorities. These media discourses tended to frame clerical contributions using neologisms such as *borantia* (volunteer), *kokoro no kea* (care for the heart/mind/spirit), the increasingly popular designation *supirichuaru kea* (spiritual care), and other categories that deliberately minimize Buddhist commitments (Berman 2018; McLaughlin 2016a). Importantly, media coverage tended to emphasize the contributions of religious individuals over sectarian organizations. This approach preserved the religious liberties of the aid providers while it anticipated, and diffused, fears that these providers represented a coordinated conversion effort. The post-3.11 religion narrative also included a marked emphasis on ecumenical cooperation, which involved repeated use of phrases along the lines of "overcoming religious boundaries" (*shūkyō no waku o koe*) or "overcoming sectarian [divides]" (*shūha o koe*) in descriptions of Buddhist, Shintō, Christian, and other religious practitioners coming together to work with one another and with non-religious experts. There was a tendency to highlight praiseworthy efforts by innovative religious activists who were marginalizing their sectarian identities in favor of working with academics, medical professionals, and other nominally non-religious actors. In these accounts, religious action took the form of scientifically verifiable treatment that has immediate, this-worldly relevance – in other words, treatment appropriate for the needs of unaffiliated individuals rather than parishioners.

This carefully mediated post-3.11 religion narrative provided an alternative to images of religion as a threat to constitutional divides. The narrative's emphasis on individual caregivers who side-lined their sectarian identities coheres with specific constitutional wording, notably of Article 20, which asserts that "No religious *organization* [emphasis added] shall receive any privileges from the State, nor exercise any political authority." Ironies abound as clerics rely on organizational support to foster professionalization in clinic-based care that requires them to "overcome" their sectarian affiliations. The Institute for Interfaith Chaplaincy began in 2012 as the Kokoro no Sōdanshitsu, or "Consultation Room for the Spirit," an aid outreach initiative in Sendai that relied on funding from a host of Buddhist and Christian denominations and other religious associations. Donations from religious juridical persons enabled the establishment of the Department of Practical Religious Studies at Tōhoku University. Presentations by the Department and its advocates nonetheless affirm Interfaith Chaplaincy as non-sectarian and driven by individual activists rather than religious organizations, and concern for constitutional divides is palpable in Interfaith Chaplaincy training. Taniyama emphasizes that "religious care" (*shūkyōteki kea*) requires chaplains to be ready to provide whatever services the recipient requires.[34] This means that a Buddhist priest should be ready to join an evangelical Christian hospital patient in a bedside prayer, and a Protestant minister must be prepared to chant "all praise the Amitābha Buddha" (*namu amida butsu*) with a Pure Land Buddhist hospice care recipient. The public sphere, Taniyama stresses, should be seen as an "away game" for the religious professional, while the professional's own temple or church is home field. At home, clergy can make presumptions about how to lead services, and practitioners enjoy constitutional protection of freedom of religion. Because Article 20 stipulates that no person can be compelled to take part in a ritual or teaching, the chaplain must wait to be asked

[34] An example of Taniyama's instruction is available in English in McLaughlin 2019b.

to perform the service in a public setting: following Taniyama's metaphor, he must be invited to play. The Interfaith Chaplaincy training materials insist that clear confirmation is required from all recipients before any religious act is performed in a caregiving situation outside sectarian boundaries.

Post-disaster activism confirmed for these instructors that the survival of their enterprises depends on how their actions are perceived in the public sphere. Retaining a place for Buddhist care providers in public forums remains a delicate balancing act, as indicated by the challenges these programs faced during the Covid-19 era. This precarity remains strongly determined by postwar constitutional mandates.

12.4 HOW CONCERNS ABOUT CONSTITUTIONAL LAW STEERED A BUDDHIST PARTY INTO "NORMAL" POLITICS: SOKA GAKKAI AND KOMEITO

Claiming a Japanese membership of 8.27 million households, Soka Gakkai (the "Value Creation Study Association") is a dominant presence in Japanese Buddhism.[35] It also exerts a significant influence in education, finance, publishing, and numerous other spheres. With a declared membership of close to two million Soka Gakkai International (SGI) adherents in 192 countries and territories, it may be Japan's most successful religious export, in terms of adherent numbers. In Japan, Soka Gakkai is perhaps best known for its affiliation with Komeito, the political party it founded in 1964.[36] The Gakkai's move into electoral politics invited heated critique from religious and political rivals. Much of this discourse has been informed by constitutional concerns. In turn, many of Soka Gakkai's and Komeito's institutional features have been shaped by attention to Japan's national constitutions.

Soka Gakkai is a lay association following Nichiren (1222–1282), a Japanese Buddhist reformer who confronted the temple-based traditions of his day to propagate the belief that only exclusive faith in the *Lotus Sūtra*, the putative final sermon delivered by Śākyamuṇi before a retinue of beings from across the Buddhist realms, serves as an effective means of salvation during *mappō*, the degraded Latter Day of the Buddha's dharma. The Gakkai maintains Nichiren Buddhist liturgies, such as chanting sections of the *Lotus* and repeatedly invoking its seven-syllable title,

35 Discussions of Soka Gakkai's history, institutional makeup, member activities, and other details in this section rely on these sources and others cited below: Aera Henshūbu 1996; Asano 1974; Asayama 2017; Higuma 1971; McLaughlin 2019a; Nakano 2016; Nishiyama 1975; Shimada 2004; Sōka Gakkai Nenpyō Hensan Iinkai 1976; Sōka Gakkai Yonjūshūnenshi Hensan Iinkai 1970; Tamano 2008; and White 1970.

36 Details regarding Komeito in this section rely on Asayama 2017; Ehrhardt et al. 2014; Hori [1973] 1999; Klein 2015; Kōmeitō Shi Hensa Iinkai 2014; McLaughlin 2015 and 2019a; Nakano 2016; Suzuki 1970; Tsukada 2015; White 1970; sources cited below.

namu-myōhō-renge-kyō, and members rely on Nichiren's writings as their primary Buddhist scriptural base. However, as the name "Value Creation Study Association" indicates, the group did not begin as a religion. It started as an educational reform movement, first called Sōka Kyōiku Gakkai ("Value Creation Education Study Association"), founded on November 18, 1930. The Gakkai's first president was Makiguchi Tsunesaburō (1871–1944). He was a schoolteacher and intellectual who in 1928, with his fellow teacher and disciple Toda Jōsei (1900–1958), converted to lay affiliation under Nichiren Shōshū, a minority temple-based sect that reveres Nichiren as the Buddha of the *mappō* era. From the late 1930s, Makiguchi and Toda's exclusivist convictions hardened, and Sōka Kyōiku Gakkai shifted away from educational reform to focus primarily on Nichiren Buddhist practices, including *shakubuku*, a forceful conversion tactic Nichiren prescribed for lands (such as Japan) that slander the *Lotus*. Conducting *shakubuku* led to conflicts with the wartime Japanese state, as did the group's opposition to the governmental mandate that all religions enshrine *kamifuda* (deity talismans) from the Grand Shrine at Ise. Makiguchi and Toda were among very few adherents in wartime Japan to maintain Nichiren's strict rejection of heterodox teachings and objects. They refused to enshrine the Shintō talismans and even encouraged converts to burn them, deeming them *hōbō*, or "slander to the dharma," as they persisted in carrying out *shakubuku* conversions. The Gakkai leaders were arrested in July 1943 for violating the terms of the 1925 Peace Preservation Law. Both were incarcerated, and Makiguchi died of malnutrition in prison on November 18, 1944, on the anniversary of the Gakkai's founding.

After World War II, Toda reformed the group as Soka Gakkai and drove institutional growth through a particularly hard-sell version of *shakubuku*. By the time of his death in April 1958, the religion had expanded to over one million adherent households. Converts were largely poor and socially atomized people who moved from the countryside into Japan's rapidly growing cities. While the Gakkai's aggressive proselytizing produced a massive surge in membership, it also created a negative public image. Public opposition to Soka Gakkai was driven in large part by the religion's move into electoral politics from the mid-1950s, which led to the founding in 1964 of the political party Komeito, often glossed as the "Clean Government Party." Today, Komeito qualifies as a "normal" political party, in the sense that it gathers votes by promoting policies that appeal to its constituents (Klein and McLaughlin 2022). Though it has wielded policy influence in national coalition with Japan's majority Liberal Democratic Party (LDP) since 1999, there is no evidence that Komeito has pursued an explicitly religious agenda in government, nor has it worked to undermine or otherwise transform Japan's political structure. It nonetheless grew out of a Soka Gakkai campaign to satisfy a millenarian Nichiren Buddhist objective: the construction of a *honmon no kaidan*, or "true ordination platform." This was to be a temple facility constructed at the Nichiren Shōshū sect headquarters at Taisekiji, near Mount Fuji, at which the sect's (and then also Soka

Gakkai's) principal object of worship was to be enshrined. This enshrinement would celebrate the conversion of the populace to exclusive worship of the *Lotus Sūtra*, a goal interpreted by the group as the nation's conversion to Soka Gakkai. Following Nichiren Buddhist dictates, a governmental decree ordering the construction of the ordination platform would be required. In postwar Japan, this entailed a majority vote in the Japanese Diet (Stone 2003). The Diet decree requirement appeared to violate the Article 20 prohibition on religious organizations exercising political authority or receiving privileges from the state, as well as the Article 89 proscription on public expenditure for the benefit of any religion.

Concern about potentially violating the then-recently promulgated Constitution did not stifle members' enthusiasm for institutional expansion in the immediate postwar years. From the early 1950s, as Soka Gakkai grew by leaps and bounds, Toda drove members to work toward the *kaidan* goal by sending them into politics. The group first fielded independent candidates for local elections in 1955. In 1956, three Gakkai administrators were elected to the House of Councillors (Upper House), and a surge of local- and national-level electoral victories followed. Members in early Gakkai campaigns transgressed multiple times against elections law, driven as they were by the objective to convert the populace to realize their Nichiren Buddhist aim. Murakami Shigeyoshi surmised that Soka Gakkai's *shakubuku*-driven efforts to gain a majority Diet vote and bring about the ordination platform was a case of substituting wartime refuge in the Emperor for a postwar effort from the ground up to install Nichiren Shōshū as Japan's national religion (1967, 155). In July 1957, Ikeda Daisaku (1928–), a Toda disciple who was then a Young Men's Division leader, was arrested alongside other young leaders, not on constitutional grounds, but for violating elections law prohibitions against house-to-house campaigning. Soka Gakkai came to eulogize Ikeda's legal tribulations as the "Osaka Incident," an episode they treat as the now honorary president's *hōnan*, or "persecution [for defending] the dharma." He was cleared of all charges in January 1962. By this time, Ikeda Daisaku was third president of Soka Gakkai, having taken the office on May 3, 1960.

May 3 has become one of Soka Gakkai's most significant commemorative dates. The importance of the Gakkai's May 3 memorials is emblematic of an ethic of constitutionalism that underlies the religion and, to a lesser extent, its affiliated political party. Both Toda and Ikeda ascended to the Gakkai presidency on May 3, the same day that the 1947 Constitution went into effect, and Japan's annual May 3 Constitutional Memorial Day also serves as Soka Gakkai's "Mother's Day," as well as the wedding anniversary of Ikeda and his wife Kaneko. A survey of other Gakkai and Komeito events on May 3 reveals the deep importance of the date for the religion and the party. This became particularly apparent under Ikeda's leadership, when the Gakkai's political engagement increased dramatically, keeping pace with the lay sect's explosive membership growth and institutional diversification. Between 1960 and 1970, Soka Gakkai in Japan grew from just over one million to over seven million households, and the organization began to gain significant numbers of followers in countries overseas. On November 27, 1961, Gakkai politicians in the Diet organized as Kōmei Seiji Renmei (or Kōseiren), the "League for Just and Fair Politics," enacting a new political body following a May 3, 1961 announcement at Soka Gakkai headquarters that established an institutionally distinct "culture bureau" (*bunkakyoku*) that would oversee political engagement (Kōmeitō Shi Hensa Iinkai 2014, 35–36). On May 3, 1964, Ikeda declared that henceforth Soka Gakkai would be a purely religious organization, that politics would be left to Kōmei politicians, and that the religion would soon establish an independent political party (Kōmeitō Shi Hensa Iinkai 2014, 35–41). This declaration, falling as it did on Constitutional Memorial Day, resonates with the constitutional guarantee separating religion and government. On November 17, 1964, the day before Soka Gakkai's founding anniversary, Ikeda announced the dissolution of Kōseiren and the establishment of Kōmeitō.

Initially, Komeito did not separate religious and political objectives. Just as Soka Gakkai is heir to the twin legacies of Nichiren Buddhism and humanism, Nichiren Buddhist priorities and a modern ideal of securing world peace through democracy inform Komeito's official founding statement. It reads (in part):

> We hold the firm conviction that it is only through the singular path of the Buddhist philosophy of absolute pacifism – that is, the superior path of a harmonious fusion of government and Buddhism (*ōbutsu myōgō*) – that the world will attain salvation from the horror of war. The Clean Government Party, through the founding ideals of a harmonious fusion of government and Buddhism and Buddhist democracy (*buppō minshūshugi*), will fundamentally cleanse Japan's political world, confirm the basis of government by parliamentary democracy, put down deep roots in the masses, and realize the well-being of the common people. (Kōmeitō 1964)[37]

From August 1, 1956, Toda Jōsei had issued an essay titled "*Ōbutsu myōgōron*" ("On the Harmonious Union of Kingship and Buddhism") in which he asserted that this utopian goal was to be realized through conversion of the populace and construction of the ordination platform (Toda 1956, 204). Ikeda's use of *ōbutsu myōgō* in Komeito's November 1964 founding statement reaffirmed the goal to unite Buddhism and government, and members continued to be inspired by this millenarian aim as they worked for Komeito campaigns. From 1964, Komeito fielded candidates in both the Lower and Upper Houses, and it expanded its presence in local legislatures across Japan. By June 1969, Komeito was the third-largest party in the National Diet, and its proportion of votes in national and regional elections was still increasing. However, Komeito's fortunes shifted abruptly. On May 3, 1970, following a scandal the previous year surrounding a failed attempt to quash the

[37] Printed transcript of founding statement. See also Ehrhardt et al. 2014, 67–68.

publication of a book titled *I Denounce Soka Gakkai*, Ikeda announced a formal institutional separation between Soka Gakkai and Komeito. The religion renounced its ordination platform plans, and Komeito eliminated its references to Buddhism and replaced them with a pledge to uphold the 1947 Constitution.

The party gained its largest-ever proportion of Diet seats in 1983, but suffered setbacks thereafter, and while Gakkai members have continued treating electioneering for Komeito candidates (and their allies) as a component of their regular practice, the party struggled to define its raison d'être until it entered into coalition with the LDP in 1999. In the meantime, constitutionalism grew into something of a Soka Gakkai constant. While Komeito began to prevaricate on its commitment to strict constitutional observance, Soka Gakkai consistently supported constitutional preservation. In particular, reverence for Article 9 continued to inspire Gakkai events and organizations. Early examples include the Youth Division's 1974 "May 3 Memorial Peace Constitution Preservation Central Committee Event" in Setagaya Ward, Tokyo, at which the Committee leadership asserted the need to protect the Constitution for its guarantee of religious liberty (Kiuchi 1974, 169).

A fierce loyalty to constitutionalism drove Gakkai institution-building and member dispositions over the course of Ikeda's leadership. Except for a small and rapidly diminishing number of elderly pioneers who converted under Toda, the present-day majority of the Gakkai's adherents, and almost all members who power Komeito's campaigns today, came of age as Ikeda disciples. From early in his presidency, Soka Gakkai transformed from an organization run *by* Ikeda into a group dedicated *to* him, and after Soka Gakkai split from Nichiren Shōshū in November 1991, member reverence for Ikeda grew ever more intense. Having left behind the Nichiren Buddhist ordination platform objective, Soka Gakkai clarified its commitment to the constitutional ideals Ikeda cherished, and the religion focused to an increasing extent on cultivating Ikeda's profile as an international statesman who reached across cultural and national boundaries to advance peace, in keeping with Japan's postwar international stance as pacifist exemplar.[38]

During Ikeda's most vigorous decades, from the 1960s into the early 2000s, members engaged in a tireless mix of peace-promoting activities. The group became famous for its "world peace culture festivals" (*sekai heiwa bunkasai*) in which thousands of costumed members swirled through stadiums in complex dance numbers as marching bands performed triumphal Gakkai anthems and attendees in the stands held up placards bearing peace messages. From January 1983, Ikeda began issuing annual *Peace Proposals*, treatises with detailed recommendations for multilateral action in the interest of resolving global conflicts. Nichiren Buddhism's

[38] For analyses of Japan's shifting security positions from the postwar into the present, see Le 2021; Midford 2020. For discussions of Buddhist pacifism and attitudes toward the peace clause of the 1947 Constitution, including those of Soka Gakkai members under Ikeda, see Kisala 2000.

status inversed, shifting from the group's guiding framework into a foundation undergirding Soka Gakkai's "three pillars": peace, culture, and education.

Even as Ikeda rallied Gakkai members around a peace platform that upheld the Japanese postwar Constitution's ideals, Komeito began to compromise on its support for pacifism. After its May 3, 1970, separation from Soka Gakkai, the party at first emphasized the absolute pacifism of its founding charter. It asserted that Japan should maintain neutrality and should establish alternatives to the 1960 US–Japan Security Treaty and maintenance of the Japan Self-Defense Forces (Kōmeitō 1973, 44–45). From 1978, however, the party came to acknowledge the legality of the US–Japan Treaty and the JSDF. Komeito's next significant adjustment came in 1992, when it supported the LDP decision to include JSDF troops in UN peacekeeping operations. After it entered into coalition government with the LDP from 1999, Komeito made more concessions, going along with Prime Minister Koizumi Jun'ichirō's decision to send troops to the Persian Gulf (2002) and Iraq (2004).[39] This policy shift inspired some of the first protests against Komeito by Soka Gakkai members (Nakano 2016, 68–69). On January 21, 2004, a group of adherents called the "Society for Preserving the Peace Constitution Opposed to the Iraq Troop Dispatch" (Irakku Hahei ni Hantai Shi Heiwa Kenpō o Mamoru Kai) submitted 1,800 signatures to Komeito headquarters protesting the party's policy reversal (Asahi Shinbun 2004; Nakano 2016, 67–69). The largest anti-Komeito protests by Gakkai adherents were triggered by the party's support of eleven security bills sponsored by Prime Minister Abe Shinzō that were rushed through the National Diet in September 2015. These laws allow Japan the "right of collective self-defense," which includes the ability for the JSDF to come to the aid of Japan's military allies. This is a security posture that radically reinterprets the Article 9 pledge to "forever renounce war as a sovereign right of the nation and the threat or use of force as a means of settling international disputes." Observers in summer 2015 were struck by the presence of protesters waving Soka Gakkai flags and bearing signs emblazoned with strident Nichiren Buddhist and Soka Gakkai slogans in demonstrations before the Diet and at other locations across the country. These were Gakkai adherents who endured harsh rejection by their fellow members as they rebuked the party their religion founded for abandoning its foundational pacifism (McLaughlin 2015).

Komeito now sidesteps clear-cut policy commitments when it comes to constitutional interpretation or revision. The party manifesto for the 2017 general election, for example, only included a short discussion in the final section that mentioned the potential for adding a third clause that acknowledges the legality of the JSDF, should this be supported by a majority of Japanese voters (Kōmeitō 2017). In the 2019 election manifesto, the only mention of the Constitution appeared as an appendix and simply stated that revision "should be discussed carefully from now on" (Kōmeitō 2019), and the manifesto for the October 2021 election only dedicated

[39] For a chronicle of Komeito's peace concessions, see Lindgren 2016.

the penultimate page of its seventy-two-page "Policy Compilation" (Seisakushū) to constitutional matters (Kōmeitō 2021). However, while constitutional fidelity as a Komeito priority seems to be fading, the party remains well known for its historical success as a brake against LDP constitutional revision attempts. Adam Liff and Ko Maeda compared the LDP's 2012 constitutional revision draft to proposals made on May 3, 2017 by Prime Minister Abe (2019). Instead of pursuing the 2012 LDP amendment strategy of *kaiken* (wholesale revision), Abe's 2017 proposal followed a modest plan first outlined by Komeito in 2005 to potentially add a third clause to Article 9 to acknowledge the legality of the JSDF, while leaving the first two clauses unchanged, should public opinion indicate approval for this course of action. Without at least 80 percent Komeito voter support for LDP politicians running in Single-Member Districts, the LDP would fall below a simple majority in both Houses of the National Diet and would lose the two-thirds super-majority typically retained by the coalition. So long as Komeito holds a significant number of Diet seats, and so long as Gakkai members continue to electioneer on behalf of LDP politicians, Gakkai member dedication to pacifist principles ensures that the LDP-Komeito coalition remains unlikely to revise or replace the 1947 Constitution.

As Komeito has shied away from explicit engagement with constitutional matters, Soka Gakkai has deepened its commitment to constitutionalism. One way the religion expresses its constitutional focus is by enacting its own constitution, which looks very much like its Japanese national constitutional predecessors. The Gakkai's promulgation of a constitution is in keeping with how the group models itself explicitly along the lines of Japanese state institutions. Elsewhere, I have characterized Soka Gakkai as a "mimetic nation-state" to explain the comprehensive extent to which the religion replicates state and state-affiliated institutions within its own parameters (McLaughlin 2019a). These replicated institutions include a massive bureaucracy modeled on a civil service, doctrinal instruction and other forms of study derived from standardized education, de facto sovereign territory at its headquarters and other facilities protected by trained cadres and bedecked by a tri-color flag, and collective memory of the organization preserved in anthem-like songs and a massive and ever-expanding published record that functions akin to a national literature. The group also mandates donation practices labeled *zaimu* (finances, or taxes) and offers singular reverence to its apotheosized Honorary President Ikeda Daisaku.

A written constitution numbers among the Gakkai's nation-like appurtenances. Announced on November 18, 2017, on the anniversary of the group's founding in 1930, the "Constitution of the Soka Gakkai" establishes an orthodox understanding of its history and confirms the transcendent authority of its "eternal mentors," the three founding presidents Makiguchi, Toda, and Ikeda.[40] Aspects of this document follow standards set out in Japan's 1947 Constitution. For example, Article

[40] English text is available at The Constitution of the Soka Gakkai 2017.

15 stipulates that a vote of two-thirds of the members of Soka Gakkai's Constitution Amendment Committee is required to make any changes to the document, a rule that appears similar to Article 96 of the 1947 national Constitution, which requires a two-thirds vote in both Houses of the Diet and a referendum of 50 percent plus one vote in order to carry out a constitutional amendment. Notably, the Gakkai version of this clause makes no room for the voice of an electorate. Overall, Soka Gakkai's constitutional mimesis arguably takes its cue less from the postwar constitution than its 1890 predecessor. Like that of the Meiji Constitution, the preamble of the Gakkai equivalent outlines a genealogy that confirms the constitution's basis in primordial and transcendent authority. Where the 1890 Constitution speaks in the voice of the Emperor who "ascended the throne of a lineal succession unbroken for ages eternal," the Gakkai Constitution declares a "profound karmic connection" from Śākyamuṇi Buddha to Nichiren to Makiguchi and Toda, culminating in Ikeda. The Meiji Constitution repeatedly confirms the supremacy of the Emperor while deferring to the need for the populace to create and interpret appropriate laws. Similarly, the Gakkai's 2017 Constitution affirms the primacy of the three founding presidents while empowering the religion's administrative bodies to generate and oversee its internal regulations.

Ironically, Soka Gakkai's mimetic equivalent of a national constitution appears closer to the document upheld by the wartime state that martyred its founding leader and destroyed the wartime-era Gakkai. Soka Gakkai's 2017 Constitution appears to call for a utopian version of the very polity that victimized its originators.

12.5 CONCLUSION: "CONSTITUTIONAL BUDDHISM" AS A COUNTERPOINT TO "BUDDHIST CONSTITUTIONALISM"

On May 3, 1970, on the tenth anniversary of his appointment as third president of Soka Gakkai, Ikeda Daisaku affirmed the religion's policy of *seikyō bunri*, or "separation of politics and religion," the principle upheld in the Japanese Constitution that came into effect on the same day in 1947. In his address, Ikeda postulated that Soka Gakkai might adopt conventions from the Japanese political system and institute a practice of soliciting votes from the religion's membership. He suggested that, in the future, Soka Gakkai might put in place a term limit of three or four years for an elected Gakkai president (Kiuchi 1974). The 2017 Gakkai Constitution, however, stands as the culmination of decades spent solidifying Ikeda Daisaku as the religion's absolute authority. Its content and tone suggest that the referents for the Gakkai's mimetic processes are drawn not only from the postwar constitutional order and its defenses of pacifism and unconditional freedom of religion, but also from the prewar, Emperor-centric constitutional nation-state. Komeito has needed to compromise on constitutionalism in order to survive as a small party within Japan's postwar political system. Soka Gakkai has remained free to promote utopian visions inspired by multiple Japanese constitutional precedents.

While its 2017 Constitution may stand as the example that hews most closely to national models, Soka Gakkai is not the only Japanese Buddhist organization to promulgate a constitutional equivalent. Sōtō Zen, for instance, formulates its denominational regulations as a multi-article "Sōtō Sect Constitution" (Sōtōshū Shūken), and other temple-based denominations present their guiding rules in similar formats, albeit not always in documents that bear the title "constitution." One might also posit that an ethic of constitutionalism is identifiable across the broad spectrum of Japanese Buddhism, whether or not an institution maintains a set of internal rules that functions in a de facto manner as a constitution.[41] The case study of post-disaster clerical aid makes clear that Buddhists in Japan formulate their public conduct and institutional practices to comport with national constitutional norms. This widely shared ethic is certainly the result of Buddhism's fraught position in modern and contemporary Japan and is indicative of the need for Japan's Buddhists to defend their continued relevance to the nation.[42] Soka Gakkai's mimesis of a national constitution can also be read as a defensive posture adopted in response to being targeted by political rivals and the threat of legal challenges mounted within a state based in constitutional law. It is a distinctive instance of what is otherwise a widely shared Japanese Buddhist convention to internalize and manifest concern for the nation's constitutional authority.

This chapter's introduction included a brief discussion of Benjamin Schonthal's theory of "Buddhist constitutionalism" that describes processes in Southeast Asia in which "Buddhist ideas and institutions figure prominently as topics of constitutional negotiation."[43] In Southeast Asian nations, lawmakers, monastics, and other power-holders work to secure Buddhism as a foundation for the state, maintaining a principle of enshrining religious teachings and institutions that Schonthal compares convincingly with Islamic and other religiously informed state-building enterprises. I suggest that the cases in this chapter exemplify a contrasting ethic of constitutionalism that has emerged as a response to the comparatively precarious position Buddhism has occupied in Japan since the nineteenth century. There is an observable urge on the part of contemporary Japanese Buddhists to foster "constitutional Buddhism," Buddhist constitutionalism's opposite. The Japanese Buddhist cases, perhaps especially the case of Soka Gakkai's constitutional mimesis, represent a countercurrent within what Schonthal identifies as global Buddhist fluidity between two putatively heterogeneous categories of religions and constitutions. In many Buddhist-majority countries, Buddhism persists as a foundational influence on the

[41] See Schonthal 2021.

[42] In his discussions of Japanese Buddhist prison chaplaincy, Adam Lyons describes this as a "statist" approach on the part of clergy who must observe constitutional divisions in their work within state institutions (Lyons 2021).

[43] Schonthal 2017, 707.

formation of national constitutions. By contrast, influence flows in the opposite direction in Japan, where Buddhist organizations take their cue from constitutions that set out an explicit religion/state divide. A full account of Buddhism as a lens through which to approach comparative constitutional law must account for Buddhism's circumstances in Japan.

REFERENCES

Abe, Keisuke Mark. 2011. "Separation of Church and State in Japan: What Happened to the Conservative Supreme Court?" *St. John's Law Review* 85 (2): 447–72.

Abe Shunsuke. 2021. "Kōshibyō tochi shiyōryō menjo wa iken seikyōbunri soshōde saikōsai." *Asahi Shinbun*, February 24. Accessed on November 15, 2021. www.asahi.com/articles/ASP2S54RJP2KUTIL018.html

Aera Henshūbu, ed. 1996. *Sōka gakkai kaibō*. Tokyo: Asahi Shinbun.

Agency for Cultural Affairs. *Shūkyō nenkan 2020*. Accessed on November 15, 2021. www.bunka.go.jp/tokei_hakusho_shuppan/hakusho_nenjihokokusho/shukyo_nenkan/index.html

Asano Hidemitsu. 1974. *Watashi no mita sōka gakkai*. Tokyo: Keizai Ōraisha.

Asayama Taichi. 2017. *Uchigawa kara miru Sōka gakkai to Kōmeitō*. Tokyo: Discovery Twenty-One.

Avenell, Simon. 2010. *Making Japanese Citizens: Civil Society and the Mythology of the Shimin in Postwar Japan*. Berkeley: University of California Press.

Baffelli, Erica and Reader, Ian. 2012. "Editor's Introduction: Impact and Ramifications: The Aftermath of the Aum Affair in the Japanese Religious Context." *Japanese Journal of Religious Studies* 39 (1): 1–28.

2019. *Dynamism and the Ageing of a Japanese 'New' Religion: Transformations and the Founder*. London: Bloomsbury.

Benn, James A., and Balkwill, Stephanie. 2021. "Buddhist Statecraft." In *Oxford Bibliographies*. Accessed on November 15, 2021. www.oxfordbibliographies.com/view/document/obo-9780195393521/obo-9780195393521-0269.xml

Berman, Michael. 2018. "Religion Overcoming Religions: Suffering, Secularism, and the Training of Interfaith Chaplains, in Japan." *American Ethnologist* 45 (2): 228–40.

Blacker, Carmen. 1975. *The Catalpa Bow: A Study of Shamanistic Practices in Japan*. London: Allen & Unwin.

Buddhist NGO Network, ed. 2013. *Ji'in to chiiki no kizuna de takameru ji'in bisai gaidobukku*. Tokyo: BNN.

Covell, Stephen G. 2005. *Japanese Temple Buddhism: Worldliness in a Religion of Renunciation*. Honolulu: University of Hawai'i Press.

Dower, John W. 1999. *Embracing Defeat: Japan in the Wake of World War II*. New York: W.W. Norton.

Ehrhardt, George, Klein, Axel, McLaughlin, Levi and Reed, Steven R., eds. 2014. *Kōmeitō: Politics and Religion in Japan*. Berkeley: Institute of East Asian Studies.

Field, Norma. 1991. *In the Realm of a Dying Emperor: Japan at Century's End*. New York: Vintage Books.

Fujiyama Midori. 2020. *Rinshō shūkyōshi: shi no bansōsha*. Tokyo: Kōbunken.

Genron Shuppan no Jiyū o Mamoru Kai, ed. 2012. *Fujiwara Hirotatsu Sōka gakkai o kiru 41-nen no kenshō*. Tokyo: Nisshin Hōdō.

Gill, Tom, Steger, Brigitte and Slater, David H., eds. 2013. *Japan Copes with Calamity: Ethnographies of the Earthquake, Tsunami, and Nuclear Disasters of March 2011*. Bern: Peter Lang.

Global Religious Futures Project. 2016. "Japan." Accessed on November 15, 2021. www.globalreligiousfutures.org/countries/japan#/?affiliations_religion_id=0&affiliations_year=2050&region_name=All%20Countries&restrictions_year=2016

Gordon, Andrew, ed. 1993. *Postwar Japan as History*. Berkeley: University of California Press.

Graf, Tim. 2016. "Buddhist Responses to the 3.11 Disasters in Japan." In *Disasters and Social Crisis in Contemporary Japan: Political, Religious, and Cultural Responses*, edited by Mark Mullins and Koichi Nakano, 156–81. Basingstoke: Palgrave Macmillan.

Hardacre, Helen. 1989. *Shinto and the State, 1868–1988*. Princeton: Princeton University Press.

2002. *Religion and Society in Nineteenth-Century Japan: A Study of the Southern Kantō Region, Using Late Edo and Early Meiji Gazetteers*. Ann Arbor: University of Michigan Press.

2017. *Shinto: A History*. New York: Oxford University Press.

Hardacre, Helen, George, Timothy S., Komamura, Keigo and Seraphim, Franziska, eds. 2021. *Japanese Constitutional Revisionism and Civic Activism*. Lanham: Lexington Books.

Higuma Takenori. 1971. *Toda Jōsei/Sōka gakkai*. Tokyo: Shin Jinbutsu Ōraisha.

Hori Yukio [1973] 1999. *Kōmeitōron*. Tokyo: Nansōsha.

Horie Norichika and Takahashi Hara. 2021. *Shisha no chikara: tsunami hisaichi "reiteki taiken" no shiseigaku*. Tokyo: Iwanami Shoten.

Horii, Mitsutoshi. 2018. *The Category of 'Religion' in Contemporary Japan: Shūkyō and Temple Buddhism*. Palgrave Macmillan.

Hur, Nam-lin. 2007. *Death and Social Order in Tokugawa Japan: Buddhism, Anti-Christianity, and the Danka System*. Cambridge: Harvard University Press.

"Hyōgoken nanbu jishin kara ichinen zadankai." 1996. *Chūgai Nippō*, January 1.

Ishii Kenchi. 2008. *Dētā bukku: gendai Nihonjin no shūkyō*. Tokyo: Shin'yōsha.

Josephson, Jason Ānanda. 2012. *The Invention of Religion in Japan*. Chicago: University of Chicago Press.

Kasai, Kenta. 2016. "Introducing Chaplaincy to Japanese Society: A Religious Practice in Public Space." *Journal of Religion in Japan* 5 (2–3): 246–62.

Ketelaar, James. 1989. *Of Heretics and Martyrs in Meiji Japan: Buddhism and Its Persecution*. Princeton: Princeton University Press.

Kingston, Jeff. 2012. *Natural Disaster and Nuclear Crisis in Japan: Response and Recovery after Japan's 3/11*. London and New York: Routledge.

Kisala, Robert. 2000. *Prophets of Peace: Pacifism and Cultural Identity in Japan's New Religions*. Honolulu: University of Hawai'i Press.

Kiuchi Hiroshi. 1974. *Kōmeitō to Sōka gakkai*. Tokyo: Gōdō Shuppan.

Klautau, Orion. 2014. "Nationalizing the Dharma: Takakusu Junjirō and the Study of Buddhism in Taishō Japan." *Japanese Religions* 34: 53–70.

Klautau, Orion and Krämer, Hans Martin, eds. 2021. *Buddhism and Modernity: Sources from Nineteeth-Century Japan*. Honolulu: University of Hawai'i Press.

Klein, Axel. 2015. "Kōmeitō: Rock 'n' Row the Coalition Boat." In *Japan Decides 2014*, edited by Robert Pekkanen, Steven R. Reed, and Ethan Scheiner, 72–86. London, New York: Palgrave Macmillan.

Klein, Axel and McLaughlin, Levi. 2022. "Kōmeitō: The Party and Its Place in Japanese Politics." In *The Oxford Handbook of Japanese Politics*, edited by Robert J. Pekkanen and Saadia M. Pekkanen, 201–22. New York: Oxford University Press.

Kōmeitō. 1964. "Printed transcript of founding statement."

ed. 1973. *Kōmeitō handobukku*. Tokyo: Kōmeitō.

2017. *Shūinsen jūten seisaku*. Accessed on January 5, 2021. www.komei.or.jp/campaign/shuin2017/manifesto/manifesto2017_l.pdf

2019. *Shūinsen 2019 manifesuto*. Accessed on November 15, 2021. www.komei.or.jp/campaign/sanin2019/policy

2021. *Shūinsen seisakushū*. Accessed on January 5, 2021. www.komei.or.jp/special/shuin49/wp-content/uploads/manifesto2021.pdf

Kōmeitō Shi Hensa Iinkai, ed. 2014. *Kōmeitō 50 nen no ayumi*. Tokyo: Kōmeitō Kikanshi Iinkai.

Kurata Takuji et al. 2002. *Hanketsu, soken no ranyō: danzai sareta gyōgen soshō*. Tokyo: Nihon Hyōronsha.

Kuroda Toshio. 1996. "The Imperial Law and the Buddhist Law." *Japanese Journal of Religious Studies* 23 (3–4): 271–85.

Kuroda Nobuyuki and Tsuganesawa Toshihiro, eds. 1999. *Shinsai no shakaigaku: Hanshin/Awaji daishinsai to minshū ishiki*. Kyoto: Sekai Shisōsha.

Kyodo. 2021. "Top Court Says Free Land Offer for Confucian Temple was Unconstitutional." *The Japan Times*, February 24. Accessed on November 15, 2021. www.japantimes.co.jp/news/2021/02/24/national/crime-legal/okinawa-temple-land/

Larsson, Ernils. 2017. "Jinja Honchō and the Politics of Constitutional Reform in Japan." *Japan Review* 30: 227–52.

2020. *Rituals of a Secular Nation: Shinto Normativity and the Separation of Religion and State in Postwar Japan*. PhD thesis, Uppsala University, Sweden.

Le, Tom Phuong. 2021. *Japan's Aging Peace: Pacifism and Militarism in the Twenty-First Century*. New York: Columbia University Press.

Liff, Adam and Ko Maeda. 2019. "Electoral Incentives, Policy Compromises, and Coalition Durability: Japan's LDP-Komeito Government in a Mixed Electoral System." *Japanese Journal of Political Science* 20 (1): 53–73.

Lindgren, Petter. 2016. "Kōmeitō's Security Ideals and Collective Self-Defense: Betwixt Pacifism and Compromises." *East Asia* 33: 233–54.

Liu, Cuilan. 2020. "The Fall of a Chinese Buddhist Monk: Law and State Governance of State Buddhism in Post-Imperial China." *Journal of Law and Religion* 35 (3): 432–49.

LoBreglio, John. 1997. "The Revisions to the Religious Corporations Law: An Introduction and Annotated Translation." *Japanese Religions* 22 (1): 38–59.

Lyons, Adam J. 2021. *Karma and Punishment: Prison Chaplaincy in Japan*. Cambridge: Harvard University Press.

McLaughlin, Levi. 2015. "Komeito's Soka Gakkai Protestors and Supporters: Religious Motivations for Political Activism in Contemporary Japan." *The Asia-Pacific Journal* 13 (41/1): 1–28. Accessed on November 15, 2021. https://apjjf.org/-Levi-McLaughlin/4386

2016a. "Hard Lessons Learned: Tracking Changes in Media Presentations of Religion and Religious Aid Mobilization after the 1995 and 2011 Disasters in Japan." *Asian Ethnology* 75 (1): 105–38.

2016b. "Religious Responses to the 2011 Tsunami in Japan." In *Oxford Handbooks Online*. Accessed on November 15, 2021. www.oxfordhandbooks.com/view/10.1093/oxfordhb/9780199935420.001.0001/oxfordhb-9780199935420-e-29

2019a. *Soka Gakkai's Human Revolution: The Rise of a Mimetic Nation in Modern Japan*. Honolulu: University of Hawaiʻi Press.

2019b. "Using Buddhist Resources in Post-disaster Japan: Taniyama Yōzō's 'Vihāra Priests and Buddhist Chaplains." In *Buddhism and Medicine: An Anthology of Modern Sources*, edited by Pierce Salguero, 164–76. New York: Columbia University Press.

Matsumoto Katsuya. 1973. *Soshō sareta Sōka gakkai*. Tokyo: Gendai Burēnsha.

Midford, Paul. 2020. *Overcoming Isolationism: Japan's Leadership in East Asian Security Multilateralism*. Stanford: Stanford University Press.

Miki Hizuru, ed. 2001. *Fukkō to shūkyō: shinsaigo no hito to shakai o iyasu mono*. Osaka: Tōhō.

2012. "Hanshin Awaji daishinsai hisaichi ni okeru shūkyō no 'tōji' to 'ima.'" *Shūkyō kenkyū* 86 (2): 421–46.

Mullins, Mark R. 2021. *Yasukuni Fundamentalism: Japanese Religions and the Politics of Restoration*. Honolulu: University of Hawai'i Press.

Murakami Shigeyoshi, 1967. *Sōka gakkai = Kōmeitō*. Tokyo: Aoki Shoten.

Nakai, Kate Wildman. 2017. "Between Secularity, Shrines, and Protestantism: Catholic Higher Education in Prewar Japan." *Japan Review* 30: 97–127.

Nakano Jun. 2016. *Sōka gakkai/Kōmeitō no kenkyū: jiko renritsu seiken no naizai ronri*. Tokyo: Iwanami Shoten.

National Diet Library. "The Constitution of the Empire of Japan." Accessed on November 15, 2021. www.ndl.go.jp/constitution/e/etc/c02.html

NHK Broadcasting Culture Research Institute. 2020. *Gendai Nihonjin no ishiki kōzō* (9th ed.). Tokyo: NHK Books.

Nishihonganji Hanshin and Awaji Daishinsai Fukkō Shien Renraku Kyōgikai, ed. 1998. *Hanshin/Awaji daishinsai fukkō shien katsudō hōkoku: rokkōan monogatari*. Kyoto: Nishihonganji.

Nishiyama Shigeru. 1975. "Nichiren shōshū sōka gakkai ni okeru 'honmon kaidan' ron no hensen: Seijiteki shūkyō undō to shakai tōsei." In *Nichirenshū no shomondai*, edited by Takashi Nakao, 241–75. Tokyo: Yūzankaku.

O'Brien, David and Yasuo Ohkoshi. 1996. *To Dream of Dreams: Religious Freedom and Constitutional Politics in Postwar Japan*. Honolulu: University of Hawai'i Press.

Okamoto Masahiro. 2014. "Higashi Nihon daishinsai ni okeru 18 shūkyō kyōdan no hisaisha/chi shien katsudō chōsa ni tsuite: chōsa hōkoku ni, jakkan no kōsatsu o kuwaete." JANPORA: Japan NPO Research Association Discussion Papers.

Okkotsu Masao. 2003. *Kōmeitō = Sōka gakkai no shinjitsu 2: "Ji/sō" gōseiken o utsu*. Kyoto: Kamogawa Shuppan.

Ooms, Herman. 2008. *Imperial Politics and Symbolics in Ancient Japan: The Tenmu Dynasty, 650–800*. Honolulu: University of Hawai'i Press.

Pew Forum on Religion & Public Life, ed. 2012. *The Global Religious Landscape: A Report on the Size and Distribution of the World's Major Religious Groups as of 2010*. Washington DC: Pew Research Center.

Piggott, Joan R. 1997. *The Emergence of Japanese Kingship*. Stanford: Stanford University Press.

Prime Minister of Japan and His Cabinet. 1946. "The Constitution of Japan." Accessed on November 15, 2021. https://japan.kantei.go.jp/constitution_and_government_of_japan/constitution_e.html

Rots, Aike P. 2017. *Shinto, Nature and Ideology in Contemporary Japan: Making Sacred Forests*. London: Bloomsbury.

Rowe, Mark M. 2011. *Bonds of the Dead: Temples, Burial, and the Transformation of Contemporary Japanese Buddhism*. Chicago: University of Chicago Press.

2017. "Charting Known Territory: Female Buddhist Priests." *Japanese Journal of Religious Studies* 44 (1): 75–101.

Ruoff, Kenneth J. 2020. *Japan's Imperial House in the Postwar Era*. Cambridge: Harvard University Press.

Sakurai Yoshihide and Kawamata Toshinori, eds. 2016. *Jinkō genshō shakai to jiin: sōsharu kyapitaru no shiza kara*. Kyoto: Hōzōkan.
Sango, Asuka. 2015. *The Halo of Golden Light: Imperial Authority and Buddhist Ritual in Heian Japan*. Honolulu: University of Hawai'i Press.
Sawada, Janine Tasca. 2004. *Practical Pursuits: Religion, Politics, and Personal Cultivation in Nineteenth-Century Japan*. Honolulu: University of Hawai'i Press.
Schonthal, Benjamin. 2017. "Formations of Buddhist Constitutionalism in South and Southeast Asia." *International Journal of Constitutional Law* 15 (3): 705–33.
2021. "The Case for Religious Constitutions: Comparative Constitutional Law among Buddhists and Other Religious Groups." *Law & Social Inquiry* 20: 1–29.
Shields, James Mark. 2017. *Against Harmony: Progressive and Radical Buddhism in Modern Japan*. New York: Oxford University Press.
Shimada Hiromi. 2004. *Sōka gakkai*. Tokyo: Shinchō Shinsho.
Shimada Hiromi et al. 2007. *Ikeda Daisaku nakiato no Sōka gakkai*. Tokyo: Takarajimasha.
The Constitution of the Soka Gakkai. 2017. Accessed on November 15, 2012. www.sokanet.jp/info/constitution.html
Sōka Gakkai Nenpyō Hensan Iinkai, ed. 1976. *Sōka gakkai nenpyō*. Tokyo: Seikyō Shinbunsha.
Sōka Gakkai Yonjūshūnenshi Hensan Iinkai, ed. 1970. *Sōka gakkai yonjūshūnenshi*. Tokyo: Sōka Gakkai.
"Sōka Gakkai yūshi 'iraku hantai shomei' o kōmei ni teishutsu." 2004. *Asahi Shinbun*, January 21.
Starling, Jessica. 2019. *Guardians of the Buddha's Home: Domestic Religion in Contemporary Jōdo Shinshū*. Honolulu: University of Hawai'i Press.
Stone, Jacqueline I. 2003. "'By Imperial Edict and Shogunal Decree': Politics and the Issue of the Ordination Platform in Modern Lay Nichiren Buddhism." In *Buddhism in the Modern World: Adaptions of an Ancient Tradition*, edited by Steven Heine and Charles Prebish, 193–220. Oxford and New York: Oxford University Press.
Suzuki Hiroshi. 1970. *Toshiteki sekai*. Tokyo: Seishin Shobō.
Takahashi, Hara. 2016. "The Ghosts of Tsunami Dead and *Kokoro no kea* in Japan's Religious Landscape." *Journal of Religion in Japan* 5: 176–98.
Takahata, Eiichiro. 2007. "Religious Accommodation in Japan." *BYU Law Review* 2007 (3): 729–50.
Tamamuro Fumio. 2001. "Local Society and the Temple-Parishioner Relationship within the Bakufu's Governance Structure." *Japanese Journal of Religious Studies* 28 (3–4): 261–92.
Tamano Kazushi. 2008. *Sōka gakkai no kenkyū*. Tokyo: Kōdansha.
Thal, Sarah. 2005. *Rearranging the Landscape of the Gods: The Politics of a Pilgrimage Site in Japan, 1573–1912*. Chicago: University of Chicago Press.
Thomas, Jolyon B. 2019. *Faking Liberties: Religious Freedom in American-Occupied Japan*. Chicago: University of Chicago Press.
Toda Jōsei. 1956. *Toda Jōsei-sensei kantōgenshū*. Tokyo: Sōka Gakkai.
Tōyō Tetsugaku Kenkyūjo, ed. 1993. *Yūjinsō o kangaeru: Nihon ni okeru bukkyō to girei*. Tokyo: Daisan Bunmeisha.
Tōyō Tetsugaku Kenkyūjo, 2006. *Yūjinsō no genzai: kawariyuku sōsō girei*. Tokyo: Tōyō Tetsugaku Kenkyūjo.
Tsukada Hotaka. 2015. *Shūkyō to seiji no tentetsuten*. Tokyo: Kadensha.
Victoria, Brian. 2006. *Zen at War* (2nd ed.). Lanham: Rowman & Littlefield.

White, James W. 1970. *The Sōkagakkai and Mass Society*. Stanford: Stanford University Press.
Williams, Duncan Ryūken. 2004. *The Other Side of Zen: A Social History of Sōtō Zen History in Tokugawa Japan*. Princeton: Princeton University Press.
Yasumaru Yoshio. 1979. *Kamigami no meiji ishin: shinbutsu bunri to haibutsu kishaku*. Tokyo: Iwanami Shinsho
Zhong, Yijiang. 2016. *The Origin of Modern Shinto in Japan: The Vanquished Gods of Izumo*. London: Bloomsbury.

13

Governing Buddhism in Vietnam

Ngoc Son Bui

13.1 INTRODUCTION

This chapter explores the Vietnamese state's constitutional framework for governing Buddhism. The framework includes: (1) principles in the big-C Constitution (the formal, written Constitution of 2013); (2) small-c constitutional rules, including broader legislation enacted to implement the formal Constitution, particularly the 2016 Law on Religions and Belief; and (3) the Buddhist constitution, a body of governing law of the Buddhist community, particularly the Charter of the Buddhist Sangha of Vietnam (on the religious constitutions, see Schonthal 2021; on small-c constitutions, see Chilton & Versteeg 2021). This chapter argues that the constitutional framework for Vietnamese Buddhism is both facilitative and regulatory. On the one hand, the constitutional framework facilitates the development of Buddhism due to its historical role, the state's reformist commitment, and the state's universalist outlook toward religions. On the other hand, the same constitutional framework places Buddhism under state control, so as to prevent Buddhist opposition to the socialist regime and to rally the support of Buddhist followers for state-building.

Some historical context is helpful before we begin the analysis. Buddhism is the second-largest organized religion in Vietnam (after Catholicism) with 4,606,543 followers according to the government's official 2019 report (General Statistics Office of Vietnam 2019). Historians debate whether Buddhism came to Vietnam in the third or second century BCE from India, or in the first to second century from China, but in any case, it is well established with deep roots (Taylor 2018). In the Ly dynasty (1009–1225) and Tran dynasty (1225–1400), Buddhism was a state religion and played an important institutional and legal role, including legitimizing royal authority (Anh 2002). The Le dynasty in the fifteenth century endorsed Confucianism as the official ideology, but Buddhism, Confucianism, and Daoism coexisted within the framework of the harmony of three religions. In the period of the French colonial rule, the influence of Buddhism declined due to the spread of

Christianity. During the Vietnam war from 1945 to 1975, Vietnam was divided into North and South: Ngo Dinh Diem, President of the Republic of Vietnam in the South, was a Catholic and launched an anti-Buddhist policy, which triggered protests by Buddhists against the government (Roberts 1965). After national unification, the socialist state supported the unification of Buddhist organizations under a body called the Buddhist Sangha of Vietnam (BSV, Vietnamese: *Giáo hội Phật giáo Việt Nam*) (Trần Thị Hằng 2020). Another Buddhist organization called the Unified Buddhist Sangha of Vietnam (UBSV, Vietnamese: *Giáo hội Phật giáo Việt Nam Thống nhất*) rejected joining the BSV, was banned by the state, and operates in exile (for an overview of the history of Buddhism in Vietnam, see Soucy 2017).

This chapter is organized as follows. The first part from Section 13.2 explores the constitutional framework for Vietnamese Buddhism, Section 13.3 explains the facilitative and regulatory elements of the constitutional framework, and finally, Section 13.4 offers a conclusion.

13.2 THE GOVERNING FRAMEWORK

13.2.1 *The Big-C Constitution*

The 2013 Constitution does not mention Buddhism. However, it includes the principles of the Communist Party of Vietnam and the Vietnamese Fatherland Front, of representative institutions, and of religious freedom, all of which are relevant to the framework for the state's governance of religions in general and Buddhism in particular.

First, the Constitution provides for the leadership of the Communist Party of Vietnam over "the state and society" (Article 4). Society includes Buddhism, which means – at least in theory – that the religion is under the Party's leadership. In fact, responding to the increase in complaints and disputes involving religious facilities, and protests carried out by religious believers, among others, in 2003 the Party issued a resolution which laid down political directives to guide the state's management of religious affairs. This included creating the conditions for religions operating within the law (such as the commitment to religious freedom), promoting patriotism among religious followers, and preventing the use of religions to oppose the state and the socialist regime (Resolution on Religious Affairs 2003). These political directives deal with religions in general and are thus applicable to Buddhism, along with other faiths. Buddhist groups as well as other religious groups are required to operate within the Party policy regarding religious affairs. In relation to religious policies, the Constitution confirms Marxism–Leninism as the Party's official ideology (Article 4). As the Party plays the leading role in society, its ideology prevails thanks to the Party's propaganda and indoctrination. Following this framework, Marxism–Leninism is secular, while Buddhism is sacred, and this generates an ideological tension between the Party and Buddhism. To deal with the tension, the Party tolerates Buddhism but also seeks to ensure that the religion will serve the Party's political goal to build socialism in Vietnam. As a response, the quasi-official BSV aligns with Marxist ideology, as evident in its motto "Dharma, Nation, and Socialism."

The second constitutional principle of note concerns the Fatherland Front. The Constitution provides that "The Vietnamese Fatherland Front is a political alliance and a voluntary union of the political organization, socio-political and social organizations, and prominent individuals representing their class, social strata, ethnicity or religion, and overseas Vietnamese" (Article 9). As the Fatherland Front is an ally of the Party, the BSV, as a member of the Front, is presumed to support the Party and submit to the Party's control. In addition, like other member organizations, the BSV must perform the constitutional duties and functions of the Fatherland Front, including promoting national unity and social consensus, supervising state activities, and participating in state institutions (Article 9).

The third constitutional principle affecting Buddhism relates to the place of religion in representative institutions. Article 22 of the Constitution provides for the right to stand for election to the National Assembly. Article 69 of the Constitution defines the National Assembly as "the highest representative body of the People." Thus, even in the context of a one-party state, Buddhists are represented in the legislature. To illustrate this, after the last election in June 2021, five Buddhist leaders (compared with one Catholic leader) were elected to the National Assembly (Thanh Trà 2021). Although the national elections are under the Party control through the Fatherland Front's multiple rounds of nominations, the National Assembly represents different sections of the society, including religion. As Buddhism is a major religion, with the BSV allied with the party and the state, the representation of Buddhists in the National Assembly is understandable. The inclusion of Buddhist leaders in the legislature may help to ensure the support of Buddhist organizations for the state and law.

A fourth constitutional principle to note is that of religious freedom. The Constitution stipulates that:

> 1. Everyone has the right to freedom of belief and religion, and has the right to follow any religion or to follow no religion. All religions are equal before law. 2. The State shall respect and protect the freedom of belief and religion. 3. No one may violate the freedom of belief and religion, nor may anyone take advantage of a belief or religion in order to violate the law. (Article 24)

Under these provisions, Vietnamese citizens are free to adhere to Buddhism as well as any other religions. There is no state religion in Vietnam: although Buddhists are practically an ally of the party and the state, the Constitution does not provide for any state support for Buddhism or any other religion. This is due to the constitutional commitment to the equality of religions. The last clause in the religious freedom provisions, regarding the manipulation of religion for illegal purposes, justifies state's regulation of religious activities, including the practice of Buddhism.

Buddhist groups played no role in shaping the constitutional framework governing its activities. However, Buddhist monks sometime engage in public constitutional debate in defence of religious autonomy, as well as for other issues. For example, when the state released a draft constitution for public debate in 2013, a Buddhist monk called for the constitutional recognition of religious organizations as legal entities so that they could enjoy more autonomy (Tá Lâm 2013). More recently, in April 2021, the BSV submitted a petition to the relevant authorities opposing a draft regulation by the Ministry of Finance which provides that the state will manage the "merit money," meaning funds donated to religious institutions. As reported by mass media, the BSV argued that the term "merit money" was not clearly defined, and in practice the term is mainly used to refer to money donated to Buddhist institutions rather than to those of other religions. The BSV also invoked Article 53 of the 2013 Constitution to affirm that "merit money" does not belong to public property managed by the state (Thiên Điểu 2021). In this case, Buddhists employed constitutional argumentation to strengthen their demand for financial autonomy, as a response to the state's attempt to place Buddhism under greater control.

13.2.2 *The Small-c Constitution*

The small-c constitution refers to a body of legislative rules issued by the Vietnamese state to regulate religions and to implement relevant provisions in the big-C Constitution (Vu Hoang Cong 2016). In 2004, the National Assembly's Standing Committee enacted the Ordinance on Belief and Religion. The Ordinance was recently replaced by the Law on Belief and Religion (hereinafter, the Law) enacted by the National Assembly in 2016 and implemented in 2018. The Law, however, retains the substantive contents of the Ordinance (Bui 2019).

The Ordinance and the Law do not specifically mention Buddhism but articulate a general legal framework for the state's management of religion which is applicable to Buddhism. The Ordinance and the Law influence Buddhist activities in two modes: facilitative and regulatory. First, the Law recognizes religious freedom, and therefore facilities the freedom of Buddhist practices (as well as other religious practices). This has enabled the development of Vietnamese Buddhism after national unification. The development is manifested in various aspects, such as: an increase in the number of Buddhist followers; numerous Buddhist festivals; the creation of four Buddhist academies for Buddhist teachings at Hanoi, Ho Chi Minh City, Hue, and Can Tho; the publication of numerous Buddhist texts (around 1,000 titles with around 6,000,000 copies published by the Religion Publishing House since 1999); the engagement of the BSV in international Buddhist activities; and the holding of the United Nations Vesak Cerebrations in Vietnam in 2008, 2014, and 2019 (Nguyen Thanh Xuan 2012, 77–84).

The religion Law is also an instrument for the state to regulate Buddhist activities. Regulation of religion refers to "the state's intentional intervention into the religious activities of the target believers and followers and their organizations and groups" (Bui 2019, 149). Using this definition, one can identify three regulatory aspects: setting binding standards (legal rules); state monitoring to ensure the implementation of these rules (monitoring); and using coercive sanctions (sanctioning) to guarantee compliance (Bui 2019, 149). Below I will illustrate the application of this general regulatory framework to Buddhism in Vietnam.

First, regarding setting standards, the government applies to Buddhist groups general legal rules prohibiting certain types of religious activities and religious organizations. The Law prevents religious organizations, including Buddhist organizations, from undermining national unification or conducting propagation campaigns in contravention of the state's laws and policies. In addition, annual programs for Buddhist activities (among other religious activities) must be approved by local governments. Local authorities may suspend Buddhist activities if they believe that they endanger national security and public order. Moreover, Buddhism – as with all other religions in Vietnam – must be officially recognized by the state. The BSV, like other religious organizations, must be formally approved and registered with the state. The congresses of the BSV and the establishment and operation of Buddhist schools must also be approved by the authorities.

Second, there are different state institutions at both central and local levels responsible for monitoring the implementation of legal rules regarding religions in general, including Buddhism. At the central level, according to a decision taken by the prime minister in 2018, the Department of Buddhism in the Government Committee for Religious Affairs plays a role in governing Buddhism. There are also committees for religious affairs in local governments, which are responsible for managing religions, including Buddhism, at the local level.

Third, the Ordinance and the Law do not provide for formal sanctions of unapproved religious activities and organizations. However, authorities have employed informal mechanisms to deal with unapproved religious activities and organizations, including those involving Buddhists. For example, Thích Huyền Quang and Thích Quảng Độ, patriarchs of the Unified Buddhist Sangha of Vietnam, were placed under house arrest because of their opposition to the government (Johnson 2007).

13.2.3 *The Buddhist Constitution*

The Charter of the Buddhist Sangha of Vietnam (hereinafter, the Buddhist Charter) was first adopted by the Sangha in 1981 and has been amended six times, with the last amendment in 2017. The Buddhist Charter can be considered a kind of constitution for Buddhism in Vietnam. It lays down fundamental principles for the Buddhist community, the structural institutions of the Sangha, the distribution of the authority and duties among Buddhist leaders, and amendment rules. Beyond being a religious document, the Buddhist Charter operates as an instrument for the state to manage Buddhism. In this regard, its formal structure and substantive contents share several features of the state's Constitution.

13.2.3.1 Formal Structure

The Buddhist Charter's formal structure is similar to those of the state's Constitution. It includes a preamble and thirteen chapters divided into seventy-one articles. It includes the titles below:

Chapter I: Name, Badge, Flag, Song, Headquarter
Chapter II: Aims, Components
Chapter III: Principles of Operation and System of Organization
Chapter IV: Patriarch Council
Chapter V: Executive Council
Chapter VI: The Buddhist Sangha of Vietnam at Provinces and Cities
Chapter VII: The Buddhist Sangha of Vietnam at County, District, Town, and Provincial City
Chapter VIII: Congress, Conference
Chapter IX: Clergy
Chapter X: Monastery and Members
Chapter XI: Finance, Property
Chapter XII: Praise of Merit and Discipline
Chapter XIII: The Validity of The Charter and Amendments to The Charter

13.2.3.2 Expression

Like the state's Constitution, the Buddhist Charter has an expressive function. Descriptively, the Buddhist Charter's preamble provides a narrative of the history of Vietnamese Buddhism and the birth of the Buddhist Sangha of Vietnam:

> In more than two thousand years of presence in Vietnam, accompanying the nation, Buddhism has become the religion of the nation. Throughout the history of nation building and nation defence, in the cause of national liberation, national unity, as well as building and protecting the Socialist Fatherland of Vietnam today, Vietnamese Buddhism has always been a reliable and strong member of the national unity bloc … Since 1975, the Fatherland has been united, the whole country unites for the goals of "prosperous people, strong country, democratic, equitable, and civilised society," Vietnamese Buddhism fully has the opportunity to fulfil the aspiration to fully unify church organizations, associational organizations, and Buddhist denominations, and to establish the Buddhist Sangha of Vietnam on November 7, 1981. (Charter of The Buddhist Sangha of Vietnam, Preamble)

The Buddhist Charter describes Buddhism as an ally of Vietnam generally and of the socialist state in particular. In describing modern Vietnamese history, the Buddhist Charter's preamble uses similar language of the state Constitution's preamble, such as "to liberate the nation, reunify the country, defend the Fatherland" (The Constitution of The Socialist Republic of Vietnam 2013, preamble). The Buddhist Charter's preamble also aligns the creation of the BSV with the Vietnamese socialist state's goals ("a prosperous people and a strong, democratic, equitable and civilised country") which are confirmed in the state Constitution's preamble (The Constitution of The Socialist Republic of Vietnam 2013, preamble). The parallel between the preambles of the Buddhist Charter and the state Constitution aims to establish a constructive relationship between Vietnamese Buddhism, the BSV, and the Vietnamese socialist state.

Prescriptively, the Buddhist Charter expresses the aspirations and commitments of the Buddhist community. Its preamble declares the motto "Dharma, Nation, and Socialism" (Charter of The Buddhist Sangha of Vietnam, preamble). The BSV's stated aims are to develop Buddhism and to contribute to building Vietnamese socialism, a commitment also confirmed in the preamble of the state's Constitution (The Constitution of The Socialist Republic of Vietnam 2013, preamble). In addition, Article 6 of the Buddhist Charter expresses the Buddhist, nationalist, and internationalist commitments: "The purpose of the Buddhist Sangha of Vietnam is to promote Buddhism, develop the Buddhist Sangha of Vietnam at home and abroad, participate in building and protecting the Fatherland, serve the nation, [and] contribute to building peace and peace for the world" (Charter of The Buddhist Sangha of Vietnam, Article 6). Particularly, beyond religious aspirations, the Charter commits the Buddhist community to contributing to nation building. The nationalist commitment aims to align Vietnamese Buddhism with the state's societal and institutional development.

13.2.4 *Buddhist Institutions*

Apart from the expressive function, the Buddhist Charter operates as a blueprint to structure and coordinate powers within Buddhist institutions and with regard to their relationship with state institutions. It stipulates the Leninist organizational principle of democratic centralism: "The Sangha leads according to the principle of democratic centralism, collective leadership, individual responsibility, majority decisions and unity of action" (Charter of The Buddhist Sangha of Vietnam, Article 10). Democratic centralism aims to combine democratic discussions and centralized actions, confirmed in the state's Constitution (The Constitution of The Socialist Republic of Vietnam 2013, Article 8). On the basis of democratic centralism, the Buddhist Charter creates a hierarchical Buddhist institutional system, relatively similar to the state's constitutional system.

At the central level, the BSV includes the Patriarch Council and the Executive Council (Charter of The Buddhist Sangha of Vietnam, Chapters IV and V). The institutional functions and relationship of these two bodies have some features in common with those of the National Assembly and government provided in the state's Constitution. The Patriarch Council, created with a five-year term by BSV's congress, is a collective decision-making body, while the Executive Council is an administrative institution. Some language of the state's Constitution is used to describe the functions of these Buddhist institutions. For example, the Charter provides that the Patriarch Council is "the supreme leading organ" of the BSV and its Standing Committee enjoys the power of "supreme supervision" over the activities of the Sangha and the Executive Council (Charter of The Buddhist Sangha of Vietnam, Articles 15 and 16). This echoes the state Constitution's description of the National Assembly as "the supreme organ of state power" which has the power of "supreme supervision" over the government and other state organs (The Constitution of The Socialist Republic of Vietnam 2013, Article 69).

Apart from the central institutions, the structural hierarchy of the Buddhist organizations includes provincial and communal sanghas. The local sanghas are comprised of the Patriarch committee and executive committee, modelled after the structure of the central Sangha. The communal sanghas work under the guidance of the provincial sanghas which in turn work under the guidance of the central Sangha (Charter of The Buddhist Sangha of Vietnam, Articles 31 and 38). Thus, the Buddhist Charter provides for a hierarchical relationship within Buddhist institutions, consistent with the broader principle of democratic centralism.

The local sanghas are structured in line with the state's local administrative system. Additional Buddhist sanghas can be created at the local levels subject to the approval of the local governments at the same levels (Charter of The Buddhist Sangha of Vietnam, Articles 29 and 37). The parallel administrative arrangement places Buddhist institutions at various levels under the management of the state institutions at the same levels. This allows state authority to closely monitor the activities of Buddhist institutions.

13.2.4.1 Buddhist Constitution and State Institutions

According to the Law on Belief and Religion, the Buddhist Charter is only implemented after it is approved by the state. The state's approval ostensibly ensures that the Buddhist Charter will serve the state's management of Buddhism. In addition, in consistence with the Law on Belief and Religion, various activities regarding implementation of the Charter (such as the elections of the Patriarch Council and Executive Council, and the holding of the BSV's congress) must be approved by state authorities. In this way, the state can keep Buddhism firmly under its control.

The Buddhist Charter also seeks to coordinate the relationship between the state and Buddhist institutions. For example, the Charter provides that BSV's Executive Council must be "responsible for coordinating with competent state agencies in dealing with organizations and individuals speaking out and disseminating information with distorted, inaccurate, and unorganized content related to Buddhism in general and to the organizations of the Vietnam Buddhist Sangha at all levels and to its members" (Charter of The Buddhist Sangha of Vietnam, Article 19). The Charter requires Buddhist institutions and members to cooperate with state institutions in the management of Buddhism. Moreover, the Charter stipulates that:

> If members of the Buddhist Sangha of Vietnam have activities and acts that hurt the reputation, harmony, and interests of the Sangha or members of the Sanga, and harm the great unity of the whole nation, the peace, independence, and unity of the Fatherland, the Sangha shall deal with canon law [Vinaya], and depending on the extent of violations, the Sangha shall request the competent state agency to consider and handle it in accordance with the [state's] law. (Charter of The Buddhist Sangha of Vietnam, Article 64)

This provision enables the punishment of members of the BSV for their actions against not only the interests of the Buddhist community but also the interests of the state. The provision also allows the Sangha to request the state authority to apply legal remedies. The Sangha is, therefore, an ally of the state in its internal management of Buddhism.

13.3 FACTORS OF GOVERNING BUDDHISM

The state constitutional framework has facilitated the development of Buddhism in Vietnam, shaped by factors internal and external to the Vietnamese context. The internal factors include the historical role and nature of Vietnamese Buddhism and the state's reformist commitment. As Buddhism has a long tradition in Vietnam and deep roots in the Vietnamese culture, the constitutional framework needs to accommodate its continuing development.

In addition, during the Vietnam war, Buddhist monks played an important role in opposing the Diem government and advocating for peace. As Topmiller states: "Some Buddhists perceived the deep distress in South Vietnamese society over the war and responded with calls for peace. Sensing significant war-weariness after a quarter-century of conflict, Thich Nhat Hanh introduced a resolution calling for an end to the fighting during a conference of monks early in 1964" (2002, 7). The fact that Buddhist monks resisted the South government to struggle for peace would make the socialist state less hostile to Buddhism after national unification.

Another internal factor involves the socialist party-state's reformist commitments. The reform program known as *Doi moi* (Renovation) introduced by the Communist Party of Vietnam in 1986 has resulted in the implementation of several liberal policies, which include policies that not only support economic liberalization but also those which facilitate religious freedom. For example, different to the previous dogmatic belief that religions would soon disappear in a new socialist society in Vietnam, in 1990 the Communist Party of Vietnam issued a resolution announcing reformist views and policies regarding religion. The resolution recognized three points: "religion is a long-standing issue"; "belief and religion are spiritual needs of a part of the people"; "religious ethics has many things suitable for the construction of a new society." (Nguyễn Nguyên Hồng 2018). These reformist views have facilitated the development of religion in general and Buddhism in particular.

Another internal factor concerns the political leaders' discourse which recognizes the positive contribution of Buddhism to state-building and social and economic development in Vietnam. John Gillespie observes that "Hồ Chí Minh is credited with saying that the values underlying Buddhism and Christianity are fundamentally the same as the party's objectives. According to this theory, the party should remain staunchly atheist, but acknowledge that in the transition to socialism, religion promotes social order and enriches lives" (2014, 143). More recently, President of State Nguyễn Xuân Phúc has said, "Over the past forty years, many Buddhist monks and nuns have made contributions and sacrifices for the revolution. The Buddhist Sangha has always been at the forefront of national unity." (Nguyễn Phan 2021). Such political rhetoric indicates the positive view of the state toward Buddhism, which has constituted a necessary political condition for the development of the religion in Vietnam.

Apart from internal factors, the constitutional space for Buddhism in Vietnam has been animated by external factors beyond the Vietnamese context. Globalization has led the Vietnamese state to engage with international legal regimes, and sign major international human rights treaties. This international engagement has resulted in the party-state's turn toward a universalist approach to religion, including Buddhism. As Gillespie points out, "Party leaders have developed a more cosmopolitan outlook and expanded their loyalties to include a wide range of religious beliefs and practices. A consensus is emerging that the party should recognize and promote religiosity in Vietnamese society" (2014, 141–42). This approach to internationalization enables the development of religions in general – and Buddhism in particular – in Vietnam.

As noted above, the constitutional framework of Vietnam places Buddhism under the state's control. As Buddhism has enjoyed a significant place in Vietnamese culture and society, the socialist state has recognized the importance of turning it not into an enemy but a supporter of the state. The regulative constitutional space is, therefore, animated by both preventive and constructive political motivations. The preventive motivation is that the state needs to preclude Buddhism from becoming a force inimical to the socialist regime.

This preventive motivation may have been inspired by the Unified Buddhist Sangha of Vietnam's continued opposition to the socialist regime. For example, in 2013, a leader of the UBSV issued a letter opposing the Vietnamese government's imprisonment of Cu Huy Ha Vu for his subversive actions, including his call to delete Article 4 of Vietnam's Constitution, which mandates the leadership of the Communist Party of Vietnam (Thich Vien Dinh 2013). One of the leaders of UBSV stated: "The United Buddhist Sangha of Vietnam has a clear goal of serving the nation and the dharma, not socialism" (Gia Minh 2015). The UBSV's goal is resistant to the BSV's goal and the Vietnamese socialist state's goal. The state, therefore, is motivated to prevent Buddhist groups from cooperating with dissidents who oppose the socialist regime.

The constructive motivation in the constitutional regulations of religion is that the state needs to mobilize social forces, including Buddhist followers, for state-building and socioeconomic development. As Buddhists are an important social force, the state needs their support for state-building and the implementation of state policy. This explains why Buddhists have been included in state institutions and involved in national affairs, for example, supporting state authority in the fight against the spread of the Covid-19 virus in Vietnam (Hồ Phúc 2021).

13.4 CONCLUSION

This chapter has explored the multiple constitutional framework employed by the state to govern Buddhism in Vietnam. It has illustrated the elements and functioning of such a constitutional framework, consisting of the principles and rules in the formal Constitution, the small-c constitution or legislations, and the Buddhist constitution or Charter of the Buddhist Sangha of Vietnam. On the one hand, the constitutional framework facilitates the development of Vietnamese Buddhism due to the nature and role of Buddhism in Vietnamese history, to the state's reformist policy regarding religious freedom, and to the party-state's universal perspective on religious freedom. On the other hand, the state places Buddhism firmly under its control to ensure that it supports the Party and its programs of state-building and socioeconomic development.

To some extent, the Vietnamese case illustrates unique features compared to other countries in terms of the relationship between Buddhism and constitutional law. These peculiar aspects are mainly due to the presence of Vietnamese socialism, as in the case of the mimicry of the Vietnamese socialist political principals visible in the BSV Buddhist constitution, the BSV's replication of national socialist institutions in its organizational structure, and the general intimacy between Buddhism, Communist Party, and the Fatherland Front.

However, the Vietnamese case also reveals commonalities with the other Buddhist contexts analysed in this volume. One comparable aspect is the relation between Buddhism and constitutional design. A written constitution may not directly refer to Buddhism, but its general provisions on human rights, religious freedom, and the broader institutional setting will undoubtedly affect the practice of Buddhism. Another element that can be compared is the distinction between Buddhist constitutionalism and the legal regulation of Buddhism. While the former concerns how Buddhist fundamental norms and principles hold state authorities accountable, the latter deals with how states use law to regulate Buddhism. A third dimension that can suggest similarities across national contexts is the presence of Buddhist constitutions, other examples of which can be found in this volume. The Charter of the Sangha of Vietnam provides a good example for the comparative study of constitution-like Buddhist texts, which in this case, draws heavily on the structure of state constitutions. What the analysis of the Vietnamese case in this chapter can suggest is that a comparative study of Buddhist constitutions needs to explore the *relational* similarities between Buddhist constitutions and state constitutions, which are echoed in similar content patterns in the guiding charters of both states and Buddhist groups. The exploration of these similarities may help to highlight the important interaction that takes place between Buddhist and state constitutional regimes.

REFERENCES

Anh, NT. 2002. "From Indra to Maitreya: Buddhist Influence in Vietnamese Political Thought." *Journal of Southeast Asian Studies* 33 (2): 225–41.

Bui, Ngoc Son. 2019. "Legal Regulation of Religion in Vietnam." In *Regulating Religions in Asia*, edited by Jaclyn Neo, Arif Jamal, and Daniel P. S. Goh, 146–68. Cambridge: Cambridge University Press.

Chilton, Adam and Versteeg, Mila. 2021. "Small-c Constitutional Rights." *International Journal of Constitutional Law*. https://doi.org/10.1093/icon/moac004.

Gia Minh. 2015. "Tự do tôn giáo và Giáo hội Phật giáo Việt Nam Thống Nhất [Religious Freedom and The United Buddhist Sangha of Vietnam]. *RFA*, August 23. Accessed on December 15, 2021. www.rfa.org/vietnamese/in_depth/freed-of-religion-unifi-buddhist-08232015053404.html

Gillespie, John. 2014. "Human Rights as a Larger Loyalty: The Evolution of Religious Freedom in Vietnam." *Harvard Human Rights Journal* 27: 107–49.

"Hiến chương Giáo hội Phật giáo Việt Nam." 2017. [Charter of The Buddhist Sangha of Vietnam, amended through 2017.]

Hồ Phúc. 2021. "64 tăng ni, phật tử Đồng Nai tham gia tuyến đầu chống dịch" [64 Buddhists Monks and Nuns at Dong Nai Join the Front Line to Fight the Epidemic]. *Bien phong*, September 10. Accessed on December 15, 2021. http://baodongnai.com.vn/tintuc/202109/64-tang-ni-phat-tu-phat-giao-dong-nai-len-duong-vao-tuyen-dau-chong-dich-dot-2-3078106/

Johnson, Kay. 2007. "The Fighting Monks of Vietnam." *Time*, March 2. http://content.time.com/time/world/article/0,8599,1595721,00.html

"Luật Tín ngưỡng, tôn giáo năm 2016, Luật số 02/2016/QH14" [2016 Law on Belief and Religion, No. 02/2016/QH14].

"Nghị quyết số 25-NQ/TW công tác tôn giáo 2003" [Resolution on Religious Affairs 2003, No. 25-NQ/TW].

Nguyễn Phan. 2021. "Chủ tịch nước Nguyễn Xuân Phúc tiếp đoàn Giáo hội Phật giáo Việt Nam" [President Nguyen Xuan Phuc Welcomes the Delegation of the Buddhist Sangha of Vietnam]. *Nguoi Lao Dong*, May 13. Accessed on December 15, 2021. https://nld.com.vn/chinh-tri/chu-tich-nuoc-nguyen-xuan-phuc-tiep-doan-giao-hoi-phat-giao-viet-nam-20210513160920032.htm

Nguyễn, Nguyên Hồng. 2018. "Quan điểm đổi mới của Đảng về tôn giáo, tín ngưỡng" [The Party's Renovative Opinions on Religions and Belief]. *Tuyen Giao*, December 3. www.tuyengiao.vn/nghien-cuu/ly-luan/quan-diem-doi-moi-cua-dang-ve-ton-giao-tin-nguong-117039
Nguyen, Thanh Xuan. 2012. *Religions in Vietnam*. Hanoi: The Gioi Publishing House.
"Pháp lệnh Tín ngưỡng, Tôn giáo 2004 21/2004/PL-UBTVQH11" [2004 Ordinance on Belief and Religion, No. 21/2004/PL-UBTVQH11].
"Quyết định số 32/2018/QĐ-TTg ngày 03 tháng 8 năm 2018 của Thủ tướng Chính phủ" [Decision No. 32/2018/QD-TTg dated August 3, 2018, of the Prime Minister].
Roberts, Adam. 1965. "Buddhism and Politics in South Vietnam." *The World Today* 21 (6): 240–50.
Schonthal, Benjamin. 2021. "The Case for Religious Constitutions: Comparative Constitutional Law among Buddhists and Other Religious Groups." *Law & Social Inquiry*: 1–29. doi:10.1017/lsi.2021.36.
Soucy, Alexander. 2017. "Contemporary Vietnamese Buddhism." In *The Oxford Handbook of Contemporary Buddhism*, edited by Michael Jerryson, 177–95. Oxford: Oxford University Press.
Tá Lâm. 2013. Chức sắc tôn giáo góp ý sửa Hiến pháp [Buddhist Monks Comment on Amending the Constitution]. *Vietnamnet*, January 30. Accessed on December 15, 2021. https://vietnamnet.vn/vn/thoi-su/chuc-sac-ton-giao-gop-y-sua-hien-phap-107730.html
Taylor, KW. 2018. "What Lies Behind the Earliest Story of Buddhism in Ancient Vietnam?" *The Journal of Asian Studies* 77 (1): 107–22.
Thanh Trà. 2021. "5 chức sắc tôn giáo trúng cử đại biểu Quốc hội khóa XV" [Five religious dignitaries elected to the National Assembly]. *Vietnam News Agency*, June 14. Accessed on December 15, 2021. https://baucuquochoi.vn/infographics-5-chuc-sac-ton-giao-trung-cu-dai-bieu-quoc-hoi-khoa-xv/1159.vnp
"The Constitution of The Socialist Republic of Vietnam." 2013.
Thich, Vien Dinh. 2013. "Letter from Leader of UBCV's Institute for the Dissemination of Dharma on Attorney Cu Huy Ha Vu's Hunger Strike in Prison." *WordPress*, June 19. Accessed on December 15, 2021. https://saveubcv.wordpress.com/2013/06/19/letter-from-leader-of-ubcvs-institute-for-the-dissemination-of-dharma-on-attorney-cu-huy-ha-vus-hunger-strike-in-prison/
Thiên Điểu. 2021. "Giáo hội Phật giáo kiến nghị Nhà nước không nên quản lý tiền công đức" [Buddhist Sangha recommends state not to manage merit money]. *Tuổi Trẻ Online*, June 17. Accessed on December 15, 2021. https://tuoitre.vn/giao-hoi-phat-giao-kien-nghi-nha-nuoc-khong-nen-quan-ly-tien-cong-duc-20210617151806168.htm
Tổng cục Thống kê Việt Nam [General Statistics Office of Vietnam]. 2019. "Kết quả toàn bộ Tổng điều tra Dân số và Nhà ở Việt Nam năm 2019" [The Results of the 2019 Vietnam Population and Housing Census]. Accessed on December 15, 2021. www.gso.gov.vn/du-lieu-va-so-lieu-thong-ke/2020/11/ket-qua-toan-bo-tong-dieu-tra-dan-so-va-nha-o-nam-2019/
Topmiller, Robert J. 2002. *The Lotus Unleashed: The Buddhist Peace Movement in South Vietnam, 1964–1966*. Lexington: University Press of Kentucky.
Trần Thị Hằng. 2020. *Tổ chức và hoạt động của Giáo hội Phật giáo Việt Nam hiện nay* [Organization and Operation of The Buddhist Sangha of Vietnam Nowadays]. PhD dissertation, Vietnam National University, Hanoi.
Vu Hoang Cong. 2016. "Religious Policies in the Socialist Law-ruled State of Vietnam." *Political Theory*, December 2. Accessed on December 15, 2021. http://lyluanchinhtri.vn/home/en/index.php/theory-research/item/396-religious-policies-in-the-socialist-law-ruled-state-of-vietnam.html

14

The Buddhist Association of China and Constitutional Law in Buddhist Majority Nations

The International Channels of Influence

André Laliberté

14.1 INTRODUCTION

This chapter looks at the Buddhist Association of China (BAC), which claims authority over the largest Buddhist community in the world, as it has tried in recent years to assert itself as an influential actor on the global stage. The BAC has acted with the full support of the Chinese Communist Party (CCP), via one of its key instruments for influence in Chinese societies and abroad, the United Front Work Department (UFWD, herein United Front) (Brady 2019). The goal of this chapter is to understand how the emergence of the BAC affects constitutional law in countries where Buddhism plays an important role in the political and legal system.

I will introduce the BAC as the main institution representing Buddhists today in the People's Republic of China (PRC) and examine the relationship between the BAC and the CCP United Front. Next, I assess the BAC efforts to establish itself as one of the prime movers among Buddhist international organizations and interpret the significance of this increasing visibility. The chapter dovetails with a broader research agenda headed by Yoshiko Ashiwa and David Wank (2020), examining how the United Front operationalizes Buddhist activities outside China.

14.2 THE BUDDHIST ASSOCIATION OF CHINA

The BAC claims authority over the largest Buddhist community in the world. Estimating the precise size of the community is difficult, in part because, as in other East Asian societies, many people practice what Michael Carrithers calls "polytropy," which means that they simultaneously practice more than one religion (2000). The BAC estimates – which err on the conservative side and are reproduced routinely by the official media – of the total number of Buddhists in China suggest that there are around 100 million adherents (ZFX 2017a). Recently conducted sociological surveys, however, point to widely divergent numbers, depending on the methodology used by the investigators (Wenzel-Teuber 2017, 27). For example, the China Family Panel Studies (CFPS), a survey created in 2010 by the Institute of Social Science Survey (ISSS) in Beijing University, reported vastly different numbers in 2012 and 2014, depending on whether people were asked about their religious affiliation or their beliefs in deities. Wenzel-Teuber (2017, 27) also quotes from the 2012 survey by sociologists Lu Yunfeng and Zhang Chunni, undertaken for the CFPS, which showed that about 6.5 percent of respondents disclosed an affiliation to Buddhism; two years later, over 15.8 percent of respondents mentioned their belief in the Buddha and bodhisattvas. Whether one chooses the more conservative figure of 91 million or that of 212 million, however, more Buddhists live in China than in Thailand, the country with the second largest number of Buddhists, projected to number 67 million by 2020 (Pew-Templeton 2016).

This large Buddhist community, relative to other countries, represents only a minority of the Chinese population, and not a sizable proportion, even though there are more Buddhists than there are followers of other religions in China. In a country where 90 percent of the population in 2012 professed no religious affiliation, and 73 percent admitted in another survey two years later that they have no religious beliefs, the cultural influence of Buddhism in Chinese society – while significant in aesthetics, the practice of popular beliefs, and ethics – does not reach as deep as it does in societies where Buddhism represents the religion of the majority, let alone countries in which it is the state religion. There are significant differences, moreover, when one considers the specific forms of Buddhism practiced by different ethnic groups, known in China as national minorities (*xiaoshu minzu* 小数民族) (Borchert 2017). While a small minority of the Han population practices Buddhism of the Mahāyāna school, the influence of the Vajrayāna school is more prevalent among most of the Tibetan and Mongol minorities (Charleux 2017). The Theravāda school, which is also practiced among some of the minority populations in the Southern parts of the country, is not practiced to the same extent (Sasas 2020). Still, China is the only country in the world with significant numbers of adherents to all three major branches of Buddhism.

The leadership structure of the BAC reflects these realities, albeit in a way that does not reflect the relative proportion of the three Buddhist schools. Its official documents distinguish between Han (*hanzhuan* 漢傳), rather than Mahāyāna (*dacheng* 大乘); Tibetan (*zangzhuan* 藏傳), rather than Vajrayāna or esoteric (*mizong* 密宗); and Southern (*nanzhuan* 南傳) Buddhism, rather than Theravāda (*shangzuobu* 上座部) (ZFX 2017b). For 2017, the State Administration for Religious affairs (SARA) provided the following numbers of registered sites for the three branches of Buddhism: 28,270 sites for the Han tradition; 3,862 for the Tibetan sites; and 1,705 for Southern sites (Wenzel-Teuber 2018, 34). In 2014, SARA counted 148,000 ordained Tibetan clergy, but only half that number among Han monastics, and only 2,000 clerics among Southern Buddhists (Wenzel-Teuber 2018, 35). Only in the first years of its existence did the BAC governance structure reflect this reality.

During the first congress between 1953 and 1957, only one among the four honorary chairs was Han; the others were the Dalai Lama, the tenth Panchen Lama, and the spiritual leader of the Mongol orders. Of the seven vice-directors who assisted the BAC director, only one was a Han, four represented the Tibetan school, and one the Southern school. The governance structure of the BAC has since changed significantly: today, the majority of the thirty-three vice-presidents represent Han Buddhism.

The state's rigid definition of what constitutes an acceptable religion makes the enumeration of religious believers even more difficult. If sociological surveys can count those who mention an affiliation to a religion or a belief in a deity, they often miss those whose beliefs belong to what the sociologist of religion Yang Fenggang (2006) called the "black market" of religions. By this, Yang means those religions opposed by the state, in contrast to the "red market" of religions recognized by the CCP. For obvious reasons, people who follow religions that the state opposes are not likely to admit they do so. The population is aware of the religions the CCP opposes as well as those it labels "evil cults" (*xiejiao* 邪教), but there is another category of tolerated practices in the liminal space between religion and culture, belief, and heritage. Yang Fenggang (2006) describes these as "gray market" practices, for which people may not fear sanction. People affiliated with Falun Gong know about this too well: their practice was legal before the state imposed a ban in the summer of 2000 (Palmer 2007).

The established sangha fears this kind of competition from the margins of the official Buddhist associations, and over the years it has expressed its opposition to new religious movements that use the name or the symbols of Buddhism, such as Falun Gong, or the Guanyin 观音 Method of Master Qinghai 青海 (Irons 2018). The BAC also fears sources of division within its own ranks, like the ethnic and linguistic cleavages mentioned above. A primary source of concern is the unrest in the Tibetan Autonomous Region and in the prefectures where ethnic Tibetans live (Powers 2016). Moreover, tensions exist even within the Han clergy. Anonymous sources allege that Jingkong (Chin Kung 净空), a well-known overseas monastic who claims to speak in the name of the Chinese tradition and has established a large following abroad and in China, has seen his writings condemned as "pornography" in 2019 (Wang 2020). Tensions within the BAC also broke out in the open with the downfall of its President Xuecheng 学诚 in 2018, following allegations of sexual misconduct (Johnson 2018).

The association has looked after the interests of the sangha and lay devotees since its founding in 1954, often against great odds. Most Buddhist monastics chose not to move outside China after 1949 and showed loyalty to the new regime (Xue 2009). That attitude did not serve them well, however: Buddhism went through what historian Hou Kunhong (2012) described as a stage of "calamity" for three decades. While full collectivization happened only in the late 1950s (Clarke 2017), the most zealous CCP cadres had earlier confiscated landed property of religious institutions to meet the state objectives of modernization, as documented by Jan Kiely (2016) in the case of Suzhou. During the Cultural Revolution (1966–76), the BAC faced near extinction, as much property was destroyed and monastics had to return to lay life, while lay followers were forced to hide their beliefs (Welch 1969). The pressure on Buddhists was disproportionately felt among Tibetan and Mongol minorities: Buddhism represented a key element of their social organization, and they viewed religious persecution by Red Guards in ethnic terms as an attack by the Han majority against minority nationalities. These disruptions did not last long, but they left a legacy of suspicion toward the CCP and the Han that never dissipated among Tibetans and Mongols (Woeser 2020).

After 1978, with the policy of economic reform and opening which favored foreign investment and support from overseas Chinese communities, the BAC began to recover. From 1980 until 2002, Zhao Puchu, a lay Buddhist, served as its director. Known for his organization of relief for refugees during the war of resistance against Japan, Zhao was one of the key founders of the Chinese Association for the Promotion of Democracy (CAPD) in 1945, a group that brought together intellectuals and CCP members (Ji 2017). One of the key themes that Zhao sought to develop as BAC president was demonstrating that Buddhism was compatible with socialism, a process that Ji (2004) divided into three stages. First, in the early 1980s, the BAC promoted the idea of "combining Chan with agricultural work" (*nong chan bingzhong* 农禅并重), to ensure that monasteries would be self-reliant. Second, in the 1990s, as more monasteries reopened, traditional aspects of religious exchange revived, and lay followers made offerings in return for spiritual benefits, a practice known as "cultivating the good earth" (*zhong futian* 种福田) or "making merit" (*zuo gongde* 做功德). In the third stage, as many local governments sought to attract investment from abroad, the BAC emphasized the use of Buddhist cultural capital for tourism, under the slogan "culture builds the stage and the economy performs (*wenhua datai, jingji changxi* 文化搭台，经济唱戏)" (Chang 2016).

The above account of the close relationship between the CCP and the BAC does not deny that the latter has some agency, as Yoshiko Ashiwa (2009) demonstrated in her case study of Xiamen Buddhists: clerics, she showed, use existing institutions to preserve their autonomy. Although the BAC is subordinated to the state apparatus according to the mechanism described below, it shares with the CCP some concerns about influence from its competitors. Even if the BAC has become a powerful institution that can serve the state by rallying its followers behind the CCP – the essence of United Front work – it can also protect the interests of the Buddhist sangha against forces that can undermine its authority from within. For these tasks, lay and monastic Buddhist milieu (*fojiaojie* 佛教界) relied on many institutions. Hence, Buddhist academies developed for the training of monastics also served the social reproduction of the monastic orders (Ji 2019, 171). The householder groves (*jushilin* 居士林), where devotees meet for their religious practice and socialization, played a key role in the life of lay Chinese Buddhists. Destroyed at the time of Mao, these institutions have since been revived, according to Jessup (2016, 69). Other revived institutions include vegetarian restaurants, publishing houses, and merit societies (*gongdehui* 功德会) that provide relief to people in need. Simply because these groups can promote moral activism does not mean that lay Buddhists have built a social movement (Fisher 2017). These developments have all happened in the context of an unpredictable and potentially repressive legal system.

14.3 CONSTITUTIONAL LAW IN THE PRC: SERVING THE CCP UNITED FRONT WORK

There is no constitutional law in the PRC that compares to what one observes in the West or in the liberal democratic societies of East Asia: Japan, South Korea, and Taiwan (Dowdle 2018). The CCP concept of rule of law, inherited from the experience of the former Soviet Union, also draws on ancient Chinese ideas of Legalism (*fajia* 法家), as distinct from the moral tenets of Confucianism (*rujia* 儒家). The CCP draws on the Legalist idea that the state ruler is supreme over the judiciary; this old idea fits nicely with the superimposed practice from the Soviet Union that assigned to the Communist Party the role of vanguard institution above the law (Li 2015). Many aspects of social life, including religious beliefs and practices, are accordingly subjected to the paternalistic guidance of the Party. The basic political supremacy of the CCP has not changed in any fundamental way, even with legal reforms in recent decades. Mao had denounced constitutionalism as a bourgeois invention and deprived the Chinese judiciary of independence. Although the policy of economic reform and opening by Deng Xiaoping has led outsiders to believe that the CCP has relinquished totalitarian ambitions, it never gave up its authority in the realm of religious affairs. If anything, under Xi Jinping, the CCP regime is moving towards a new phase of control, as it seeks to nullify any restraining influence from constitutional law (Delisle 2017; Minzner 2015).

The weakness of constitutional law in China is rooted deep in its history, and the Buddhist tradition has only marginally influenced this development (Beydon 2015, 527ff.). Although the status of Buddhism, as a social force and as a religion, has changed over the course of centuries and imperial dynasties, the dominance of Confucianism and Legalism in the legal system endured until the end of the Qing Dynasty (1644–1911), when reformers promoted the introduction of Western norms of constitutionalism in their project to modernize China (Piquet 2005). These attempts failed during the Republican era (1911–49) as the country was divided politically between different warring factions and suffering from the Japanese invasion; no central government had the will or the capacity to reform the legal system. Moreover, neither the concept of the rule of law derived from the Germanic–Roman legal code nor Common Law judicial thought managed to leave a good impression among Chinese patriots. Introduced in the treaty ports during the Qing Dynasty, Western legal forms were associated with the unequal treaties that protected the Western and Japanese privileges of extraterritoriality (Scully 2000). It was only near the end of the Civil War, in 1947, that the Nationalist Party (*Kuomintang* 國民黨, or KMT) promulgated a constitution for the Republic of China (ROC). This green shoot of constitutionalism vanished from China after 1949 when the CCP took control and would be suspended for thirty-eight years in Taiwan, where the KMT relocated the ROC government. In the absence of constitutional law, the unfettered power of the state can impose its will on society. In the PRC, however, the state itself serves as an instrument for the CCP, an organization that sees itself as the vanguard of society, guiding all social forces, including religions.

Although internal reforms have erased some of the most extreme language used at the time of Mao, its charter still asserts that the CCP stands above the legal system enforced by the government (Holbig 2018). China's system differs starkly from the legal regimes prevalent in Western societies and most other societies where the rule of law prevails: the state is not an impartial arbiter between different political factions, but an instrument in the service of the political line determined by the CCP. This conception of the law, implemented in the Soviet Union and other Leninist regimes (as well as by the fascist regimes in Italy and Nazi Germany), found acceptance in the CCP because it resonated with some of the characteristics of China's own legal system that had remained in place after the fall of the *ancien régime* in 1911: most importantly, the idea of a strong state led by a vanguard elite (Zheng 2015). The CCP United Front represents a key instrument in that renewed assertiveness, both domestically and on the international stage.

Once the CCP gained power in 1949, it formalized the United Front with the creation of the Chinese People Political Consultative Conference. That deliberative assembly included representatives of "people's organizations" from a wide variety of sectors: broad categories of the population such as youth, women, and returned overseas Chinese; economic groups such as chambers of commerce, trade unions, and a variety of other associations, federations, and foundations representing different corporations and guilds (Sagild and Ahlers 2019). Our focus is on the religious component of the broader United Front. Although they remained committed to the view that religion would whither under socialism, CCP leaders initially avoided precipitous actions against religious believers during campaigns against "sects" and foreign missionaries, lest they oppose the new regime. To that end the CCP United Front sought to nurture "patriotic" religious leaders who were supportive of socialist ideals, and relied on them to ensure that they would obtain compliance with government directives from their followers (Wickeri 2011). The Religious Affairs Bureau – which would later become SARA – and the BAC emerged in that context in 1954. That period of relative openness did not last long.

The failing attempt in 1954 at establishing constitutional law became increasingly apparent between 1956 and 1976. Meanwhile the United Front went into what Gerry Groot (2004) called its phase of "hibernation." Religious associations had by then become targets of attacks by young "red guards," and even after the peak years of the Cultural Revolution began to subside in 1969, the radical factions of the "Gang of Four" maintained their restrictions on religion. The period covered by these political vicissitudes may appear short, but the damage to a generation has proven enduring and long-lasting. The aging monastic leaders who had survived the political persecution found few successors, and it would take years before the BAC recovered lost ground. The political struggle initiated by Mao Zedong had led to the abolition of the 1954 Constitution and its replacement by the 1975 Constitution, which instituted the principle of the CCP as the paramount source of power. Although that document did not last more than three years, the 1978 Constitution, which brought back some of the elements of the more lenient 1954 Constitution, such as checks on executive power and guarantees for religious beliefs, maintained the principle that citizens must support CCP leadership and the socialist system.

After Deng took charge as paramount leader of the CCP, the new leadership revived the United Front and expanded the scope of its activities to include Taiwan, Hong Kong, and overseas Chinese communities. In 1982, the CCP enunciated "The basic viewpoint on the religious question during our country's socialist period," known as Document 19. This political statement spelled out the limits in which religious freedom can be exercised (Potter 2003). The SARA resumed its duties as monitoring agency for all religious activities and the BAC reestablished itself as a key component of the apparatus of state control for Buddhism, albeit in a subordinate position. Under Deng's successor, Jiang Zemin, the priority of the government was to deepen the policy of reform and opening. The CCP United Front, however, focused more openly on Taiwan, and it encouraged religious exchanges, along with trade, business, and tourism, to serve the goal of "re-unification." This approach included the pilgrimage to the goddess Matsu, but also the humanitarian work of Taiwanese Buddhist associations across the Taiwan Strait. The strategy also included an effort to support the rebuilding of Buddhist temples. These efforts paid off, as Buddhist leaders rallied behind the regime in denouncing Falun Gong in 1999 (Tong 2009). During the administration of Hu Jintao, the situation in Tibet became a major target of attention for the CCP United Front. Near the end of Hu's tenure as CCP secretary-general in 2012, the United Front encouraged the development of charity by religious organizations to serve the public interest (cishan gongyi shiye 慈善公益事业), a policy which the BAC endorsed enthusiastically.

Under the instruction of the CCP Secretary-General Xi, the United Front again changed its approach vis-à-vis religion after 2014, when Xi expressed his wish to see Chinese religions becoming more "Chinese," a goal that has left many people perplexed, since all the five recognized religions in China have been going through a process of acculturation for centuries (Cook 2017). A speech in 2016 clarified further the meaning of this "Sinicization" (*zhongguohua* 中国化): religion must serve the interests of the state and the value of the CCP (Vermander

2019). In 2018, the CCP passed new regulations that implemented these ideas, with the incorporation of SARA under the umbrella of the CCP United Front (Joske 2019). These policies reveal the wish of the party to monitor religious affairs more closely than ever before. Two aspects of this policy stand out. Firstly, the CCP reverted to a policy which was more hostile to religion in general, and seemed to target, in particular, Christians and Muslims. Secondly, the CCP redefined religions such as Buddhism and Daoism as "culture," promoting them at the expense of the others.

The new reorganization of the CCP United Front deepens some of the trends observed under the administration of Hu. When Xi took power, SARA was divided into four bureaus, one for Buddhist and Daoist affairs; one for Christians; another for Muslims; and one for all the other types of religions inside or outside China about which the regime wanted to know. The incorporation of SARA's four branches into the United Front suggests greater integration and coordination with its other key missions: communication with like-minded people in Hong Kong, Macau, and Taiwan (Third Bureau), and liaison with people among overseas Chinese (Ninth and Tenth Bureaus). Recent efforts by the CCP United Front to promote its interests on the international stage via the promotion of the BAC has added a layer of complexity to the issue of Buddhist institutions and constitutional law throughout contemporary societies. In the framework of its strategy of "soft power" to support the project of "One Belt One Road," the CCP has promoted the transnational expansion of Chinese temples and sponsored the organization of international Buddhist meetings that serve to establish the presence of the BAC on the global stage (Raymond 2020). The next section looks at the achievements of the CCP in making Chinese Buddhism more visible.

14.4 FROM THE WORLD FELLOWSHIP OF BUDDHISTS TO THE WORLD BUDDHIST FORUM

The BAC stood little chance of being admitted into international Buddhist associations after its founding in 1954 and has faced difficulty for half a century. This exclusion rested on three rationales reinforcing each other: the context of the Cold War (1954–91); the influence of the BAROC (Buddhist Association of the Republic of China) in Buddhist international associations (Jones 1999); and the CCP's continued insistence on rejecting the legitimacy of the Dalai Lama. During the Cold War, as recent evidence confirms, the US diplomacy service sought to enlist Southeast Asian Buddhists to support its policies against the PRC (Ford 2017). In contrast to the PRC's admission to the United Nations (UN) in 1971, the BAC had to wait another three decades before achieving the same feat in the major international Buddhist associations. The difficulties experienced by the BAC within the PRC through the end of the 1970s, which undermined its credibility to represent Chinese Buddhism, may explain this delayed admission.

Another causal factor behind the late recognition of the BAC may lie with the nature of the two most important international Buddhist organizations: the World Fellowship of Buddhists (WFB 2021a) and the World Buddhist Sangha Council (WBSC 2021). Although both advertise their activities, there is little academic study in the English language about their activities (Schedneck 2016). The WFB included mostly representatives of the Theravāda tradition, practiced by a minuscule minority in the PRC. And while the WBSC leadership includes a greater proportion of the Mahāyāna clergy than the WFB, a disproportionate number of them were based in Taiwan. As the latter endured a regime of martial law from 1949 to 1987 which limited freedom of expression, the independence of the BAROC from the government in Taipei may seem theoretical. However, as Jones (1996) showed, the BAROC clergy had agency and could defend the interests of Buddhists in Taiwan. Moreover, it had its own reasons to support the authoritarian regime in Taiwan: it shared with the KMT a hostility to the CCP regime and did not fear religious persecution under the culturally conservative Chiang Kai-shek. These facts, in their view, only added credibility to the BAROC claim of representing Chinese Buddhism in Taiwan.

The WFB, founded in 1950 in Colombo, relocated its permanent headquarters to Bangkok in 1969. Although based in the Theravāda world, since 1986, countries where the Mahāyāna tradition prevails have hosted most of its conferences (WFB 2021b). The BAC tried unsuccessfully to gain admission and asked for the first WFB conferences to exclude the delegation from Taiwan (Abbott 1966). The exclusion of the BAC from the WFB until then mirrored the exclusion of the PRC from the UN until 1971. The BAROC gained legitimacy in representing Chinese Buddhism when the BAC stopped activities in China from 1966 to 1978, but that position appeared vulnerable and open to challenge with the reform and opening policy that followed. The WBSC, also established in 1966 in Colombo and relocated in Taipei in 1981, stood out as primarily an association of monastics and their organizations. It worked to harmonize the three traditions of Mahāyāna, Theravāda, and Vajrayāna, and includes representatives from all traditions; its leadership counts a larger proportion of Taiwanese than the WFB, and its third, fifth, and seventh conferences were held in Taipei.

The admission of the PRC to the UN and the extension of diplomatic recognition by the US in 1979 did not lead to an improvement in the BAC situation within the international Buddhist organizations. More research needs to be done to fully understand why national Buddhist associations waited so long before agreeing to extend an invitation to the BAC to join them in international Buddhist organizations. The process took years, if not decades, after most of their governments extended recognition to the PRC. The opposition of the BAROC alone – although understandable – does not suffice to explain this delay. Certainly, the BAROC played a disproportionate role in the WBSC, but not in the WFB. The BAC's staunch opposition to the spiritual authority of the Dalai Lama, who is much respected by his peers, has certainly complicated relations between Buddhists from the PRC and their counterparts abroad, at least until 2008 (Repp 2008). However, that motive does not suffice.

When Deng Xiaoping sought to open China to foreign investors, the revival of Christian institutions such as the YMCA and the Amity Press mattered more to the CCP than supporting Buddhist institutions because of the connections of Christian institutions to their counterparts in North America (Carino 2016). Showing good will toward religions sent a message that China was now open to international cooperation. That approach toward religion also affected Buddhism, although it was limited mostly to Japan and South Korea. This changed with the sixteenth WFB conference held in 1988. That event was remarkable for two reasons. Convened in Los Angeles, this was the first such conference held outside of Asia. Under the sponsorship of the Hsi Lai (literally "Coming to the West") Temple, it resulted from the initiative of Hsing Yun, a Chinese monastic who had established in Southern Taiwan a major monastic order, the Buddha Light Mountain (Foguangshan) (Chandler 2004). This mattered to the BAC because Hsing Yun has never hidden his wish to promote Chinese Buddhism on the international stage. Moreover, although he did not express sympathy for the CCP, he shared with the latter an opposition to Taiwanese demands for self-determination.

The eighteenth general conference, held in 1992, took place in Kaohsiung, in Taiwan, also under the cosponsorship of Foguangshan. In the same year, another event occurred that went unnoticed outside of Taiwan, but with significance to relations with China and the future of Buddhism in that country. The Tzu Chi Foundation, the largest philanthropical organization in Taiwan, received from the CCP the authorization to deliver relief to victims of flooding in eastern China that year, and to contribute to the rehabilitation of villages. This case of relative openness represented an example of CCP United Front work directed at the Taiwanese, promoting the idea of "reunification" with China (Laliberté 2003). Despite these cases of rapprochement between Chinese and Taiwanese Buddhists, the exclusion of the BAC from the WFB remained in place. As the WFB organized its events without it, the BAC sought to work around its exclusion from Buddhist international associations by creating its own international institution, the World Buddhist Forum (WBF), with an international conference held every three years (Ramachandran 2019).

In 2006, the Religious Culture Communication Association of China, a CCP United Front organization, worked with the Hong Kong Buddhist Association, and two prominent Buddhist leaders in Taiwan, Hsing Yun and Wei Chueh, to set up the first WBF in the province of Zhejiang, the first religious event of its kind since the establishment of the PRC (Zongwen 2006). The second WBF, held three years later in both China and Taiwan, promoted a CCP priority: the "re-unification" between China and Taiwan at a time when the political climate in Taipei seemed to favor that possibility. However, the United Front work achieved mixed results, as Taiwanese Buddhists preferred to leverage their own networks to serve broader interests outside the PRC (Brown and Cheng 2012). Held in 2012, the third WBF showcased the eleventh Panchen Lama, promoting the CCP preference for the spiritual leadership of Tibetan Buddhism. Held in Hong Kong, that conference suffered from the same limitation as the previous ones: it was a China-centric event, with limited international participation that went unnoticed outside the Sinosphere (Xinhua 2012). Even as the United Front has shifted again to a new strategy directed at other genuinely international Buddhist associations, the global landscape of Buddhism has become more complicated: in addition to the WFB and WBSC, a new association has emerged in New Delhi, the International Buddhist Confederation (IBC 2021).

The IBC, which began in 2010, resulted from the initiative of an Indian monastic, Lama Lobsang. Convening for the first time in 2013, the IBC could not benefit from the Indian government's patronage, because of the Indian state's constitutional (if not actual) commitment to secularism. However, with the arrival into power of the Bharatiya Janata Party in 2014, its leader, Prime Minister Narendra Modi, adopted a strategy that mirrors the United Front's, promoting events such as the IBC meetings on Indian soil, as examples of Indian "soft power" projection in the international arena (Ranade 2017). For the CCP, the IBC represented the same problem as the WSBC: its governing structure included monastics from associations that were politically close to governments whose relations with China were difficult. Moreover, the participation of the Dalai Lama made the participation of any member of the BAC problematic. In the same year, however, the United Front efforts to ensure the BAC joins the WFB finally bore fruit: not only was the BAC admitted into the WFB, but the latter met for the first time in the PRC (Ma & Liang 2014).

When the fourth WBF convened again in Wuxi in 2015, it had lost one of its main *raisons d'être* because the situation in Taiwan the year before had taken a turn less favorable to the CCP, following popular rejection of a cross-strait service trade agreement between Taiwan and China submitted by the KMT (Ho 2019). When the WBF convened for the fifth time in Putian, Fujian, three years later, it experienced a confirmation of these setbacks (Xinhua 2018). The Taiwanese general election held in 2016 had brought to power Tsai Ying-wen and delivered most of the seats in the legislature to the party led by her, the Democratic Progressive Party, whose policy opposes PRC rule over Taiwan. The WBF promoters have not issued any announcement about a sixth meeting in 2021; it is unclear if this is because the CCP has realized that the organization has lost its purpose, or because of the Covid-19 pandemic. Likewise, the other major venue through which the PRC could perform its "religious diplomacy," the WFB, did not meet in 2020, and had no plans to meet in 2021.

14.5 INTERPRETING THE SIGNIFICANCE FOR BUDDHISTS WORLDWIDE OF THE BAC "GOING OUT OF CHINA"

Why would the CCP choose to rely on Buddhism for its "soft power"? The CCP recognizes the growing relevance of religion in global affairs – not necessarily in China itself, but abroad. In the current nationalist turn of the Chinese government, Christianity – whether Protestant or Catholic – has no appeal for the regime: the evidence of its presence in China evokes the "century of humiliation." Moreover, many Chinese political dissidents have over the years converted to Christianity and attracted the sympathy of foreign governments (Wright and Zimmerman-Liu 2015). Islam presents the regime with a thorny dilemma: on the one hand, the supply to China of energy from Muslim-majority countries may lead one to believe that the CCP would seek to cultivate the goodwill of Islamic countries by promoting an image of good relations with Islamic minorities within the country. On the other hand, the security concerns of the regime, whether they are real or manufactured (as a justification ex post facto for its policies targeting the Muslim minorities, mostly Uyghurs and Kazakhs) appear to trump the wish to cultivate good relations with Islamic regimes. Daoism is a less valuable asset than Buddhism for a different reason: apart from ethnic Chinese minorities living overseas, few people outside China practice that religion.

When the CCP acknowledges the international influence of Buddhism, it can harness the importance of that religion in neighboring countries, as seen above, as well as its popularity for many other people living outside Asia. These include not only those with Chinese heritage, but also others disenchanted with their own religious tradition who are seeking answers in their search for meaning (Scott 2016). Moreover, from the perspective of the CCP leaders who have a more nationalist orientation, the authorities can evoke important precedents in Chinese history, for example when Buddhism constituted a crucial element of governance during the two "foreign dynasties." In those periods, the Mongol rulers of the Yuan Dynasty (1279–1368) and the Manchu rulers of the Qing Dynasty, who had maintained good relations with Buddhist clerics, incorporated into one realm the people of Central Asia alongside the Chinese. Although the patronage of Buddhist monastic hierarchies under the Yuan and the Qing favored Tibetan and Mongol Buddhists and not the Han Chinese hierarchies, the present regime nevertheless relies on these historical precedents to reinforce its legitimacy in international fora.

For three decades after 1949, the multi-denominational composition of the BAC leadership structure suggests that the CCP recognized the legacy bequeathed to the Republican regime by the imperial regime. Under Mao and his successor Deng, a sizable proportion of the leaders of the BAC were still representing the Tibetan tradition. Under the two more recent administrations of Jiang and Hu, however, the BAC has moved away from that, with the voices of Tibetan Buddhism within its leadership structure increasingly drowned out by those of the Han tradition. To what extent this reflects the tense relations between the Han central government and the restive Tibetan minority in the Greater Tibetan area is not clear. There could also be another rationale: Mahāyāna Buddhist leaders have worked hard since 1995 to improve relations between China, Japan, and South Korea (Zhang 2012, 28; Yang and Cheng 2010).

In more recent years, many in the CCP would certainly welcome a "softening" of PRC diplomacy at a time when "warrior diplomacy" has put off many governments and people around the world (Martin 2021). However, a few obstacles stand in the way of this strategy of "soft power" through Buddhist diplomacy. In Western societies particularly, most people know little about the Chinese Buddhist tradition, but many are already familiar with the leaders of the Tibetan, Japanese, or even Theravāda traditions. Many in the West who already associate the Buddhist tradition with a message of peace and non-violence attribute those qualities to the Dalai Lama, and they have not failed to notice that the CCP has targeted him for decades. The strategy of the CCP on this matter has backfired. Unless the CCP ceases the rhetoric that demonizes the Tibetan leader in exile and unless the BAC demonstrates a sincere attempt to enter into dialogue with him, it will be difficult to convince outsiders in the West of its goodwill.

The United Front reliance on the BAC also faces some serious limitations in Asian countries, on several grounds. A major obstacle to overcome is the tarnishing of Buddhism by the violent actions of extremist leaders such as Ashin Wirathu in Burma and movements such as the Bodu Bala Sēnā in Sri Lanka (Keyes 2016; Reny 2020), that claim to defend their religion against its enemies. These movements have little to do with the CCP, but they matter to its United Front strategy with the BAC, as it targets societies where most of the population is Buddhist. These movements horrify democratic societies, and engagement with them may cancel out the effectiveness of any projection of soft power by the PRC via the BAC on the global stage. One way to preempt such an outcome would be to take a principled stand and publicly speak out against extremist violence. However, the BAC abides by the CCP principle of non-interference in other countries' domestic affairs and has so far kept quiet.

Of course, the political leanings of Buddhists in Southeast Asia are diverse. Without denying there are hyper-nationalist movements, pro-democratic and non-violent groups have arisen in the region, which are associated informally in what scholars have defined as engaged Buddhism (Sivaraksa 2005; Queen and King 1996). New groups of Buddhist democratic activists, such as the All-Burma Monks' Alliance founded by U Nat Zaw have also emerged (Lehr 2019). As targets of authoritarian regimes themselves, these Buddhists are not likely to support the BAC because of its close relationship with a regime that is an accomplice to their tormentors. Although the differences between the schools are not sources of conflict in the way sectarian differences can be between Christian denominations and the

Sunni and Shi'a branches of Islam, it is not clear how Buddhists in Theravāda countries view China, considering the minority and marginal status of Theravāda in China (Yang 2017).

The CCP United Front must also overcome formidable obstacles in societies where most Buddhists identify with the Mahāyāna tradition in East Asia. As religious minorities in Japan, South Korea, and Taiwan, Buddhists in these three countries are unlikely to sway most of the population to their side. Moreover, reflective of the political pluralism that prevails there, no government-licensed corporation holds a monopoly on the representation of Buddhists, which means that there is competition between Buddhist leaders and their followers (Watts 2004; Nathan 2017; Laliberté 2004). In other words, even if the BAC were successful in swaying a national Buddhist association's leadership to espouse the policies of the CCP, its rank-and-file members may not follow suit. For instance, although the monastic Hsing Yun, founder of the popular Taiwan-based Buddha Light International Association promotes the improvement of relations with China, aligning him with some high-ranking members of the KMT and allied political parties, many lay Buddhists in the same association do not agree with the views of their leaders on matters of politics.

If the CCP were to succeed in overcoming these obstacles and bringing into a United Front the BAC and other national Buddhist associations in countries with Buddhist majorities to influence their respective governments, the international community would face a serious conundrum. Such a convergence could reinforce trends already unfolding in most of Southeast Asia, where authoritarian governments either support the PRC as a fellow authoritarian regime or depend on its promise of developmental support (Soong 2018). As demonstrated by the deafening silence of many authoritarian governments in Muslim-majority countries over the genocide committed in the Xinjiang Uyghur Autonomous Region (Kelemen and Turcsányi 2020), we should not be surprised if the authoritarian governments of countries where most people identify as Buddhists support the PRC policy against the Dalai Lama. Buddhist actors who seek to shape, interpret, and reformulate constitutional law in their respective countries based on their spiritual tradition will have to keep in mind that the international organizations that represent them face the prospect of being influenced by a fellow Buddhist association, one that cannot come close to achieving that in its own country.

There is even a risk that Buddhists in Southeast Asia who want cooperation with their Chinese counterparts may have to fulfill some conditions. One telling example, taken from Buddhists in Canada, gives us a sense of what is in store. Even though Canada is a country where the rule of law prevails and Buddhists can express their views without fear of retribution, key actors in that milieu have shown remarkable deference to the CCP United Front perspective that "there is one China in the world" and that "Taiwan is part of China." Hence, the online directory of the Canadian Buddhist associations, which numbers over 450 associations and groups them by national origins, ranks branches of Taiwanese associations in Canadian cities as Chinese, mirroring the practice that the PRC is imposing on governments, international organizations, private corporations, and even civil society organizations (Sumeru n.d.). If Canadian Buddhists fear upsetting the CCP United Front on a matter such as the sovereignty of Taiwan, there is little reason to believe that Buddhists in countries more dependent on China's largesse will be more assertive in the affirmation of their own views.

14.6 CONCLUSION

What are the implications of the above for constitutional law? Different Buddhist traditions have shaped and influenced the legal systems of the countries in which they have evolved but China stands out from its neighbors in that respect: although Buddhism represents a vital element of its religious tradition, philosophy, and culture writ large, it has left no important trace on its legal system, let alone its constitutional law. Constitutionalism – or more specifically the idea of an independent judiciary – has been declared one of the seven forbidden topics that Chinese academics should not address, following orders issued by the General Office of the CCP Central Committee to institutes of higher education in 2013 (the others are universal values, press freedom, civil society, civic rights, historical mistakes by the CCP, and elite cronyism). Since the establishment of the PRC, Buddhist elites have failed to leave a mark on the evolution of constitutionalism, leaving the field open to "rights protection lawyers" (*weiquan lushi* 维权律师) and other legal activists – many of whom, such as Gao Zhisheng 高智晟, are Christians (Xi 2013). The promotion by the CCP of Buddhism in a variety of international associations does not mean a new-found appreciation for religion, but a return to a purely instrumentalist strategy of using a United Front work to convince Buddhists in Southeast Asia that they share the same ideals as the CCP for harmonious coexistence, peace, and development. Human rights and self-determination are improper topics in that kind of "dialogue." In democratic and open societies like Japan, South Korea, and Taiwan, the public can see through the ulterior motives behind the projection of "sharp power" by the Chinese state. On the other hand, the non-democratic regimes in Thailand, Burma, Sri Lanka, Cambodia, and Laos, prone to soliciting the acquiescence, if not the legitimation, provided by Buddhist monastic orders in their own countries, may welcome this source of support from a Buddhist association sponsored by a fellow authoritarian state. Buddhist actors who seek to shape, interpret, and reformulate constitutional law in their respective countries will have to come to terms with the reality of a fellow Buddhist association that may wield considerable influence abroad if its sponsors support it, but little capacity to push back at home if it wants to express dissent.

REFERENCES

Abbott, Arthur. 1966. "World Buddhists Under Pressure." *World Affairs* 129 (2) (July, August, September 1966): 101–8.

Ashiwa Yoshiko. 2009. "Positioning Religion in Modernity: State and Buddhism in China." In *Making Religion, Making the State: The Politics of Religion in Modern China*, edited by Ashiwa Yoshiko and David Wank, 43–73. Stanford: Stanford University Press.

Ashiwa Yoshiko and Wank, David. 2020. "The Chinese State's Global Promotion of Buddhism." *Geopolitics of Religious Soft Power*, Policy Brief 4 (November 11). Washington, DC: Georgetown University's Berkley Center for Religion, Peace & World Affairs and Brookings Institution.

Beydon, Olivier. 2015. *Introduction à la pensée juridique chinoise*. Bruxelles: Larcier.

Borchert, Thomas A. 2017. *Educating Monks: Minority Buddhism on China's Southwest Border*. Honolulu: University of Hawai'i Press.

Brady, Anne-Marie. 2019. "On the Correct Use of Terms for Understanding 'United Front Work.'" *China Brief* 9 (9): 1–5.

Brown, Deborah A., and Cheng Tun-jen. 2012. "Religious Relations across the Taiwan Strait: Patterns, Alignments, and Political Effects." *Orbis* 56 (1): 60–81.

Carino, Theresa. 2016. "Faith-based Organisations Between Service Delivery and Social Change in Contemporary China: The Experience of Amity Foundation." *HTS Theological Studies* 72 (4): 1–10.

Carrithers, Michael. 2000. "On Polytropy: Or the Natural Condition of Spiritual Cosmopolitanism in India: The Digambar Jain Case." *Modern Asian Studies* 34 (4) (Oct.): 831–61.

Chandler, Stuart. 2004. *Establishing a Pure Land on Earth: The Foguang Buddhist Perspective on Modernization and Globalization*. Honolulu: University of Hawai'i Press.

Chang Kuei-min. 2016. *Spiritual State, Material Temple: The Political Economy of Religious Revival in China*. PhD dissertation, Columbia University.

Charleux, Isabelle. 2017. "Chinese, Tibetan and Mongol Buddhists on Mount Wutai (China) from the Eighteenth to the Twenty-first Century." In *Pilgrimage and Ambiguity: Sharing the Sacred*, edited by Thierry Zarcone, Pedram Khosronejad and Angela Hobart, 87–118. Herefordshire: Sean Kingston Publishing.

Clarke, Donald. 2017. "Has China Restored Private Land Ownership? The Implications of Beijing's New Policy." *Foreign Affairs*, May 16. www.foreignaffairs.com/articles/china/2017-05-16/has-china-restored-private-land-ownership

Cook, Sarah. 2017. *The Battle for China's Spirit: Religious Revival, Repression, and Resistance under Xi Jinping*. Lanham: Rowman & Littlefield.

Delisle, Jacques. 2017. "Law in the China Model 2.0: Legality, Developmentalism and Leninism under Xi Jinping." *Journal of Contemporary China* 26 (103): 68–84.

Dowdle, Michael W. 2018. "Infrastructural Power and Its Possibilities for the Constitutional Evolution of Authoritarian Political Systems: Lessons from China." In *Authoritarian Constitutionalism: Comparative Analysis and Critique*, edited by Helena Alviar García and Günter Frankenberg, 76–94. Northampton: Edward Elgar.

Fisher, Gareth. 2017. "Lay Buddhists and Moral Activism in Contemporary China." *Review of Religion and Chinese Society* 4 (2): 247–70.

Ford, Eugene. 2017. *Cold War Monks: Buddhism and America's Secret Strategy in Southeast Asia*. New Haven: Yale University Press.

Groot, Gerry. 2004. *Managing Transitions: The Chinese Communist Party, United Front Work, Corporatism and Hegemony*. New York: Routledge.

Ho Ming-shi. 2019. *Challenging Beijing's Mandate of Heaven: Taiwan's Sunflower Movement and Hong Kong's Umbrella Movement*. Philadelphia: Temple University Press.

Holbig, Heike. 2018. "China After Reform: The Ideological, Constitutional, and Organisational Makings of a New Era." *Journal of Current Chinese Affairs* 47 (3): 187–207.

Hou Kunhong 侯坤宏. 2012. *Haojie yu chongsheng: yijiusijiu nian yilaide dalu fojiao* 浩劫与重生：一九四九年以来的大陆佛教. Tainan: Miaoxin 妙心.

IBC (International Buddhist Confederation). 2021. "International Buddhist Confederation." Accessed June 3, 2021. www.ibcworld.org/

Irons, Edward A. 2018. "On sects in China." *The Journal of CESNUR* 2 (1) (January–February): 33–57.

Jessup, Brooke. 2016. "Buddhist Activism, Urban Space, and Ambivalent Modernity in 1920s Shanghai." In *Recovering Buddhism in Modern China*, edited by Jan Kiely and J. Brook Jessup, 37–78. New York: Columbia University Press.

Ji Zhe. 2004. "Buddhism and the State: The New Relationship." *China Perspectives*, 55 (September–October 2004). Accessed May 31, 2021. http://journals.openedition.org/chinaperspectives/408

2017. "Comrade Zhao Puchu: Bodhisattva under the Red Flag." In *Making Saints in Modern China*, edited by David Ownby, Vincent Goossaert and Ji Zhe, 312–46. New York: Oxford University Press.

2019. "Schooling Dharma Teachers: The Buddhist Academy System and Sangha Education." In *Buddhism after Mao: Negotiations, Continuities, and Reinventions*, edited by Ji Zhe, Gareth Fisher and André Laliberté, 171–209. University of Hawai'i Press.

Johnson, Ian. 2018. "#MeToo in the Monastery: A Chinese Abbot's Fall Stirs Questions on Buddhism's Path." *New York Times*, September 15. Accessed May 31, 2021. www.nytimes.com/2018/09/15/world/asia/metoo-china-monastery.html

Jones, Charles B. 1996. "Relations Between the Nationalist Government and the Buddhist Association of the Republic of China (BAROC) since 1945." *Journal of Chinese Religions*, 24 (1): 77–99.

1999. *Buddhism in Taiwan: Religion and the State, 1660–1990*. Honolulu: Hawai'i University Press.

Joske, Alex. 2019. "Reorganizing the United Front Work Department: New Structures for a New Era of Diaspora and Religious Affairs Work." *China Brief* 19 (9): 6–14.

Kelemen, Barbara and Turcsányi, Richard Q. 2020. "It's the Politics, Stupid: China's Relations with Muslim Countries on the Background of Xinjiang Crackdown." *Asian Ethnicity* 21 (2): 223–43.

Keyes, Charles. 2016. "Theravāda Buddhism and Buddhist Nationalism: Sri Lanka, Myanmar, Cambodia, and Thailand." *The Review of Faith and International Affairs*, 14 (4): 41–52.

Kiely, Jan. 2016. "The Communist Dismantling of Temple and Monastic Buddhism in Suzhou." In *Recovering Buddhism in Modern China*, edited by Jan Kiely and J. Brooks Jessup, 216–53. New York: Columbia University Press.

Laliberté, André. 2003. "'Love Transcends Borders' or 'Blood is Thicker than Water'? The Charity Work of the Compassion Relief Foundation in the People's Republic of China." *European Journal of East Asian Studies* 2 (2): 243–61.

2004. *The Politics of Buddhist Organizations in Taiwan, 1989–2003: Safeguarding the Faith, Building a Pure Land, Helping the Poor*. London: Routledge.

Lehr, Peter. 2019. *Militant Buddhism: The Rise of Religious Violence in Sri Lanka, Myanmar and Thailand*. New York: Palgrave Macmillan.

Li Ling. 2015. "Chinese Characteristics of the 'Socialist Rule of Law': Will the Fourth Plenum Cure the Problems of the Chinese Judicial System?" *Asia Policy* 20 (July): 17–22.

Ma Xiaojun and Liang Jun. 2014. "27th General Conference of the World Fellowship of Buddhists Kicks Off in Famen Temple in Baoji." *People's Daily*, October 24. Accessed July 16, 2022. http://en.people.cn/n/2014/1024/c204459-8799435.html

Martin, Peter. 2021. *China's Civilian Army: The Making of Wolf Warrior Diplomacy*. Oxford: Oxford University Press.

Minzner, Carl. 2015. "Legal Reform in the Xi Jinping Era." *Asia Policy* 20 (July): 4–9.

Nathan, Mark A. 2017. "Contemporary Korean Buddhist Traditions." In *The Oxford Handbook of Contemporary Buddhism*, edited by Michael Jerryson, 100–21. New York: Oxford University Press.

Palmer, David. 2007. *Qigong Fever: Body, Science, and Utopia in China*. New York: Columbia University Press.

Pew-Templeton (Global Religious Futures Project). 2016. "Countries Profiles: Thailand." *Religion and Public Life Project*. Washington: Pew Research Center. www.globalreligiousfutures.org/countries/thailand#/?affiliations_religion_id=0&affiliations_year=2020&region_name=All%20Countries&restrictions_year=2016. Accessed July 16, 2022.

Piquet, Hélène. 2005. *La Chine au carrefour des traditions juridiques*. Bruxelles: Bruylant.

Potter, Pittman. 2003. "Belief in Control: Regulation of Religion in China." *The China Quarterly* 174: 317–37.

Powers, John, 2016. *The Buddha Party: How the People's Republic of China Works to Define and Control Tibetan Buddhism*. New York: Oxford University Press.

Queen, Christopher S. and King, Sallie, eds. 1996. *Engaged Buddhism: Buddhist Liberation Movements in Asia*. Albany: State University of New York Press.

Ramachandran, Sudha. 2019. "Rivalries and Relics: Examining China's Buddhist Public Diplomacy." *China Brief* 19 (5): 15–20.

Ranade, Jayadeva. 2017. "Buddhism: A New Frontier in the China–India Rivalry." *Carnegie India* 17. Washington: Carnegie Endowment of International Peace.

Raymond, Gregory V. 2020. "Religion as a Tool of Influence: Buddhism and China's Belt and Road Initiative in Mainland Southeast Asia." *Contemporary Southeast Asia* 42 (3): 346–71.

Reny, Marie-Eve. 2020. "Myanmar's Transition and the Resurgence of Buddhist Nationalism: How Incumbents Seek to Hold on to Power." *Asian Survey* 60 (6): 1072–89.

Repp, Martin. 2008. "HH The 14th Dalai Lama and Japanese Buddhists: An Account and Analysis of Complicated Interactions." *Japanese Religions* 33: 103–26.

Sagild, Rebekka Åsnes and Ahlers, Anna Lisa. 2019. "Honorary Intermediaries? The Chinese People's Political Consultative Conferences in Theory and Practice." *China Perspectives* (2): 9–16.

Sasas, Roger. 2020. "Monastic Intimacies: An Anthropology of Good and Bad Buddhism Among the Tai Lue of Sipsong Panna (P.R. China)." *Journal of Global Buddhism* 21: 153–69.

Schedneck, Brooke. 2016. "Buddhist International Organizations." In *The Oxford Handbook of Contemporary Buddhism*, 398–416. Oxford: Oxford University Press.

Scott, David. 2016. "Buddhism in Current China–India Diplomacy." *Journal of Current Chinese Affairs* 45 (3): 139–74.

Scully, Eileen P. 2000. "Historical Wrongs and Human Rights in Sino-Foreign Relations: The Legacy of Extraterritoriality." *Journal of American–East Asian Relations* 9 (1–2): 129–46.

Sivaraksa, Sulak. 2005. *Conflict, Culture, Change: Engaged Buddhism in a Globalizing World*. New York: Simon & Schuster.

Soong Jenn-Jaw. 2018. "China's One Belt and One Road Initiative Meets ASEAN Economic Community: Propelling and Deepening Regional Economic Integration?" *The Chinese Economy* 51 (4): 291–97.

Sumeru. n.d. "The Sumeru Guide to Canadian Buddhism." Ottawa: Sumeru Press. Accessed May 31, 2021. www.directory.sumeru-books.com/tag/chinese/

Tong, James. 2009. *Revenge of the Forbidden City: The Suppression of the Falungong in China, 1999–2005*. New York: Oxford University Press.

Vermander, Benoît. 2019. "Sinicizing Religions, Sinicizing Religious Studies." *Religions* 10 (2): 1–23.

Wang Yichi. 2020. "Buddhist Books Seized as 'Pornography and Illegal Publications.'" *Bitter Winter* (January 22). Accessed May 31, 2021. https://bitterwinter.org/buddhist-books-seized-as-pornography-and-illegal-publications/

Watts, Jonathan, S. 2004. "A Brief Overview of Buddhist NGOs in Japan." *Japanese Journal of Religious Studies* 31 (2): 417–28.

Welch, Holmes. 1969. "Buddhism Since the Cultural Revolution." *The China Quarterly* 40: 127–36.

Wenzel-Teuber, Katharina. 2017. "Statistics on Religions and Churches in the People's Republic of China – Update for the Year 2016." *Religions & Christianity in Today's China* 7 (2): 26–53.

2018. "Statistics on Religions and Churches in the People's Republic of China – Update for the Year 2017." *Religions & Christianity in Today's China* 7 (2): 26–51.

WFB (World Fellowship of Buddhists). 2021a. "Welcome to the World Fellowship of Buddhists." Accessed May 31, 2021. http://wfbhq.org/index.php

2021b. "General Conference." Accessed May 31, 2021. http://wfbhq.org/general-conference.php

Wickeri, Philippe. 2011. *Seeking the Common Ground: Protestant Christianity, the Three-Self Movement, and China's United Front*. Eugene: Wipf and Stock.

Woeser, Tsering. 2020. *Forbidden Memory: Tibet During the Cultural Revolution*. Lincoln: University of Nebraska Press.

World Buddhist Sangha Council (WSBC). 2021. "Introduction," *WBSC*. Accessed May 31, 2021. www.wbsc886.org/en/aboutus-142

Wright, Teresa and Teresa Zimmerman-Liu. 2015. "Atheist Political Activists Turned Protestants: Religious Conversion Among Chinese Dissidents." *Journal of Church and State* 57 (2): 268–88.

Xi Lian. 2013. "'Cultural Christians' and the Search for Civil Society in Contemporary China." *The Chinese Historical Review* (May) 20 (1): 70–87.

Xinhua (staff writer). 2012. "Third World Buddhist Forum Closes in HK." *China Daily*, April 27. www.chinadaily.com.cn/china/2012-04/27/content_15164025.htm. Accessed July 16, 2022.

(staff writer). 2018. "World Buddhist Forum Opens in Fujian." *China Daily*, October 28. https://global.chinadaily.com.cn/a/201810/28/WS5bd5b67ca310eff303285046.html. Accessed July 16, 2022.

Xue Yu. 2009. "Buddhist Contribution to the Socialist Transformation of Buddhism in China: Activities of Ven. Juzan during 1949–1953." *Journal of Global Buddhism* 10: 217–53.

Yang Fenggang. 2006. "The Red, Black, and Gray Markets of Religion in China." *The Sociological Quarterly* 47 (1) (Winter): 93–122.

Yang Zeng-wen, trans. Janet Mei-kee Cheng. 2010. "The Contribution of Buddhist Scholars Toward the Friendship of China and Japan." *Journal of Oriental Studies* 20: 155–70.

Yang Zi. 2017. "The Soft Power Limits of Chinese Theravāda Buddhism." *The Diplomat*, August 15. https://thediplomat.com/2017/08/the-soft-power-limits-of-chinese-theravada-buddhism/

ZFX (Zhongguo fojiao xiehui 中国佛教协会). 2017a. "Zhongguo fojiao xiehui jianjie 中国佛教协会简介." *Benhui jieshao* 本会介绍. Accessed May 31, 2021. www.chinabuddhism.com.cn/e/action/ListInfo/?classid=540.

2017b. "Zuzhi jigou 组织机构," *Benhui jieshao* 本会介绍. Accessed May 31, 2021. www.chinabuddhism.com.cn/e/action/ListInfo/?classid=533.

Zhang, Juyan. 2012. *Buddhist Diplomacy: History and Status Quo*. USC Center on Public Diplomacy at the Annenberg School, Paper, 7.

Zheng Qi. 2015. *Carl Schmitt, Mao Zedong and the Politics of Transition*. New York: Palgrave Macmillan.

Zongwen 宗文 (ed.). 2006. *Hexie shijie: Congxin kaishi* 和谐世界, 从心开始 [*A Harmonious World Begins in the Mind*]. Beijing: Zongjiao wenhua chubanshe 宗教文化出版社.

15

Governing "Lamaism" on the "Frontier"

Buddhism and Law in Early Twentieth-Century Inner Mongolia

Daigengna Duoer[*]

15.1 THE CASE OF INNER MONGOLIA IN THE STUDY OF BUDDHISM AND LAW[1]

Since Rebecca French declared Buddhist legal studies a "missing discipline" in 2004, this interdisciplinary subfield has been slowly but surely growing. However, as Benjamin Schonthal and Tom Ginsburg have pointed out, most of these advances focus on the ancient, premodern, and early modern periods, and on Buddhists sources relating to Buddhist conduct (Schonthal and Ginsburg 2016). This chapter addresses this gap in the "missing discipline" by focussing on the state regulations of Buddhism in Inner Mongolia in the early twentieth century.

The early twentieth-century regimes considered in this chapter are the Republic of China (1912–49), the Japanese puppet states of Manchukuo (1932–45), and the Mengjiang United Autonomous Government (1939–45). These three modern states competed to make claims of sovereignty over Inner Mongolia, the southern half of Qing-era Mongolia after the northern half (Outer Mongolia) declared independence under the Bogda Khan[2] government in 1911. Under the leadership of Bogda

[*] I am grateful for the insightful comments I was able to receive on this chapter from the editors, Benjamin Schonthal and Tom Ginsburg, and from their research assistant, Paride Stortini. I am also thankful for the valuable feedback I received throughout writing this chapter from Vesna Wallace, José Cabezón, Kate McDonald, Matthew King, Rory Lindsay, Anran Wang, James Meador, Yiming Ma, and Yanshuo Zhang. All translations are by the author, unless specified.

[1] By "Inner Mongolia" (M: *Dotogadu Monggol*, and later 1947, *Öbör Monggol*, C: *neimenggu* 内蒙古, J: *uchi mongoru* 内モンゴル), this chapter refers mostly to the geographical regions included in Qing-era Inner Mongolia. The idea of "Inner Mongolia" however, has taken on different shapes and forms in the various spatial imaginations of modern states since the Qing, resulting in different systems of administrative divisions.

[2] In this chapter, all terms in Mongolian have been transliterated according to the system used in Christopher P. Atwood's *Encyclopedia of Mongolia and the Mongol Empire* (2004), except for

Khan, who was also the Eighth Jebtsundamba Khutugtu[3] (1870–1924), Outer Mongolia operated as a theocratic state until the establishment of the socialist Mongolian People's Republic in 1924.[4] Inner Mongolia, on the other hand, never became politically independent and was subject to the influences of the competing nation-building and empire-building projects of modern China and the Japanese empire. This period between the fall of the Qing empire (1912) and the establishment of the People's Republic of China (1949) was formative not only for the Inner Mongolia Autonomous Region as we know it today, but also for the state regulations of Buddhism in the region. During this period, Chinese and Japanese policymakers considered the Buddhist tradition in Inner Mongolia as ethnically and geopolitically relevant for their frontier policies. In the same way that Buddhism was understood to be the solution to the "Tibetan Problem" for the Republic of China (Tuttle 2005, 11), Buddhism was also taken as the key to winning the support of Inner Mongolia and beyond for nation-building and empire-building projects.

This chapter argues that early twentieth-century Inner Mongolia makes a fascinating case for the study of Buddhism and law in the modern East Asian context because it was governed by multiple states and empires, which drew upon parallel and overlapping policies toward Buddhism as part of their competing projects of nation-state construction and imperialism. As a religion that is neither fully foreign nor domestic for the Chinese and Japanese policymakers, Buddhism in Inner Mongolia also provides an important case study for the understanding of how religions on the "ethnic frontier" were understood and governed by modern East Asian nation-states that were built on ethno-nationalist foundations. While Buddhism and law in Asia is often discussed in national terms, the Inner Mongolia case exposes the fact that different legal structures sometimes exist for people of different ethnic groups belonging to different Buddhist traditions living under one nation or empire, and that legal practices directed at the peripheries may look very different from those directed at the center.

One reflection of this distinctive context is that the terms used to discuss Buddhism in Inner Mongolia in the legal discourses of the Republic of China, Manchukuo, and Mengjiang were not *fojiao* or *bukkyō*, terms more commonly used

the term "Jebtsundamba," as this spelling has become more commonly used than "Jibzundamba."

3 The Jebtsundamba Khutugtus belong to a lineage of incarnate lamas in Tibeto-Mongolian Buddhism and were one of the most revered Buddhist leaders among the Khalkha Mongols in Qing Outer Mongolia, comparable to the Dalai Lamas in Tibet. The Eighth Jebtsundamba Khutugtu (1870–1924) was born in Tibet into the family of an official of the Dalai Lama's estate. Despite his Tibetan birth, the Jebtsundamba identified strongly with Khalkha Mongolia and consistently supported Mongolian independence from the Qing. On the Jebtsundamba Khutugtu and his lineage, see "Jibzundamba Khutugtu" in Atwood's *Encyclopedia of Mongolia and the Mongol Empire* (2004).

4 By "theocratic state," this chapter refers to the fact that the Eighth Jebtsundamba was proclaimed the "holy emperor" (Bogda Khan) and "dual ruler of religion and state" on December 29, 1911.

to refer to Buddhism in the Chinese and Japanese languages. Instead, the type of Buddhism in Inner Mongolia was mostly referred to as "Lamaism" (C: *lamajiao*; J: *ramakyō*),[5] or sometimes as "Mongolian-Tibetan Buddhism" (C: *mengzang fojiao*), or "Manchu-Mongolian Buddhism" (J: *manmō bukkyō*).[6] In contrast to the Buddhist traditions of China and Japan, "Lamaism" was understood as spatially, temporally, racially, and morally distinct in the legal languages of these modern East Asian states. More specifically speaking, "Lamaism" was imagined to be an "exotic" Buddhism practiced by ethnic groups on the "frontiers" of nations and empires built on Sinocentric and Japan-centric foundations. "Lamaism," with its maintenance of the reincarnated lamas and traditional monasticism, was deemed "backwards," "superstitious," and even morally "degenerate" for the modern nation-state, when compared to Chinese and Japanese Buddhism that had been open to modern reforms.

Situating this "Lamaism" on a spatial and temporal frontier, the legal practices of the three modern states of Republican China, Manchukuo, and Mengjiang aimed to exploit Buddhism in Inner Mongolia for their multiethnic nation-building and empire-building projects and strived to discipline the religion as a political-economic issue that needed to be depoliticized, modernized, and reformed. On the one hand, these three modern states supported Buddhism and the *tulku* system of reincarnated lamas under "religious freedom" legislated in their constitutions and emphasized Buddhism as a commonly shared heritage that could link culturally diverse regions in post-Qing Inner and East Asia together into new modern nation-states. In these discourses, the three modern states would replace the Manchu rulers of the Qing empire as the new patrons in the priest–patron relationship with the *tulku*s of Inner Mongolia. These renewed alliances would not only help justify the three modern states' claims over disputed land on the "frontiers" of post-Qing Inner Mongolia, but they would also help to create coalitions to combat Soviet influences and Euro-American imperialism.

5 Donald S. Lopez, Jr. has written on the history of the term "Lamaism" in "'Lamaism' and the Disappearance of Tibet" (1996) and in *Prisoners of Shangri-la* (1998). He points out that the first official usage of the Chinese term *lamajiao* 喇嘛教 to talk about Tibetan Buddhism can be dated to 1775 during the reign of the Qing Qianlong emperor and argues that the later European usages of the term "Lamaism" served as a trope in the Orientalist historicism of late Victorian colonialism. How the post-Qing Chinese states and modern Japan came to use the term (喇嘛教・ラマ教), however, is not discussed in Lopez's works. The author of this chapter finds that the usages of "Lamaism" in the early twentieth-century East Asian context offers two additional points to consider: first, "Lamaism" in modern China and Japan referred not only to Tibetan Buddhism, but to Buddhism in Mongolia and Manchuria as well; second, the Orientalist usages of the term in modern East Asian discourses suggest that modern East Asian states and empires similarly engaged with colonialist imaginations toward the "Other." Jason Ānanda Josephson has argued that although Japanese scholars writing about Asia and its religions could position themselves as liberating Asian religions from European colonialism, they did so as the colonizer rather than the colonized (Josephson 2012, 247).

6 蒙藏佛教; 満蒙仏教.

On the other hand, in the actual articles of the regulations, Buddhism in Inner Mongolia was governed and disciplined as a political-economic issue. Politically, "Lamaism" in Inner Mongolia and the substantial authority of its *tulku* system was deemed inappropriate for the modern states that operated on centralized power. Thus, monastic involvement in politics was restricted in legislations that attempted to challenge existing Buddhist structures. The management of monastic affairs, such as reincarnations and monastic exams, became centralized, and monastic organizations were restructured with new centers of authority. Economically, "Lamaist" monasticism in Inner Mongolia was understood to be one of the major causes of the decline in population in the region and the culprit for the shrinkage of prime-age male labor forces. Laws were thus created to curb the growth of monasticism so that an "unproductive" male population could be redirected toward more economically "productive" endeavors. It also became necessary for monastic assets, such as land, property, monastic population, and lay subjects, to be regularly registered with and surveilled by the central governments.

This rather contradictory promotion and limitation of Buddhism in Inner Mongolia in the laws of the Republic of China, Manchukuo, and Mengjiang shows that instead of completely revoking the Qing policies on Buddhism among the Mongols, the modern East Asian states chose to maintain a certain kind of continuity with Qing-era practices so that they could continue to make claims of sovereignty over Qing-occupied territories. As Gray Tuttle has argued for modern Tibet, the Inner Mongolia case examined in this chapter also shows us that religion can serve as "a crucial link between the social organization of dynastic empire and that of the nation-state" (2005, 3). The Inner Mongolia case examined in this chapter demonstrates that Buddhism indeed served as a "crucial link" through which the three modern East Asian states competed to make sense of remnant ethnopolitical, economic, and labor structures from the Qing era. This formative period between the fall of the Qing to the end of World War II eventually established a legacy of governance and legal precedents on which the People's Republic of China's frontier policies would be built later.

15.2 BUDDHISM IN INNER MONGOLIA AT THE TURN OF THE TWENTIETH CENTURY

Similar to Tibet, Inner Mongolia at the turn of the twentieth century was a significantly Buddhist society. Toward the end of the Qing era, there were around 1,600 monasteries and temples and 100,000 Buddhist monks in the region, which comprised around 10 percent of the entire male population (Delege 1998, 452). In certain regions, this percentage was even higher: in the Xilingol League, for example, in the 1940s the total monastic population was 20 percent of the entire population in the region and 42 percent of the entire male population (Delege 1998, 219). On the steppes of Inner Mongolia, where life remained largely nomadic for centuries, Buddhist monasteries were often the only architectural structures that dotted the landscape. Many of the larger monastic institutions also functioned as colleges that taught languages, medicine, and astrology. For centuries, monasteries in these regions of Mongolia were the sole providers of education, health care, and social mobility.

In Inner Mongolia, as was in the case of Tibet, Buddhism was intimately linked with political power. Since the second conversion of the Mongols to Buddhism in the late sixteenth century, Mongolian society operated under the principle of dual law (*qoyar yosu*, Tib., *lugs gnyis*), which maintained that both the state and the Buddha Dharma were fundamental sources of spiritual refuge and the most sacred domains of one's social duties (Wallace 2014, 321). This principle of dual law was said to have originated in India and refers to the conjoining of Dharma and rule (Tib., *chos srid zun 'brel*) and the sharing of authority between religion and the state. Buddhist teachings and state laws were regarded as complementary and equal, occupying distinct social domains. However, under certain circumstances one or the other could be regarded as preeminent, and in some cases both orders could be concentrated in a single person (Ruegg 2014, 68). Under this principle, both the Buddha Dharma and the state would endure as long as they continued to be consolidated and interdependent; conversely, crimes committed against either the state or Buddhism entailed serious karmic consequences (Wallace 2014, 321). This system of dual law encouraged the formation of priest–patron relationships between powerful rulers and monastic networks not only in Inner Mongolia, but all across Inner Asia.[7] In this relationship, the lama, especially incarnate ones, served as the donee (*takhil-un oron*, Tib., *mchod gnas*), while the state ruler served as the donor (*öglige-yin ejen*, Tib., *yon bdag*). The lama offered religious teachings and spiritual protection for the state, and the state ruler promised to defend monastic properties and the socioeconomic privileges of the lamas. In this arrangement, offenses committed against the state entailed serious karmic consequences; on the other hand, the state also had the duty to regulate the conduct of the monastic community and their interactions with lay communities and state authorities (Wallace 2014, 324).

Economically, Buddhist institutions in the Mongolian regions in the Qing period also possessed enormous wealth. Monasteries, especially the larger ones, and the incarnate lamas received sizeable incomes through donations and contributions from elite patrons and *shabinar* – lay disciples and subjects of a monastery, or a reincarnated lama. The *shabinar* were required to pay services, such as corvee labor to maintain temples and monasteries, as well as taxes in kind and in currency (Moses 1977, 131–32). For example, in 1918, the Eighth Jebtsundampa Khutugtu had 8,833 *shabinar* families, 21,180 lamas, for a total of 49,878 individuals under his jurisdiction (Moses 1977, 127). The annual tax income from the *shabinar* subjects alone for the

7 On these monastic networks in Inner Asia and their political history, see Sullivan 2021.

Jebtsundamba ranged from 500,000 to one million *lans*[8] of silver per year (Moses 1977, 132). The total wealth of the Jebtsundamba's personal estate was estimated at 57 million gold rubles or one fifth of the total wealth of Outer Mongolia in 1921 (Moses 1977, 125). Although the khutugtus of Inner Mongolia were not as wealthy as the Eighth Jebtundamba at the turn of the twentieth century, they similarly received significant donations and contributions from patrons and *shabinar* subjects, in addition to accumulating wealth from herds, land, land rentals, and money lending (Miller 1959, 97–105). For example, in some regions of Inner Mongolia, such as in the Jalaid banner,[9] the lamas (4 percent of the population) reportedly held 7 percent to 23 percent of the cattle and horses in the entire banner (Miller 1959, 116). Monasteries in the Kharachin banner alone were able to collect at least 100 million *wen*[10] from their hundreds of *qing*[11] of leased land in 1835 (Huricha 2013, 230). Being the only permanent structures on the vast steppes in Inner Mongolia also allowed the monasteries to become trade centers and key economic hubs. Often located on major trade routes, the monasteries held regular fairs where markets, trade, and large-scale public rituals took place (Miller 1959, 109; Huricha 2009, 202–3).

Therefore, to say that Buddhism was a formidable political, social, and economic force in Inner Mongolia at the turn of the twentieth century is an understatement. The power of the tradition of dual law and the influence of Buddhist economy in both local and transregional terms was not lost on the modern states and empires in the post-Qing that were vying to gain control of the region for their nation-building and empire-building projects. It is their attempts at governing the powerful Buddhist institution in Inner Mongolia that is the focus of this chapter.

15.3 QING REGULATION OF BUDDHISM IN INNER MONGOLIA

Prior to the twentieth century, Mongolian society operated under a kind of legal pluralism in addition to the dual law tradition that allowed the regulation of Buddhism to be managed from afar, regionally, and within specific monastic settings. In the Yuan period (1271–1368), the administration of local religious affairs in the empire was delegated by the Khan to Tibetan clerics (Barrett 2014, 214). After the second conversion of the Mongols to Buddhism in the late sixteenth century, multiple types of laws were instituted within Mongolian territories to regulate Buddhism,

8 According to the Mongolbank, the central bank of Mongolia, *lan* was introduced as a temporary monetary unit to function as a medium of exchange in August 1921. One *lan* equaled one Chinese silver *Yanchaan* and 1.42 Russian gold coins. See "History of Mongolian currency," (Mongolbank n.d.). www.mongolbank.mn/eng/listbanknote.aspx?id=15

9 A banner (*khoshuu*) is an administrative division first used in Inner Mongolia in the Qing. The banner system remained the basis for local administrative units under the Republic of China.

10 *Wen* 文 is a standard unit of currency used in the Qing period. Approximately 1,000 *wens* equals one *liang* 兩(tael of silver) (Harris 2018, IX).

11 *Qing* 頃 is a unit of area for measuring land in the Qing period. One *qing* is approximately 16 acres (Harris 2018, IX).

including banner laws, state laws, the laws of individual monasteries, and the laws of governing the Great Shabi (Ikh Shav'), the personal estate of the Jebtsundamba Khutugtus (Wallace 2014, 320). Buddhist monasteries, especially the large network of Geluk Buddhist monasteries in Inner Mongolia, also had their own internal monastic regulations in the form of *bca' yig*, or monastic constitutions that instituted administrative procedures, curricula, and financial protocols, among other things.[12]

During the Qing period, Mongolia was understood by the Mongols to be a constituent realm or *ulus* within the Qing empire that existed not as a part of but alongside China (*Khitad*) and Tibet (*Töbed*), so in this view, Mongolia had its distinctive way of life and government system that the Manchu Qing rulers preserved and nourished (Atwood 2002, 37–38). Governed separately from the rest of Qing China, Buddhist affairs in Mongolia were regulated from Beijing by the Lifanyuan, or the Court of Colonial Affairs that oversaw issues of the Qing Empire's frontiers. In governing Buddhism in Inner Mongolia, the Lifanyuan acted on behalf of the Manchu emperors in the dual law structure and was mostly responsible for codifying and promulgating regulations that were intended to bind all Buddhist monastics throughout Mongolia. Among other things, these regulations established administrative posts for monasteries, managed their salary schedules, handled requests that the emperor grant a name to a temple or contribute toward a temple's repair, planned visits of high-level lamas to the capital, regulated pilgrimages, prohibited certain groups of Mongols from becoming lamas, and restricted the right of lamas to be buried at the sacred site of Mount Wutai (Miller 1959, 76). The Lifanyuan also managed the titles and positions of prominent Mongolian and Tibetan Buddhist monastics, and even prevented high-level incarnate lamas from being identified among the Mongols, in order to curb their influence, although Mongolian incarnate lamas became more common in the late Qing (Atwood 2002, 36). As we will see in the next paragraphs, the regulation of Buddhism in the post-Qing attempted to preserve and maintain these Qing-era policies based on the dual law and priest–patron arrangements before more intrusive reforms were introduced.

15.4 REPUBLICAN CHINA'S REGULATIONS OF BUDDHISM IN INNER MONGOLIA

With the fall of the Qing empire in 1912, the Lifanyuan was abolished. Taking its place to govern the religious affairs of Inner Mongolia was the Mengzangju (Mongolian and Tibetan Affairs Bureau) of the Republic of China, which was later reorganized into the Mengzangyuan (Mongolian and Tibetan Ministry) in 1914 (Lin 2006, 32). This time, instead of a government agency managing the affairs of the Mongols and the Tibetans for the multicultural Manchu Qing empire, the Mengzangju and Mengzangyuan were agencies that served a modern nation-state

[12] On *bca' yig*, see Jansen 2018 and Sullivan 2021.

built on Sun Yat-sen's vision of "Five Races Under One Union" (*wuzu gonghe*). Under this vision, the Republic of China connoted a single nation formed through the union of the Han Chinese, the Manchus, the Mongols, the Tibetans, and the Muslims. Unlike the Qing Manchus that had created racial hierarchies that placed themselves at the top, the Republic of China pledged to treat all five races as equal before the law, eliminate any special status, and represent all five races in the new parliament (Atwood 2002, 39). However, in practice, the new Republic did not dare to eliminate the special ethno-legal statuses that these different ethnic groups had enjoyed under Qing rule (Atwood 2002, 40). To woo the support of the Inner Mongolia nobility, the President of the Republic, Yuan Shikai (1859–1916), maintained the privileges that the Mongol nobles had enjoyed in the Qing period, increased their salaries, and gave them prestigious posts in the capital (Atwood 2002, 40). For high-ranking Buddhist lamas, the same strategy of preserving Qing-era treatment was deployed (Boyan Mandu 1979, 109).

On the other hand, the new Republic was also aware of the large monastic presence in Inner Mongolia, which posed potential threats to the central authority and placed economic strain on the nation. Considering this, members of the Mengzangyuan, or the Mongolian and Tibetan Ministry, proposed the "Legislation for Limiting Mongols on Becoming Lamas"[13] in 1924. The six-article document proposed to prohibit the only child or the sole living heir of any given family from joining the Buddhist monastic order. Parents of children who did not wish to join the monastic order would be unable to force their children to become lamas, especially when they were underage. Those who wished to join the monastic order were required to report to their banner officials first and could only be ordained if the banner leaders had found that none of the articles had been violated (Mengzangyuan 1924, 43). This proposal expressed concern over the decline of the Mongols since the Qing and the decrease in population due the growth of Buddhist monasticism, and it argued that Buddhist monasticism must be limited if the Mongolian population was to bounce back (Mengzangyuan 1924, 42–43). A report carried out by the Mengzangyuan revealed that the proposal gained unanimous support within the Ministry, even though the Republic of China's Constitution at the time promised freedom of religion. On this point, the report explains that although the twelfth article of the Constitution of the Republic of China promised freedom of religion to its citizens, this proposed legislation was based on "the utmost of good intentions,"[14] because it was aimed at preventing a further decrease in the Mongolian population (Mengzangyuan 1924, 44–45). The report also reminded members of the Ministry to "not openly limit" monasticism and instead use the words of "respect and support" (Mengzangyuan 1924, 45).[15]

[13] 限制蒙人充當喇嘛案.

[14] 用意至善.

[15] 不必明白限制應改為尊崇黃教. *Huangjiao* 黃教, or "yellow religion," here refers to "Lamaist" Buddhism.

Similar limitations were imposed on Buddhist monasticism in Inner Mongolia when the Nationalist Government under Chiang Kai-shek was established, ushering in a period of political tutelage beginning in 1928. One of the first things that the Kuomintang (KMT) did when they came to power was to divide the central part of Inner Mongolia into the four new provinces of Rehe (Jehol), Chahar, Suiyuan, and Ningxia. Other Mongol regions were then incorporated into the provinces of Gansu, Ningxia, Heilongjiang, Liaoning, and Jilin (Lin 2006, 25). On this disfiguration of Inner Mongolia under the KMT, Hsiao-ting Lin writes, "The newly established provincial boundary cut ruthlessly across the traditional Mongol tribal and league or banner boundaries, contributing further to the Mongols' disunity and facilitating their ultimate colonization by the Han Chinese" (2006, 25).

Unlike the treatment of Buddhism in Inner Mongolia during the Yuan Shikai period, the state regulation of Buddhism in the Republic of China after the KMT came into power was more intrusive. Buddhist affairs were managed by the Mengzang weiyuanhui (Mongolian and Tibetan Affairs Commission, MTAC), which had to approve most decisions, such as the appointment of important lamas' reincarnations, the granting of monastic certifications, and the handling of *shabinar*. In June 1931, the KMT government issued the "Statutes for the Supervision of Mongolian Lama Monasteries"[16] where it stated that all "Lama" monasteries in Inner Mongolia must release all *shabinar*[17] from monastic possessions and that all monasteries report their registers and budgets annually to the MTAC (Wuliji 2015, 300–1). In December 1935, the "Statutes for the Management of Lama Monasteries"[18] were announced by the Republican government. The statutes further required all "Lamaist" monasteries and lamas to register with the MTAC, and stipulated that only the reincarnation identifications, appointments, and remunerations approved by the MTAC would be recognized (Zhongguo di'er lishi dang'an guan 1994, 13). In a supplementary directive to the statutes announced in January 1936 and entitled, "Measures for the Awards and Punishments of Lamas,"[19] lamas were rewarded with elevated titles and monetary prizes if "meritorious services"[20] were performed for the nation, and were punished through forced secularization, demotion of titles, and monetary fines if they did not register with the MTAC as prescribed (Zhongguo di'er lishi dang'an guan 1994, 14–16).

It is unclear whether these Republican Chinese regulations were enforced on the ground. Scholars of the Republic of China, such as Hsiao-ting Lin, have pointed out

16 蒙古喇嘛寺廟監督條例.

17 *Shabinar* are referred to as "black disciples" 黑徒 in Chinese. In contrast to this legislation in Inner Mongolia, the Mongolian People's Republic (Outer Mongolia) legislated to abolish the *shabinar* from the lama's estates following the death of the lama-emperor Bodg Khan in 1924 (Atwood 2004, 47).

18 管理喇嘛寺廟條例.

19 喇嘛獎懲辦法.

20 有大勳勞於國家.

that it should not be assumed that Chiang Kai-shek's asserted policies on China's frontier and minority affairs reflected what he and his regime intended to achieve, especially given the fact that the Nationalist Government, which emerged as a localized regime in Nanking, only had alleged authority over the vast border regions of Qing China (Lin 2006, 32). Lin argues that the KMT's assertion of sovereignty over the frontier was based on a political imagination that was engineered to maintain its nationalist façade and legitimacy (Lin 2006, 13). In fact, Lin reminds us that frontier policies were more important for internal power struggles within the Nationalist Party and that "regional militarists and politicians also capitalized on frontier and ethnopolitical issues to criticize and oppose their political enemies in Nanking" (Lin 2006, 32). In any case, the regulation of Buddhism in Inner Mongolia merged with a much broader set of political goals emanating from Nanking, namely, to create the impression of taming the frontier in order to consolidate the nation.

15.5 MANCHUKUO REGULATIONS OF BUDDHISM IN INNER MONGOLIA

While Buddhism in Inner Mongolia was being regulated in the laws of the Republic of China, the Japanese puppet states of Manchukuo and Mengjiang were also drafting competing regulations of Buddhism for the area under their control. Although Manchukuo encompassed most of northeast China, a significant Mongol population lived in the eastern part of the state, especially the Xing'an Province, which the Republic of China also claimed for itself. According to a 1940s study, the Xing'an region included 32 percent of the geographical area of Manchukuo and contained 64 percent of the Mongol population in all of Manchukuo (Qi 2016, 14). Connecting Manchukuo with the Soviet Union, Outer Mongolia, and the northern part of the Republic of China, the Xing'an region was considered to be geopolitically critical to Manchukuo and the "lifeline" (J: *seimei-sen*) of the Japanese Empire. In this crucial region, the presence of Mongolian Buddhism was dominant. Official statistics from the Manchukuo government records 29,697 lamas and 985 Buddhist monasteries in the region in the 1940s (Manzhou diguo zhengfu 1969, 830). A total of 61 percent[21] of these lamas were located in the Xing'an area alone (Manzhou diguo zhengfu 1969, 828–29).

In contrast to Republican Chinese laws, Manchukuo regulations of Buddhism in its Mongol regions attempted to separate Buddhism from political activities to reform Buddhist monasticism and to create transnational Buddhist organizations

[21] The population of lamas in the Xing'an region was as follows: Xing'an South Province 興安南省: 7,280; Xing'an West Province 興安西省: 7,566; Xing'an North Province 興安北省: 3,528. The total lama population in the Xing'an region was 18,374, which was 61.87 percent of the total lama population in Manchukuo, according to the statistics compiled by the Xing'an Bureau 興安局 in 1940.

and education programs. Nine months after the creation of Manchukuo, in December 1932, the Xing'an Provincial government issued a directive called "On the Prohibition of Lamas' Involvement in Politics."[22] This directive stated that the practice of dual law in the Inner Asian Buddhist tradition was incompatible with the new nation-state of Manchukuo, which was built on the foundations of "scientific development"[23] (Guowuyuan fazhichu 1936, 2).[24] The directive recognized that although religion (C: *zongjiao*, J: *shūkyō*) offered moral teachings and bonded people for the unity of societies, it had only been necessary in the past when humanity was "ignorant,"[25] and lacked the organizational units of families and nations (C: *jiaguo*, J: *kakoku*). With the establishment of bureaucratic structures and legal processes, the directive contends, the nation was able to use politics (C: *zhengzhi*, J: *seiji*) to regulate morality and discipline wrongful behaviors, rendering religion relevant only in the realm of spiritual salvation (Guowuyuan fazhichu 1936, 2). Thus, for Manchukuo, a modern state operating under the ideology of the "kingly way"[26] (C: *wangdao*, J: *ōdō*), the mix of politics with "Lamaism" was considered to be not only inappropriate but an unacceptable "immoral practice"[27] (Guowuyuan fazhichu 1936, 2). In other words, the directive made it apparent that Manchukuo now operated under a centralized authority of the "kingly way" in the Confucian model of sage rulership, and not in the model of the dual law that had been supported by the Manchu rulers of the Qing.

In August 1940, the Manchukuo government issued another, more comprehensive collection of policies regarding the regulation of Buddhism. Entitled, "Outline for the Reformation of Lamaism,"[28] this document contained policies to address the "problems" of Lamaism for the welfare of the Mongolian people (Manzhou diguo zhengfu 1969, 825). These "problems" were the "low quality" of lamas, the heavy economic burdens that lamas and monasteries had created for the Mongolian people, and the issue of depopulation caused by regional overpopulation of monastics (Manzhou diguo zhengfu 1969, 825). To solve these "problems" of Mongolian Buddhism in Manchukuo, the Outline lists the following seven articles of reform.

The first article of reform was the creation of the Manchukuo Empire Lamaist Group[29] that would unite all the lamas in the nation under one organization. This

[22] 關於禁止喇嘛干政之件/喇嘛ノ政治干涉禁止ニ関スル件.

[23] 科學發達.

[24] The specific location of this document in the *Manzhouguo faling jilan*, vol. 2 is in the fourth section on religion.

[25] 無知無識.

[26] The idea of the "kingly way" was based on the Confucian concept of sage rulership in which the ruler governed with the mandate of heaven. Policymakers of Manchukuo used the idea to justify the restoration of the last Qing emperor, Pu Yi (1906–67), as the emperor of the state (Young 1998, 286).

[27] 弊端.

[28] 喇嘛教整頓綱要/喇嘛教整備に就て.

[29] 滿洲帝國喇嘛教宗團/満洲帝国喇嘛教宗団.

new organization would not only centralize followers of Tibeto-Mongolian Buddhism into a nationwide religious reform movement, but it would also prevent "blind dependency"[30] on khutugtus from outside the nation.

The second article claimed to remedy the imputed fact that many of the 30,000 lamas within Manchukuo were uneducated, illiterate, and unaccomplished. In order to "improve" the situation, public secular education programs would be established within major monasteries and reeducation programs introduced for underage lamas. These public education programs were aimed at inserting modern knowledge into existing monastic curricula to cultivate the future leaders of Mongolian Buddhism. Monastic study-abroad programs were also initiated where young Mongolian lamas would be sent to Buddhist monasteries in Japan to study, where "the most correct Buddha Dharma flourished."[31]

Third, the ranks, titles, and posts of Mongol lamas that had been preserved in the region needed to be organized and centralized under the approval of the Manchukuo Empire Lamaist Group, which implied yet another intervention at restructuring the monastic organization systems established since the Qing.

Although the Tibetan language was the *lingua franca* among Mongol Buddhists in the region, the fourth article encouraged Mongols to use Buddhist texts in Mongolian language in their daily practices and liturgies. Showing awareness that changing the language of religious rituals overnight is not an easy task, the article recommended a gradual promotion of Mongolian Buddhist texts.

Articles five and six addressed perceived deficiencies in monastic infrastructure. Article five promised that, in addition to establishing the Manchukuo Empire Lamaist Group, the Manchukuo government would found a national head temple (J: *sōhonzan*) for all the lamas of Manchukuo at a suitable location headed by a respectable khutugtu. Article six promised that the economic management of Buddhist monasteries in the state was to be systematized. Specifically, a clear financial management system needed to be set in place to oversee the assets of the monasteries and the daily spending of the monastic community.[32]

Seventh, regarding the Mongol lay Buddhist population, an emphasis was put on the development of secular public education, especially for the cultivation of "a critical stance toward the superstitious elements within Lamaism"[33] (Manzhou diguo zhengfu 1969, 825–27). Interestingly, what entailed "superstitious elements" was not elaborated on in the document.

As with the regulation of Buddhism in Inner Mongolia under Republican Chinese laws, it is unclear how these Manchukuo policies directed at reforming Mongolian Buddhism were implemented on the ground. The Manchukuo Empire

30 盲目的依存性.
31 世界に於て最も正法の興隆せる日本佛教.
32 Notably, in contrast to the Republican Chinese regulations of Buddhist assets in Inner Mongolia that prescribed the abolition of *shabinar* subjects, these Manchukuo articles did not.
33 喇嘛教が多分に有する迷信的要素に対する批判力の養成.

Lamaist Group was indeed created on December 5, 1940, in Xinjing, the capital of Manchukuo, and was headed by the Chagan Khutugtu, a high-ranking Mongolian lama, and the Japanese vice director Satō Tomie (Narangoa 2003, 501). About two hundred Mongol lamas were also sent to Japan to study between 1932 and 1945, funded by Japanese Buddhist organizations such as the Jōdo, Shingon, and Tendai schools (Narangoa 2003, 500). However, these policies did not seem to spark significant discussions of Buddhist reform among the Mongols themselves.[34] On the effects of these policies toward Mongolian Buddhism, Narangoa Li writes:

> In general, the response of the Mongol leaders in Manchukuo to Japanese reform efforts was selective. They were happy with the introduction of modern facilities such as health care and medical training and they were generally willing to accept the broadening of the education system and the promotion of Mongol culture. But especially on more strictly doctrinal issues, the Mongolian lamas and politicians saw little reason to change their established beliefs and practices at the behest of the Japanese. (Narangoa 2003, 501)

Interestingly, Thomas DuBois has found that as in the case of codified laws of Manchukuo, case records were largely silent on the topic of Buddhism and religion in general (DuBois 2017, 126), which again raises the issue of the actual implementation and enforcement of Manchukuo regulations on Buddhism. DuBois adds, "such silence on the topic of religion notably contrasts not only with the activism displayed in government ordinances, but also with the pivotal role that other judiciaries have subsequently played in the interpretation of religion" (2017, 127–28). Similar to how Buddhism in Inner Mongolia was governed under the Republic of China with an "imagined sovereignty" over the frontier region, the Manchukuo policies were probably more active on paper than in practice.

15.6 MENGJIANG REGULATIONS OF BUDDHISM IN INNER MONGOLIA

As Japanese influence expanded from Manchuria to Inner Mongolia following the establishment of Manchukuo in 1932, the puppet state of the Mengjiang United Autonomous Government was created in 1941 under the military leadership of Demchugdongrub (1902–66), a Mongol prince who also spearheaded an independence movement in Inner Mongolia. At first, the same policies toward Buddhism created in Manchukuo were to be implemented in Mengjiang (Hirokawa 2007, 92). However, being a Qing-era Mongol noble and a devout Buddhist sandwiched between rising Chinese, Japanese, and Soviet powers, Demchugdongrub looked

[34] Narangoa contends that "Although many monasteries sent young lamas to Japan to study, most of the lamas remained faithful to their belief in the tenets of Mongolian Buddhism. Only a few of the lamas who studied in Japanese Buddhist temples and schools were attracted to the religious forms they were introduced to in Japan" (2003, 505).

to the past to the traditions of the Qing for inspiration in his management of Buddhist affairs in his state. As a result, the Office of Lama Seals and Services (C: *lama yinwuchu*), a Qing-era administrative agency overseeing Buddhist affairs in Mongolia and Tibet, was revived (Hirokawa 2007, 92). However, the prince was not unreceptive to the suggestions of modern reforms of Buddhism suggested by the policies of Manchukuo. As Hirokawa has pointed out, Demchugdongrub was supportive of the Buddhist reform measures aimed at solving the depopulation issue among his fellow Mongols (2007, 92). Thus, at the Xilingol League Conference of 1942, the administration under Prince Demchugdongrub promulgated regulations to limit monasticism. These regulations prohibited the only son of any family from joining the monastic order, and put a cap of four as the maximum number of monastics a given family could have (Narangoa 2003, 503).

By the end of 1942, qualifying monastic examinations were carried out in the various leagues in Mengjiang, promoting the secularization of Buddhist lamas in the region. For example, after lama qualifying examinations were instituted in the Ulanqab League, only 375 individuals out of 525 passed.[35] Out of the remaining 150 individuals, 55 joined the army, and 95 joined other forms of secular occupations (Hirokawa 2007, 92). In 1943, the Mengjiang government further tightened its grip on the growth of monasticism. Newspapers at this time began criticizing the tradition of child lamas and blamed Tibetan Buddhism for the decrease in the Mongolian population (Hirokawa 2007, 94).

As for how these reform policies toward Buddhism were received by the Mongols, Narangoa suggests that there was neither enthusiastic support nor significant protest. She argues that Mongolian Buddhist resistance to Japanese policies in the puppet states of Manchukuo and Mengjiang was weaker than that of colonial Korea, and there were no active Mongolian Buddhist attempts to protest Japanese invasion and war, nor cases of entire monasteries converting to Japanese Buddhism, as had occurred in colonial Korea and Taiwan (2003, 506).

15.7 GOVERNING BUDDHISM ON THE FRONTIERS OF THE NATION AND THE EMPIRE

To summarize, the regulation of Buddhism in Inner Mongolia in the post-Qing by the Republic of China, Manchukuo, and the Mengjiang governments began with a continuation of Qing-era policies. In the early years of the Republic of China, the socioeconomic statuses that high-level Buddhist leaders in Inner Mongolia had enjoyed in the Qing were maintained and even further elevated in service of political alliance-making. Considering the amount of political, religious, social, and even emotional capital that the Buddhist institution was able to maintain in Inner

[35] For these qualifying examinations, monastics were tested on their knowledge of Buddhist doctrines and practices.

Mongolia, all three of these modern East Asian states chose not to drastically disrupt the status quo of dual law that respected the Buddhist clergy as much as (if not more than) the state. As a result, although the policymakers of these modern states saw Buddhism in Inner Mongolia as an outdated "superstitious" institution that caused the decline of Mongolian society both demographically and economically, the reforms that they wanted to see had to be planned gradually and diplomatically.

Beginning in the mid-1920s, the policies of these three modern states toward Buddhism in Inner Mongolia began to limit monasticism and Mongolian Buddhist agency. To diminish the power of Buddhist monasticism in Inner Mongolia and to increase the non-monastic population in the form of mobilizable labor forces for the nation and the empire, the tradition of "monk taxes," which required families sending at least one male child to the Buddhist monastic system, was restricted in various ways. As an alternative to the Buddhist monastery, which had served as one of the only venues for education in Qing Inner Mongolia, modern public secular education was offered to children and young adults, often on the sites of large monasteries. In the 1930s, Buddhism in Inner Mongolia was regulated to be separated from political involvement, and the management of monastic affairs was given to new structures of monastic organizations created by these modern states to deal specifically with ethnic religious matters on the frontiers. In this period, Buddhism in Inner Mongolia was increasingly the subject of biopolitics and governed as a political-economic issue for the state. Monastic assets, such as property, income, herds, and monastic population were required to be registered with the central government. The practice of holding *shabinar*, or lay subjects at monasteries for labor, was also abolished.

But as we have discussed in the previous paragraphs, how these regulations were implemented on the ground, if they were indeed implemented at all, is rather murky. Situating Buddhism in Inner Mongolia spatially on the frontiers of Sinocentric and Japan-centric nation-states, these regulations of Buddhism were mostly top-down elite legal practices directed from metropolitan centers at the periphery. As Hsiao-ting Lin has contended, frontier policy for the Republic of China was a form of "imagined sovereignty" (Lin 2006, 15), which I argue the Japanese puppet states of Manchukuo and Mengjiang similarly participated in, given the fact that both puppet states did not stay in power long enough for their policies to be implemented effectively on the ground. Observing how these post-Qing modern East Asian states made competing claims of "imagined sovereignty" over Inner Mongolia, we can see that overlapping legal structures were created that competed to govern Buddhism in the region. These competing regulations and frontier policies may have played a role in the internal power conflicts of these modern states, such as in the case of the Kuomintang, but they were also useful for nation-building and empire-building projects. For the policymakers of the Republic of China, Manchukuo, and Mengjiang, Buddhism was one of the only trans-Asian threads that could link ethnic groups with different languages and cultures together under one nation and/or empire. Therefore, having the power to manage and govern Buddhist institutions meant the ability to tap into and mobilize the political, economic, and social capital of the religion, and to do so transnationally.

As tools of nation-building and empire-building, these elite regulations assumed a linear temporality and a teleology of "progress" and "modernization" for Inner Mongolian Buddhism deemed "unproductive" and "backwards." I argue that this is a form of epistemic violence inflicted on the religious bodies (especially the non-tulku ones) on the peripheries of modern national and imperial projects. In her well-known essay, "Can the Subaltern Speak?" Gayatri Spivak states that "The clearest available example of such epistemic violence is the remotely orchestrated, far-flung, and heterogeneous project to constitute the colonial subject as Other" (Spivak 2003). The state regulations of Buddhism in our Inner Mongolia case are examples of this colonial project remotely orchestrated to constitute the Other through competing and overlapping frontier policies.

It is important to remember that the practice of epistemic violence through legal processes preceded actual violence in the Mongolian case. In post-Qing Outer Mongolia, similar limitations were created to curb Buddhist monasticism in the region, especially after the fall of the theocratic Bogda Khan government when the socialist Mongolian People's Republic (1924–92) came into power. Under the leadership of Khorloogiin Choibalsan (1895–1952), approximately 18,000 lamas were killed in a socialist purge lasting eighteen months from late 1937 to mid-1939, and all but a handful of Buddhist monasteries were destroyed across the country (Kaplonski 2014, 5). Before the carnage took place, however, modern legal and bureaucratic frameworks existed to "know and control the population and the lamas, to introduce measures of governmentality, and to rule through the economic deployment rather than the blunt application of power" (Kaplonski 2014, 226). As Christopher Kaplonski shows, for the Mongolian socialist state, the problem of the lamas was "not that they were religious but that they possessed substantial economic, political, and ideological power" (2014, 227). The way that the socialist state chose to solve this "lama question" was first through accommodation, symbolic violence, structural violence, and proactive measures before choosing direct physical violence (Kaplonski 2014, 226). Indeed, state violence for modern Mongolia was not an event but a process that involved multiple modes of violence.

In Inner Mongolia, although the Republic of China and the Japanese puppet states of Manchukuo and Mengjiang did not manage to stay in power long enough to purge Buddhism on a similarly massive scale,[36] their legacy of governing

[36] The monastic population in Inner Mongolia declined gradually throughout the decades after the fall of the Qing Empire. Compared to the Qing period which had about 100,000 lamas and 1,600 monasteries and temples in the region, there were about 60,000 lamas and 1,366 monasteries and temples after 1945 (Delege 1998, 452–53). This translates to an approximate 40 percent decrease in monastic population and a 15 percent decrease in Buddhist sites between 1912 and 1945.

Buddhism and the infliction of epistemic violence through legal practices would later be inherited by the Chinese Communist Party in its policies toward ethnic minorities' religions in the People's Republic of China. In May 1947, the Inner Mongolia Autonomous Region was established under the leadership of the Chinese Communist Party, two years before the establishment of the People's Republic of China itself in October 1949. In the "Policy Guidelines for the Inner Mongolia Autonomous Government,"[37] announced on April 27, 1947, "freedom of religion" was promised to the Mongols in the region. However, in the same document, "separation of religion from the state"[38] was to be instituted. Lamas were also persuaded to "voluntarily" participate in secular industries and join the larger labor force (Zhonggong zhongyang tongzhanbu 1991, 1111–13).[39]

By the early 1960s, there were about 17,000 Buddhist monks in Inner Mongolia, compared to 100,000 at the end of the Qing period (Delege 1998, 761). According to a 1961 survey, 11,584 lamas out of 13,000 surveyed participated in forms of secular labor. Of these, 354 individuals were involved in mining, 2,330 in agriculture, 6,400 in husbandry, 1,200 in medicine, and 1,300 in other industries (Delege 1998, 761). During the Cultural Revolution in the late 1960s and 1970s, Buddhism in Inner Mongolia experienced brutal repressions similar to that of the Mongolian People's Republic in the 1930s and was one of the worst affected areas within the People's Republic of China. According to official statistics, the Cultural Revolution resulted in over 22,000 deaths and 300,000 injuries in Inner Mongolia (Brown 2007). The Buddhist community was heavily affected in the campaign to remove "the Four Olds." It is unclear how many Buddhist monastics in Inner Mongolia were killed or injured during this period, but according to official statistics, only 5,000 lamas were found in the region after the Cultural Revolution in 1984, and 3,854 out of these 5,000 lamas reported no sources of income (Delege 1998, 779). The number of Buddhist monasteries still standing in the area was also reduced from at least 1,600 at the end of the Qing period to less than 500 after the storm of the Cultural Revolution (Delege 1998, 777). Only seventy-two monasteries received renovation funds from the government and were reopened to the public between 1985 and 1995 (Delege 1998, 777).

15.8 WHAT CAN THE INNER MONGOLIA CASE TELL US ABOUT CONSTITUTIONAL LAW AND BUDDHISM?

The Inner Mongolia case discussed in this chapter can tell us at least four things about the relationship between constitutional law and Buddhism in the modern

[37] 內蒙古自治政府施政綱領.

[38] 實行信教自由與政教分立.

[39] 提倡喇嘛自願投資經營農工商業與各種合作事業，獎勵喇嘛自願入學與參加勞動，行醫，識字.

East Asian context. First, although the constitutional practices of modern East Asian states were mostly influenced by western law,[40] they contained considerable continuities with the laws of imperial China when it came to the regulation of Buddhism in Inner Asia. Western constitutional ideas such as "freedom of religion" were present in the modern East Asian constitutional discourses discussed in this chapter, but they had to be mediated through previously existing political formations and structures, such as the tradition of dual law that allowed Buddhism to play key roles in legitimating or resisting political and legal orders.

Secondly, when we observe how Buddhism in Inner Mongolia was regulated in post-Qing East Asia, we begin to see that there were parallel, overlapping, and competing legal structures in place. Different laws were created to regulate different traditions of Buddhism in different geographical regions practiced by people of different ethnicities. This can be seen in the varieties of legal vocabulary developed to govern Buddhism. For example, while institutional Buddhism was regulated as *fojiao* in the Republic of China, Buddhism in Inner Mongolia was regulated as *lamajiao*, or "Lamaism," which was understood as an ethnic religious tradition that needed uniquely designed modernizing reforms. Thus, the regulation of religion on the frontier regions, which was more often informed by frontier policies, can look very different from the regulation of religion in the rest of the nation. At the same time, the Inner Mongolia case shows that in the modern East Asian context, there could be overlapping and even competing legal structures – competing constitutions – operating simultaneously when it comes to the regulation of religion. Competing claims of sovereignty over the region of Inner Mongolia allowed modern states backed by very different political ideologies to "flex their legal muscles" in religion governance in overlapping and competing ways.

Thirdly, the state governance of religion in modern East Asia reveals its teleological dimension. Situating the region of Inner Mongolia and its people in a particular spatiality and temporality, namely, the "frontier" and the "pre-modern," Buddhism and Buddhist monasticism in Inner Mongolia came to be understood as "uncivilized," "backwards," and even morally "degenerate" in the reform policies of the Republic of China and the Japanese puppet states of Manchukuo and Mengjiang. Following this logic, Buddhism in Inner Mongolia was governed and disciplined in these state regulations as a political-economic and biopolitical problem. As DuBois has pointed out in his study of religion in early twentieth-century northeast Asia, "[l]awmaking and social policy are not merely a passive platform for the expression of religious ideas, but a realm of ethical and theological exploration in their own right" (2017, 109).

40 Maria Adele Carrai has shown in her work on the governance of Tibet in Republican China that strategies of empire are not only a prerogative of the West but were also adopted by both the Republican China and later the People's Republic of China, to assert themselves in the international domain as sovereign states and pursue their fictional claims over Tibet (Carrai 2017, 801).

Lastly, these parallel, overlapping, and competing regulations of religion created paradigms of constitutional practice that created a legacy of religion governance and frontier policies that would be inherited by subsequent nation-states, even if the new state operated under a different political ideology. I argue that this legacy of the governance of religion on the frontiers exemplifies a legacy of epistemic violence carried out through the processes of law-making. This legacy has been passed on from the Qing to the People's Republic of China. As Ilana Feldman argued in her book *Governing Gaza*, the authority of any governmental bureaucracy is reiterative; it has to be enacted through practice as an ongoing process and cannot simply be established once and for all (2008, 15).[41] Interestingly, the legacy of reiterative authority examined in this chapter only reveals the contingent nature of these modern East Asian states, be it the Republic of China, Manchukuo, Mengjiang, or the People's Republic of China.

REFERENCES

Atwood, Christopher. 2002. *Young Mongols and Vigilantes in Inner Mongolia's Interregnum Decades, 1911–1931*. Leiden: Brill.

2004. *Encyclopedia of Mongolia and the Mongol Empire*. New York: Facts on File.

Barrett, Timothy Hugh. 2014. "Buddhism and Law in China: The Emergences of Distinctive Patterns in Chinese History." In *Buddhism and Law: An Introduction*, edited by Rebecca R. French and Mark A. Nathan, 201–16. Cambridge: Cambridge University Press.

Boyan Mandu. 1979. "Huiyi xinhai geming." In *Neimenggu Xinhai Geming Shiliao*, 74–76. Hohhot: Neimenggu renmin chubanshe.

Brown, Kerry. 2007. "The Cultural Revolution in Inner Mongolia 1967–1969: The Purge of the 'Heirs of Genghis Khan'." *Asian Affairs* 38 (2):173–87.

Carrai, Maria Adele. 2017. "Learning Western Techniques of Empire: Republican China and the New Legal Framework for Managing Tibet." *International Legal Theory* 30: 801–24.

Delege. 1998. *Neimenggu lamajiao shi*. Hohhot: Neimenggu renmin chubanshe.

DuBois, Thomas David. 2017. *Empire and the Meaning of Religion in Northeast Asia: Manchuria 1900–1945*. Cambridge: Cambridge University Press.

Feldman, Ilana. 2008. *Governing Gaza: Bureaucracy, Authority, and the Work of Rule, 1917–1967*. Durham and London: Duke University Press.

French, Rebecca R. 2004. "The Case of the Missing Discipline: Finding Buddhist Legal Studies." *Buffalo Law Review* 52 (3): 679–700.

Guowuyuan fazhichu, ed. 1936. *Manzhouguo faling jilan, vol. 2*. Xinjing: Manzhou xingzheng xuehui.

Harris, Lane J. 2018. *The Peking Gazette: A Reader in Nineteenth-century Chinese History*. Leiden: Brill.

Hirokawa, Saho. 2007. "Mōkyō seiken no tai-Mongoru seisaku – Manshūkoku to no hikaku wo tsūjite." In *Nihon no Mōkyō senryō: 1937–1945*, edited by Tomoyuki Uchida and Yoshimasa Shibata. Tokyo: Kenbun shuppansha.

Huricha. 2009. *Qingdai Neimenggu diqu siyuan jingji yanjiu*. Shenyang: Liaoning minzu chubanshe.

Qingdai Menggu simiao guanli tizhi yanjiu. Shenyang: Liaoning minzu chubanshe.

[41] I am grateful for Kaplonski's *The Lama Question* (2014) for introducing me to Feldman's work.

Jansen, Berthe. 2018. *The Monastery Rules: Buddhist Monastic Organization in Pre-Modern Tibet*. Oakland: University of California Press.
Josephson, Jason Ānanda. 2012. *The Invention of Religion in Japan*. Chicago: University of Chicago Press.
Kaplonski, Christopher. 2014. *The Lama Question: Violence, Sovereignty, and Exception in Early Socialist Mongolia*. Honolulu: University of Hawaiʻi Press.
Lin, Hsiao-ting. 2006. *Tibet and Nationalist China's Frontier: Intrigues and Ethnopolitics, 1928–49*. Vancouver: University of British Columbia Press.
Lopez, Donald S. 1996. "'Lamaism' and the Disappearance of Tibet." *Comparative Studies in Society and History* 38 (1): 3–25.
1998. *Prisoners of Shangri-La: Tibetan Buddhism and the West*. Chicago: University of Chicago Press.
Manzhou diguo zhengfu, ed. 1969. *Manzhou jianguo shinian shi*. Tokyo: Hara shōbō.
Mengzangyuan. 1924. *Mengzangyuan zhaoji Mengshi huiyi yishilu*. Publisher unknown.
Miller, Robert. 1959. *Monasteries and Culture Change in Inner Mongolia*. Wiesbaden: Otto Harrassowitz.
Mongolbank. n.d. "History of Mongolian Currency." Accessed October 4, 2021. www.mongolbank.mn/eng/listbanknote.aspx?id=15.
Moses, Larry William. 1977. *The Political Role of Mongol Buddhism*. Bloomington: Asian Studies Research Institute, Indiana University.
Narangoa, Li. 2003. "Japanese Imperialism and Mongolian Buddhism, 1932–1945." *Critical Asian Studies* 35 (4): 491–514.
Qi, Baishun. 2016. *Riben qinzhan shiqi "Xing'an sheng" jingji tongzhi zhengce yanjiu*. Shenyang: Liaoning chubanshe.
Ruegg, David Seyfort. 2014. "The Temporal and the Spiritual, and the So-called Patron–Client Relation in the Governance of Inner Asia and Tibet." in *Patronage as Politics in South Asia*, edited by Anastasia Piliavsky. Cambridge: Cambridge University Press.
Schonthal, Benjamin and Tom Ginsburg. 2016. "Setting an Agenda for the Socio-Legal Study of Contemporary Buddhism." *Asian Journal of Law and Society* 3: 1–15.
Spivak, Gayatri Chakravorty. 2003. "Can the Subaltern Speak?" In *Colonial Discourse and Post-Colonial Theory*, edited by Patrick Williams and Laura Chrisman. New York: Columbia University Press.
Sullivan, Brenton. 2021. *Building a Religious Empire*. Philadelphia: University of Pennsylvania Press.
Tuttle, Gray. 2005. *Tibetan Buddhists in the Making of Modern China*. New York: Columbia University Press.
Wallace, Vesna. 2014. "Buddhist Laws in Mongolia." In *Buddhism and Law: An Introduction*, edited by Rebecca R. French and Mark A. Nathan. Cambridge: Cambridge University Press.
Wuliji Taogetao, ed. 2015. *Minguo zhengfu youguan Menggu de falv*. Chifeng: Neimenggu kexue jishu chubanshe.
Young, Louise. 1998. *Japan's Total Empire: Manchuria and the Culture of Wartime Imperialism*. Berkeley: University of California Press.
Zhongguo di'er lishi dang'an guan, ed. 1994. *Zhonghua minguo shi dang'an ziliao huibian: vol. 5, no. 1*. Nanjing: Jiangsu guji chubanshe.
Zhonggong zhongyang tongzhanbu. 1991. "Neimenggu zizhi zhengfu shizheng gangling." In *Minzu wenti wenxian huibian*, 1111–13. Beijing: Zhongguo zhongyang dangxiao chubanshe.

16

Buddhist Constitutional Battlegrounds

Using the Courts to Litigate Monastic Celibacy in South Korea (1955–1970)

Mark A. Nathan

16.1 INTRODUCTION

On November 24, 1960, at around three o'clock in the afternoon, six young monks (all between the ages of 21 and 35) surreptitiously entered the Supreme Court building in Seoul, South Korea. Upset about a ruling that had been handed down earlier that day, they demanded to see the Chief Justice, but upon learning that he was out, they went to the office of the presiding judge, Ko Chaeho. Although the young monks were told that the presiding judge, too, was not in his office, they barged in anyway, announcing their intention to wait for him. At least some of the monks present that day were familiar with this office, having visited just one day prior with their senior monastic leader, Chŏngdam *sŭnim*, who had lectured Ko about the righteousness of their cause. The leader had also apparently warned the judge that if the Court ruled against their side in the pending case, the monks seated before him were prepared to become martyrs for the cause.

Thus, the next day, after delivering a short message explaining their opposition to the Court's ruling, each of them pulled out a knife and, as promised, attempted to disembowel themselves right there in the judge's office. When the crowd of some four hundred Buddhist monks, nuns, and laity who had gathered outside the courthouse to demonstrate heard a rumor that the young monks had killed themselves to protest the decision, they stormed the Supreme Court building. This chain of events resulted in over three hundred arrests, including the six young men who had tried unsuccessfully to commit suicide, as well as Chŏngdam himself, who was accused of orchestrating the events from behind the scenes.[1]

[1] Ninety-three nuns and four laywomen were among those taken into custody. Most of those initially detained were eventually let go, and of the fifty-two who were prosecuted, only twenty-four were ultimately sentenced. This included, it should be noted, the six monks who had disemboweled themselves. Although Chŏngdam was initially taken into custody, the charges against him were dropped and he was even allowed to testify at the trial of the younger monks (Pak 2007).

This incident remains as shocking to learn about today as it was for those hearing about it just over six decades ago when it occurred. Although those protesting at the Supreme Court that day were roundly condemned in the press for their extreme actions, public opinion at the time was decidedly in their favor when it came to the larger goals of their so-called purification movement (*chŏnghwa undong* 淨化運動). The monks who snuck into the Supreme Court building ostensibly to commit *hara-kiri* were part of a minority group of monastics who had sought to restore the vow of celibacy in post-colonial South Korea as a necessary qualification for membership in the Korean monastic order. They had managed to wrest control of the Chogye Order (Chogyejong 曹溪宗) from the dominant faction that permitted monks to marry and eat meat, but only with the heavy support of the president at the time, Syngman Rhee.

This story of married monks and attempted disemboweling may seem like an odd way to start a chapter on Buddhism and constitutional law, but the emotionally charged events described above also involve an important set of legal disputes that help to illuminate the mechanics of Buddhism and constitutional law in Korea. The purification movement has been studied from a wide variety of perspectives, but few studies have fully appreciated what one might call the "clash of constitutions" that lies at its core. Celibacy may have been the most visible theme in the legal battles over control of the Chogye Order, but the court cases and extra-judicial conflicts were not really about celibacy per se. Rather, litigants and judges in these cases focussed instead on the legal justifications for revising the Chogye Order's own constitution (*chonghŏn* 宗憲) or, by extension, the legality of the meeting or gathering in which these changes were authorized.

Neither the Vinaya, nor any traditional temple regulations that predated the colonial period, represented legitimate sources of authority under the law. The courts were concerned only with the written constitution, rules, and regulations of an organization composed of members who self-identified as Buddhist. At the same time, the Korean courts – guided as they were by their own national constitution – were unwilling to wade into the doctrinal disputes over celibacy due to the provisions contained in Article 12 of the 1948 Constitution that guaranteed freedom of religion and the separation of religion and the state.[2] Ultimately then, the clash between unmarried and married monks – between supporters of monastic "purification" and proponents of the status quo – became a contest over the respective legitimacy of two rival Buddhist monastic constitutions written by and representing the rival factions. And that contest was enabled, even encouraged, by legal mandates stemming from state law.

[2] South Korea's first constitution was adopted on July 17, 1948. Article 12 reads "All citizens shall enjoy freedom of faith and conscience. No state religion shall exist. Religion shall be separated from politics."

16.2 PRELUDE TO THE PURIFICATION MOVEMENT: TEMPLE LAWS AND MONASTIC MARRIAGES IN THE COLONIAL PERIOD

The origins of the above events can be traced to the period of Japanese colonial rule (1910–1945), when clerical marriages among Korean monks became normalized and increasingly common. Korean monks who may have had wives or concubines, and sometimes families, could certainly be found prior to Japan's colonial takeover of Korea, but such relationships were usually kept secret. Exposure to Japanese Buddhism in the late nineteenth and early twentieth centuries, however, introduced the idea that monks could legally marry. Clerical marriage in Japan had been decriminalized in 1872 during the early years of the Meiji period (1868–1912). In Korea during the mid-1920s, celibacy was removed from the requirements necessary to become the abbot of a temple according to Korean own temple laws (*sabŏp* 寺法), which were then approved by the government-general.[3] The colonial government claimed the sole legal power to approve or certify revisions to the temple laws, but did not assert the power to enforce (or, conversely, to abrogate) the Vinaya precepts that ostensibly underpinned monastic conduct. These powers had been formalized through the creation of the Temple Ordinance (*sach'allyŏng* 寺刹令) in 1911, after the start of colonial rule, as a way for the Japanese government-general to regulate the entire Korean monastic community.[4] This law mandated the creation of temple laws, which were legal rules laying out the administrative authorities and regulations to be observed by monks living at a particular temple. When the long-standing desire to create a centralized monastic order finally brought about the creation of the Chosŏn Pulgyo Chogyejong in 1941, a constitution (*hŏn* 憲) for the monastic order (*chong* 宗) that superseded the individual temple laws was written, which set out the qualifications to become a monk or a temple abbot, as well as other positions within the monastic order.[5] However, with no way to adjudicate the propriety or impropriety of allowing monks to marry and eat meat based on the Vinaya or other sources of Buddhist law, court rulings in this matter necessarily revolved around the issue of who had the power to revise the monastic order's constitution (*chonghŏn*) and whether the actions taken to do so were in accordance with the organization's own governing procedures.

Discussions of law and Buddhism during the Japanese colonial period (1910–1945) typically begin (and often end) with a discussion of the Temple Ordinance (*sach'allyŏng*) mentioned above. Studies of colonial-era Korean Buddhism have

3 Kue-jin Song has persuasively argued recently that the colonial government's approval of these changes to the temple regulations was granted reluctantly in response to the growing presence of married Korean monks and demands for change (Song 2019).

4 The Temple Ordinance was promulgated as Law No. 7 on June 3, 1911 (Meiji 44).

5 Disputes over the monastic constitution and attempted revisions led to further strife in the 1990s, although by that time authoritarianism had given way to democracy in South Korea and the number of monastic orders had multiplied significantly.

comprehensively traced the law's broader implications for the exercise of state power and colonial control over the Buddhist community, and the practical impact of the law on Buddhism has been widely examined. The law itself, though, is actually rather short, consisting of just seven articles, only five of which actually contain substantive content. Briefly, the Temple Ordinance required government approval for the disposal of any temple property (Article 5), for merging, relocating, closing, or renaming temples (Article 1), and for any activities taking place at temples and monasteries other than those specified by this law (Article 2).[6] In addition, Article 4 mandated the appointment of an abbot (*chuji* 住持) to act as the legal representative of the temple. The abbot had to assume responsibility for administrative duties, including managing all property and assets of the temple, and for carrying out ceremonies and rituals at the temple. Article 3 stipulated the creation of temple laws (*sabŏp*), which had to be officially approved by the Japanese governor-general, and these regulations not only detailed the relationship between head or main monasteries (*ponsan* 本山) and branch temples (*malsa* 末寺), but also set forth the necessary qualifications for becoming an abbot.[7] These temple laws came to play an important role in the question of clerical marriages during the colonial period since the revisions approved by the government-general in 1926 removed celibacy from the list of required qualifications to assume the duties of abbot, which seemed to open the door to legal recognition of monastic marriages.[8]

In addition to these seven articles, the Temple Ordinance also came with a set of enforcement rules that further spelled out the legal regulations and rules to which monasteries and temples would be subjected.[9] The enforcement rules mainly elaborated on the third and fourth articles of the Temple Ordinance concerning, respectively, the temple laws, especially the head-branch temple structure, and the role and duties of the abbot as the legal representative of a temple. Article 1 stated that the temple laws must explicitly address the procedures for selecting and replacing an abbot or otherwise handling a vacancy in the post, but Article 2 gave the ultimate power to decide who would serve as abbot to the colonial state, negating the independence that Article 1 seemed to promise. In the case of the thirty head monasteries (later increased to thirty-one), the abbot had to be approved

6 A copy of the law (in Korean) can be found in Yi [1918] 2003, 249–51.

7 The last two articles of the law merely spell out the penalties for the failure to comply with the law (Article 6) and empower the government-general to enact any further provisions as needed (Article 7).

8 In fact, as Jeongeun Park has convincingly shown, the temple laws did not actually determine the legality of monastic marriages. Her careful study of the archives demonstrates that household registers, which the Japanese had instituted in 1909, were the actual avenues that monks used to gain legal recognition for their marriages, often under their secular names (Park 2016; Park 2017, 131–63).

9 The *Sach'allyŏng sihaeng kyuch'ik* (寺刹令施行規則), Law No. 84, was promulgated on July 8, 1911. Comprised of eight articles in total, it contained additional rules and regulations that were needed for the actual implementation of the law. Both the Temple Ordinance and its enforcement rules took effect on September 1 that same year.

directly by the governor-general, while the branch temples could obtain the consent of provincial officials when filling the post. The remaining articles dealt mostly with matters pertaining to the position of abbot.

Article 3 of the Temple Ordinance instructed the thirty "head temples" to compose "temple laws," which were designed to cover a wide range of monastic operations and activities related to the structure, organization, offices, and finances of the head monasteries and their branch temples.[10] The laws appear to have been based in part on the sectarian regulations and temple laws found contemporaneously in Japan, and they generally follow a similar pattern of 13 chapters and roughly 100 articles.[11] Jeongeun Park points out, however, that through "a clever blend of Korean Buddhist practices and Japanese Buddhist customs," the Korean temple laws were largely accepted by the Korean Buddhist community. Park further posits that the laws "successfully stabilized the entire Korean Buddhist monastic community on the heels of the Japanese annexation of Korea" (2017, 146). Unlike the laws and regulations for many Japanese Buddhist institutions at the time, however, the early iteration of temple laws adopted by Korean monasteries explicitly stated that individuals who marry or eat meat are not eligible for bhikkhu (*pigu* 比丘) ordination or for taking the bodhisattva precepts.[12] This was a problem mainly for those monks who sought higher positions within the monasteries, such as the abbot, because they were more closely scrutinized; even those who were empowered to vote in the elections for abbot had to have received bhikkhu ordinations. Nevertheless, the colonial state retained ultimate supervisory powers over the temple codes because the ratifying of those laws required the approval of the governor-general.

After being exposed around the turn of the twentieth century to the practice of marriage among Buddhist clerics in Japan, some within the Korean Buddhist community wanted to permit Korean monks to enjoy similar opportunities (Jaffe 2001). For many progressive-minded Korean monks, Japanese Buddhism at the time seemed to represent a modernized form of the religion, which should be emulated to strengthen their own tradition and secure its place in contemporary society. As early as 1910 the monastic reformer Han Yongun expressed strong support for clerical marriage when he submitted formal petitions on two separate occasions to

[10] The legal adoption of the temple laws was contingent, of course, on the approval of the governor-general. The first monastery to submit a set to the colonial authorities and receive approval was Haein-sa on July 2, 1912, and most others followed the same basic template (Kim 2003, 53).

[11] The Japanese temple laws and sectarian regulations were apparently consulted by a bureaucrat named Watanabe Akira who worked for the government-general in order to generate a rough draft, which was then sent to the abbots of the thirty main monasteries in Korea. For more on this matter, see Han 2006, 127–28, and Park 2016, 89–91. For the process leading to the adoption of temple laws and regulations among Japanese Buddhist schools and sects in the late nineteenth century, see Ikeda 1998.

[12] The language regarding marriage and meat-eating can be found in Chapter 8, Article 58 of the temple laws, a copy of which is reproduced in Yi (Yi 2003, 284–85).

the Japanese authorities, asking them to remove any restrictions on monks and nuns that would prevent them from marrying.[13] Han even appended the text of these petitions to his *Treatise on the Restoration of Korean Buddhism* (Chosŏn Pulgyo yusillon 朝鮮佛教維新論), published in 1913, where he further explained his position on the topic of monastic or clerical marriages. From a practical point of view, Han feared that maintaining the precepts on celibacy would hinder the modernization and reform of Korean Buddhism, leading to a steady decline in the number of people willing to join the monasteries. He also argued that it would make it exceedingly difficult for monks to effectively carry out propagation (*p'ogyo*), further jeopardizing the future viability of the religion in the peninsula.[14]

These types of arguments in favor of clerical marriage did not result in any changes to the laws and regulations governing the monastic community during the first decade of colonial rule. Yet they did bear fruit in the following decade.[15] In October 1926 the governor-general approved the revised temple laws that had been submitted by some abbots of the head monasteries, thereby lifting the restrictions on certain monks needing to have bhikkhu ordinations, namely the abbots themselves. The reality on the ground, of course, is that a good many monks were already married by this time, and some even had families of their own. According to some estimates, roughly half of all monks were married during the mid-1920s (Kim 2014, 213).[16] By the end of the colonial period in 1945, a clear majority of Korean monks had taken advantage of the relaxed rules to find marriage partners.

Despite being a small minority, a committed core of mostly senior monks sought ways to restore the vow of celibacy to its rightful place among the Vinaya precepts required for ordination, and many of these individuals were affiliated with the Sŏn hagwŏn (Sŏn Study Center). This important organization was formed in the 1920s as a conservative, practice-oriented monastic organization that operated independently of the colonial-recognized Dual Sŏn-Kyo Order of Korean Buddhism (and later from its successor, the Chogye Order). It served as the institutional base for the

[13] An English translation of both of these petitions can be found in Tikhonov and Miller 2008. Hwansoo Kim points out that, even though this seems early, Han was actually the second Korean known to have submitted petitions to the Japanese seeking permission for monks to marry, although he was the first to do so from within the monastic community as a monk (Kim 2012, 265).

[14] In addition to these practical reasons based on social concerns, Han also tried to support his position with appeals to doctrine. Philosophically, Han pointed to the doctrine of *sasa muae* 事事無碍 (unimpeded interpenetration of all phenomena) to argue that the difference between celibacy and marriage does not exist at the absolute level of truth. For a discussion of both lines of argument, both the practical and philosophical, in Han's writings, see Buswell 1992, 27–30.

[15] For a discussion of other arguments and viewpoints put forward in favor of clerical marriage within the Korean Buddhist community prior to the 1926 revision of the temple laws, see Park 2016, 149–62.

[16] Jeongeun Park's estimate of the ratio of married to unmarried monks at the famous monastery T'ongdosa in 1926, based on historical documents relating to an investigation conducted by the Japanese colonial authorities, shows similar parity (Park 2017, 153).

celibate faction of Buddhist monks for the remainder of the colonial period, and it was also pivotal, organizationally speaking, for carrying out the purification movement after liberation (Taehan Pulgyo Chogyejong Kyoyug'wŏn 2001, 195–200).

16.3 THE UNCONSTITUTIONAL LONGEVITY OF THE TEMPLE ORDINANCE AFTER LIBERATION

After liberation from Japanese rule, the Korean people soon learned that they would not immediately be given the right to govern themselves. In the southern half of the peninsula, where the Americans established a military government (USAMGIK) to rule the country, one might reasonably have expected them to eliminate the Japanese laws regarding religion, especially onerous ones like the Temple Ordinance that so blatantly infringed the religious rights and freedoms of the monastic community. Unfortunately, that turned out to be a false assumption. The law was never overturned during the period of American military rule that ended in 1948. This is perhaps less surprising when we consider the fact that the Americans mostly left the Japanese legal system intact in order to facilitate the daunting task of running a country about which they knew next to nothing (Hahm 1996, 70; Henderson 1991, 139). The Pacific Command (AFPAC) under General MacArthur gave vague assurances to the Korean people in Proclamation No. 1, promulgated the day before the commander of USAMGIK and his troops landed in Korea, about protecting their "personal and religious rights" (Cho 2013, 153; Kim 2007, 301). This was followed about a month later with the public announcement of Ordinance 11, which eliminated various laws regarding the Japanese emperor, Shintō shrine worship, and related matters, as well as containing in Section II a blanket repeal of all laws that "would cause discrimination on the grounds of race, nationality, creed or political opinion" (Henderson 1991, 140).

The Temple Ordinance, however, was not among those laws that were explicitly struck down. The following month, Ordinance 21, issued on November 2, stipulated that "all laws which were in force, regulations, orders, notices or other documents issued by any government of Korea having the force of law as of August 9, 1945, will continue in force until repealed by [a] competent authority" (Henderson 1991, 139). Beginning with this declaration, the Temple Ordinance, which gave state actors a degree of control over internal monastic affairs, would remain in force throughout the period of American military occupation and beyond.

Although the American military government claimed to be upholding the principle of religious freedom in Korea, the Buddhist and Christian communities were treated very differently by the state, and there was very little doubt about which group was favored.[17] Christmas, for instance, was designated a national holiday in

[17] As Don Clark notes, "Koreans understood the Americans to be promoting a package of democracy, capitalism and Christianity in their country" (Clark 2004, 24).

October 1945, despite the fact that Christians represented only a small fraction (perhaps two to three percent) of the total population at that time (Cho 2013, 155; Kim 2007, 307). The Buddha's birthday, by comparison, did not become a national holiday in Korea until thirty years later in 1975 (Kim 2011, 237). Other examples could be cited, but most important, as long as the Temple Ordinance remained in effect, the Buddhist monastic community would be subject to government oversight and interference through the imposition of legal constraints that did not apply to Christian organizations. The Temple Ordinance clearly gave the Americans a powerful tool that enabled them to keep a watchful eye on Buddhist temples and monastic leaders and to exercise substantial control over them. At the same time, the American military government relied heavily on native Koreans who could speak English, which disproportionately favored Christians who had been educated in mission schools, where English language instruction was guaranteed.[18] The unfairness of maintaining the colonial-era law that regulated the Korean monastic community was repeatedly emphasized.

Buddhist leaders from around the country made repealing the Temple Ordinance a priority when they gathered at the first national monastic conference (*chŏn'guk sŭngnyŏ taehoe*) which was held after liberation on September 22 and 23, 1945 and headed by Kim Pŏmnin (Kim 2011, 213–14). All thirty-one head temples under the Japanese system were asked to send representatives, and all but a few in the northern half of the peninsula did so.[19] At the gathering, steps were immediately taken to eliminate this head-branch temple system and to abolish the temple laws since they were both deemed colonial creations. In place of these governing structures, the Buddhist leaders set out to erect a more centralized monastic order (*chongdan*) that used a type of parish system (*kyoguje* 教區制) with a central administrative affairs office (*ch'ongmuwŏn*) at T'aego-sa, the headquarters monastery, that would oversee various regional offices (*kyomu*) in the provinces (Kim 1997, 102–3). They also formed a Central Assembly (*chung'ang chonghoe*) which met in early 1946 and passed a constitution for the order. Although a monastic constitution was technically created when the monastic community received permission to establish a temple headquarters of the newly renamed Chogye Order in 1941 during the late colonial period, the one created in 1946 was the first to be drafted free from state interference. Despite the fact that the current constitution of the Chogye Order is considered a revision of an original passed in 1962 (for reasons that will be discussed), the 1946 monastic constitution was the basic template that was later revised during the course of the purification movement.

The continued existence and enforcement of the Temple Ordinance, however, remained a major obstacle to fully implementing these institutional changes and other reforms. Kim Kwangsik has noted that multiple requests for the repeal of this

[18] This fact has led some to refer to USAMGIK as the "interpreters' government" (Clark 2004, 24).

[19] Of the seventy-nine invitees to the conference, sixty were actually present (Kim 2006, 24).

law in the summer of 1946 were all ignored. He also points out that in March of the following year, the Order formally submitted a written petition to the newly created South Korean Interim Legislative Assembly (SKILA), and its demands even received the backing of twenty-five of its members (Kim 2011, 214–15). Although this body unanimously passed a piece of legislation on August 8, 1947 that would have abolished the Temple Ordinance – not to mention other Japanese laws regarding religion – and created in its place a temporary law dealing only with the protection of Buddhist property, the American military government refused to approve it (Kim 2007, 304; Kim 2011, 215; Mun 2011, 224).[20] Thus, despite their best efforts, Buddhist leaders within the Chogye Order never managed to convince the Americans to do away with the Temple Ordinance, which remained in effect when Syngman Rhee took over from the Americans at the helm of a new government in 1948, giving him undue powers to intervene in the internal affairs of the Buddhist monastic community.[21]

16.4 THE BATTLE OVER CELIBACY AND CONTROL OF THE CHOGYE ORDER

Not long after the conclusion of the Korean War, President Syngman Rhee (Yi Sŭngman), the first president of the Republic of Korea (ROK), in power from 1948 until he was forced out by the people in 1960, began issuing a series of presidential messages or specifically "admonitions" (*yusi* 諭示), that were highly critical of clerical marriage among the Buddhist monks in Korea. These public statements are widely seen as sparking the purification movement that quickly consumed much of the time and energy of the Buddhist community for the rest of the 1950s and into the 1960s. Rhee's motivations for wading into this matter are opaque and his sincerity may be questionable, but the impacts of his actions on Korean Buddhism are profound and undeniable.[22]

[20] The USAMGIK, of course, exercised veto power over SKILA. While the former issued 352 ordinances from its inception through to August 1948, when the Republic of Korea (ROK) came into existence, this quasi-legislative body managed to pass a mere twelve laws during its year and half in operation, none of which were particularly significant (Henderson 1991, 140).

[21] Land and Buddhist property rights were central to this issue. Kim Kwangsik points out that there were 857 Japanese Buddhist temples or propagation stations, 593 of which were located in the South. Although initially the rights to manage these temples were given to the Korean monastic community (the Sŏn Hagwŏn and then the Chogye Order's *ch'ongmuwŏn*), in 1947 this policy changed and the Americans took direct control of the Japanese Buddhist temples (Kim 2011, 218–19).

[22] In addition to the oft-noted fact that Rhee was a devout Christian who wanted to see South Korea become a majority Christian country, there were possible political calculations at work in his actions. In 1954, Rhee could have been looking ahead to the upcoming elections, and among his opposition in the National Assembly were several married monks who had won local elections.

After the Korean War ended, stories began circulating about President Rhee's visits to various Buddhist temples. In one case, he claimed to have seen women's undergarments hanging out to dry; in another anecdote, he supposedly witnessed a Korean monk with not one, but two wives! It was also rumored that he encountered a monk who had studied in Japan for a long time and who had a Japanese wife, alongside written placards of praise for the Japanese emperor. True or not, these stories served to conveniently illustrate the main thrust of Rhee's rhetorical attack on the married monks.[23] Rhee cast the practice of monastic marriage as a vestige of Japanese colonialism, which amounted to a corruption of traditional Korean Buddhist monasticism, and he bemoaned the lack of morality and patriotism among these monks. Therefore, he instructed married monks (and their wives, of course) to vacate the precincts of Buddhist temples and to turn over the running of the Chogye Order and its temples to the monks who adhered to the vow of celibacy. It is important to keep in mind what a bold statement this must have been: at the time of his first public pronouncement on this issue in 1954, celibate monks constituted an estimated ten percent of the total number of Korean monks and controlled not even one monastery in all of Korea.

Despite the constitutional guarantees separating religion from the state, Rhee was able to utilize his authority under the Temple Ordinance to justify his intervention into the internal affairs of the monastic community. Because the law was not abolished during the period of American military rule after liberation, Rhee could use this powerful legal tool to maintain control over the monastic community. Eventually, the Supreme Court invalidated certain parts of the law and its accompanying enforcement rules, but this did not take place until 1956, and even then, the justices did not strike down the law entirely.[24]

The disputes over control of the Chogye Order and its temples initiated by Rhee would eventually turn not only litigious, but also violent.

16.5 CONTENTIOUS DEBATES AND RIVAL CONSTITUTIONS

The minority of unmarried monks argued against clerical marriage by drawing both on religious grounds and appeals to tradition. By not following the precepts outlined in the *Four-Part Vinaya* that had been used in Korea traditionally, which clearly prohibited sexual activity as a major transgression, they argued that the monastic

[23] These stories are recounted in Kang and Pak 2002, 208–9. Some or all of them may be apocryphal since they appear to be uncorroborated, as far as I can tell, but their veracity cannot be discounted nor dismissed out of hand.

[24] The parts that were challenged in court and overturned concerned the legal requirement to obtain government approval for the selection of abbots to individual monasteries. This had been perhaps also the most damaging and widely opposed provision of the Temple Ordinance during the colonial period. The decisions in these cases are found in Supreme Court Judgment on March 30, 1956, 4288 Haengsang 21 and Supreme Court Judgment on April 20, 1956, 4289 Hyŏngsang 1 (Taehan Pulgyo Chogyejong Ch'ongmuwŏn 1996, 25–27).

community had become corrupted. Syngman Rhee's intervention, however, added a strong undercurrent of nationalist arguments to the debate, assigning blame for the supposedly degenerate state of Korean Buddhism to the corrupting influence of Japanese Buddhism and the legacy of colonialism. In response, the married faction "argued that they practiced *taejung Pulgyo* (Buddhism for lay people) and modern Buddhism" (Park 2007, 135). In other words, they maintained that monks who married could better understand the everyday lives of the laity and thus were better suited to carry out propagation. They also claimed that if they were not monks, then neither were the unmarried monks since they did not adhere to the entire Vinaya either. Although the leadership of the Chogye Order attempted to make concessions by offering to give the celibate monks possession of some monasteries, the unmarried faction forged ahead with its plan to cleanse the order completely of married monks.

To this end the celibate monks convened their own first national conference at the Sŏn Hagwŏn in August 1954, at which they resolved to revise the order's constitution. The revised constitution, which reinstituted celibacy as a necessary qualification for ordination and maintaining one's status as a monk, would be adopted at a second national conference held in late September of the same year (Mun 2011, 245–53). The unmarried monks were steadfast in their refusal to recognize married clerics as legitimate members of the monastic order, insisting instead that they be classified simply as lay people or as a special group of (lay) Dharma protectors (*hobŏp chung* 護法衆).[25] The married monks had earlier that summer already revised their own constitution, passed in 1946, presumably to legally identify two types of monks – those that maintained the vow of celibacy as well as those that entered into marriages – as both belonging to the order (*chongdan*).

President Rhee continued to periodically issue presidential messages supporting the unmarried monks and denouncing the married clerics, with his second appearing on November 4, 1954, after the unmarried monks had produced and passed their revised version of the order's constitution at their first two monastic conferences (*Sinmun ŭro pon Han'guk Pulgyo kŭnhyŏndae sa* 1995, 185–87). The impasse between the two sides soon sparked violent confrontations in the temples as well as litigation in the courts, and Rhee issued yet another *yusi* on November 19 (*Sinmun ŭro pon Han'guk Pulgyo kŭnhyŏndae sa* 1995, 188). The Rhee administration directly intervened at the ministerial level, bringing the leaders of each faction together repeatedly for face-to-face meetings to seek a resolution. At one of these meetings on December 22, 1954, held at the National Police Headquarters, representatives of the two sides were presented with a document outlining the government's basic position on the dispute and containing a concrete proposal for how to resolve it. Of particular interest is the assertion that the married clerics should

[25] Park 2007, 136; *Tong'a ilbo*, September 10, 1954 (*Sinmun ŭro pon Han'guk Pulgyo kŭnhyŏndae sa* 1995, 185).

be classified as propagation monks, which is very close to the position taken by the married monks who had already revised their constitution in accordance with this same basic approach:

> The monastic order is composed of two groups, ascetic monks and propagation monks. The ascetic monks, constituting celibate monks and nuns, and monastics of more than 10 years after making a divorce, should concentrate on one or two practices in the following five practices: (1) the preservation of precepts, (2) the practice of Seon [Sŏn meditation], (3) the chanting of the titles of Buddhas and Bodhisattvas, (4) the reading of scriptures, and (5) the chanting of spells. They should live and practice Buddhism in the praxis compounds, follow the teachings of the Seon patriarchs, and obey the monastic rules. The propagation monks should preserve the ten precepts and can practice Seon, chant the titles of Buddhas and Bodhisattvas, read scriptures, or chant spells. They are also able to accomplish the mission of Mahāyāna Buddhism by dedicating themselves to propagation, education, and social affairs and to take charge of all administrative and accounting affairs. (Mun 2011, 267)

Although this compromise would have technically allowed married monks to remain in the order, the proposal further specified that the so-called propagation monks had to remove their families from temple grounds and that any private homes within the boundaries of the temple should either be removed or taken over by the temple, but only after financially compensating the married monks (Mun 2011, 268). The government's proposal was completely rejected by the three representatives of the celibate monks who were present at the meeting, and the conflict, violence, and court battles continued unabated. Lay Buddhists and the general public for the most part supported the celibacy faction, and with public opinion on their side and the president's office exerting pressure on lower-level ministers and possibly the courts, the celibates eventually gained the upper hand and took control over most of the Buddhist temples in the country.

16.6 CONTROVERSIES AND THE COURT

The controversy continued into the following year as more seizures of temples, more frequent and intense fighting, and more lawsuits in the secular courts dominated the news. There were further meetings between the two sides and efforts by government officials and agencies to mediate the dispute. By the summer of 1955, however, the unmarried monks were ready to hold another national conference for celibate monastics. This time they wanted explicit government authorization for their gathering, allowing them to ostensibly establish a legal basis for a newly revised monastic constitution that placed power in the hands of those who had received the traditional bhikkhu ordinations and to reinstitute celibacy as a condition for monkhood. Two conferences were thus held in quick succession in the first two weeks of August, with a newly revised constitution created at the first, which would then be passed and confirmed at the second. Government officials from the Ministry of Education who were present at the conference could thus grant approval and permission for the celibate faction's version of the monastic constitution, their selection of executive and administrative officers, and their control over the appointment of abbots to the country's roughly 1,000 temples (Mun 2011, 296–97; Park 2007, 238).

In terms of the subsequent court battles that eventually came before the Supreme Court on that day in late November 1960, the central legal question the Court had to consider was whether this celibate monastic conference was, in fact, authorized and sanctioned in accordance with the rule of law. The only reason this fact mattered at all was because of the monastic constitution that was passed that day: the changes to the Chogye Order constitution, if approved by the courts, would legally establish a definition of monkhood that excluded married individuals.

The situation remained tense, however, and the married monks did not willingly step aside. Nor, for that matter, did the celibate monks have enough qualified monks to complete the takeover of every Buddhist temple in the country. Accommodations were eventually made to allow some of the married monks to resume their positions at many of the smaller temples and monasteries. The married faction also refused to hand over the management of key business interests and corporations affiliated with the Chogye Order. However, the lower courts eventually validated the monastic conference, thus approving the celibates' revised constitution and handing power to the unmarried faction of monks, which they maintained through the remainder of the 1950s.

In April 1960, facing growing protests over political corruption and his government's widespread human rights abuse, Syngman Rhee was forced to resign from office. His departure reignited the internal conflict within the monastic community, as unmarried monks lost their most important backer and the married monks sought to retake many of the temples they had previously lost, often through force. With the Supreme Court set to rule later that year on the case concerning the government's recognition of the national conference of unmarried monastics in August 1955, tensions were extremely high. The non-married faction continued to demonstrate to publicly press their case, with the Ven. Ha Dongsan, who was the Supreme Patriarch of the celibate faction of monks, even leading a procession of demonstrators to the Supreme Court while sitting cross-legged on the roof of an automobile. As noted earlier, while the ruling merely sent the case back to a lower court, it was interpreted as favorable to the married monks since they had prevailed in the pending case.

16.7 LEGAL AFTERLIVES UNDER PARK CHUNG HEE

While that case was pending, a new political leader emerged, and the new regime that came to power in May 1961 following a military coup took immediate steps to quell the disorder that had engulfed the monastic community by forcing the two sides to come together and form a "unified order" (*t'onghap chongdan* 統合宗團) in early 1962.[26] The new leader, Park Chung Hee, moved fairly quickly to push through a new law to replace the colonial-era Temple Ordinance, which had remained in effect for more than a decade and a half after liberation from Japanese rule. Less than six months after the married and unmarried monks were forced to come together and create the unified order, Park repealed the Temple Ordinance and replaced it with the Buddhist Property Management Law (*Pulgyo chaesan kwalli pŏp* 佛教財産管理法) in May 1962.[27] While the long-overdue elimination of the despised colonial-era Temple Ordinance was certainly welcomed by the Buddhist community, its replacement unfortunately followed many of the former law's precedents.[28] Despite being challenged in court on constitutional grounds, the Supreme Court held in 1969 that the Buddhist Property Management Law did not violate the constitution and its guarantee of religious freedom and neutrality toward religion, a dubious verdict that some legal scholars and others have repudiated.[29] After democratization in 1987, this law was finally replaced with the Traditional Temple Preservation Law (*Chŏnt'ong sach'al pojon pŏp* 傳統寺刹保存法) which went into effect in late May the following year with the promulgation of its accompanying enforcement rules. It has remained in place since that time.[30]

Park's forced alliance between the two factions failed to completely quell the unrest and discord, and feeling disadvantaged by the new arrangement, the married monks once again turned to the secular courts to resolve the issue. Once again, the courts failed to address the necessary qualifications for monkhood and the question of celibacy, and concentrated instead on matters pertaining to the rules and regulations regarding the number of people needed to validate and certify decisions made by the administrative leaders of the organization. In the end, though, after they had lost the last of their court appeals in 1969, the leaders of the married faction broke away and formed a separate order, officially named the T'aego Order of Korean Buddhism (Han'guk Pulgyo T'aegojong 韓國佛教太古宗).[31] Other Buddhist orders

26 For more information about the origins of the *t'onghap chongdan*, see Kim 2002, 338–39.

27 Law No. 1087, promulgated on May 31, 1962.

28 For instance, it was established through non-democratic means under authoritarian rule; it applied exclusively to Buddhist temples and organizations, requiring them to register with the appropriate ministry (Article 6); it made disposal of temple property subject to prior government approval (Article 11); and it enabled close government supervision of the Buddhist community.

29 Supreme Court Judgment on December 23, 1969, 69 Ta 1053. See Taehan Pulgyo Chogyejong Ch'ongmuwŏn 1997, 29. For a discussion of the constitutional issues surrounding this law, see Yŏn 1987.

30 Law No. 3974, November 28, 1987. The law has undergone numerous revisions, beginning in 1993. See Korean Law Information Center, www.law.go.kr/ (last accessed July 29, 2022).

31 The T'aego Order remains the second largest Buddhist order in Korea today. Despite the formal schism, litigation involving the T'aegojong and Chogyejong did not end in 1970 as the two monastic orders continued to fight in court over temples, property, and assets.

were formed and also gained legal recognition in the 1960s under the Buddhist Property Management Law; each of these possessed the right to determine whether monks needed to adhere to a vow of celibacy or could get married in order to become a member.

16.8 CONCLUSION

While much more could be said about the historical episodes described above, the details show clearly the complex entanglements of Buddhism and constitutional law in Korea, both historically and in the present. At issue was not one type of constitution but two – state constitutions and monastic constitutions – which themselves existed in various relationships fraught with tensions. During the Japanese colonial period, the Temple Ordinance required that each head temple create its own set of rules and regulations, known as temple laws, to govern individual monasteries. These temple laws, while notionally autonomous, were nonetheless open to state intervention, and that dynamic gave rise to one sort of tension between monks and state authorities. After the advent of American military rule on the peninsula and continuing after the creation of a South Korean state, these constitutional tensions took a slightly different form. Where the constitution for the Republic of Korea mandated a separation between state and religion, the constitutional conflicts among rival factions of Chogye monks drew state leaders and courts into the fray.

Through all of this, notions of Buddhism and state authority were not resolved or stabilized but multiplied and were increasingly contested. Rather than narrowing or "stabilizing" discourses around internal governance and administrative regulation of the monastic community, these nested constitutional conflicts opened up new spaces for intense disagreement and instigated an internal schism among monks and lay Buddhists alike. At the same time, constitutional guarantees of religious freedom and separation of church and state forced the Supreme Court to sidestep any determination about the Vinayic propriety disputes of allowing monks to marry – ultimately the Court sidestepped the matter, sending the dispute back to a lower court on technical, procedural matters.[32] In other words, the Court could not pronounce on the content of monastic constitutions, but only on the question of who had the right to amend or draft them. In fact, one of the biggest differences between the colonial and post-colonial contexts may have been the greater judicial recourse that was available to members of the monastic community in the 1950s and 1960s, as well as the litigiousness that came to characterize the purification movement as a result. While Buddhist actors were able to use colonial courts to press certain claims relating to internal monastic disputes, these judicial avenues were

[32] For similar examples of civil courts evading substantive questions of Vinaya or Buddhism civil course in Sri Lanka, see Schonthal 2017–18.

highly constrained under colonial authorities. The establishment of the Republic of Korea and its constitutional guarantees of religious freedom and the separation of religion and the state, on the one hand, allowed for increased judicial recourse on the part of Buddhist actors, but on the other hand, it simultaneously restricted the ability of the courts to adjudicate doctrinal disputes, including whether monks had to take a vow of celibacy to be considered monks.

The case of the purification movement in Korea highlights an important aspect of Buddhism's interlinking with constitutional law in Asia. Not only does it highlight the significance of history, sectarianism, and change in national constitutions, but it also calls attention to the importance of non-state constitutions – Buddhist monk constitutions – in the legal, political, and religious histories of this complex part of the world.

REFERENCES

Buswell Jr., Robert E. 1992. *The Zen Monastic Experience: Buddhist Practice in Contemporary Korea*. Princeton: Princeton University Press.

Cho, Kyuhoon. 2013. *The Appropriation of Religion: The Re-formation of the Korean Notion of Religion in Global Society*. PhD dissertation, University of Ottawa.

Clark, Donald N. 2004. "Protestant Christianity and the State: Religious Organisations as an Example of Civil Society in South Korea." *Papers of the British Association for Korean Studies* 9: 19–32.

Hahm, Pyong-choon. 1996. "Korea's Initial Encounter with the Western Law, 1910–1948 A.D." In *Korean Law in the Global Economy*, edited by Sang-hyun Song, 61–74. Seoul: Bak Young Sa.

Han, Tongmin. 2006. "*Sach'allyŏng* ch'eje ŭi yŏksa jok paegyŏng kwa ŭimi." In *Pulgyo kŭndaehwa ŭi chŏngae wa sŏnggyŏk*, edited by Taehan Pulgyo, Chogyejong Kyoyug'wŏn and Pulhak Yŏnguso, 93–134. Seoul: Chogyejong Ch'ulp'ansa.

Henderson, Gregory. 1991. "Human Rights in South Korea, 1945–1953." In *Human Rights in Korea: Historical and Policy Perspectives*, edited by William Shaw, 125–69. Cambridge: Harvard University Asia Center.

Ikeda Eishun. 1998. "Teaching Assemblies and Lay Societies in the Formation of Modern Sectarian Buddhism." *Japanese Journal of Religious Studies* 25 (1–2): 11–44.

Jaffe, Richard M. 2001. *Neither Monk nor Layman: Clerical Marriage in Modern Japanese Buddhism*. Princeton: Princeton University Press.

Kang Sŏkchu and Pak Kyŏnghun. (1980) 2002. *Pulgyo kŭnse paengnyŏn*. Seoul: Minjoksa.

Kim, Hwansoo Ilmee. 2012. *Empire of the Dharma: Korean and Japanese Buddhism, 1877–1912*. Cambridge: Harvard University Asia Center.

Kim Kwangsik. 2002. *Sae Pulgyo undong ŭi chŏn'gae*. Ansŏng, South Korea: Top'i ansa.

2006. *Han'guk hyŏndae Pulgyosa yŏn'gu*. Seoul: Pulgyo Sidaesa.

2011. "1945–1980 nyŏn kanŭi Pulgyo wa kukga kwŏllyŏk." *Pulgyo hakbo* 58: 209–43.

Kim Pŏmjun. 2007. "Haebang konggan migunchŏng ui Pulgyo ch'ŏngch'aek yŏn'gu." *Sŏnmunhwa yon'gu* 3: 295–334.

Kim Sunsŏk. 2003. *Ilche sidae Chosŏn ch'ongdokbu ŭi Pulgyo chŏngch'aek kwa Pulgyogye ŭi taeŭng*. Seoul: Kyŏngin Munhwasa.

Kim Ŭngch'ŏl. 1997. "Chung'ang chonghoe ŭi yŏkhalpyŏnhwa wa unyŏngsilt'ae e kwanhan yŏn'gu." In *Chogyejong chung'ang chonghoe hwaldong yŏn'gu*, 95–146. Seoul: Silch'ŏn Pulgyo Chŏnguk Sŭnggahoe.
Kim, Yeong-tae. 2014. "Korean Buddhism's Efforts to Establish Itself as a Modern Religion, and Its Political Subjugation to Authorities in the Process." In *The State, Religion, and Thinkers in Korean Buddhism*, edited by Robert M. Gimello, Robert Evans Buswell and Richard D. McBride, 192–232. Seoul: The Institute for Buddhist Culture, Donnguk University.
Korean Law Information Center. Accessed on December 15, 2021, www.law.go.kr/
Mun, Chanju. 2011. *Purification Buddhist Movement, 1954–1970: The Struggle to Restore Celibacy in the Jogye Order of Korean Buddhism.* Honolulu: Blue Pine Books.
Pak Puyŏng. 2007. "Taebŏbwŏn yukpi'gu halbok sa'gŏn." *Pulgyo p'yŏngnon* 33. Access on December 15, 2021. http://www.budreview.com/news/articleView.html?idxno=92.
Park, Jeongeun. 2016. *Clerical Marriage and Buddhist Modernity in Early Twentieth-Century Korea.* PhD dissertation, University of British Columbia.
2017. "Re-thinking Married *Bhikṣu*: Examination of *Bhikṣu* Ordinations and Clerical Marriage in 1920s Korean Buddhism." *Seoul Journal of Korean Studies* 30 (2): 131–63.
Park, Pori. 2007. "The Buddhist Purification Movement in Postcolonial South Korea: Restoring Clerical Celibacy and State Intervention." In *Identity Conflicts: Can Violence be Regulated?* edited by J. Craig Jenkins and Esther E. Gottlieb, 131–45. New Brunswick: Transaction Publishers.
Schonthal, Benjamin. 2017–2018. "Litigating Vinaya: Buddhist Law and Public Law in Contemporary Sri Lanka." *Buddhism, Law & Society* 3: 69–111.
Song, Kue-jin. 2019. "The Real Face of Korean Buddhism under Japanese Colonial Rule." *Journal of Korean Religions* 10 (2): 275–99.
Sŏnu Toryang Han'guk Pulgyo Kŭnhyŏndaesa Yŏn'guhoe, ed. 1995. *Sinmun ŭro pon Han'guk Pulgyo kŭnhyŏndae sa*. Seoul: Sŏnu Toryang Ch'ulp'anbu.
Taehan Pulgyo Chogyejong Ch'ongmuwŏn, ed. 1996. *Pulgyo p'allyejip*. Seoul: Taehan Pulgyo Chogyejong Ch'ongmuwŏn Ch'ulp'ansa.
Taehan Pulgyo Chogyejong Kyoyug'wŏn, ed. 2001. *Chogyejong sa: kŭnhyŏndae p'yŏn*. Seoul: Taehan Pulgyo Chogyejong Kyoyug'wŏn.
Tikhonov, Vladimir and Miller, Owen. 2008. *Selected Writings of Han Yongun: From Social Darwinism to Socialism with a Buddhist Face*. Kent: Global Oriental.
Yi Nŭnghwa. (1918) 2003. *Chosŏn Pulgyo t'ongsa: kŭndae p'yŏn*. Seoul: Hyean.
Yŏn Kiyŏng. 1987. "Pulgyo chaesan kwallibŏp ŭi munjejŏm (wan)". *Pŏmnyul Sinmun* 1671.

PART V

Comparative Perspectives

17

On the Familiar Pleasures of Estrangement

*Deepa Das Acevedo**

17.1 INTRODUCTION

Anthropological analysis, at any rate the kind that has been emanating from Euro-American departments for the last fifty years or so, is grounded in the discovery of difference. Anthropologists look closely, watch patiently, think critically, and engage in a kind of concentrated musing – what others have more elegantly called "cultivated attentiveness" – all in the hopes of seeing new colors in the rainbow.[1] We are the science, if one cares to use that word, of human specificity. And yet, as much as anthropology trades in human difference, it also delights in sameness. Nineteenth-century anthropologists of the armchair variety, turn-of-the-century fieldworkers of a functionalist persuasion (as well as their structuralist others), postmodernists, and even twenty-first century anthropologists ever so gingerly attempting an ontological turn are all committed to seeing what can, and what cannot, be considered true of humankind writ large. In the face of difference, we are fascinated by similarity.

The chapters in this collection are, therefore, not only a source of incredibly rich insight on the relationship between Buddhism and constitutional law; they are, additionally, the source of a peculiarly *anthropological* pleasure because they offer a charming lesson in the interpretive possibilities of sameness. For those of us who are not scholars of Buddhism and are only very tenuously students of constitutional law, the chapters cast into stark and provocative relief the assumptions that we may carry about the wide swath of Buddhist contexts examined by the chapter authors. What that means, of course, is that the chapters also reveal the assumptions we as scholars carry about ourselves and our own areas of work.

* My thanks to Tom Ginsburg and Benjamin Schonthal for including me in this fantastic project, to all of the participants for sharing their work, and to my colleagues on the April 15, 2021, roundtable for a truly enjoyable conversation.

[1] This phrase comes from the syllabus for a graduate anthropological methods class taught at The University of Chicago in 2015 (Sunder Rajan 2015).

In the rest of my own short chapter, I will tease out a few moments where the thematic concerns addressed by some of the authors with respect to Buddhism speak powerfully to concerns that have animated the study of *Hinduism* and constitutional law as undertaken by myself and others. I focus on three chapters in particular: Mark Nathan's analysis of monasticism and celibacy in Korea; Richard W. Whitecross' reflections on dual sovereignty in Bhutan; and Krishantha Fedricks' writing on language ideology in Sri Lanka. This selection both is and is not random. I read Nathan's chapter first and was so struck by the way its central concerns resembled issues that I have repeatedly engaged with in my own work on Hinduism in India, that I decided to cast about the series collection for geographical and thematic variety. I landed on the chapters by Whitecross and Fedricks and realized that, together with Nathan's, they constituted an excellent triad. Each of them showed me, thoughtfully but unequivocally, how themes I had only considered with respect to India and Hinduism were applicable and generative far beyond those contexts. As with all anthropological endeavors, my hope is to unsettle assumptions about one thing via an exploration of another. But first, a little background.

17.2 HINDUISM AND CONSTITUTIONAL LAW

What I am about to say certainly does not apply to all Hindus or all Buddhists. But, just as certainly, it *does* capture the way a particularly significant constitutional law system – India's – understands the contours and content of Hinduism. It also seems to capture elements of Buddhism as it is understood by the legal systems of several countries. Two points of divergence between Hinduism and Buddhism seem especially important for the task of regulating them constitutionally.

First, everyday Hinduism is deeply tied to temple worship. There are caveats, of course: not all Hindus worship in temples; those who do so worship for different reasons and at different frequencies; and, finally, both the experience and the perceived merits of temple worship vary widely. Nevertheless, the importance of *darśanam* ("auspicious sight") necessarily makes temples, whether they are roadside altars, pilgrimage centers, or precolonial royal masterpieces, central to the practice of Hinduism. Moreover, Hindu temples are not primarily or even significantly associated with religious elites in the vein of bhikkhus and bhikkhunis – although, again, there are many such elites and many of them are linked with specific temples.

Second, it is difficult to identify stable communities or hierarchies within Hinduism of the sort generally associated with the Buddhist sangha – for the most part. Communities that are generally (and certainly judicially) considered Hindu range from the tens of thousands in the Ramnami Samaj to the tens of millions in the Radha Soami Satsang. The various *mathas* that control many of Indian Hinduism's most venerated temples are nothing if not hierarchical. And castes are both hierarchical and communitarian, even if their membership boundaries and religious bona fides have long been up for debate. Despite these and other reasonable caveats, it remains the case that Hinduism writ large lacks a standing religious elite that is hierarchically structured.

Both of these features suggest that the challenges precipitated by "Hinduism and constitutional law" ought to be markedly, albeit not entirely, different from those triggered by the confluence of "Buddhism and constitutional law." And yet, as the rest of this chapter shows, that is not the case. The three chapters I will discuss below demonstrate that, despite these seemingly foundational religious differences between Hinduism and Buddhism (as well as innumerable legal differences between the countries in question), the puzzles to be solved – or not – are in many ways the *same*.[2] That lesson is, in itself, striking in the extreme.

17.3 MONASTICISM AND CELIBACY IN KOREA

In his chapter, Mark Nathan uses a longstanding dispute over monastic celibacy to argue that South Korea's modern constitutional framework opened up spaces for disagreement over Buddhist institutions, rather than having a consolidating, stabilizing, or homogenizing effect, as we might have expected. In November 1960, a group of young monks stormed into the Supreme Court and threatened to commit suicide because the Court had not definitively supported their side in a battle over whether Korea's national Chogye Order mandated monastic celibacy. Rather than ruling on this core issue, the justices relied on procedural reasons to send the case back to a lower court (where the protestors' pro-celibacy side had won). Indeed, despite repeated and contentious litigation, Korean courts never actually made a determination as to the religious necessity of monastic celibacy. As Nathan observes, they remained unwilling to wade into doctrinal disputes and were "concerned only with the written constitution, rules, and regulations of an organization composed of members who self-identified as Buddhist" (2022).

Self-governance within a framework of intense state oversight is, as Nathan argues, a characteristic feature of Foucauldian governmentality, and it is a thread that runs through the historical period he discusses. The Temple Ordinance published in 1911 by Korea's colonial Japanese government comprised just seven short articles, and it required Korean monastics to formulate the laws that would govern their own behavior as well as the procedures by which their leaders would be chosen. These temple laws were, however, subject to the colonial government's approval, and as such they became an important avenue for indirect state involvement in the reshaping of Korean Buddhism. In 1926, for instance, revisions that won Japanese approval "removed celibacy from the list of required qualifications to assume the duties of abbot, which seemed to open the door to legal recognition of monastic marriages" (Nathan 2022). Because the colonial approach both *depended on* and *reinforced* the appearance of Korean Buddhist autonomy in matters of religious life, disputes over

[2] Readers should note that I use the authors' own transliterations of non-English terms.

religious practice – including over the issue of monastic celibacy – became disputes over which religious faction had the authority to issue behavioral mandates, rather than disagreements over which practice better reflected Buddhist tenets.

I confess that what initially drew me to this chapter was its focus on religiously motivated celibacy. For the last ten years, my own work in India has centered on the Hindu temple at Sabarimala, Kerala, whose presiding deity, Ayyappan, is most famous for being a permanent celibate who is unable or unwilling to receive fertile women devotees. But the dynamics that Nathan explores – of state involvement under cover of religious autonomy, and of state involvement that facilitates (rather than erases) uncertainty and contestation – were also immediately recognizable to me, as indeed they would be to any student of religion-state relations in India. Like so many other public Hindu temples, Sabarimala is subject to intense and statutorily mandated state oversight that is often presented as, and sometimes actually is, the product of citizens' preferences. Similarly, although there is no organizational constitution at play in the women's entry dispute, an earlier phase of the dispute required courts to determine "who had the power to revise ... the rules of governance": the temple's chief priest, its advisory committee (a non-governmental body of local elites), or governmental overseers (Nathan 2022; Das Acevedo 2018).

There is, to be sure, a key difference: namely, the willingness of Indian courts to wade enthusiastically into religious doctrinal waters. Scholars disagree about whether or not these forays reflect indigenous or foreign interpretive styles, about whether they are democratically defensible given the unelected nature of the judiciary, and even about whether they negate India's ostensibly secular character – but there is little disagreement over whether or not Indian courts do, in fact, pronounce on the validity of religious beliefs and practices (Das Acevedo 2013; Dhavan 2001; Fuller 1988; Galanter 1971; Mehta 2005; Smith 1963). At various points during the women's entry dispute, for instance, Indian courts have declared both that Sabarimala's ban on women is an "essential" aspect of Ayyappan worship (making it eligible for more robust constitutional protections) and that it is a non-essential aspect of Hinduism that gives way to other constitutional guarantees of equality and non-discrimination (Das Acevedo 2020).

But what Nathan's chapter makes beautifully clear to outsiders like me, aside from the similarities and differences I've just described, is that we may need to reexamine our often too-quick assumptions about the traditions and countries we study. Scholarship on religion-state relations in India has generally rationalized extensive state involvement in the management of Hindu temples by pointing to the lack of religious hierarchy and congregational identity within Hindu tradition. If the state *didn't* step in, this thinking goes, there would be no one to coordinate resources, resolve disputes, or pursue reforms. While Nathan's chapter on Buddhism in Korea does not by itself unravel this way of understanding Hinduism in India, it does – given the existence of religious hierarchy within most iterations of Buddhism and the importance of the sangha – suggest that we may need to more carefully examine its explanatory power.

17.4 DUAL SOVEREIGNTY IN BHUTAN

In his chapter on Bhutan, Richard W. Whitecross argues that the Dual System implemented in Bhutan by the Zhabdrung, Ngawang Namgyal (d. 1651), and further entrenched by the 2008 Constitution, has had unexpected and not always positive consequences. The Zhabdrung himself embodied both religious (*chos*) and secular (*srid*) authority but he separated these two aspects of his authority among his subordinates – most relevantly, between a secular regent (the *Druk Desi*) and a chief abbot (the *Druk Je Khenpo*). This Dual System "functioned reasonably well until the last quarter of the eighteenth century when the rivalry emerged between the regional governors who vied for the post of *Desi*" (Whitecross 2022, 7). The 2008 Constitution, which was largely the achievement of Bhutan's Fourth King but only came into force during the reign of his son, the Fifth King, simultaneously embraces and resists the Dual System.

On the one hand, the 2008 Constitution provides, for the first time, that the Dual System will be embodied in the person of the monarch (Whitecross 2022). Whitecross notes that "[t]he coronation rituals created for the enthronement symbolically presented the monarch as the legitimate successor, the Zhabdrung," who was, it should be remembered, the last ruler of Bhutan to personify both forms of authority. More explicitly, Article 2(2) of the Constitution states that the Dual System "shall be unified in the person of the [king] who, as a Buddhist, shall be the upholder of the [Dual System]."

At the same time, the Constitution takes significant steps to separate religious and secular authority because of the drafters' belief that "ethnic and religious differences are the main causes of problems in this world" (Whitecross 2022). Article 3(1) calls Buddhism the country's "spiritual heritage," rather than its state religion. Article 3(3) obliges "religious institutions and personalities" to ensure "that religion remains separate from politics" and even declares that "[r]eligious institutions and personalities shall remain above politics." And finally, there is no formal role for the Zhung Dratshang (Central Monk Body) within any central governing bodies, as had been the case since 1953. Thanks to these provisions, Whitecross argues that the 2008 Constitution has led to a decidedly "un-dual" outcome, which is "the exclusion of religious practitioners from engaging in local level politics" (2022).

Once again, there are plenty of similarities with the Indian – and specifically, Hindu – context. A primary and well-documented worry of India's constitutional framers was that "left to itself, religion could permit orthodox men to burn widows alive on the piers [sic] of their deceased husbands ... coerce indulgence in social evils like child marriage or even crimes like human sacrifice ... or relegate large sections of humanity to the sub-human status of untouchability and inferiority"

(Bhagwati 2005, 43). Likewise, India still formally – although the hollow formality of this statement is becoming every day more extreme – lacks an established state religion. At the same time, and apart from political developments that have made India a Hindu state in all but name, the Constitution accords considerable cultural and legal dominance to Hinduism over other religious traditions. It identifies India by a name, *Bharat*, with largely Hindu connotations; it authorizes reforms respecting Hindu temples that are widely understood to have been motivated by a desire to consolidate Hindu identity and prevent an exodus of Dalit Hindus through conversion; it includes the prohibition of cow slaughter among its non-justiciable Directive Principles; and, perhaps most unambiguously, it treats Buddhism, Jainism, and Sikhism as legally equivalent to Hinduism.[3]

Notwithstanding these considerable similarities between the Bhutanese and Indian contexts, what is most striking to me about Whitecross' study is the way in which it acknowledges, even *embraces*, the inescapable ambiguity of the Dual System of sovereignty. For some time now I have been arguing – and I think the "women's entry" dispute demonstrates – the extent to which India's Constitution reflects allegiance to two very different visions of democratic sovereignty. Many of the Constitution's more striking elements reveal an understanding of sovereignty as something that is shared between citizens and the state; conceptualizing sovereignty this way "enables the state to undertake the kind of broad and often unpredictable reforms required to construct a more equitable society" (Das Acevedo 2016, 579–580). At the same time, and often within the very same constitutional articles, India's charter also promises traditional liberal protections that are predicated on the state's obligation, as a mere agent of citizens' (wholly owned) sovereign authority, to stay out of various spheres of activity. What other commentators have discounted, I've argued, "is the possibility that this tension is an intentional and productive feature of Indian constitutionalism writ large (and by extension, of Indian democracy) rather than being accidental, pathological, or specifically about religion" (Das Acevedo 2016, 579). Even as it explores the unintended consequences of the Dual System, Whitecross' chapter encourages us to take seriously the tensions baked into it in both its original formulation by the Zhabdrung and its interpretation in the 2008 Bhutanese Constitution.

17.5 LANGUAGE IDEOLOGY IN SRI LANKA

Krishantha Fedricks' chapter argues that the religio-political Mahamevnāwa movement is shaped by a Sinhala-centered language ideology in a way that is responsive to both nationalist and constitutionalist idioms. Since its establishment in 1999,

[3] Constitution of India, Art. 1(1) ("Bharat"); Art. 48 ("cow slaughter"); Art. 25, Explanation II (regarding Buddhism, Jainism, Sikhism). On the Hindu nature of India's constitution see Singh (2005).

Mahamevnāwa has founded seventy branches within Sri Lanka as well as international outposts in countries like the United States, India, Germany, England, and Dubai. The movement is both nationalist and transnationalist. On the one hand, Mahamevnāwa challenges the liturgical primacy and sonic sacredness of Pāli, and it also embraces popular aesthetic and religious forms to a degree that is unusual within "mainstream nationalist monastic politics" (Fedricks 2022). On the other hand, Mahamevnāwa is intentionally transnational in its orientation and technologically diversified in its methods, so much so that Fedricks considers it to be "the first televangelist Buddhist group in Sri Lanka" (2022). Similarly, the movement is both constitutionalist and anti-constitutionalist. Its faith in the power of correct language and form, like its emphasis on a philosophical orientation or set of principles – the *dhamma* – as a guiding charter for the true Buddhist state, means that Mahamevnāwa incorporates the foundational premises of constitutional law within its own structure and strategy. At the same time, the movement is firm in its disavowal of secular constitutions and its critique of monastic participation in politics, on the grounds that both have led to the decline of Buddhism in contemporary Sri Lanka.

Fedricks' inversion of the usual question – how religion impacts law – is familiar and familiarly productive to anyone studying the impact of constitutional law on Hinduism in India. The Indian Supreme Court's religious freedom jurisprudence is regularly applauded or derided (or both) for its construction of a Hinduism that coheres remarkably well with the Constitution's more progressive impulses. In the mid-twentieth century, for instance, some of the Court's most famous adjudicative efforts argued that, properly understood, neither Hindu texts nor Hindu principles required that temples absolutely exclude Dalit individuals from their premises; instead, what they required was "insignificant participation" on par with many other Hindu constituencies. More recently, the Supreme Court held that neither the tenets of Ayyappan worship nor those of Hinduism as a whole require the exclusion of women aged ten to fifty from Sabarimala's premises. "It is a universal truth," wrote Chief Justice Dipak Misra in 2018, "that faith and religion do not countenance discrimination" – because, in the end, he said, "[a]ll religions are simply different paths to reach the Universal One" (*Indian Young Lawyers Association* v. *State of Kerala*, at para. 4). Scholars of Indian religious freedom jurisprudence, myself included, have thus become accustomed to pointing out how, to paraphrase Fedricks, "notions of constitutional law find their way into [Hindu] institutions" (2022).

But what is striking is that Fedricks begins his account with a brief history of ethnolinguistic nationalism before he ever gets to constitutional law, and even after discussing constitutional concerns he returns to language ideology as it is marshalled by Mahamevnāwa. The bidirectional nature of this dynamic is just as evident in the Indian context: Chief Justice Misra's comment about different paths riffs off a well-known line from the *Ṛg Veda* that was arguably mistranslated by Swami

Vivekananda, and that now makes cameo appearances in both legal and popular discourse with such frequency that it is impossible to accurately parse the direction of flow (Doniger 2014, 18). What Fedricks' chapter reminds us of, in other words, is not simply the value of occasionally fronting law as subject rather than object in conversations about religion and constitutionalism, but the need to always remember the chicken-and-egg nature of that relationship.

17.6 CONCLUSION

As I began by suggesting, the chapters in this volume offer a rare opportunity: the chance to learn substantively about a fascinating new area of interdisciplinary legal scholarship while also learning, thematically and analytically, about one's own. For the anthropologist who seeks difference, there is nuanced, granular analysis that teases out the unique dimensions of both Buddhism and constitutionalism as they manifest across several contexts. And for the anthropologist who delights in sameness, there is an invitation, subtly different in each chapter but present in them all, to consider how these lessons about a particular religious tradition (and several countries) are also lessons about *other* traditions and *other* countries.

For the scholar of comparative constitutional law – who is, after all, one of the primary readers of this volume – these chapters offer a distinct yet related provocation: how are the chapters' shared points of emphasis, Buddhism and constitutionalism, best thought of? Is it Buddhism *and* constitutional law, Buddhism *as* constitutional law, or even the preposition-free *Buddhist constitutional law*? Too often, comparative constitutional law scholarship has rested on the easy assumption that what is being compared is most relevantly thought of in political and geographic terms – the nation-state – and, consequently, that the third of these formulations is best: American constitutional law versus Indian constitutional law, and so on. That assumption may always have been problematic, but it is now even less defensible given the rapid ascendance of movements that are populist, transnational, and very often ethnoreligious in nature. By troubling the premise that the objects of comparison and analogy in comparative constitutional law are easily identifiable, these chapters open up a space for thinking more creatively about the intersection of religion and law.

REFERENCES

Bhagwati, P. N. 2005. "Religion and Secularism Under the Indian Constitution." In *Religion and Law in Independent India* (2nd ed.), edited by Robert D. Baird, 35–50. New Delhi: Manohar.

Das Acevedo, Deepa. 2013. "Secularism in the Indian Context." *Law & Social Inquiry* 38 (1): 138–67.

2016. "Temples, Courts, and Dynamic Equilibrium in the Indian Constitution." *The American Journal of Comparative Law* 64 (3): 555–82.

2018. "Gods' Homes, Men's Courts, Women's Rights." *International Journal of Constitutional Law* 16 (2): 552–73.
2020. "Just Hindus." *Law & Social Inquiry* 45 (4): 965–94.
Dhavan, Rajeev. 2001. "The Road to Xanadu: India's Quest for Secularism." In *Religion and Personal Law in Secular India*, edited by Gerald Larson, 301–29. Bloomington: Indiana University Press.
Doniger, Wendy. 2014. *On Hinduism*. New York: Oxford University Press.
Fedricks, Krishantha. 2022. "Guardians of the Law: Sinhala Language and Buddhist Reformation in Post-war Sri Lanka." In *Buddhism and Comparative Constitutional Law*, edited by Tom Ginsburg and Benjamin Schonthal, X–X. Location: Cambridge University Press.
Fuller, C. J. 1988. "Hinduism and Scriptural Authority in Modern Indian Law." *Comparative Studies in Society and History* 30 (2): 225–48.
Galanter, Marc. 1971. "Hinduism, Secularism, and the Indian Judiciary." *Philosophy East and West* 21 (4): 467–87.
Indian Young Lawyers Association *v.* State of Kerala, Writ Petition (Civil) No. 373 of 2006, 2018 SCC OnLine Sc 1690.
Mehta, Pratap Bhanu. 2005. "Reason, Tradition, Authority, Religion and the Indian State." In *Men's Laws, Women's Lives: A Constitutional Perspective on Religion, Common Law and Culture in South Asia*, edited by Indira Jaising, 56–86. New Delhi: Women Unlimited.
Nathan, Mark A. 2022. "Buddhist Constitutional Battlegrounds: Using the Courts to Litigate Monastic Celibacy in South Korea, 1955–1970." In *Buddhism and Comparative Constitutional Law*, edited by Tom Ginsburg and Benjamin Schonthal, X–X. Location: Cambridge University Press.
Singh, Pritam. 2005. "Hindu Bias in India's 'Secular' Constitution: Probing Flaws in the Instruments of Governance." *Third World Quarterly* 26 (6): 909–26.
Smith, Donald E. 1963. *India as a Secular State*. Princeton: Princeton University Press.
Sunder Rajan, Kaushik. 2015. Syllabus: ANTH 42000: Anthropological Fieldwork Methods.
Whitecross, Richard W. 2022. "The Zhabdrung's Legacy: Buddhism and Constitutional Transformation in Bhutan." In *Buddhism and Comparative Constitutional Law*, edited by Tom Ginsburg and Benjamin Schonthal, X–X. Location: Cambridge University Press.

18

Buddhism and Constitutionalism

A Comparison with the Canon Law

Richard H. Helmholz

18.1 INTRODUCTION

Readers of this volume may be wondering, as I myself have wondered, why a person with only the most rudimentary knowledge of Buddhism and only a smattering of knowledge about constitutionalism itself should be involved in a discussion devoted to both subjects. I have considered this question as a likely one among you, and I want to offer two possible justifications for my appearance.

One is Tom Ginsburg's invitation. An offer from him was something I hesitated to reject. Tom stands at the top of the field of comparative constitutionalism, and I figured: If *he* asked me, there must be a plausible reason. You can make your own decision on this. The other is my own interest in the character of religious law – not just Christian law but the law of other religions. Both this volume and my research involve the possible connection between the two. I thought – I still think – that organized religion may, by its inherent nature, be connected with constitutionalism. Both stand upon a conviction that there are certain fundamental rules and principles that must be respected. They stand outside our own volition, indeed our own full understanding, and they shape our law. Perhaps the easiest example from the perspective of Christianity is that of the Ten Commandments. Its commands are not subject to repeal or amendment, though our adherence to them will never be perfect and their exact reach may be controversial. They are "constitutional" in that sense. Containing no penalties for violation, they cannot be considered positive law, but they invite legislators to provide more definite enactments to secure their enforcement.

In contributing to this volume, I was motivated by a desire to discover whether another religion – Buddhism – shared this feature with Christianity. Does what I have described make an intellectual connection with what exists in the practice of Buddhism? For purposes of comparison, this short chapter contains four examples that show how the canon laws, which regulated life in Christian churches, were understood and treated in practice.

18.2 DEFINITIONS

I begin with two definitions. Canon law means the law of the medieval church. In its definitive form, it was the product of the twelfth to the thirteenth centuries, fashioned from decrees of church councils, papal rulings, biblical texts, the ancient laws of Rome, and the dictates of natural law. It lasted in its medieval form for a long time: in the Catholic church until the twentieth century, and in Protestant lands, in what might be called a secularized but still substantially similar form, until about the same time. It was part of the European *ius commune*, the general law of European lands that supplemented and directed the scope of local customary laws. Constitutionalism is a more contested term. If I may borrow from what I remember from a talk given by the dean who first invited me to come to the University of Chicago, Gerhard Casper, later president of Stanford University, it is not simply a set of laws that preempted other laws. He wrote: "Constitutionalism does not refer to having a constitution but to structured and substantive limitations on government" (Casper 1987, 16). He did not mean that only a democracy could have such constitutional limitations. As Tom Ginsburg has himself shown, even authoritarian regimes may leave room for institutions that check the exercise of despotic powers (2008). The significant question is not where we place any particular category of rights, but how close they are to being unlimited. Almost all the rights we hold are subject to limitations. They cannot be absolute, and it is more useful to examine what the limitations are than it is to attempt to place those rights into one box or the other. In what follows, I shall assume that the reader knows only slightly more about the medieval canon law than I do about Buddhist law.

18.3 FIRST: STATUS-BASED RIGHTS OF THE CLERGY, INCLUDING MONKS AND NUNS

A foundational principle of the canon law was that the clergy should be treated as a class and separately in law than were other men and women. Most famously, this principle was the basis for "benefit of clergy" in England, a privilege that allowed clerics accused of serious crimes to escape prosecution in the royal courts. Instead, they were to be remitted to the hands of their bishop, who would deal with them as he saw fit – no mean privilege in an age when the ordinary punishment for those found guilty of a felony was death at the gallows. This was only the most famous application of what the church itself considered a matter of right ordering in a world where clergy stood apart from the laity. The claim, canonists said, was one that no secular ruler had authority to reverse. The temporal law itself recognized this principle, as in Magna Carta's first clause – the English church shall be free. This arrangement had consequences. It meant that physical attacks against a cleric were to be dealt with differently from similar attacks against the laity – an offender was to be tried in an ecclesiastical court and, if found guilty, required to undertake a journey to the papal court in Rome to seek absolution from the Roman pontiff. It also required special disposition of the property of clerics at their death, much like the situation of Buddhist monks.

Of course, it was also true that the clergy was bound by stricter rules in some respects. Requirements in their dress, limitations on the right to own property, and of course the burden of celibacy – the issue we learned about in the context of Korean Buddhism presented by Mark Nathan in this volume – were all regarded as consequences of this part of the canon law. I should add that some of these assertions were contested in specific situations – just as the reach of provisions in the US Constitution today sometimes become matters of dispute. Allowing claims to freehold land to escape secular jurisdiction simply because it came into the hands of an ecclesiastic seemed an abuse of the right ordering of society to most English common lawyers for instance, and they developed ways to prevent it. However, that there existed a basic and permanent difference between the spiritual and the temporal spheres of life those lawyers did not dispute, and this fundamental difference had in effect constitutional consequences.

18.4 SECOND: FREEDOM OF RELIGIOUS CHOICE

Surprising as it may seem to find any mention of freedom of choice in matters of religious faith in the law of the medieval church – the architect of the Inquisition – the canon law did in fact contain such a principle. No unwilling person was to be required to embrace Christianity. Jews were permitted to raise their children in the Jewish faith, even where the government of a land was in the hands of orthodox Christian bishops and magistrates. The same was true of other religions. This is, however, an example of a fundamental freedom that was reduced to a very small corner of human life as it was put into practice, and the medieval church cannot pretend to have been a champion of religious freedom. This is because the canon law also held that, although the choice to accept baptism or to refuse it was a real one, once baptism had been chosen freely, it was final. No freedom to renounce Christianity was available, and since in practice most baptisms were conducted while the person was an infant, in fact, this freedom of choice largely disappeared. It was akin to circumcision among the ancient Israelites; it could not be undone, and it obliged the circumcised to keep the Mosaic Laws. The constitutional freedom to choose one's religion, found in the texts of the medieval canon law, would thus have to wait to become fully effective – just as in the history of the common law, freedom of speech in English had to wait until it could be expanded from the privileged floor of the Houses of Parliament to the streets of London.

18.5 THIRD: A RIGHT TO REMAIN SILENT

Known commonly in modern legal parlance as the "privilege against self-incrimination," this constitutional principle was commonly stated by the legal maxim *Nemo tenetur prodere seipsum*: No one is obliged to proceed against himself. Included in Amendment V to the US Constitution (1791), the principle is also found in several of the canonical texts as understood in the Middle Ages. It was buttressed also by the principle, stated in the same basic texts, that *De occultis non judicat ecclesia*: The church does not pass judgment on matters that are hidden. The proper place for these private matters was the private forum of confession to God, not the public forum of a court of law. As Panormitanus, the greatest of the late medieval canonists, stated in this argument, buttressing it with citations from the Bible and the *Decretum*, "It seems that no one is required to answer an interrogation or an incriminating charge, because *Nemo tenetur prodere seipsum*" (Panormitanus 1615). Like the concept of religious freedom, however, this constitutional right turned out in practice to mean less than it does today. This happened because public fame was accepted as raising a legitimate presumption of a person's guilt, requiring him to swear a compurgatory oath of his innocence if he wished to squelch the rumor's effect. In other words, he could not be required to incriminate himself, but he could be required to rebut public fame against him if it was held by good and substantial members of the community. Parallels to this situation may be seen today – most recently in the reputation of "inappropriate behavior" that has been fastened on many men in respect of women they admired. Had this been 1250, in the absence of definitive proof of their offenses, they might have been obliged to undergo canonical purgation, and I think it is fair to say that this would be an inroad on the presumption of innocence and the privilege against self-incrimination.

18.6 FOURTH: WELFARE RIGHTS

Article 25 of the Universal Declaration of Human Rights declares that "Everyone has the right to a standard of living adequate for the health and well-being of his family." It may be surprising to discover that the medieval canon law contained a similar, though not identical, provision. However, it was based not upon noble aspirations, but rather upon dictates canon lawyers found in the law of nature. Before society was organized, their argument ran, all things on Earth had been held in common. So it was in the Garden of Eden. Private property depended upon a general agreement to forgo common ownership in favor of individual incentives to make productive use of what they possessed. It would reward effort and protect against thievery. However, that agreement did not extend to times of extreme want. When those times arrived and social organization fell apart, the poor could take from the wealthy without scruple. In a sense, they were simply taking what was already theirs – held in common perhaps – because they were entitled to it under the agreement made at the time. It followed also that governments had the ability to organize efforts in this direction to avoid the chaos and public disquiet that would accompany a regime of pure self-help. This point may also be amusing. Of course, the idea that there had actually once been a "world parliament" that agreed to this system requires a stretch of the imagination. William Blackstone, the great eighteenth-century English lawyer, described it as "too wild" to be believed (Blackstone 1979). But he did not reject the conclusions that lawyers had always drawn from it. Undoubtedly more limited in scope than what is now found in the Universal Declaration, it has been claimed that it stands as a worthy ancestor of today's aspirations.

18.7 CONCLUSION

There is a good deal more that could be said on this subject. More examples could be provided, more rights and limitations expanded upon. My hope, however, is that there may be some parallels in Buddhist thinking that relate to what I have described. I picked my four subjects because I thought there might be, and there are, indications in the chapters from this volume to encourage my hopes on this score. Clerical privileges, for instance, might be just such an area which Buddhist thought held to be off limits from meddling and change by secular authorities. Berthe Jansen's very helpful chapter on monastic constitutional law certainly encourages this approach. Perhaps another example would be Martin Mills' discussion of Songtsen Gampo's royal law based on the Buddhist ten virtues, or Iselin Frydenlund's chapter on events in Myanmar. Seemingly, it also resembles what D. Christian Lammerts wrote about the *dhammasattha* law of precolonial Southeast Asia and his wonderful example of the exchange of a bunch of bananas for a coconut filled with gold. Richard W. Whitecross' treatment of constitutionalism in Bhutan encouraged the same thought, as did Krishantha Fedricks' intriguing introduction to televangelist Buddhist monks. On the other hand, some of the contributions seem to me to suggest the opposite – that the real problem has been simply the treatment of Buddhists by avowedly secular governments rather than the place of constitutional ideas within Buddhism itself. Levi McLaughlin's considerations on the impact of the 1951 Religious Juridical Persons Law on Japanese Buddhists is an example. This chapter and a few others have addressed the treatment of Buddhism under current law, not constitutionalism itself as part of religious law. Valuable and interesting as they are in themselves, they have suggested to me the absence of Buddhism as a likely source of constitutional principles. If that is what we must conclude the evidence shows, I will be wiser, but also sadder.

REFERENCES

Blackstone, William. [1765–1769] 1979. *Commentaries on the Laws of England: A Facsimile of the First Edition of 1765–1769*. Chicago: University of Chicago Press.

Casper, Gerhard. 1987. *Constitutionalism*. Occasional Papers from the Law School, n. 22. Chicago: University of Chicago Law School.

Ginsburg, Tom. 2008. "Administrative Law and the Judicial Control of Agents in Authoritarian Regimes." In *Rule by Law: The Politics of Courts in Authoritarian Regimes*, edited by Tom Ginsburg and Tamir Moustafa. Cambridge: Cambridge University Press.

Panormitanus (Nicolaus de Tudeschis). 1615. *Commentaria super decretalium libros*, f. 137 (X 2.18.2, no. 16). Venice.

19

Islam and Constitutional Law

Insights for the Emerging Field of Buddhist Constitutional Law

Clark B. Lombardi

19.1 INTRODUCTION

In the hope of encouraging the enormously valuable project of developing a field of Buddhism and law that can interact symbiotically with the young field of Islam and constitutional law, this chapter will try briefly to do three things. First, it will ruminate upon the surprisingly long delay in commencing a study of the relationship between Islam and constitutional law, and upon the political and academic developments that eventually inspired the academic field to focus its energies productively onto studies in this area. Second, it will discuss some of the central findings produced by scholars over the past twenty-five years as they started, belatedly, to explore the complex relationships between Islam and constitutional law around the world. This part of the chapter will focus on the conclusions that have been drawn by scholars of the Sunni tradition. The study of Islam and constitutional law makes clear that when one is dealing with a global, internally plural tradition such as Islam or Buddhism, it is sometimes necessary to generalize first about particular sects or regional instantiations of a religious tradition, before one can draw broader conclusions. Scholars of Islam and constitutional law have largely, though not exclusively, focussed on the Sunni world and its "constitutional imaginary."[1] Third, this article will very cautiously draw upon the contributions in this volume to highlight some ways in which patterns found in the Sunni Muslim world seem to be absent in a number of Buddhist countries. The claims made in this section are cautious and the ambitions of the discussion modest. Hopefully, though,

[1] Martin Loughlin defines the constitutional imagination as "the manner in which constitutions can harness the power of narrative, symbol, ritual and myth to project an account of political existence in ways that shape – and re-shape – political reality. The phrase draws our attention to the capacity of constitutions to offer alternative perceptions of reality, revealing new ways of conceiving the boundaries of practical political action" (2015, 3).

this discussion will highlight some possible areas for productive future research for scholars in the new field of Buddhism and constitutional law.

19.2 THE RISE OF THE STUDY OF "ISLAM AND CONSTITUTIONAL LAW"

In retrospect, it should have been obvious that the introduction of constitutions into the Muslim world would have profound effects upon the constitutional imagination of people around the world, Muslims and non-Muslims alike.

From a very early period, Islamic thinkers have been interested in questions of ethical governance and about how government should be structured, both to ensure that the ruler acts morally and that he creates a society in which morality is encouraged. Scholars of Islamic thought have long been interested in this subject. Furthermore, almost from the time that they were first introduced in the nineteenth century, constitutions in majority Muslim states have generally made at least some reference to Islam. Over time, the references to Islam have become more widespread and more elaborate. Furthermore, in countries where the constitution explicitly carved out a role for Islam or Islamic values, governments began to feel significant pressure to honor the constitutional obligation to respect Islam. As a result, national administrative legislation was adopted to organize (and control) the institutions that had historically interpreted Islam for the people. A number of scholars, particularly political scientists focusing on Islamic politics in post-colonial countries, have discussed these developments.

Hiding in plain sight within this literature were questions that begged to be answered. Why over the course of the twentieth and twenty-first centuries, were polities throughout the heterogeneous Muslim world demanding that constitutional systems carve out a role for Islam in shaping state practices and state law? What was the role of religious mentalities in the shaping of these demands? What were the effect of debates about constitutionalizing Islam on Muslims' understanding of their own religion? Were they causing Muslims fruitfully to revisit the works of Islamic religious and intellectual history? If so, should their findings cause the Western academy to rethink some of its accepted wisdom about Islamic intellectual and political history? Were these debates inspiring them to develop viable alternatives to classical liberal constitutionalism? If so, what was (or should be) the effect of this development of the constitutional imaginary *outside* the Muslim world?

The Islamic tradition, like many global religious traditions, presents itself differently in different parts of the world and, indeed, within a single majority Muslim country, different classes or communities may express their commitment to Islam in different ways.[2] After World War II, scholars focusing on the Islamic tradition

[2] Variations are so large that after World War II, some scholars of religious studies in the Euro-American academy suggested that it was misleading even to talk about a single religion of Islam

started to emphasize the importance of describing the way that Muslims in a particular region experienced and understood their religion. Less attention was focussed on the task of identifying transregional patterns in Muslim religious discourse or practices.[3] During this same period, many sociologists of religion were under the thrall of a secularization thesis, a commitment that likely led them to discount the possible significance of religious language in political discourse or in new constitutional texts.

By the 1980s, however, global events were forcing policymakers and academics to admit and address the obvious. Islamist discourse was becoming an increasingly important factor in politics all over the Muslim world. This discourse often involved a common demand that national governments recognize (and honor) a constitutional obligation to respect supposedly "Islamic" traditions of government. In 1979 alone, the world watched as a military government in Pakistan continued to impose a program of Islamic constitutional reforms accompanied by massive legal reforms; Iran completed a dramatic Islamic revolution against a dictatorial ally of the US; Afghanistan was convulsed by an Islamically inflected war of resistance against a Soviet puppet regime; and oil-rich Saudi Arabia experienced a shocking armed takeover of the Grand Mosque in Mecca by Islamist radicals, who believed that the seemingly conservative monarchy was insufficiently respectful of Islamic traditions of moral governance. Within two years, the president of Egypt had been assassinated by Islamist radicals and in Sudan, a military junta decided to shore up its flagging popularity by embracing a radical program of Islamic constitutional and legal reform.

By the early 1990s, scholars studying different parts of the Muslim world through a variety of disciplinary lenses were beginning to think about how best to approach the phenomenon of Islamic political discourse in a world of nation-states and of Islamic language embedded into national constitutions. As they did so, these scholars began

(see e.g., Al-Azmeh 1993). Although few people adopted the strong form of this argument, it nonetheless had an impact on the way that Islam was studied. The study of "Islam" continued to accept at face value Muslims' shared description of themselves as partners engaged in a common project – the project of engaging with, interpreting, and obeying the divine message revealed in a shared set of scriptures.

3 The post-war academy began increasingly to react against a long "orientalist" tradition of Islamic studies in the West, one that had very justly been accused of developing simplistic generalizations about Islam, generalizations that had shaped in unfortunate ways Western attitudes towards Muslims as well as colonial (and post-colonial) policies toward Muslim populations. After World War II, academics began consciously and systematically to challenge old generalizations about Islam and began specifically to focus on highlighting the rich diversity of different ways in which a commitment to "Islam" could be manifested in different countries or communities. Helping to push this trend were structural shifts. Many scholars who focused on Islam were placed into newly formed "area studies" departments, so that scholars working on Islam in South Asia had far more contact with scholars of Hinduism in South Asia than with scholars of Islam in the Middle East. And even scholars located in traditional methodological departments tended more than in the past to focus on exploring the nuances of Islamic belief, practice, and institutions as they developed in a particular region, rather than trying to look for broader patterns in Islamic beliefs and practices.

to identify some new questions. Among them: When and where did the impulse to constitutionalize Islam first emerge? Did it really grow organically (as some modern Islamist thinkers asserted) out of a premodern tradition of political thought that had incubated a latent commitment to constitutionalism even before the age of written constitutions? Why was the wording of the constitutional provisions that referenced Islam so idiosyncratic? How did a decision to integrate Islam into a constitutional text (or into the interpretation of a formally secular constitution) actually affect the people who lived under that constitution? This last issue involved two distinct but symbiotic questions. First, did the decision to bring Islam into constitutional discourse change the way that Muslims understood and engaged with their religion? Second, did the decision to bring Islam into the constitutional order change the practices of the state and/or the experiences of its subjects?

To answer all these questions scholars had to draw upon a multitude of disciplines that had not hitherto existed in regular dialogue. Historians of classical Islam had to revisit the accepted wisdom in their field about both Islamic thought and state practices, while historians, anthropologists, sociologists, and political scientists with expertise in one or more parts of the Muslim world had to explore the evolution of modern ideas about constitutions and constitutionalism. Building on these microstudies of constitutional (or proto-constitutional) thought and of religious developments, scholars could attempt to draw broader conclusions about the way in which ideas and practices traveled and evolved across space and time, and about the nature of the impact in the Muslim world both of Islam on constitutional law and, conversely, of constitutional law upon Islam.

As scholars have begun to answer some of these questions, the promise of a greater prize has appeared. Some scholars began tentatively to draw hypotheses about the broader lessons that evolving studies of Islam and constitutional law might teach the world about the role religion can and often does play in the modern world and, more specifically, about the roles that religion can play in the constitutional orderings of modern states (Brown 2002, Hirschl 2010). For some of the more ambitious hypotheses to be tested, scholars needed access to studies that could help establish whether patterns in the Muslim world were analogous to patterns in other parts of the world, especially parts in which a person's identity was understood in terms of a religion other than Islam. For example, were majority Buddhist countries constitutionalizing Buddhism? If so, was the process being driven by factors similar to those driving constitutional Islamization? Was the process proceeding in a fashion similar to that unfolding in the Muslim world? Was the constitutionalization of Buddhism enshrined in constitutional provision similar to that being drafted in the Muslim world? And finally, was the constitutionalization of Buddhism affecting governance in the Buddhist world in a manner similar to the way it was affecting governance in the Muslim world?

The present volume provides hope that some of the answers to these questions may start to be answered in the coming years. Contributions to this volume demonstrate that Buddhism, like Islam, has clearly engaged from a very early period with questions about how rulers should act and about how political actors should interact with religious actors to ensure that ethical behavior is encouraged in society. Buddhism does show up, albeit sometimes obliquely, in modern constitutional texts and/or commentaries. And Buddhist actors are active politically, sometimes in ways that affect constitutional politics directly and sometimes in ways that significantly affect the political dynamic and political expectations and thus, albeit indirectly, shape the constitutional order of the state.

The study of Buddhism and constitutional law seems to be at an even earlier stage in its development than is the now quite robust study of Islam and constitutional law. Possessing only the most cursory knowledge about the history of Buddhist studies in the modern world, I cannot say whether the delay grows out of the institutional structures and academic trends that postponed the arrival of a robust community focussed on studying Islam and constitutional law. Looking at the wealth of material produced in this volume, one can only be grateful that scholars in the field of Buddhist studies have, like scholars of Islamic studies, identified the study of religion and constitutional law as a fruitful area for research. Already in this pathbreaking volume, the editors and contributors have demonstrated that they have a great deal to work with. For anyone who is interested in generating robust comparative work on the phenomenon of "religion and constitutions," "constitutionalization of religion," or something that might be described as the "religification of constitutions," the contributions to this volume, taken together are eye-opening and provocative. One can only hope that scholars of Buddhism and constitutional law will be interested in actively engaging with scholars focusing on the study of Islam and constitutional law and vice versa.

19.3 THE STATE OF "ISLAM AND CONSTITUTIONAL LAW" STUDIES

As the intellectual project of "Buddhism and constitutional law" begins, the participants in that project might productively bear in mind some of the insights that scholars of "Islam and constitutional law" have to date developed as they have sought to describe the evolving constitutional imaginary for the vast number of Sunni Muslims who today want their state simultaneously (i) to satisfy the obligations of an "Islamic state" and (ii) at the same time to operate as a modern state under a modern constitution.

Over roughly the past twenty-five years, scholars interested in the broader connection between Islam and constitutional law have produced and slowly begun to synthesize a wide variety of findings from a myriad of different academic fields including, among others, religious studies, political history, social history, contemporary Islamic politics, anthropology, sociology, and area studies. As a result of this work, scholars have begun to develop a new understanding of Sunni Islamic intellectual and political history – one that tries to explain patterns in Islamic thought and behavior, that scholars of Islam until recently tended to see as counter-intuitive and problematic.

19.3.1 *The Rise of Classical Sunni Institutions and Theories of Islamic Law*

Islam is a global religion growing out of the experiences of a man, Muhammad, who lived in Western Arabia in the late sixth century and early seventh centuries CE. His revelations lay the basis for the *shari`a* (literally the "path"), God's moral code that was simultaneously the path to individual salvation for an individual Muslim and the path to material welfare for a Muslim community. When the Prophet died without a designated successor, the young Muslim community lost both its moral guide and its political leader. Henceforth the community's access to God would come through texts, which provide a record of the signs given to the community in the special prophetic moment both in direct revelation and in the exemplary practices of its messenger. Since the secrets were recorded in scriptural texts, the community needed to identify people who could help them understand these texts, and it also needed to identify the people who could be trusted effectively to govern the expanding Islamic empire and its growing Muslim populations, protect its borders, and establish an order which allowed people to enjoy the material benefits that God had revealed to be "goals of the *shari`a*."

Muslims after the death of the prophet faced two questions: Who should engage with scripture to find information about God's moral command? Who should be trusted to develop and impose rules that realize the social benefits that God commands Muslim societies to enjoy? While some suggested that the roles of moral guide and political leader should be held by the same person, the group that would become the "Sunni" community ultimately concluded that the two roles could be divided and that, in many circumstances, dividing these roles was not only manageable but inevitable. The thinkers who developed Sunni Islam decided to begin with the first question. They believed that if they first identified people who could be trusted to uncover in the scriptures reliable information about God's moral expectations for individuals and for the community, those figures could then explain how the community should select the proper leaders.

Some Muslims, including the group that would evolve into the Shiite sect of Islam, suggested that people were not all born with the same capacity to understand scripture. According to them, God had granted to certain men known as "Imam" special abilities and insights. At any one point in time, there would be one Shiite Imam, and the community should defer to his interpretations of God's law. Upon his death, the Imam's unique insight and authority would transfer to a designated successor.

The community that would become the Sunni sect took a more democratic view of human capacities in the area of moral reasoning. According to the formative

Sunni thinkers, it was impossible to identify one person who was destined always to interpret scripture correctly; all humans were born with the ability to do this. While most Muslims would remain untrained, a self-selected group of Muslims could and should take on the responsibility for providing moral guidance. After enormous training and effort, a person gained the right to try and demonstrate their command of scriptures and logic and to try and shape the views of other scholars – and, thus, of all the followers that those scholars had amassed among the untrained.

An aspiring scholar of God's law must not only demonstrate mastery of texts and language but must bear in mind God's assurance that his laws always promoted human welfare. This was tricky because, in some cases, it could be hard to understand how accepting and following one interpretation of God's command (as opposed to another) might promote the goals of the *shari`a*. The successful moral reasoner would have to develop a compelling interpretation of God's command from texts. Some texts could be accepted at face value. Ambiguous text needed to be interpreted in a sophisticated manner, drawing on tools adapted from Greek logic, where analogical reasoning was influenced in subtle (and often tentative) ways by utilitarian calculations in which "the good" was defined as communal enjoyment of the *shari`a*'s goals.

Recognizing the need to develop a robust system of education in which particularly talented scholars could develop and distinguish themselves, Muslim communities began to encourage and support scholarly guilds. Those guilds devoted themselves to the task of training people to elaborate law from scripture and reason and to credential people whose opinions should be considered probative (if not dispositive) on questions of God's law. These guilds were not created and regulated by rulers. Rather, they emerged organically within communities committed to the goal of living according to God's law. The power of a guild depended upon its ability to attract students and to produce scholars whose interpretations of God's law were judged compelling.

Over the course of several centuries, the Sunni community came to prefer certain guilds of religious law over others. The four which ultimately survived, the Hanafi, Maliki, Shafi`i, and Hanbali are often described as the "four Sunni schools of law." For roughly 1,000 years (very roughly from 900 until 1900) these four Sunni juristic guilds, or "schools of law," functioned as self-governing institutions that controlled the teaching of Islamic law and the credentialing of scholars. Their opinion could be sought by anyone, ruler or subject, who needed an informed opinion about how God wanted people to behave. Aspiring scholars underwent training from a senior jurist recognized as a master of one among the Sunni schools of law. Upon receiving their own credentials as a master jurist of the guild/school's doctrines, they were deemed to be member of the Sunni *fuqaha'*, the profession of Islamic jurists who were understood almost uniformly to be the only trustworthy sources for reasonable opinions on the *shari`a*.

To understand the evolution of Islamic political thought, it is important to note that four guilds taught slightly different variations on the classical approach to legal interpretation and taught different versions of God's law. Each guild could trace its origin back to a founding scholar. Each founder employed moderately different tools of interpretation and left a record of answers to questions about the morality of particular types of behavior. Members of a guild assumed axiomatically that the answers provided by the founder were correct, at least at the precise time and under the specific circumstances in which the question was posed to him. To be recognized as a member of the *fuqaha'*, a Sunni Muslim would have to study with a master jurist from one of the guilds/schools and would have to demonstrate command of the guild's preferred methodology and precedents. The successful student would receive a certification from the master stating that he was now a *faqih*, able to and, indeed, with a moral duty to provide informed opinions (*fatwas*) to anyone who had questions about God's law. Those opinions could be trusted reasonably to approximate the answer that the founder of the guild would most likely have provided were that founder alive today. As he issued these opinions, the master jurist was supposed to familiarize himself as far as possible with the opinions that his contemporaries in the guild were issuing on similar topics. To be a "Hanafi" jurist then was by definition, (i) to be formally recognized by one or more masters of the Hanafi guild, (ii) to commit to answering questions about God's law as one reasonably believed the school's founder, Abu Hanifa, would have done, and (iii) to continue to engage in dialogue with other Hanafi scholars and to allow one's understanding of the law, over time, to evolve in line with the views of thinkers that one found compelling.

The credentialed jurists trained within the Sunni schools of law represented within premodern Islamic society a distinct professional class of religious experts who were independent of the political authorities, although, as will be discussed shortly, they were constantly in dialogue with political authorities. In short, they represented a religious "establishment" distinct from the political establishment. While it is tempting to analogize them to members of the Buddhist sangha (or to members of the Catholic priesthood), one should recognize some ways in which the credentialed jurists of the guilds, the *fuqaha'*, as professionals, differ from the members of religious orders who constituted a special class of human within society.

First: the members of the Sunni schools of law, masters and apprentices alike, considered themselves to be members of society similar in crucial ways to all other members and generally subject to the same moral commands. Interpreting God's law was seen as a job among other jobs in society. God expected certain things from credentialed scholars that he did not expect from others, and God had also established rules that required scholars to follow certain procedures when they issued Islamic legal opinions. Outside of their professional duties, however, a credentialed scholar understood themselves to be a person like other people. Food that God had made permissible for a layman was also permissible for a credentialed scholar. Words that would form a contract for a layman would also form a contract that bound a scholar. Scholars could own property to the same extent that other members of Muslim society could, and like all adult Muslims, they were permitted (indeed encouraged) to marry according to the same rules as non-jurists. When they did, they understood that their obligations to their spouse were no different than the obligations of a married layperson.

Second, when they acted in their particular area of expertise – issuing opinions about God's law – the credentialed jurists refused to establish a formal hierarchy of interpretive authority. While the community of scholars could identify some rules upon which they agreed and about which the Muslim community could know with certainty to be rules of *shari`a*, the community also recognized those areas of jurisprudence in which they had come to equally reasonable but fundamentally different understandings of God's law. Given the guilds' disagreements on questions of proper interpretive methodology and their decision to look to a competing body of precedents, the different guilds/schools of law inevitably taught slightly different versions of God's law. Each of these versions was described as a body of *fiqh*: literally, a well-reasoned "understanding" of God's law. Furthermore, the scholars within a single guild might disagree on questions of first impression, meaning that on some issues there would be different versions of *fiqh* within a single guild. Rather than try to establish a hierarchy of scholars who were empowered to make arbitrary and potentially incorrect judgements about which of the guild's interpretations was best, the guilds concluded that it was morally better just to "agree to disagree." Outside of the small number of rules that the guilds jointly recognized as those that were indubitably rules of *shari`a*, they acknowledged that it was impossible to say which of the competing interpretations of God's law was correct and all things being equal, humans had the right to choose for themselves which of the competing interpretations they wanted to follow. This was a concession that would come to impact in important ways classical Sunni political philosophy and the practice of premodern Islamic states. This would in turn shape profoundly the ways in which modern Muslims engaged with the idea (and realities) of constitutions.

19.3.1.1 Classical Sunni Discussions about Whether (and How) to Develop a Body of Predictable and Uniform State "Law"

Classical Sunni Islamic political thought developed in this very particular conceptual and institutional context. It was assumed that (i) God had laid down a code which dictated how every human was to act, and thus dictated how a ruler was to act when he laid down rules to govern his society; (ii) following this code would result not only in the salvation of individuals but also in the production of material benefits for the community (the so-called "goals of the law"), of which the most important were the protection within the society of religion, life, children, reason, and wealth; (iii) the secrets to the moral code were embedded in scripture (and to some extent in nature), and although all humans were given equal access at birth to scriptural secrets, their meaning could be properly discovered only by people who were trained both in the arts of scriptural analysis and of logical reasoning; (iv) those who are trained to seek and acquire skills in the art of scriptural moral interpretation remain, in almost all respects, members of society like any other and subject to the same moral rules as anyone else; (v) among the many people who are recognized (and credentialed) as experts in the arts of Islamic moral interpretation, none can claim unquestioned superiority over another, thus Sunni society must accept that there are moral questions for which there is no indisputably correct answer. It follows that, although the answers to some moral questions are obvious to any trained scholarly mind (and are known with certainty to be part of God's *shari`a*), there will always be questions on which trained minds will disagree and about which the community will be given a range of answers, any of which might turn out to be correct. With respect to these rules-about-which-we-can-only speculate, no one can say with certainty which of the competing interpretations is definitively the best. Indeed, no one can preclude the possibility that the correct rule of *shari`a* will turn out to be "none of the above," a rule that is yet to be proposed.

God's *shari`a* surely required that a ruler establish and impose a uniform body of social laws that was consistent with what the scholars had discovered about God's law and would also demonstrably promote communal welfare. Notwithstanding the default rule that allowed Muslims generally to select for themselves which guild's version of *fiqh* to follow, that freedom disappeared when the ruler had established within the areas of behavior that could not be regulated with absolute moral certainty, stable rule of law not inconsistent with what scholars had discovered about the *shari`a*'s rules and goals. At that point (though only at that point) every Muslim was required by God to abandon her preferred interpretation of God's *shari`a* and act as if the ruler's positive law accurately reflected God's will. Paradoxically, God would at that point reward in heaven the person who followed a ruler's ultimately incorrect laws to the exclusion of their own ultimately correct understanding of what God wanted to do. And God would punish in hell the person who did not. So much was known with certainty. But agreement on those basic principles raises its own questions.

The *fuqaha'*, the scholars credentialed by one of the four Sunni schools of law, struggled to understand who had the right to serve as the ruler who established order, what methods that figure should use when selecting rules to impose, and, of course, what the substance of that law should be. Although members of the *fuqaha'* touched upon such questions in a variety of different scholarly genres, many seem to have directed their energies towards developing theories that defined the legitimately "Islamic" body of state law as a body of law created by a special type of ruler.

19.3.1.2 Classical Caliphal Theories

For a time, leading Sunni thinkers such as al-Mawardi, a famous jurist of the Shafi`i school of law, proposed that Sunni societies should ideally be ruled by a person who combined, among many other extraordinary characteristics: credentials as a master scholar within one of the four Sunni schools of law, expertise in matters of governance, and the military power to impose his command. Once a person with such qualities was recognized as "Caliph" by the leading religious and military notables, he was allowed (indeed required) to draw upon his scholarly training as a *faqih* to fill in the gaps where the scholars had not identified with certainty all the rules necessary to regulate life efficiently and to ensure communal thriving. When he did so, Muslims were divinely commanded to set aside their respect for scholars who had urged humans to act in a way other than that favored by the Caliph, and to obey the Caliph's laws. According to this theory the legitimacy of state law depends upon the quality of the ruler who produces it.

19.3.1.3 *The Emergence of the Classical Doctrine of* Siyasa Shari`iyya

By the thirteenth century, many Sunni scholars had concluded that it was unrealistic to expect any proper Caliph to appear. As a result, some including Ibn Taymiyya, a famous jurist of the Hanbali school, proposed a new theory about the type of ruler that God permits. This theory, sometimes called the theory of *siyasa shar`iyya* (literally "governance" that is consistent with the *shari`a*), is far more radical in its implications than might at first be obvious.

The theory asserts that a ruler's right to impose his laws, and his subjects' duties to obey them (at the risk of divine punishment), do not depend upon the ruler's personal qualities. Under some circumstances, a ruler can be untrained in Islamic law and even personally impious and yet can produce, in the areas where God's law is not known with certainty, a set of legitimate positive laws, laws that God expects all the ruler's subjects to obey. The one quality a figure must always have if he is to be recognized as one-qualified-to-create-legitimate-positive-law-for-an-Islamic-state is simply the ability to project hard power and compel people to act in accordance with his preferred rules.

When such a person establishes himself, then irrespective of his personal qualities and irrespective of whether he has been "appointed" through the process of investiture that marked the rise of a Caliph, this "possessor of power" (*wali al-`amr*) is authorized to enact uniform rules. Each of these rules will be legitimate – meaning that God will punish people who fail to act in accord with them – so long as that rule satisfies two conditions. First, the rule must not require any Muslims to act in a way that violates a rule of *fiqh* that is known with certainty. Second, the ruler must be able to make a plausible argument that his rule will promote the social benefits that God wants his believers to enjoy. So long as a ruler's *siyasa* (the rules that he enforces in society) meet the conditions necessary to be recognized as *siyasa shar`iyya*, his laws are legitimate and deserve to be obeyed even in cases where they conflict with a subject's preferred interpretation of *fiqh*.

The doctrine of *siyasa shar`iyya* thus inverts the logic of Caliphal theories. Caliphal theories assume that the legitimacy of a ruler's law depends upon the quality of a ruler and, in particular of his possessing certain qualities. By contrast, the doctrine of *siyasa shar`iyya* assumes that the legitimacy of a ruler depends upon the quality of his positive laws. For the purpose of comparing Sunni and Buddhist intuitions about governance, it is important to note that according to the jurists who embraced the doctrine of *siyasa shar`iyya* (a group that came over time to include the vast majority of jurists), a legitimate positive state law binds all of a ruler's subjects. So long as a ruler's orders satisfy the twin requirements, credentialed jurists and lay-people alike, *fuqaha'* and non-*fuqaha'*, are required to obey them. Unless the ruler voluntarily chooses, by edict, to treat the *fuqaha'* differently, a member of the *fuqaha'* is obliged to obey the same contracts, pay the same taxes, and litigate in the same courts as lay-people.

19.3.1.4 *The Incorporation of* Siyasa Shar`iyya *into the State Practice in Premodern and Early Modern Empires*

In the wake of the Mongol invasions of the thirteenth century CE, the theory of *siyasa shar`iyya* came to be embraced by jurists and rulers alike in a number of empires around the world. Among the largest, longest-lived and most influential empires to establish its legitimacy in terms of this theory was the Ottoman Empire. The Ottoman sultan established a cabinet with a central role for a leading member of the *fuqaha'*, invariably a master jurist trained in the Hanafi guild. The bureaucracy of this appointed jurist, the *Shaykh al-Islam*, was tasked with the duty to review every statutory pronouncement and to confirm that it did not violate clear scriptural commands. The *Shaykh al-Islam* also stood as head of a judiciary staffed entirely by guild-trained jurists, which was instructed to approach cases that could not be resolved by statute by reference to the rules of *fiqh* (scholarly interpretations of God's moral law). The legitimacy of the Ottoman Empire came very much to be understood in terms of its adherence to the theory of *siyasa shar`iyya*, a theory whose own authority expanded as the empire that had adopted it thrived, and this success seemed to confirm God's promise that obedience to his command would allow a community to enjoy the goals of the law.[4]

4 Although in the nineteenth century the Ottoman sultan began to assert that he should be recognized as a "Caliph," he did not claim to have the qualities of a Caliph in the classical Mawardian sense. Rather, he claimed to be a person whose rule was legitimate unlike, he said, the rule of Western colonialists and of their puppets. His rule alone was morally binding according to the doctrine of *siyasa shar`iyya*. By applying a body of rules that were either (i) statutes approved by scholars as being consistent with juristic *fiqh*, or (ii) judge-made rules grown of the *fiqh* tradition, the Ottomans could legitimately claim to be governing according to the doctrine of *siyasa shar`iyya*.

19.3.2 *Initial Muslim Engagements with Written Constitutions*

The tradition of *siyasa shar`iyya* and the Ottoman instantiation of that tradition gave many Muslims a conceptual lens through which they viewed the modern innovation of a written constitution. The Sunni tradition as mediated through the Ottomans proved to be a vernacular that could easily translate the normative claims of liberal constitutionalism and see them as cognates of at least some ideas and institutions already present in the Islamic tradition.

As scholars like Nathan Brown have described, during the nineteenth century, many states in the Muslim world, both colonial and independent states trying to strengthen themselves to fend off would-be colonizers, began to borrow tools of Western governmental organization to expand the power of the state at the expense of its citizens and of civil society (Brown 1997; 2002). Ironically, as Brown points out, the first written constitutions in the Muslim world, including the Ottoman Constitution of 1876, were part of this state-empowering process. They were promulgated by unaccountable rulers in order to establish the procedures by which rulers would henceforth come to power and make decisions. Naturally, they did not include many provisions which explicitly defined substantive limits on the government's discretion with respect to lawmaking or policy.

What Brown calls "non-constitutionalist" constitutions were increasingly challenged, however, by constitutionalist movements in Muslim societies, which demanded reforms that would rewrite constitutions to include substantive constraints on the government's legislative discretion, and in some cases also include institutions which could enforce those constraints. Increasingly these were characterized, sometimes explicitly and sometimes implicitly, as calls to integrate into constitutions provisions which required the state to respect the traditional logic of *siyasa shar`iyya*.

It is easy to see in the doctrine of *siyasa shar`iyya* some areas of overlap with modern European theories of liberal constitutionalism. Rereading scriptures and classical texts in light of modern constitutionalist theories, an influential group of Islamic intellectuals – many but not all of whom were based in the Ottoman Empire – argued that there was built into Islam a sophisticated theory of constrained government in the service of the public good that, when implemented properly, was superior to the liberal constitutionalism that Europeans had developed far later using their reason alone. Accepting that liberal constitutionalism reflected a meaningful, if imperfect way of guaranteeing constrained government, Islamic constitutionalists saw constitutions as useful tools to help reinvigorate traditional Muslim commitments to the ideal of an Islamically constrained state. Islamic constitutionalists were thus eager participants in constitutional politics in the late nineteenth and twentieth-century Middle East, and backed many of the demands of liberal constitutionalists, such as rights guarantees and demands for judicial review. They demanded, however, the addition of further provisions which would require the state to respect the core principles of Islamic law.

The earliest successful call for Islamic constitutionalism of this type appeared in majority Shiite Persia (soon to be renamed "Iran"). Persia/Iran was a neighbor of the Ottoman Empire, with its population close observers of its powerful Sunni neighbor. Over the course of 1906 and 1907, a diverse group of liberal and Islamic constitutionalists in Iran forced the king of Iran to enact constitutional documents that required the state both to respect some fundamental liberal rights and also to forswear the adoption of any law that was inconsistent with principles announced in Islamic scriptures. This Iranian Constitution, as amended in 1907, also established what was for all practical purposes a constitutional council staffed by credentialed Shiite clerics. It was empowered to exercise preenforcement review of legislation and had the power to void any draft law that its members deemed to be inconsistent with Islam. Notwithstanding their success in having this constitution enacted, the Iranian king later reasserted his power and thereafter he and his successors ignored entirely their constitutional commitments. But the Iranian revolution of 1979 ushered in a new constitution which reiterated the requirement that Iran enact only legislation that conformed to Islamic law as understood by credentialed clerics.

In Istanbul and the Anatolian heartland of the Ottoman Empire, incipient Sunni Islamic constitutionalism associated with the Young Ottoman movement was supplanted during the early decades of the twentieth century by the militantly secularist and non-constitutionalist Young Turk movement, leading to the dissolution of the Ottoman Empire and the formation of modern Turkey and a multitude of other nation-states. Yet Sunni Islamic constitutionalism thrived in the Arab-speaking states that had formerly been part of the Ottoman Empire as well as in parts of the British Empire, where Pakistan was about to emerge as a new state that would be a homeland for the Muslims of the subcontinent.

Harnessing the tools of mass communication and mass political organization and finding around the world a community of Sunni Muslims whose scriptural studies had equipped them to read in Arabic, a number of Sunni thinkers were able to transmit these ideas and this particular framing of constitutionalism to a global audience. Among the influential Arab thinkers were activists like Rashid Rida, the founder of a publication with a global audience, and the founders and early leaders of the Egyptian Muslim Brotherhood, a group that inspired like-minded organizations around the Muslim world. Their ideas of such thinkers and groups were reframed by local thinkers, some of whom expanded upon the idea of Islamic constitutionalism in ways that, themselves, were transmitted globally. A notable example of such a thinker was Maulana Maududi, an Islamist thinker in India – and later Pakistan – whose ideas on Islamic law and Islamic constitutionalism were transmitted back to the Middle East, where they influenced the ongoing evolution of the ideology of the Muslim Brothers.

The development of a transnational ideology of Islamic constitutionalism helped to shape the way in which Sunni Muslims around the world engaged with the phenomenon of written constitutions and the constitutional demands of liberal colonial legal elites, many of whom had been trained abroad and were using their influence to push for the adoption of liberal constitutionalism. In the hands of thinkers like Rida, al-Banna, Qutb, Maududi, and many others, a Sunni Islamic constitutionalism reframed classical Sunni Islamic texts, including those that were connected with the doctrine of *siyasa shar`iyya*, as texts which (if properly understood) embraced constitutionalist ideas long before European liberals had reasoned out their own arguments in favor of constrained governance. They saw European constitutionalism as an area in which the ideal end-state embraced values that overlapped in some but not all ways with Islamic values, and more importantly as a source of ideas about institutional design that would permit those with moral insight to constrain executive power.

Today it seems plausible to define an "Islamic constitution" as a constitution that contains a provision prohibiting the state from enacting legislation that is inconsistent with Islamic values (a provision almost invariably read to require the state to govern only by *siyasa shar`iyya* which is consistent both with all clear scriptural rules and with the quasi-utilitarian requirement that government rule to advance the spiritual and material welfare of the people).[5]

19.3.2.1 Pressures of Modernity

As noted earlier, during the classical period when it came to the question of who could be trusted to interpret the *shari`a*, the *fuqaha'* established for themselves a monopoly on interpretive authority. Their initial claim was, however, a humble one. Interpretive authority, they claimed, belonged to those who could develop the most compelling interpretation of God's law. Jurists associated with the four Sunni schools of law had developed the most compelling method of interpreting God's law, as proved by its ability to attract the leading intellects of the day and to inspire compliance on the part of rulers and masses alike, and by its ability to generate a society that thrived as God had promised its law, properly understood and obeyed, would do.

The colonial era represented for many Muslims a humiliation which suggested that if classical Islamic legal theory as applied by the *fuqaha'* had once been a trustworthy source of information about God's law and about how to integrate God's law into the governance of a state, that situation no longer held true. Either the

[5] Some constitutions that contain these two types of provision contain other provisions as well. Depending upon the nature of the additional provisions, one could probably identify a number of different types of "Islamic constitution." Nonetheless, the presence of the two core provisions is the only near constant in the constitutions of states that seek to define themselves as Islamic states.

methodology was appropriate only for an earlier period and was now obsolete or, alternatively, the *fuqaha'* misunderstood and were misapplying the method that their forebears had used. Sharing these intuitions, many of the twentieth-century champions of Sunni Islamic constitutionalism accepted these institutions. It was instrumental in another development as an extraordinary attack on the authority of the *fuqaha'* and an insistence that Muslims who were not trained within the four Sunni schools of law should be able to opine on an equal footing with classically trained jurists. This was the second development that would shape the ongoing evolution of Sunni Islamic constitutionalism in subtle but significant ways and would create new possibilities for thinkers who wanted to harmonize the new Islamic constitutionalism with liberal constitutionalism.

For a myriad of reasons, many of the early theorists and champions of Islamic constitutionalism came to question the value of the highly complex, often formalistic methods of Islamic legal interpretation that were associated with the four Sunni guilds/schools of law. These Sunni "modernists" argued that people without credentials as *fuqaha'* could and should reengage with scriptures using the new quasi-utilitarian methods of reasoning. As they did so, modern thinkers should not defer excessively, if at all, to the conclusions that had been reached in the past by scholars associated with the classical Sunni schools of law. Going back to the scriptures and applying their new methods of interpretation, modernist champions of Sunni Islamic constitutionalism, including Maududi in Pakistan and the Muslim Brothers in Egypt, argued that if a modern Sunni state was to be effectively constrained by Islamic values, it could not rely upon institutions that measured compliance according to the views of classically trained jurists steeped in the methodologies and worldviews of the four Sunni schools of law.

Anti-clerical movements fleetingly appeared in Shiite Persia, but they had little success, relative to those in the Sunni world.[6] While some in the Sunni Middle East, Pakistan, Southeast Asia, and Africa continued to defer to classically trained scholars, many did not. The growing number of dissenters accepted the "modernist" position that if Islam created constraints on governmental power and should be a source of guidance for humans when they acted in private areas not governed by law, then Islam had to be interpreted not by classically trained jurists, but rather by people who were pious, fluent in Arabic, trained in modern sciences, including modern social sciences, and usually committed to less formalistic, more utilitarian modes of interpreting God's law.

The rise of "lay" Islamic legal interpretation created new spaces for discussion about the possible overlaps between Islamic constitutionalism (seen as a modern

[6] Where Sunni jurists were divided among four guilds, Shiite jurists all belonged to one Shiite guild. The jurists centralized the procedures by which they trained jurists and by which they recognized hierarchies of authority among the credentialed jurists. The reorganized, newly centralized body of Shiite ulama were able to maintain their prestige within Persia (soon to be renamed Iran).

corollary of the doctrine of *siyasa shar`iyya*) and liberal constitutionalism. Modern Sunni ideas of constitutionalism, as a reframing of the classical doctrine of *siyasa shar`iyya* declares un-Islamic (and thus constitutionally invalid) state laws that either unambiguously violate clear scriptural commands or impede the public welfare. Classical jurists had historically defined "the good" as the enjoyment of five core values (religion, life, children, reason, and wealth) and they were very deferential to the ruler's judgement as to whether a law was likely to advance one or more of those benefits. Modernist lay intellectuals, by contrast, tended to consider a far larger number of possible benefits and harms, and they tended to be less deferential to a government official's conclusions about a law's impact. Depending on how a utilitarian lay Islamic modernist defined "the good," she might, in theory, conclude that a law was invalid because it violates internationally recognized human rights or principles of equitable social distribution. Conversely, if she were a social reactionary, she might strike down a law as violating the public good simply because it indirectly led to the subversion of traditional gender roles.

The assault in the Sunni world on the authority of a single self-regulating profession of scholars forced Muslims to think in a new way about what sort of institution could be trusted to mediate between the growing number of competing interpretations of Islam and establish one interpretation that would be binding on the state (Lombardi 2013). As Sunni political theorists and activists tried to answer these questions, new possibilities opened up, in theory, for the possible fusion of the proto-constitutionalism inherent in the doctrine of *siyasa shar`iyya*, on the one hand, and on the other, the democratic versions of liberal constitutionalists.

Andrew March has recently described the process by which a number of influential modernist Sunni Islamist thinkers moved in the direction of democratic popular constitutionalism (2019). In a world where every Muslim must be trusted to engage with scripture and to bring her own insights to bear upon questions of interpretation and in which on most questions no individual could ever be trusted with inevitable certainty to have superior insight to another, then one must trust "the wisdom of the [Islamically committed] crowd." According to this line of thought, in a modern era where every Muslim could be expected to be literate, the demos did not need to defer to a special scholarly class. Potentially each member of the demos could come to his or her own understanding of what moral rules a ruler must respect and could, through democratic institutions, identify and develop an official understanding on the point. It would then enforce the constitutional boundaries of moral governance through popular constitutionalism (March 2019). Since at least some members of the demos are likely to be reactionaries and other liberals, democratically defined versions of Islam will involve compromises between the two.

Alternatively, other modern Islamic intellectuals suggested that a modern, educated demos should not be asked to interpret God's law or to identify the boundaries it placed on rulers. The demos could, however, be trusted to set up systems that would appoint people to carry out this task on their behalf. In other words, they argued that a constitution should provide some process by which judges would be appointed to perform a special type of judicial review: Islamic review. These judges should then be trusted to police the moral boundaries of the *shari`a* alongside other further constitutionally specified boundaries, such as liberal boundaries or socialist boundaries (Lombardi 2013). In this alternative mode of Sunni Islamic constitutionalism, constitutional benches (which might be staffed, in part or in whole by lawyers without classical training) would have the power to determine whether a state law was consistent with the core principles of Islamic law, by satisfying the twin obligations of (i) being consistent with clear scriptural commands, and (ii) plausibly advancing the public welfare.

Islamic review has, in fact, been adopted in many countries with Islamic constitutions. Depending on the process by which judges were appointed to the court, the training, and the character of the judges, a court could sometimes serve as a mediator between traditional understandings of Islamic law and the demands of modern liberalism. Among the judges who have exercised Islamic review in constitutional courts in the Muslim world some have been judges with degrees from secular law schools and of these some have apparently, a commitment to the modern, liberal rule of law. In some countries that have institutionalized the practice of Islamic review, including Egypt and Pakistan, constitutional courts have issued decisions that see Islam not merely as tolerating a liberal state but as affirmatively requiring the state to respect liberal values. Sometimes judges have tried to accomplish this through creative reading of Islamic scriptures.[7] In other cases, they have argued that in modern times, the traditional requirement that a ruler never enact a law that fails to serve the public good must be understood to preclude a court from upholding a law that manifestly violates internationally recognized human rights (Lombardi & Brown 2006).[8]

19.3.3 *A Note Regarding the Recent Evolution of Authoritarian Islamic Constitutionalism in Shiite Iran*

The doctrines of Sunni Islam, historical patterns of governance (which has shaped popular expectations regarding government behavior), and the increasingly fragmented nature of Sunni religious authority have combined to facilitate not only the embrace of constitutions, but more specifically the embrace of constitutions as a tool to promote "constitutionalism." It also has, in at least some places, created opportunities for thinkers to argue, sometimes controversially, that the substantive demands of Sunni Islamic constitutionalism might overlap significantly with the

7 For example, in Pakistan, *Hazoor Bakhsh* v. *Federation of Pakistan* [1981] PLD 145 (FSC) but compare with *Federation of Pakistan* v. *Hazoor Bakhsh* [1983] PLD 255 (FSC).

8 For a particular case, see Egypt, Supreme Constitutional Court of Egypt Case No. 8 of Judicial Year 17 (May 18, 1996) as published in Brown & Lombardi 1996.

demands of liberal constitutionalism. This is to say that Sunni Islam seems in the grand scheme of things to have helped mediate the entry of modern constitutionalism into the public discourse of modern Muslim societies, and has, at the same time, resulted in creative new thinking about the different types of constitutionalism that might meaningfully constrain a state. During a period of ongoing religious revival, the presence of good faith arguments has had an impact, and a handful of Muslim states have, even if tentatively, tried to implement liberal or liberal-leaning versions of Islamic constitutionalism.

This has not been the case over the past fifty years in Iran, the largest Shiite nation in the world. In Shiite-dominated Iran, Islamic thinkers and, it appears, the people remained committed to the ideal of Islamic constitutionalism. The 1979 Islamic revolution was designed to overthrow an unabashedly secular nationalist authoritarian regime. Yet the constitutional regime evolved in a direction that was distinctly illiberal. One reason appears to be that the Shiite *fuqaha'*, jurists trained and credentialed in the one Shiite guild/school of law, retained an extraordinary degree of popularity and religious authority and, furthermore the scholars had established for themselves an internal hierarchy of religious authority, subordinated to a "Supreme Leader." Unlike the Sunni *fuqaha'* who in most parts of the Sunni world had lost their monopoly on religious authority, the Shiite *fuqaha'* of Iran retained in the eyes of most Iranians a monopoly on the right to opine on questions of Islamic law. Because the 1979 constitution only required the state to respect the principles of Islamic law as interpreted by clerics and because the Supreme Leader was, for all practical purposes, the highest-ranking clerical authority in the country, the "Islamic" constraints on his authority were largely ineffective (Künkler and Law 2021).

Iran's constitutional experiment has, sadly, expanded the constitutional imaginary of Muslims outside the Shiite community. For some reactionary Sunni Muslims who decry the space that modernist Islam has created for liberal values, the Shiite example is inspiring. In Afghanistan, the Taliban regime from 1997 to 2001 clearly aspired to construct a clerical regime ruled by credentialed jurists from the Hanafi school that represented an embryonic reimagining of the clerical Iranian regime. It is quite likely that after the Taliban's recent military conquest of Kabul and the restoration of a second Taliban regime they intend to continue in this project (Lombardi and March 2022).

19.4 ISLAM AND BUDDHISM AND CONSTITUTIONAL LAW

Looking at the contributions to this volume, it seems clear that scholars of Buddhism and law are making progress toward some broader hypotheses about the relationship of Buddhism to constitutional law at different times and places. It is exciting to think that one may soon be able to do comparative studies of Islamic and Buddhist constitutional ideals, and it will be fascinating to see whether these potentially quite different conceptualizations may have led Muslims and Buddhists to use constitutions (and constitutional law) in different ways. Many of the contributors to this volume describe ways in which the nature of Buddhist concepts and intuitions may have led Buddhists to embrace a different understanding to Muslims about what religion is, what the role that religious law and religious institutions should play in a modern state, and thus, in the modern world, what types of constitutional provision a religious constitution should include.

In the Sunni Muslim world, Islamic ideas have to date tended to facilitate the rise of a "constitutionalist" ethos in Sunni Muslim polities, albeit one that does not necessarily understand "constitutionalism" to require state respect for liberal values. This in turn has led to the widespread adoption of constitutional provisions that are explicitly constitutionalist and which announce that government discretion is broadly constrained by some moral principles that are announced in scripture. In these cases, the boundaries on moral governance are to be interpreted in the final instance by people outside the control of the ruler and whose authority comes, ultimately, from their recognition as scholars by the community as a whole. This pattern, already present in the premodern period, sounds in a "constitutionalist" key. It has led to the rise of Islamic constitutions that are marked by their consistent concern with identifying Islam as a source of *restraint* on state power, and with the identification of a system that can guarantee that the executive is not given control of the definition of Islam to such an extent that it is left to be the judge of its own power, notwithstanding the different assumptions about religious authority in the Shiite context of Iran.

19.4.1 *Some Questions for Scholars of Buddhism and Constitutional Law Going Forward*

As scholars in the still-congealing field of Buddhism and constitutional law go forward, I for one will be interested to see further exploration into a number of questions.

19.4.1.1 Is the Buddhist Tradition More Fragmented than the Muslim Tradition?

Based on the contributions to this volume, it seems possible that since the passing of the Buddha, the Buddhist tradition may have fragmented in a more complete way than the Muslim tradition did after the death of Muhammad. If so, this raises questions about how broadly one can generalize about "Buddhism" and constitutional law.

The possibility of fragmentation is suggested primarily by the fact that the Buddhist tradition is developed in any particular country by thinkers and activists who are often divided linguistically from thinkers and activists in another. By contrast, throughout the Muslim world, Muslims engage with scriptures that are written in Arabic, and the tradition is developed largely by people who read and write in this common language. Thus, from the beginning of Islamic history, one has been able to find in every country religious authorities and religious-minded people who read and teach in Arabic. Notwithstanding regional variations in Islamic thought and practice, people throughout the Muslim world (or at least educated people with a command of the Arabic language) have been able to engage with each other's ideas about Islam, and in the twentieth century the spread of literacy, the rise of mass media, and the phenomenon of religious revival have together increased the set of people able to engage with common ideas. This may explain why one finds transregional patterns in Sunni thought about constitutional law and in the structure of self-consciously Sunni constitutional regimes.

This core of Arabic speakers around the world has also facilitated communication and productive discourse across sectarian divides. Notwithstanding the differences between Sunni and Shiite ideas and between Sunni and Shiite institutions, the two sectarian traditions have evolved in an environment where religious scholars (in the past) and a large number of literate pious lay Muslims (in the present) have access to views developed among members of the rival sects. Sunni Muslims in the modern era seem generally to have developed a different view on questions of governance and "constitutional law" than have Shiite Muslims, with Sunnis embracing a more decentralized understanding of religious authority than Shiites, one that might be analogized to Protestant Christian views that plant themselves in opposition to more hierarchical and bureaucratic views held by, for example, members of the Catholic or Orthodox church. Even here more work needs to be done to determine if this is in fact true and if so, whether there is any reason to believe that one or both of the traditions will change in ways that causes the two to converge. There was a time when it seemed possible that Shiite understandings of religious authority might move in a "Sunni" direction and the example of the Taliban suggests that at least some Sunnis might embrace a more centralized view.

Looking at the contributions to this volume, a specialist in Islamic intellectual and social history is led to wonder whether the Buddhist tradition has over the centuries, atomized in a deeper way than the Islamic tradition. Because the core scriptures of different sects and/or different regions seem to be written in different languages, there may not be in each country a religious elite capable of engaging with the ideas that are developing in other sects or religions, and thus around the word, Buddhism may see fewer broad transregional trends than Islam with respect to its constitutional imaginaries. If so, scholars of Buddhism may find it more difficult than scholars of Islam to develop a holistic view of the global religious tradition and constitutional law. While scholars of Islam need to be careful to avoid hasty and unnuanced generalizations, the scholarship to date suggests that it is possible to talk meaningfully about "Islam and constitutional law." Scholars of Buddhism may find it necessary to talk instead about "Buddhisms and constitutional law."

19.4.1.2 Does Sunni Thought Tend to Incorporate and Build Upon a More Egalitarian View of Humanity than Buddhist Thought?

Sunni Islam has reflected, from the start, fairly egalitarian intuitions about humanity. All humans are born equal, and each is given an equal opportunity to succeed or fail, with success being rewarded in heaven and failure punished in hell. God has created a moral law to which all humans are subject in the same way; the rules apply to everybody. Everybody must pray in the same fashion, irrespective of one's social status or profession. Other rules govern certain activities. As a result, a ruler (when acting as a ruler) is subject to rules that do not apply to the subject (when acting as a subject), a trader (when carrying on his trade) must obey rules that are simply not relevant to a shepherd (and vice versa). Being a ruler or a scholar does not imply that one is morally superior to a subject or uneducated person, or that one is subject to different moral rules when it comes to the vast majority of one's daily life. One has distinct moral obligations only insofar as one is acting in one's professional capacity, whatever that profession may be. This intuition has consequences for the constitutional ordering of the state, as it tends to promote the idea that state laws too should tend to apply equally to all people. If a particular activity is regulated, then all people who engage in that activity should be subject to the same regulation. And if there are limits to the ruler's ability to regulate an activity, then those regulations provide space for every one of his subjects.

By contrast, Buddhism asserts that humans are not all born equally far along the path to salvation. In the contributions to this volume, one finds suggestions that this belief in the inequality of humankind may impact Buddhist intuitions about the way in which a Buddhist society should be structured and the goals that a Buddhist government should pursue – intuitions that might in turn affect the drafting and interpretation of constitutions in a Buddhist state. Buddhist societies are divided, in one way, between the members of the sangha and lay-people. At least in some contexts, it is suggested that members of the sangha are farther along the path to enlightenment, deserving of special solicitude and, therefore, should be allowed to govern themselves without governmental interference.

If this is correct, it would be interesting to see more work exploring whether Buddhist constitutions are generally drafted (or understood) that might be considered almost "federal" or even "confederal" insofar as they identify a country in which one community, the sangha, which is subject primarily to rules established by its own governing institutions; and a second community, the laity, which is subject to a second layer of national government.

19.4.1.3 Does Sunni Thought Tend to Incorporate and Build Upon a More Egalitarian View of Human Capacity to Understand the Higher Law than Buddhist Thought?

Sunni Islam posits that all humans are born to develop the same ability to discern their obligations under the law. Ultimately, everyone who wants to do so can seek training to work in the profession of Islamic jurist; and if they do, their success or failure is not to be assumed based on the circumstances of their birth. Rather, it is to be judged by their ability to convince people that their interpretation of God's law is to that of other interpreters. More striking still, Sunnis believe that if they are to maintain their monopoly on religious authority, religious institutions must also continue to justify themselves to the public by producing compelling interpretations of God's law that society – rulers and masses alike – find convincing. When in the nineteenth and twentieth centuries, intellectuals without guild training were able to produce compelling interpretations of God's law, the *fuqaha'* lost their monopoly on religious authority. This development had significant consequences for the way in which Sunni societies decided, constitutionally, to design the institutions that would interpret and police a constitutional obligation for the executive and legislature to respect all limits established by the *shari`a*. (Shiism, it should be noted, seems to have been less consistently enthusiastic about the idea that all humans have an equal capacity to understand God's scriptural command and the implications of God's promise that obedience to His law will inevitably promote social flourishing.)

The embrace of egalitarian views about humanity's capacity to engage with the law seems to have impacted subtly but significantly the way in which constitutions are drafted and interpreted. Egalitarian understandings of human capacity to understand God's law implies egalitarian understandings about human capacity to understand the constraints that God has placed on a ruler (or government's) discretion in social regulation. It facilitates intriguing discussions about the institutional structure of a state, and about who should have ultimate authority to determine whether government laws or policies are Islamic and thus deserving of obedience. As Andrew March has demonstrated (2019), it has facilitated in many Sunni Muslim countries arguments in favor of democracy as a moral obligation. If the Muslim community as a whole might be conceptualized as the ultimate arbiters of Islamic-ness, society must be structured to allow the community regularly to express its views on the matter. In other countries, it has facilitated the discussion on what sorts of institution should be trusted to speak for the public when it comes to interpreting constitutional guarantees that the state will govern in accordance with core Islamic principles, and in many countries, this has led Islamic constitutionalists to ally with liberal constitutionalists in clamoring for strong independence of the judiciary. (That said, the degree to which Islamic and liberal constitutionalists agree on the qualities that they would like to see judges possess may, in some countries, differ significantly.)

For a person familiar with Islam and constitutions, it is striking that some contributions to this volume suggest that some strains of Buddhism seem to have taken a non-egalitarian position and that this has affected the structure of governments in Buddhist societies over the years, and more recently seems to have impacted the drafting/implementation of constitutions. For example, it seems that a great deal of Buddhist thought suggests that not only is the sangha best suited to understanding what members of the sangha themselves are supposed to do as they pursue enlightenment (a fact that requires that the sangha be given autonomy within society), but it also assumes that with respect to the regulation of lay-people, some members of lay society, by virtue of their advanced position at birth on the path to enlightenment, have more of an innate capacity to understand how they and their fellow lay-people are supposed to behave. In short, if I understand these contributions correctly, in some Buddhist societies, rulers are assumed to be, by virtue of the fact that they have accumulated enough merit to be born as rulers, people who are likely to have unique insights into the secrets of moral behavior. Rulers are thus uniquely prepared to develop laws that can be trusted to encourage the acquisition of merit.

19.5 CONCLUSION

These are only an initial set of questions that comes to mind from comparing my own field of specialty, in Islam and constitutional law, with the incipient subfield of Buddhism and constitutional law, as apparent in the contributions to this volume. The study of Islam and constitutional law has emerged only recently, but it has already produced provocative work that has challenged some long-held assumptions in the fields of Islamic studies and in comparative constitutional law alike. The study of Buddhism and constitutional law promises on its own to do similar things for the academy. More exciting yet, the work produced by scholars of Buddhism and constitutional law creates the possibility of meaningful comparative study in a broader field of "religion and constitutional law."

REFERENCES

Al-Azmeh, Aziz. 1993. *Islams and Modernities*. London and New York: Verso.

Brown, Nathan J. 1997. *The Rule of Law in the Arab World: Courts in Egypt and the Gulf*. Cambridge and New York: Cambridge University Press.

2002. *Constitutions in a Nonconstitutional World*. Albany: State University of New York Press.

Brown, Nathan J. and Lombardi, Clark B. 2006. "The Supreme Constitutional Court of Egypt on Islamic Law, Veiling and Civil Rights: An Annotated Translation of Supreme Constitutional Court of Egypt Case no. 8 of Judicial Year 17 (May 18, 1996)." *American University International Law Review* 21: 437.

Hirschl, Ran. 2010. *Constitutional Theocracy*. Cambridge: Harvard University Press.

Künkler, Mirjam and Law, David S. 2021. "Islamic Constitutionalism: Iran." In *Constitutionalism in Context*, edited by David S. Law, 449–73. Cambridge: Cambridge University Press.

Lombardi, Clark B. 2013. "Designing Islamic Constitutions: Past Trends and Options for a Democratic Future." *International Journal of Constitutional Law*, University of Washington School of Law Research Paper No. 2013–18. Available at SSRN: https://ssrn.com/abstract=2258089

Lombardi, Clark B. and Brown, Nathan J. 2006. "Do Constitutions Requiring Adherence to *Sharīʿa* Threaten Human Rights? How Egypt's Constitutional Court Reconciles Islamic

Law with the Liberal Rule of Law." *American University International Law Review* 21 (3): 379–435.

Lombardi, Clark B. and March, Andrew F. 2022. "Afghan Taliban Views on Legitimate Islamic Governance. Certainties, Ambiguities, and Areas for Compromise." *United States Institute of Peace*, February 28. www.usip.org/publications/2022/02/afghan-taliban-views-legitimate-islamic-governance

Loughlin, Martin. 2015. "The Constitutional Imagination." *Modern Law Review*, 78 (1): 1–25.

March, Andrew F. 2019. *The Caliphate of Man: Popular Sovereignty in Modern Islamic Thought*. Cambridge: Harvard University Press.